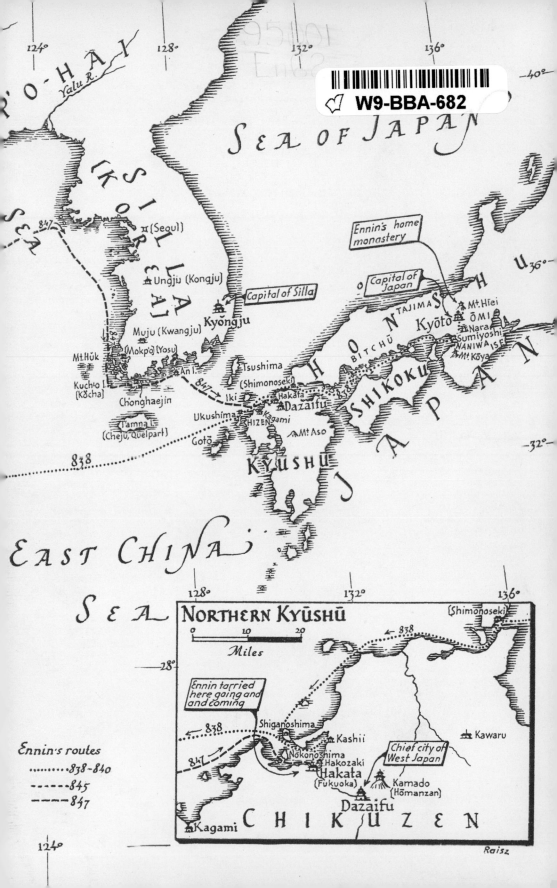

P'O-HAI

Yalu R.

124° 128° 132° 136° —40°

SEA OF JAPAN

[SI
(KOREA]
LLA]

SEA

847

Ennin's home
monastery

36°

U

日 (Seoul)

Capital of Japan

Ungju (Kongju)

Capital of Silla

o

TAJIMA
H
O
N
S
Mt. Hiei

Kyŏngju

Kyōto ŌMI

BITCHŪ

Nara
Sumiyoshi
NANIWA
ISE

Muju (Kwangju)

Mt. Hŭk

(Mokp'o) [Yosu]

An I.

Tsushima
(Shimonoseki)

H
O
N

Mt. Kōya

Kuch'o I.
(Kŏcha)

Iki

Hakata
Dazaifu

SHIKOKU

J

A

P

A

N

Ch'ŏnghaejin

847

Kagami

Ukushima

CHIZEN

Mt. Aso

32°

(T'amna I.
(Cheju, Quelpart)

Gotō

KYŪSHŪ

J

838

EAST CHINA

SEA

NORTHERN KYŪSHŪ

128° 132° 136°

(Shimonoseki)

0 10 20

838

Miles

28°

Ennin tarried
here going
and coming

838

Shiganoshima

Kashii

Kawaru

847

Nokonoshima

Chief city of
West Japan

Hakozaki

Hakata
(Fukuoka)

Kamado
(Hōmanzan)

Dazaifu

Kagami

CHIKUZEN

124°

Raisz

Ennin's Diary

THE RECORD OF A PILGRIMAGE TO CHINA
IN SEARCH OF THE LAW

ENNIN'S DIARY

The Record of a Pilgrimage to China in Search of the Law

TRANSLATED FROM THE CHINESE BY

EDWIN O. REISCHAUER

PROFESSOR OF FAR EASTERN LANGUAGES

HARVARD UNIVERSITY

The RONALD PRESS COMPANY New York

LIBRARY OF CONGRESS CATALOG CARD NUMBER: 55–5553

TO

Serge Elisséeff

Preface

THIS BOOK is a complete translation of the diary written in Chinese by the Japanese Buddhist monk Ennin 圓仁, or Jikaku Daishi 慈覺大師 (793-864), during his travels in China between the years 838 and 847. The Japanese name of this work, though susceptible to several variant pronunciations, is generally read *Nittō guhō junrei gyōki* 入唐求法 巡禮行記,[1] which literally means *The Record of a Pilgrimage to T'ang in Search of the Law*. T'ang (618-907) was the ruling Chinese dynasty, and "the Law" was a term frequently used by Buddhists for their religion.

The real Introduction to this translation is to be found in a separate volume entitled *Ennin's Travels in T'ang China*. In that volume I have discussed Ennin's life as a whole and the historical value of his diary. I have also brought together in it the materials from the diary and a few other sources on certain of the more significant aspects of the life of the time, such as the Japanese embassy to China which Ennin accompanied, Korean traders in T'ang China, travel conditions, festivals, popular Buddhism, and the great persecution of Buddhism which Ennin encountered at the Chinese capital. This Preface, therefore, is devoted primarily to a discussion of the text itself and some of the problems encountered in translating it.

Ennin's diary exists in two manuscripts and four printed editions. The earliest manuscript, now classified in Japan as

---

[1] A conceivable though highly improbable reading of the name of the text, indicating some of the major variant pronunciations, would be *Nyūtō kyūhō junrai kōki*.

a " National Treasure," is owned by the Tōji 東寺, a great Kyōto monastery. It was copied in a shaky hand by a seventy-two-year-old monk, Ken'in 兼胤, in Kyōto in 1291, four and a half centuries after the diary was originally written. The manuscript was collated by a second monk whose name may have been Kan'en 寬圓, though he wrote it in such a modestly tiny scrawl that almost all scholars who have attempted to decipher it have done so differently. Another monk, Gembō 賢寶, has also noted on the manuscript that he received it in the year 1391, though Gembō was probably not aware that this was exactly a century after its completion, since Japanese until very recently always counted time by irregular year periods and not by centuries. The Tōji manuscript was made available to the scholarly world in 1926 in a photographic reproduction published by the great Japanese Sinologist, Okada Masayuki 岡田正之, as a supplement to No. 7 of the *Tōyō bunko ronsō* 東洋文庫論叢 series.

The other manuscript, which was owned by Ikeda Chōden 池田長田, a priest in a monastery of the Tendai 天台 Sect in Nagano-ken, was made in 1805 by a monk named Chōkai 長海 from a manuscript then in the possession of the great monastic headquarters of the Tendai Sect on Mt. Hiei 比叡, near Kyōto.[2]

The differences between the two manuscripts are very minor. Practically all of the points on which the Ikeda text differs from the Tōji appear to be merely corrections of obvious errors of a sort which could have been made by any intelligent student of the text. Furthermore, the Ikeda manuscript has nothing new to offer in many places where the Tōji text is obviously wrong, but where there is no way to guess what the original may have been. In a few cases the Ikeda text makes corrections which seem reasonable at first glance but after careful study prove to be miscorrections. I

---

[2] The colophons of the Tōji manuscript will be found at the end of this translation. Okada Masayuki in the introduction to his photographic reproduction of the Tōji manuscript gives the essential information on both manuscript texts.

have, therefore, come to the conclusion that the Ikeda manuscript, which most Japanese scholars have treated as though it were an entirely independent transmission of the diary, is merely a slightly emended copy of either the Tōji manuscript itself or at least of an almost identical manuscript which has since been lost.

The first printing of Ennin's diary was in the *Zoku zoku gunsho ruijū* 續續群書類從 (Tōkyō, 1907) 12.165-258 (abbreviated hereafter as *ZZGR*). This printing was based on the traced copy of the Tōji manuscript in the possession of the Office of Historical Compilation (Shiryō Hensan Jo 史料編纂所) at Tōkyō University. It is a pioneering effort at deciphering a difficult manuscript and consequently contains many erroneous interpretations of characters and several blank spots. However, its variant readings are still of use on doubtful points as are also its punctuation and its analysis of the grammatical structure of the text through the addition of *kaeriten* 返り點 markings, indicating the sequence in which the Chinese characters should be read in translating the text into Japanese.

The second printing was made in 1914 in a supplement to the now defunct publication, *Shimei yoka* 四明餘霞. This edition, which I have never seen, is said to be based on the Ikeda text with corrections from the *ZZGR* edition.

The third printing is in the great collection of Buddhist works, the *Dainihon Bukkyō zensho* 大日本佛教全書 (Tōkyō, 1918) 113.169-282 (abbreviated hereafter as *DBZ*). This edition is based on the Tōji manuscript, but it has corrections from the Ikeda text as printed in the *Shimei yoka* edition. This text is also punctuated and provided with *kaeriten* markings.

The fourth printing is in the *Kokuyaku issai kyō* 國譯一切經 (Tōkyō, 1935) A24.1-154 (abbreviated hereafter as *KIK*). This edition is presented as a translation into Japanese, but it is a translation in only a very limited sense. It is apparently based on the printed text in *DBZ*, for it contains virtually all of the misinterpretations and accidental misprints found in that edition. Moreover, it simply presents the original Chinese characters in the order called for by the

kaeriten markings in *DBZ*, filling out, in the Japanese phonetic script, the necessary Japanese grammatical elements,
such as verbal endings and postpositions. This, of course,
leaves all the actual words of the original text in exactly the
same character form they had before, even though many of
these ninth-century Chinese words convey little or no meaning to the modern Japanese. Often enough the really difficult
passages are just strings of characters printed in the original
Chinese order. The two editors of this text, Kubota Ryōen
久保田量遠 and Hori Ichirō 堀一郎, however, have added
quite a few helpful notes.[3]

The present translation has been based primarily on the
photographic reproduction of the Tōji manuscript and the
printed edition in *DBZ*. My first draft of the translation was
made from the latter text with reference on all dubious
points to the reproduction of the manuscript and to the
printed texts in *ZZGR* and *KIK*. The whole translation was
then checked word by word against the reproduction of the
Tōji manuscript. Textual notes have been limited for the
most part to suggested corrections of the Tōji manuscript,
errors in characters (but not in punctuation or *kaeriten*
markings) in the *DBZ* text, variant interpretations of
dubious characters in the three printed texts consulted, and
significant differences in characters between the Tōji and
Ikeda manuscripts as noted in *DBZ*.

---

[3] Arthur Waley devotes pages 138-159 of *The Real Tripitaka and
Other Pieces* (Allen and Unwin, London, 1952) to a discussion
of Ennin and the translation of a few scattered passages from his
diary. There is a translation into Japanese with copious foot-
notes of about one-eighth of the diary, dealing with Ennin's
pilgrimage to the Buddhist center of Mt. Wu-t'ai, in the volume
entitled *Godaisan* 五臺山 (Tōkyō, 1942; pp. 289-339) by Ono
Katsutoshi 小野勝年 and Hibino Takeo 日比野丈夫. Okada
Masayuki in a series of articles entitled "Jikaku Daishi no nittō
kikō ni tsuite" 慈覺大師の入唐記行に就いて in the journal
Tōyō gakuhō 東洋學報 (11.461-486, 12.147-186, 273-295, 13.1-
28) has published detailed studies of some of the more histori-
cally important parts of the text, which were extremely helpful
to me in making this translation.

Ennin's diary as it now exists is a long work of about seventy thousand characters, which, because of the conciseness of the Chinese language, is the equivalent of an English text of about a hundred thousand words. The diary is divided into four booklets or scrolls, as they are called in Chinese. Of these the second is slightly longer and the fourth considerably shorter than the other two. While the greater part of the text is in day-by-day diary form, there were long periods during the latter part of Ennin's stay in China when he allowed his diary to lapse and only jotted down an occasional entry or summarized the major happenings of a period of several months in one long entry.

The language of the diary is classical Chinese with a liberal admixture of ninth-century colloquialisms, which are of considerable interest to the student of the development of the modern vernacular. However, one cannot place full reliance on Ennin's use of the colloquial, for Chinese was a foreign tongue to him and many of the linguistic peculiarities of the text are no doubt the result of his own imperfect command of the language. The diary also contains many verbatim texts of documents, which are rare examples of the curious " officialese " of the petty bureaucrats of the time.

Textual inaccuracies in Ennin's diary as it exists today offer far more serious problems than the somewhat mixed style of the original. The shaky and abbreviated calligraphy of Ken'in, the copyist of the Tōji manuscript, raises many doubts about the correct interpretation of individual characters, and the inevitable wormholes in a manuscript of this age have partially obliterated other characters. Still more troublesome are the many obvious textual corruptions. Either Ken'in or some earlier copyist of the text must have transcribed it without a full understanding of what he was writing, for there are numerous characters that are obvious errors for others which they closely resemble. Moreover, what little paragraphing the Tōji manuscript has, usually in connection with inserted documents, has been made with little discrimination. There are also several sections in the first two scrolls where the text is out of order, although these places are usually quite obvious because of the date nota-

tions. More perplexing than misplacements are missing
sections. There seems to be a lacuna near the beginning of
the diary which seriously confuses the story of Ennin's
original landing in China, and I suspect that there are a
few other similar lacunae which are all the more misleading
because they are not so obvious.

Another corruption of the text is the overlapping of the
final part of the second scroll and the first part of the third.
These two sections present somewhat variant versions of
the diary for an eighteen-day period, indicating clearly that
at least parts of the text once existed in more than one form.
I have concluded from this fact that at least certain sections
of the diary, as we now have it, may not be the original
document compiled from day to day by Ennin while in
China, but an edited form of his diary, perhaps as stylistic-
ally revised by himself after his return to Japan.

This conclusion is also suggested by the fairly consistent
stylistic level of the work. It is clear from the diary that
Ennin when he first went to China, while well versed in
written Chinese, did not speak the vernacular at all. However, he seems to have learned spoken Chinese and probably
improved his command of the written language as well
during his nine years in China. One would expect, therefore,
that if the diary had never been revised, colloquialisms
would be lacking in the early part and would become pro-
gressively more frequent as Ennin picked up the vernacular.
This, however, is not the case. While I feel that the early
pages are somewhat more clumsily written than the rest of
the text, the combination of classical and colloquial Chinese
that Ennin employs remains fairly consistent throughout
the diary. This suggests that at least the early parts of the
diary were revised in style at some later date.

The possibility that the diary was rewritten to some extent
by Ennin after his return to Japan and the certainty that
many errors have crept into the text because of faulty
transmission, make the document somewhat less reliable as
a historical source than if we had Ennin's original text as he
first wrote it down in China, but the loss in reliability is
actually very slight. Whatever the revision made by the

author and the errors introduced by others, the document as a whole remains unquestionably a real diary and the vast bulk of its contents rings true. When Ennin quotes hearsay the text is full of inaccuracies, but when he records what he himself did or saw there is an extremely high degree of accuracy in details of a sort that could not have been remembered for long by the author or supplied at some later date except from the best of modern reference libraries. There are hundreds of names of obscure places, distances between obscure points, titles of obscure officials, and the like, which are verifiable by the modern scholar and which attest the extraordinary degree of factual accuracy of the text, despite all its obvious errors of transmission. Even these errors help to confirm the reliability of the text, for in almost every case they are quite understandable and identifiable miscopyings of what must have been the original, and in no case do they suggest subsequent tampering with the facts of the diary by either the author or later copyists.

I feel certain that anyone who reads Ennin's diary, even in this translated form, will be struck by the high degree of reliability of the text remaining to us. I must warn the reader, however, that, while I have cleared up many textual errors in the Chinese text of the diary, many other inaccuracies have unquestionably been introduced in the process of converting Chinese characters into English words. I have, of course, done my best to make the translation as exact and accurate as possible, but I am fully aware that it must contain numerous errors and inconsistencies, some of which may be more obvious in this final printed form than they were in the successive manuscripts with which I worked.

One problem, common to all translations from Chinese into a Western language, is the necessity of making the translation more specific at points than the original. For instance, number and tense are commonly not specified in Chinese, but an English sentence must always be precise on these points. Another problem common to all premodern Chinese texts is that there is no punctuation or any division between phrases and sentences or, for that matter, any indications of which groupings of characters form names or polysyllabic

words and which do not. Slight changes in the divisions
made between words, phrases, or sentences of the original
undivided and unpunctuated text can result in startling
differences in meaning.

In addition to these usual hazards of the translator, I
have encountered other more specialized ones in this particular work. There are, for example, many points on which
no one can be absolutely certain of the exact meaning of
the text as we have it, either because of mistakes made by
Ennin himself or because of imperfect transmission. Many
more portions of the diary require a great variety of specialized technical knowledge for thorough comprehension. The
translator of this diary ideally should have a deep understanding of such widely separated fields as Buddhist the-
ology, T'ang political administration, Korean history, Far
Eastern diplomatic relations, Shintō mythology, Chinese historical geography, ninth-century maritime navigation, and a
host of other equally complicated and sometimes esoteric
subjects. I need hardly say that my grounding in most of
these fields is far less adequate than it should be for the
burden I have shouldered. And finally, there are no doubt
many places where I have erred in my translation simply
because of the inadequacy of my command of the Chinese in
which Ennin wrote or because of the inevitable careless slips
which creep into a work of this size.

For these various reasons I am the first to urge the research scholar to verify with the original Chinese text any
point of special interest to himself which he may find in my
translation. But even for the research scholar I trust that
this translation will serve a useful purpose, first through its
index which gives a key to the vast store of detailed information in Ennin's diary and second through the notes which
may help him around some of the pitfalls which abound in
the text. The notes make no attempt to follow the many
byways into which the diary invites the reader and are
limited merely to those points which need explanation for a
more complete understanding of the original. The points
covered for the most part are the significant textual problems, the corresponding dates in the Western calendar for

the first day mentioned by Ennin in each moon of the Chinese lunar calendar, and the identification and necessary elucidation, in so far as possible, of all proper names and technical terms. For the benefit of the scholar making piece-meal use of this translation, I have repeated footnote num-bers to indicate where he can find an earlier identification of a name or term repeated later in the text. All references to the diary are by date (with the moon written in Roman numerals between the year and day), and for this reason the date has been used as the running head on each printed page.

While I hope that this translation will prove a useful tool for the research scholar, its primary value, like that of the original text itself, does not lie in the individual facts it con-tains but rather in the over-all picture it gives of life in ninth-century China. My chief purpose has been to make this unique account of T'ang China more accessible to the general scholarly world than it has been before, and I feel confident that the individual errors of my translation, though they may be misleading on details, have not seriously distorted or dimmed the clarity of this picture as a whole.

One element of confusion which unfortunately cannot be remedied is the vast number of proper names and official titles mentioned throughout the diary. I have, however, sought to make the titles somewhat less confusing for the Western reader by translating them into English, attempting where possible to indicate something of the holder's duties as well as the literal meaning of the title.[4] Japanese, Chinese, Korean, and Indian names of persons and places, though uni-formly written in Chinese characters, I have rendered accord-ing to the generally accepted transcriptions for the respective languages. A difficult problem was presented by the many Buddhist scriptures, deities, and technical terms Ennin

---

[4] I have been greatly aided in my treatment of the complex and manifold official T'ang titles of rank and office by the great two-volume work of Robert des Rotours, *Traité des fonctionnaires et traité de l'armée, traduits de la nouvelle histoire des T'ang* (*Chap. XLVI-L*), Leiden, 1947 and 1948.

mentions, for these could be rendered with almost equal validity according to the original Sanskrit, the Chinese character translations or transliterations of the Sanskrit, or the Japanese or even Korean pronunciations of the Chinese characters. Except for a few terms and texts which have well accepted English equivalents derived from the Sanskrit, I have put all these Buddhist names and terms into their Japanese forms, because it is only the Japanese religious and scholarly tradition which has kept alive the type of Buddhism which Ennin knew.

While many errors, no doubt, remain in this translation, the degree of accuracy it does achieve is in large part the result of the generous aid given me by many friends. I cannot mention all those who in one way or another contributed to this work, but I wish to take this opportunity to express my heartfelt thanks to all of them and especially to the Trustees of the Harvard-Yenching Institute for the financial support that has made this project of research and publication possible; to Professor Serge Elisséeff for his constant aid and encouragement in this work from its inception until its accomplishment; to Professor Paul Demiéville of Paris for having first suggested the subject to me; to Katsuno Ryūshin 勝野隆信, a monk of the Tendai Sect, who aided me in my first faltering attempts at translating Ennin's diary in the autumn of 1935; to Professor L. S. Yang and Mr. Achilles Fang for invaluable aid on many difficult points; to Professor Kenneth Ch'en for checking the Sanskrit names and terms in the notes; to Mrs. Susan Guttman and Mrs. Marilyn Abels for endless editorial and typing assistance; to Mrs. Achilles Fang for preparing the index; to Mr. W. A. Dwiggins and Miss Dorothy Abbe for designing the whole of this volume; and finally to my wife, whose aid from first to last has been invaluable and whose discipleship under Ennin, therefore, has been as long and almost as arduous as my own.

E. O. R.

Cambridge, January, 1955

Contents

PREFACE   vii

FIRST SCROLL   1

SECOND SCROLL   118

THIRD SCROLL   226

FOURTH SCROLL   329

CHARACTER GLOSSARY   411

INDEX   415

BIBLIOGRAPHICAL ABBREVIATIONS

USED IN THE NOTES

Adachi—Adachi Kiroku 足立喜六, *Chōan shiseki no kenkyū* 長安史蹟の研究 (*Tōyō bunko ronsō* 21), Tōkyō, 1933.

Coates and Ishizuka—Harper Havelock Coates and Ryugaku Ishizuka (translators), *Honen the Buddhist Saint, His Life and Teaching*, Kyōto, 1925.

CTS—*Chiu T'ang shu* 舊唐書.

DBZ—*Dainihon Bukkyō zensho* and specifically the edition of this diary in that collection (113.169-282).

Des Rotours—Robert des Rotours, *Traité des fonctionnaires et traité de l'armée, traduits de la nouvelle histoire des T'ang (Chap. XLVI-L)*, Leiden, 1947 and 1948.

HTS—*Hsin T'ang shu* 新唐書.

Ikeda—the Ikeda manuscript of this text.

KIK—the edition of the diary printed in the *Kokuyaku issai kyō* (A24.1-154).

Okada—Okada Masayuki, " Jikaku Daishi no nittō kikō ni tsuite," *Tōyō gakuhō* 11.461-486, 12.147-186, 273-295, 13.1-28.

Ono and Hibino—Ono Katsutoshi and Hibino Takeo, *Godaisan*, Tōkyō, 1942.

SNK—*Shoku Nihon kōki* 續日本後紀 (references by date).

TCTC—*Tzu-chih t'ung-chien* 資治通鑑.

Tōji—the Tōji manuscript of this diary.

TTLCT—*T'ang ti-li-chih t'u* 唐地理志圖 of 1911 in *Li-tai yü-ti yen-ko hsien-yao t'u* 歷代輿地沿革險要圖.

Waley—Arthur Waley, *The Real Tripitaka and Other Pieces*, London, 1952.

ZZGR—the edition of the diary printed in the *Zoku zoku gunsho ruijū* (12.165-258).

ENNIN (Jikaku Daishi)
An Idealized Portrait of the Twelfth Century

Ennin's Diary

THE RECORD OF A PILGRIMAGE TO CHINA
IN SEARCH OF THE LAW

RECORD OF

A Pilgrimage to China in Search of the Law

I

First Scroll

OF THE RECORD
OF A PILGRIMAGE TO CHINA
IN SEARCH OF THE LAW

JŌWA · FIFTH YEAR

SIXTH MOON: 13*th* DAY [1] At noon the embassy boarded the first and fourth ships, but because we did not have a
favorable wind, we waited for three days.

17*th* DAY In the middle of the night, profiting from
a stiff wind, we hoisted sail and set the ships in motion. At
10 A. M. we reached the sea east of Shiganoshima.[2] Because
we did not have reliable winds, we stopped for five days.

---

[1] July 8, 838. Jōwa 承和 is a Japanese year period. Ennin states
in a document of 840 III 2 that he boarded ship on 838 IV 13
and repeats in a document of 840 VIII 24 that it was in the
fourth moon.
[2] 志賀嶋, the tip of the peninsula which forms the landlocked
harbor of Hakata Bay 博多灣 on the north coast of Kyūshū. In

22nd DAY   At 6 A. M., profiting from a northeast wind, we set out. We did not again seek a cove, and on into the night we went in the dark.

23rd DAY   At 10 A. M. we reached Ukushima.[3] A northeast wind was blowing. Those going and those staying behind took farewell of one another. At 6 P. M. we hoisted sail and set out across the sea. The northeast wind was blowing, and on into the night we went in the dark. The two ships were in contact with each other by fire signals.

24th DAY   We saw at a distance the fourth ship going ahead of us, separated from the first ship by about thirty *li* [4] and going far to the west. The Ambassador [5] for the first time made a drawing of the Bodhisattva Kannon,[6] and the

---

ancient times this was the most important port in western Japan, being close to the great administrative center of Dazaifu 太宰府 a few miles to the south, and it still retains its importance as the harbor for the modern city of Fukuoka 福岡. Since a ten-hour run with a stiff breeze brought them to this point, they must have started some distance to the east and possibly as far away as the Shimonoseki 下關 area.

[3] 有救嶋, now written 宇久, at the northern end of the Gotō 五島 Archipelago off the northwest coast of Kyūshū and about 120 km. southwest of the mouth of Hakata Bay.

[4] The traditional Chinese *li* 里 is usually considered to be a little over a third of a mile (about 600 meters). Ennin invariably gives his longer distances in terms of *li*. As is all too common, he tended to overestimate distances with the result that, in the cases in which his estimates can be checked, his *li* averaged around 500 meters. As he himself writes on IX 13, " the people's [use of the] word *li* is not consistent." The Japanese *ri*, written with the same character, is 2.44 miles or 3.93 km., but Ennin never uses this term.

[5] *Taishi* 大使. This was Fujiwara no Tsunetsugu 藤原常嗣 (796-840), who was known for his knowledge of Chinese literature, which Waley (p. 138) assumes was in part the reason for his appointment as Ambassador.

[6] 觀音 (Ch. Kuan-yin; Skr. Avalokiteśvara), one of the most popular deities of Far Eastern Buddhism. A Bodhisattva (J. Bosatsu 菩薩, commonly abbreviated 井) is a Buddhist deity

Scholar and Student Monks [7] together read scriptures and prayed. At 10 P. M. [the ships] were in contact by fire signals, which were like stars in appearance, but when dawn came [the fourth ship] was not to be seen. Although there had been a shift of the wind from the northeast to the southeast, we were not afraid of drifting from the course. Great bamboos,

---

who, though ready for Buddhahood, has postponed entry into Nirvana in order to help his fellow creatures achieve salvation. Ennin sometimes writes Kanze 觀世 (short for Kanzeon) in place of Kannon. The drawing of this picture of a Buddhist deity presumably was a pious act meant to aid them in the crossing.
[7] *Shōyaku Ryūgaku Hosshi* 請益留學法師. *Hosshi* (Ch. *Fa-shih*) is a term of respect for a monk, which I have translated in titles as "Ecclesiastic." Among the members of Japanese embassies to China were long-term student monks called *Ryū-gaku-sō* 僧 and, ranking above them, short-term student monks usually called *Gengaku-sō* 還學僧 (also pronounced *Kangaku-sō*). The former I have translated "Student Monk," but Ennin uses the term *Shōyaku-sō* (also pronounced *Shin'eki*, etc.) in place of the latter, and this I have rendered "Scholar Monk." By this term he usually means himself, while the term "Student Monk" he usually uses for Ensai 圓載, who like Ennin was a monk of the great Tendai 天台 Sect and was his constant companion during the early part of the trip.

Ensai figures prominently in the *Gyōryakushō* 行歷抄 (*DBZ* 113.286-295), a fragmentary account by the monk Enchin 圓珍 (814-891) of his travels in China between 853 and 858. Enchin later became a successor of Ennin as Abbot of the Enryakuji 延曆寺 on Mt. Hiei 比叡山 near Kyōto, the central monastery of the Japanese Tendai Sect. He also was a founder of a rival branch of the sect to that of Ennin. Not only did Enchin see a great deal of Ensai while in China, but he was repeatedly annoyed and inconvenienced by the latter's unfriendliness, suspicion, troublemaking, duplicity, and open flouting of the rules of his religion. Ensai, at an advanced age, finally attempted to return to Japan in 877 but was lost on the way together with all the scriptures and secular works he had collected. Waley (pp. 159-168) has a rather detailed account of Ensai's relations with Enchin, as recorded in the *Gyōryakushō*. Cf. also Ono and Hibino 296.

roots of reeds, cuttlefish,[8] and the like drifted along with the billows. Dropping hooks, we caught and inspected them. Some were living; others were withered. The color of the sea was light green. The men all said that we were close to land. At 4 P. M. large fish followed the ship, disporting themselves.

27th DAY   The " flat irons " [9] were struck by a wave and all fell off. Exhausted [egrets][10] settled down [on the ship] for the night and did not leave. Two or three would fly off to the west and then again return and perch. They did this several times. The sea is whitish green. All night men were ordered to mount the mast to look for mountains or islands, and they would always [10a] call out that they saw none.

28th DAY   Early in the morning the egrets flew off in pairs toward the northwest. Since the wind was still unchanged, we trimmed sail and headed southwest. At 10 A. M. we reached whitish water, the color of which was like yellow mud. The men all said that this perhaps was water flowing from the Great River of Yang-chou.[11] They had a man

---

[8] *Wu-tsei-pei* 烏賊貝, probably standing for *wu-tsei-yü* 魚.

[9] 平鐵. These may have been pieces of iron used as reinforcements on the sides of the ship or else an error for 平金 (or 扁鉦), read *hiragane* in Japanese and meaning " gongs," that is, the ship's bells. The absence of records for the twenty-fifth and twenty-sixth indicates a possible lacuna in the text at this point.

[10] Obviously some words have also been lost from the text at this point, which comes at the start of a new page in *Tōji*, but the egrets mentioned the next day must be meant.

[10a] *DBZ* and *KIK* omit 悉.

[11] 揚州, the modern Chiang-tu 江都, which in T'ang times was one of the two subprefectures into which the city was divided. Yang-chou is located on the Grand Canal about twelve km. north of the Yangtse 揚子 River and about 240 km. from the river's present mouth. At the time it was the greatest city in the lower Yangtse valley and the capital of Huai-nan-tao 淮南道, the province lying north of the lower reaches of the Yangtse River. It was, therefore, quite natural for the Yangtse itself to have been known as the " Great River of Yang-chou," though it is called by its modern name on 839 IV 2.

mount the mast to see, and he reported that [the whitish water] flowed from the northwest [12] directly toward the south and that its width was over twenty *li* but that when one looked far along the way ahead the water again became light green. After we had proceeded for a short time, it turned out just as he had said. The Ambassador was greatly surprised that the color of the sea again became light green. The Korean Interpreter,[13] Kim Chŏngnam 金正南, stated that he had heard it said [14] that it was difficult to pass through the dug channel of Yang-chou [15] and that, since we had already passed the whitish water, he suspected that we may have passed by the dug channel.

At 2 P. M. the water was again whitish, and the men were all amazed. A man was ordered to mount the mast to look for the mainland or islands, but he still called out that he saw nothing. The wind blew steadily. The sea was shallow and the waves high, and they crashed down like thunder. A piece of iron tied to a rope was submerged, and it only went down fifty feet. After a little while the iron was [again]

---

[12] 戊亥, as printed in *DBZ* and *KIK*, should be 戌亥.

[13] *Shiragi Osa* 新羅譯語. Silla, which the Japanese pronounce Shiragi, at the time comprised the greater part of the Korean Peninsula, and I have translated it throughout as "Korea." Korean Interpreters, who apparently knew both Chinese and Japanese, were of great importance to the Japanese embassies.

[14] 導 is an error for 導, which appears in comparable phrases later in the text.

[15] By the "dug channel" (*chüeh-chiang* 掘港) Ennin means the waterway which he tells us on VII 18 was dug by the Sui Emperor Yang-ti 隋煬帝 (605-617) and on which he subsequently traveled to Yang-chou by way of Ju-kao-chen 如皋鎮 (the modern Ju-kao-hsien, about 105 km. due east of Yang-chou and 35 km. north of the Yangtse) and Hai-ling-hsien 海陵縣 (the modern T'ai-hsien 泰, about 45 km. east and a little north of Yang-chou). A waterway is still to be found connecting these towns, continuing on to Chüeh-chiang-chen (about 65 km. east of Ju-kao-hsien), in which the ancient name of this waterway appears to have been preserved. See note 45.

lowered to measure the ocean's depth. It was only five fathoms.[16] The envoys were afraid. Some said that we should drop anchor and stop, going on again tomorrow. Others said that we should lower sail halfway and send out boats to learn the depth of the way ahead and only then gradually advance. The proposal to stop seemed inadvisable.

Before we had decided the problem it was already 7 P. M., and the east wind was blowing fiercely, and the waves were raging high. The ship was suddenly dashed up onto a shoal. In trepidation we immediately lowered sail, but the corners of the rudder [17] snapped in two places, while the waves from both east and west battered the ship and rolled it [back and forth]. Since the blade of the rudder was stuck in the ocean floor, and the ship was about to break up, we cut down the mast and cast away the rudder. The ship straightway floated with the waves. When the waves came from the east, the ship leaned over to the west, and when they came from the west, it inclined to the east. They washed over the ship [to a number] beyond count. All on board put their faith in the Buddha and in the [Shintō] deities, and there was none but did pray. The men were desperate, and all from the head of the mission down to the sailors stripped and bound their loin cloths fast about them. Since the ship was about to break in the middle, we rushed to stern and bow, and each of us looked for a place that remained intact. Because of the shock of the waves the structural joints [of the ship] were all pulling apart, so they fastened ropes to the right and left railings and pulled them together, striving to find a way to survive. Bilge water filled [the ship], which thereupon settled onto the sand bottom, and the official and private goods [in the hold] washed about in the bilge water.

29th DAY   At dawn the tide went out, and consequently the bilge water also dried out. They had men inspect the bottom [of the ship]. It was completely smashed, and

---

[16] *Hsün* 尋, defined as eight feet.

[17] 柂角, perhaps meaning " tiller," although part of the rudder itself would be more apt to break under these circumstances.

the . . .[18] was covered with sand. The group made plans. Now that the ship was already wrecked, if it again encountered the rise of the tide, we feared that it might be further broken up. We therefore took down the mast and cut down the left and right bow planking [19] and erected poles at the four corners of the ship and bound together . . . .[18]

[A section of the original text apparently has been lost somewhere near this point, but some of its contents can be reconstructed from later references to these days. It probably stated that it was decided that the Ambassador and an accompanying group of officers and men should attempt to reach shore in one or more of the lifeboats. Accordingly, the Ambassador and his group left at 2 P.M. on the twenty-ninth. When those left on board received no word of the Ambassador and his party, they seem to have become worried and sent out a second but probably much smaller expedition, including the archer, Mibu no Kaisan 壬生開山, which set out on the 1st DAY of the SEVENTH MOON [20] to seek aid. The text apparently continues that evening with the story of the thirty-odd men left on board the ship.]

At 10 P.M. far to the west we saw the light of a fire. The men faced toward it, and there was none but did rejoice. Throughout the night we gazed at it. We saw no mountains or islands, but only the light of the fire.

---

[18] 栖辱栈, a term repeated a few lines later. The first character is read *nou* and means " a hoe." Obviously the term refers to some part of the hull of the ship, but it is either a copyist's error or a technical term no longer understood. *DBZ* suggests that the characters might stand for 栿伏.

[19] Literally " sheds " (J. " shelves ") 棚, but some sort of superstructure is clearly meant. See VIII 8.

[20] July 25, 838. There were only twenty-nine days in the preceding moon. The lack of the words " seventh moon " and the absence of any account of the first day, despite the perilous situation, are the clearest proof that part of the text is missing.

2nd DAY   Early in the morning the tide rose, and we
were carried off some several hundred *chō*.[21] To the west we
saw islands which looked like two ships side by side. After
advancing for a short time we knew it to be the mainland.
Before we had floated very long, we encountered a whirlpool
[caused by] two currents, and we floated sideways for over
fifty *chō*. [Then] the ship sank and settled in the mud, and
we could not advance or withdraw. The current, which was
strong and swift, then dug out the mud at the side of the
ship, and the mud boiled up. The ship eventually fell over
and was about to be submerged. The men were terrified and
struggled to climb onto the side of the vessel. All bound their
loin cloths about them and tied themselves with ropes here
and there [to the ship]. Tied thus in place, we awaited death.
Before long the boat again fell over, [this time] to the left,
and the men consequently shifted to the right side [of the
ship]. When [the ship] would fall over, we would change
place, and in time [these shifts] mounted up in number.
Furthermore, the second covering [22] on the ship's bottom
broke up and floated away. The men lost heart and wept
and made vows.

   In the northwest we saw at a distance something floating
along with the waves. The men all said that it perhaps was a
boat come to meet us. While we were speculating, it came
on towards us against the wind, and at last we knew that
it was a boat. We saw [it to be] a " small store ship " 小倉船
with men on board. The archer, Mibu no Kaisan, who had
been sent out the day before, and six Chinese rushed up to
the front of the boat. Then,[23] the Secretary [24] and his sub-

----

[21] 町, a distance of 119 yards (109 meters) in modern Japan.
On 840 V 20 we find the flat summit of a mountain described as
about a *li* and a half in radius and something over 100 *chō* in
circumference. This would indicate a distance of more like 50 or
60 yards for a *chō*, but Ennin's statistics are not to be taken that
literally.
[22] 第二布材, possibly part of the repair work of the twenty-ninth.
[23] *DBZ* and *KIK* have 爭 misprinted for 爰.
[24] *Rokuji* 錄事, of which there were several on the embassy, were

ordinates asked first of all where the Ambassador had landed, but [the archer] replied that he did not yet know where he had landed. On hearing this, we were distressed and found it hard to suppress our tears.

We straightway drew up to the boat and moved the national tribute articles [25] to it. The Secretary, the two Ship's Masters,[26] the Monks of Learning,[27] Ensai and others, and twenty-seven subordinates [28] also transshipped to it and set out for shore. At noon we reached the mouth of a river, and at 2 P. M. we arrived at Tung-liang-feng-ts'un 東梁豊村 in Sang-t'ien-hsiang 桑田鄉 in Pai-ch'ao-chen 白潮鎮 in Hai-ling-hsien in Yang-chou.[29] The second day of the seventh moon of the fifth year of Jōwa in Japan turned out to be the

---

the fourth-ranking category of officers. This particular Secretary we learn later was Yamashiro no Ujimasu 山代氏益, and he apparently had been left in charge of the ship.

[25] From the various references to 國信, 國信物, or 信物 in this text and the trading functions of the officer in charge of them (see note 351), it would seem that these were terms for articles brought ostensibly as tribute, but which included goods intended for sale. In time it became the standard practice for tributary embassies to bring " supplementary " goods for sale on the open market. The term has been interpreted in the Japanese histories as *kuni tsu mono*, " national products."

[26] *Chijōsenji* 知乘船事, abbreviated below to *Chijō*, who, according to Wada Hidematsu 和田英松, *Shūtei kanshoku yōkai* 修訂官職要解 (Tōkyō, 1929) 172, ranked next to the Secretaries.

[27] *Gakumon-sō* 學問僧, a term which Ennin uses for both *Shō-yaku-sō* and *Ryūgaku-sō* (see note 7) and, therefore, for himself and Ensai together.

[28] The whole party is described as " over thirty " on VII 3.

[29] *Chou* 州, or prefectures, were divided into *hsien* 縣 (as in Hai-ling-hsien), or subprefectures, which in turn were subdivided into *hsiang* 鄉 (as in Sang-t'ien-hsiang), or cantons. The sub-divisions of cantons were villages, for which *ts'un* 村 (as in Tung-liang-feng-ts'un) was a common name in some parts of China. A *chen* 鎮 (as in Pai-ch'ao-chen) was a frontier garrison (cf. Des Rotours 785-86), but came to be simply a common final element in local place names in some parts of China.

second day of the seventh moon of the third year of K'ai-ch'eng 開成 in China. Although the year periods were different, the moon and the day were the same. The Student Monk and others went to the house of Chi Pin 季賓, a soldier of the military detachment,[30] and lodged there.

We heard that, while the Ambassador's [boat] was floating along after leaving the ship on the twenty-ninth of the sixth moon at 2 P. M., the wind was strong, and the waves were fierce, and they feared that the boat was about to sink, so they threw away the anchor and cast out the goods. With their mouths they called upon Kannon [6] and Myōken,[31] and with their minds they sought for a way to survive. The wild wind then subsided, and at midnight they floated to the edge of a reed-covered plain south of the mouth of a great river.

At dawn on the 1st DAY of the SEVENTH MOON the tide went out, and they could not go on. They had a man climb to the top of the mast to look for mountains or hamlets. Far to the south there were three mountains, whose names they did not yet know. The villages were far off, and there was no one with whom to talk. If they waited until the tide rose, they feared that it would be too long, and night would have fallen, and they would be unable to save the boat and refloat it. Accordingly, they tied ropes to the boat and dragged it out seawards, but, since the men were extremely few in number, they could not budge it. [All] from the Administrative Officers [32] on down seized the hawsers and pulled on them. At 2 P. M. they refloated the skiff and proceeded along [33] the seacoast. They kept looking for a river mouth and at last came upon the mouth of a great river. The opposing current flowed swiftly, and they could not

---

[30] Military detachments (*shou-cho* 守捉) also were one of the categories of border guard units. Cf. Des Rotours 785.

[31] 妙見 (Skr. Sudarśana), another Bodhisattva.

[32] *Hangan* (also pronounced *Hōgan*) 判官 was a general term for the third-ranking category of officers in various administrative posts in Japan as well as in an embassy to China.

[33] *DBZ* suggests 從 for 徒.

move forward, but, since the river was rather shallow, they had the sailors get out and pull the boat along.

They looked for people and had difficulty finding any, but by chance they met with some reed-sellers [34] and straightway questioned them about the region. They replied that this was the mouth of the Great River in Huai-nan-chen [35] in Hai-ling-hsien in Yang-chou in China. They then told two of the merchants to board their boat and headed for Huai-nan-chen. They had gone halfway, following a waterway, [when it developed that] the two men did not know [the whereabouts of] the garrison offices, so they again returned to the mouth of the river. Since it was late in the day, they spent the night at the mouth of the river.

2nd DAY   The [previous] evening the two men had gone home. Near at hand there was a salt bureau,[36] and when they dispatched the Administrative Officer, Nagamine no Sukune Takana 長岑宿禰高名, and the Acting Secretary,[37] Takaoka no Sukune Momooki 高丘宿禰百興, with orders to proceed to the garrison offices and sent with them a docu-

---

[34] Presumably men gathering reeds in the marshes in order to sell them later.

[35] Huai-nan-chen is an alternate name for the command of the *Chieh-tu-shih* 節度使 (or Regional Commander) of Huai-nan, who had military control over the greater part of Huai-nan-tao (see note 11) with his capital at Yang-chou. (For Regional Commanders cf. Des Rotours 656 ff.) Hai-ling-hsien of course was in Huai-nan-chen and not the reverse. Probably the Japanese at this point were confused, supposing that some small local military post under the control of Huai-nan-chen had that name itself. The " great river " referred to may have been the Yangtse, but it may also have been one of the many lesser rivers in the region. To a Japanese any Chinese river would probably seem " great."

[36] *Yen-kuan* 鹽官. This part of the Chinese coast has always been a salt-producing region.

[37] *Jun-rokuji* 准錄事, which might be more accurately translated " of the provisional rank of a Secretary."

ment, the Administrative Officer[38] of the salt bureau, Yüan Hsing-ts'un 元行存, came at once by a small boat to inquire after them. The envoys conversed by brush[39] with him about the customs of the land, and the Ambassador presented him with Japanese products.

They again started off for Huai-nan-chen and reached the garrison offices[40] after proceeding northward from the river's mouth some fifteen *li*, but the garrison soldiers told them they should turn back again toward a station on the dug channel,[41] so, taking two garrison soldiers with them, they returned to the mouth of the river. Just before they reached the mouth of the river, [they saw] the Administrative Officer [of the salt bureau], Yüan Hsing-ts'un, beside the waterway, and he told them to spend the night there, because it was already late in the day. They followed his suggestion and stopped, and he inquired after them with special concern and also gave them a guide.

3rd DAY At 2 A. M. the tide rose, and, with the guide boat leading the way, they headed toward the station on the dug channel.[41] At 10 A. M. they reached the mouth of the Pai-hu.[42] The opposing current was extremely swift, but the

---

[38] Des Rotours 310, 658-669, 890, etc., cites several cases in which the title *P'an-kuan* 判官 (see note 32) was used for military and civilian officers in the capital and provinces, but Ennin uses the term for several other officials, indicating that at this time it may have been a title used quite widely, if not always accurately, for various local officials. On 840 III 4 and 5 we find that Administrative Officers ranked above Secretaries (see note 696) as they did in the Japanese system (see notes 24 and 32).

[39] Meaning, of course, " in writing." *KIK* follows *Ikeda* in correcting 筆上 to 筆言.

[40] *Tōji* has 字 (*DBZ* and *KIK* read 孚) in place of 家. See also note 35.

[41] The character, which is produced in different ways in the printed texts, may be a variant for an abbreviation of *ti* 遞 and perhaps should be regarded simply as part of a place name, Chüeh-chiang-ti.

[42] 白湖, meaning " White Lake." Since Pai-hu and Pai-ch'ao,

three Chinese together with the Japanese sailors pulled the boats across the current, and when they reached the [opposite] bank, they tied [the boats] up and waited for a while for the tide to rise. At this point they heard that the fourth ship had floated across the North Sea.[43] At noon, scarcely had they reached the village of the soldiers of the military detachment,[44] under the jurisdiction of Pai-ch'ao-chen in Hai-ling-hsien, when the Secretary, Yamashiro no Ujimasu,[24] and others, [in all] over thirty men, from whom they had previously parted on the sea, came out to meet them. Once more we saw each other. Sorrow and joy were crowded together, and with flowing tears we told our stories. Then, all together, we lodged there.

We hired small boats to transport the national tribute articles,[25] and we also washed and dried in the sun the articles, official and private, which had been damaged by the water. Although we spent several days there, we still had no solicitous messages from the prefecture or subprefecture. The men all looked around for convenient lodgings, encountering no little difficulty. The Scholar Monk lodged in the same place with the Student Monk. Eighteen *li* from Tung-liang-feng-ts'un was Yen-hai-ts'un 延海, and in this village there was a monastery called the Kuo-ch'ing-ssu.[45] The Ambassador and others lodged there in order to recuperate from the fatigue of the voyage.

---

which occurs as a place name above and again below, are graphically very similar, one or the other is probably a copyist's error. In a document of 840 VIII 24 we find Pai-hu-chen given as the place where Ennin first landed, instead of Pai-ch'ao-chen, as stated above.

[43] Pei-hai 北海 was usually used for the Gulf of Pohai (Chihli), but here it is obviously being used more loosely for the whole Yellow Sea, for we learn on VIII 17 and 21 that men from the fourth ship were at Ju-kao-chen and Chüeh-chiang-chen (see note 15), indicating that they too had landed not far north of the mouth of the Yangtse.

[44] Meaning Tung-liang-feng-ts'un. See note 30.

[45] 國清寺, probably the monastery of this name founded during

9th DAY   At 10 A. M. a Commissioner [46] from Hai-ling-chen,[47] Liu Mien,[48] came and inquired after the envoys. He presented them with wine and cakes and also organized music [for them]. In attendance were eight government soldiers [49] and personal attendants. This Liu Mien wore purple court clothes, and the village Guard Captain [50] likewise wore purple clothes. After completing their tour of inspection, they returned to the subprefectural offices.

12th DAY   They transported [my] baggage by the waterways from Tung-liang-feng-ts'un and placed it in the monastery.[51] At noon on the same day they sent the Interpreter,[52] Ōyake no Toshio 大宅年雄, and the archer, Ōyake no Miyatsugu 宮繼, by the waterways to the subprefectural offices to hasten on the boats coming to meet us. At 4 P. M. it thundered. The Student Monk and some others are staying in Tung-[liang]-feng-ts'un and have not yet come here.

---

the Yüan-ho 元和 period (806-820) at Chüeh-chiang-ying 營, in the Chüeh-chiang-chen area (see note 15). Cf. *Ju-kao-hsien chih* 如皋縣志 (1808) 3.100a and 2.38a. See also note 93.

[46] *Ta-shih* 大使 (the same characters as for Ambassador) is used throughout this text as a title for a chief representative of some higher authority or for an officer who has been delegated supreme local authority.

[47] Ennin probably means Ju-kao-chen rather than Hai-ling-hsien (see note 15), for on VII 20 and 21, where he calls the man "the Garrison Commissioner," he clearly indicates that he was stationed at Ju-kao-chen.

[48] 劉勉. Throughout most of *Tōji* the copyist's usual writing of the common surname Liu has resulted in the printing of 劉 in *DBZ, KIK,* and *ZZGR*. In the last part of the fourth scroll, however, 劉 appears several times in a name apparently written 劉 before.

[49] *Kuan-chien* 官健. Cf. Des Rotours 672 and see note 1322.

[50] *Ya-kuan* 押官. Cf. Des Rotours 741.

[51] Meaning that he himself moved to the Kuo-ch'ing-ssu. See note 45.

[52] *Osa*, written 通事, is normally used in this text for the Japanese as opposed to the Korean Interpreters (see note 13), although on 839 VI 9 it is used for one of the latter.

13*th* DAY It was very hot. At 2 P. M. it thundered. Ever since we first floated ashore, the mosquitoes [53] have been very numerous. They are as large as flies. When night comes, they torment the men, who suffer limitlessly. At 4 P. M. the Student Monk came and stayed with us in the monastery. He was suffering from dysentery.

14*th* DAY At 8 A. M., because the boats coming to meet us from the subprefecture and prefecture had not come, the Ambassador, two Administrative Officers,[32] one Secretary,[24] one Ship's Master,[26] one Scribe,[54] and some archers and sailors, in all thirty men, started for the subprefectural offices by the waterways.

Just then the monk Yüan-yü 元昱 of the K'ai-yüan-ssu [55] came and communicated with us by brush. He was well versed in composition. We asked him about the national customs and also gave him Japanese products. The monk gave us peaches and the like. His cloister [56] is close beside

[53] 蚊 and a second character which may be 蚋, but is printed 蛳 by *DBZ* and *KIK* and 虻 by *ZZGR*.

[54] *Shijo* 史生, later sometimes abbreviated to 史.

[55] A K'ai-yüan-ssu 開元 was ordered to be established in each prefecture by the Emperor Hsüan-tsung 玄宗 in 738, the twenty-sixth year of K'ai-yüan. Many of these were merely older monasteries renamed and given special government status at this time. We learn later that there was a K'ai-yüan-ssu at Yang-chou, from which Yüan-yü may have come. The *Ch'ung-hsiu Yang-chou-fu chih* 重修揚州府志 (1810) 28.3a-b says that the K'ai-yüan-ssu of Yang-chou was built in the T'ang period and was located fifty *li* east of the city before it was moved in 1661. This same work 28.26b also mentions a K'ai-yüan-ssu on the shores of Lake Pai-mao 白茆湖, forty-five *li* northeast of Yang-chou (cf. *ibid*. 8.14a-b), stating that this is said to be the K'ai-yüan-ssu mentioned in T'ang poetry. The book refers to still another K'ai-yüan-ssu in Chiang-tu-hsien (see note 11). In any case the many notices given the K'ai-yüan-ssu in our text indicate that it was either in the city of Yang-chou or else very close to it (see 838 IX 13).

[56] *Yüan* 院, originally meaning "courtyard," is a term for a small monastery or a subdivision of a larger one.

the monastery. After conversing a short while, he returned home.

At sunset it thundered, and we had a heavy rain. We felt all the more depressed.

17*th* DAY   At noon the archer, Ōyake no Miyatsugu, the Guard Captain,⁵⁰ and others, [in all] over ten persons, came from the offices of Ju-kao-chen, bringing over thirty " grass-boats." ⁵⁷ We then heard that the Ambassador had arrived the day before at the [Ju-kao]-chen offices. At 4 P. M. the Ship's Master, Haru[michi],⁵⁸ and the Secretary, Yama[shiro], and some archers came from Tung-liang-feng-ts'un and stayed in the monastery.

18*th* DAY   Early in the morning they moved the official and private property on board the craft.⁵⁹ At 10 A. M. all of us, from the Secretary down to the sailors, started for the prefectural [capital] by water. Two water buffalo were tied to over forty boats, with either two or three of the latter joined to form a single craft and with these connected in a line by hawsers. Since it was difficult to hear from the front to the rear [of the train of boats], there was much shouting back and forth. Our progress was rather swift. The dug canal ⁶⁰ is over twenty feet wide and is straight, without bends. It was dug by Yang-ti of the Sui [dynasty]. We suffered in the rain. After floating along for over thirty *li*, we arrived at Kuo-pu-ts'un 郭補 at 4 P. M. and stopped for the night. When night came, there were many mosquitoes, which hurt like needle pricks, and we were much bothered. All night drums were beaten. It is the custom of this land to

---

⁵⁷ 草船, possibly meaning small boats used by reed-gatherers. See note 34.

⁵⁸ On 839 II 20 we hear of a Harumichi no Sukune Nagakura 春道宿禰永藏, who, although given a different title at one point, appears to be the Ship's Master referred to later on the same day. Moreover, in *SNK* 839 VIII 25 he is called a Ship's Master.

⁵⁹ *Fang-ch'uan* 舫船, a term for two or more boats bound together to form a single craft. See Ennin's description below.

⁶⁰ Here *chüeh-kou* 掘溝 instead of *chüeh-chiang*. See note 15.

have watchmen who, when night comes, beat drums in order to guard government [61] property.

19*th* DAY   At 4 A. M. we started off with the water buffalo pulling in front. It was dark and cloudy, but it did not rain. At 6 A. M. we heard cocks crowing. For the first time we encountered groves of black bamboo [62] and growing millet and " small horn beans " 小角豆.

At 10 A. M. a letter from the Ambassador arrived.[63] We examined it and found it to say that the ship injured on the trip across was to be examined by the officials in charge [64] at their convenience and that the local military detachments [30] were to take charge of guarding it, while the ship's sailors were all [65] to be ordered to come on and were not to be left behind. We at once sent the Acting Ship Captain,[66] Yamato no Itomaru 矢俟糸丸, and some others back to where the ship was.

At noon we arrived at a storehouse facing on the river,[67] but we pushed on all night.

20*th* DAY   At 7 A. M. we reached Ch'ih-an-ts'un.[68] When we asked the natives, they told us that Ju-kao-chen was 120 [*li*] [69] from here. After we had gone a short distance,

---

[61] *DBZ* corrects 宮 to 官.

[62] *Kuretake* 吳竹 (" Chinese bamboo "), is a Japanese name for a species of black bamboo (*phyllostachys puberula*).

[63] The second 來 in *DBZ* is a misprint.

[64] *So-yu* 所由. Cf. J. J. L. Duyvendak's review of Des Rotours, *T'oung pao* 38.299.

[65] 依數 appears again on VIII 18.

[66] *Jun-senshi* 准船師. For further comment on the man's name see note 114.

[67] Probably meaning the canal, for they are often called rivers in China.

[68] 赤岸. An embankment of reddish earth called the Ch'ih-an (" Red Bank ") extends for sixty or seventy *li* to the northeast of Ju-kao. Cf. *Ju-kao-hsien chih* 2.6a.

[69] An obvious overestimate, for they covered the distance in seven hours.

there was an obstruction,[70] but we dug through this solid obstruction and proceeded on.

On past the obstruction there was a public office 院 of Ju-kao. The officer in charge, without investigating the reasons why the boats were going too slowly, gave up the water buffalo and formed the crafts into units of three, to each of which units were apportioned seven sailors who were ordered to pull the boats along. After going a little while the men were exhausted, so we again tied [the boats] in a long line, with the water buffalo pulling them along. All had been at their wits' end and had become more and more exhausted. Where a large number of men had pulled [the boats] with difficulty, the harnessed water buffalo hastened along. The men all remarked that the strength of one water buffalo was equal to that of a hundred men.

At noon [we came upon] willow trees standing in a row along the north bank of the waterway, and at 2 P. M. we reached the teashops of Ju-kao and stopped a short while. Along the north shore of the dug canal stretched stores and houses. The archer, Hasetsukabe no Sadana 丈部貞名, and some others came from where the Ambassador was and told us that the garrison offices were a half *li* from here on the west side [of the waterway] and that the Ambassador, Administrative Officers, and the others were there and had not yet gone on to the subprefectural offices. When they had heard that we were coming with the tribute articles, they had had their boats loaded in order that they might go on to the prefectural city.

They also told us that a representative of the prefecture had come today and that for the first time they had been supplied with living provisions. [He had told them that] they had previously conducted [71] a Korean embassy, and,

---

[70] A character of unusual appearance occurs three times in rapid succession and each time in slightly different form. The last occurrence somewhat resembles 堰, and the printed editions assume that these are graphic variants of that character.

[71] *Tōji* has 導 with 噵 as a gloss.

since [Korea] was in the same place as our country, the present tributary embassy had been called a Korean embassy, and consequently [the Chinese officials] had been remiss in their attentions. Now, since the Ambassador and the others had come before us to the garrison offices, they had already established the fact that our country is different and far distant from Korea. The subprefecture and the prefecture had at once accepted this, and word had already been sent up [to the throne that a Japanese embassy was on its way]. Hearing this, we were delighted, and our weary spirits were greatly comforted.

At 4 P. M. the Garrison Commissioner,[47] Liu Mien, came on horseback with about seven or eight grooms and attendants to where the boats were tied up and, after inquiring into the state of affairs, departed again. The Secretary and the others [in our group] debarked and paid a visit to the Ambassador. Since it was late in the day, we did not go on but stayed the night there.

21st DAY   At 6 A. M. all of us from the Ambassador on down started out together. The waterway was lined on both sides with rich and noble houses quite without a break, but, before we had gone very long, the homes gradually thinned out. Before this the garrison offices. . . .[72] The Commissioner escorted us about three or four *li* and then returned to his own garrison.

From the garrison offices it was 220 *li* to the subprefectural town. At 10 A. M. the water buffalo were let go, and [the boats] were divided up into individual craft, which were poled along. There were no houses at all. At 5 P. M. we arrived at Yen-hai-ts'un [73] in Yen-hai-hsiang and stopped for the night. There were very many mosquitoes, and we suffered without limit.

We started out [again] in the middle of the night. Boats

---

[72] Possibly 四圍, but *ZZGR* prints 四國 and *DBZ* and *KIK* 囘國.

[73] The same characters but clearly not the same place as the Yen-hai-ts'un mentioned on VII 3. For *hsiang* see note 29.

of the salt bureau laden with salt, with three or four, or again, four or five boats bound side by side and in line, followed one after the other without a break for several tens of *li*. This unexpected sight is not easy to record. It was most extraordinary.

22nd DAY   At dawn the boats were tied to the water buffalo, which pulled them along. At times there were many white ducks and white geese, and there were houses in rows, but from 10 A. M. on we would sometimes go thirty *li* before coming on three or four houses. Sometimes there were some and sometimes not. On into the night we went in the dark and at midnight arrived at a village, the name of which I do not know. The boats stopped there for the night.

23rd DAY   At 6 A. M. we started. The natives told us that it was twenty *li* from here to the subprefectural town. Before going long, we encountered men tending waterfowl beside the waterway. They were herding them together, preventing them from scattering. In a single place there would be over two thousand [fowl] which they were tending. This sort of thing was to be found at the bends of the river.[74] Groves of bamboo were to be found everywhere. The bamboo was some forty feet in height.

We went along northwards. Since the day we had first boarded the boats we had been going west for the most part and at times north, northeast, or northwest.[75]

At 8 A. M. we saw a pagoda ahead of us. We at once inquired of the natives, who replied that this was the Hsi-ch'ih-ssu 西池 (" West Pond Monastery "), that its pagoda was an earthen one of nine stories, and that it was one of the seven official monasteries.[76] After going on for a little while,

---

[74] The canal, hitherto often referred to as 河 (see note 67), is here called 江. Possibly bends in the waterway, where two sides of a piece of land were bordered by water, were considered particularly satisfactory places for raising waterfowl.

[75] The reference presumably is only to the canal trip, not the ocean crossing, which was in a southwesterly direction.

[76] 七所官寺, probably seven monasteries under the special pa-

we reached the eastern end of Hai-ling-hsien. The officials of the subprefecture are a Chief Official,[77] an Administrative Officer,[38] and a Commissioner of Troops,[78] and others, in all seven men. I have not yet ascertained their ranks.

Proceeding a little further, we reached the river south of the subprefectural town. The Subprefect [77] and others came out to meet us in front of the bridge over the river south of the Hsi-ch'ih-ssu. The Ambassador, Administrative Officers, and Secretaries went ashore from the boats and, entering the monastery, spent the night there. The subprefectural officials presented them with coins. We Scholar and Student Monks, however, remained on board the boats. All the people of the subprefectural town crowded around, struggling to look at us. The Student Monk was having stomach trouble.

24th DAY   At 8 A. M. the Hsi-ch'ih-ssu held a lecture on the *Kishinron*.[79] The Abbot [80] was kind enough to come on board [our boat] together with the former and present officers of the monastery.[81] He inquired kindly after us two

---

tronage of the prefecture or regional commandery. See below XI 24.

[77] *Chang-kuan* 長官 (cf. Des Rotours 228) was not the official title of a Subprefect (*Hsien-ling* 縣令 , *ibid*. 733-34), which Ennin uses correctly below, but was probably a popular title which could be used for any local chief official.

[78] *Ping-ma-shih* 兵馬使 also does not seem to have been an official title but apparently was a popular title for the chief military officer in a local government of this sort. From its frequent appearance in this text, it would seem to have been very widely used.

[79] The *Daijō-kishin-ron* 大乘起信論 (Skr. *Mahāyāna-śraddhot-pāda-śāstra*), commonly called *The Awakening of Faith*.

[80] *Zasu* 座主.

[81] *Sankō* (also pronounced *Sangō*) 三綱 is a term for the three chief officers of a monastery and is used either individually or collectively for them. These three are listed as the *Jōza* 上座 (Superior), *Jishu* 寺主 (Rector), and *Tsuina* 都維那 (or *Tsui* or *Ina*) or again as the *Jōza* (or *Shuso* 首座), *Inō* 維那, and *Tenzo* 典座 (Controller).

monks who had come from a distance, and communicated with us, writing with a brush. These monks, after staying a while, went back.

At 10 A. M. the Ambassador and the others left the monastery and boarded the boats, and we started out together. The officials of the subprefecture, because they were lacking in hospitality, sent [only] members of the military to see us off. At 4 P. M. we reached I-ling-kuan.[82] This was a place which provided for official travelers going back and forth. Because of a sudden dysenteric discharge of the Acting Administrative Officer, Fujiwara no Sadatoshi 藤原貞敏, the boats stopped in front of this inn for the night. We two monks got off our boat and visited the sick man and then returned at once to our boat.

We heard that the Administrative Officer of the fourth ship, unable to endure the turbulent waters, had left his ship and was staying at the home of a fisherman. Before the national tribute articles [25] had been taken off, the boat broke up completely, but the official and private goods were not damaged. Because no boats had come to meet [the party], they had not been able to send [the goods] on.

25th DAY   At 4 A. M. we started out. The men were suffering from dysentery, and the boats did not progress evenly. A boat going in front would stop and thus become a unit in the rear, and men bringing up the rear would forge ahead. From Hai-ling-hsien to I-ling-kuan is fifty *li* and from [I-ling]-kuan [83] to the prefectural city sixty-five *li*. At

---

[82] 宜陵館, in which *kuan* probably means a "hostel," such as Ennin describes. I-ling-kuan by present routes is about thirty-four km. west of Hai-ling-hsien and thirty-two km. northeast of Yang-chou. On VII 25 Ennin states that it was fifty *li* from the former and sixty-five *li* from the latter.

[83] The character which *DBZ* and *KIK* interpret as 舒 and correct to 餘 on the basis of *Ikeda* is more probably an error for 舘, a variant of 館. If one accepts the *DBZ* and *KIK* interpretation, the sentence reads, "From Hai-ling-hsien to I-ling-kuan is over fifty *li* and to the prefectural city sixty-five *li*," which is a far less accurate estimate than the one actually made. See note 82.

10 A. M. we reached the Hsien-kung-kuan [84] but went straight on without resting.

At 2 P. M. we stopped on the east side of the Ch'an-chih Bridge.[85] At the north end of the bridge is the Ch'an-chih-ssu. During the Enryaku period (782-806) [86] the anniversary of the death of the Vice-Ambassador [87] was performed in this monastery.

The capital city of Yang-chou lies three *li* west of the bridge. The Ambassador sent a Guard Captain [50] and others there in order to inform the government, and when they eventually returned, we started out [again] at 4 P. M. The river was full of large boats, boats laden with reeds 積蘆 船, and small boats, too numerous to be counted. At 5 P. M. we went by the water gate of the eastern outer wall and at 6 P. M. reached the river north of the city wall and stopped there. The Ambassador and some others went ashore and lodged, but they have not yet met the government officials. We Scholar and Student Monks have not yet landed from our boat. In the night it rained, and we suffered all the more.

26th DAY   At 4 P. M. we alighted from our boat and lodged at the official inn 官店 on the south side of the river. We two [88] monks stayed in separate rooms.

---

[84] 仙宮觀. *Kuan* is the term for Taoist monasteries, just as *ssu* is the term for Buddhist monasteries.

[85] The Ch'an-chih Bridge was obviously named for the Ch'an-chih-ssu 禪智, mentioned immediately below. Also known as the Shang-fang-ssu 上方, this monastery was located five *li* northeast of Yang-chou and was originally a palace of the Sui Emperor Yang-ti (see note 15). Cf. *Ch'ung-hsiu Yang-chou-fu chih* 9.6a-7a and the map in *chüan-shou* 卷首 3b-4a. On the map the monastery is shown somewhat west of the juncture of the water route from I-ling-kuan to the east with that from the north.

[86] 延曆, a Japanese year period.

[87] This was Ishikawa no Ason Michimasu 石川朝臣道益, the Vice-Ambassador (*Fukushi* 副使) of the preceding embassy to China in 804-805, who died while on the trip. Cf. *Nihon kōki* 日本後紀 13, under the dates of 805 VII 25 and VIII 16.

[88] *DBZ* suggests 兩 for 尚.

28th DAY   After the forenoon meal [89] we hired a small boat and started for the Ling-chü-ssu 靈居, but we encountered an obstruction halfway there and could not go on to the monastery, so we returned to the official inn. Before long Ch'üan-ts'ao 全操 and other monks of the K'ai-yüan-ssu,[55] nine [in all], came and inquired kindly about the hardships of the trip.

30th DAY   Chen-shun 貞順, a monk of the K'ai-yüan-ssu, inquired kindly after us. Writing by brush, we learned the names of the monasteries of the city and the names of their monks. We also gave him Japanese products.

EIGHTH MOON: 1*st* DAY [90]   Early in the morning the Ambassador went to the prefectural offices and saw the Governor General of Yang-fu,[91] the Minister of State, Li,[92] and when this was over, he returned.

---

[89] *Sai* 齋, which means " abstinence " or " fast," is a technical Buddhist term with several shades of meaning. It was commonly used to refer to the Buddhist practice of not eating after noon, and thus came to mean the " forenoon meal " of a Buddhist monk, as in this phrase. It was also used to mean a Buddhist banquet, at which the Buddhist eating prohibitions were observed and which was held to celebrate some special occasion; in this usage I have translated it " maigre feast."

[90] August 24, 858.

[91] Governor General (*Tu-tu* 都督, cf. Des Rotours 668, etc.) was an older title for what by this time were usually known as Regional Commanders (*Chieh-tu-shih*, see note 35). Since a government general was called a *tu-tu-fu* 府 and a regional commandery a *chieh-tu-fu*, it was natural that Ennin sometimes refers to Yang-chou as Yang-fu or simply as the *fu*.

[92] This was Li Te-yü 李德裕 (787-849), a poet of note and one of the greatest statesmen of his day. He was to become the dominant political figure of the following reign after his return to the capital as a Minister of State in 840 (which Ennin records on 840 IX 5). The son of a Minister of State (see note 126), he came close to attaining this post himself as early as 829 and finally did achieve it in 833. Since he was a leading protagonist in the greatest factional feud within the Chinese bureaucracy

After the forenoon meal, we two Scholar and Student Monks sent a note to the embassy's quarters, asking [to be allowed] to go to the Kuo-ch'ing-ssu in T'ai-chou [93] and also asking for the services of the sailor, Tei Kachikomaro,[94] that he might perform the menial tasks in our search for the Law.

---

during this period, his career was full of ups and downs, one of which brought him to Yang-chou in 836. He has full *chüan* devoted to his biography in the standard histories (*CTS* 174, *HTS* 180) and is mentioned repeatedly and at length in *TCTC* 244-48. Cf. also Waley 139-141 and Herbert A. Giles, *A Chinese Biographical Dictionary* (London, 1898), No. 1211.

Here Ennin calls Li Te-yü a *Hsiang-kung* 相公, an elegant variant for *Tsai-hsiang* 宰相 or Minister of State (cf. Des Rotours 4), which was an exalted title used for any of the chief ministers of state. According to *TCTC*, the actual title Li received in 833 and 840 which entitled him to be called a Minister of State was *T'ung P'ing-chang-shih* 同平章事, which, with *P'ing-chang-shih* (more fully *Chung-shu Men-hsia P'ing-chang-shih* 中書門下平章事), might be translated " Grand Overseer of the Imperial Secretariat and Imperial Chancellery " (cf. Des Rotours 7). The Imperial Secretariat (*Chung-shu-sheng* 省) and the Imperial Chancellery (*Men-hsia-sheng*) were two of the main organs of the central government, whose respective heads were also considered to be Ministers of State (cf. *ibid.* 5, 130, 174).

[93] This was the great Kuo-ch'ing-ssu (see note 45), which was the central monastery on Mt. T'ien-t'ai 天台山 (in T'ai-chou 台 in what is now eastern Chekiang), the center of the T'ien-t'ai (J. Tendai) Sect, to which Ennin belonged.

[94] This presumably is the reading of 丁勝小麻呂, whose name is Sinicized to Tei Yūman 丁雄滿 in the document quoted on VIII 4 and thereafter. The first character is not a Japanese surname, but it does happen to be one in Chinese (Ting). This is the same person as the Tei Man 丁滿 (or 丁萬) who later traveled through China with Enchin and figures in the *Gyōryakushō* (see note 7). It is not certain whether Tei Yūman returned to China with Enchin in 853 or had remained in China all along and was found there by the latter. Enchin records that on 855 V 25 Tei

At sunset, on the order of the Ambassador, we went to the K'ai-yüan-ssu in order to fulfill the vows made at sea.[95] We saw the Ting-hsien-yüan 定閑院.[56] The monastic officers[81] and the monks, over thirty [men in all], came and inquired kindly after us. After concluding our pilgrimage, we returned to the inn 店館.

3rd DAY The embassy sent a letter to the Yang-fu [authorities] asking that the Scholar Monk and the others[95a] be allowed to go to T'ai-chou.

We had an artist[96] go to the monastery to draw pictures of the Bodhisattva Myōken[31] and the Four [Heavenly] Kings,[97] but for some reason the regulations do not allow foreigners to enter monastery buildings at will, and the officers of the monastery would not allow him to draw the pictures. The embassy, therefore, sent a letter to the Minister of State, but there has as yet been no reply.

4th DAY Early in the morning there was a reply, and the Ambassador presented Japanese products to the Minister of State, Li, but the latter would not accept them and returned them. Beginning with this day, there were deficiencies in all the things supplied us for our daily needs. After the forenoon meal they brought a reply from Yang-fu. The [original] document had said:

Man was asked by a Chinese monk in Ch'ang-an 長安, the Chinese capital, if he had not been Ennin's attendant, and he answered in the affirmative (*DBZ* 113.291a-b). Enchin describes Tei Man as being forty-nine in 853 (*ibid*. 288b). This age notation, like all those in this text, is in Far Eastern count, which is from one to two years higher than the corresponding Western count. Waley (146 ff.) refers to Tei Kachikomaro (alias Tei Yūman or Tei Man) as Komaro.

[95] See VI 24, 28, and VII 2.

[95a] *Tōji* has 寺 in place of 等. These two characters are frequently confused in *Tōji*.

[96] *Gashi* 畫師, who presumably was a member of the embassy.

[97] *Shi[ten]nō* 四天王, militant protecting deities of Buddhism.

The Scholar Monk,[7] Ennin, the novices, Ishō and Igyō,[98] and the sailor, Tei Yūman.[94]

The above ask to go to the Kuo-ch'ing-ssu of T'ai-chou to seek teachers and to reside in T'ai-chou and, on leaving T'ai-chou, to go to the capital.

The Student Monk, Ensai, the novice, Ninkō 仁好, and Ban Shiman.[99]

The above ask to go to the Kuo-ch'ing-ssu of T'ai-chou to seek teachers and to reside in T'ai-chou and, on leaving T'ai-chou, to go to the capital.

Now the reply [100] stated:

The Scholar Monk, Ennin.

The above asks to go to the Kuo-ch'ing-ssu of T'ai-chou to seek teachers and to resolve some doubts and, if that prefecture is without teachers, then to go to the capital and to pass through the various prefectures.

The Student Monk,[101] Ensai.

The above asks to go to the Kuo-ch'ing-ssu of T'ai-chou to study under teachers and, if this prefecture is entirely without [learned] men or the Law, perhaps to go to the capital in search of the Law and to pass through the various prefectures in search of it.

We received an announcement from the embassy saying that they had given up the drawing of the pictures because divination [102] had shown that there was a taboo against it, but that next year when we were about to depart for home,

---

[98] Ishō 惟正 and Igyō 惟曉 are given the alternate and more complicated readings of Yuijō and Yuigyō by Waley (146 ff.). Ennin 圓仁 here and usually elsewhere in *Tōji* is abbreviated to 圓イ.

[99] 伴始満, another Sinicized name. No doubt he was Ensai's servant.

[100] The so-called reply, however, is merely a revised and shorter form of the same request. Apparently the Chinese officials, disapproving of the tone or composition of the original, corrected the petition before forwarding it to the throne.

[101] *Ryūgakumon-sō.* See notes 7 and 27.

[102] *DBZ* corrects 卜蓥 to 卜筮.

we were to attend to the drawings and make offerings. Accordingly, we went to the great gate of the K'ai-yüan-ssu at 8 P. M. and prayed about the matter.

7th DAY We rushed a letter to the officers of the K'ai-yüan-ssu to inquire [about the matter] and also gave them Japanese products. They sent a letter [103] of thanks together with their reply.

8th DAY We heard that the fourth ship was still [stuck] in the mud and had not yet reached an anchorage and that the national tribute articles [25] had not yet been sent on. The ship's planking 廣棚 [19] had opened up, and it was quite full of bilge water. The hold was dry or submerged depending on whether the tide was in or out. It was not fit to be a vessel for crossing the sea. The monks in search of the Law had not yet landed, but the Commander [104] Administrative Officer had landed and was staying at the house of a fisherman. Five of the men on board had died of body swellings. About ten Chinese boats sent to meet them had come, and once each day they would take off some of the national tribute articles, but when the waves were like mountains and the wind blew, they could not transport them, and they suffered all the more severely. I heard that yesterday Yangchou issued a document [stating that] boats were to be sent to meet them and that these had already been dispatched, but I do not yet know the details.

9th DAY At 10 A. M. the Regional Commander,[91] the Minister of State, Li, wrote to the K'ai-yüan-ssu, authorizing the drawing of the Buddhist pictures.

At 2 P. M. the Commissioner in Charge of the Japanese Embassy,[105] Wang Yu-chen,[106] came to the official inn and

---

[103] *DBZ* corrects 唐 to 書.

[104] 頭 is used here as an abbreviation of *Sendō* 船頭, "Commander," a term used on VIII 25 and in the *SNK* for the official in command of a ship.

[105] *Kou-tang Jih-pen-kuo Shih* 勾當日本國使, referred to below as *Shih*, *Ta-shih* (see note 46), and *Kou-tang* (translated as Manager).

[106] Written here as 主支眞, but elsewhere in *Tōji* as 王友眞.

inquired kindly after us monks and also consulted with us about our being allowed to go soon to T'ai-chou, after which he went back. The Scholar Monk gave the Commissioner Japanese products.

Just then a merchant, Wang K'o 王客, came. Writing with a brush, we asked for information about the Kuo-ch'ing-ssu, and he did much to dispel our anxieties. He also gave us some knives and the like.

10th DAY   At 8 A. M. we recorded the weight of the baggage of the two Scholar and Student Monks and reported it to the embassy's quarters. We then heard that the second ship had reached Hai-chou.[107] The Korean Interpreter of the second ship, Pak Chŏngjang 朴正長, had sent a letter to Kim Chŏngnam.[108]

At noon Commissioner Wang [Yu-chen] came and told us that the Minister of State had already petitioned the throne [on our behalf] and that we should await the arrival of an Imperial order before starting out for T'ai-chou.

The Ambassador again sent a letter to the Minister of State saying that, while the Student Monk might stay for a while in Yang-fu, the Scholar Monk should be allowed to go to T'ai-chou without waiting for the Imperial credentials.[109] Two or three days later the Minister of State replied that I was not permitted to start yet and that they were waiting for the [arrival of the Imperial] credentials to decide whether we were to go or to remain; in the meantime we monks were to be quartered in a monastery.

---

[107] 海, the modern Tung-hai 東海, near the eastern end of the Lung-hai Railway. The departure of this ship from Japan was recorded in the SNK on VII 29. Since the departure of the other two ships was recorded on VII 5, seventeen days after they left the Hakata area, we can assume that the second ship's actual departure was around VII 12.

[108] The Korean Interpreter mentioned on VI 28.

[109] The reason for this request was probably that Ensai, as a long-term student, could better afford to wait a few months than could Ennin, who was scheduled to return with the embassy to Japan the following year.

The Ship Captain,[66] Saeki no Kanenari 佐伯金成, has been suffering from dysentery for several days.

16th DAY   At 8 A.M. we two monks offered prayers on the transiency [of life],[110] but [Kanenari's] life has not yet come to an end. At sunset the Commissioner in Charge of the Japanese Embassy, Wang Yu-chen, came to the official inn with a representative[111] of the Minister of State and made a record of Kanenari's baggage.

17th DAY   At 4 P.M. we heard that the Administrative Officer of the fourth ship had reached Ju-kao-chen[15] and that the various goods, official and private, had also all been transported to the garrison[29] offices. At present they are marshaling small boats, intending to go to Yang-fu.

In the night at 2 A.M. the ailing Kanenari died.

18th DAY   Early in the morning Guard Captains[50] came to investigate the matter. In accordance with the decision of the Japanese embassy, Kanenari's baggage was all[65] handed over to his retainer, Sei Kyūtai.[112] At 2 P.M. the Guard Captains attended to the buying of a coffin and to the burial.

21st DAY   The Commissioner to Inspect the Ship[113] and the Acting Ship Captain, . . . no Itomaro,[114] came in haste, and then we heard that the boatswain, Saeki no Matatsugu 全繼, had died in Chüeh-chiang-chen.[15]

22nd DAY   Commissioner Wang brought a letter from the Minister of State, which on examination proved to say that we two monks and our followers were permitted to live in the K'ai-yüan-ssu.[55]

---

[110] *Mujō jugan* 无常呪願, offered on behalf of the dying Kanenari.
[111] *DBZ* and *KIK* overlook the character 一 written as an interlinear gloss between 使 and 人.
[112] 井俠替, presumably a Sinicized name. *KIK* interprets the last character as a word in the sentence.
[113] 撿挍舶之使, obviously a Chinese official.
[114] 楊集糸麿, who very probably is the Acting Ship Captain called Yamato 矢侯 no Itomaro on VII 19. Arthur Waley, in a letter to me dated September 24, 1950, suggests that his real surname was Yoko 楊侯.

23rd DAY   In the evening a letter was brought from the K'ai-yüan-ssu, and we sent it to Commissioner Wang who is in charge [of the Japanese embassy].

24th DAY   At 8 A. M. the Administrative Officer of the fourth ship and his subordinates arrived by small boats. The total number of boats was thirty or less.

After the forenoon meal, we sent a messenger to the monastery to examine the guest rooms, and at 2 P. M. we two monks with our followers left the official inn and proceeded to the K'ai-yüan-ssu. After entering the monastery from a point north of the east pagoda, we passed through two walls and lodged in the central rooms of the third corridor. At once the officers and monks [115] of the monastery and the [Monastery] Supervisor [116] monk came crowding around. The Superior [81] monk, Chih-ch'iang 志強, the Rector,[81] Ling-cheng 令徵, the *Tsu[ina]* monk,[117] Hsiu-ta 修達, the Monastery Supervisor, Fang-ch'i 方起, and the Monastery Steward,[118] Ling-tuan 令端, inquired kindly after us. Our baggage also was brought into the monastery.

25th DAY   Early in the morning, on the invitation of the Monastery Administrator,[119] we went to the monastery living quarters and ate gruel.[120] At noon the Sanron Student

---

[115] 和上 is a variant of 和尙, a polite term for a monk, pronounced *Ho-shang* in Chinese but *Kashō* (Tendai), *Oshō* (Zen 禪), or *Wajō* (Ritsu 律 and Shingon 眞言) in Japanese, depending on the sect. In titles I have translated it " Priest."

[116] *Kan* is an abbreviation of *Kansu* 監寺 (also pronounced *Kanji*), an official whose function is described on 839 I 18.

[117] 都師 is probably a contraction of *Tsuina Hosshi*. See notes 81 and 7.

[118] *Kōshi* 庫司, the monk in charge of the monastery living quarters.

[119] *Kōi* (or *Kōyui*) 綱維, an administrative officer in a monastery, sometimes identified with one or more of the *Sankō* (see note 81).

[120] *Chou* 粥, " rice gruel," which Ennin consistently records as his breakfast fare in China.

Monk, Jōgyō [121] [Hos]shi,[7] came, and we consoled each other.
The monastery arranged provisions,[122] and we had our forenoon meal together. Jōgyō [Hos]shi made a tour of inspection
and then returned to his inn. I sent Ishō to inquire after
him, and the Shingon Scholar [Monk] [123] sent me a reply,
consoling us. At the same time, the Commander [104] Administrative Officer of the fourth ship and the Magistrate of Kibi
and the Magistrate of Sanuki [124] graciously inquired after us.

The fourth ship had been carried away by high waves and
had run aground again on a high shoal. It could not be
refloated easily. Sailors had boarded small boats to go to the
ship, but before they had gone halfway, the current pushed
them back, and they could not reach it, nor did they know
where they were going. An archer fell into the tide and was
submerged in the current, but a fisherman pulled him out.

26th DAY   Minister of State Li's military aide, the
Raiding General,[125] Shen Pien 沈弁, came and inquired after
us. He also told us that the Minister of State avoided using

---

[121] Jōgyō 常曉, whose name is written 常晈 here, but correctly
on XII 28, had presumably crossed on the fourth ship. Sanron
三論 is the name of a Japanese Buddhist sect.

[122] 供, an abbreviation of kuyō 供養, "offering," a term used for
food provided for monks.

[123] This is probably Engyō 圓行, who is referred to by this title
on X 4. Shingon is the name of a sect (see note 115).

[124] Magistrates (Jō 掾) were the third-ranking category of officers in a Japanese province. Kibi 吉備, which at this time had
already been divided into the four provinces of Bizen 備前,
Bitchū 備中, Bingo 備後, and Mimasaka 美作, was an ancient
name for a region lying on the north shore of the Inland Sea,
and Sanuki 讚岐 was the province opposite it in Shikoku. The
Magistrate of Sanuki probably was Tajihi no Takanushi 丹墀
高主, an Acting Secretary of the embassy, who was the Provisional Magistrate (Gon no Jō 權掾) of Sanuki, and the Magistrate of Kibi was probably Tomo no Sugao 伴須賀雄, who was
a Provisional Magistrate of Bingo. Cf. SNK 839 VIII 25; see
also note 182.

[125] Yu-chi-chiang-chün 游擊將軍, one of the many honorary

four characters, *fu* 府, *chi* 吉, *fu* 甫, and *yün* 云. His grandfather's taboo name was Yün. His father's taboo name was
Chi-fu 吉甫.[126] At sunset Shen Pien sent a messenger to give
us a bowl of honey.

The Scholar Monk, in order to provide [a meal] for the
monks of the monastery, called the Monastery Steward
monk, Ling-tuan, and asked him the number of the monks
in the monastery. In all there are one hundred, so the
Scholar Monk devoted two small ounces [127] of gold dust 沙金
to provisions [128] for the monks. The Student Monk also gave
two ounces. The total was four small ounces, which we sent
to the monastery offices. The Monastery Administrator [119]

---

titles without specific function for military officials. This one was
for officials of the fourth class of the fifth rank. Cf. Des Rotours
101.

[126] See note 92. It was customary to avoid the use of characters
in the personal names of one's father and grandfather. He
probably avoided the first *fu* 府 as well, because it was a common
homonym of 甫. His grandfather's name actually was Hsi-yün
栖筠, but 云 was probably singled out for mention because it
was a very common homonym of the second character. If Ennin
has made no mistake in transmitting this information, we may
assume that his informant was simply telling him the common
characters among those which Li Te-yü avoided, together with
a few common homonyms, which were best avoided in any
communications addressed to him.

[127] The *liang* 兩 (or tael) is estimated as having been about 37.3
grams ever since T'ang times. The Chinese pound (*chin* 斤 or
catty), which was sixteen *liang*, is 596.8 grams. In the T'ang
dynasty, however, a small ounce, which was the continuation of
a Sui measure, was also used. This amounted to about 13.92
grams and was considered to be one-third the size of the larger
ounce. Cf. Lien-sheng Yang, "Numbers and Units in Chinese
Economic History," *Harvard Journal of Asiatic Studies* 12.221-
22 and Wu Ch'eng-lo 吳承洛, *Chung-kuo tu-liang-heng shih*
中國度量衡史 (Shanghai, 1937) 74.

[128] 籵 appears in this text as a graphic variant of 料.

and Monastery Supervisor [116] monks met together and determined the weight to be one large ounce and two and one-half *fen*.[129] At once we received a statement from the monastery to the effect that we should record the quantity of gold and also inform the officials to take the necessary steps so that we might arrange a maigre feast.[130]

> *Four small ounces of gold dust.*
>
> We monks in search of the Law, having succeeded in avoiding [the perils of a voyage of] ten thousand *li* and having come through alive and being lodged for awhile in the monastery, where we have formed affinities even in this brief contact,[131] respectfully present the gold dust for food for the monks.[132] Humbly we ask you to undertake the labor of arranging for this and to use [what we present] for a maigre feast for the assembly of monks in the monastery. The time is to be tomorrow.
>
> *Eighth moon, 26th [day].*
>
> *The Scholar [Monk] of the Dentō-hosshi [Rank] and*

---

[129] *Fen* 分 in modern Chinese is a term for the hundredth part of a *liang* or the tenth part of a *ch'ien* 錢, but from this passage and the mention on X 14 we see that this is not the meaning here. While Ennin seems to use *ch'ien* in its proper sense, he also appears to use *fen* to mean a tenth of a *liang*, utilizing the term "two and a half *fen*" (*erh-fen-pan* 二分半) to mean a quarter of a *liang* and a "large (*ta*) two and a half *fen*" to mean three-quarters (see X 14). Cf. Yang, *op. cit.* 222, note 22, but Waley (p. 183) does not follow Yang's interpretation.

[130] The context here and elsewhere where the term *k'ung-fan* 空飯, "empty meal," is used and the use of *sai* in the phrase "maigre-feast essay" on VIII 29 indicate that this is a substitute term for *sai*. See note 89.

[131] 結泉樹因, a highly abbreviated Buddhist cliché, implying the forming of karma relationships in such chance occurrences as a pause beneath a tree or in drawing water from a spring.

[132] *Kōshaku* 香積 is a term for food for monks, being a comparison with the "nectar" of a Buddhist paradise known as the Shukō-kokudo 衆香國土, the "Land of Incense."

the Student Monk of the Dentō-man Rank [133] *of the Tendai
Lotus Sect* [134] *of Japan.*

29*th* DAY   We provided [a meal] for the monks of the
monastery. All sorts of things were set forth in great abundance. The monks numbered over one hundred. Ch'ang-
chien 常簡, a monk of this monastery, on the request of the
Monastery Administrator, made a maigre-feast essay.[135] This
document is [recorded] separately.

30*th* DAY   Hsing-tuan 行端, a monk of the Ch'ien-fu-
ssu [135a] of Ch'ang-an, came and, speaking by brush, communicated his sympathy. At the same time we inquired and
obtained information about Ch'ang-an, the capital of China.[136]

NINTH MOON: 1*st* DAY [137]   Nothing special happened.
To the west across the river from the K'ai-yüan-ssu stands
the Wu-liang-i-ssu 無量義, where there is an old monk named
Wen-hsi 文襲, who is seventy years old and has recently
written a commentary to the *Yuima-kyō* in five scrolls.[138]

---

[133] *Dentō-hosshi-i* 傳燈法師位 and *Dentō-man-i* 滿位 were the
fifth and sixth ranks respectively of the six honorary ranks of
the Buddhist Church in Japan. They were held by Ennin and
Ensai respectively, who are, of course, the two indicated by
these titles.

[134] Tendai Lotus (*Hokke* 法花), a fuller name for the Tendai
Sect.

[135] 齋文. See also XI 24.

[135a] 千福 in the northwestern corner of the T'ang capital. Cf.
Adachi, map opposite 136.

[136] 唐 appears to be misplaced in this sentence.

[137] September 23, 838.

[138] More fully the *Yuimakitsu-shosetsu-kyō* 維摩詰所說經 (Skr.
Vimalakīrti-nirdeśa-sūtra), which tells of the famous early
Indian Buddhist layman, Yuima (Vimalakīrti). The *Bussho
kaisetsu daijiten* 佛書解說大辭典 11.124 lists a *Yuima-kyō
kanchū shoki* 關中疏記 by Wen-hsi in five scrolls as being no
longer extant. Jōgyō (see note 121) is said to have brought a
copy of this work back to Japan. Ennin calls it a *Yuima-kyō ki*
記 here, but a *shoki* below.

At present he is lecturing on his commentary in the [lecture] hall [of the monastery]. He makes much use of the doctrines of [Seng]-chao, [Tao]-sheng, [Tao]-jung,[139] and T'ien-t'ai [Ta-shih].[140] The monks of neighboring monasteries assemble to listen to him. In all there are thirty-eight listeners, who all revere Wen-hsi Ho-shang.[115]

2nd DAY The Monastery Supervisor monk, Fang-ch'i, and others arranged a maigre feast [130] in the monastery living quarters.[141]

9th DAY The Minister of State arranged a farewell banquet for the Japanese [142] embassy. The Ambassador did not go, but the Administrative Officers and their subordinates all went.

11th DAY We heard that the Vice-Ambassador [143] had not come [to China] but had stayed in Japan and that the Administrative Officer, Fujiwara no Toyonami 豊竝, had come as Commander of the ship.

13th DAY We heard that a reply to the petition of

---

[139] These three, Seng-chao 僧肇, Tao-sheng 道生, and Tao-jung 道融, together with Seng-jui 僧叡, were the four most famous disciples of Kumārajīva (*ca.* 344-413), the great Central Asian missionary of Indian parentage, who was the author of the *Yuima-kyō*. They were called the "four sages of Kuan-chung" (*Kuan-chung ssu-sheng* 關中四聖). All three men listed here wrote commentaries on the *Yuima-kyō*.

[140] 天台大師, a title for Chih-i 智顗 (538-597), the founder of the Tendai Sect in China. He wrote the *Yuima-kyō gengi* 玄義, the *Yuima-kyō monsho* 文疏, and other commentaries on the *Yuima-kyō*. *Ta-shih* (J. *Daishi*) means "Great Teacher" and was commonly bestowed on a monk as a posthumous title.

[141] 庫頭, apparently the same as *kuri* 庫裡.

[142] 大國 is probably an error for 本國, the usual term for Japan in this text.

[143] The Vice-Ambassador (see note 87) was Ono no Takamura 小野篁, who, angered because the Ambassador changed ships with him, feigned illness and refused to go to China and as a result was sent into exile. Cf. *SNK* 838 VI 22 and XII 15.

the Minister of State [on our behalf] had come to Yang-fu,
but we do not yct have the details.

After the forenoon meal, Hsün Nien-i-lang, a Registrar of
the Military Inspector's Bureau,[144] came and told us the
statistics of the prefecture. The Regional Commander of
Yang-chou controls seven prefectures:[145] Yang-chou, Ch'u-
chou,[146] Lu-chou,[147] Shou-chou,[148] Ch'u-chou,[149] and Ho-

---

[144] *Chien-chün-yüan* 監軍院 (but *Chien-chün-men* 門 on 839 I
18). Military Inspectors were high officials who were direct
Imperial appointees sent out to keep check on the important
local officials. In the second half of the T'ang period eunuchs
were used for this office. The Military Inspector at Yang-chou
at this time was Yang Ch'in-i 揚欽義, whom Ennin was to
mention in his text on 843 VI 3, though apparently without
realizing that he had met the man in Yang-chou on 838 XI 18.
Cf. *TCTC* 246 under the date of 840 VIII. Yang Ch'in-i, perhaps because of his association with Li Te-yü in Yang-chou,
was to become a close collaborator with the latter at court in
later years. Cf. Waley 142 and Okada 11.479-82.

Registrars (*Yao-chi* 要籍) were minor officials under a Regional Commander (cf. Des Rotours 660). Hsün 薫 is not a
standard Chinese surname, but cognomens such as Nien-i-lang
卄一郎 appear occasionally in this text.

[145] *Ikeda* has "six," and only six are listed. During the T'ang,
however, the actual number of prefectures under the Regional
Commander of Yang-chou was normally more, not less, than
seven, and on 839 I 17 Ennin refers to eight prefectures under
Yang-chou. Ennin quite frequently names fewer geographical
units than he says existed, perhaps because their names slipped
his memory. For example, below he names only six of the seven
subprefectures and five of the ten provinces.

[146] 楚, which, as we see from the text (839 II 24 and III 22-24),
was located at the northern end of the canal system connecting
the Yangtse near Yang-chou with the Huai 淮 River. *TTLCT*
41a shows it some distance northeast of the present town of
Huai-an 淮安, but the location of the monasteries either in or
near Ch'u-chou (see notes 375 and 378) and the travel distances
recorded by Ennin (see note 372) indicate that the T'ang
Ch'u-chou was not far from the modern Huai-an.

chou.[150] Yang-chou has seven subprefectures:[151] Chiang-yang-hsien, T'ien-ch'ang-hsien,[152] Liu-ho-hsien,[153] Kao-yu-hsien,[154] Hai-ling-hsien,[15] and Yang-tzu-hsien.[155] At present the K'ai-yüan-ssu is in the area of jurisdiction of Chiang-yang-hsien. [The city of] Yang-fu is eleven *li* from north to south, seven *li* from east to west, and forty [155a] *li* in circumference. Straight north of the K'ai-yüan-ssu are [the offices of] Yang-fu. Ch'ang-an, the capital, is 3,000 *li* north of Yang-chou, and T'ai-chou [93] is 1,450 *li* south of Yang-fu. Some say it is about 3,000 *li*. The people's [use of the] word *li* is not consistent. At present Yang-chou is in Huai-nan-tao,[11] and T'ai-chou is in Western Chiang-nan-tao.[156] In Yang-fu there are forty-nine monasteries and convents. In [Yang]-chou there are 20,000 soldiers, and in the seven prefectures [145] under its control there are a total of 120,000 troops. China has ten provinces, [including] Huai-nan-tao 14 prefectures, Kuan-

---

[147] 廬 (miswritten 盧 and not corrected in *DBZ* or *KIK*), the modern Ho-fei 合肥 in Anhwei, 150 km. west of Nanking.

[148] 壽, in Anhwei, 200 km. west and somewhat north of Nanking.

[149] 滁 (miswritten Hsü-chou 徐), 55 km. northwest of Nanking.

[150] 和, on the north bank of the Yangtse River in Anhwei, 55 km. southwest of Nanking.

[151] Again *Ikeda* has " six," and only six are listed, but this is one of several points at which *Ikeda* shows reasonable but mistaken corrections of what I assume to have been the original text. Yang-chou in the T'ang did have a seventh subprefecture, Chiang-tu-hsien (see note 11), which with Chiang-yang-hsien 江陽 were the two subprefectures in the city of Yang-chou.

[152] 天長, in Anhwei, 55 km. northwest of Yang-chou.

[153] 六合, 60 km. west of Yang-chou.

[154] 高郵, on the Grand Canal 40 km. north of Yang-chou.

[155] 揚子, which was on the Yangtse south and a little west of Yang-chou.

[155a] *DBZ* and *KIK* misprint " thirty."

[156] 江南道, covering most of China between the Yangtse and the modern Kwangtung. In 733, when the provinces were increased from ten to fifteen, Chiang-nan-tao was divided into an eastern and a western section, and T'ai-chou actually was in the eastern and not the western half, as Ennin says.

nei-tao 24 prefectures,[157] Shan-nan-tao 31 prefectures,[158] Lung-yu-tao 19 prefectures,[159] and Chien-nan-tao 42 prefectures,[160] with a total of 311 prefectures.[161] Yang-chou is 2,500 *li* and T'ai-chou 4,100 *li* from the capital. T'ai-chou is in Ling-nan-tao.[162]

16*th* DAY The Administrative Officer Naga[mine] told us that they had received a notice from the Minister of State saying that, with regard to the Scholar Monk's being allowed to go to T'ai-chou, the Ambassador, on reaching the capital, should present a petition and when a [favorable] reply to this had been received, the Scholar Monk and the others would then be permitted to go to T'ai-chou. I have not yet received the document.

19*th* DAY Kuang-yo Fa-shih[163] of the Hui-chao-ssu[164] came and we met and conversed. The monks of this monas-

---

[157] 關內, for the most part the modern Shensi, the capital area of the T'ang. Materials given in small type occur in *Tōji* as glosses written in small characters.

[158] 山南, for the most part the modern Hupeh.

[159] 隴右, for the most part the modern Kansu.

[160] 劍南, for the most part the modern Szechwan.

[161] Since there was, of course, some fluctuation in the number of prefectures during the T'ang, most of Ennin's statistics may have been correct for his time. The *Li-tai chiang-yü piao* 歷代疆域表 lists 14 prefectures for Huai-nan-tao, 22 for Kuan-nei-tao, 33 for Shan-nan-tao, 20 for Lung-yu-tao, but only 26 for Chien-nan-tao and a grand total of 293 or 294.

[162] 嶺南, for the most part the modern Kwangtung and Kwangsi. The statement is, of course, a gross error, contradicting what he has already recorded.

[163] Apparently 廣礿, but interpreted by *DBZ* and *KIK* as 唐虳 (or 初). For Fa-shih, see note 7.

[164] There was a Hui-chao-chiao-ssu 惠照教, built in the Ching-lung 景龍 period (707-710), three *li* north of Yang-chou (cf. *Ch'ung-hsiu Yang-chou-fu chih* 28.18b) and a Kan-ch'üan-ssu 甘泉, which during this very period was renamed the Hui-chao-ssu, on Mt. Kan-ch'üan, seventeen km. by road northwest of Yang-chou (cf. *ibid.* 28.19a).

tery tell me that he is a " Lotus Abbot " [165] and is lecturing
on Tz'u-en's [166] commentaries.

20*th* DAY   I copied the Minister of State's letter,
which said that among the members of the Japanese tributary embassy, the monk, Ennin, and others, seven men [in
all], had asked to go to the Kuo-ch'ing-ssu of T'ai-chou to
search for teachers, but that an Imperial order had been
received to the effect that the monks were not to be allowed [167] to go to T'ai-chou until [168] the tributary embassy
had reached the capital and that they should wait until the
Japanese credentials had arrived before they were to be
permitted to start. The details are to be found in the
document.[169]

21*st* DAY   Shen-wan 神玩 Ho-shang,[115] a venerable
monk [170] of the Pagoda Monastery,[171] came and met us and
inquired kindly after us.

23*rd* DAY   It was the great festival of Yang-fu. About
two hundred horsemen and about six hundred foot soldiers,

---

[165] *Hokke Zasu* could conceivably mean an Abbot of the **Tendai**
Lotus Sect (see note 134), though more probably the first two
characters refer to the famous *Lotus Sutra* (*Hokke-kyō* or more
fully *Myōhō-renge-kyō* 妙法蓮華經, Skr. *Saddharma-puṇḍarīka-
sūtra*).

[166] Tz'u-en 慈恩 Ta-shih is the posthumous title of K'uei-chi
窺基 (632-682), a disciple of the great Hsüan-tsang 玄奘 (602?-
664) and himself a famous translator and commentator who
wrote on the *Lotus Sutra* among other works. (See note 1156.)

[167] 未入可允許 is somewhat doubtful.

[168] 未 may be a better interpretation of the character printed
來 by *DBZ* and *KIK*.

[169] Meaning that the above is merely an abridgment of the
original document, which must be the notice Nagamine had
spoken of on the sixteenth.

[170] *Rōsōshuku* 老僧宿, more commonly *rōshuku*.

[171] Possibly the " White Pagoda Monastery " (Pai-t'a-ssu 白
塔) of XI 29. According to the *Ch'ung-hsiu Yang-chou-fu chih*
28.19a, there was a Pai-t'a-ssu dating back to T'ang times near
I-ling (see note 82).

in all one thousand cavalry and infantry, [participated]. This affair corresponds to the " Target-Shooting " Festival of the fifth day of the fifth moon in Japan.[172]

28*th* DAY His Excellency, the Ambassador, gave me ten handfuls of tangle and one bundle of seaweed.[173]

29*th* DAY His Excellency, the Ambassador, gave me ten large ounces [127] of gold dust for our support [128] in our search for the Law. The Minister of State arranged a farewell banquet at the " Water Inn " [174] for the envoys going to the capital.

I received instructions from the Ambassador, saying:

With regard to your going early to T'ai-chou, I received a letter from the Minister of State, saying that after I reach the capital, I am to petition the throne, and, after I receive an Imperial permit, then you are to be allowed to proceed to T'ai-chou. I thereupon sent the Minister of State a personally sealed letter, but yesterday I received his reply stating that a separate petition had already been made on this matter and that we might get a reply in a day or two, and, if he does receive Imperial permission, he will let you start out quickly

I hear that the present Emperor, because of someone's plotting,[175] killed the Crown Prince. The reason for this was that the Crown Prince had intended to kill his father the ruler and become Emperor, and therefore his father the ruler killed his own son.[176]

---

[172] 射的之節, the Boys' Festival, usually called *Tango* 端午, *Gogatsu Sekku* 五月節句, or *Kisha no Setsu* 騎射節 (" Festival of Mounted Shooting ").

[173] *Kombu* (or *kobu*) 昆布 and *miru* 海松.

[174] 水館, though there is some doubt about the first character.

[175] *DBZ* follows *Ikeda* in substituting 計 for 許.

[176] Both *CTS* 17B and *TCTC* 246 record on 838 IX 7 that the Emperor, Wen-tsung 文宗, wished to remove the Crown Prince, Yung 永, but was persuaded by his ministers to give him another chance, though many of his attendants were executed. Then on X 16 both sources record the Crown Prince's sudden death. Ennin may have heard a false rumor, but it is not implausible

TENTH MOON: *3rd* DAY [177]　In the evening we two, the Scholar Monk and the Student Monk, went to the P'ing-ch'iao Inn [178] and took leave of the Ambassador and Administrative Officers, since they were going to the capital, and consulted with them. The Administrative Officer Naga-[mine] said that, if he had statements of our sincere desires, he would take them to the capital, petition the throne and quickly obtain permits [for us].

4th DAY　After the forenoon meal we two monks wrote out on separate sheets statements of our sincere desires and sent them to the Administrative Officer. These documents are as separately [recorded].

The officials going to the capital are the Ambassador, the Administrative Officer Nagamine, the Administrative Officer Sugawara,[179] the Secretary Takaoka,[180] the Secretary Ōmi-wa,[181] and the Interpreter Ōyake. In addition, there are the Scholar, Tomo no Sugao,[182] the Shingon Scholar [Monk], Engyō,[123] and thirty-five minor officers [183] and subordinates. There are five official boats.

---

that the Crown Prince was actually executed by his father and the deed glossed over in the official records.

[177] The first day was October 22, 838. The previous moon had only twenty-nine days.

[178] 平橋館. The *Ch'ung-hsiu Yang-chou-fu chih, chüan-shou* 2b, shows a T'ai-p'ing-ch'iao 太平橋 "T'ai-p'ing Bridge" in the western part of the modern city.

[179] Sugawara no Yoshinushi 菅原善主. Cf. *SNK* 839 VIII 25.

[180] Here 高岳 but correctly on VII 2.

[181] Ōmiwa no Muneo 大神宗雄. Cf. *SNK* 839 VIII 20 and 25.

[182] See note 124. Here he is called a *Shōyaku-shō* 請益生 (see note 7), with the second character miswritten 基. He probably was not the Tomo called an Administrative Officer on 839 III 22, but may have been the man in charge of the eighth ship of the return voyage on 839 IV 4. Since he was still alive in 882 (cf. *Sandai jitsuroku* 三代實錄 882 I 7), he was probably quite young at this time.

[183] *Zasshiki* 雜職, probably the same as 雜色, minor officers without court rank.

The Administrative Officer Naga[mine] has entrusted me with the record of rank of the Vice-Ambassador [87] to China of the Enryaku period [86] and with a memorial essay and also with ten packages [184] of silk floss. I have received a statement from the Administrative Officer saying:

> The Vice-Ambassador to China of the Enryaku period, Ishikawa no Ason Michimasu, died in Ming-chou.[185] Now, there has been an Imperial order promoting him to the fourth rank,[186] which has been entrusted to this embassy to present before his [grave] mound. You should make inquiries regarding the route to T'ai-chou,[93] and, if you should reach the borders of Ming-chou, you should then read the memorial essay and with fire burn up the record of rank.

The Sanron Student [Monk], Jōgyō,[121] will still stay at the Kuang-ling Inn [187] and will not be able to go to the capital.

5th DAY   At 7 a.m. the Ambassador and the others boarded the boats and set out for the capital. It rained all day and all night.

6th DAY   It was cold for the first time.

7th DAY   There was a light freeze.

9th DAY   For the first time we had the *san'e* [188] made

---

[184] *T'un* (J. *mochi*) 屯, equal to six ounces. Cf. Des Rotours 472.

[185] 明, the present Ning-po 寧波 in eastern Chekiang.

[186] According to the *SNK*, he had been promoted posthumously from the lower grade to the upper grade of the junior fourth rank on 836 V 10.

[187] Kuang-ling 廣陵 was an old name for the Yang-chou region, and the *Ch'ung-hsiu Yang-chou-fu chih*, *chüan-shou* 3b, shows a Kuang-ling-i 驛 across the canal south of the city wall.

[188] 三衣 (also pronounced *sanne*), the three *kesa* 袈裟 (Skr. *kaṣāya*), or Buddhist scarves worn by monks. The simplest of these is made up of five strips of cloth, each divided into two pieces, and is called the *gojō* 五條; the next is of seven strips, each divided into three pieces, and is called the *shichijō* 七條; the finest is usually of nine, fifteen, or twenty-five strips, each divided into four pieces, and is called the *daie* 大衣. Ennin

for Igyō [189] and the others. The *gojō* [took] 28 feet and 5 inches [190] of silk, the *shichijō* 47 feet and 5 inches of silk, and the *daie* in 25 strips 40 feet of silk, a total of 116 feet of silk. The tailor's charge for making the *daie* of 25 strips was one string of cash,[191] for making the *shichijō* 400 cash, and for making the *gojō* 300 cash, in all one string and 700 cash. We had Chen-shun, a monk of the K'ai-yüan-ssu, attend to the matter.

13*th* DAY   At noon the Scholar [Monk's] attendant, Igyō, and the Student [Monk's] attendant, Ninkō, both shaved their heads.

14*th* DAY   I had two large ounces [127] of gold dust changed at the market. The market determined the weight to be one large ounce and seven *ch'ien* and let the seven *ch'ien* be counted as three-quarters [of an ounce].[129] It was worth nine strings and 400 cash. I also bought two bolts [192] of white silk for two strings of cash and had two Buddhist scarves, a *shichijō* and a *gojō*,[188] made. Again I had the monk Chen-shun attend to this.

After the forenoon meal thirteen Zen [115] and other monks came to see us. [They were] Hui-yün 惠雲 of the Tendai Sect from the Ch'ien-fu-ssu [135a] of Ch'ang-an and the Zen Scholar Monks: Hung-chien 弘鑒, Fa-tuan 法端, Shih-shih 誓實, Hsing-ch'üan 行全, Ch'ang-mi 常密, Fa-chi 法寂, Fa-chen 法眞, Hui-shen 惠深, Ch'üan-ku 全古, Ts'ung-shih 從實, Chung-ch'üan 仲詮, and T'an-yu 曇幽. They wrote by brush:

---

specifies in a small-character gloss that the *daie* was of twenty-five strips.

[189] 曉 is written 皎. By "the others," Ennin means Ishō and Ninkō.

[190] The Chinese foot, which is slightly shorter than the English foot, has only ten inches.

[191] A string (*kuan* 貫) of cash, or copper coins (*ch'ien* 錢, counted with the auxiliary *wen* 文), consisted of 1,000 cash and was the common unit for large sums of money.

[192] *P'i* (J. *hiki* 疋), a measure of cloth equal to almost forty feet. Cf. Des Rotours 471.

Together, quite idly and without attachments, like clouds floating about the landscape, we descended from Wu-feng [193] and wandered to Ch'u [146] and Ssu.[194] Now, having reached this region, we are particularly happy to pay you our respects. It is most extraordinary, and great is our rejoicing. We now intend to go to [Mt.] T'ien-t'ai, and so we take leave of you and depart.

Our great esteem.

Writing by brush, we then replied:

We Japanese monks now meet with you monks because in the past we had important affinities with you. We know for certain that one must dwell in the emptiness which is the nature of the Law.[195] [Our meeting] is most fortunate. If we reach [Mt.] T'ien-t'ai, we shall certainly see you.

Our great esteem.

19*th* DAY In order to have Ishō and Igyō ordained, I wrote a letter to the Administrative Officer and Secretary [still in Yang-chou].[196] Because there had been many secret ordinations in the prefectures, since the second year of T'ai-ho (828)[197] in China orders had been issued to the prefectures forbidding the people to shave their heads and become monks. There are only the ordination platform[198] of Mt.

---

[193] 五峯 ("Five Peaks"), the name of a mountain center of Buddhism in northwestern Kiangsi, a little northwest of I-feng 宜豐 and about 600 km. southwest of Yang-chou.

[194] Ssu-chou 泗, which was located on the Huai River in the vicinity of the modern Hsü-i 盱眙 in Anhwei, about 115 km. northwest of Yang-chou and some distance southeast of the modern Ssu-hsien. The area has since been inundated in large part by Lake Hung-tse 洪澤湖. See note 1417.

[195] *Hosshōjakkū* 法性寂空. Cf. *Hosshōkū.*

[196] See XII 2.

[197] 太和. Here as frequently elsewhere in the text the first character is written 大.

[198] *Kaidan* 戒壇, a platform on which the novice "received the rules" of a monk and was ordained.

Wu-t'ai [199] and the lapis lazuli [200] ordination platform of Chung-shan in Lo-yang.[201] Aside from these two, all have been banned. Because of this, I asked that the matter be reported and appropriate action taken.

    22nd DAY   Early in the morning we saw a comet about a *hsün* [16] in length in the southeastern corner [of the heavens]. Clouds covered it, and not much was visible. The Rector [81] monk, Ling-cheng, told us that this star is like a shining sword [202] and that it appeared day before yesterday, yesterday, and tonight, these three nights. Each day the Minister of State has marveled at it, and each day he has ordered seven monks to read the *Nirvana* and *Hannya* [*Sutras*] [203] for seven days. The same is true in the [other] monasteries as well. Furthermore, last year in the third moon this star also appeared and was extremely bright and long. The Emperor was alarmed and would not stay in his palace but placed himself apart in a lowly seat and clothed himself in

---

[199] 五臺山, a famous Buddhist center in the high mountains northwest of Wu-t'ai-hsien in northeastern Shansi near the Hopeh border.

[200] *Ruri* 瑠璃, a term much used in Buddhism and suggestive of beauty and elegance.

[201] 洛陽, the Eastern Capital of the T'ang and the modern Ho-nan-fu 河南府 in northern Honan. Chung-shan 終山 would seem to be the "mountain name" of a monastery in Lo-yang, but I cannot identify it. Perhaps the Chung-nan Mountains 終南 are meant, for they were the site of a famous Buddhist center some seventy km. southwest of Ch'ang-an, where there was an ordination platform.

[202] *Chien-kuang* 劍光, literally "a sword's light."

[203] *Nehan-gyō* 涅槃 (Skr. *Nirvāṇa-sūtra*) and *Hannya-kyō* 般若 (Skr. *Prajñāpāramitā-sūtra*), each of which exists in several different forms. "Read" is *tennen* 轉念. Cf. *tengyō* 轉經, meaning to scan scriptures rapidly as an act of religious devotion, reading out only the beginning, middle, and end of each chapter. In places Ennin shortens the expression simply to *ten*. The following sentence shows that these seven monks were from the K'ai-yüan-ssu only and that similar groups were ordered to do the same elsewhere.

thin garments. There were prolonged fasts [204] and an amnesty. It is believed that this year it will be similar. On hearing this, I figured out that what I had seen while in Japan tallied with what the Rector said.[205]

23rd DAY   Shen Pien came and said, " When comets appear, the nation greatly declines and meets with military disturbances. The Lords of the East Sea, the leviathan and the whale, these two fishes, have died. The auguries are very alarming. Blood will flow, forming torrents. Military revolutions will break out all over and will lay low the empire. If it be not Yang-chou, then [this augury] will apply to the capital. Previously, on the night of the twenty-third day of the third moon of the ninth year of Yüan-ho (814),[45] a comet appeared in the east, and in the tenth moon of that year there was, accordingly, a revolt of the Ministers of State. Wang, a Minister of State, and others plotted, and some Ministers of State and great officials, in all twenty men, were killed. More than ten thousand persons were killed in the disturbances." Although the matter is not clear to us monks,[206] I have recorded it for later reference.[207]

From nightfall until dawn I left my room to look at the

---

[204] *Chōsai* 長齋, prolonged periods of strict observance of the ban on eating after noon. See notes 89 and 1302.

[205] *CTS* 17B mentions the comet of 838 on X 21 and ff., but a great deal more is told about that of the preceding year on 837 III 2 and ff. The 837 comet, I am informed by Dr. Dorrit Hoffleit of Harvard University, was Halley's comet, which closely approached the earth in April, 837.

[206] 寺 is corrected to 等 without comment by *DBZ* and *KIK*.

[207] The matter obviously was not clear to Ennin, as he says. No comet or disturbance of 814 fits the description, but we may have here a garbled account of the ninth year of T'ai-ho (835), for in the tenth moon of that year Wang Shou-ch'eng 王守澄, a powerful eunuch who had murdered the Emperor Hsientsung in 820, was himself murdered by a nephew of a Minister of State and an accomplice. In the eleventh moon a plot of some of the leading officials to do away with the eunuchs misfired and resulted instead in a massacre of the officials, including a

comet. It was in the southeastern corner [of the heavens], and its tail pointed to the west, shining very distinctly. Seen from a great distance, the length of its tail might be estimated at over a hundred feet. People all said that it definitely was a shining sword.[202]

24th DAY I hired a man to make two mats [208] for Ishō and the other. Chen-shun, a monk of this monastery, again attended to this. The material for one mat consisted of twenty-one feet of coarse silk—eight feet and four inches for the top surface, eight feet and four inches for the bottom surface, and four feet and two inches for the border. The material for the two mats was forty-two feet in all. The maker's charge for one was 250 cash, and the total was 500 cash.

30th DAY It hailed before the forenoon meal.

ELEVENTH MOON: 2nd DAY [209] I bought the *Yuima-kanchū-sho* [138] in four scrolls. It cost 450 cash.

There is an Imperial order prohibiting [the use of] copper, and throughout the land the sale or purchase of it is not allowed. It was explained that there was [such a regulation] as a rule once every six years. The reason for the prohibition is that they fear that, if the people of the empire always make copper utensils, there would be no copper for minting cash.

ELEVENTH MOON: 7th DAY Chen-shun, a monk of the K'ai-yüan-ssu, privately sold broken pots to a merchant

---

certain Wang Yai 王涯 . Cf. *TCTC* 245 and O. Franke, *Geschichte des Chinesischen Reiches* (Berlin and Leipzig, 1936) 2.488.

[208] *Zagu* 坐具 (or 座具), literally "sitting-mats," but at this time they were used by monks for beds as well. They are twice as long as they are wide, and the central surface of cloth is surrounded by a border of even width. The second mat was probably for Igyō. The "three chairs with rope seats" mentioned by Waley on pp. 143-44 appears to be a mistaken reference to these "two mats."

[209] The first day was November 21, 838.

to the amount of ten pounds weight. When the merchant went out with his iron, he ran into some police inspectors [210] at the monastery gate and was arrested and brought back. The five inspectors came and said, " Recently the Minister of State has prohibited [the use of] iron, and one is not allowed to sell or buy it. How then is it that you have sold some? " Chen-shun replied that he did not know that its sale was prohibited. Then the officer in charge and Chen-shun prepared documents asking for a decision, and the officials pardoned him. Thus we learned that within the jurisdiction of Yang-chou the sale or purchase of iron is not permitted.

After the forenoon meal three police guards [211] from before the Minister of State's official residence came especially [212] to see us and communicated with us by brush. The Minister of State, beginning on the third day of [this] moon, is having a three-foot white sandalwood [213] image of the Buddha Shaka [214] carved in the Jui-hsiang Balcony [215] of this monastery. As for this Jui-hsiang Balcony, in the time of Yang-ti of the Sui, four sandalwood images of Shaka came flying from India to the balcony, and accordingly Yang-ti himself wrote the four characters *Jui-hsiang-fei-ko* (" Balcony of the Auspicious Images "), which were hung on the front of the balcony.

8th DAY   Before the forenoon meal the Minister of State came into the monastery. After worshiping the Buddha, from the stone pavement in front of the hall he summoned the two of us Scholar and Student Monks. Thus we met, and

---

[210] *Hsün-chien* 巡撿.

[211] *Yü-hou* 虞候. Cf. Des Rotours 647 and see note 1358.

[212] *DBZ* suggests 特 for 持.

[213] *Pai-t'an* 白檀.

[214] Shakamuni 釋迦牟尼 (Skr. Śākyamuni), the historical Buddha.

[215] Jui-hsiang-ko, below called the Jui-hsiang-fei-ko 瑞像飛閣, " Balcony of the Auspicious Images." At the end of this passage it is called a *lou* 樓, showing clearly that it was a building of more than one story.

he asked us whether or not we were comfortable. I estimated that he had around him in attendance about two hundred foot soldiers and over forty police guards. At the gate were eighty-odd [216] cavalry. All were dressed in purple garments. He also had attendant civil officials, all of whom were dressed in watery blue-green. They were all mounted, presenting a scene not easily described. After the Minister of State had finished inspecting what the monks were doing, he squatted on a large chair within the monastery and was carried out. He has donated in all one hundred bushels [217] of rice to defray the costs of repairing the monastery.

16th DAY   We wrote a letter of thanks to the Minister of State for coming to the monastery and inquiring after us. We also gave him a few things—two rosaries of rock crystal, six knives decorated with silver, twenty assorted brushes, and three conch shells. We made a separate list of the gifts and put it into the envelope with the message, and we entrusted it to the Minister of State's military aide, the Ta-fu [218] Shen Pien, to transmit.

17th DAY   At 10 A. M. Shen Pien returned and gave us a message from the Minister of State to the effect that he thanked us for our letter and that he would keep only the large conch shell without the end cut off 不截尻 and that he was giving the two small conch shells with the ends cut

---

[216] DBZ misprints 計 for 許.

[217] The hu 斛 was in theory 10 tou 斗 (or 㪷) or 100 sheng 升. According to Wu Ch'eng-lo, op. cit. 71, the tou was 5.944 liters and the sheng .5944 liters in T'ang times, making a hu a trifle over one and two-thirds bushels. When Ennin used the term "large sheng" he was probably referring to the T'ang sheng as opposed to the earlier Sui sheng, which was less than half as large (see note 127). Later in the text Ennin uses shih 石 ("stone") and its homophone 碩 in place of hu. DBZ and KIK print 惣 for 物 in this sentence.

[218] 大夫, an honorary title for various officials and a traditional term for any officer of the fifth rank, which was Shen Pien's actual rank (see note 125).

off, the rosaries,[219] the knives, and the brushes to his messenger to return to us. He also sent a police guard to give us two bolts [192] of white silk and three bolts of white silk damask.[220] We at once wrote a letter of thanks and sent it by a return messenger.

The present Chinese Emperor's taboo name is Ang [221] which is called his personal name. The taboo names of his ancestors are Shun 純 Shun 淳, Chao 詔 Sung 誦, Kua 括, Yü 譽 Yü 豫 or Yü 預, Lung-chi 隆基, Heng 恆, Chan 湛, Yüan 淵, Hu 虎 Chieh 戒, and Shih-min 世民.[222] [Characters] of the same sound are all tabooed. In this country they avoid these characters and never write them in any documents. This is what was told to us by Tsung-jui 宗叡 Fa-shih, a monk of the Hsi-ming-ssu.[223]

---

[219] *Tōji* has 餘珠, *Ikeda* 念珠.

[220] *Ling* 綾.

[221] The character more closely resembles Po 帛 than Ang 昻, Wen-tsung's actual taboo name.

[222] In this listing the names in small type (small characters in the original) are meant to be those which, because of resemblance in sound, appearance, or meaning to the tabooed names, were substituted for them in writing. Ennin, of course, was wrong in saying further on that all homophones were tabooed, and he was obviously confused over some of the tabooed names and their substitutes. Shun was the eleventh T'ang ruler, Hsien-tsung 憲宗; Sung, which has been reversed with Chao, its substitute, was the tenth emperor, Shun-tsung 順; Kua is a graphic substitute for Kua 适, the ninth ruler, Te-tsung 德; Yü 豫, for which 預 was a tabooed equivalent and 譽 a substitute, was the eighth ruler, Tai-tsung 代; Lung-chi was the sixth emperor, Hsüan-tsung; Heng was Wen-tsung's father, the twelfth ruler, Mu-tsung 穆; Chan was Wen-tsung's brother and predecessor, the thirteenth emperor, Ching-tsung 敬; Yüan was the first T'ang emperor, Kao-tsu 高祖; Hu was the latter's grandfather, and the substitute character in *Tōji* may be Wu 武 instead of the Chieh in the printed texts; and Shih-min was the second ruler, T'ai-tsung 太.

[223] There was a Hsi-ming-ssu 西明 in the western half of Ch'ang-an, but I find none in this area.

18*th* DAY   The Minister of State came to the monastery and worshiped the " auspicious images " in the balcony
and inspected the newly made image. Presently, his military
aide, the *Ta-fu* Shen Pien, rushed up to us and said that the
Minister of State invited us monks [to join him]. On hearing
this, we climbed up to the balcony with the messenger. The
Minister of State and the Military Inspector,[144] together with
Senior Secretaries,[224] Deputy Secretaries,[225] and Administrative Officers [38] of the prefecture, all were seated on chairs
drinking tea. When they saw us monks coming, they all
arose and paid us respect by joining their hands and standing. They called out to us to sit down, and we all seated ourselves on the chairs and sipped tea. There were the Minister
of State and his attendants from the Senior Secretaries down
to the Administrative Officers, eight men in all. The Minister
of State wore purple, the three Senior Secretaries and Deputy
Secretaries wore dark red,[226] and the four Administrative
Officers wore green.[227] The police guards, foot soldiers,
cavalry, and honor guards [228] were just as before.

The Minister of State, who sat directly in front of us,
asked if it were ever cold in our country, and the Student
Monk replied that the summers were hot and the winters
cold, at which the Minister of State remarked that this was
the same as hereabouts. The Minister of State then asked
whether or not we had monasteries, and we replied that
there were many, and he further asked how many monasteries there were, and we replied that there were about 3,700.
He also asked whether or not we had convents, and we

---

[224] Des Rotours 34-129 lists Senior Secretaries (*Lang-chung* 郎
中) as the chiefs of the various bureaus of the six ministries
under the Department of State (*Shang-shu-sheng* 尚書省) at
the capital, but none in a provincial administration of this sort.
[225] *Lang-kuan* 郎官. Cf. Des Rotours 667.
[226] *Fei* 緋, worn in T'ang times by officials of the fifth rank and
higher.
[227] Followed by 衩, for which *DBZ* suggests 衫, " jackets."
[228] *Chang-jen* 丈人. Cf. 仗 in Des Rotours 84, etc. The reference
is to XI 8.

replied that there were many. He further asked whether or not we had Taoist priests, and we replied that there were no Taoist priests. The Minister of State also asked how many *li* in area was the capital of our country, and we replied that it was fifteen *li* from east to west and fifteen *li* from south to north.[229] He also asked if we observed summer retirement,[230] and we replied that we did. The Minister of State then conversed with us a little longer, and, in consoling us, communicated to us his sympathy. After that, we bowed to each other and descended from the balcony. He also went to the Kuan-yin-yüan (" Kannon [6] Cloister ") [56] to inspect the repair work.[231]

19*th* DAY In order to provide for a maigre feast on the anniversary of the death of T'ien-t'ai Ta-shih [140] on the twenty-fourth day, we gave four bolts of silk and three bolts of silk damask [220] to the monastery offices, the Student Monk [giving] two bolts of silk and the Scholar Monk three bolts of silk damask and two bolts of silk. We prepared a letter and sent it to the monastery offices. It is recorded on a separate sheet. They sold [the goods] for more than six strings of cash.[191]

24*th* DAY The maigre feast was arranged in the [dining] hall. The assembly of monks [numbered] over sixty. Huan-ch'ün 幻羣 Fa-shih performed the rite of . . . of the maigre feast.[232] The assembly of monks entered the hall to-

---

[229] Actually Kyōto was not 9 by 9 km. as the monks claimed, but was laid out 5.25 km. north to south by 4.8 km., and not all of this area was built up. The number of monasteries claimed for Japan was no doubt a similar exaggeration on the part of the monks.

[230] *Zage* 坐夏, the same as *ango* 安居 (Skr. *varṣa*), a period from the middle of the fourth moon to the middle of the seventh when Buddhist monks were supposed to stay within their monasteries and study. The practice arose in India because of the summer rainy season.

[231] 修法之事 , " matters of religious practice," I suspect is an error for 修理之事. See the last sentence under XI 8.

[232] 作齋難人食儀式 , literally, " to perform the rite of ' to be

gether and sat down in order, and a man performed [the rite of] purification by water.²³³ We patron monks stood in front of the hall. One of the assembly of monks beat a wooden mallet, and another monk chanted a Sanskrit [hymn].²³⁴ The Sanskrit hymn was, "How through this scripture is one eventually to reach the other shore? ²³⁵ We desire the Buddha to open to us the subtle mystery and to explain it in detail for all creatures." It sounded most beautiful.

During the chanting of the Sanskrit a man was passing out scriptures. After the Sanskrit, the assembly together recited scriptures, about two pages of each. Then a wooden mallet was struck, and the reading of scriptures ²⁰³ came to an end. Next, a monk chanted, " Reverence the three eternal treasures," ²³⁶ and the assembled monks all got down from their benches and stood. Then the first master of Sanskrit chanted in Sanskrit a one-line text, " The body of the *Nyorai* is without exhaustion," etc.²³⁷

During the reciting of the Sanskrit, the Monastery Administrator ¹¹⁹ had the Scholar Monk and the others enter [the hall] and burn incense,²³⁸ and [this was done for] every one of the monks. The rite of incense burning is the same as

---

difficult long to eat ' of the maigre feast." The sequence 齋難 久, however, closely resembles 齋歎文, " maigre-feast essay in praise [of the Buddha]," which occurs below.

²³³ *Gyōzui* 行水.

²³⁴ 作梵, but 梵頌 below. Part of this same hymn is again quoted on 839 XI (or XII) 22.

²³⁵ *Higan* 彼岸, a term for Nirvana, the Buddhist concept of salvation.

²³⁶ *Jōjū sambō* 常住三寶, which were the Buddha, the Law (*Dharma*), and the Church (*Saṃgha*), or more strictly the " monastic community."

²³⁷ *Nyorai* 如來 (Skr. *Tathāgata*) is one of the ten appellations of the Buddha, and *shiki* probably stands for *shikishin* 色身, " the visible body," a term occurring in a comparable phrase on XII 8.

²³⁸ *Gyōkō* 行香. The term itself means " to pass out incense " to monks, for them to burn in worship.

in Japan. The monks who had arranged the maigre feast for the others, preceding [239] the congregation, rose and went to the left side of [the image of] the Buddha, where they stood facing south and burned incense.

After that, they then gave praise to the Buddha. This did not differ in wording from the praise of the Buddha at the beginning of a prayer in our country. After giving praise to the Buddha, they made known the document in which we patrons [240] had first requested that a maigre feast be arranged. Then they read the maigre-feast essay in praise [of Buddha]. After reading the maigre-feast essay, they chanted, " The Buddha, Shakamuni," [214] the great assembly calling out the Buddha's name in unison. After that they chanted praises. These were the same as what we call in Japan hymns for the eight classes of demi-gods [241] and the good spirits and kings.[242] They chanted these praises while standing, and then all together climbed onto their benches and seated themselves.

The monk who had read the maigre-feast essay, the Monastery Supervisor,[116] the Monastery Administrator,[119] we patron monks, and others, [in all] more than ten of us, left the dining hall and went to the living quarters, where we had our maigre feast. The other monks and the novices all had their maigre feast in the dining hall. In the living quarters we separately made offerings on behalf of the monks of Nan-yo and T'ien-t'ai.[243]

---

[239] *DBZ* suggests 先 for 矣.

[240] *Dan'otsu* 檀越, more commonly *danna* 檀那 (Skr. *dānapati*).

[241] *Tenryū-hachibu*, standing for *hachibushū* 八部衆, the eight classes of demi-gods, of which the *ten* 天 (" heavenly beings," Skr. *deva*) and the *ryū* 龍 (" dragons," Skr. *nāga*) are the first two.

[242] 善神王, the local spirits and demons which were considered to be protecting deities of Buddhism.

[243] Nan-yo 南岳, " the southern peak," is an alternate name for Mt. Heng 衡, a little west of the town of Heng-shan in central Hunan. The monk referred to here by this name is Hui-ssu 慧思 (515-577), who from the point of view of doctrine is

When the assembly of monks holds a maigre feast, two Monastery Steward [118] monks arrange matters. The custom in China is that, each time a maigre feast is held, in addition to [purchasing] food, they set aside some of the money provided, and when the maigre feast is about to end, they divide it equally among the monks in accordance with how many cash there are and the number of the assembled monks.[244] For the monk who has made the maigre-feast essay, however, they especially augment the number of cash. If they give thirty cash to each of the monks, they give four hundred cash to the one who has made the maigre-feast essay. Both are called alms cash, which I believe is the same as what is called " charity " [245] in Japan. After the maigre feast, we all rinsed out our mouths together and returned to our rooms.

An established custom of all monasteries is that, when a patron intends on the next day to boil gruel [120] and serve it to the monks, at sunset he sends a man around to inform them that on the following morning there will be gruel, but, when a man is arranging a maigre feast, he does not inform them in the evening but sends around a man early in the morning of that day to inform them that there will be food in the [dining] hall. When a man comes to the monastery and asks that scriptures be read, they also have a man announce that they are going up to the hall to recite scriptures.

In Yang-fu there are over forty monasteries. When one monastery arranges a maigre feast, it invites the monks of other monasteries in turn to come and receive the maigre feast and alms, rotating [the invitations] in this manner. Each time they hold a maigre feast, they record the names of the monasteries [whose monks have been invited], and

---

considered to be the second patriarch of the Tendai Sect in China. He was the teacher of the third patriarch, Chih-i, the real founder of the sect, with whom he is coupled in this passage (see note 140).

[244] DBZ suggests 依 for the first 僧.

[245] Fuse 布施. The term translated above as " alms cash " is ch'en-ch'ien 儭錢.

in turn then invite the monks of the remaining monasteries. Thus, they determine the sequence of monasteries and take the monks in turn. When this has been done for one monastery, they then do the same for the other monasteries, each taking the other monasteries in order and the monks [of each monastery] in turn. The [number of] monks invited varies in accordance with the quantity of [provisions for] the maigre feast. When a monastery one day arranges a maigre feast, it counts together the list of monks of that [246] monastery and the list of monks of the other monasteries [invited].

There are [in China] "Ecclesiastics Who Convert Laymen," who are the same as what we call "Evangelists" [247] in Japan. Those who expound the principles of impermanence, suffering, and emptiness in this world and convert men and women disciples are called "Ecclesiastics Who Convert Laymen." Those who lecture on the *sūtra*, *śāstra*, *vinaya*, and commentaries are called Abbots,[80] Priests,[115] and Reverences.[248] Those who wear clerical robes and master their hearts are called Masters of Meditation or again *Dōsha*.[249]

---

[246] *DBZ* suggests 當 for 堂.

[247] *Hikyōkeshi* 飛教化師. The Chinese term is *Hua-su Fa-shih* 化俗法師 (see note 7). Neither term has become a generally accepted one.

[248] *Daitoku* 大德, literally "Great Virtue," an honorary title for a monk. The *sūtra* (Ch. *ching*, J. *kyō* 經), *śāstra* (Ch. *lun*, J. *ron* 論), and *vinaya* (Ch. *lü*, J. *ritsu* 律) are the three main divisions of the Buddhist Tripitaka (Ch. *San-tsang*, J. *Sanzō* 三藏) or body of holy writings. As we see below, these terms were combined with *Daitoku*, etc. to form religious titles such as "Reverence of the *Vinaya*" (*Ritsu-daitoku*), as also on 839 I 18.

[249] "Master of Meditation" (*Zenji* 禪師, Ch. *Ch'an-shih*) was an honorary title for those versed in meditation practices, but *Dōsha* 道者 is not a usual Buddhist term. By the clause "those who wear clerical robes and master their hearts" 衲衣收心, Ennin probably meant to distinguish between Buddhist practitioners of meditation and Taoists and other non-Buddhist mystics.

Those who are particularly strong in the observation of the rules are called Reverences of the *Vinaya*. [Those who] lecture [on the *vinaya*] are called Abbots of the *Vinaya*. The [other] titles are comparable to these.

Since the tenth moon there have been several long rainy spells, so the Minister of State wrote to the seven monasteries [76] that each was to have seven monks seek good weather by reciting scriptures over a period of seven days. When this was finished, the skies cleared. The custom in China is that when seeking good weather they close the north end of the roads,[250] and when seeking rain they close the south end of the roads. The tradition says, " When, seeking good weather, you block the north, *yin* is obstructed, and *yang* [251] then pervades, and the skies should clear. When, asking for rain, you block the south, *yang* is obstructed, and *yin* then pervades, and rain should fall."

26th DAY   This night no one sleeps. It is the same as New Year's Eve and the nights of *Kōshin* [252] in our country.

27th DAY   It is the festival of the winter solstice. Monks and laymen all offer congratulations. Those who are laymen pay their respects to the officials and congratulate them on the festival of the winter solstice. When they see the Minister of State, they say, " Moving by degrees, the sun has reached its southern extremity. We humbly hope for a myriad of blessings for the Minister of State's honored self." Officials of high and low rank and the common people all offer one another congratulations when they meet. Clerics offer each other congratulations when they meet, uttering phrases about the winter solstice and making obeisance to

---

[250] That is, the north gates of a city.

[251] *Yin* 陰, the female principle, represents the north, darkness, and rain; *yang* 陽, the male principle, represents the south, brightness, and good weather.

[252] On the nights of *Kōshin* (Ch. *Keng-shen*) 庚申 , the fifty-seventh day of the hexagenary cycle, the ancient Japanese traditionally held a wake called *Kōshin-machi* 待. In this case the wake was being held on the eve of the winter solstice and had nothing to do with the days of the cycle.

one another. Laymen on entering the monastery also show the same courtesy.

The congregation of monks said to us foreign monks, "Today is the festival of the winter solstice. May you have a myriad of blessings; may the propagation of the lamp [of the Law] be without end; and may you return soon to your own land and long be National Teachers." [253] After we had all paid our respects to one another, they remarked that it was extremely cold. One monk came and said, "This being the winter solstice, may you have a myriad of blessings; may your scholarship illumine the 'three learnings'; [254] may you soon return to your homeland and for long be National Teachers." There were all sorts of [such] speeches.

This festival is exactly the same as New Year's Day in Japan. Each lay and monastic establishment provides rare delicacies, and all sorts of dishes are assembled. All use congratulatory phrases on the season, conforming to the tastes of the men of former times.[255] Clerics and laymen alike offer congratulations on the winter solstice for a period of three days. This monastery also arranges a three-day offering, and various sorts [of things] are gathered.

28*th* DAY   It snowed.

29th DAY   It was clear. Yang-chou has over forty monasteries. Among them is the Lung-hsing-ssu [256] where Chien-

---

[253] *Kokushi* 國師, an honorary title bestowed on certain eminent monks.

[254] *Sangaku* 三學 (Skr. *trīni-śiksani*), the three Buddhist "disciplines," which are *kai* 戒 (Skr. *adhiśīla*), the commandments or precepts, *jō* 定 (Skr. *adhicitta* or *samādhi*), meditation, and *e* 慧 (Skr. *adhiprajñā*), knowledge or wisdom.

[255] 隨前人所樂, by which Ennin probably sought to explain stereotyped expressions which may not have seemed suitable to him.

[256] The Emperor Hsüan-tsung ordered the establishment throughout the land of Lung-hsing-ssu 龍興 as well as K'ai-yüan-ssu (see note 55). For the Yang-chou Lung-hsing-ssu, cf. *Ch'ung-hsiu Yang-chou-fu chih* 28.19a-23b.

chen Ho-shang,[257] who came across the seas [to Japan], originally lived. A picture of him still exists there. The Vicar
General, Fa-chin,[258] originally lived in the White Pagoda.[171]
It was in this White Pagoda Monastery that the statesman,
[Li] Shan, compiled the *Wen-hsüan*.[259] Hui-yün Fa-shih [260]
also was a monk of the White Pagoda Monastery. Each
prefecture has a K'ai-yüan-ssu and a Lung-hsing-ssu. This
is merely the Lung-hsing-ssu of Yang-chou.

At 4 P. M. K'o-ssu 可思, a monk of Ch'ang-an who lectures
on the *Hyaku-ron*,[261] came to see us.

An Administrative Officer of the first ship, Fujiwara no
Ason Sadatoshi, has for some time been lying ill and suffering. As a special act of faith, he has resolved to make
pictures of the Bodhisattva Myōken [31] and the Four Heavenly Kings.[97] He, therefore, had the Ambassador's attendant,
Awada no Ietsugu 粟田家繼, come to this monastery today
to decide on a place for the drawing of the " Buddhas."

30*th* DAY   Early in the morning they started drawing

---

[257] Chien-chen (J. Ganjin, Kanshin, etc.) 鑑眞 (688-763) came
to Japan in 754 and established the Ritsu Sect there. The
account of his trip to Japan is translated by Takakusu as " Le
voyage de Kanshin en Orient (742-754)," *Bulletin de l'École
Française d'Extrême-Orient* 28.1-41 and 441-472 and 29.47-62.

[258] Fa-chin (J. Hōshin) 法進 (709-778) studied under Chien-
chen and accompanied him to Japan, where he eventually became a Vicar General (*Sōzu* 僧都), the second of the three
categories of general officers of the Buddhist church in Japan.
For Fa-chin cf. Takakusu, *op. cit.* 28.23.

[259] Ennin has made a serious error in attributing the *Wen-hsüan*
文選, the famous sixth-century anthology, to Li Shan 李善, who
was active during the middle years of the seventh century. The
latter, however, did write an important commentary on the
Wen-hsüan, which when later joined with a similar commentary
by five other authors came to be known as the *Commentaries
of the Six Statesmen* (*Liu-ch'en-chu* 六臣註).

[260] Presumably the Ch'ang-an monk of this name mentioned on
X 14.

[261] 百論 (Skr. *Śata-śāstra*), one of the standard scriptures of the
Sanron Sect (see note 121).

the pictures of the Bodhisattva Myōken and of the Four Heavenly Kings in the Hall of the Deity Kabira.[262]

TWELFTH MOON: 2nd DAY [263]   In order to have Ishō and the others ordained, the Japanese officials who have been left behind [in Yang-chou] again wrote to the Minister of State. They have written him about this previously, but the Commissioner in Charge [of the Japanese Embassy],[264] Wang Yu-chen, lost [the letter] on the way, so now they have written again. The letter is as separately [recorded].

   5th DAY   The drawings were finished.

   8th DAY   Today was a national anniversary day,[265] and accordingly fifty strings of cash were given to the K'ai-yüan-ssu to arrange a maigre feast for five hundred monks. Early in the morning the monastic congregations gathered in this monastery and seated themselves in rows in the flanking buildings on the east, north, and west.[266] At 8 A. M. the Minister of State and the General [267] entered the monastery by the great gate. The Minister of State and the General walked in slowly side by side. Soldiers in ranks guarded them on all sides, and all the officials of the prefecture and of the

---

[262] 迦毘羅 (Skr. Kapila), a minor deity in the Buddhist pantheon, associated with Kumārajīva (see note 139).

[263] The first day was December 21, 838.

[264] *DBZ* suggests that 等 be deleted from the middle of the term *Kou-tang* (see note 105).

[265] *Kuo-chi* 國忌, the anniversary of the death of an Emperor or Empress (cf. Des Rotours 87-88). In this case it was the anniversary of Ching-tsung, who was assassinated on 826 XII 8.

[266] As we see further on, the ceremony took place in the courtyard facing the lecture hall on the north. Alexander C. Soper, *The Evolution of Buddhist Architecture in Japan* (Princeton University Press, 1942) 28, 86-87, 146, draws certain conclusions regarding the plan of the K'ai-yüan-ssu from Ennin's description of this ceremony, but Soper does not seem to be justified in assuming that the ceremony took place inside one of the halls.

[267] *Chiang-chün* 將軍, a high military title, here possibly referring to the Military Inspector of XI 18.

regional commandery followed behind. They came as far as the foot of the steps in front of the lecture hall, and then the Minister of State and the General parted, the Minister of State going to the east [268] and entering behind a curtain on the east side [of the courtyard], and the General going to the west and entering behind a curtain on the west side. They quickly changed their slippers, washed their hands, and came out again. In front of the hall were two bridges.[269] The Minister of State mounted the eastern bridge and the General the western bridge, and thus the two of them circled around from the east and west and met at the center door of the hall. They took their seats and worshiped the Buddha.

After that, several tens of monks lined up in rows at both the east and west doors of the hall. Each one held artificial lotus flowers and green [270] banners. A monk struck a stone triangle and chanted, " All be worshipful and reverence the three eternal treasures." [236] After that the Minister of State and the General arose and took censers, and the prefectural officials all followed after them, taking incense cups. They divided, going to the east and west, with the Minister of State going towards the east. The monks who were carrying flowered banners preceded him, chanting in unison a two-line hymn in Sanskrit, " The wonderful body of the Nyorai," etc.[237] A venerable monk [170] followed first [behind the Minister of State] and then the soldiers guarding him. They went along the gallery under the eaves. After all the monks had burned incense,[238] they returned toward the hall by this route, chanting Sanskrit hymns without cease. The General went to the west and burned incense, performing the same rite as [that performed by the Minister of State] in the east, and [the two of them] came [back] simultaneously and met in their original place [before the central door of the hall].

During this time, there was beautiful responsive chanting

---

[268] *DBZ* follows *Ikeda* in correcting 行人 to 東行.
[269] Large courtyards in China frequently have small streams, crossed by stone bridges.
[270] Or blue (*pi* 碧).

of Sanskrit hymns by [the groups of monks] on the east and west. The leader of the chants, standing alone and motionless, struck a stone triangle, and the Sanskrit [chanting] stopped. Then they again recited, " Honor the three eternal treasures." The Minister of State and the General sat down together in their original seats. When they burned incense, the incense burners in which their incense was placed stood side by side. A venerable monk, Yüan-ch'eng 圓乘 Ho-shang, read a prayer, after which the leader of the chants intoned hymns in behalf of the eight classes of demi-gods.[241] The purport of the wording was to glorify the spirit of the [late] Emperor. At the end of each verse he recited, " Honor the three eternal treasures." The Minister of State and the officials rose to their feet together and did reverence to the Buddha, chanting three or four times. Then all [were free] to do as they wished.

The Minister of State and the others, taking the soldiers [with them], went into the great hall behind the [lecture] hall and dined.[266] The congregation of five hundred monks dined in the galleries. The numbers of monks invited varied in accordance with the size of the monastery. The large monasteries had thirty, the middle-sized monasteries twenty-five, and the small monasteries twenty. All were seated together as groups in long rows, and managers [271] were dispatched from each monastery to attend to the serving of their respective groups. The managers from the various places themselves did the serving. The maigre feast was not served in a single place, but was served and eaten at the same time [in all places], and then [the monks] arose and dispersed, each one going to [272] his own monastery.

On this day the Minister of State especially [272a] gave out cash and sent managers [271] to two monasteries to have water heated and the congregations of monks of the various monasteries bathed. This is to be done for three days.

---

[271] *Kou-tang.* See note 105.

[272] *DBZ* suggests 赴 for 起.

[272a] 別 is missing in *DBZ* and *KIK.*

9th DAY The Japanese Administrative Officer, Fujiwara no Ason Sadatoshi, arranged a maigre feast in the K'ai-yüan-ssu, putting out five strings and 600 cash for the food. He made offerings [of food] to the newly drawn pictures of the Buddha Amida,[273] the Bodhisattva Myōken, and the Four Heavenly Kings, and to over sixty monks. Also, on this day he had copies made of the paintings of Nan-yo Ta-shih[243] and T'ien-t'ai Ta-shih[140] which were on the walls of the Fa-hua-yüan 法花 (" Lotus Cloister ") of the Lung-hsing-ssu.[256]

18th DAY At 2 P.M. the Korean Interpreter, Kim Chŏngnam, left for Ch'u-chou[146] to settle upon the ships for the embassy's homeward voyage.

At 4 P.M. the Commissioner in Charge [of the Japanese Embassy], Wang Yu-chen, came and told us that the Ambassador had finally arrived at the capital on the third day of this moon and that he himself would soon follow the Ambassador to the capital and would send to the prefectural offices the documents he was in charge of.[274] He also [said that] the Minister of State would not permit the ordination of the novices and that, since there had been Imperial orders year after year that ordinations were not to be permitted, he could not allow it without [special] Imperial permission.

20th DAY I bought a new calendar [for the next year]. It snowed during the night.

21st DAY The snow stopped, but the sky was overcast.

23rd DAY It was clear. More than fifty artisans, porters 運, and archers from the first ship came to the monastery for a maigre feast and to have scriptures recited.

After the maigre feast, Tao-wu 道悟, a monk of the Wu-liang-i-ssu, came and we met. He told us himself that he

---

[273] 阿彌陀 (Skr. Amitābha).

[274] Presumably the requests for Ennin and Ensai to go to T'ai-chou (see XII 12). We see from this passage that it took the embassy fifty-nine days to reach the capital, but the reply came back in sixteen days or less.

understood *shingon*.[275] There is also a Wen-ch'en 文琛 **Fa-shih** of the Ch'i-ling-ssu [276] who is said to have mastered the laws of *shingon*, and recently I have heard that the Sanron Student Monk, Jōgyō, is living in that monastery and is learning the *shingon* laws in the apartment of [Wen]-ch'en Fa-shih and intends to draw the *Double Mandara*.[277]

29th DAY At sunset clerics and laymen together burned paper money,[278] and after midnight the lay households burned bamboos and as they exploded, shouted " Banzai." [279] In the streetshops there were all sorts of foods in extraordinary profusion. On this night in Japan lamps are lit everywhere—in gardens, within homes, and in front of gates. In China it is not so. Unlike our country, they only light the usual lamps.

---

[275] The word from which the Shingon Sect derives its name (see note 115), literally meaning " true words " and corresponding to Skr. *mantra*, the ritualistic formulae of Buddhism.

[276] *DBZ* and *KIK* suggest that this be corrected to Ch'i-hsia-ssu 棲霞, the name of a famous monastery near Nanking, but Ch'i-ling-ssu 棲靈 (*DBZ* and *KIK* have *hsi* 栖, a recognized substitute for the first character) was an old name for the Ta-ming-ssu 大明, located beside the present P'ing-shan-t'ang 平山堂, a short distance northwest of Yang-chou. Cf. Tokiwa Daijō 常盤大定, *Shina Bukkyō shiseki tōsa ki* 支那佛敎史蹟踏査記 (Tōkyō, 1938) 422-26 and the *Tseng-hsiu Kan-ch'üan-hsien chih* 增修甘泉縣志 9.*ssu-kuan-chih* 寺觀志 14b and *t'u* 圖 1b.

[277] 曼荼羅 (Skr. *maṇḍala*), usually meaning graphic portrayals of the Buddhist pantheon arranged to represent Buddhist cosmological principles. The so-called *Double* (*Ryōbu* 兩部) *Mandara* are those of the *Kongōkai* 金剛界 (Skr. *Vajra-dhātu*), the " Diamond Realm " or " Realm of the Indestructibles," and the *Taizōkai* 胎藏界 (Skr. *Garbha-dhātu*), the " Realm of the Womb," which underlie the metaphysics of Esoteric Buddhism.

[278] Not paper money in the modern sense, which was not developed in China until a century or more later, but imitation money such as is still used in China for similar occasions. In this case it was, of course, in celebration of New Year's Eve.

[279] Ch. *wan-sui* 萬歲.

After midnight they struck the bell in the monastery, and the congregation of monks gathered in the dining hall to pay reverence to the Buddha. At the moment for worshiping the Buddha, the whole congregation descended from their benches and, spreading out their mats [208] on the ground, worshiped the Buddha, after which they climbed back onto the benches. Then the Monastery Steward [119] and Controller [81] monks read out in front of the assembly the various account books [280] for the year for the assembly to hear. Before dawn came, they dined on gruel in front of the lamps, after which they scattered to their rooms. Late the next morning they all left their quarters and took part in a ceremony, exchanging greetings among the congregation of monks. The monastery arranged offerings [of food],[122] which lasted for three days.

K'AI-CH'ENG · FOURTH YEAR

chi-wei

WHICH IS THE SAME AS

JŌWA · SIXTH YEAR

IN JAPAN

tsuchinoto hitsuji

FIRST MOON: 1st DAY: *chia-yin* [281] This is New Year's Day. Officials and laymen have a three-day holiday, and this monastery will have three days of maigre feasts. Early in the morning the Minister of State came to the monastery and worshiped the Buddha and then went back.

---

[280] *Yung-t'u-chang* 用途帳. Cf. *yung-ch'ien-wu-chang* 用錢物帳 on 840 XII 25.

[281] January 19, 839. *Chi-wei* 己未 (*tsuchinoto hitsuji* in Japanese), referring to the year, is fifty-six in the hexagenary cycle, and *chia-yin* 甲寅, referring to the day, is fifty-one. "Sixth year (*tsuchinoto hitsuji*)" is copied twice in *Tōji* and then is set off the second time with brackets.

3rd DAY We started the drawing of three pictures [282]
each of Nan-yo and T'ien-t'ai Ta-shih. Of old, during the
Liang period, there lived [a man called] Han Kan,[283] who
was the leading painter of the Liang dynasty. When, in
painting pictures of birds or animals, he drew in their eyes,
they were able to fly or run. He investigated the appearance
of Nan-yo Ta-shih and drew a likeness of him in the Lung-
hsing-ssu of Yang-chou, which the Emperor placed on the
wall of the south gallery of the Lapis Lazuli Hall of the Lotus
Place of Ritual.[284] Now I have had the Ambassador's attendant, Awada no Ietsugu, make copies of this, which [he has
done] without a single error. Next I am having Ietsugu draw
on silk in the K'ai-yüan-ssu the visage and clothing [of Nan-
yo], entirely in the manner of Han Kan.[285]

On the walls of the same gallery in that cloister is drawn
the " Reciting of the *Lotus Sutra*," which again and again I
find quite moving. Since there are about twenty pictures of
monks, it cannot be described in detail. To the east of the
Lapis Lazuli Hall is the Hall of Fugen's [286] Counter-Wind. In

---

[282] *DBZ* prints 鋪, *KIK* 舗, and *ZZGR* 補. *Tōji* has the last, but
it is presumably an error for one of the other two.

[283] Han Kan 韓幹, who is famous for his paintings of horses, was
active in the middle decades of the eighth century. Ennin has
obviously confused one of his reputed places of origin, Ta-liang
大梁 in Honan, with the name of the Liang dynasty (502-557).

[284] *Fa-hua tao-ch'ang* (J. *hokke dōjō*) 法花道場, a place for the
performance of *hokke-zammai* 三昧, one of the four types of
religious concentration of the Tendai Sect. (Cf. Coates and Ishizuka 208.) This hall probably was part of the Fa-hua-yüan
(" Lotus Cloister ") mentioned on 838 XII 9 and below. The
term *tao-ch'ang* (*dōjō*), " place of ritual," appears frequently in
later parts of the text, and occasionally is used for the ritual itself
(see 841 II 15).

[285] Implying that Ietsugu made a sketch of the original painting
and then made final copies on silk in the K'ai-yüan-ssu.

[286] 普賢 (Skr. Viśvabhadra or Samantabhadra), a Bodhisattva
often pictured on a white elephant on the right-hand side of the
Buddha Shakamuni. The name of the building in Chinese is
普賢廻風之堂.

olden times there was a fire which destroyed the whole monastery, but, when it reached the Fa-hua-yüan,[284] the master of scripture-reciting 誦經師, Ling-yu 靈祐, recited the *Lotus Sutra*[165] in the Hall of Fugen, whereupon a great wind suddenly arose, blowing from within this cloister, and drove back the fire so that the hall was not consumed. The people nowadays accordingly call it the " Hall of Fugen's Counter-Wind."

In the Tung-t'a-yüan 東塔 (" Eastern Pagoda Cloister") there is placed a portrait of Chien-chen Ho-shang.[257] The inscription on the pavilion says, " The portrait of the monk who crossed the sea." On the eastern side within the inner gate stands a stele with an inscription to " the monk who crossed the sea." The introduction of the inscription tells how Chien-chen Ho-shang crossed the sea in the cause of Buddhism. It says, " In crossing the sea, the monk encountered evil winds. First he came to a sea of serpents, which were several tens of feet long. After proceeding a whole day, he came to the end of it and then reached a black sea, where the color of the sea was like India ink," and so on.

I hear that an Imperial document has reached the prefecture, the text of which says, " In accordance with the petition of the tributary embassy, notice is being sent to Ch'u-chou to hire ships for the Japanese embassy which then is ordered to [return home] across the sea in the third moon." The meaning of this is not yet clear.

6th DAY   The Minister of State's military aide, Shen Pien, came and reported as a message from the Minister of State that, starting the fifth day of this moon, everyone was going to collect money, on behalf of the country, in order to repair the Balcony of the Auspicious Sandalwood Images in the K'ai-yüan-ssu. They were going to hold lectures on scriptures and the raising of funds[287] at the Hsiao-kan-ssu,[288]

---

[287] *Bōen* 募緣, a Buddhist term meaning " to urge the establishment of karma affinities " by good acts such as the donation of money.

[288] 孝感, in existence since at least the beginning of the eighth century. Cf. the *Ch'ung-hsiu Yang-chou-fu chih* 28.3b.

and he asked us Japanese monks in particular to come to hear the lectures and at the same time urged the Japanese officials to establish karma affinities [289] and donate money.

7th DAY   Shen Pien came and gave us a message from the Minister of State to the effect that the officials of the prefecture and regional commandery intended to assemble on the next day at the Hsiao-kan-ssu and were going to invite us Japanese monks to come and listen [290] to the lecture. There also was a fund-raising statement [287] by the Scripture-Lecturing Priest, . . .-fan.[291] I examined the document, and it said:

[In order to] repair the Balcony of the Auspicious Images, we are lecturing on the *Diamond Sutra*.[292] What we ask for [from you] is fifty strings of cash.[293] We have petitioned the Minister of State and have had our raising of funds approved by him. Let those of like karma affinities and relationships come to the Hsiao-kan-ssu, where we shall lecture on the scriptures and await their pleasure.[294]

This document is as separately [recorded].

Shen Pien tells us that the Minister of State has donated 1,000 strings of cash, and that the lectures are to last for a period of two moons.[295] There are many persons who come daily to listen to the Law. They estimate that with 10,000

---

[289] *Kechien* 結縁. See note 287.

[290] *DBZ* suggests 聽 for 者.

[291] The title is *Kōkyō Hosshi* 講經法師. As frequently in this text, only the second character of the name (fan 璠) is given.

[292] *Kongō-kyō*, or more fully *Kongō-hannya-haramitsu-kyō* 金剛般若波羅密經 (Skr. *Vajracchedikā-prajñā-pāramitā-sūtra*).

[293] As we learn below, this was the assessment for the whole Japanese party.

[294] 候縁 (see note 289) is presumably a Buddhist variation of a typical Chinese phrase of invitation.

[295] It was concluded on Intercalary I 8 (see Intercalary I 5). In China anything lasting more than one full moon is said to have lasted two moons.

strings of cash they can repair the balcony. Persia [296] has given 1,000 strings of cash, and some men from Champa [297] have donated 200 strings. Since our national group is few in number, [only] 50 strings are being solicited from us. With their repeated urging, I feel [this sum] to be small.

8*th* DAY   A Korean, Wang Ch'ŏng 王請, came, and we met. He was a man who had been on the same boat with the Chinese Chang Chüeh-chi 張覺濟 and others who drifted to the Province of Dewa [298] in the tenth year of the Japanese [year period of] Kōnin 弘仁 (819). When we asked him the circumstances of his having drifted there, he said that in order to trade various goods, they left here and crossed the seas, but that suddenly they encountered evil winds and drifted southward for three moons, drifting ashore in the Province of Dewa. When they were about to leave, Chang Chüeh-chi and his brother together deserted and stayed in Dewa. [The others] set out from northern Dewa on the " north sea," and with favorable winds drifted to the province of Nagato [299] in fifteen days. [Wang Ch'ŏng] understands the Japanese language very well.

9*th* DAY   The copying of the pictures of Nan-yo and T'ien-t'ai [Ta-shih] was completed.

14*th* DAY   It was the beginning of spring. The towns-

---

[296] 彼期國, presumably standing for Po-ssu-kuo 波斯國 and referring to an official emissary or, more probably, some merchants from Persia.

[297] 婆國. It is likely that this stands for Chan-p'o-kuo 占婆國, or Champa, an ancient country on the southeastern coast of Indochina.

[298] 出州國 may be Dewa 出羽, the northwestern province of the main island of Japan, but in that case the subsequent statement that they drifted south to reach this area cannot be correct. *DBZ* and *KIK* believe that this may have reference to the drifting of twenty Chinese to Dewa recorded in the *Nihon kiryaku* 日本記略 on 820 IV 27. The same source also records that some Chinese arrived in Japan on board a Korean ship on 819 VI 16.

[299] 長門, the western tip of the main island of Japan.

men made orioles and sold them, and people bought them and played with them.[300]

15th DAY At night they burned lamps in the private homes along the streets to the east and west. It was not unlike New Year's Eve in Japan. In the monastery they burned lamps and offered them to the Buddha. They also paid reverence to the pictures of their teachers. Laymen did likewise.

In this monastery they erected a lamp tower in front of the Buddha Hall.[301] Below the steps, in the courtyard, and along the sides of the galleries they burned oil. The lamp cups were quite beyond count. In the streets men and women did not fear the late hour, but entered the monastery and looked around, and in accordance with their lot cast coppers before the lamps which had been offered. After looking around they went on to other monasteries and looked around and worshiped and cast their coppers.

The halls of the various monasteries and the various cloisters all vie with one another in the burning of lamps. Those who come always give coppers before departing. The Wu-liang i oou sets up a "spoon-and-bamboo lamp."[302] I estimated that it has a thousand lamps. The spoon-and-bamboo lamp is constructed like a tree and looks like a pagoda. The way in which it is bound together is most ingenious. It is about seven or eight feet in height. [This festival] lasts for a period of three nights from this night to the night of the seventeenth.

17th DAY Shen Pien came and joined us in lamenting

---

[300] This custom may have some connection with the festivals held in Kyūshū and other parts of Japan on certain days in the first moon in which man-made figures of birds are exchanged. Cf. Nishimura Shinji 西村眞次, *Nihon kodai keizai* 日本古代經濟 (*Kōkan-hen* 交換篇) 1.228 ff.

[301] *Butsuden* (Ch. *Fo-tien*) 佛殿, a hall containing Buddhist images and often the main building of a monastery.

[302] 匙燈竹燈 and below 匙竹之燈. Apparently this was a tree-like tower constructed of bamboo, with metal or pottery spoons for burning oil tied to the ends of the bamboo branches.

our late departure [for Mt. T'ien-t'ai]. Then we asked him
whether or not we could go to T'ai-chou if we were especially
to receive a document from the Minister of State. Shen Pien
wrote in reply that he, Pien, had asked the Minister of State
about this three or four times in all, explaining that we
Japanese monks wondered whether or not we could get
[something from him] like a permit in order to go to T'ai-
chou, but that the Minister of State said that, even if a
Yang-chou document were issued, it would do nothing for us
in Che-hsi-tao and Che-tung-tao [303] and that we should make
a petition to the throne. If there were an Imperial order, we
could go, but otherwise we could not. With a permit from
the Minister of State we could come and go in the eight
prefectures which the Minister of State administers, but Jun-
chou [304] and T'ai-chou [93] have other Ministers of State, [305]
who have their own areas of jurisdiction. The respective
officials have no relations with one another, and it is feared [306]
that if we have no Imperial order, we shall not be able to
go easily.

After the forenoon meal they spread out in front of the
halls of the monastery the treasures [of the establishment],
laying out forty-two portraits of sages and saints [307] and all
sorts of rare colored silks beyond count. As for the countenances of the sages and saints, some were concentrating with
closed eyes, others with faces uplifted were gazing into the
distance, others looking to the side seemed to be speaking,

---

[303] Che-hsi Province 浙西道 and Che-tung Province were late
T'ang divisions corresponding roughly to the western and eastern
halves of the modern Chekiang in the northeastern corner of the
original Chiang-nan Province (see note 156).

[304] 潤, the modern Chen-chiang 鎮江 across the Yangtse from
Yang-chou.

[305] The term is used incorrectly here, as if all Prefects or Regional
Commanders were Ministers of State.

[306] *DBZ* follows *Ikeda* in correcting 怒 to 恐.

[307] 賢聖. *KIK* suggests a possible identification of these forty-two
pictures. On 840 V 2 and 5 references are made to " seventy-two
sages and saints."

and others with lowered visages regarded the ground. The forty-two pictures had forty-two different types of countenances. As for the differences in their sitting postures, some sat in the full cross-legged position and others in the half cross-legged position.[308] Their postures thus differed. Besides the forty-two sages and saints, there were pictures of Fugen and Monju [309] and of *Gumyō-chō* and *Karyōbinga-chō.*[310]

At sunset they lit lamps and offered them to the pictures of the saints. At night they chanted praises and worshiped Buddha and recited Sanskrit hymns of praise. The monks reciting Sanskrit came in together,[311] some of them holding golden lotuses and jeweled banners, and sat in a row in front of [the pictures of] the saints and intoned together Sanskrit hymns of praise. They went through the night without resting, lighting a cup lamp in front of each saint.

18*th* DAY   At dawn they made offerings of medicines and gruel, and at the time of the forenoon meal they made offerings of food of all sorts and of all flavors. Men and women onlookers gathered in large numbers both day and night. In the [dining] hall they arranged a maigre feast for the monks. In the night they again lit lamps and made offerings and chanted Sanskrit hymns of praise. In all [this lasted] two days and two nights.

The great officials, the military, and the monks in the monasteries on this day all pick over the hulled rice. The number of days [for this work] is not limited. They bring

---

[308] The *kekkafuza* 結跏趺坐 or *kafuza*, in which the sole of each foot faces upwards in the crook of the knee of the opposite leg, is the proper sitting posture for meditation (*enza* 宴坐). In the *hankaza* 半跏坐 or *hankafuza* the sole of only one foot faces upwards, and the other foot is under the knee of the opposite leg.

[309] Monju or more fully Monjushiri 文殊師利 (Skr. Mañjuśrī), the Bodhisattva of Wisdom, often pictured riding on a lion on the left side of Shakamuni and opposite Fugen (see note 286).

[310] 共命鳥 (Skr. *Jīvaṃjīvaka*) and 伽陵頻伽鳥 (Skr. *Kalaviṅka*), both mythical Indian birds.

[311] *DBZ* and *KIK* misprint 八 for 入.

the rice from the prefectural government and divide it among the monasteries according to the size of the congregation [of monks]. The number of bushels [217] is not fixed, being either ten or twenty bushels [per monastery]. The monastery storehouse receives it and then apportions it out to the monks, either one *tou* or one *tou* and five *sheng* [217] apiece. The monks on receiving the rice select the good [312] from the bad [grains]. The broken ones are bad and the unbroken good. If one receives one *tou* of rice and divides it into the two types, the good will amount to only six *sheng*. The good [313] and the bad are put into different bags and returned to the government. All the monasteries also follow this same practice, each selecting the good from the bad, and returning both to the government, which, on receiving the two types, presents the good to the Emperor as Imperial rice and retains the bad in the [local] government.

[The work of picking] is assigned to the civil and military [officials], including monks among the civil [officials], but not to the common people. When they pick over millet [314] in the prefecture, it is harder to do. The rice selected in Yangchou is extremely black in color, but they reject unhulled and damaged grains, taking only the perfect ones. The other prefectures differ from this. I hear that the Minister of State picks over five bushels,[217] the Military Inspector's Office [144] the same, the Senior Secretaries [224] two bushels, the Deputy Secretaries [225] one bushel, and the military and monks one *tou* and five *sheng* or one *tou*.

The Minister of State recently invited Kuang-i 光義, a Reverence of the *Vinaya* [248] of the Hao-lin-ssu of Jun-chou,[315] to stay temporarily at the Hui-chao-ssu.[164] Since the Minister of State intends to make this monk the Bishop [316] of this

---

[312] *DBZ* and *KIK* correct 怒 to 好 without comment.

[313] *DBZ* follows *Ikeda* in changing the preceding 惡 to 而.

[314] *Su-mi* 粟米, which occurs occasionally in this text, appears to be a term for millet.

[315] There was a famous Hao-lin-ssu 鶴林 at Jun-chou (see note 304). *DBZ*, *KIK*, and *ZZGR* all misprint 洞 for 潤.

[316] *Sōjō* 僧正 (Ch. *Seng-cheng*), whose functions in China are

prefecture, he is now having him live at the K'ai-yüan-ssu. The Bishop will look after the affairs of the monasteries and also the monks of the Government General [91] of Yang-chou. As a rule in China there are three categories [of Buddhist officers], Archbishops,[317] Bishops, and Monastery Supervisors.[116] Archbishops control the monasteries of the whole land and regulate Buddhism. Bishops are only for the area of jurisdiction of a single Government General, and Monastery Supervisors are limited to a single monastery. Aside from these there are also the monastic officers [81] and the Monastery Stewards.[118]

At sundown the Bishop [came to] dwell in this monastery.

20*th* DAY At sunset the Bishop came, and he saw us and was sympathetic.

21*st* DAY After the forenoon meal they brought a letter of the sixth day of the twelfth moon of last year from the Ambassador and the others. I examined it, and it said that on the third day of the twelfth moon they safely reached the capital and were lodged in the Foreign Guest Court in the eastern half of the capital.[318] This document is as sepa rately [recorded]. A letter of the same date from Murakiyo 村清, an attendant of the Administrative Officer Naga[mine], said that at 8 A.M. on the third day of that moon they arrived at Ch'ang-lo Post Station [319] and were met by an

described below. In Japan this was the highest of the three categories of general officers of the church (see note 258).

[317] *Sōroku* 僧錄 (Ch. *Seng-lu*).

[318] Ch'ang-an was divided for administrative purposes into eastern and western halves, called " the streets of the left " (*tso-chieh* 左街) and " the streets of the right." Here we actually have " Eastern Capital," which was Lo-yang (see note 201), but Ennin, no doubt means the eastern half of Ch'ang-an. The Foreign Guest Court (*Li-pin-yüan* 禮賓院) was established in 754 under the Bureau of Ceremonies for Foreigners (*Hung-lu-ssu* 鴻臚寺) for the reception of foreign emissaries (cf. Des Rotours 408-417).

[319] Presumably at Ch'ang-lo Slope 長樂陂 (Ennin writes 坡 on 845 IV 15), about three km. due east of the eastern gates of

Imperial representative who transmitted to them the Imperial inquiries. The envoys went to the Foreign Guest Court and have also had their audience with the Emperor.[320] [From this] we have some idea of what has happened [at the capital].

25th DAY   Through the monk Hui-wei 惠威 of the Yen-kuang-ssu [321] I got hold of the *Hokke-enkyō* [322] in three scrolls.

INTERCALARY FIRST MOON: 3rd DAY [323]   The monastery celebrated the arrival of the Bishop, inviting the venerable monks [170] from various monasteries to the living quarters for a " maigre tea " [324] and a maigre feast. There were all sorts [of food] in profusion, and they also held a concert.

4th DAY   In response to a request from Kim Chŏng-nam,[325] they are having thirty-six master carpenters, general carpenters, ship's carpenters, and founders go to Ch'u-chou to repair the ships he has bought.

They have asked monks in this monastery to seek rain, forming groups of seven to read scriptures [for this purpose].[326]

5th DAY   It rained,[327] and in the night it thundered, lightning flashed, and there was a heavy rain. It was like a

---

the T'ang city of Ch'ang-an and near the present Shih-li-p'u 十里舗.

[320] 異 is probably a copyist's error for 畢.

[321] 延光, mentioned in the *Ch'ung-hsiu Yang-chou-fu chih* 28.20a, double column 7.

[322] 法花圓鏡, listed in the *Bussho kaisetsu daijiten* 10.17 as no longer preserved.

[323] The first day was February 18, 839. The preceding moon had thirty days.

[324] *K'ung-ch'a* 空茶. Cf. the term *k'ung-fan* " maigre feast " (see note 130) which follows.

[325] The last character is miswritten 寄 in *Tōji*. The Korean Interpreter, Kim, had left for Ch'u-chou on 838 XII 18 to procure ships for the homeward voyage.

[326] *DBZ* follows *Ikeda* in correcting to 今 the 人 which prefaces this statement.

[327] *DBZ* suggests that 下 be expanded to 雨下.

summer thunderstorm. After that it rained for seven days, clearing for the first time at the time of the full moon.[328]

The Minister of State, in order to repair the Balcony of the Auspicious Images of the K'ai-yüan-ssu, held lectures to raise funds, commencing the lectures on the first day of the first moon [329] and concluding them on the eighth day of this moon. They bought lumber for five hundred strings of cash and hauled it to the courtyard of the monastery, where managers [271] have had it planed into shape.

Over sixty embassy sailors and archers of the first Japanese tributary ship have all fallen sick and are suffering.

19th DAY The monk Ching-wen 敬文 of the Ch'an-lin-[ssu] 禪林 of Mt. T'ien-t'ai [93] came, and we met. He wrote as follows:

I, Ching-wen, live in the Ch'an-lin-ssu of Mt. T'ien-t'ai. Following my teacher, I became a monk at this mountain at the age [329a] of twenty-one. I studied Nan-shan [Ta-shih's] excerpts from the *Shibun-ritsu* [330] and studied the *Lotus Sutra Shikan* [331] of T'ien-t'ai [Ta-shih].[140] Last year on the third day of the tenth moon I left the monastery and went to Che,[303] reaching western

---

[328] That is, on or around the fifteenth.

[329] On I 6 Ennin implied that the lectures started on I 5.

[329a] A character which appears to be 夏 in *Tōji* is given as 受 in the printed texts.

[330] Nan-shan Ta-shih 南山大師 is an appellation for Tao-hsüan 道宣 (596-667), the great Chinese systematizer of the Ritsu Sect, who wrote several commentaries on the *Shibun-ritsu* 四分律 (Skr. *Catūrvarga-vinaya* or *Dharmagupta-vinaya*), a work which gave its name to the Ritsu ("Rules"), or Shibunritsu Sect. Tao-hsüan's appellation was derived from his long residence in the Chung-nan Mountains (see note 201).

[331] *Hokke-kyō shikan*, by which he no doubt means the *Maka-shikan* 摩訶止觀. This and two other works, the *Hokke-gengi* 玄義 and *Hokke-mongu* 文句, are basic works of the Tendai Sect dictated by the founder Chih-i. They are collectively known as *The Three Great Lotus Works* (*Hokke sandaibu* 法華三大部), which explains the title used here.

Su-chou.³³² I learned that Japan had sent an embassy to present tribute and that you great monks were accompanying it and have, therefore, come to visit you.

In my youth, when I, Ching-wen, followed the Priest Hsing-man, I saw Master Saichō ³³³ come and receive the Tendai teachings. After that I received no news of him for some thirty years, and then chanced to hear that his Reverence ²⁴⁸ [Sai]chō had died. How the believers must have mourned him! Before this, [Hsing]-man Ho-shang had returned to Mt. T'ien-t'ai, and he has been dead sixteen years. I, Ching-wen, chanced to hear that you two Reverences were here and therefore have come to visit you.

From the Scholar Monk he received the written statement:

I, Ennin, am a disciple of this [Sai]chō Kashō ¹¹⁵ who formerly came to China. I have come here ³³⁴ in order to visit T'ien-t'ai sites, but, because the Imperial permit has not yet come, I am residing for the time being in this monastery, unable to proceed. Please give this your consideration.

Ching-wen wrote:

Saichō Kashō came to T'ien-t'ai in the twenty-first year of Chen-yüan 貞元 (805) and later returned to his homeland. I deeply rejoice in his accomplishments. Great are the affinities of that land for the Tendai teachings, which he brought to it. The Crown Prince of that land at the time is said to have been a reincarnation of Nan-yo [Ta-shih].³³⁵ In the future, may [these

---

³³² 蘇, about eighty km. west of the modern Shanghai.

³³³ Saichō 最澄 (here abbreviated as 寂 ?, better known as Dengyō Daishi 傳教大師 [767-822]) was the founder of the Tendai Sect in Japan. He had gone to China as a *Gengaku-sō* (see note 7) with the previous embassy (804-805) and had studied at Mt. T'ien-t'ai under Hsing-man 行滿 and other Chinese Buddhist scholars. "Master" is *Ajari* 阿闍梨 (usually abbreviated as *Jari* in this text), a Buddhist title corresponding to Skr. *Ācārya*, or "Teacher."

³³⁴ *DBZ* corrects 聞 to 間.

³³⁵ Presumably referring to a popular belief about Prince Shōtoku 聖德 who had actually lived two centuries before Saichō (cf.

teachings] never be rejected. Now, you are a disciple of [Sai]chō Kashō. Why do you not go to T'ien-t'ai before the Imperial order comes and wait for it there. If you just stay here, letting time pass, when the Imperial order does come, the embassy will be returning home. How could you be content at this?

The Scholar Monk made an inquiry, [saying] that he had not yet discovered how many monks and abbots there were at the Kuo-ch'ing-ssu of T'ien-t'ai, and Ching-wen replied:

The Kuo-ch'ing-ssu normally has 150 monks in permanent residence, and in the summer period [of retirement] [336] 300 or more men stay there. The Ch'an-lin-ssu usually has 40 men in residence and in the summer period over 70 men. The Kuo-ch'ing-ssu has as Abbot, Wei-chüan 維蠲, who commonly lectures on the *Shikan*.[331] He perfected himself under the Abbot Kuang-hsiu 廣修. At the Ch'an-lin-ssu there is this Abbot Kuang-hsiu, who for long has lectured on the *Lotus Sutra Shikan* and *Gengi*,[331] both summer and winter without fail. There are several Abbots who have studied under him.

We talked a great deal. At present, he is staying at the Ch'an-lin-yüan 禪林 of the Hui-chao-ssu of this prefecture, and at sunset he went back there.

21st DAY Ching-wen came again, and we communicated with each other by brush. Thereafter, he repeatedly came and conversed with us.

Through the Devotions Priest,[337] Ch'üan-ya 全雅, of the Sung-shan-yüan,[338] I borrowed several tens of scrolls of

---

Ono and Hibino 307). The belief is referred to again by Ennin on 840 V 16. For Nan-yo see note 243.

[336] 夏節. The second character is miswritten 郎 below in *Tōji*. See note 230.

[337] *Jinen Kashō* 持念和尙 is not a recognized title. *Jinen*, which I have translated throughout as " devotion," is a technical term meaning " to maintain and keep in mind the Law."

[338] 嵩山, possibly an earlier institution on the site of the Sung-shan-ssu on the north bank of the Yangtse directly south of Yang-chou. The latter is said to have been erected in the thirteenth century. Cf. the *Ch'ung-hsiu Yang-chou-fu chih* 28.6a.

giki [339] on the deities of the *Kongōkai* [277] and copied them. This Ch'üan-[ya] Ho-shang is in possession of the two *mandara* [277] of the *Taizō[kai]* and the *Kongō[kai]*, and he also understands the principles of making *dan*.[340]

SECOND MOON: 5th DAY [341] The monk Ch'üan-ya came to our rooms and made a *dan* to Nyoirin.[342]

6*th* DAY The prefectural government, in accordance with an Imperial order, gave us official salaries. I saw the document from the Imperial Regional Inspector,[343] which said:

In accordance with an Imperial order of the second day of the intercalary first moon, five bolts [192] of silk are to be given to each of the 270 men of the embassy who went to the capital, making a total of 1,350 bolts. It is in accordance with an Imperial order of the sixth day of the second moon of the twenty-first year of Chen-yüan (805),[344] that each person is given five bolts. There is no precedent for giving official salaries to monks, but they are to be given to the monks this time when official salaries are being issued. Each of the men who did not go to the capital but remained behind, from the Administrative Officer on down to the sailors, is to be given five bolts and no more nor less.

8*th* DAY We received a letter of the thirteenth day of the intercalary first moon from the Administrative Officer

---

[339] 儀軌, the regulations and rituals of Esoteric Buddhism and the texts which explain them.

[340] 壇, small tables or raised trays bearing the image of a deity of Esoteric Buddhism surrounded by the proper symbols and adornments in the proper positions. The art of preparing *dan* is called *dan'yō* 壇樣. See IV 5.

[341] The first day was March 19, 839.

[342] 如意輪 (Skr. *Cintāmaṇicakra*), one of the six forms of Kannon (see note 6).

[343] *Kuan-ch'a-shih* 觀察使 were first appointed in 758. It was a new title for an older office, which was one of the chief ones in the T'ang local administration. Cf. Des Rotours 669.

[344] This was the time of the preceding embassy from Japan. See notes 87 and 333.

Naga[mine], which said[345] that on the day they had an audience with the Emperor they had vigorously presented in person [my request] but had not received permission [for me to go to Mt. T'ien-t'ai], for which they were deeply grieved.

Because an archer and two sailors from the fourth ship had physically mistreated some Chinese, they were arrested the other day and taken to the prefectural [offices] and pilloried. They have not yet been released.[346]

14*th*, 15*th*, and 16*th* DAYS These three days were "cold" days. On these three days no smoke is produced throughout the empire, and only cold food is eaten.[347]

17*th* and 18*th* DAYS They loaded all our official and private goods onto boats in order to go to Ch'u-chou.[348]

18*th* DAY After the forenoon meal we Scholar and Student Monks left the K'ai-yüan-ssu and resided in the P'ing-ch'iao Inn[178] awaiting the boats. The officials have not yet boarded the boats.

---

[345] *DBZ* corrects 使 to 僐.

[346] Beyond this point the text is clearly out of order. What purports to be a continuation of the record of the eighth day is more probably the last part of the record of the twentieth and is followed by the entries for the twenty-first to the twenty-seventh days before the record of the days between the fourteenth and the first part of the twentieth appears. *KIK* has noted the confusion, but the rearrangement of the manuscript it suggests is clearly wrong. I have attempted to correct the order of the text by inserting *DBZ* 21a3-b4 (*Tōji* 107.1-109.6) at this point. This revision cannot be made with complete certainty, and it seems probable that some of the original text has been lost.

[347] This was the so-called Chinese "Lent" (*Han-shih* 寒食, "Cold Eating"), which comes 105 days after the winter solstice. See also 840 II 23, 842 II 17, and 845 I 3.

[348] In the missing part of the text (see note 346) there may have been the statement that the members of the embassy remaining in Yang-chou had been ordered to go to Ch'u-chou to meet the party returning from the capital and to board the ships which Kim Chŏngnam had been preparing there for the embassy's return voyage.

19*th* DAY   Early in the morning the officials went to the prefectural [offices] to take leave of the Minister of State, and at 4 P. M. we boarded the boats and took on board our personal belongings.[349] There are ten boats in all. We spent the night east of P'ing-ch'iao Inn.

20*th* DAY   Because official matters had not yet been fully arranged,[350] we could not start out. At noon the Supervisor of the National Tribute Articles [351] Harumichi no Sukune Nagakura,[58] the Officer at Large 雜使 Yamashiro no Yoshinaga 山代吉永, the archer Kami no Noritsugu 上教繼, and Shiratori 白鳥, Murakiyo, and [Kiyo]mine 清岑,[352] the attendants of the Administrative Officer Naga[mine],[353] [in all] over ten men who earlier had been with the envoys who went to the capital, arrived [354] on board a boat. We then learned that the Ambassador and the others had arrived at Ch'u-chou on the twelfth day of this moon and were staying there. Because they had not been able to buy or sell at the capital, the men mentioned above had been sent [355] here to buy various things. We also learned that all from the Ambassador on down had been sick in bed and had suffered extremely, but that later they had gradually recovered. The Administrative Officer of the second ship, Fujiwara no Toyonami, had been sick on the way and, unable to endure his suffering, had died.[356] The others were all well. The

---

[349] *DBZ* and *KIK* correct 惣 to 物.

[350] Possibly referring to the arrest of the three men on II 8.

[351] *Kan-kokushin* 監國信. See note 25.

[352] See the variant listing of their names later this same day. Murakiyo was mentioned previously on I 21.

[353] *DBZ* and *KIK* print Chōshū 長州, an alternate name for the province of Nagato (see note 299). The second character in *Tōji*, however, appears to be 別 and may represent a duplication of the 判 of *Hangan* (see note 32), which follows immediately, for usually the three characters 長判官 stand for Nagamine.

[354] *KIK* corrects 未 to 來. Failing to make this correction, *DBZ* and *ZZGR* mispunctuate at this point.

[355] *DBZ* corrects 着 to 差.

[356] The implication is that Toyonami had made the trip to the

Shingon Scholar Monk, Engyō Hosshi, had gone to the Ch'ing-lung-ssu [357] and had been able to hire twenty scribes for twenty days to copy texts and commentaries. The Hossō Scholar Monk [358] was not allowed to enter the capital, and they forced his disciple monk Gichō 義澄 to become a lay official [359] and to be a retainer of one of the Administrative Officers and had him enter the capital. Wang Yu-chen, the Manager [105] and Military Officer,[360] accompanied them to Ch'u-chou and would not allow Nagakura and the others to sell [things and, when they were about to trade,] would strike the drums [361] and start forth.

The Supervisor of the National Tribute Articles transmitted a message from the Ambassador to the effect that, after arriving at the capital,[362] the Ambassador petitioned several times regarding the Scholar Monk's going to T'ai-chou, but in the end he did not receive permission for this.[363]

At 2 P.M. we went out the Tung-lang [364] Water Gate, but before long, men came from the Minister of State to summon

---

capital, suggesting that a group from the second ship too had gone to Ch'ang-an.

[357] 青龍, a famous Ch'ang-an monastery where Kūkai 空海 (Kōbō Daishi 弘法大師), the founder of the Shingon Sect in Japan, had studied when in China from 804-806. It was located just inside the Yen-hsing Gate 延興門, the southernmost of the three eastern gates of the T'ang city. Cf. Adachi 220-21 and map opposite 136.

[358] Probably Kaimyō 戒明, a Scholar Monk of the Hossō 法相 (Skr. Dharmalakṣana) Sect, mentioned on IV 8 and VI 9.

[359] Literally, "to don a hat."

[360] 軍將, which appears as a title several times on 840 III 5 and again on 840 IV 21. Since it is not used again for Wang Yu-chen, it may be a copyist's error for T'ung-shih-chiang, which is used for him on II 26 (see note 379).

[361] As a signal that they were about to depart.

[362] DBZ corrects 宣 to 京.

[363] This is the end of the transposed section, and we return to DBZ 19a15 and Tōji 97.7.

[364] Here 東郎, but on II 23 東廊, as printed both times in DBZ, KIK, and ZZGR.

the Supervisor of the National Tribute Articles and the Interpreter of the fourth ship, because they had bought some items under Imperial prohibition, and they went off with the officers to the prefectural [offices]. The boats stopped on the east side of the Ch'an-chih-ssu,[85] and we entered the monastery and made a tour of it.

At dawn the Interpreter and Ship's Master [58] of the fourth ship were released and hastened back. The attendants of the Administrative Officer Nagamine,[365] Shiratori, Kiyomine, Nagamine,[352] and a Student,[366] these four, debarked from the boats and went to the market place to buy incense and medicines, but because local officials [64] questioned them, they fled, abandoning over two hundred strings of cash, and only three of them got back.

21st DAY   Early in the morning we started out. The Ambassador's [attendant], Awada no Ietsugu, had left the boats the other day and had gone to the market place to buy things, and the local officials [64] had arrested him and had detained him at the prefectural [offices]. Today he was released and came back. An archer of the fourth ship also was released and came back.

We reached the Hui-ch'uan Dam [367] in Chiang-yang-hsien [151] and spent the night there.

22nd DAY   At 8 A. M. we started. An archer, Myūtobe no Sadakiyo 身人部貞淨, who had bought things in the market place and had been arrested the other day and locked up in the prefectural [offices], was released today and came back. He did not lose the things [he had bought]. Before long an archer and sailor [368] of the fourth ship were released

---

[365] Here abbreviated to 長官. See note 353.

[366] *Ryūgaku*, presumably standing for *Ryūgaku-shō* 留學生. See note 7.

[367] 廻船堰, meaning "Send-back-the-ships Dam," perhaps a barrier beyond which deep-draft vessels could not proceed.

[368] The second character of 水手 is missing in *Tōji*. These two and the archer released on II 21 may be the archer and two sailors whose arrest was reported on II 8, though here they appear as a sailor and two archers.

and came back. The Scribe Ochi no Sadahara 越智貞原 had gone the other day to the market place and bought things, and the local officials [64] had informed the prefectural [government] and had asked for a judgment. Today he hastened back.

We proceeded for a little while to the Ch'ang-pai Dam 常白堰 and stopped under the Ch'ang-pai Bridge. At sunset we again started out, going on in the night in the dark. At 10 P.M. we reached Lu-chin-i [369] and stopped for the night.

23rd DAY Early in the morning we started out and at 8 A.M. stopped for a short time at Kao-yu-hsien.[154] It is fifty-five *li* from the borders of Pao-ying-hsien [370] of Ch'u-chou on the north and thirty-three *li* from the borders of Chiang-yang-hsien on the south. We have been heading north since we went out of the Tung-lang [364] Water Gate and passed east of the Ch'an-chih-ssu. At 8 P.M. we passed Hsing-ho 行賀 Bridge in the jurisdiction of Pao-ying-hsien. After proceeding a little while longer, we stopped and then started out again at 2 A.M.

24th DAY At 6 A.M. we reached the Pai-t'ien Market [371] in Pao-ying-hsien. At the southern end of the bridge at the market place stands the Fa-hua-yüan (" Lotus Cloister "). At 8 A.M. we reached Pao-ying-hsien and stopped. Nearby is the An-lo-kuan 安樂館 .[82] It is 120 *li* from Kao-yu-hsien of Yang-chou to the south and 80 *li* from [Ch'u]-chou to the north.[372] At noon we reached Shan-yang-hsien,[373]

---

[369] 路巾驛, probably the modern Lu-chin-chen 露筋鎮, on the Grand Canal about twenty-seven km. air-line north of Yang-chou.

[370] 寶應 on the Grand Canal sixty-nine km. by water north of Kao-yu.

[371] 白田市. A Pai-t'ien-p'u 舖 (*p'u* also means market) is located ten *li* south of Pao-ying. Cf. *Ch'ung-hsiu Pao-ying-hsien chih* 重修寶應縣志 (1840) 1.8a.

[372] If Ennin is correct in his figures, Ch'u-chou could not have been farther north than Huai-an, which is forty-six km. by water north of Pao-ying. See note 146.

[373] 山陽, the subprefecture located in the city of Ch'u-chou.

which is 65 *li* from [Ch'u]-chou. At 5 P. M. we reached the walled city of Ch'u-chou.

The Administrative Officer, Secretary, and others left the boats and entered the post station inn to pay their respects to the Ambassador. We Scholar and Student Monks went to the inn at sunset and saw the Ambassador, the Administrative Officer, and the others. The Ambassador said to me, " On the day I reached the capital I made petitions regarding the Scholar Monk's going to T'ai-chou and our hiring nine ships and having them repaired, but the Commissioner for Foreign Guests [374] said that no petitions could be made before our audience [with the Emperor]. I repeatedly urged that petitions be presented, and they did permit us to hire ships and repair them, but did not allow us to send you to T'ai-chou. I received an Imperial statement which said, ' The day for the return of the envoys to their land is close at hand. It is a long way from Yang-chou to T'ai-chou, and, if the monks were to go there, it is felt that they would not be [back] in time for the date of your departure. How then, when the embassy casts off hawsers [and departs], will they be able to return to their homeland? They are, therefore, not permitted to go to T'ai-chou. But the Student Monk is permitted to go to T'ai-chou and is to be completely provided with subsistence for a period of five years.' On the day of our audience, I again petitioned, but received a flat refusal from the Emperor, and later I again petitioned, but in the end did not receive permission. It is very disappointing."

After the conversation we went to the K'ai-yüan-ssu [375]

Since Ennin says it was sixty-five *li* from Ch'u-chou, he must have meant the borders of Shan-yang-hsien. The borders of the present Huai-an-hsien, which may correspond roughly to those of Shan-yang-hsien of T'ang times, commence only about ten km. north of Pao-ying.

[374] *Li-pin-shih* 禮賓使. See note 318.

[375] According to *Shan-yang-hsien chih* (1873) 2.12a, there was a K'ai-yüan-ssu west of the present town of Huai-an. It was given this name in 717 and was rebuilt in the Yüan period. See note 146.

and lodged in the western pavilion of the storerooms 厨庫
西亭.

25th DAY   We met Engyō Hosshi, the Shingon Scholar
[Monk], who said that the Ambassador, while at the capital,
petitioned several times that the [Shingon] Scholar [Monk]
be allowed to reside in a monastery, but this was not permitted by the Emperor. Later, they again petitioned and
managed to receive Imperial permission for him to lodge at
the Ch'ing-lung-ssu.[357] For fifteen days he received [376] [in-
struction in] the principles of the *Taizō[kai]*[277] at the quarters
of the Abbot I-chen,[377] and he provided [a feast for] one
hundred monks, but he did not receive [instruction in] the
principles of the *Kongōkai*.

26th DAY   Early in the morning Ch'üan-ya came.
Because the officials in charge 總官 would not let him live
in [this] monastery, he moved to the Lung-hsing-ssu [378] five
li away. He had letters from Yang-chou to Ch'u-chou, to
the Manager Wang Yu-chen, and to the Japanese tributary
embassy. I examined the letters, and they said:

"The tributary embassy petitioned that the Student
[Monk] Ensai, the novice Ninko, and the attendant Shiman [99] [be allowed to] go to T'ai-chou to study, and an
Imperial order has been received granting this request. The
said Ensai and the others wrote us asking [to be allowed] to
go to Ch'u-chou to take leave of the tributary embassy and
then to return to Yang-chou and to proceed to T'ai-chou.
A decision was received from the Minister of State approving
this. Now, when they have taken leave of the tributary
embassy, it is proposed that they be sent to T'ai-chou and

[376] *DBZ* and *KIK* misprint 取 for 受.

[377] 義眞, who later was to become one of Ennin's teachers in
Ch'ang-an (see 840 IX 6, X 23, 841 IV 28 ff.), was a disciple
of Hui-kuo 慧果 (d. 805), who himself was a disciple of Amoghavajra (see note 948) and had taught Kūkai when he was in
Ch'ang-an (see note 357).

[378] According to *Shan-yang-hsien chih* 2.12a, there was a Lung-
hsing-ssu northwest of Huai-an. See notes 146 and 256.

that Manager Wang Yu-chen, the Assimilated Colonel,[379] take charge of the monks, and hire a small boat and escort them here quickly, while the prefectural office [380] awaits their departure to supply them with provisions. A decision has been received from the Minister of State approving this, and the prefecture [380] is to act in accordance with it."

The details are to be found in the [original] texts. Wang [Yu]-chen urged them on and would not let them take their time.

The Japanese Ambassador Plenipotentiary [381] of senior third rank,[382] Acting Controller of the Left of the Council of State,[383] Provisional Governor General of Kyūshū,[384] and Consultant [Counselor] [385] Consultant Counselors are Grand Overseers [92] here

---

[379] *T'ung-shih-chiang* 同十將, apparently meaning " of the same rank as the ten *Chiang* (Generals)," appears too often in widely scattered parts of the text to be simply a copyist's error. It is translated "Assimilated Colonel" merely to suggest the possible tone of the title. See note 360.

[380] Presumably Ch'u-chou, which was under the control of Li Te-yü, the Minister of State.

[381] *Jisetsu-daishi* 持節大使, "Ambassador Bearing the Sword of Authority" (*settō* 節刀), which was the sign of the delegation of authority from the Japanese Emperor. This whole paragraph consists merely of the Ambassador's Japanese and Chinese titles, the latter probably having been conferred upon him at the time of his audience with the Chinese Emperor.

[382] 正三位, his Japanese court rank.

[383] Under the Council of State (*Dajōkan* 太政官), the supreme administrative organ of the Japanese government, there was a Controller of the Left (*Sadaiben* 左大弁) in charge of liaison with four of the eight ministries. The prefixed *gyō* 行 (" acting ") indicates that the office was not commensurate with his rank, since a Controller was usually of junior fourth rank, upper grade.

[384] *Chinzeifu-tōtoku* 鎮西府都督 was not a regular Japanese office and possibly was especially created to enhance the Ambassador's prestige in China. *Chinzeifu* was the name of the government of Kyūshū. The prefixed *shu* 守 (Ch. *shou*) indicates a " provisional " appointment (cf. Des Rotours 3).

[385] There were eight Consultant Counselors (*Sangi* 參議; the

[in China], Cloud Banner General [386] of China this is of the second rank, Acting President of the Bureau of Imperial Sacrifices [387] this is a civil post of the senior third rank, and concurrently General of the *Chin-wu* Imperial Palace Guards of the Left [388] this is a military post of the senior third rank given to relatives [of the ruler] of a first-class country, [389] and an auxiliary official, corresponding [in status] to a regular official.[390]

27th DAY The Student Monk packed his baggage in order to go to Yang-chou. After the forenoon meal the Japanese embassy gave the Student Monk thirty-five bolts of "eastern rough silk," ten pads of silk floss, sixty-five packages [184] of long silk floss,[391] and twenty-five large ounces [127] of gold dust for his study expenses. The tributary embassy gave wine to the Manager, Wang Yu-chen, which was drunk in sad farewell. After the forenoon meal the

---

second character is missing in *Tōji* but is printed in *DBZ* and *KIK*) who, together with the regular Counselors (*Nagon* 納言), were members of the Council of State.

[386] *Yün-hui Chiang-chün* 雲麾将軍, a title for Generals of the third class of the third rank (according to *ibid.* 100) and not of the second rank (*p'in* 品) as stated here. This and the following titles are all Chinese.

[387] *T'ai ch'ang-ch'ing* 太常卿, the highest post in the *T'ai-ch'ang-ssu* 寺 and, according to *ibid.* 315, a post of the first class of the fourth rank and not of the third rank as recorded here. The text has *tai* for *t'ai* (see note 197). "Acting" here is *chien-chiao* 撿挍 (cf. 檢校 in *ibid.* 3).

[388] Two Generals (*Chiang-chün*) were the third-ranking officers of the *Tso Chin-wu Wei* 左金吾衞, one of the sixteen groups of Imperial Palace Guards. The Grand General (*Ta-chiang-chün*) mentioned on 841 I 6 was the second-ranking officer of this body. Cf. *ibid.* 530 ff. *Chin-wu* was the name of a mythical bird.

[389] The exact meaning of *Ti-i-kuo-ch'in* 第一國親 is not certain.

[390] *Yüan-wai-chih T'ung-cheng-yüan* 員外置同正員. Cf. *ibid.* 2-3. On 840 III 22 we find simply *Yüan-wai* for *Yüan-wai-chih*.

[391] These are merely guesses for the three terms 東絁, 帖綿, and 長綿. The "eastern" may refer to East Japan, still the chief silk-producing region.

Japanese Consultant Counselor [392] summoned the Student Monk in order to give him the gold dust and bade him a tearful farewell.

Enchō [393] told me that they started back from Ch'ang-an on the fourth day of last moon [394] and that on the thirteenth, when they reached Kan-t'ang-i in T'ien-chou,[395] they decided to stay at Ch'u-chou and not to go on to Yang-chou. The officials had been very sick and ailing ever since they had arrived at the capital. Thus, on the thirteenth day of the previous moon, the Secretary did not get to accompany the twenty-five men who went to the Imperial Palace. In all five foreign [embassies] were gathered there. Nan-chao [396] came first, and Japan was placed second. The princes from the other [lands] did not wear headgear and were crooked and ugly in appearance and dressed in furs and blankets. None of the students, whether monks or laymen, are being allowed to remain here [in China], and Ensai Zenji [249] alone has received Imperial permission to go and stay in T'ai-chou. We others are all to return home. I, the Scholar Monk, am not to be allowed to go to T'ai-chou. They tried everything

---

[392] From this point on Ennin often calls the Ambassador the Shōkō 相公 (the same characters as for the Chinese " Minister of State "), which in Japan was an alternate name for Saishō 宰相, an elegant substitute title for a Consultant Counselor (see note 385), the Ambassador's highest post in Japan.

[393] Possibly an error for Engyō, since there is no other mention of an Enchō on the embassy. Enchō could be a copyist's error influenced by the reference below and on III 3 to another Enchō. See note 399.

[394] The trip from Ch'ang-an to Ch'u-chou, thus, took thirty-nine days.

[395] 甘堂驛 might be Kan-t'ang 甘棠 in the neighborhood of I-yang 宜陽 on the Lo 洛 River west of Lo-yang (see note 201), but I cannot identify T'ien-chou 塡.

[396] Nan-chao 南照, correctly written 南詔, was a native Thai kingdom in modern Yunnan.

they could but did not receive permission [for me], for which they are very sorry.[397]

I have entrusted to the Student Monk the letter and the Buddhist scarf of variegated colors[398] from the Great Abbot[399] to Mt. T'ien-t'ai as well as the "Questions from the Monastery" and the "Questions from the Shuzen'in."[400]

28th DAY After the forenoon meal the Student Monk and his two attendants boarded a boat with the Manager Wang Yu-chen and started for Yang-chou. We parted most sorrowfully.

THIRD MOON: 1st DAY[401] The Japanese Consultant Counselor had three Japanese painters draw pictures of the

---

[397] At this point one must skip to *DBZ* 20b4 (*Tōji* 109.6). See notes 346 and 363.

[398] *Nōgesa* 衲袈裟. See note 188.

[399] Presumably Enchō 圓澄, who was the second Abbot of the Enryakuji (see note 7). The date of Enchō's death is variously given in the different sources. The two most frequent dates cited are 836 X 26 (as given in the *Tendai zasu no ki* 天台座主記, in *Gunsho ruijū* 群書類從 [1893 edition] 3.622) and 837 X 26 (as given in chapter five of the *Honchō kōsō den* 本朝高僧傳, in *DBZ* 102.108), but *SNK* records it on 833 X 20. The references here and on III 3 suggest that Ennin supposed Enchō to be still living or at least that he was alive when Ennin himself had first been appointed to go to China, which may have been around the time of the first announcement of the embassy on 834 I 19 (cf. *SNK*).

[400] *Jika-miketsu* 寺家未決 and *Shuzen'in-miketsu* 修禪院未決, obviously two sets of questions being referred by the Japanese Tendai Sect to the mother church in China. Shuzen'in, the name of part of the Enryakuji, is also an appellation for Gishin 義直, who accompanied Saichō to China in 804 (see note 333), was appointed the first Abbot of the Enryakuji in 824, and died in 833. The second set of questions, thus, had probably been drawn up originally by Gishin, accounting for the letter sent to him in reply by the Chinese (see III 3). The first set of questions probably was from Enchō (see note 399).

[401] April 18, 839. There were thirty days in the preceding moon.

Bodhisattva Myōken and of the Four Heavenly Kings in the K'ai-yüan-ssu. This is what he had vowed to do while shipwrecked on the high seas.[402]

2nd DAY   In the evening the work was completed.

3rd DAY   The Consultant Counselor arranged a maigre feast in the K'ai-yüan-ssu for over sixty monks, spending seven strings and 500 cash for the maigre feast and for alms. After the maigre feast the monk Ching-wen [403] of the Ch'an-lin-ssu of Mt. T'ien-t'ai arrived from Yang-chou with a letter for Mugyō Hosshi [404] of Japan and a letter for the Abbot, Enchō. Ching-wen had not met Master Ensai on the way from Yang-chou. On arrival, he had intended to go to the K'ai-yüan-ssu, but the gatekeepers [405] would not let him enter, so he went to the Ts'ui-chia-ch'an-ssu 崔家禪 (" Meditation Monastery of the Ts'ui Household ") and lodged there. I sent Ishō to inquire after him and to give him powdered tea 細茶 and the like.

In the night the Japanese Consultant Counselor, in order to fulfill the vow he had made on the sea, lighted one thousand cup lamps in a hall of the K'ai-yüan-ssu and offered them to the Bodhisattva Myōken and to the Four Heavenly Kings. Then he renewed his vow [saying], " Last year, when shipwrecked, I vowed that on the day I reached land I would draw ten pictures of the Bodhisattva Myōken, one of the Buddha Yakushi,[406] and one of the Bodhisattva Kanze,[6] of the same height as my own body, but after reaching shore my public duties were numerous, and while traveling it was difficult to arrange for all this, and so I was unable to make them. On the day I reach Japan I shall certainly draw these pious [pictures]." [407]

---

[402] See 838 VI 24 and VII 2.

[403] Here and again below, 入 has been written for 文, an extremely easy error for a copyist to make.

[404] 无行, another name for Gishin (see note 400 and cf. Ono and Hibino 312).

[405] *DBZ* corrects the second character in 統者門人 to 看.

[406] 藥師 (Skr. Bhaiṣajyaguru), the Buddha of Healing.

[407] *Kudoku* 功德, literally " good works."

This prefecture does not observe the festival of the third day of the third moon.

4th DAY   After the forenoon meal Ching-wen Ch'an-shih [249] left for Yang-chou. He told me [408] that when he reached Yang-chou, he would go on from there to Mt. T'ien-t'ai with Master Ensai and that he would transmit to the Abbot of [Mt.] T'ien-t'ai the letter already entrusted to him from Mugyō Kashō.[409]

5th DAY   After the forenoon meal. They have already drawn five copies of the *Taizō[kai] Mandara*, but they have not yet colored them.

I presented a letter to the Ambassador Consultant Counselor, [saying that] I should remain in China because I was having difficulties in accomplishing my search for the Law. The full document is as separately [recorded]. The Consultant Counselor notified me saying, " If you desire to remain, that is for the sake of Buddhism, and I dare not stand in the way of your determination. If you wish to stay, then do remain. The government of this land, however, is extremely severe, and, if the officials learn of this, it will [entail] [410] the crime of disobeying an Imperial order, and you will probably have trouble. You should think it over."

17th DAY   I moved my baggage to the second ship.[411] I am to be on the same ship as the Administrative Officer Naga[mine]. The officials are divided among the nine vessels, each one as a Commander in charge. Besides the Japanese sailors under their command, they have also hired over sixty Koreans who are familiar with the sea routes. Each ship has either seven, six, or five of them.

The Korean Interpreter Chŏngnam has been ordered to

---

[408] 語云 is mistakenly printed twice in *DBZ* and *KIK*.

[409] *DBZ* and *KIK* print 無行 (see note 404). Ennin presumably meant the " Questions " mentioned on II 27 (see note 400) and below 840 V 18.

[410] *Tōji* has 導, *Ikeda* 道.

[411] That is, the second of the nine newly hired ships, not of the original four vessels from Japan.

devise some scheme whereby I can stay [in China], but it is not yet certain whether or not anything can be done.

19th DAY   The Prefect [412] of the prefecture held a farewell wine party and invited the Consultant Counselor. The Consultant Counselor did not go, but those who wore dark red,[226] from the Administrative Officers on down, went to the prefectural [offices] and participated in the party.

After the forenoon meal I, the Scholar Monk, left the monastery and went to the ship.

22nd DAY   Early in the morning I sent two large ounces of gold dust and an Ōsaka girdle [413] to the Korean Interpreter, Yu Sinŏn 劉愼言 .[48]

At 6 A. M. the tributary embassy left the inn and went to where the ships were. All from the Military Attachés [414] on up were on horseback, and there were eight men to clear the roads for them. At 10 A. M. we purified ourselves and boarded the ships,[415] and worshiped the Great God of Sumiyoshi.[416] I, the Scholar Monk, and [my followers] boarded the second ship. The Ship's Commander is the Administrative Officer

---

[412] *Tz'u-shih* 刺史. Cf. Des Rotours 721 ff.

[413] 大坂腰帶. Ōsaka may indicate the place of manufacture in Japan, but one cannot tell which Ōsaka is meant. These gifts may have been in payment for the assistance of the Koreans in seeking means to keep Ennin in China.

[414] *Sangun* 參軍. The corresponding Chinese term, *Ts'an-chün,* was the name of a large category of minor officials which Des Rotours (636, 699, etc.) calls " administrateurs," but the Military Attaché mentioned on IV 8 was clearly a Japanese. Since *Sangun* in Japan was an elegant term for Lieutenants (*Shōgen* 將監) of the Imperial Bodyguards (*Konoe* 近衞), this may refer to a specific man with that post in Japan, or it may be a title for a category of officers attached to the embassy.

[415] 解除 (*kaijo* or *gejo* in Japanese). See also IV 13 and V 27.

[416] 住吉大神. The famous shrine of Sumiyoshi (also pronounced Suminoe) is in the southern part of what is now Ōsaka and is dedicated to the sea deities to whom travelers on the sea once prayed for protection. See 847 XI 29.

Nagamine, that of the first ship the Ambassador,[417] that of the third ship the Administrative Officer Suga[wara], that of the fourth ship the Administrative Officer Fuji[wara no Sadatoshi], and that of the fifth ship the Administrative Officer Tomo.[182] The Vice-President [of the Tribunal of Censors][418] sent[355] a General to oversee the departure of the nine ships, and Imperial orders were sent to Hai-chou,[107] Teng-chou,[419] and the [other] prefectures and subprefectures on our route, [commanding them] to provide for [the embassy].

Koshiki no Inamasu 甑稲益, a sailor of the first ship, is not allowed to board the ships during the moon, because at the inn in Ch'u-chou he had relations with[420] Tobimo 飛喪, the attendant of the Scribe Ochi no Sadahara. The Ambassador has decided that he should be put on the ship of the General overseeing our departure.

At 6 P. M. we poled out into the river and stopped for the night on the south side of the Great Huai [River].[146]

23rd DAY At 2 P. M. Yu Sinŏn came and gave me, the Scholar Monk, ten pounds of powdered tea and some pine nuts.[421]

At 4 P. M. we heard from a Chinese that the second ship[422]

---

[417] *Sekka* 節下. See note 381.

[418] Two *Chung-ch'eng* 中丞 were the second-ranking officers of the Tribunal of Censors (*Yü-shih-t'ai* 御史臺, cf. Des Rotours 281). This probably was a former post of the local Prefect (see note 412), for Vice-Presidents were of the second class of the fourth rank and Prefects were of this same rank or else of the second class of the third rank, depending on the size of the prefecture.

[419] 登, at the northernmost point of the Shantung Peninsula. It is now called P'eng-lai 蓬萊, which in T'ang times was the name of the subprefecture located in the city.

[420] 逢. Presumably the act had made him ritually impure. See note 415.

[421] Probably a courtesy gift in return for the large payments he received on III 22. "Pine nuts" is a guess for 松脯.

[422] The second ship of the original four, which was reported on

had set out from Tung-hai-hsien [423] in Hai-chou on the four-teenth of this moon. We are not yet sure whether this is true or false.

North of Ch'u-chou is the Great Huai [River] flowing from west to east. The so-called " crossway " 橫涉 of the Great Huai leads to the East Sea.

In the night I, the Scholar Monk, entrusted to the Am-bassador's attendant, the Ōmi Professor,[424] Awada no Ie-tsugu, a letter of information to the Enryakuji.[7]

24*th* DAY   At 6 P. M. they struck the drums, and we started out, coming out onto the Huai from a [side] stream and spending the night there.

25*th* DAY   At 6 A. M. we started. The wind blew from due west, and we went east on the Huai. At 2 P. M. we reached a point south of Lien-shui-hsien [425] under the ad-

---

838 VIII 10 as having landed in Hai-chou. It, too, was now on its way home. See III 26.

[423] See note 107. *TTLCT* 32a shows Tung-hai-hsien on the east-ern side of an island consisting of what is now a mountainous part of the mainland northeast of Hai-chou (Tung-hai) and between it and the sea. Ennin's account of his travels in this region of IV 5-8 indicates that the subprefectural capital lay instead on the west side of this mountainous area and opposite Hai-chou across a shallow bay, which must have occupied the present lowlands immediately east of Hai-chou. This would suggest that Tung-hai-hsien was either the modern Nan-ch'eng 南城 or near that town. Ennin's statements that it was 100 *li* (III 29) or 120 *li* (IV 7) across three mountain ranges from the northeastern tip of Tung-hai-hsien to the subprefectural town correspond reasonably well with the air-line distance of about thirty km. from this point to Nan-ch'eng.

[424] *Hakase* 博士, a Professor of the Government University (*Daigaku* 大學). Ōmi 近江 presumably was Ietsugu's province of origin. On VII 21 he is called the " Provisional (see note 124) Professor from Ōmi." *Tōji* omits the second character of 傔從 (attendant), and *Ikeda* has added it in place of the first char-acter of Ōmi.

[425] The modern Lien-shui 漣水 is about thirty km. northeast

ministration of Hsü-chou [426] and stopped for the night on the Huai. The wind had not changed, but, because the Korean sailors and helmsmen [427] of the first ship had left the ship and had not yet come back, the ships were held up on account of this and could not proceed. All night long the favorable wind continued.

26th DAY   Early in the morning the wind changed to the southwest. They beat drums, and we started out, but, since the tide was against us [428] and the wind was from the side, we went a little while and then stopped. At 1 P. M. we started again. At 2 P. M. the first, third, and the other ships, eight [in all], entered a canal from the Huai and stopped in front of Ch'iao-lung-chen 橋籠鎮 . The second ship did not enter the canal but went straight down the Huai and stopped on the Huai southwest of [Ch'iao-lung]-chen, about five or six *li* from the other ships. The wind blew from the southeast, and in the night it [shifted] gradually to due east.

A boat came from the river mouth. We asked them where they came from, and the boatmen replied that they had come from Hai-chou and that on the twenty-fourth day of this moon the second Japanese ship had left Hai-chou and gone to Tung-hai-hsien and that yesterday they had noticed that it had not yet set out [for Japan].

At midnight we heard that the first ship had sounded the drums and started out, so the second ship weighed [429] anchor and went on ahead.

27th DAY   At 6 A. M., when we were over seventy *li* from the mouth of the Huai, we ran into the incoming tide and stopped for a while, and the other ships came up from behind. The wind blew from the southwest, but the men all said that the wind only appeared to be changing, because the

---

of Huai-an, but the old town was farther north and across the Huai outside of Ch'u-chou and Huai-nan-tao.

[426] 徐, the modern railway junction in northwestern Kiangsu.

[427] 稍功, more correctly written 梢工 on 842 V 25.

[428] Indicating that the Huai was tidal at least as far up as Lien-shui-hsien.

[429] *DBZ* suggests 舉 for 奉.

Huai is sinuous, and that today we should have only a west wind. At 10 P. M. we went on, but at noon a northeast wind blew and we dropped anchor and stopped a little over twenty *li* short of the mouth of the Huai. At sunset the northeast wind was [still] blowing, and we had a thundershower.

28th DAY   It was clear. At 10 A. M. in order to get a favorable wind, we worshiped the Great God of Sumiyoshi.[416] At 1 P. M. the wind shifted to southeast, and in the night it shifted to southwest.

29th DAY   At dawn the nine ships hoisted sail and set out. At 7 A. M. we went out of the mouth of the Huai [430] onto the sea and headed straight north. The General seeing us off could not accompany us [farther] because the waves were wild and high, so the sailor Inamasu boarded a passing ship to go to Hai-chou.

We saw the ocean stretching far and mysterious to the east and south, but mountains and islands were strung out starting in the northwest. This is the eastern extremity of the area under Hai-chou. At 4 P. M. we arrived east of the Tung-hai Mountains in Tung-hai-hsien in the area under Hai-chou and entered a cove and stopped. Just east of the cove is Hu-hung Island.[431] The south wind blew hard, and we rocked beyond compare. These Tung-hai Mountains are a mass of lofty crags and cliffs. On the sea side they are precipitous, and the pines are very beautiful. It is a most moving [sight] indeed. From these mountains there is a road to Tung-hai-hsien, a distance of one hundred *li*.

---

[430] The old mouth of the Huai is sometimes identified with the old mouth of the Yellow River, about ninety km. southeast of the eastern tip of the Tung-hai region, but this is a little far for the nine-hour run recorded below. Probably the mouth of the Huai was closer to what is now known as the mouth of the Kuan 灌, about forty km. southeast of the Tung-hai hills, as is indicated on the map in *Chia-ch'ing Hai-chou chih-li-chou chih* 嘉慶海州直隸州志 1.37a.

[431] 胡洪島, possibly the modern Ying-yu-shan 鷹遊山, also known as Hsi-lien Island 西連.

FOURTH MOON: 1st DAY [432]   It was clear, but clouds [soon] swirled about. At 2 p. m. the Ambassador and his subordinates went ashore and sacrificed to the deities of heaven and earth. Before long it rained, and the northeast wind grew rather strong. The waves raged, and the ships bobbed up and down. Since there were many ships in the small cove, they often bumped one another, and our fears were great.

I have passed on to the Student of History,[433] Nagamine no Sukune, to take back to our country, the four letters and the black horn scepter [434] entrusted to me at Ch'u-chou for delivery to Mt. [Hi]ei by the Student Monk.

After the officials had made their sacrifices, they conferred together about crossing the sea. The Korean sailors said that Mt. Ta-chu [435] on the east coast of the area under Mi-chou [436] is a day's trip north of here and that, since we now had a south wind, it would be safest for us to proceed to this mountain and repair our ships and then cross the sea from there. The Ambassador agreed to this, but the other officials objected.

2nd DAY   The wind shifted to southwest. The Ambassador called together the officials from the various ships to confer again about setting out, and he had them speak their minds. The Commander of the second ship, Nagamine no Sukune, said, " This Mt. Ta-chu, I believe, is due west of Korea. If we go there and start out [from there for Japan],

---

[432] May 17, 839. The previous moon had only twenty-nine days.

[433] *Kiden-ryūgaku-shō* 記傳留學生 .

[434] *Nyoi* 如意, a Buddhist emblem said to have developed from a back-scratcher.

[435] 大珠, on the Shantung coast about forty-five km. southwest of Tsingtao. There is a large bay immediately west of it. Ta-chu is miswritten 人珠 here and 大朱 on 847 Intercalary III 17, but correctly elsewhere in *Tōji*.

[436] 密, the modern Chu-ch'eng 諸城 (which in T'ang times was the name of the local subprefecture), about eighty km. west of Tsingtao. Mi is miswritten 蜜 on 840 III 17.

our misfortunes will be innumerable.[437] Moreover, Korea is having troubles with Chang Pogo [438] and is at war with him. If we have a west wind, a northwest wind, or a southwest wind, we shall certainly land in the territory of the bandits.

---

[437] Japan and Silla (see note 13) had been traditional enemies for several centuries.

[438] Chang Pogo 張寶高 was an extraordinary Korean adventurer of the time, whose name crops up several times in the histories of China and Japan as well as those of Korea. He is said to have got his start as a military officer in Hsü-chou in China, though what Ennin records on 845 VII 9 and elsewhere suggests that the town of Lien-shui in Hsü-chou (see notes 425 and 426) was his old headquarters. Subsequently he returned to Korea and in 829 persuaded the King to appoint him Commissioner of Ch'ŏng-haejin 清海鎮大使 with the mission of curbing slaving depra-dations in that region, of which he had become aware while in China. Ch'ŏnghaejin was on Wando 莞島, an island just east of the southwestern tip of Korea and a key place at this time in the trade between China, Korea, and Japan. From this vantage point Chang Pogo became a merchant-prince with extensive holdings and commercial interests in China (as Ennin indicates on VI 7 and elsewhere) and with trade contacts with Japan. He also became a kingmaker in his homeland. In 837 one of the Princes of Silla fled to him for protection, and the next year he was persuaded to support by arms the Prince's claim to the throne. After a decisive victory over the forces of the reigning King in the intercalary first moon of 839, he placed the Prince on the throne as Sinmu 神武, the forty-fifth King of Silla, and probably was influential in winning speedy recognition for his candidate from the Chinese Emperor (see below IV 24). Chang Pogo was of course richly rewarded for these services. Nagamine obviously was aware of the war of succession in Korea, but not of Chang Pogo's victory, word of which first reached Ennin only on IV 20.

In Chang Pogo's name the last character is miswritten 亮 here and again on IV 20, but correctly on VI 7 and VI 28. This is the form of the name which appears in *SNK* (840 XII 27, 841 II 27, and 842 I 10), but Pogo is written 保臯 in *HTS* 220 (4150a in the K'ai-ming edition) and in the Korean history known as the *Samguk sagi* 三國史記 (10.10-13; 11.1-2; 44.7-9

According to old precedents, ships which have set out from Ming-chou [185] have been blown to Korean territory, and ships which have set out from the Yangtse River [11] have also landed in Korea. This time these nine ships have already gone far north, and we know we are close to the bandits. How much the more, if we go on to Mt. Ta-chu, shall we be going right into bandit territory. Therefore, let us cross the sea from here. We need not go to Mt. Ta-chu."

Five of the ships agreed with this opinion, but the Ambassador did not concur, and they argued back and forth a great deal. At 8 P.M. a letter was sent from the first ship to the Administrative Officers and the others, saying, " The second, third, fifth, seventh, and ninth ships may, as their Commanders wish, cross the sea from here. The decision is as stated above." [439] In accordance with [the instructions of] the letter, the word was passed around.

In the night the wind blew variably from the north and the south.

3rd DAY They had the five Ships' Commanders, the Administrative Officer Naga[mine] and the others, sign the letter of decision from the first ship last night. On the second ship the name of a Scribe was signed, but on the other four ships they would not list their signatures.

I received a letter from Kim Chŏngnam saying that, since the second, third, fifth, seventh, and ninth [ships] were crossing the sea from here, I should transfer to the seventh [440] or eighth ship.

---

in the Chōsen Shi Gakkai 朝鮮史學會 edition of 1928). The latter also gives his original name as Kungpok 弓福, and it is presumably a variant of this which appears as Kungp'a 弓巴 in the Korean history known as the *Samguk yusa* 三國遺事 (2.18-19 in the Chōsen Shi Gakkai edition of 1928). Ennin's various references to Chang Pogo are exhaustively discussed in connection with all the other materials on his life in Okada 13.14-28 and Imanishi Ryū 今西龍, *Shiragi shi kenkyū* 新羅史研究 (Keijō [Seoul], 1933) 303-330.

[439] *DBZ* corrects 石 to 右 .

[440] " Seventh " is obviously an error.

4th DAY   At 6 A. M. I, the Scholar Monk, Ishō, Igyō, and Tei Yūman left the second ship and transferred to the eighth ship, in order to go to Mi-chou with the Consultant Counselor and stay there. The west wind did not change. The Commander of the eighth ship, Tomo no Sukune, informed the Consultant Counselor [of our move] and asked for a decision, and received the Consultant Counselor's decision that he should accede to the monks' wishes.

The Commander of the second ship, Nagamine no Sukune, visited the Consultant Counselor's ship and again asked about crossing the sea. His opinion was still as it had been before. The Consultant Counselor told him that tonight they will observe the nature of the wind, and, if it does not change, early tomorrow morning they will cross the sea from here, but, if there is a change of wind, then they will simply go to the Mi-chou district.

5th DAY   At dawn the favorable wind had not changed. A letter from the first ship said, " The first, fourth, sixth, and eighth ships, in order to change their fittings, previously intended to go to the Mi-chou district and repair the ships and then cross the sea from there. But now, since a favorable wind blows, let us strengthen the weak points and supplement what is missing and cross the sea from here. Pass on the word to all the ships."

I, the Scholar Monk, while at Ch'u-chou, had planned with the Korean Interpreter Kim Chǒngnam that, when we reached the Mi-chou region, we would stay in a private house, and, when the tributary embassy departed, we would live in hiding in the mountains and would then go to [Mt.] T'ien-t'ai and also to Ch'ang-an. The Ambassador had not opposed this scheme, but now the ships were crossing the sea from here and were not following the Ambassador's decision to go to the Mi-chou district. Moreover, the favorable wind had not changed day after day, and consequently the first ship was simply following the proposal to cross the sea from here and, loosing its hawsers, was about to start out. I therefore entrusted to Tomo no Sukune, the Commander of the eighth ship, a bamboo box of Buddhist teachings 法門 and the two *mandara* and the *dan'yō* [441] placed in a large leather box, which I had obtained [in China], and I also gave him our baggage. [Then], the Scholar Monk, Ishō, Igyō, and the sailor Tei Yūman, we four, left the ship and settled on shore. The Ambassador gave me twenty large ounces [127] of gold. Faced with this parting, there was none of us that did not grieve. At 8 A. M. the nine ships hoisted [442] sail and started out, going with the wind straight northeast. We climbed up the shore and gazed at the white sails moving in a row over the sea.

We monks, the four of us, remained [behind] on the mountainous shore. When it came time for our forenoon meal, we entered a deep valley in search of water, and presently we heard many voices. We gazed about in fright and saw that a ship had arrived at the anchorage with more than ten [443] men. They dropped anchor and stopped [the ship and then] came from the ship and asked us monks how we happened to be here. We replied, " We monks originally were Koreans, and we formerly lived in Ch'u-chou. In order to go to Mi-chou, having matters on which to confer [there], we briefly took passage on the ship of a tributary embassy, and came here on it. But, since the ship of the tributary embassy today crossed the sea, we left the ship and are staying here."

The boatmen said, " We have come from Mi-chou with a load of charcoal on board and are going to Ch'u-chou. Originally we [also] were Koreans, and there are over ten of us. Now, you monks are in these deep mountains, which are completely devoid of human habitation. At present there is no boat going to Mi-chou. Are you going to spend the night here or not? Are you going off to look for a village? If you stay here for long, we do not know where you will find shelter when it blows or rains."

Here we monks were in this isolated valley, suddenly encountered by this situation. We did not know what to do.

---

[441] See note 340. *DBZ* corrects 寺 to the pluralizing 等.
[442] 上 is supplied by *Ikeda*.
[443] *Ikeda* corrects 合 to 拾.

We gave all the baggage and even the food we had brought with us to the boatmen, not keeping back a single thing. We feared that, if we said that we had gold, they would agree among themselves to kill us. We therefore said that we would go to a village.

The boatmen said [444] that if we went over twenty *li* south from here across a mountain range, we would reach a village, and that they would have a man accompany us. We then started with one of them accompanying us. The rocky cliffs were precipitous, and we descended into ravines and climbed up ridges. We still did not know if the men were good or evil at heart, and our doubts and worries were unbounded.

Fording inlets and walking through slime, we reached the home of a Korean in Su-ch'eng-ts'un [445] at 4 P. M. and rested briefly. They then [446] asked us how we Korean monks happened to come here from Mi-chou.[447] We monks replied, " We Korean monks, Kyŏngwŏn 慶元, Hyeil 惠溢, and Kyohye 教惠, came here on a chance ship and shall stay here a day or two. We ask you to take charge and in your compassion let us stay." The village elder, Wang Liang 王良, wrote, saying:

You monks have come here and call yourselves Koreans, but I see that your language is not Korean, nor is it Chinese. I have been told that the ships of the Japanese tributary embassy stopped east of the mountains to wait for [favorable] winds, and I fear that you monks are official visitors [to China] who have fled to this village from [448] the ships of your own country. I dare not let official visitors stay. I ask you to tell the truth and

---

[444] The repetition of 云從 in *Tōji* is clearly a copyist's error.

[445] A Su-ch'eng 宿城 is shown in *Chia-ch'ing Hai-chou chih-li-chou chih* 1.39a, south of a range of hills which extends along the northeastern coast of the hilly area of Tung-hai (see note 423). This would indicate that Ennin's party landed somewhere in the vicinity of Sun-chia-shan 孫家山 or Lao-yao 老窰, at present the last two stations on the Lung-hai Railway.

[446] *DBZ* and *KIK* misinterpret 便 as 使.

[447] An obvious error for Ch'u-chou.

[448] 從 is repeated in *Tōji*.

not make up falsehoods. This village has just had a communication from the prefecture, and three or four representatives 使下 of the Guard Officer [449] are here investigating, so I fear that they will see you monks and arrest you and take you to the prefectural [capital].

While we were thinking this over, three men, Chang Liang 張亮, Chang Mao 張茂, and another, who were military police [450] under the Police Commandant [451] of the four sub-prefectures of Hai-chou, arrived with bows and asked us where we came from. We monks intended to reply with the truth, but we still feared that people would say that we had committed a crime and we would be arrested, and so, as an expedient, we devised a scheme and . . .[452] replied to them, " We monks really are from the Japanese ships, but, because we were sick, we left the ships for a little while and spent the night [ashore] and were not aware that the ships had started out. We hired a man and came here. We ask that you send a representative to accompany us on our way."

The soldiers then realized the situation and accordingly [453] had us monks go to the house of the village headman, Wang Liang. In response to a request from the soldiers that we write out in detail for the Guard Officer the reasons for our being left behind, we monks made out a document to inform them. It said:

> The nine ships of the Japanese tributary embassy anchored back of an island east of the mountains of Tung-hai and waited for a [favorable] wind. Because I had a stomach ailment and was suffering from beriberi, I left the boat on the third day of this moon. My two attendant monks and my servant left the boat with me. We went up into the mountains to search for

---

[449] *Ya-ya* 押衙. Cf. Des Rotours 225. See also note 50.
[450] *Tzu-hsün chün-chung* 子巡軍中 is not a known term.
[451] *Tu-yu-chiang* 都遊將, called a *Tu-yu-i* 奕 below and a *Tu-yu-i-shih* 使 on IV 7. None of these are known titles.
[452] *DBZ* interprets a character defaced by wormholes as 書, but this reading is doubtful.
[453] *DBZ* corrects 僧 to 依.

water. Day and night I cared for myself 將理, but I have not yet recovered. The ships of the tributary embassy [sailed] last night, because there was a favorable wind. When early in the morning we went to where the ships had been and looked for them, we did not see them. We had been left behind on this isolated shore. While we were lamenting over this, a ship laden with charcoal arrived with ten men on board. They inquired in detail about the matter and then informed us of the village. We monks insisted on hiring one of them and came through the mountains here to Su-ch'eng-ts'un. The baggage we have brought with us [consists of] robes and clothing, begging bowls and cups, small bronze bells,[454] writings, water bottles,[455] over seven hundred cash, and straw rain hats. We now intend to go to where the Japanese ships are and return to Japan on them.[456] We ask you to send a representative to accompany us.

The military police [450] added a separate letter [to ours] and sent them off to inform the office of the Guard Officer and Police Commandant.[451]

In the night from 10 P. M. on it thundered and a downpour fell. The wind blew fiercely, the thunder was deafening, and the violent rain and fierce wind were quite beyond compare. At 2 A. M. the thunder and rain both stopped, and the wind shifted. When early in the morning I inquired, many said it had been a north wind.

6th DAY   It was clear. A general representative of the subprefecture 縣家都使 came and asked for a written statement. I made one like that of the night before and gave it to him. The officer of the military police 子巡將 [450] has sent two men to where the ships were anchored to see if they have gone or not, and since they are late in returning, we have not been able to start out [from Su-ch'eng-ts'un]. Chang Liang, the officer of the military police, has told me that he is now going to send a man with our baggage and clothing to where the second ship [422] is. When he gets south of the

---

[454] *DBZ* corrects 鋼鋺 to 銅鐃, as given on VII 28.

[455] 澡瓶, literally meaning "washing-bottles."

[456] Ennin, however, had no reason to think that the ships would again touch at a Chinese port.

mountains, he will look for a baggage donkey, because there
are no places that rent donkeys here.

In the evening the general representative of the subprefecture came and said, " I am going today,[457] and tomorrow,
south of the mountains, I shall make noodles and hire a
donkey and wait for you monks to arrive. Early tomorrow
morning you should come quickly, after eating only some
gruel, and get there before the forenoon meal and eat
there." [130] After saying this, he departed.

A little later Li Shun 李順, a Guard Captain [50] of the prefectural government who had been sent by the Guard Officer,
came hastening with a letter, which said, " You have especially gone to the island to determine the truth about whether
or not those nine ships have departed. Send someone this
very night to inform me." In accordance with the report of
those commissioned to look for the ships, Chang Liang of
the military police then made out a document [stating that]
the ships had already set out and nothing had been seen of
them, and he sent a man to inform the office of the Guard
Officer.

7th DAY At 6 A. M. the military policemen, Chang
Liang and another, these two men, hired men to carry our
baggage and went off with us monks. It was dark and cloudy.
We went through the mountains, crossing two rocky ranges
and wading through places where salt is gathered. The mud
was deep and the road long. At 10 A. M. we reached the home
of the general representative of the subprefecture and had
our forenoon meal, after which we proceeded, with me riding
a donkey and my attendants all walking. After a little while
a soldier came out to meet us and said that, because we
monks were so slow coming, the Guard Officer had especially
sent him to urge us on.

At 2 P. M. we reached the Hsing-kuo-ssu.[458] The men of

---

[457] Followed by a character interpreted by *DBZ*, *KIK*, and
ZZGR as 旦 , "morning," but this does not agree with the
" evening ". above.

[458] According to the *Chia-ch'ing Hai-chou chih-li-chou chih* 29.

the monastery said that the Guard Officer had been there, but had been unable to await our late arrival and had just left. The Rector [81] boiled tea [for us]. Then, hiring three donkeys, we mounted them and started out. The charge for one donkey to go twenty *li* is 50 cash, and the three came to 150 cash. We went twenty *li* to the Hsin-ching-ssu 心淨, which is a convent. The Guard Officer was there, so we went into the convent and met him and told him in detail about the situation. The offices, rank, and name of the Guard Officer are: the Guard Officer of Hai-chou and concurrently the *Tso-erh-chiang-shih-chiang*,[459] the Police Commandant [451] of the four subprefectures, the Manager of Foreign Guests 勾當蕃客, official of the first class of the sixth rank,[460] and the probationary 試 [member of] the *Chin-wu* Imperial Palace Guards of the Left,[388] Chang Shih 張實.

After we had sipped our tea, we left for the subprefectural office. Again we hired a donkey. From the convent to the subprefecture is twenty *li*. We arrived there in the evening, and, going to the house of Wang An 王岸, the Secretary of the Guard Office,[461] spent the night. We gave 20 cash for the hire of the donkey. For a single person to go one hundred *li* [it had cost] 120 cash.[462]

8*th* DAY Early in the morning, after we had eaten our gruel, the Guard Officer went to the subprefectural [offices] and soon returned accompanied by Li I-fu 李夷甫 the Subprefect,[77] who is a Provisional [384] Subprefect of the

---

14b, there was a Hsing-kuo-ssu 興國 of T'ang date in Hsin-hsien 新縣, which is shown in *ibid*. 1.38b as Hsin-hsien-hsün 汛, about midway between Su-ch'eng and Nan-ch'eng. The actual date of the founding of this monastery is given as the twentieth year of Yüan-ho, but this year period lasted only from 806 to 821.

[459] 左二將十將, evidently a military title. See note 379.

[460] *Ch'ao-i-lang* 朝議郎 was a title for officials of that rank. Cf. Des Rotours 36.

[461] *Ya-ssu Lu-shih* 押司錄事. See note 696.

[462] Probably meaning that the three donkeys he had ridden that day had cost a total of 120 cash, 50 each for the first two and 20 for the third.

fourth class of the sixth rank,[463] Ts'ui Chün-yüan 崔君原 the Assistant Subprefect,[464] who is a substitute 攝 Assistant Subprefect of the second class of the ninth rank [465] and was a former probationary Secretary in Charge of Rites [466] of the Bureau of Imperial Sacrifices,[387] Li Teng 李登 the Superintendent of Registers,[467] who is a Provisional Superintendent of Registers of the fourth class of the ninth rank,[468] Hua Ta 花達 the Chief of Employees of the subprefecture,[464] who is a Chief of Employees of the third class of the ninth rank,[469] and Lu Liao 陸僚 the Catcher of Bandits 捕賊 官, who is a Chief of Employees of the third class of the ninth rank.[469] They met us and talked with us monks. Our host prepared wine and food for the Subprefect and the others, and after eating, they went back.

After the forenoon meal the Guard Officer and we monks left the house of Wang the Secretary and went to the harbor. The Guard Officer and eight soldiers put a small boat in order, and we boarded it and started out together. The Subprefect Li I-fu entrusted two tou [217] of fresh flour to Chang the Guard Officer to give to the Prefect of the prefecture.

The second ship [422] was ahead of us in a bay 小海. The Guard Officer said, " This subprefecture is on the east shore [of the bay] and the prefectural [capital] on the west shore. Because the Administrative Officer Yoshi[mine] [470] is sick,

---

[463] *T'ung-chih-lang* 通直郎. Cf. *ibid.* 36.

[464] 竝, for which *DBZ* suggests *Wei* 尉, Chief of Employees, the fourth category of officials of a subprefecture, but which is more probably an error for *Ch'eng* 丞, the second category of subprefectural officials. Cf. *ibid.* 731-35.

[465] *Teng-shih-lang* 登仕郎. Cf. *ibid.* 37.

[466] *Feng-li-lang* 奉禮郎. Cf. *ibid.* 320.

[467] *Chu-pu* 主簿, the third category of subprefectural officials. Cf. *ibid.* 731-33.

[468] *Chiang-shih-lang* 將仕郎. Cf. *ibid.* 37. For his post, he should have ranked at least one class higher.

[469] *Wen-lin-lang* 文林郎. Cf. *ibid.* 37.

[470] Yoshimine no Nagamatsu 良岑長松 (the second character is

he has [left] [471] the ship. On the west shore of this bay stands
the Hai-lung-wang-miao ('Temple of the Dragon-King of
the Sea'). [472] At present the Administrative Officer Yoshi-
[mine] has been placed in this temple, and I propose now to
go where he is and have you meet him."

We hoisted sail and went straight ahead, right past the
[Japanese] ship. We monks wished to board it, but the Guard
Officer would not let us. At 2 P. M. we reached the Hai-lung-
wang-miao and saw the Administrative Officer Yoshimine,
Awa[da] [473] the Secretary, Ki the Interpreter, [474] and Kami
. . . 神 the Military Attaché. [414] I explained in detail why
we had remained behind and also told them about our hardships. When the Administrative Officer and the others heard
the story, they both grieved and rejoiced. Here, the Secretary Wa[ke] [475] has been sick on board the ship, and the
Hossō Scholar [Monk] Kaimyō Hosshi [358] and the Korean

---

sometimes written 峯) is called an Acting Administrative Officer
on 840 IV 15 and elsewhere in *SNK*. He was in command of the
second ship, since Fujiwara no Toyonami had died, as reported
on II 20.

[471] The text has 上.

[472] 海龍王廟, *miao* being the term for Taoist and certain other
temples. *Chia-ch'ing Hai-chou chih-li-chou chih* 29.13a-19b lists
no less than six temples in Hai-chou with similar names, but
none corresponds in location with the temple mentioned here.
Cf. M. W. de Visser, *The Dragon in China and Japan (Ver-
handelingen der Koninklijke Akademie van Wetenschappen te
Amsterdam*, 1913) for a detailed discussion of the relationship
between the dragon and water, and the Indian influence through
Buddhism on the Chinese and Japanese concepts of the dragon.

[473] *Ikeda* has Awada 粟田 throughout, but *Tōji* has only the
first character, forming an apparently incomplete surname.

[474] Probably Ki no Harunushi 紀春主, a former monk who,
according to *SNK*, had been appointed Interpreter on the embassy on 836 Intercalary V 13.

[475] Possibly the Acting Secretary who, according to *SNK*, was
given the family name of Wake 和氣 on 836 II 9.

Interpreter Tohyŏn [476] are likewise on board. Thus, we arrived and met one another.

The Guard Officer said that it would be proper for us three monks to go to the prefectural [offices] and briefly meet the *Ta-fu*.[477] We three monks accompanied the Guard Officer to the prefectural [offices], going about three *li* west from the temple to the gate of the prefectural [offices]. The Guard Officer and some officers 將 went in first to report, and soon we monks were summoned into the presence of the Prefect. He had us sit on chairs and asked us how we happened to be abandoned. We had the Guard Officer tell him. The Prefect's surname is Yen 顏 and his given name is Ts'o 措. He has a rough understanding of Buddhism and discoursed on it himself to us monks. After our conversation, we returned to the temple. The Prefect, Yen the *Ta-fu*, sent a military officer to accompany us three monks and our servant. We stayed for a little while in the Hai-lung-wang-miao.

From Su-ch'eng-ts'un of Mt. Tung-hai to Tung-hai-hsien is more than one hundred *li*. The whole way was mountainous, but we were able to cover it by riding and walking in a single day.

Since the sixth day a northeast wind has been blowing day after day without change. I fear that the nine ships, after encountering the thunderstorm and bad winds [of the night of the fifth], may have been unable to cross the sea. I am sad at heart.

In order to search for the Buddhist Law, we monks have several times made schemes, but we have not yet been able to carry out these plans. On the point of returning to Japan, we with difficulty devised a plan for staying behind, but again it did not work, and we were discovered by them. We have tried every idea, but we cannot stay. The officials are vigilant and do not permit the slightest [irregularity]. Therefore, I have decided to board the second ship and return to

---

[476] 道玄, who we learn from references on IV 10 and VI 29 was a Buddhist monk, as his name suggests.

[477] Obviously referring to the Prefect. See note 218.

Japan. I left on the eighth ship all the Buddhist teachings and the materials which I had previously sought out in Yang-chou and Ch'u-chou,[478] and I gave to others between Hu-hung Island and the prefecture all the baggage we took with us when we expected to be left behind, so we board the ship empty-handed.[479] But my sighs are caused entirely by our failure to accomplish our search for the Law.

9th DAY   The wind still was from the northeast, but in the night it shifted[480] to the west.

10th DAY   [The wind] again sprang up in the west. At 2 P. M. the Administrative Officer Yoshimine left the temple and boarded the ship. We monks accompanied him on board and saw Kaimyō Hosshi and Master[333] Tohyŏn. Awa[da] the Secretary and Ki the Interpreter, because they are attending to some matters, have not yet come on board.

11th DAY   At 6 A. M. Awa[da] the Secretary and the other came on board, and then we started. Hoisting sail, we went straight ahead. A southwest wind was blowing. We intended to go west of [Tung]-hai-hsien, but, because we were blown by the wind straight onto a shallow beach, we lowered sail and rowed. When we passed across shallows, we proceeded haltingly 趑, measuring [the depth of] our course with poles. We had a hard time of it all day and just managed to reach the subprefecture. [Then] the tide went out, and the ship stuck in the mud unable to move.

We stayed the night there, and [someone][481] came on

---

[478] Miswritten in *Tōji* as Yang Ch'u Yang-chou.

[479] *Ikeda* corrects 年 to 手.

[480] 受 may be a copyist's error for 變.

[481] The omission of a name at this point and the improbability of the statement about the Guard Officer and the Subprefect in the letter from Su-ch'eng, as well as the hour mentioned, all suggest that we have a corruption of the text here and that it should be rearranged to read:

"At 4 P. M. the Guard Officer and the Subprefect came on board to see if we monks had returned 却歸 to the ship, and they told us that a letter had come today from Su-ch'eng-ts'un saying that the third of the nine Japanese ships had drifted to

board and told us that a letter had come today from Su-ch'eng-ts'un saying that the third of the nine Japanese ships had drifted to Mt. Ta-chu in Mi-chou. At 4 P. M. the Guard Officer and the Subprefect had come to Su-ch'eng-ts'un to seek the place where we monks had left 却歸 the ships. Now, the ship had drifted to the district of Lai-chou [482] and then had drifted with the current to Mt. Ta-chu in Mi-chou. It had lost the eight [other] ships on the sea and did not know where they had gone.

At 10 P. M. we hauled on hawsers, intending to pull [the ship] out, but we still were unable to refloat it.

12th DAY At dawn the wind [was blowing] fitfully from the east and west, and the ship was not yet refloated. There was a letter from the subprefecture to the Administrative Officer Yoshimine and the others informing them that the third ship of the tributary embassy, which had drifted to the territory of the said subprefecture,[483] had started out again the other day. I have not yet seen the real letter. The wind shifted and was not steady.

13th DAY Early in the morning the tide rose, and we intended to start out, but because the wind was not steady, we advanced and returned several times. At 1 P. M. a wind sprang up, shifting from southwest to west. At 2 P. M. the tide rose, and the ship of itself floated off to the east, so we hoisted sail and set forth. From in front of Tung-hai-hsien we headed east.[484] We purified ourselves for being on

---

Mt. Ta-chu in Mi-chou. Now, the ship had drifted to the district of Lai-chou," etc.

[482] 萊, the modern I-hsien (or Yeh-hsien) 掖, which was the name of the local subprefecture in T'ang times. It is located on the northwestern side of the Shantung Peninsula, but its territory stretched across the peninsula to the southern side in the vicinity of Chi-mo 卽墨, northeast of Kiaochow Bay, and it was undoubtedly in this area that the third ship first came ashore.

[483] Presumably the Mt. Ta-chu region in Mi-chou.

[484] Implying that there was enough water between the Tung-hai hills (see note 423) and the mainland to allow a ship to sail

shipboard [415] and also worshiped the Great God of Sumi-yoshi,[416] and only then started across the sea. A rather stiff wind was blowing. Not far out at sea, a sailor who had been sick in bed for some time died at 5 P. M. They wrapped him up in a mat and lowered him into the sea, and he floated away with the waves. The color of the sea was fairly clear. In the night the wind was stiff, and we went straight ahead.

14*th* DAY   At dawn the water again became white and muddy, but the direction of the wind was unchanged. We looked in all directions without seeing mountains or islands. At noon the wind died. The water was a light green. At 2 P. M. a south wind blew, and trimming our sail, we headed northeast by north 丑. At 8 P. M., in order to get a favorable wind, we arranged offerings of the five grains to the Dragon-Kings of the five directions in accordance with the *Kanjō-gyō*,[485] and we recited scriptures and incantations.[486] The wind changed to the southwest and in the middle of the night to due west, and we turned our prow with the wind.

15*th* DAY   At dawn the ocean water was deep blue in color. A due-west wind sprang up, and we headed towards the point where the sun was rising. At 10 A. M. the wind died. At 2 P. M. a southeast wind blew, and trimming our sail, we went north. A sailor died of an illness and they lowered him into the sea. At 4 P. M. they had the diviner foretell about the wind without much avail, but he divined with regard to the way ahead [and said that], even though it be Korean territory, we need have no fears.

---

south of these hills and straight east from the Hai-chou Nan-ch'eng region to the open sea.

[485] The ninth chapter of the *Kanjō-gyō* 灌頂經 (cf. *Taishō daizōkyō* 大正大藏經 21[No. 1331].521-523) tells of how a terrible epidemic in India was checked by calling on the *nāga*, or dragon protecting deities, of the five directions (the fifth direction being the center). See notes 241 and 472. One of the rites of Buddhism is to burn the five grains in a small brazier as an offering. The usual list of the five grains in Buddhism consists of barley, wheat, rice, red beans (*azuki* 小豆), and sesame seeds.

[486] *Darani* 陀羅尼 (Skr. *dhāraṇī*).

The officials on board, in order to stop the contrary winds, together made vows and prayed for a favorable wind. We saw the point where the sun set right in the middle of the " great oar " 大櫂.[487] In the night we made offerings of the five grains, recited the *Hannya-[kyō]*,[203] the *Kanjō-[gyō]*,[485] and other scriptures, prayed to the [Shintō] deities, and put our faith in the Buddha, asking for a favorable wind. At midnight the wind changed to southwest and before long to due west. We saw that the point where the moon set was back of the stern rudder house 艫柂倉 .

16*th* DAY At dawn it was foggy and rainy, and we could see in no direction. We discussed the wind, but without agreement. Some said that it was a west wind, others a southwest wind, and still others a south wind. We saw the morning sun through the oarlock (?) 腋門 of the small oar of the prow,[488] and then we knew we were going northeast, so, trimming the sail, we proceeded. Some suspected it might be a south wind. Although the sky above us was clear, in all directions on the sea a heavy fog closed us in, and we could not see through it.

Today for the first time the officer in charge of the water 主水司 apportioned the water of the water tank among the men on board, two *shō* [489] daily for each man [ranking as] an official or below, and one and a half *shō* daily for each man from attendants down to sailors.

Later on in the afternoon we saw that the wind for the most part was from the southeast and we were cutting across it toward the north. The fog cleared, but the sky was cloudy, and from the northeast and north to the southwest there

---

[487] Since they were going north, this was obviously somewhere on the port side of the ship.

[488] 舳 means either stern or prow but here must be the latter since Ennin records below that they were sailing northeast. *DBZ* and *KIK* are incorrect in stating that *Tōji* has 舶 in place of this character.

[489] The modern Japanese *shō* is 1.8 liters (more than one and a half quarts), but here we presumably have the corresponding T'ang *sheng* of .5944 liters (a little over a pint). See note 217.

lay a wall of clouds. Since I, the Scholar Monk, was indisposed and not feeling well, I did not take food or drink. In the night there was a downpour, and we were very uncomfortable.

17th DAY   Early in the morning the rain stopped, but the fog was heavy,[490] and we did not know in what direction we were going. The color of the sea was light green. We could not see the sun and wandered aimlessly. Some said that we were going northwest, others that we were going due north, and still others said that they saw islands ahead. After we had advanced for some time, the ocean waves looked like [those in] shallow water, so we lowered a rope and measured it, and there were eight fathoms. We wished to drop anchor and stop, not knowing how far we were from land. Someone said that, now that we had discovered that the ocean was shallow, it would be best to drop anchor and stop for a while and wait for the fog to clear and then decide whether to go on or stop. All agreed with this, and we dropped anchor and tied up.

We could just make out below the fog the dashing of white waves, and then we saw something black, so we knew it was an island. It was very indistinct. Before long the fog lifted a trifle, and the shape of the island became clear, but we did not yet know what country it was. They lowered a skiff and sent two archers and five sailors to search for the mainland and to ask the name of this place.

The fog cleared somewhat, and in the north [could be seen] mountains and islands in a row. Beginning in the northeast,[491] they extended in an uninterrupted line to the southwest. Some said that this was the southern part of the land of Korea. They had the diviner divine upon it, and he called

---

[490] The indistinct spot in *Tōji*, which *DBZ* and *KIK* print as 云, perhaps should be interpreted as a sign to repeat the preceding character 重, as it is printed in *ZZGR*.

[491] Actually " southeast " in the text, but the preceding sentence and their position on the southern coast of Shantung indicate that this is a copyist's error.

it China and then later said that it was Korea. The matter
rested between these two alternatives,[492] and we still did not
know for certain.

While we were in doubt, the sailors and archers whom they
had dispatched returned with two Chinese, who said that
this is the southern part of T'ang-yang-t'ao-ts'un 唐陽陶
in Mou-p'ing-hsien [493] in Teng-chou.[419] It is 160 *li* from the
subprefectural [capital] and 300 *li* from the prefectural [capital].
East of here is the land of Korea, which can be reached
with a good wind in two or three days. The officials on board
gave them wine and silk floss and then made out letters to
inform the prefecture and subprefecture [of our arrival].

Because the sky had not yet cleared, the tops of the mountains were not yet clearly visible in the distance. An east
wind blew. At sunset the fog closed in on us, and it was dark.

18*th* DAY The food regulations were changed. Each
man daily [is to receive] one *shō* [489] of food and one *shō* of
water. The east wind did not change.

It is said that this prefecture grows millet, and rice is
very expensive.

I, the Scholar Monk, in order to return quickly to Japan
to fulfill the vows made in recent years, had the diviner pray
to the [Shintō] gods and offered a fire crystal [494] to the Great
God of Sumiyoshi, a rosary of rock crystals to the Dragon-
King of the Sea,[472] and a razor to the patron deity of ships
主舶之神, in order to pray for our safe return to Japan.

[END OF] FIRST SCROLL OF THE RECORD OF A PILGRIMAGE

---

[492] 盈 may be an error for its homophone 楹.

[493] 牟平 (also known as Ning-hai 寧海) on the north coast of
Shantung about a hundred km. west of the tip. Its present
administrative area includes a thirty-km. strip of coast on the
southern side of the peninsula just west of Wu-lei-tao 五壘島
Bay.

[494] 火珠 (*hitorutama* in Japanese), a crystal which can ignite
a fire by focusing the rays of the sun.

RECORD OF

A Pilgrimage to China
in Search of the Law

II

Second Scroll

OF THE RECORD
OF A PILGRIMAGE TO CHINA
IN SEARCH OF THE LAW

NINETEENTH DAY At dawn it was clear, and a north wind was blowing. We raised anchor and headed out southward. At 2 P.M. the wind died, so we rowed towards the southwest. At 4 P.M. we reached the inlet at Shao-ts'un 邵村浦 and dropping anchor, tied up. It is southwest of [T'ang-yang]-t'ao-ts'un. We intended to enter the bight, but the opposing current flowed fast, and we could not advance against it.

20th DAY Early in the morning a Korean came in a small boat, and we then heard that Chang Pogo had plotted with a Korean Prince against the country and had made this Prince the Prince of Korea.[495]

There was a rather stiff south wind. Because the current

---

[495] See note 438. Ennin may have used the term " Prince 王子 of Korea " both here and on IV 24 because Sinmu had not yet been invested as King by the Chinese Emperor.

flowed swiftly against us, we could not hold still, but swung back and forth from east to west and were tossed about a great deal.

21st DAY   It was foggy. At noon a south wind blew hard.

22nd DAY   It was cloudy and rainy. At 4 P. M. a . . .[496] died. They put him in a skiff and took him to an island.

23rd DAY   It was cloudy, and the wind was from the south.

24th DAY   It was foggy and rainy. Hawsers were holding us in our place of anchorage, but some of them broke. The wind was blowing and the waves were high. The last few days we have lowered eight hawsers [with anchors], but three of the hawsers and anchors have snapped and sunk, and very few remain. If we were to encounter a storm, they could not hold fast. We are extremely worried.

24th DAY [497]   A west wind blew. At sunset a mounted man came to the shore north of us. The Korean Interpreter Tohyŏn [476] was sent from the ship to meet him. Tohyŏn returned and reported that the man who had come was an Administrative Officer [38] of the Guard Officer.[449] While at the subprefecture, he had heard that a ship of the Japanese embassy had anchored here for many days and, consequently, had come to meet us. Because it was night, he had gone back, and [Tohyŏn] did not get to meet him, but tomorrow he will make a special point of coming on board. He had a Korean remain on the beach to pass on this information to Tohyŏn, who in turn had [the Korean] tell the officer how we happened to come here.

We also learned that the Japanese tributary envoys on board five of the Korean ships had drifted to the vicinity of Mt. Lu 廬 in Lai-chou.[498] We do not know where the remain-

---

[496] 挾抄, possibly meaning a scribe or servant.
[497] *DBZ* suggests that this might be an error for " 25th day," but it is simply an unnecessary repetition of " 24th day."
[498] See note 482. Chou here is miswritten 明.

ing four ships have gone. Although we have learned this, we do not yet know which of the ships these are. We also heard that the Chinese Emperor was sending an embassy to Korea in order to bestow the title of King on the Prince of Korea.[438] They have put the ships in order and also arranged for the official pay [for those making the trip].

25th DAY   The wind blew unsteadily, and the fog did not clear. At noon the Administrative Officer of the Guard Officer, who yesterday retired from the beach,[499] sent [a man called] Wang Chiao-yen 王敎言 to give wine and fish to the officials [on board]. Wang Chiao-yen himself also gave them wine and cakes, and the officials gave him floss silk and the like.

This anchorage[500] has many submerged reefs. Each time we are carried by the waves, they cut the hawsers. We have lowered anchors five or six times. At 3 P. M. we rowed towards Mt. Ju[501] going out of the inlet of Shao-ts'un onto the open sea, but before we had gone halfway, a dense fog suddenly arose, and it became dark in all directions. Since we did not know from which direction the wind came or which way we were going, we threw out the anchors and stopped. The wind and waves vied with each other in tossing us about and tormenting us, and they did not let up all night long.

26th DAY   Early in the morning the fog lifted a little, and we saw Mt. Ju not far to the west. A wind sprang up in the northeast, and hoisting sail, we proceeded. At 10 P. M. we reached the west inlet of Mt. Ju, anchored the ship, and stopped. We are protected by both mountains and islands, surrounding us like a wall. This Mt. Ju is steep and lofty with a summit rising like a spear and skirts falling away in

---

[499] 後 is probably an error for 從, which it often closely resembles in *Tōji.*

[500] *DBZ* suggests 泊 for 舶.

[501] 乳, about midway between Kiaochow Bay and the tip of the peninsula, with a large and well-protected inlet lying to the east of it and a bay called Mt. Ju Bay to the south.

all directions from the peak. On the west side of the bight there is another rocky mountain, with precipitous peaks forming a ridge and soaring halfway to heaven. Although there is a range of hills [stretching] from the east to the north, they are only gently sloping.

At 2 P. M. over thirty Koreans came mounted on horses and donkeys and told us that the Guard Officer intended to come to see us when the tide ebbed and that they had, therefore, come on ahead to await him. Among them was a commoner who said that he had come from Mt. Lu yesterday and had observed that the nine ships of the Japanese tributary embassy had all arrived at Mt. Lu. The men and goods were uninjured, and the officials had all landed, erected tents to stay in, and were at their leisure waiting for a [favorable] wind.

Before long the Guard Officer came on board a Korean boat and debarked on the shore. There were many young women 娘子 [with him]. The Administrative Officer of the tributary embassy sent the Korean Interpreter Tohyŏn to explain the situation. Subsequently,[502] the Secretary Awa[da] left the ship and went to the Guard Officer in order to meet him. He also wrote a request for food, [stating], " Previously while we were in Tung-hai-hsien, we were given [503] provisions for crossing the sea, but this ship, while crossing the sea, was driven back by contrary winds and drifted ashore here. It would not be right for us to consume our provisions for the ocean crossing while here, so we ask for fresh provisions." The Guard Officer took the document and said that he would inform the prefectural officials to take action. In the evening he returned home. All day a northeast wind blew.

27th DAY It was cloudy and rainy, and a north wind blew.

28th DAY It was clear. The Guard Officer came and met the officers [of the embassy].

---

[502] *DBZ, KIK,* and *ZZGR* all misprint 已後 as 巳後 (11 A. M.). By this time it must have been late afternoon.
[503] 但 is probably a copyist's error for 供 or some similar verb.

29th DAY   A north wind blew. I had the Korean Interpreter Tohyŏn scheme to see whether or not I could safely stay here [in China]. Tohyŏn consulted with some Koreans about the matter and came back and said that I could safely stay.

FIFTH MOON: 1st DAY [504]   They sent [someone] to buy provisions for the ocean crossing at the house of Wang Hsün 王訓, the village manager,[271] and to ask about my staying in this village. Wang Hsün and the others said that, if I wished to live there, they would arrange everything, and we monks would not have to return to Japan. Because the matter is not right, I have not yet been able to make up my mind. All day a west wind blew.

2nd DAY [505]   A west wind blew, so we loosed hawsers to leave the cove, but because the wind was very stiff and our way lay close to the reefs, we were unable to go out [of the bay]. At 6 P.M. the wind died, so we drifted with the current to the mouth of the bay 海口 and stopped there. [Men] were sent to draw fresh water. At sunset on board the ship we worshiped the deities of heaven and earth and made offerings of official and private silks, tie-dye cloth,[506] and mirrors to the Great God of Sumiyoshi which is on board the ship.

A sailor who had been seriously ill for some time and was on the point of death was wrapped up while still alive at 2 A.M. and put in a barque and abandoned beside a mountain. The men who had taken him returned and said that, when they left him on shore, the invalid was not yet dead, but asked for food and water and said that, if he recovered

---

[504] June 15, 839. The preceding moon had only twenty-nine days.
[505] *Ikeda* corrects " 20th " to " 2nd."
[506] *Kōkechi* 纐纈 (sometimes pronounced *kyōkechi*), a patterned dyed cloth in which the pattern has been made by tying up parts of the cloth with thread at the time of dyeing. It is written 夾纈 on 845 VI 9.

from his illness, he would look for a village. There was none on board but did grieve.[507]

3rd DAY   The wind blew unchanged, and raising sail, we set forth from the mouth of the bay southwest of Mt. Ju. The wind gradually lightened, and at noon it died down. Presently an east wind blew, and we reversed sail and returned to the mouth of the anchorage at Mt. Ju and stopped for the night.

4th DAY   At 8 A. M. we went about four or five *li* southwest from the mouth of the anchorage and tied up on the north side of Sang Island 桑島 in the east inlet of Wang-hai-ts'un.[508]

5th DAY   We left the ship and went up on shore and performed the festival of the fifth moon.[172] We also bathed ourselves and laundered our clothing. In the evening a letter was brought from the ship, which said, " Since we are having difficulties getting a favorable wind and are not accomplishing a successful crossing, the Commander [104] Administrative Officer has discussed [the matter] with the group, and the whole ship is to observe ritual purity.[509] We invite you monks for three days beginning tomorrow to read scriptures, call on the Buddha's name,[510] and pray

---

[507] The heartless treatment of this sailor was presumably in order to avoid the ritual defilement which a death on board would have entailed and which, it was thought, might have an adverse influence on the crossing. See V 5 and note 415.

[508] There is a Wang-hai-k'ou 望海口 in the vicinity of the bay now called Ch'ang-hui-k'ou 長會口, southeast of Wen-teng-hsien 文登, which itself is in the center of the Shantung Peninsula only about fifty km. west of the tip. Cf. *Wen-teng-hsien chih* (1922), *chüan-shou* 17b, *Tseng-hsiu Teng-chou-fu chih* (1881), introductory maps 3b, and *Shan-tung t'ung-chih* 山東通志 (1911), map preceding 2B.19. At this point, however, Ennin appears to have been quite some distance southwest of this particular Wang-hai-k'ou.

[509] *Kessai* 潔齋, a Buddhist term for the avoidance of evil and abstinence from meat and wine.

[510] *Nembutsu* 念佛.

for a favorable wind. May [the Buddha] look upon us and grant us his glorious grace." [511] Because it was night, we did not go at once, but spent the night on shore.

6*th* DAY   Early in the morning we went on board the ship and had our forenoon meal there. The Korean Interpreter Tohyŏn went to the Guard Officer's residence. After the forenoon meal we again went ashore and, setting up a tent, arranged for the service. In the evening we worshiped the Dragon-Kings of the five directions.[485] Kaimyō Hosshi managed the affair.

7*th* DAY   It rained.

9*th* DAY   Early in the morning we concluded our reading of scriptures.

11*th* DAY   We worshiped the deities of heaven and earth of China. From this day until the 13*th* DAY the skies were alternately dark and clear, and the wind was unsteady.

14*th* DAY   The Guard Officer of the prefecture came on board and asked us how many men were on the ship. Then he returned to the village. The Manager of Shao-ts'un, Wang Hsün, and others came to see us, and we learned that the nine ships of the Japanese Consultant Counselor [392] and the others had earlier set out across the sea from Mt. Lu but meeting with adverse winds, had drifted back again to Mt. Lu and since then had anchored there. In the night it thundered and rained heavily.

15*th* DAY   In the morning the clouds were wildly confused, and the rain was rather heavy. The Guard Officer of the prefecture came on board the ship and asked for the number of men on board. Our officials recorded the number in detail and wrote informing the prefectural offices of it. In the evening, when the Guard Officer returned home, the tributary embassy rewarded him with such things as coarse silk cloth and floss silk.

16*th* DAY   The heavens were dark. A messenger from the Guard Officer came and asked for a letter from the tribu-

---

[511] 照察幸垂光儀, possibly a quotation from a Buddhist text, which cannot be interpreted with certainty out of context.

tary embassy to the subprefecture. I, the Scholar Monk, wrote a letter about my remaining behind and sent it by the merchant Sun Ch'ing 孫清 to the residence of Lin 林 the Commissioner.[46] The officials on board sent two archers and two sailors together to the Guard Officer of the prefecture to ask for provisions, but the Guard Officer would not give any to us, on the grounds that no local (i. e., Japanese) products had been given to the prefecture and subprefecture. The above-mentioned men returned from shore.

17th and 18th DAYS The wind alternated between northwest and west. The men were of divided opinion [about setting sail].

19th DAY During the night until 2 A. M. there was thunder and lightning, and there was a heavy rain and a great wind, which were unbearable. The bow hawsers all snapped, and the ship at once started to float off. In consternation we dropped anchor and thus managed to stop it. The planks covering[512] the shrine 神殿 at the stern were blown off by the great wind, and we could not find them. The men all trembled with fear and could not control themselves.

20th DAY A west wind was blowing, and we decided to cross the sea. We put the sailcloth in order and brought aboard those on shore. At noon the wind shifted to southwest, and we thought that we could not get out of the anchorage, so we did not set out. In the night the thunder and rain were again severe.

21st DAY At 10 A. M. a west wind was blowing, so we loosed our hawsers and started, but the wind died down and would not blow. After we had waited awhile for the wind, a south wind blew faintly, so we could not raise our sail and returned to the anchorage and tied up. The diviner on board has been sick for a long time, and in the evening he left the ship.[507]

22nd DAY Early in the morning we heard that the

---

[512] *Tōji* has 葢揖, *Ikeda* 葢葺.

diviner had died on shore. All day it was dark and rainy, and an east wind blew.

23rd DAY   The clouds cleared a little. In the night the wind and rain vied with each other in fierceness.

24th DAY   A west wind blew briskly, but since the rain has not yet cleared, we still did not start out. In the evening the officials conferred together and [decided that], since the wind has not changed all day, we shall start out tomorrow.

25th DAY   Early in the morning we loosed our hawsers, but the wind died, and we were unable to start. At 4 P. M. a Korean ship with white sails passed across the entrance of the bay, but before long it reversed sail and came on in. In the evening it drifted with the current toward the Mt. Ju anchorage. The men all wondered whether it were [one of the nine ships of] the tributary embassy, coming from Mt. Lu, so they sent a skiff in haste to find out, but the Korean ship sped away, and because it was night, the skiff returned without obtaining any information.

26th DAY   We intended to depart, but the wind gradually became unfavorable. In the evening lightning flashed brightly in the west and north, and the clouds lowered darkly. In the night the ship was suddenly tossed about, and we were extremely frightened. At 8 P. M. we moored [the ship] on the northwest shore. The howling of foxes resounded far and continuously. Before long thunder and lightning roared forth. It was deafening to our ears, and the flashes of lightning were too dazzling to look at. The rain fell in torrents, and we were afraid and distressed.[513] Everybody on board was unable to move.

27th DAY   At dawn a thunderbolt fell, cleaving the prow side of the mast and splitting it obliquely. The piece torn off it is over four inches deep, about six inches wide, and over thirty feet long. Besides this, five other fragments have been torn off, some four fathoms [16] [long] and others five feet or less. The fragments were scattered about, but

---

[513] *DBZ* suggests 辛艱 for 章難.

we gathered them together and tied them onto the ship's
. . . .[514]

We also made offerings[515] [to the gods, vowing that] on
the day we arrived in Japan we would especially erect a
shrine and for a long time perform sacrifices and prayers
there. Burning a tortoise shell,[516] we divined regarding this
curse. [The oracle] said that the ship's diviner, Morokimi
諸公, had been buried in front of the local deity, and consequently we had incurred the anger of the deity, who had
brought down this disaster upon us, but, if we could purify
ourselves,[415] we might then be safe. Therefore, we purified
ourselves on Sang Island, and on board the ship we worshiped the local deity.

Some said of the riven mast that it was broken and should
be replaced, but others said it would be difficult to find
quickly in this area lumber with which to make a mast and
that, if we were to replace it, they thought that we could
not cross the sea this year, and therefore we should bind
together the broken places, so that we could set forth quickly.
The men accepted the latter opinion, and so we decided to
start. A wind sprang up in the northwest, rolling the ship a
little, but then it died down. The men were at variance in
their views, and the officers and men were not in harmony.[517]
A fresh breeze blew a little, and we loosed hawsers and
started out anyway, but because there was no sign of a
favorable wind, we dropped anchor after going a short time.
In the night a fresh breeze blew a little, so we hoisted sail
and proceeded gradually, but hardly [had we reached] the

---

[514] 角, literally " horns." See note 17.
[515] *Heihaku* 幣帛, originally cloth hung up as offerings to the
gods, in time became a general term for any such offering, including paper pendants substituted for cloth.
[516] A form of divination, practiced at a much earlier age in North
China and neighboring areas, had been to apply a heated rod
to a tortoise shell and to read the future from the resultant
cracks in the shell.
[517] For 瞳, *DBZ* suggests 睦 and *KIK* 壹.

island mouth [of the bay] when the wind died, and we could not start out, so we dropped anchor and tied up.

28th DAY   At 8 A.M. it was foggy and dark, and since the "stone-god" [518] shook and sounded, we raised anchor and returned. It was raining, and we suffered. We rowed into a bay southeast of Sang Island, where there is an island to which we moored the ship.

30th DAY   It was clear. According to the Japanese calendar it is the first day of the sixth moon. A wind sprang up in the northwest, but it shifted around and was not steady. For the past several days I have been requesting to be allowed to live in this village, but the officials will not permit it. Today I asked again, but have not yet received permission.

SIXTH MOON: 1st DAY [519]   The sky cleared a trifle. Because of the matter of my staying, I asked for a dinghy [520] for a little while, but did not [get to] [521] leave the ship.

2nd DAY   It was clear. Although we did not have a favorable wind, the men sorely wished to return home, so we hauled up anchor [522] and started out anyway. All day long we tried to get out [of the bay]. In the evening when we were raising sail to take the ship back, we were suddenly caught in a current and were about to pile up on the rocks. We dropped anchor and, exerting all our efforts, just managed to save ourselves.

3rd DAY   A west wind blew lightly, sometimes blowing and sometimes not. We raised and lowered sail three or

---

[518] 石神, meaning the "thunder-god," presumably because of the identification in Japan of certain stones, particularly neolithic weapons, with thunderbolts. See my article on "The Thunder Weapon in Ancient Japan," *Harvard Journal of Asiatic Studies* 5.137-141.

[519] July 15, 839.

[520] Printed 舟遊艇 in *DBZ, KIK,* and *ZZGR* and written this way on VI 23, but written with 舟斿 for the first character at this point in *Tōji.* This unusual term is also to be found in *SNK* 836 VII 25.

[521] *Ikeda* has 失, *Tōji* apparently 天.

[522] 步矴. The second character is misprinted 叮 in *DBZ.*

more times. Alternately sailing and rowing, we headed for
distant Mt. Ch'ih,[523] going out of the inlet of Shao-ts'un
with the current. When we had almost reached the mouth
of the inlet, the current caught us sideways, and the ship
suddenly ran onto a reef. We lowered poles to push it off,
but were unable to control it. There were submerged rocks
on the bottom, against which we struck, and we bumped up
against the rocks along the shore. The ship was about to
break up, but the men pushed together on the poles and at
the same time hauled on [522] the anchors, and we managed
to extricate ourselves. We went out with the current and
stopped on the open sea. At sunset there was a great wind
and heavy rain, and the thunder was deafening and the
lightning blinding. All on board waved spears, axes, and
swords and shouted [524] with all their might in order to fend
off the thunderbolts.

4th DAY Early in the morning we raised sail and
proceeded. After we had gone along a little while, the wind
died, and we dropped anchor and tied up.

---

[523] Ch'ih-shan 赤山 (now more commonly written 斥山), standing near the southeastern extremity of the Shantung Peninsula
and straddling the present border between Wen-teng-hsien and
Jung-ch'eng-hsien 榮成 (close to the northeastern tip of the
peninsula). It is immediately west of Shih-tao 石島 Bay in the
vicinity of the present village of Ch'ih-shan-chi 集 and 100 *li*
southeast of Wen-teng-hsien. (Ennin estimated this distance at
130 *li* on IX 1.) Cf. *Wen-teng-hsien chih* (1922) 1A.13b. The
newer name appears on maps in *ibid., chüan-shou* 22b; *Tseng-
hsiu Teng-chou-fu chih*, introductory maps 3b and 13a; and
Jung-ch'eng-hsien chih (1840), *t'u* 2a. The older name appears
on maps in *Teng-chou-fu chih* (1660), *t'u* 1b and 11b, but the
newer name also appears in the text at 2.22b. The Mt. Ch'ih
inlet, where the ship subsequently anchored, appears to be Shih-
tao Bay or some part of it (see VI 29). *Tseng-hsiu Teng-chou-fu
chih* 3.31b records that this bay can hold five or six hundred
vessels.
[524] 呼 and a second character printed 川 in *DBZ, KIK,* and
ZZGR, but in *Tōji* the stroke on the left is written as if it might
be the "mouth" radical.

5th DAY   Just before dawn we hoisted sail and went on, and at noon we arrived west of Mt. Ch'ih. As the tide was against us, we stopped for a little while and then abruptly started again, gradually entering [the bay] south of the mountain. Suddenly masses of clouds closed in on us, and an opposing wind struck us, reversing our spread sail. While we were lowering the sail, a black bird flew up and circled the ship three times and then returned to perch on an island. The group was afraid, and all said that this was a divine spirit which would not let us enter the anchorage, so we turned the ship about and left, going some distance from the mountain and tying up on the open sea.

We heard thunder to the north, shaking the clouds and roaring towards us. The officials on board were extremely afraid and all the more suspected that these were signs of the displeasure of the mysterious deities. Together we made vows, purified ourselves, and prayed to the god of the thunderbolt on board the ship.[525] We also worshiped the Great God of Sumiyoshi which was on board and made vows to Hachiman [526] and the other great deities of Japan, to the Dragon-King of the Sea,[472] and to the deities of the mountains and islands of Teng-chou. The thunder gradually died away, and a wind sprang up in the . . . east.[527] We dropped anchor and tied up. The ship has been away from land for many days, unable either to cross the sea or to enter a cove. For many days and nights we have tossed about on the sea. The movement [of the ship] is unbearable, and our spirits have been worn down.

6th DAY   A northwest wind blew briskly, and we intended to enter the Mt. Ch'ih anchorage. Since the wind was

---

[525] Possibly the spot made sacred by the thunderbolt which had struck the ship on V 27.

[526] 八幡, a popular Japanese deity, whose principal shrine at this time was at Usa 宇佐 in northeastern Kyūshū. Although a Shintō deity, he is sometimes called the Bodhisattva Hachiman by the Japanese.

[527] " East and west " is presumably an error for " northeast " or " southeast."

favorable we raised the submerged anchor and arranged the
sailcloth, but the wind died, and the waves became rough,
so we again put down an anchor. We are not yet certain
about going into [the anchorage]. The winds and waves are
irregular, and the way ahead is not to our liking. Never
have we been more miserable than this.

7th DAY   At noon a northwest wind blew, and we
raised sail and proceeded. At 3 P. M. we arrived east of Mt.
Ch'ih and anchored the ship. The northwest wind was very
stiff. This Mt. Ch'ih is a lofty mass of crags. It is in Ch'ih-
shan-ts'un in Ch'ing-ning-hsiang [528] in Wen-teng-hsien. In
the mountains there is a monastery called the Fa-hua-yüan
("Lotus Cloister") of Mt. Ch'ih. It was originally built by
Chang Pogo.[438] Chang [529] has an estate from which he provides it with food. This estate brings in five hundred bushels [217]
of rice a year. In winter and summer they hold lectures, lecturing in winter on the *Lotus Sutra* [165] and in summer on the
eight-scroll *Konkōmyō-kyō*.[530] For long years they have
lectured on them. To the north and south [of the cloister]
are precipitous peaks, and water flows through the cloister
courtyard from west to east. The sea can be seen spreading
out far to the east. On the south, west, and north, rows of
peaks form a wall, but in the southwest corner they merely
slope down gently. At present the Korean Interpreter Guard
Officer, Chang Yŏng,[531] together with the Commissioner [532]
Lin and Wang Hsün are in complete charge.[533]

---

[528] Here 清寧鄉, but with the first character usually written 青
in documents in later parts of this diary.

[529] *Ikeda* corrects 長 to 張.

[530] The *Konkōmyō-saishōō-kyō* 金光明最勝王經 (Skr. *Suvarṇa-
prabhāsottama-rāja-sūtra*), the standard Chinese translation of
which was made by I-ching 義淨 (see note 1147) in 703 in ten
scrolls.

[531] 張詠, whom he calls a 新羅通事押衙 here, but a "Military
Guard Officer of this prefecture" on 840 I 20 and the "Guard
Officer Chang in charge of Korean Embassies" on 840 II 19. See
also 845 VIII 27.

[532] Here *T'ai-shih* 太使 for *Ta-shih*. See V 16 and note 46.

8th DAY   At sunset I, the Scholar Monk, Ishō, and Igyō climbed up to the monastery and casually visited the monastery living quarters. We met over thirty monks and sipped tea with them, and we spent the night in a vacant room [in the monastery].

9th DAY   Before the forenoon meal, the Hossō Scholar Monk Kaimyō Hosshi, with his attendant monks following him, came up [to the monastery]. We ate our forenoon meal together in the dining hall. After the forenoon meal, the Secretary Awada, the Korean Interpreter Tohyŏn, and others came up together [to the monastery] and spent the night.

10th DAY   After the forenoon meal, the Secretary Awa[da] went back to the ship, but we seven Japanese monks are to stay in the mountain monastery for seven days.[534] The southwest wind blew very hard, not stopping for a moment.

22nd DAY   There was a great wind and violent rain, which did not stop all night.

23rd DAY   Early in the morning we went on a tour of inspection of the mountain monastery. [As a result of the storm], trees had been uprooted, branches had been broken, cliffs had fallen, and stones had crashed down. A sailor came running from the anchorage to say that the ship had run onto rough rocks and had been badly damaged and that a pair of dinghies [520] had been completely smashed to pieces. On hearing this, our fears knew no bounds, and we sent a special messenger to where the ship lay to see if this were true or false. [We learned that] the ship had been blown by the wind onto rough rocks, the rudder board [535] had been

---

[533] The implication here seems to be that they were in charge of the cloister, but later statements indicate that Ennin may have meant only his own relations with the cloister or with the government officials.

[534] Actually Ennin does not record ever having returned on board the ship.

[535] *DBZ* and *KIK* print 柂板 and *ZZGR* 柂放 for two indistinct characters in *Tōji*. On VI 26 the manuscript has 柂 (printed as 柂 in *DBZ* and *KIK*), presumably referring to the same thing,

broken off, and a pair of dinghies had been completely smashed. The ship struck on the rocks three or four times. The huge waves were like mountains. The hawsered anchors did not hold, but dragged with the waves [536] from the west shore to the east shore [of the anchorage]. The wind blew ever stronger, and [the ship was] tossed about most severely. They dropped . . . 鏘 as anchors, and only then did the anchor ropes hold. [537] [The ship] was close to the shore, where they tied it fast. The men on board were out of their minds and had not eaten. They were as if half dead. Two days later they returned to the old anchorage and patched up the dinghies.

26th DAY   They divided the men up 分頭 and had them select anchor stones and search for materials for the rudder. [535] Ever since the recent fourth moon, the clouds and fogs have been dark and enveloping, and the winds and rains have not ceased. For a day or two it would be clear, and then the clouds would again close in.

27th DAY   I hear that two commerce [538] ships of the Commissioner [46] Chang have arrived at Mt. Tan inlet. [539]

28th DAY   Wu Tzu-ch'en 吳子陳, the Commissioner of Troops [78] of Ch'ing-chou, [540] who is the envoy being sent to Korea by the Emperor of China to inquire after the newly

---

so the mast may be meant. However, the rudder fits the situation better.

[536] *DBZ* corrects 彼 to 波.

[537] 沈, that is, sink to the bottom and stay. See IV 25.

[538] For 灾關 *DBZ* suggests 交關, used on 839 VIII 13 in a similar context. The embassy to Korea mentioned the next day and previously on IV 24 was probably on board these vessels. The Chang mentioned here would seem to be Chang Pogo rather than Chang Yŏng.

[539] 旦山浦. *DBZ* suggests that Tan is an error for Ch'ih. In any case, it was obviously close to the cloister where Ennin was staying.

[540] 青州 (the characters are reversed in *Tōji*), also known as I-tu 益都, the name of the local subprefecture in T'ang times, is in central Shantung about midway between Tsingtao and Tsinan.

enthroned King, and the Vice-Ambassador Ts'ui 崔, the
Administrative Officer [38] Wang 王, and others, over thirty
men [in all], came up to the monastery, where we met them.
In the evening the military official 兵馬司 Ch'oe,[541] who is
an agent sent by Chang Pogo to China to sell things, came
to the monastery and inquired after us.

29th DAY   Just before dawn, I went with Master[333]
Tohyŏn into the guest room and consulted about the matter
of my staying [in China]. Then he went back to the
anchorage.

Southeast of Mt. Ch'ih inlet, across a small stretch of
water 少海, is an island close to the east shore. This is where
Kan Chiang[542] of Wu made his sword. The people nowadays
call it Mo-yeh Island, but Mo-yeh is only the name of
the island, and Kan Chiang is the name of the metal founder.

SEVENTH MOON: 10th *and* 11th DAYS[543]   There was
no wind on the sea, but the waves rose fiercely and dashed
against the bottom and boiled and bubbled up. The waves
sounded like thunder. The ship tossed about, and the fears
[of those on board] were not slight.

---

[541] This is the Korean form of the surname given above in Chinese as Ts'ui. This man apparently was the Korean called Ch'oe
Un Sibirang whom Ennin was to meet again in Lien-shui on
845 VII 9 and whom he calls a Guard Officer on 840 II 15.

[542] Mo-yeh 莫耶 (or 鏌鋣) Island is a large island forming the
eastern side of Shih-tao Bay. (On 847 IX 2 Ennin writes the
second character as 琊.) A famous sword of Chinese myth, made
by Kan Chiang 干將 of the feudal state of Wu 吳 in the lower
Yangtse valley, was named Mo-yeh for his wife. *Jung-ch'eng-
hsien chih* 1.8a and *Tseng-hsiu Teng-chou-fu chih* 3.31a repeat
the tradition that this island was so named because a fisherman
found a sword there, but they add that really the name may be a
corruption of Mu-chia 慕家, since many people with the surname
Mu live there. Ennin's idea that Kan Chiang actually worked
on this island is a surprising elaboration of the tradition.

[543] August 13 and 14, 839. The preceding moon had only twenty-
nine days.

14*th* DAY   At 8 A. M. I left the mountain cloister and, going to the anchorage, took leave on shore of Kaimyō Hosshi, the Secretary Awa[da], and the Secretary Wa[ke].[475] I went to the T'ien-men-yüan 天門 ("Heaven's Gate Cloister") in Chen-chuang-ts'un 眞莊 and saw Master Fak'ung 法空. This priest had once gone to Japan, and had returned twenty years ago. I spent the night in this cloister.

15*th* DAY   At the mountain cloister they ate new millet [314] for the forenoon meal.[544]

16*th* DAY   Early in the morning I descended from the mountain cloister, but on the road we heard from a man that the ship had left yesterday. On reaching the anchorage, I looked for the ship but could not see it. After I had been on the beach a short while, a group of monks from the Mt. Ch'ih Cloister came and consoled me, and together we climbed up to the Mt. Ch'ih Cloister and ate.

I then saw four representatives of the prefecture, who had come earlier and were in the cloister. They had brought seventy bushels [217] of rice as provisions for the Japanese tributary embassy. They cannot accept it now in this village, because the tributary embassy has already left, so they sent word to the subprefectural offices.

Both old and young in the cloister have been much surprised at our being abandoned [by the embassy], and they are consoling us most kindly.

21*st* DAY   At 4 P. M. the nine ships under the Japanese Consultant Counselor [392] came and anchored in Mt. Ch'ih inlet and stopped, so I sent Ishō to inquire after the Consultant Counselor and to ask about the Administrative Officers and Secretaries. The Consultant Counselor sent the Provisional Professor from Ōmi,[424] Awada no Ietsugu, and the archer Hasetsukabe no Sadana of the *Sakon'e* [545] to

---

[544] Probably in connection with the All Souls' Festival observed annually on this day. See note 1007.

[545] 左近衞, the Imperial Body Guard of the Left, one of the six Japanese Imperial guard groups. This man was first mentioned on 838 VII 20.   .

inquire after us and to ask about the perils encountered by the second ship.

22nd DAY   They did not start out.

23rd DAY   Early in the morning I looked at the anchorage from the mountain, but nothing was to be seen of the nine ships, so we knew that they had started out together in the night. A northwest wind was blowing.

Northeast from Mt. Ch'ih more than a hundred *li* across the sea a mountain can be seen in the distance. It is called Mt. Ch'ing.[546] Three peaks stand in a row indistinctly in the distance. This was the place where the First Emperor of the Ch'in built 修 a bridge over the ocean. From this mountain the First Emperor also saw to the east Mt. P'eng-lai, Mt. Ying, and Mt. Hu.[547] He died here,[548] and his hemp sandals of that time still exist. I met an old man who told me this, and thus I came to know it.

In order to go to T'ien-t'ai, we three monks have given

---

[546] There is a Mt. Ch'ing 青 sixty *li* south of Jung-ch'eng (cf. *Jung-ch'eng-hsien chih* 1.7a and *Tseng-hsiu Teng-chou-fu chih* 3.29b), which may have been visible from Mt. Ch'ih, but what follows indicates that Ennin meant Mt. Ch'eng 成, the eastern-most extremity of the Shantung Peninsula just east of Jung-ch'eng and approximately sixty km. northeast of Shih-tao Bay. The First Emperor of Ch'in climbed this mountain promontory in 219 B.C. and may have visited it again in 218 and 210 (cf. Édouard Chavannes, *Les mémoires historiques de Se-ma Ts'ien* 2.143, 157, 191; *Jung-ch'eng-hsien chih* 1.5a; *Tseng-hsiu Teng-chou-fu chih* 3.29a). A chain of rocky islets extending eastward from Mt. Ch'eng into the sea is known as the Bridge of Ch'in or the Bridge of the Ch'in Emperor 秦皇橋 (cf. *Jung-ch'eng-hsien chih* 1.10a and *t'u* 1b and *Tseng-hsiu Teng-chou-fu chih* 4.8a and introductory maps 3b and 12b); this name obviously gave rise to Ennin's story of a bridge below.

[547] 蓬萊山瀛山胡山, clearly a different version of the names of the three islands of the immortals (P'eng-lai, Fang-chang 方丈, and Ying-chou 瀛洲) which the First Emperor sought in the Eastern Sea (cf. Chavannes, *op. cit.* 2.152).

[548] Actually he died in modern Hopeh after a trip around Shantung. Cf. *ibid.* 2.191-92.

up the idea of returning home and are staying at the Mt.
Ch'ih Cloister. Whenever we ask about the trip,[549] [we are
told that] it is an extremely long way to the south, but we
hear that, if we were to make a pilgrimage toward the north,
we would find Mt. Wu-t'ai[199] about two thousand-odd *li*
from here. Thus, the south is distant, but the north is close.
I also hear that there are monks of the Tendai Sect with
the religious names Chih-yüan 志遠 and Abbot Wen-chien
文鑒, who are both disciples of Abbot Hsüan-su 玄素 of
[Mt.] T'ien-t'ai and are at present practicing *hokke-zammai*[284]
at Mt. Wu-t'ai. They are transmitting the Tendai tradition.
They formerly practiced *hokke-zammai* on the northern terrace at the Sung Valley Monastery[550] and attained the Way.
Recently a certain . . .-chin 進 Ch'an-shih,[249] a monk of the
Lung-hsing-ssu[378] of Ch'u-chou, took 1,000 copies[551] of the
Nirvana Sutra[203] to Chih-yüan Ch'an-shih of Mt. [Wu]-t'ai
and received the *hokke-zammai*. He entered the hall for the
practice [of *hokke-zammai*] in order to " seek " Fugen,[286] and,
while there practicing the Way, he succeeded in seeing His
Holiness.[552] That was some twenty years ago. I have recorded
this in accordance with the verbal statement of the Korean

---

[549] *Hsing-li* 行李. Cf. Ku Yen-wu 顧炎武, *Jih-chih-lu* 日知錄
(Hupeh Ch'ung-wen shu-chü 崇文書局 edition, 1872) 32.15b
and *Yu-yang tsa-tsu* 酉陽雜俎 13.1a-b (in the *Ssu-pu ts'ung-
k'an* 四部叢刊 edition) by the ninth-century author Tuan
Ch'eng-shih 段成式. Later in the text Ennin uses this word for
" baggage " as well as for " travel."

[550] " Monastery " here is [*a*]*rannya* 阿蘭若 (Skr. *āraṇya*). The
" northern terrace " 北臺 is one of the five terraces or peaks of
Mt. Wu-t'ai, a name which means " Five Terraces." On 840 V 21
Ennin, describing the wonders of the northern terrace, says
that Sung Valley 宋谷 lies on its northern side and was the
scene of a miracle. Cf. Ono and Hibino 319.

[551] 一千部, possibly printed extracts.

[552] *Daishō* 大聖, literally " Great Sage," a term for Buddhas
and important Bodhisattvas. Here it apparently is used for
Fugen, but later in the text it usually refers to Monju (see
note 309).

monk, Sŏngnim Hwasang.[553] This monk wandered for some twenty years, going to Mt. Wu-t'ai and to Ch'ang-an, before coming to this mountain cloister.

In the course of conversation, I continually hear how wonderful are the holy sites of Mt. [Wu]-t'ai. I deeply rejoice that we are close to this holy region. For the time being I am giving up my plan to go to T'ien-t'ai and have decided to go to Wu-t'ai. Thus, I have changed my previous plan and intend to spend the winter at the mountain cloister and, when spring comes, to wander forth on a pilgrimage to Mt. [Wu]-t'ai.

28*th* DAY   At 4 P. M. two representatives of the sub-prefecture, Tou Wen-chih 竇文至 and another man, came with a letter from the subprefecture. This letter said:

The subprefecture notifies Ch'ing-ning-hsiang:
We have received a report from the *Pan-t'ou* [554] Tou Wen-chih about the three men abandoned by the Japanese ship.

The dossier on this case reveals 右撿案内 that we have received the above-mentioned report from the *Pan-t'ou,* inform-ing us that the ship left on the fifteenth day of this moon and that the three abandoned men are to be found at the Korean Cloister of Mt. Ch'ih. This report is as stated above.

In accordance with our investigation of the said per-sons,[555] when they were abandoned by the ship, the *Ts'un-pao* [556] and *Pan-t'ou* should have informed us on that very day. Why have they allowed fifteen days to pass before informing us? Furthermore, we do not find the surnames and given names of the abandoned men or what baggage [549] and clothing they have. Also there has been no report at all of your having checked

---

[553] 聖琳. The second character is written 林 here and on 840 I 15 but correctly on 839 XI (or XII) 16 and in *Ikeda.* Hwasang is the Korean pronunciation of the Chinese Ho-shang (see note 115). This is Ennin's first clear statement of oral communication with a Korean or Chinese.

[554] 板頭, an unidentified title.

[555] 依撿前件人. A stereotyped phrase of this nature usually introduces the decision in the documents found in this text.

[556] 村保, probably the head of the village mutual guarantee system.

with the Monastery Administrator [119] and Supervisor [557] monks
of the Mt. Ch'ih Cloister on their having foreigners living there.
The canton elders [558] are hereby notified to investigate the
matter. On the very day this notice reaches you, report on the
matter in detail. If anything does not tally in your investigation, or if there are any falsifications,[559] you will be called in and
held responsible, or if in your eventual report on the investigation you disregard the time limit, or if the investigation is
not careful enough, the original investigators will most definitely
be judged severely.

    *Notice of the twenty-fourth day of the seventh moon
of the fourth year of K'ai-ch'eng by the Intendant* [560] *Wang Tso*
王佐.

    Hu Chün-chih 胡君直, *the Superintendent of Regis-
ters* [467] *and the Vice-Chief of Employees* 副尉.[464]

    [Signed] *the substitute Subprefect, Ch'i Hsüan-yüan*
戚宣員.

We monks in search of the Law then wrote a letter to
inform them of our reasons for staying. This letter is as
follows:

    *The reasons why the Japanese monk, his two dis-
ciples,*[561] *and his servant are staying at the mountain cloister.*
    The said monk, in order to search for the Law of
Buddhism, has come far across the sea. Although he has reached

---

[557] *Chiji* 知事, a general term for the various supervisory officers
of a monastery, such as the *Inō, Tenzo* (see note 81), and *Kansu*
(see note 116).

[558] 鄉專老人, possibly a copyist's error for *hsiang ch'i-lao* 耆老
(see note 29). Cf. Des Rotours, "Les grands fonctionnaires
des provinces en Chine sous la dynastie des T'ang," *T'oung pao*
25.277.

[559] 妄有拒改. The last character is not clear as written in *Tōji*
and is interpreted as 注 by *DBZ, KIK*, and *ZZGR*.

[560] *Tien* 典, a title not listed by Des Rotours for this sort of
provincial post. The first two names are presumably those of
the actual drafters, the last that of the official signer.

[561] *Shōshi* 小師, a term used for disciples, novices, and monks
during their first ten years after ordination.

China, he has not yet fulfilled his long-cherished vow. His original intention in leaving his homeland was to travel around the holy land [of China], seeking teachers and studying the Law. Because the tributary embassy returned early, he was unable to accompany it back to his country and in the end came to reside in this mountain cloister. Later he intends to make a pilgrimage to some famous mountains,[562] seeking the Way and performing [Buddhist] practices. His baggage [consists of] one iron alms bowl, two small bronze bells,[454] one bronze jug, more than twenty scrolls of writings, clothes against the cold, and nothing else. Undergoing an investigation by the subprefectural government, he fully presents his reasons as above and gives his statement as above. Respectfully written.

A statement made on the twenty . . .[562a] day of the seventh moon of the fourth year of K'ai-ch'eng by the Japanese monk Ennin and humbly presented by the attendant monk Ishō, and the monk Igyō, and the servant Tei Yūman.

A statement presented by the Mt. Ch'ih Cloister at Ch'ing-ning-hsiang in the inquiry into the reasons why the Japanese monk did not return home on board the ship.

The said Japanese monk, Ennin, his disciples [561] Ishō and Igyō, and a servant, in all four men, say that they heard from afar that China 重花 has made Buddhism prosper, and therefore they have come and have given themselves over to the study of the sacred doctrine. They intend to visit in turn the famous mountains and holy sites, making pilgrimages in various regions, but, because it is hot now, they are staying for the time being in this mountain monastery to escape the heat, waiting for it to become cool, after which they will start.[563] Consequently, they did not obtain [564] their [travel] documents from the subprefectural government.

---

[562] The word "mountains" in this and following documents refers to monasteries and Buddhist holy sites, which commonly were in the mountains.

[562a] A partly obliterated character has been omitted by *DBZ*.

[563] A plausible excuse, since it was still early in September, but they actually stayed through the winter.

[564] *DBZ* suggests 得 for 早.

We have examined in detail the clothes and bowls this monk and the others have brought with them, and there is nothing else [besides what they have declared]. If this communication subsequently proves to be inaccurate, I, Pŏpch'ŏng 法清, and my colleagues are guilty of lying. Respectfully written and presented. The matter is as stated above.

A statement of a day in the seventh moon of the fourth year of K'ai-ch'eng by Pŏpch'ŏng, the Prior [565] *of the Mt. Ch'ih Cloister.*

EIGHTH MOON: 13th DAY [566]   I have heard that the nine ships under the Consultant Counselor are in Mt. Ch'ing inlet [546] and also that a P'o-hai [567] commerce [538] ship likewise is anchored in that inlet. A man came from there to inform the subprefectural offices. I do not yet know whether this is true or false or how it happened. Ever since the nine ships started out from the Mt. Ch'ih inlet the northwest wind has been blowing continuously day after day, and it still is now, so what could there have been to prevent them from going? It must be a false report by this man.

15th DAY The monastery prepared noodles, cakes, and so forth, and observed the festival of the fifteenth day of the eighth moon. Such a festival is not held in other countries, and Korea alone observes it. The old monks tell me that, when of old Korea (Silla) [19] was fighting with P'o-hai, they won a victory on this day, so they have made it a festival and make music and gaily dance. This has gone on without interruption for many generations. They prepare all sorts of food and drink, and sing, dance, and play instrumental music for three days before stopping, continuing from the daylight hours into the night. Now, in this mountain cloister, in memory of their homeland, they are today observing this festival. When P'o-hai was chastised by Korea (Silla), a mere one thousand men [managed to] flee to the

---

[565] *Inju* 院主.

[566] September 24, 839.

[567] 渤海, a Tungus state in eastern and northern Manchuria and northern Korea, which existed from about 713 to 927.

north, and later they again formed a state, and this is what is now called the country of P'o-hai.[568]

16*th* DAY   On behalf of Ishō and Igyō we read for the first time the commentaries to the *Immyō-ron*.[569]

Under the jurisdiction of the Government General [91] of Ch'ing-chou [540] are four prefectures, Lai-chou, Teng-chou, and Tzu-chou.[570] All are in Shantung Province.[571] The four subprefectures of Teng-chou are Mou-p'ing-hsien,[493] Wen-teng-hsien, P'eng-lai-hsien,[419] and Huang-hsien.[572] P'eng-lai-hsien is in the prefectural city. This mountain cloister is in Ch'ih-shan-ts'un (Mt. Ch'ih Village) in Ch'ing-ning-hsiang in Wen-teng-hsien. From the southern extremity of Ch'ing-ning-hsiang, one can look across the sea to Mo-yeh Island. This was where Kan Chiang of Wu made his sword.[542] It is southeast of Mt. Ch'ih, separated from it by a small stretch

---

[568] This story has reference to the crushing of the kingdom of Koguryŏ 高句麗 in northern Korea by the combined forces of the T'ang and Silla in 668, for remnants of the Koguryŏ forces subsequently joined with the Tungusic Mo-ho 靺鞨 tribesmen of Manchuria to form the state of P'o-hai. Mishina Akihide 三品 彰英, in his article "Shiragi Karō no genryū to sono hatten" 新羅花郎の源流とその發展 (*Shigaku zasshi* 史學雜誌 45. 1326), identifies this festival with one known from other Korean sources.

[569] 因明論 (Skr. *Nyāya-śāstra*), not the name of a work but of a class of *śāstra*, such as the *Shōrimon-ron* 正理門論 and *Nyū-shōri-ron* 入正理論, which explain *immyō* (Skr. *hetuvidyā*), a system of logic, classed as one of the *gomyō* 五明 or five fields of knowledge.

[570] The modern Tzu-ch'uan 淄川 about forty-five km. due west of Ch'ing-chou. The character for *Tzu* is followed by an unclear character which may be an error for the *Ch'ing* of Ch'ing-chou.

[571] 山東道. Actually Shantung became an official administrative title only under the Chin dynasty in the twelfth century, and this area was at the time part of Honan 河南 Province, but, unless "Shantung" is a later copyist's interpolation, this statement would indicate that the name was already in unofficial use for at least the eastern part of the modern Shantung.

[572] 黃, about thirty km. southwest of Teng-chou.

of water. One can reach it by land by going north from Mt. Ch'ih and then turning east.

NINTH MOON of thirty days: 1st DAY *chi-mao* [573] I asked a traveler [549] who had gone to Mt. [Wu]-t'ai the names of the prefectures [he traversed] and the distance in *li* and recorded [his answers]. He passed through eight prefectures to reach Mt. Wu-t'ai, a total distance of about 2,990 *li*. From Ch'ih-shan-ts'un to Wen-teng-hsien is 130 *li*, from the sub-prefecture to Teng-chou 500 *li*, from Teng-chou to Lai-chou 220 *li*, from Lai-chou to Ch'ing-chou 500 *li*, from Ch'ing-chou to Tz'u-chou 180 *li*, from Tz'u-chou to Ch'i-chou [574] 180 *li*,[575] from Ch'i-chou to Yün-chou [576] 300 *li*, from Yün-chou across the Yellow River to Wei-fu [577] 180 *li*, from Wei-fu to Chen-chou [578] about 500 *li*, and from Chen-chou into the mountains to Mt. Wu-t'ai a five-day trip of about 300 *li*. I recorded this in accordance with the verbal statement of the Korean monk Yanghyŏn 諒賢.

3rd DAY At noon a representative of the subpre-

---

[573] October 11, 839. *Chi-mao* 己卯 is the sixteenth pair in the hexagenary cycle. Ennin indicates that this was a long moon of thirty days by adding 大 after " ninth moon."

[574] 齊, the modern Tsinan, the capital of Shantung.

[575] Actually " 108 *li*," but the total distance Ennin cites of 2,990 *li* and the actual distance between Tz'u-chou and Ch'i-chou make it clear that this is an error for " 180 *li*."

[576] 鄆, a city which no longer exists but which was located a short distance northwest of the modern Tung-p'ing 東平 and about a hundred km. southwest of Tsinan.

[577] 魏府, officially Wei-chou at this time, located a short distance north of the modern town of Ch'ao-ch'eng 朝城, which is near the Hopeh-Shantung border and about 140 km. southwest of Tsinan. As Ennin tells us on 845 XI 3, it was the seat of a regional commandery, and it was consequently known as Wei-fu.

[578] 鎮, the modern Cheng-ting 正定, a little north of the railway junction of Shih-chia-chuang 石家莊 in west central Hopeh. It too was the seat of a regional commandery (see 845 XI 3).

fecture came with letters from the subprefecture, which are as follows: [579]

The subprefecture notifies Ch'ing-ning-hsiang:

We have received a report that three monks and one servant abandoned by the Japanese ship are at the Mt. Ch'ih Cloister.

The dossier on this case reveals that we have received a statement saying that you have presented a full statement of the matter of the said monks, but, fearing that the prefectural government will subsequently wish to have a further investigation, you have asked us to notify the Harbor Master 海口所由,[64] the *Pan-t'ou* [554] of the village, and the Monastery Administrator of the Mt. Ch'ih Cloister to keep constant track of their whereabouts and have asked us to decide on the matter. The decision received [from higher authorities] approves this, and we are notifying the officials in charge.[64]

In accordance with our investigation of the case, we hereby notify the Harbor Master, informing him and the monastery officers to keep constant track of their whereabouts. If later the prefectural government investigates further and you say that they have gone somewhere [580] and you do not know where they have gone, you will certainly be severely judged.[581] On the very day this notice reaches you, you are to make this known and are to assemble statements to be forwarded to the prefecture.[582]

Notice of the thirteenth day of the eighth moon of the fourth year of K'ai-ch'eng by the Intendant Wang Tso.

Hu Chün-chih, the Superintendent of Registers and the Vice-Chief of Employees.

[Signed] *the substitute Subprefect Ch'i Hsüan-yüan.*

---

[579] The first letter, dated VIII 13, obviously was a copy of the original, which, we learn from the second letter, had been lost in transmission.

[580] 有東西. The last two characters (*tung-hsi*) are used repeatedly in the documents which follow, apparently with the meaning of " to go east or west."

[581] The character preceding 追 is obliterated by worm holes.

[582] The whole passage 告示畜取狀州狀上者 is not very clear, even with the emendation of 畜 to 審, as suggested by *DBZ*.

To the Bureau of Merits.[583]

Regarding the three monks and one servant abandoned by the Japanese ship, who have been in the Mt. Ch'ih Cloister at Ch'ing-ning-hsiang.

The prefecture and [in turn] the Commissioner [584] have already been informed about the said monks, but since it was feared that they might go somewhere, notice was sent on the fourteenth day of the recent eighth moon to the Mt. Ch'ih Cloister and to the *Ts'un-pao*,[556] the *Pan-t'ou*, and the Harbor Master to keep track of their whereabouts. When the village directors [585] of this canton were asked [about the matter], they said that the village director T'an Tan 譚亶 had lost the letter and to date they had had no information about it at all. The said T'an Tan now humbly asks for a judgment and gives his statement as above. Respectfully written.

Statement of a day of the ninth moon of the fourth year of K'ai-ch'eng by the Intendant Wang Tso.

[Signed] *the director of Ch'ing-ts'un* 靑, *(T'an Tan)*.[586]

A statement by the Japanese monk Ennin and the others.[587]

We have received a letter of inquiry regarding the movements [580] and whereabouts of the three Japanese monks and one servant who were abandoned at the Mt. Ch'ih Cloister.

---

[583] *Ssu-kung* 司功, one of the subdivisions of a subprefectural government. Cf. Des Rotours 736.

[584] 使, possibly referring here to the Regional Commander. See note 719.

[585] *Li-cheng* 里正 (but *ts'un-cheng* 村正 below). Cf. Des Rotours 72 and 733.

[586] The signature appears in *Tōji* as 狀一日員. *Ikeda* corrects the middle two characters to 宣, and another easy step would be to correct the first character to 戚, giving us the name of the substitute Subprefect, Ch'i Hsüan-yüan. In view of the title and the wording of the document, however, a safer correction would be to interpret the last three characters as an extremely elongated version of 亶 and the first a complete error for 譚.

[587] This letter was presumably written by Ennin in response to the two preceding documents.

The said monks, because of their yearnings for Buddhism, are temporarily 權 residing at the mountain cloister where they are already comfortably settled,[588] but they desire to avail themselves of the opportunity to go on a pilgrimage to various places. Because it is now about to become cold,[588a] they have not yet gone anywhere, and they are passing the winter in this mountain cloister, but when spring comes they will make a pilgrimage to famous mountains and will search out sacred sites. The monks sincerely desire to have you informed in advance, and now that they have received your inquiry regarding their movements and whereabouts, they respectfully state the matter in full. The statement is presented as above, and the facts are given as above. Respectfully written.

A notice of the third day of the ninth moon of the fourth year of K'ai-ch'eng by the Japanese monk Ennin and the others.

12th DAY   At noon it was cloudy and thundered, and hail and rain fell. After the fifth watch (5 A.M.) the " dragons " were heard fighting, hail and rain fell together, and lightning flashed in confusion. It continued for some time, but stopped at dawn. In the morning we went out to see [and found that] the hail had rolled and piled up [to a depth of] three or four inches. It was piled up like snow. The old monks say that according to an old tradition this mountain has many " dragon palaces." [589]

The Bureau of Sacrifices [590] *notifies the Korean monk Pŏpch'ŏng of the Chang-ching-ssu* [591] *of the capital:*

---

[588] 已得 has been mistakenly copied twice in *Tōji.*

[588a] In a letter copied under the date of VII 28 it was stated that they were waiting for the weather to turn cool before starting.

[589] This passage clearly indicates the close relationship thought to exist between dragons and thunderstorms. See note 472.

[590] *Tz'u-pu* (or *Ssu-pu*) 祠部 , one of the four branches of the Ministry of Rites (*Li-pu* 禮部) in the central government. It was in charge of monks and nuns as well as various other matters. Cf. Des Rotours 79-80, 87-91. Ennin apparently copied this document, dated over thirty years earlier, as a precedent for the permission to travel which he sought. The Korean monk

The said person has asked that, in accordance [591a] with the regulations, he [be allowed] as his destiny permits to wander and beg [592] everywhere.

Notice: We have received the said monk's statement saying, "At my own desire I have entered on the Buddhist life, and my spirit rejoices in wandering and begging. On famous mountains [562] I worship with devout heart, and I pass through groves [593] looking everywhere for teachers. I study the way 行門 of Kashō [594] and advance in the ideals of the Buddha. I ask that you take as a precedent [595] the Imperial edict of the twelfth day of the fourth moon of the first year of Yüan-ho (806), when the Learned Doctor monk Prajñā [596] strongly petitioned that his disciples, Ta-nien 大念 and others, [be allowed] to wander and beg, in the manner of the Buddhist teachings, and, in accordance with an Imperial edict, they [were allowed to] practice [this sort of life] and begged everywhere without discredit to the holy scriptures. Now I have overtaxed myself in my devotion [to the holy Law] 持念損心 and of late have also become afflicted with palsy 風疾, which has attacked me off and on. I need to obtain medicines for my cure 藥餌之間要須市易將息. I now wish to

---

it concerns was the Prior of the Mt. Ch'ih Cloister who signed the third letter included under VII 28.

[591] 章敬, which Ennin was to pass on 840 VIII 20 on his way into Ch'ang-an. It was located outside the T'ung-hua Gate 通化門, the northernmost of the three eastern gates of the T'ang city. Cf. Adachi, map opposite p. 136.

[591a] *DBZ* suggests 准 for 唯.

[592] *Zuda* 頭陀 (Skr. *dhūta*), a term for mendicancy on the part of a Buddhist monk. The second character somewhat resembles 陁 in *Tōji* and is sometimes so printed in *DBZ, KIK*, and *ZZGR*.

[593] *Ringe* 林下, a term for gatherings of monks for the purpose of study.

[594] An abbreviation of Makakashō 摩訶迦葉 (Skr. Mahākā-śyapa), the name of an Indian Buddhist famed for his mendicancy.

[595] *DBZ* suggests that the 乾 should be disregarded as a copyist's error. For the preceding character see note 591a.

[596] 般若, a north Indian monk, who reached China by sea in 781. The title I have translated "Learned Doctor" is *Sanzō* 三藏 (Skr. *Tripiṭaka*). It was bestowed on him, as on other great transmitters of the Tripitaka, by the Emperor in 790.

go to various mountains on a pilgrimage and to seek physicians to treat my illness, but I fear that everywhere the guards of the passes, [those] at the city gates or in the streets, the Buddhist halls in the villages or wards, the monasteries [550] in the mountains and forests, and the monasteries of the prefectures and subprefectures will not honor 練 my reasons for traveling 行由, so I ask to be given official credentials."

We have found in the archives an Imperial edict in which the names agree [with those he cites], and we have respectfully examined the regulations [and find that] there are cases of monks and nuns who have been allowed to wander and beg and to be cared for by the monasteries of the prefectures and subprefectures, without the officials concerned having to be alarmed by it.[597]

With reference to the monk Pŏpch'ŏng's request [to be allowed] to wander and beg, we have examined the matter and grant his request and, therefore, issue this document.

Statement of a day in the second moon of the second year of Yüan-ho (807) by the Scribe [598] *P'an Lun* 潘倫.

The Superintendent [598] *Chao Ts'an* 趙參.

[Signed] *the Auxiliary Secretary* [598] *Chou Chung-sun* 周仲孫.

The Japanese monks in search of the Law inform this monastery:

A document in which the monk Ennin, his attendant monks Ishō and Igyō, and his servant Tei Yūman request the monastery to write the prefecture and subprefecture to give them official credentials to wander and beg as their destiny permits.

We monks, having in mind merely our longing for the Buddhist teachings, have come from afar to this benevolent land with our hearts set on sacred places and our spirits rejoicing

---

[597] 將理不得所由恐動者. This and some other sentences in this document are of somewhat doubtful meaning.

[598] The second-ranking officer of the Bureau of Sacrifices was an Auxiliary Secretary (*Yüan-wai-lang* 員外郎), and among the lesser officers were two Superintendents (*Chu-shih* 主事) and six Scribes (*Ling-shih* 令史, miscopied in *Tōji* as 令吏). Cf. Des Rotours 86-87.

in the pilgrimage. It is said that Mt. [Wu]-t'ai and some other places are the source [598a] of the teaching and the places where the great saints have manifested themselves. Eminent monks from India [599] have visited them, crossing their precipitous slopes, and famous patriarchs of China have there attained enlightenment. We monks have admired these glorious places, and having chanced to meet with this happy destiny, have by good fortune come to this holy land. Now we wish to go to these places to fulfill our long-cherished hopes, but we fear that on the road [others] will not honor our reasons for traveling. We have heard that the Learned Doctor Prajñā petitioned for official credentials on behalf of some mendicant monks, and that they [were allowed] by Imperial edict to practice [their mendicancy. Thus,] this started of old and has continued until recent times.

We humbly hope that this monastery, in accordance with the laws and precedents of the land, will address the prefecture and the subprefecture, asking for [599a] official credentials. If it does so, the . . .[600] glorious fame of the Monastery Administrators [119] will stir foreign lands afar, their encouraging magnanimity will make gloriously manifest the sun-like Buddha,[601] and we shall be more than indebted to you.

The full statement is as above. The statement of the matter is as given above. Respectfully written.

The twenty-sixth day of the ninth moon of the fourth year of K'ai-ch'eng.

The Japanese monk in search of the Law from the Enryakuji.[7]

23rd DAY It is the beginning of winter according to the Chinese calendar. From this time on the cold winds are quite strong.

[598a] *DBZ* here misprints 原 for 源.

[599] Hsi-t'ien 西天, a Chinese term for India or the western regions in general.

[599a] *DBZ* and *KIK* misprint 給 as 經.

[600] 弘法 in *Ikeda*, but the second character appears to be 絡 or 給 in *Tōji*.

[601] *Butsunichi* 佛日, a term for the Buddha because of his sun-like qualities in dispelling the ignorance of all beings.

27th DAY   It snowed. Since the middle ten days of the ninth moon, cold winds have been blowing up. The mountains and moors are without green grass, and the streams and springs have ice.

28th DAY   This cloister for the first time gathered in its turnips.[602] The Superior [81] and all the others in the cloister went out and picked the leaves. When the monastic living quarters [141] are out of firewood, all the monks in the cloister, regardless of whether they are old or young, go out and carry firewood.

TENTH MOON: 1*st* DAY [603]   We had our first frost.

5th DAY   The springs were frozen.

10th DAY   In the middle of the night I heard the cries of a flock of geese flying south.

15th DAY   There was an eclipse of the moon in the middle of the night. The masters in the cloister all went out and cried out and struck boards. At 3 A. M. the moon gradually brightened.

ELEVENTH MOON: 1*st* DAY [604]   In response to the invitation of a Korean, Wang Changmun 王長文, I went to his house and ate the forenoon meal, after which I went with several other monks to the manor of the cloister and spent one night.

2nd DAY [605]   In the evening we returned to the mountain cloister.

9th DAY   It was the winter solstice, and the congregation of monks paid their respects to one another. At 8 A. M. we worshiped the Buddha in front of the hall.

16th DAY [606]   They commenced lecturing on the *Lotus*

---

[602] *Man-ching* 蔓菁 and *lo-po* 蘿蔔, both varieties of turnips. Possibly the monks were thinning the rows of turnips and picking the excess greens for food.

[603] November 10, 839.

[604] December 10, 839.

[605] The text has " 12th day," obviously a copyist's error.

[606] The " 9th day " above, being the winter solstice, was clearly

Sutra at the mountain cloister. The period for this will be until the fifteenth day of the first moon of next year. Monks and associated patrons 有緣施主 from all over have come and are meeting together. Among them Sŏngnim Hwasang [553] is the scripture lecturer 講經法主, and there are two debaters 論義, the monks Tonjung 頓證 and Sangjŏk 常寂. Men and women, monks and laymen, are gathered together in the cloister listening to lectures in the daytime and worshiping and repenting and listening to scriptures and the order [of worship] at night. The monks and others number about forty. The lecturing, worshiping, and repentances are all done in accordance with the customs of Korea. The worship and repentance at dusk and before dawn are in the Chinese manner, but all the rest are in the Korean language. Everyone in the assemblage, monk or layman, old or young, noble or humble alike, is Korean except for us Japanese, three monks and a servant.

17th DAY Because the lecturing in this cloister had started . . .[607] I left the monastery before the forenoon meal and went to the cloister of Master Fa-k'ung on the southern mountain,[608] but the officers of the Mt. Ch'ih Cloister sent me a letter in haste, asking me to return, because I was not permitted to go to the southern cloister. I then prepared a letter for them, asking for fifteen days leave, and they [609] finally gave their permission.

---

in the eleventh moon, and the " 29th day " recorded below, being New Year's Eve, was obviously in the twelfth moon, but it is not certain to which moon the 16th, 17th, and 22nd days belong. Since the lectures, which started on the 16th, continued until 840 I 15, they lasted for either one or two full moons, depending on whether this day was XI 16 or XII 16.

[607] An illegible character.

[608] Presumably the T'ien-men-yüan in Chen-chuang-ts'un, where he had visited Fa-k'ung on VII 14. It may have been called the " southern mountain " or " southern cloister " because of its geographic relationship to the Mt. Ch'ih Cloister.

[609] The repetition of 綱 is presumably a copyist's error.

22nd DAY Because the matter was not properly settled, I returned to my original cloister.

THE SCRIPTURE-LECTURING RITE AT THE MT. CH'IH CLOISTER

At 8 A.M. they struck the bell for the scripture lecturing, apprising the group, after which the congregation spent quite a little time entering the hall. At the moment the bell sounded for the congregation to settle down, the lecturer entered the hall and mounted to a high seat, while the congregation in unison called on the name of the Buddha. Their intonation was wholly Korean and did not resemble the Chinese sounds. After the lecturer had mounted to his seat, the invocation of the name of the Buddha stopped. A monk seated below him chanted in Sanskrit, entirely in the Chinese manner, the one-line hymn, " How through this scripture," etc.[234] When he reached the phrase, " We desire the Buddha to open to us the subtle mystery," the crowd chanted together, " The fragrance of the rules, the fragrance of meditation, the fragrance of deliverance," etc. 戒香定香解脫香. After the singing of the Sanskrit hymn had ended, the lecturer chanted the headings 題目 of the scripture and, dividing them into the three parts,[610] explained the headings. After that the *Ina* [81] came forth in front of the high seat and read out [610a] the reasons for holding the meeting and the separate names of the patrons and the things they had donated, after which he passed this document to the lecturer, who, grasping his chowry,[611] read the patrons' names one by one and made supplications for each individually.

---

[610] *Sammon* 三門, the three approaches to enlightenment through wisdom (*chie* 智慧), compassion (*jihi* 慈悲), and skill in means (*hōben* 方便), but here it may be used for *sambun* 三分, the three traditional divisions of scriptural exegesis, the introduction (*jōbun* 序分), the main thesis (*shōshūbun* 正宗分), and the propagation (*rutsūbun* 流通分).

[610a] *DBZ* misprints 談 for 讀.

[611] *Shūbi* 麈尾, a duster (traditionally made from the tail of a large species of deer) which was held by a Buddhist teacher

After that the debaters argued the principles, raising questions. While [612] they were raising a question, the lecturer would hold up his chowry, and when a questioner had finished asking his question, he would lower it and then raise it again, thank [the questioner] for his question, and then answer it. They recorded both the questions and the answers. It was the same as in Japan, except that the rite of [pointing out doctrinal] difficulties 難 was somewhat different. After lowering his hand at his side three times and before making any explanation, [a debater] would suddenly proclaim the difficulty, shouting with all his might like a man enraged, and the lecturer would accept [613] the problem and would reply without raising problems in return.

After the debate, he took up the text and read [610a] the scripture. At the end of the lecture, the congregation chanted praises together in drawn-out syllables. Among these praises were words of blessing.[614] The lecturer descended from his seat while a monk chanted the hymn, " Being in this world is like [living] in emptiness." It sounded very much the way it does in Japan. The lecturer mounted the worship platform [in front of the deities] 禮盤, while a monk chanted the three praises.[615] Then the lecturer and the congregation, singing together, left the hall and returned to their rooms.

There was also a repeat lecturer 覆講師 seated below and to the south of the high seat, who discussed the text the

---

while lecturing. It was thought of as a symbol of the cleansing of the impurities of the world or else as a sign of leadership (since the leader deer raises its tail when it leads the herd).

[612] The character printed 間 in *DBZ* is more plausibly interpreted as 聞 by *ZZGR* and *KIK*.

[613] *DBZ* suggests 蒙 for 家.

[614] *Ekōmon* 回向文 (here 廻向詞) are hymns or prayers chanted at the end of a service to bring the benefits derived from the service to others. Often, and perhaps in this case too, they were chanted specifically on behalf of the dead. Note that the ceremony described next is expressly stated to have been on behalf of a deceased person.

[615] For the Buddha, the Law, and the Church. See note 236.

lecturer had expounded the day before. When he came to phrases explaining the meaning, the lecturer had written out the explanations, and the repeat lecturer read these. After he had read the whole of the text expounded the day before, the lecturer then read the next text. Thus it went each day.

THE KOREAN RITE OF A SINGLE-DAY LECTURE

At 8 a. m. a bell was struck. After prolonged ringing,[616] the lecturer and the leader [617] entered the hall. The congregation had entered previously and was seated in rows. When the lecturer and the reader entered, the congregation together called on the Buddha's name, dragging it out. The lecturer mounted to a seat on the north and the leader to one on the south, whereupon the praising of Buddha stopped. Then a monk in a seat below them chanted in Sanskrit a one-line hymn, " How through this scripture," etc.[234] After the Sanskrit chanting had ended, the one seated to the south chanted the headings of the scripture. This so-called chanting of the scripture was drawn out, and his voice quavered a great deal. While the scripture was being intoned, the congregation scattered flowers [618] three times. Each time flowers were scattered a different hymn was sung. After the intoning of the scripture, the headings were chanted in short syllables. The lecturer expounded the scripture headings, dividing them into three parts [610] and presenting the general meaning of the scripture. After the scripture headings had been explained, the *Ina* [81] read out the reasons for holding the affair. In this document were stated the principle of the impermanency [of life], the merits of the deceased person, and the date of his death.[614]

---

[616] 擬 may be an error for 鍾.

[617] *Tokō* 都講, translated here as " leader " to distinguish him from the 講師. In the next sentence this same man appears to be called the " reader " 讀師.

[618] *Sange* 散花, a standard Buddhist rite.

The Prefect [412] who controls Teng-chou has the surname Wu 烏 and the given name of Chüeh 角. The people nowadays call him the Magistrate [619] Wu. He has three taboo characters, *ming* 明, *ch'i* 綺, and *chi* 給. Hence they say *lai-jih* 來日 for " tomorrow " (*ming-jih* 明日). The Regional Commander [35] of Ch'ing-chou has the surname of Shou 壽, and the people nowadays call him the President of the Ministry [620] Shou. He has no taboo characters.

THE KOREAN RITE OF RECITING SCRIPTURES 誦經
CALLED REPEATING SCRIPTURES 念經 IN CHINA

A bell was struck and after the congregation had settled down, a monk in a low seat arose and, striking a mallet, chanted, " Let all be worshipful and pay reverence to the three eternal treasures." [236] Then a monk chanted in Sanskrit a two-line hymn, " The wonderful body of the *Nyorai*," etc.[237] The pronunciation was about the same as in Chinese. While the Sanskrit was being chanted, a man walked back and forth in front of the seated congregation, holding up a censer. He walked quickly and then stopped, and the congregation recited together several tens of times, the title of the *Maka-hannya*.[621] Then a master stated the reasons for the gathering to recite scriptures, after which the congregation recited scriptures, sometimes distributing copies of a scripture and sometimes not distributing copies of a scripture, but reciting it from memory. Then the leader 導師 alone chanted, " Put your faith in the Buddha; put your

---

[619] *Shih-chün* 使君, an honorific term for the chief official of a local government. Ennin uses it for both Prefects and Subprefects.
[620] *Shang-shu* 尚書, the chief official of one of the six ministries of the Department of State (see note 224). Cf. Des Rotours 21, 34, etc. This presumably was a post which the Regional Commander had once held.
[621] More fully the *Maka-hannya-haramitsu-kyō* 摩訶般若波羅蜜經 (Skr. *Mahā-prajñāpāramitā-sūtra*), one of the several *Hannya-kyō* (see note 203). *Haramitsu* is sometimes rendered *haramitta* through the addition of the character 多.

faith in the Law; put your faith in the Church." Next he recited the names of the Buddhas and Bodhisattvas. The leader chanted, " Glory to the twelve great vows," [622] and the congregation replied, " The Lapis Lazuli Shining Buddha Yakushi "; the leader said, " Glory to Yakushi," and the congregation together replied, " The Lapis Lazuli Shining Buddha." The leader said, " Glory to the great compassion," [623] and the congregation replied in unison, " The Bodhisattva Kanzeon." They paid reverence to all the other Buddhas in like manner. Then the leader alone made the concluding benediction [624] and blessing.[614] The blessing was rather long. After the blessing, the leader said, " Have faith," 發心 and the congregation repeated together, " Have faith." Next the leader chanted a vow 發願, after which he prostrated himself to the three treasures.[236] Then the patrons seated themselves, holding their contributions, and the leader recited prayers [on their behalf],[110] and then they scattered.

29th DAY [606]   In the evening they lighted lamps as offerings at the Buddha Hall and Scripture Storehouse of this Korean Cloister but they did not light lamps elsewhere. They burned bamboo leaves and grass in the stoves in each of the cells, and smoke poured from their chimneys. At dusk, before midnight, after midnight, and before dawn they worshiped Buddha, and after midnight the novices and disciples [561] went around to the various cells with congratulatory words on the new year, in the Chinese manner.

---

[622] The twelve vows of the Buddha Yakushi (see note 406), below called Yakushi-ruri-kōbutsu 瑠璃光佛, a translation of his full Sanskrit title.

[623] A reference to Kannon's vow to save all sentient creatures (see note 6).

[624] *Kechigan* 結願.

K'AI-CH'ENG · FIFTH YEAR

keng-shen

FIRST MOON: 1*st* DAY *mou-yin*[625]   After worshiping Buddha early in the morning, we did not pay calls on one another, but returned to our own cells. After eating our gruel, we worshiped the Buddha in front of the hall, walking around [the images],[626] and, after worshiping thus, the monks then greeted one another in front of the hall, all mixed together and not in any order.

FIRST MOON: 15*th* DAY   I obtained a copy of the calendar for this year and copied it out as follows:

CALENDAR FOR THE FIFTH YEAR OF K'AI-CH'ENG

" stems " and " branches " the same as in the *na-yin* text [627]

Three hundred and fifty-five days in all. On *i* and . . .[628] days, one can carry earth and make repairs and construction. T'ai-sui 太歲 in *shen*,[629] Ta-chiang-chün 大將軍 in *wu*, T'ai-

---

[625] February 7, 840. *Keng-shen* 庚申 comes fifty-seventh in the hexagenary cycle and *mou-yin* 戊寅 fifteenth.

[626] *Gyōdō* 行道, a standard Buddhist rite.

[627] Assuming that the first *t'ung* should be deleted from the statement 干同支同納音本. The ten " stems " and twelve " branches " are the two sets of cyclical characters from which the hexagenary cycle is constructed. *Na-yin* is a system of numerology by which the sixty combinations in the hexagenary cycle are fitted to each of the five notes in each of the twelve keys of Chinese music.

[628] Apparently a second *i* 乙, the second of the " ten stems," which *Ikeda* corrects to *ssu* 巳, the fifth of the " twelve branches."

[629] T'ai-sui and seven of the nine terms which follow it constitute the eight deities known as the Pa-chiang-shen 八將神, whose positions were thought to have magical influence. T'ai-sui itself is also the name of the " year star," Jupiter, and the others may also correspond to planets, stars, or constellations. The two which do not belong to the Pa-chiang-shen are Sui-te (" Year's

yin 太陰 in *wu,* Sui-te 歲德 in . . . , Sui-hsing 歲刑 in *yin,* Sui-p'o 歲破 in *yin,* Sui-sha 歲殺 in *wei,* Huang-fan 黃幡 in *ch'en,* Pao-wei 豹尾 in *hsü,* Ts'an-kung 蠶宮 in *sun.*

First moon, thirty days first day *mou-yin,*[630] earth-construct;[631] fourth day stabilization achieved;[632] twelfth day "rain water";[633] twenty-sixth day "excited insects."

Virtue ") and Ts'an-kung (" Silkworm Palace "). In small characters are given the directions in which these ten were to be found, *shen* 申 being southwest by west, *wu* 午 south, *yin* 寅 northeast by east, *wei* 未 southwest by south, *ch'en* 辰 southeast by east, *hsü* 戌 northwest by west, and *sun* 巽 southeast. The direction following Sui-te may be *shen-yu* 申酉, west by southwest. In T'ai-sui and T'ai-yin the *t'ai* is miswritten *ta* (see note 197), and in Sui-hsing the *hsing* is miswritten 形.

[630] The first day of each moon is identified by its place in the hexagenary cycle of days, being 15th in the cycle for the first moon, 45th for the second, 14th for the third, 44th for the fourth, 13th for the fifth, 42nd for the sixth, 12th for the seventh, 41st for the eighth, 11th for the ninth, 40th for the tenth, 10th for the eleventh, and 40th for the twelfth.

[631] Following the two characters for the hexagenary cycle are two other characters identifying the first day of each moon according to another and somewhat similar cycle. The first character in this pair is always one of the five elements: wood, earth, water, fire, and metal. The next is one of a series of words for actions or qualities, known by the first two as the *chien-ch'u* 建除, which are supposed to determine the luck of a day. The whole series is: construct, remove, full, even, settle, grasp, break, dangerous, complete, collect, open, close 建除滿平定執破危成收開閉, and nine of these appear in this calendar. As can be seen in the earliest known example of a woodblock-printed Chinese calendar, which perhaps is from the year 877 (cf. Yabuuchi Kiyoshi 藪內清, *Zui Tō rekihō shi no kenkyū* 隋唐曆法史の研究 [Tōkyō, 1944], illustration opposite page 48), the five elements were assigned in rotation to two days at a time, with the result that the first days of successive moons would continue to have the same element until there had been two twenty-nine-day moons. Consequently, the " earth " recorded for the seventh moon is presumably an error for " fire " (the characters

Second moon, twenty-nine days first day *mou-shen* 戊申, earth-break; eleventh day sacrifice to the earth god 社, "vernal equinox"; twenty-sixth day "clear and bright."

Third moon, thirty days first day *ting-ch'ou* 丁丑, water-close; second day heavenly amnesty; [634] twelfth day . . . ; [633] twenty-eighth day "summer begins."

Fourth moon, twenty-nine days first day *ting-wei* 丁未, water-even; thirteenth day "grain fills"; twenty-eighth day "grain in ear."

Fifth moon [635] first day *ping-tzu* 丙子, water-break; fourteenth day "summer solstice"; nineteenth day heavenly amnesty.

Sixth moon, thirty days first day *i-ssu* 乙巳, fire-open; eleventh day first summer festival; [636] fifteenth day "great heat"; twentieth day [633] "autumn begins."

---

resemble each other closely as written in *Tōji*). Under the twelfth moon occurs a character which appears to be "snow" 雪, but this is clearly a copyist's error for "metal." The 877 calendar and more recent ones also show that the characters of the series of twelve were assigned to one day at a time with an occasional repetition of the same character for two days in a row. A study of Ennin's calendar will show that some months had two such repetitions, others one, and some none.

[632] 得平, of doubtful meaning.

[633] The terms in quotation marks are the regular names for the twenty-four seasons of the Chinese year, as given in Herbert A. Giles, *A Chinese-English Dictionary* 26. All but three of the seasons appear. "Spring begins" did not happen to fall in this year at all; "grain rains" 穀雨, which should have come on III 12 is miswritten *kuei-ping* 癸丙, an impossible cyclical combination; and "slight heat" which should have come around V 29 is omitted entirely. The seasons are all properly spaced from fourteen to seventeen days apart, with most of the intervals an even fifteen days, except for "autumn begins," which is misdated on VI 20 instead of VI 30.

[634] *T'ien-she* 天赦, a particularly lucky day, which was supposed to come four times each year, though only three appear in this calendar.

[635] A twenty-nine-day moon.

Seventh moon, twenty-nine days first day *i-hai* 乙亥, earth-even;[631] second day last summer festival;[636] fifteenth day "limit of heat."

Eighth moon, thirty days first day *chia-ch'en* 甲辰, fire-complete, "white dew"; fifth day heavenly amnesty; fifteenth day sacrifice to the earth god; sixteenth day "autumnal equinox."

Ninth moon, twenty-nine days first day *chia-hsü* 甲戌, fire-remove; second day "cold dew"; seventeenth day "hoar frost descends."

Tenth moon, thirty days first day *kuei-mao* 癸卯, metal-grasp; second day "winter begins"; eighteenth day "little snow"; twentieth day heavenly amnesty.

Eleventh moon, thirty days first day *kuei-yu* 癸酉, metal-collect; third day "heavy snow"; twentieth day "winter solstice."

Twelfth moon [637] first day *kuei-mao*, metal-even; [631] third day "little cold"; eighteenth day "severe cold"; twenty-sixth day winter sacrifice.[638]

The above calendar I have checked over in detail.

This day the *Lotus* [*Sutra*] Meetings at the mountain cloister came to an end.[639] The assembled men and women yesterday numbered 250 and today about 200. After the concluding benediction [624] the Rules of the Bodhisattva [640] were given to the assembled crowd, and after the forenoon meal, they all dispersed.

---

[636] *Ch'u-fu* 初伏, the first of the three *fu*. It is supposed to fall on the third *keng* 庚 day after the "summer solstice," the second on the fourth *keng* day, and the third on the first *keng* day after "autumn begins." The theory is that fire is in the ascendant in the summer and that *keng* represents metal, which is the element that overcomes fire. In this calendar, however, the first *fu* fell five days later than it should have in theory, and the last, here called *yin-fu* 陰伏 rather than *mo-fu* 末伏, four days too soon.
[637] A thirty-day moon.
[638] *La* 臘, theoretically held on the third *hsü* day after the "winter solstice," but coming six days later in this calendar.
[639] This presumably was written on I 15, since that was the date given for the termination of the lectures when they began on 839 XI (or XII) 16.
[640] *Bosatsu-kai* 菩薩戒, a category of rules for monks.

The names of the monks and novices permanently in residence at the Fa-hua-yüan of Mt. Ch'ih are the monk Tamp'yo 曇表, the monk Yanghyŏn, the monk Sŏngnim,[553] the monk Chijin 智眞, the monk Kwebŏm 軌範 Zen sect, the monk Tonjung the Rector,[81] Myŏngsin 明信 last year's Controller,[81] Hyegak 惠覺 Zen sect, Suhye 修惠, Pŏpch'ŏng last year's Prior,[565] Kŭmjŏng 金政 the Superior,[81] Chingong 眞空, Pŏphaeng 法行 Zen sect, Ch'ungsin 忠信 Zen sect, Sŏnbŏm 善範, the novices Tojin 道眞 last year's Manager,[641] Sagyo 師教, Yŏnghyŏn 詠賢, Sinhye 信惠 who lived in Japan six years, Yungnak 融洛, Sasun 師俊, Sosŏn 小善, Hoeryang 懷亮, Chiŭng 智應, three nuns, and two old women.

Ennin, the Japanese monk in search of the Law, notifies this cloister:

Requesting [permission] to make a pilgrimage to various places in order to find teachers and seek the Way.

Notice: I, Ennin, having fortunately met with your kind benevolence, have been residing in peace in the cloister. Your gracious generosity [642] has been profound, and I find it difficult to repay you. The depth of my obligation is not easily expressed in concrete metaphor.

Now, as the year moves on and the spring gradually becomes warm, I wish to go forth and make a pilgrimage to various places, seeking the Buddha's teachings. I humbly ask for a decision. My statement is as given above. Respectfully written.

A statement of the nineteenth day of the first moon of the fifth year of K'ai-ch'eng by the Japanese monk in search of the Law, Ennin.

20th DAY The officers of this cloister drew up another statement and sent Ishō and a representative of the cloister to the home of Chang Yŏng, the Military Guard Officer of this prefecture,[531] to inform him. The monk in search of the

---

[641] *Chissui* 直歲 (the second character is here abbreviated 才, not 戈 as *DBZ* prints), a term used in Zen monasteries.

[642] *DBZ* suggests 濟 for 洛. A standard abbreviation of the former closely resembles the latter.

Law made out a separate statement to be sent with the other to the Guard Officer, which is as follows:

Respectfully submitted.

With the new year here [643] and the spring all fresh, I humbly hope that much happiness will bless the Guard Officer's person and actions. I, Ennin, have received your indulgence and the other day received your benevolence and your solicitous inquiries.[644] I am your sincere admirer and am overcome with appreciation, but, limited by being a traveler, I cannot express it to you.[645] To what can I compare my great joy?

I, Ennin, being devoted to the Buddhist teaching, have stayed in China and now wish to go to various regions and seek out holy sites. I humbly hope for your all-embracing compassion and that you will grant me your gracious protection in this. I have respectfully sent my disciple monk, Ishō, to present this letter on my behalf.

Respectfully written in brief.[646]

Presented on the twentieth day of the first moon of the fifth year of K'ai-ch'eng by the Japanese monk in search of the Law, Ennin.

To the Guard Officer Chang Esquire, with humble respect. [647]

21st DAY We received a notification from the Guard Officer saying that he would send a messenger tomorrow to Wen-teng-hsien to get a statement from them and that a special messenger would speed this notice to the Mt. Ch'ih Cloister, so we should wait for it calmly.

---

[643] 展奉羊開 is of doubtful meaning. *DBZ* suggests 年 for 羊.

[644] This letter presents several problems of calligraphy and interpretation, for example the phrase 伏蒙慈流及問殊慰, in which *KIK* proposes to read 及問 as 存問.

[645] I prefer to interpret this passage as 限以旅情不獲披. See the letter on 840 IX 14.

[646] The second character of the phrase 不宣 is missing in *Tōji*.

[647] 侍者, meaning "servant," indicates that in theory this letter is addressed to the Guard Officer's servant, out of deference, and not to him directly. 謹空, originally meaning that a blank space had been left at the end of the letter to permit a simple reply, came to be merely a polite concluding phrase.

The monks of the cloister and the Guard Officer and the villagers have all told me that for the past three or four years various places on this side of Ch'ing-chou [540] have been suffering from plagues of locusts, which have eaten up all the grain, and because people are starving, there are many bandits and not a little killing and robbing. If travelers were to ask for food, no one would give it to them. If the four of us were to go there together at the present time, they feel that we would have grave difficulties and that we should stay a while longer in this cloister, passing the summer and waiting for autumn to come, and then, when the crops come in, proceed as we wish with safety. If we want to leave, we should go to the Yang-chou and Ch'u-chou region, where, when the grains have ripened we can obtain food with ease, and if we wish to carry out our original purpose, we can go straight north from Ch'u-chou and Hai-chou. What people tell me does not agree, and I am undecided in my own mind.

The Chief Official [77] of Wen-teng-hsien has *tung* 動 as a taboo and the Lesser Official [648] has *p'ing* 平 as a taboo.

27th DAY In the evening we received a notice from the Guard Officer saying that earlier he had detailed our high intentions to His Excellency the Magistrate 宰君 of this subprefecture, from whom a notice now has come, saying that he had told the prefecture of this, and that, if we would wait ten days or so, the prefectural government would take action and we could then proceed.[580]

SECOND MOON: 1*st* DAY [649] I made out another statement to importune the Guard Officer. This statement is as follows:

With mid-spring gradually bringing warmth, I humbly hope that much happiness will bless the Guard Officer's person and actions.

I, Ennin, have received your kindness and now sud-

---

[648] *Shao-fu* 少府, an unofficial term for a subprefectural Chief of Employees. See note 464.
[649] March 8, 840.

denly have been favored with a letter from you and have been informed in full of your high sentiments. Your benevolent concern for me has been profound and, lowly monk that I am, I am quite overcome by it.

I respectfully note that the statement from the subprefecture says that they have told the prefecture of this, and that if we wait ten days or so, the prefectural government will take action and then we can proceed. In my humble opinion, this is most reasonable. However, the trip [549] we have planned of more than ten thousand *li* is the private aspiration of us travelers from a distance and not official business,[650] and so I feel that the subprefectural government may not necessarily be speedy in notifying the prefecture. If they are dilatory or do nothing, our trip will come in the hot season.

I humbly ask that you again grant me your kind cooperation. I, Ennin, came from afar across many difficulties [651] and have my whole heart concentrated on the Way. Carried away by my desire to make an early start, I am unmindful of the distasteful reproof [I am bringing upon myself] and have dared to trouble my commander [652] with petty matters. Although I should be covered with embarrassment, I cannot remain quiet. Thus, because of my longing for the Guard Officer's gracious support, I humbly hope that you will redouble your efforts and that I shall be quickly granted a decision. If that transpires, your great generosity and glorious fame will stir foreign lands afar, the merit of our search for the Law will bind us in a close association, and I shall be overwhelmed with gratitude. I respectfully send my disciple Ishō to present this statement in my place.

Respectfully written in brief.

Presented on the first day of the second moon by the monk in search of the Law, Ennin.

To the Guard Officer Chang Esquire.[647]

I received an announcement from the Guard Officer saying

---

[650] In 非此公務 the reading of the last character is in doubt.

[651] 雲程踰險, another very dubious phrase in which the second character is merely *DBZ*'s suggestion for an illegible original.

[652] *Hui-hsia* 麾下, an obvious reference to the Guard Officer.

that he would again send a messenger to inform [the sub-prefecture] and he felt that [an answer] would come before long and he hoped that I would not worry and that, ever since I [653] had come under his jurisdiction and stopped here, a number of people had been doing what they could for me all day long.

7th DAY   The Superior's [81] disciple, the novice Sagyo,[654] left the monastery and went west.

11th DAY   At dusk the Rector's disciple, the novice Yŏnghyŏn, took away with him the Superior's disciple,[561] Sasun. The two plotted together and secretly ran away. No one in the cloister knew of it.

14th DAY   At the invitation of the Korean monk Sangjŏk, I went to Liu-ts'un [48] and saw a white stone image of Miroku [655] there. Earth was plastered on its body. When I inquired about this, they told me that there is a Korean here [called] Wang Hyŏn 王憲 who dreamed one night that a monk came and said to him, " I am Monjushiri.[309] An ancient Buddha hall has fallen to ruin, and for years no one has repaired it. Its Buddhas and Bodhisattvas are buried in the ground. I have observed your faith and, consequently, have come to tell you about it. If you wish to know the truth, dig [656] around the pagoda [657] southeast of your house and you will see." On awakening, he was awe-struck and told his dream to monks and laymen. Then,[657a] going to the ancient pagoda,[657] he dug up the earth with a hoe. When he had reached a depth up to his chest, he discovered the images of the Buddhas and Bodhisattvas. I now saw the one

---

[653] Here politely called " the Abbot." See note 80.

[654] 師敬 seems to be an error for 師教, which is clearly written on 840 I 15.

[655] 彌勒 (Skr. Maitreya), the Buddha of the Future.

[656] *DBZ* suggests 掘 for 抽.

[657] 寶圖 (the second character is written without the " en-velope " in *Tōji*) appears to mean " pagoda," as in the com-pound *fou-t'u* 浮圖. Below he refers to it as an " old pagoda " (*ku-t'u* 古圖).

[657a] *DBZ* misprints 遠 for 遂.

dug-up image of the Buddha Miroku, one figure of the Bodhisattva Monjushiri, one figure of the Bodhisattva Fugen,[286]
two figures of the Bodhisattva Kanzeon,[6] one figure of the
Bodhisattva Daishishi,[658] a figure of Ragora,[659] and an iron
cupboard holding the Buddha's bones of more than twenty
pounds weight. When all of us saw this, we marveled not a
little. At night we worshiped the Buddha, and monks and
laymen gathered and made donations all night long.

15*th* DAY   A maigre feast was held without any limit
of the number participating. I saw the Guard Officer Chang
there and received a notice from him saying that, with
regard to my going west, he was sending men at every
opportunity to inform the prefecture to take special action
and that I should wait patiently for three to five days, but,
if I were particularly anxious to hasten matters, I could
especially have the officials in charge [64] take me to the subprefectural government, which would pass me on up.

For fifteen days the Guard Officer Ch'oe's [541] ship from
Yang-chou has been at the Mt. Ju [501] inlet.

17*th* DAY   I left a letter for the Guard Officer Ch'oe
with this cloister and also presented with it a letter to Commissioner Chang.[438] These letters are as follows:

Since the start of the new year, I have heard from
you rarely, but have been thinking about you all the more.
With the spring already warm, I humbly hope that the Guard
Officer's person is at ease. I, Ennin, have received your kindness,
but, distant from you like the clouds, I have not been able to
meet you, though my admiration grows daily greater. To what
can I compare my esteem for you?

I, Ennin, have stayed in the mountain cloister, passing
the year with much good fortune. I have received the warm
kindness of the monks, which has greatly consoled my worries
as a traveler.[660] This is all the Guard Officer's kind doing. Your
protection has been extensive. How can I, insignificant man that

---

[658] 大師子, "Great Lion," not the name of a known Bodhisattva.
[659] 羅睺羅 (Skr. Rāhula), the Buddha's eldest son.
[660] *DBZ* suggests 旅 for 張.

I am, repay you. [Your kindness] is deeply engraved on my heart, and my gratitude grows ever greater.

I have received word from you that this spring you will especially donate a ship to take me by way of Lien-shui [661] to Huai-nan.[662] Of late I have heard of the holy sites of Mt. [Wu]-t'ai, and I yearn past all endurance [to go there]. My sole purpose is to search for the Buddhist teaching. When I have by good fortune heard of the holy land, how can I not go there? Since I have this wish, I am going there first, which means I am going back on my agreement with you, so my words and deeds do not match, for which I am deeply ashamed before you. I also fear that the men you sent will have expended their efforts for nought. Please do not blame me.

After my search for the Law, I shall return to Mt. Ch'ih and shall then go back to my homeland by way of Ch'ŏng-haejin.[438] I humbly hope then to visit the Commissioner Chang and explain the whole situation to him. I shall be going back, I estimate, about the autumn of next year. If you should have men or ships operating in that area, please be so kind as to order them to keep a special lookout for me. Our return home depends solely on your great assistance, and we shall be overwhelmed with gratitude to you.

With respect and deference.[647] Sent through another. Respectfully written in brief.

K'ai-ch'eng fifth year, second moon, seventeenth day.
The Japanese Scholar [Monk] in search of the Law, of the Dentō-hosshi Rank,[133] *Ennin.*
To the Guard Officer Ch'oe Esquire.[647]

To the Administrative Officer Nam.[663] A myriad blessings on your person. Although I have never met you, I have heard of your fame for some time, and I feel as if we had met. I humbly hope that you will keep your eye on the matter as

---

[661] Apparently miswritten 槤水, but the "water" and "cloth" radicals closely resemble each other in *Tōji*. See note 425.

[662] Miswritten 維南. See notes 11 and 661.

[663] 南判官, presumably a Korean and a subordinate or associate of Ch'oe.

stated above. Please do not become offended by me. Because [664]
I have no paper with me, I cannot write you a separate letter.
I shall be most fortunate if you will extend to me your sym-
pathy. *With humble respect.*[647]

Although I have never in my life had the honor of
meeting you, I have for long heard of your great excellence,
and I humbly respect you all the more. With mid-spring already
turning warm, I humbly hope that a myriad good fortunes will
bless the Commissioner's person and actions.

I, Ennin, have received your benevolence from afar and
am overwhelmed with gratitude. In order to carry out long-
cherished hopes, I remained in China. By great good fortune to
my insignificant self, I have been sojourning in the area blessed
by the vow of the Commissioner,[665] and I find it difficult to
express in words anything but my great happiness.

When I left home, I was entrusted by the Governor of
Chikuzen [666] with a letter for the Commissioner, but, since our
ship unexpectedly sank in a shallow part of the sea and our
things floated away, the letter with which I had been entrusted
sank in the waves, which causes me greater sorrow every day.
I humbly beseech you not to blame me.

I do not know when I shall have the honor of meeting
you, but in my humble way I think of you all the more from
afar. Respectfully I write to inquire after you. Respectfully
written in brief.

*Presented on the seventeenth day of the second moon
of the fifth year of K'ai-ch'eng by the Japanese monk* [666a] *in
search of the Law, of the Dentō-hosshi Rank,*[133] *Ennin.*

---

[664] Interpreting the two characters printed together as 辨緣
in *DBZ* as 弁緣 and belonging to two different sentences.
[665] Meaning the Mt. Ch'ih Cloister, which Chang Pogo had built
and endowed. See 839 VI 7.
[666] " Governor " here is 大守 (correctly 太守), a term normally
reserved for an Imperial Prince serving in such a capacity. Cf.
Wada, *op. cit.* 140-41. Chikuzen 筑前 (the first character is very
doubtful as written in *Tōji*) was the province in northern Kyūshū in which Hakata and Dazaifu were located.
[666a] An extra 傳 before the 僧 in *Tōji* is not printed in *DBZ*.

To Chang, the Commissioner of Ch'ŏnghaejin [458]

His Excellency, [652] *with humble respect.* [647]

Ennin, the Japanese [monk] in search of the Law has respectfully received your kind grants of considerable public goods.[667] Insignificant man that he is, he is overcome with gratitude. How can Ennin, an ordinary foreign monk, dare presume to such great largess? It will indeed be hard for him to repay his debt to you, and he is all the more embarrassed before you.

He is humbly aware that the Magistrate's [619] integrity draws the Imperial attention and your renown serves as a bulwark of the state. Your pure character forms a lofty [standard]; [667a] your benevolence is all-pervading; your military establishment is peaceful; and monks and laymen are all indebted to you.

In order to seek the Buddha's teaching, Ennin has come here from afar, moved by your virtue, and has tarried in your region. He has been fortunate enough to enjoy your benevolence. Being a mere nobody, he is overcome with gratitude.

K'ai-ch'eng fifth year, second moon, nineteenth day.[668]

After the forenoon meal, we left the Korean Cloister at Mt. Ch'ih and started for the subprefecture. The Prior [565] monk Pŏpch'ŏng accompanied us to the home of the Guard Officer Chang in charge of Korean Embassies.[531] The Guard

---

[667] This document, dated II 19, appears to be an incomplete draft of a letter of thanks by Ennin to the local Subprefect, written after he had learned that his petition had been granted by the local officials (see below). It is preceded (*Tōji* 77.7-79.7; *DBZ* 212b-213a) by another letter from Ennin dated III 3, which is omitted from the translation at this point because it is repeated verbatim (except for certain minor stylistic differences) on III 5. Possibly the letter as it appears here was the original draft for the later document.

[667a] *DBZ* prints 標, which appears in a similar passage in the document of III 5.

[668] In *Ikeda* the next line reads, " Presented by the Japanese monk in search of the Law, of the *Dentō-hosshi* Rank, Ennin " (the same signature as in the letter of II 17 to Chang Pogo), and the next paragraph begins with " nineteenth day."

Officer met us and said that he had just received a notice
from the subprefecture and was about to send a man to
inform me, and that, since I had come here myself, it was
clear that I indeed had divine favor [669] in my travels and
that he heartily congratulated me [on the outcome]. He then
showed me the subprefectural notice [which said]:

> *Wen-teng-hsien notifies the office of the Guard Officer
> in charge of Korean [affairs]:*
> The matter of the traveling monks from the Japanese
> ship, Ennin and three others, previously reported by this sub-
> prefecture [to the prefecture].
> *Notice*: We have consulted the dossier, and their [670]
> statement says that the said traveling monks have been staying
> at the Mt. Ch'ih Cloister and that, because of the spring warmth,
> they now [671] wish to go to various places on a pilgrimage, but
> they fear that [the local officials] will not honor their reasons.
> They now wish to be free to travel, but they have not dared [672]
> to do so on their own, and so have notified us.

We have received a decision granting them permission
to go. They do not yet have a written permit, and we are writing
to the office of the Guard Officer Chang in charge of Korean
[affairs] to take care of this. Thus, we are writing the Guard
Officer Chang in accordance with the document. Respectfully
written.

> *Notice of the tenth day of the second moon of the fifth
> year of K'ai-ch'eng by the Intendant* [560] *Wang Tso.*
> *Hu Chün-chih, the Superintendent of Registers* [467] *and
> the Vice-Chief of Employees.* [673]

The subprefectural seal appears at three places.

---

[669] 感應, implying responsiveness on the part of the gods.

[670] *DBZ* suggests 彼 for 被.

[671] 全 in *DBZ* and *ZZGR* and 舍 in *KIK*, but probably a copyist's error for 今.

[672] *DBZ* suggests 敢 for 最.

[673] 判尉 is probably an error for 副尉, the title this man has in
a letter under 839 VII 28. See note 464.

Wen-teng-hsien of the Government General [91] *of Teng-chou notifies the Japanese traveling monks Ennin and three others.* [674]

The monk Ennin, his disciples Ishō and Igyō, his servant Tei Yūman, and the clothing, alms bowls, etc., which they have with them.

Notice: On examination of the dossier, we find the statement of the said monk, [saying that] in the sixth moon of the recent fourth year of K'ai-ch'eng, they came on a Japanese tributary ship to the Korean Cloister of Mt. Ch'ih in Ch'ing-ning-hsiang in Wen-teng-hsien and stayed there and that they are now free to travel and wish to go to various places on a pilgrimage, but that they fear that everywhere in the prefectures and subprefectures, the barriers and fords, the passes and market places, and along the road, their reasons for travel will not be honored, and so they humbly seek to be granted official credentials as evidence and ask for a decision. [674a]

In accordance with our examination of the afore-mentioned traveling monks, we find that they still have no written permit and that they ask for something to be done about granting them official credentials. In accordance with the said statement, they are given official credentials as evidence. Respectfully written.

Notice of the twenty-third day of the second moon of the fifth year of K'ai-ch'eng by the Intendant Wang Tso.

Hu Chün-chih, the Superintendent of Registers and the Vice-Chief of Employees. [673]

We spent the night at the Guard Officer's home.

20th DAY The Guard Officer entrusted Ennin and the others with a letter for the subprefectural government

---

[674] The preceding document implies that the Guard Officer was to make out Ennin's travel permit, but this document, which appears to be the credentials Ennin was seeking, is signed by two subprefectural officials. Ennin apparently was not satisfied with the original decision and, as we see below, went himself to the subprefecture on II 20. This document presumably was the one which he states he received on II 24.

[674a] *DBZ* corrects the order of 處請分 without comment.

asking that the official credentials be issued, and he also assigned a functionary,[64] Li Ming-ts'ai 李明才, to accompany us there. We then parted from the Guard Officer, and, after taking leave of Pŏpch'ŏng, the Prior monk of Mt. Ch'ih, and the others, we went twenty *li* north to the home of a certain Wang 王 in Wang-hai-ts'un,[508] where we took our midday rest.[675] After the forenoon meal, we went fifty *li* north and by night reached Wen-teng-hsien, spending the night at the cloister of Master[333] Chi-lo 極樂 in the Hui-hai-ssu 惠海.

21st DAY   Early in the morning we went to the Hui-chü-ssu 惠聚 to look for living quarters and were placed in the north cloister. At the time of the forenoon meal, we went to the cloister of Master Chi-lo in the Hui-hai-ssu and took our midday rest. Li Ming-ts'ai went early in the morning to the subprefecture and, at the time for hearings, handed over the Guard Officer's letter, but the Chief Official[77] made no decision, and so he has not yet got the official credentials for us.

According to Chinese usage, officials, in governing, hold hearings twice a day, a morning hearing and an evening hearing. They wait until they hear a roll of drums and then go to their seats and hold hearings. Official or private visitors must wait until the time for hearings to see officials.

22nd DAY   We ate gruel in this monastery. Because the Chief Official has asked for a holiday and did not go [to his office today], I have not yet received the official credentials.

I hear that the K'ai-ch'eng Emperor (Wen-tsung) died on the third day of the first moon of this year[676] and that for three days the empire was in mourning and wore mourn-

---

[675] Ennin repeatedly uses 斷中, especially during his travels afoot, to mean a midday pause, usually for the purpose of eating the "forenoon meal."

[676] Ennin has the date wrong by a day. *CTS, HTS,* and *TCTC* all record Wen-tsung's death on 840 I 4, and Ennin himself mentions the anniversary of his death on 841 I 4.

ing garb. I also hear that the new Emperor, on ascending the throne, killed over four thousand persons in the capital who had been favored in the time of the preceding Emperor.[677]

23rd DAY   It is the Cold Food Festival and for three days fires are not allowed.[347]

After the forenoon meal the subprefecture sent the Superintendent of Registers Hu and the Superintendent of Registers Cheng 鄭 with several tens of men to the monastery to see us and inquire after us, and I told them in detail about our purpose in having come so far and in having stayed on here. Wen-teng-hsien is at the western edge of the Yellow Sea [678] and forms the eastern boundary of China. The Emperor of Ch'in deigned to come here and accordingly erected a monastery and named it [the Monastery of] " Blessings Accumulated " (Hui-chü).[679] At present it is south of the subprefecture.

24th DAY   Early in the morning we received the official document from the subprefecture. The text is as given elsewhere.[674] Since the functionary Li Ming-ts'ai had completed his work of arranging for the official credentials, he returned to the office of the Guard Officer Chang.

25th DAY   At 10 A.M. I went to the subprefecture and took leave of the Chief Official and then went back to the monastery. After the forenoon meal, we started out. The Monastery Administrator and the Controller [81] and others went to the moor west of the subprefecture to say farewell. We went [west from] the subprefecture for thirty li to Chao-

---

[677] The number may be exaggerated, but *TCTC* 246 does record that the infamous Wu-tsung, who succeeded his brother Wen-tsung, at once executed many courtiers who had been favored by the latter.

[678] P'o-hsieh 渤澥, an equivalent for P'o-hai 渤海, now designating the Gulf of Chihli, but here obviously referring to the whole Yellow Sea.

[679] The association of the founding of the monastery with the visits of the First Emperor of Ch'in to Shantung is a curious bit of historical nonsense. See note 546.

hsien-kuan 招賢館 [82] and spent the night. The innkeeper, Kao Shu,[680] lives in the inn and makes a very cordial host.

26th DAY   It was clear, and early in the morning we left Chao-hsien-kuan and went thirty li to Hsieh-shan-kuan 斜山 [82] in Lung-ch'üan-ts'un [681] and took our midday rest. The innkeeper, Liang Kung-tu 梁公度, lives in the inn. He was neither particularly good nor particularly bad, but, because our feet hurt, we could not start out again and accordingly spent the night in the inn.

27th DAY   Early in the morning we started out and reaching the home of Sung Jih-ch'eng [682] in Fan-ch'e-ts'un 牽車, took our midday rest. We asked for soy sauce, vinegar, and pickled vegetables, but he had none at all, and we could not eat either soup or rice. We went seven li northwest along the sea to a point one-half li east of the walled town of Mou-p'ing-hsien [493] where there stands the Lu-shan-ssu.[683] We entered the monastery at 2 P. M. and spent the night there. There were only the three chief officers of the monastery,[81] the Controller, and the Manager,[641] these five, and no other monks at all. The Buddha halls were dilapidated, and the monks' living quarters were all occupied by laymen and had been converted into ordinary living quarters. The walled town of the subprefecture is one li and a half from east to west and more than two li from north to south.

28th DAY   The Lu-shan-ssu arranged a maigre feast [sponsored by] the Prefect of Teng-chou, His Excellency Wu, for two monks of the monastery, the Rector [81] I-hsing 一行 and the Manager Ch'ang-piao 常表 and for us three Japanese monks, five persons in all.[683a] More than twenty villagers,

---

[680] 高恕. The second character is *DBZ*'s correction of 怒.

[681] There is a Lung-ch'üan-t'ang 龍泉湯 about thirty km. north-west of Wen-teng-hsien.

[682] 宋日成, but *DBZ*, *KIK*, and *ZZGR* all print the surname as 采.

[683] There is a Mt. Lu (Lu-shan) 廬山 a short distance west of Mou-p'ing-hsien. Cf. *Tseng-hsiu Teng-chou-fu chih*, introductory maps 3b and 10b.

[683a] There is an erroneous duplication of 有 in *Tōji*, not shown in *DBZ*.

in accordance with their respective abilities, prepared the food in their own houses and brought it to us. The Rector I-hsing expressed our appreciation. The villagers in front of the hall likewise partook of what they each [had brought].[684]

29th DAY   We left early and went northwest for thirty *li* to Chih-yang-kuan [685] and took our midday rest. After the forenoon meal we went twenty *li* to the home of Kao An 高安 in Mou-ch'eng-ts'un 牟城 and spent the night. Our host was not unpleasant.

THIRD MOON: 1*st* DAY [686]   We started out at dawn and went ten *li* to Ku-hsien-kuan [687] and then twenty *li* northwest to the home of Sun Hua-mao 孫花茂 in Shu-t'ai [688] and took our midday rest. We went right into the house without announcing ourselves and frightened our host, but he was very cordial. After the forenoon meal we went thirty *li* northwest to a monastery in Wang-t'ing-ts'un 王庭 in Wang-hsien-hsiang 望仙鄉 in the area of jurisdiction of P'eng-lai-hsien [419] and spent the night. In the night it thundered and rained.

In China at a distance of five *li* they erect a lookout [689] and at a distance of ten *li* they erect another lookout. They construct them as square mounds of earth pointed at the

---

[684] The sentence breaks off abruptly without the final verb in *Tōji* 98.3. The section which seems to follow this, and is so printed in *DBZ* and *KIK*, is to be found between 111.1 and 113.6.
[685] The *Shan-tung t'ung-chih*, map following 2B.13, shows a Mt. Chih-yang 芝陽 just east of the modern town of Fu-shan 福山 about thirty km. northwest of Mou-p'ing-hsien.
[686] April 6, 840.
[687] 故縣 (" the old subprefecture "), about forty-five km. northwest of Mou-p'ing-hsien. It is now written 古現, but appears with the other characters in *Tseng-hsiu Teng-chou-fu chih*, introductory maps 3b, and *Shan-tung t'ung-chih*, maps following 1A.12 and 2B.13.
[688] 竪泰, but the second character is of doubtful reading.
[689] *Hou-tzu* 候子, which apparently were merely distance markers.

top and broader below, varying from four to five or six feet in height, and they call them *li* posts.

2nd DAY   We started out at dawn and went twenty *li* to the home of T'ing Yen 庭彦 in An-hsiang-ts'un [690] and had our forenoon meal. Then we went twenty *li* to Teng-chou and went to the K'ai-yüan-ssu [55] and spent the night there. Teng-chou is 400 *li* from Mt. Ch'ih inlet. Tramping across mountains and hills, we had worn out our feet and had gone, staff in hand, on our knees. Ch'iao Kai 喬改, a local official [64] of the southern area of the city, came and asked us our reason for traveling, so I wrote out our travel schedule as follows and gave it to him:

> *The Japanese monk in search of the Law, Ennin, his disciples Ishō and Igyō, and his servant Tei Yūman.*
>
> The said Ennin and the others, accompanying a tributary embassy, boarded ship on the thirteenth day of the fourth moon [691] of the fifth year of the Japanese [year period] Jōwa and left our homeland. On the second day of the seventh moon of the third year of the Chinese [year period] K'ai-ch'eng we arrived in Pai-ch'ao-chen in Hai-ling-hsien in Yang-chou and on the twenty-eighth day of the eighth moon, reached Yang-chou, where we resided in the K'ai-yüan-ssu. [692] On the twenty-first day of the second moon of the fourth year of K'ai-ch'eng we started out by boat from Yang-chou and on the seventh day of the sixth moon reached Ch'ing-ning-hsiang in Wen-teng-hsien where we resided in the Korean Cloister of Mt. Ch'ih, passing one winter. On the nineteenth day of the second moon of this year we started out from the Mt. Ch'ih Cloister and at dusk on the second day of this moon reached [693] this K'ai-yüan-ssu,

---

[690] The map following *Shan-tung t'ung-chih* 2B.11 shows an An-hsiang-tien 安香店 near the An-hsiang River about twenty-five *li* southeast of Teng-chou (see note 419).

[691] The diary as we have it, however, only starts with 838 VI 13. See below the document dated 840 VIII 24.

[692] Actually they had arrived at Yang-chou on VII 25, but they had moved to the K'ai-yüan-ssu on VIII 24.

[693] At this point the misplaced section (see note 685) ends, and one must return to *Tōji* 98.3. *DBZ* mistakenly includes the re-

where we are lodging. The matter is respectfully stated in full as above.

    Written on the second day of the third moon of the fifth year of K'ai-ch'eng by the Japanese monk in search of the Law, Ennin.

The walled city of the Government General of Teng-chou is one *li* from east [to west] and one *li* from north to south. On the southwestern edge of the city stands the K'ai-yüan-ssu,[694] on the northeast the Fa-mo-ssu 法膜, and on the southeast the Lung-hsing-ssu.[256] There are no other monasteries. Outside the city walls are clustered private homes. P'eng-lai-hsien is in the city.[419]

The K'ai-yüan-ssu has quite a few cells for monks, but they are all occupied by official travelers, and none are vacant. When monks come, they have nowhere to put them.

North of the city one *li* and a half is the ocean, and on its shores stands the Ming-wang-miao 明王廟,[472] facing the sea in solitary splendor. In the eastern part of the city is a market place, where a *tou*[217] of millet[314] [costs] thirty cash and a *tou* of non-glutinous rice seventy cash. East of the south street of the city there is a Korean Inn and a P'o-hai Inn.[695] Houses were scarce along the way from Mt. Ch'ih on the borders of Teng-[chou] to Teng-chou itself, and the whole area consisted of mountains and moors. From Mou-p'ing-hsien to Teng-chou we went along the North Sea. For successive years there have been insect plagues, and the peasants are starving and are using acorns for food.

3rd DAY Early in the morning a representative of the Chief Official[77] of the subprefecture came and invited us to go to see the Chief Official. We went to the prefectural

---

mainder of the document in the misplaced section, and *KIK* follows this but omits the signature.

[694] *P'eng-lai-hsien chih* (of 1673), *t'u* 3b, shows it in the southwestern corner of the city, next to the south wall.

[695] Presumably official establishments to accommodate embassies from Silla and P'o-hai (see note 567), which usually passed through Teng-chou on their way to and from the Chinese capital.

[offices] and saw a Secretary.[696] We also went to the office of the Administrative Officer [38] and saw him, and then we went in through a gate [697] to see the Magistrate.[698] They took us into the audience hall, and we sipped tea. The Magistrate wrote out a statement bestowing on us two bushels [217] of rice, two bushels of flour, one *tou* [217] of oil, one *tou* of vinegar,[699] one *tou* of salt, and thirty sticks of firewood as provisions for our travels.

4*th* DAY   It was a national anniversary day.[700] The Magistrate, the Administrative Officer, the Secretary, and the subprefectural officials all came to the K'ai-yüan-ssu and burned incense. The Magistrate, the Administrative Officer, and the others then drank tea in the monastery living quarters,[141] and they summoned us monks in search of the Law, presented us with tea, and asked us about the customs of our country.

At the time of the forenoon meal we three Japanese monks and the Controller monk of this monastery went to the Chang 張 household at their invitation and had our midday rest.

5*th* DAY   Early in the morning I presented a letter thanking the Magistrate for the provisions he had given us, and in a separate letter I asked for official credentials. These letters are as follows:

The Japanese monk in search of the Law, Ennin, has gratefully received your kind gift of two bushels of rice, two

---

[696] *Lu-shih* 錄事, a category of officers in government generals, prefectures, subprefectures, and various other offices. Cf. Des Rotours 705, 725, 731. See also notes 38 and 461 above.

[697] 㦿門 may mean " a second gate," that is, an inner gate.

[698] See note 619. The context suggests that he meant the Subprefect, but from what follows, especially on III 5 and 8, we see that he was using the term for the Prefect.

[699] Here *ts'o* 酢, but *ts'u* 醋 in the document on III 5.

[700] See note 265. The only person this date seems to fit is one of the consorts of Shun-tsung, the great-grandfather of Wutsung. Cf. *T'ang-hui-yao* 唐會要 (Chiang-su shu-chü 江蘇書局 edition of 1884) 3.10b.

bushels of flour, one *tou* of oil, one *tou* of vinegar, one *tou* of salt, and thirty sticks of firewood. Insignificant man that he is, he is overwhelmed with gratitude. How can Ennin, being an ordinary foreign monk, dare accept such magnanimity? It will indeed be difficult for him to repay his debt to you, and he is all the more embarrassed before you.

He is humbly aware that the Magistrate's loyalty draws the Imperial attention and that your glory is worth a myriad cities. Your pure character forms a lofty standard; your benevolent administration is all-pervading; your military establishment is peaceful; and monks and laymen respect you.

In order to seek the Buddha's teachings, Ennin has come here from afar, moved by your virtue, and has tarried [701] in your region. He has been fortunate enough to enjoy your benevolence. You have been particularly benevolent to him and have cared for him on his arduous travels. Unworthy that he is, he is overwhelmed with gratitude. Humbly he presents this letter, stating his thanks. Respectfully written in brief.

Presented on the fifth day of the third moon of the fifth year of K'ai-ch'eng by the Japanese monk in search of the Law, Ennin.

To the Magistrate His Honor, [702] with humble respect. [647]

Presented by the Japanese monk in search of the Law, Ennin.[703]

Requesting official credentials to go to Wu-t'ai and other famous mountains and places in order to make a pilgrimage of holy sites, to seek teachers and to study the Law, for the monk Ennin, his disciples Ishō and Igyō, his servant Tei Yūman, and the razors and alms bowls they have with them.[704]

The said Ennin and the others are solely devoted to the

---

[701] *Ikeda* corrects 屆遊 to 留遊, in conformity with the wording of the letter of II 19, which shows many close parallels with this letter.

[702] *Chieh-hsia* 節下.

[703] This is the document which also appears in the text between the letters dated II 17 and II 19. See note 667.

[704] The razors and alms bowls may come in for special mention here and again in the document of III 9 because they were contraband articles. See 838 XI 2 and 7.

Buddhist teaching and to practicing the Buddha's Way. From afar they heard of Wu-t'ai and other places in China. These are the sources of the Buddhist Law, the places where the great saints have manifested themselves. Eminent monks of India have come there from afar, crossing precipitous slopes; famous patriarchs of China have there obtained enlightenment. Ennin and the others of old have admired [these places] and, crossing the sea, have come to visit them, but they have not yet accomplished their long-cherished wish. In the sixth moon of the fourth year of K'ai-ch'eng they reached the Korean Cloister at Mt. Ch'ih in Ch'ing-ning-hsiang in Wen-teng-hsien, separated by the ocean wastes from the land of their birth and forgetting their beloved land on this ocean shore. Fortunately they were free to travel and were able to come to the Magistrate's enlightened territory.

They now wish to go to various regions to worship at the holy sites and to seek teachers and to study the Law, but they fear that everywhere in the prefectures and subprefectures, the barriers and fords, the passes and market places, and the monasteries and temples, their reasons for traveling will not be honored, so they humbly hope that the Magistrate, out of his magnanimity, will especially grant them official credentials to serve as verification, and they humbly ask for a decision regarding this. The said matter is as stated above. Humbly written.

Presented on the third day of the third moon of the fifth year of K'ai-ch'eng by the Japanese monk in search of the Law, Ennin.

I received a notice from the Magistrate saying that his office had looked into the matter.

An Imperial Rescript by the new Emperor has arrived from the capital. Two carpets were spread in the court in front of the gate of the mansion 第門 inside the city walls, and above the steps on the north side of the great gate was placed a stand, on which was spread a purple cloth, and on this was placed the Imperial Rescript, written on yellow paper. The Administrative Officers and Secretaries of the prefecture, the Subprefect and the Superintendents of Registers of the subprefecture, the Commissioner of Troops,[78] the military officers,[360] the military officials 軍中行官, the common people, and the monks, nuns, and Taoist priests stood in ranks according to their posts on the east side of the court facing west. The Magistrate came out from within [his mansion], preceded by twenty military officers, ten each leading the way on the left and the right. When the Secretaries, the subprefectural officials, and the others saw the Magistrate come out, they bowed their heads almost to the ground.

The Magistrate called out, " The common people," and they chanted a response all together. The Magistrate stood on one of the carpets and an Administrative Officer stood on the other, both of them facing west. Then a military officer called out the titles of the various officials, and the row of Secretaries and subprefectural officials chanted their response in unison. Next he called out to the row of Military Guard Officers, Generals,[267] and Commissioners of Troops, and the row of military men chanted their response in unison. He also said, " The various guests," and the official guests and clients [705] chanted their response. Next he said, " The common people," and the common people, both old and young, chanted their response together. Then he said, " The monks and Taoist priests," and the monks, nuns, and Taoist priests chanted their response all together.

Next, two military officers brought the stand with the Imperial Rescript and placed it in front of the Magistrate, who bowed once and then picked up the Imperial Rescript in his hand and lowered his head, touching it to his forehead. A military officer knelt and received the Imperial Rescript on his sleeve and, holding it up, went into the court and, standing facing north, chanted, " An Imperial order has arrived." The Magistrate, Administrative Officers, Secretaries, and the military, all together bowed again. A military officer called out, " Let the common people bow," and the people bowed again, but the monks, nuns, and Taoist priests did not bow. They had two Assistant Judges [706] spread out

---

[705] 酢太. The term is used again on 845 VI 9.
[706] *Ya-kuan* 衙官, which were officials serving under a Prefect who was at the same time a Regional Commander. Cf. Des Rotours 729.

the Imperial Rescript. These two men wore green coats. Two other Assistant Judges read it alternating with each other. Their voices were loud, as when government decisions are announced in our country. The Imperial Rescript was some four or five sheets of paper long, and it took quite a long time to read, while no one sat down.

After the Imperial Rescript had been read, the Magistrate and the others bowed again. Next a Secretary and a military officer came out into the court and voiced their thanks to the Magistrate and then hastened back to their original posts and stood there. The Magistrate announced to the officials, " Let each be diligent in his charge," and the Administrative Officers and the others [707] all chanted their response. Next a general representative [708] called out, " The monks and Taoist priests," and the monks, nuns, and Taoist priests chanted their response. Next he said, " The common people," and they chanted their response. Then the Commissioner who had brought the Imperial Rescript 詔書使 walked up in front of the Magistrate and bowed again, whereupon the Magistrate stepped off his carpet and stopped him with his sleeve.[709] Several tens of officials and guests went up in front of the Magistrate and stood with their bodies bowed toward the ground. A military officer called out, " You may leave," and they all chanted their response in unison. The officials, the military, the monks and Taoist priests, and the common people thereupon dispersed.

We served the rice and flour given to us by the Magistrate on the fifth day [710] in the monastery living quarters.

---

[707] Since the Administrative Officers ranked next to the Magistrate, 巳上 is probably an error for 巳下.

[708] *Tu-shih* 都使, a descriptive title which appears again on III 22. On 839 IV 6-7 it was used with reference to a subprefectural officer.

[709] This may have been a gesture of courtesy or of deference to the man's role as the bearer of an Imperial Rescript.

[710] Presumably a copyist's error for " third day."

Five tou of rice, one bushel of flour, vinegar, salt, and oil as needed, and thirty sticks of firewood.[711]

Not daring [712] to receive alone the gracious benevolence of the Magistrate, I am donating the said articles to the cloister where I have been living in order to hold a maigre feast, which is to be provided tomorrow for the congregation of monks of the whole monastery. Respectfully stated.

Third moon, sixth day.
The Japanese monk in search of the Law, Ennin.
To the officers of the monastery
Their Reverences 法前.

6th DAY   At noon we provided for the more than ten monks in the monastery and then had our midday rest. At 4 P. M. Wang Ch'ang-tsung 王長宗, a Military Guard Officer of this prefecture, gave us a donkey to carry our supplies.

7th DAY   I had the forenoon meal at the home of the Guard Officer Wang. On the north wall inside the Seng-chieh-ho-shang-t'ang 伽和尙堂 (" Hall of Monks and Priests ") outside the western corridor of the Buddha Hall in this K'ai-yüan-ssu are painted [representations of] the Western Paradise and the Potalaka Paradise.[713] These were [drawn] at the wish of a Japanese embassy, and the story is written on the wall. It is all obliterated, but one can make out the three characters for Japan. To the left and the right of the figures of the Buddhas are written the names of the sponsors. They all are ranks, surnames, and given names of Japanese:

---

[711] This is the heading of the document through which Ennin announced to the monastery officers his intention of holding a feast for his hosts. It will be noticed that he used only one-quarter of the rice and one-half of the flour, but all of the firewood.

[712] *DBZ* suggests 敢 for 取.

[713] The Western Paradise is that of Amida, while Potalaka (J. Fudaraku 補陀落) is the name of a mountain in India where Kannon is supposed to reside.

The Secretary of the Senior Sixth Rank, Upper Grade, Tate Hikkan; [714] the secretary of the Senior Sixth Rank, Upper Grade, Hane Hōshō 羽豐翔; the Officer at Large of the Junior Eighth Rank, Lower Grade, Hata Sodatsu; [715] the Officer at Large of the Junior Eighth Rank, Lower Grade, Shiro Ushigai 白牛養; the Functionary 諸吏 of the Junior Sixth Rank, Lower Grade, Hata Umiuo 秦海魚; the Attendant 使下 of the Junior Sixth Rank, Lower Grade, without corresponding office 行散位, two characters missing . . . do 度; the servant of the Junior Seventh Rank, Lower Grade, Muraji Takesada; [716] the servant of the Junior Eighth Rank, Lower Grade, Ki no Ason Sada . . . 紀朝臣貞 character missing.

I inquired about this, but no one could explain the origin of it. I do not know what year it was that this tributary embassy reached this prefecture.

8th DAY   Early in the morning I prepared a letter and presented it to the Prefect, and at the same time I urged him [to give us] official credentials.

The end of spring has turned very warm, and I humbly hope for a myriad blessings for the person and actions of the Magistrate.[717]

I, Ennin, have received your benevolence, but since the way of a monk has its limitations, I have not been able to come to pay my respects for several days. Unworthy that I am, I am overcome with trepidation and respectfully send my disciple monk Ishō to present this letter. Respectfully written in brief.

Presented on the eighth day of the third moon of the fifth year of K'ai-ch'eng by the Japanese monk in search of the Law, Ennin.

To the Magistrate His Honor, [702] with humble respect. [647]

---

[714] 建必感. Since none of the names can be identified, we know no more about this embassy than Ennin did. Most of the names appear to be incomplete, having apparently been Sinicized and shortened to the usual three-character length of Chinese names.
[715] 秦育, though the second character looks more like Mutsuki 六月 ("six months") in *Tōji*.
[716] 連雄貞. Muraji actually was a title rather than a surname.
[717] *DBZ* suggests the deletion of 尋 between the two characters for "Magistrate." See note 619.

The Japanese monk in search of the Law, Ennin.

The said Ennin deeply desires to go to Mt. [Wu]-t'ai to spend the summer and after that to go to various places in order to make a pilgrimage of holy sites, but he fears that eventually the general situation will put a stop to his trip. In a previous letter, he bothered the Magistrate about official credentials, and he humbly asks for a decision. The matter is as stated above. Respectfully written.

Presented on the eighth day of the third moon of the fifth year of K'ai-ch'eng by the Japanese monk in search of the Law, Ennin.

The Prefect sent word that [the credentials] would come right away. At the time of the forenoon meal, in response to an invitation from the Guard Officer Chiang 姜, I went with four monks of this monastery to his house for the forenoon meal.

9th DAY   I received a notice from the *Yüan-chang*,[718] saying that the notice from the prefecture should come tomorrow and that I was to ask the [Regional] Commander [719] for a decision and that, by taking the letter myself to the Regional Commandery of Ch'ing-chou,[540] I should be able to get my official credentials.

At noon I went to the home of Liu Tzu-cheng 劉自政 for the forenoon meal.

10th DAY   It rained. I went to the Chang household for the forenoon meal.

11th DAY   At 10 A.M. I received two [720] documents from the prefecture, one for the Base Officer [721] and one to be taken to the [Regional] Commander.[719] I went to the

---

[718] 院長, perhaps the Prior (see note 565) or possibly a government official.

[719] Here only *Shih*, but the term, *Chieh-tu-fu*, is used immediately below. See note 91.

[720] 道 is used three times in this sentence in place of 通, the more usual numerary adjunct for documents.

[721] *Liu-hou-kuan* 留後官. Cf. the use of *Liu-hou* and *Liu-hou-*

prefecture and thanked the Prefect and also took leave of him. Then a copy was made for me of the text of the prefectural document:

The Government General of Teng-chou notifies the Commissioner in Charge of the Two Barbarian Peoples: [722]
With reference to the statement of the Japanese monk Ennin asking for official credentials to go to Wu-t'ai and other famous mountains and various regions in order to make a pilgrimage of holy sites and to seek teachers and to study the Law, for the monk Ennin, his disciples Ishō and Igyō, his servant Tei Yūman, and the razors and alms bowls they have with them.[704]
Notice: Consulting the dossier, we find the said monk's statement that his only interest is his devotion to the Buddhist teachings and the practicing of the Buddha's Way. From afar he heard of Wu-t'ai and other places in China. These are the sources of the Buddha's Law, the places where the great saints have manifested themselves. Eminent monks of India have come [to these places] from afar, crossing precipitous slopes; famous patriarchs of China have there obtained enlightenment. Ennin and the others of old have admired [these places] and, crossing the sea, have come to visit them, but they have not yet accomplished their long-cherished wish. In the sixth moon of the fourth year of K'ai-ch'eng they reached the Korean Cloister at Mt. Ch'ih in Ch'ing-ning-hsiang in Wen-teng-hsien, separated by [723]

---

shih 使 in Des Rotours 670 and 825. From the use of this term on III 28 and of *Chih-hou-yüan* 知後院 ("Base Office") on III 22, we may assume that the Base Officer was the representative of Teng-chou at Ch'ing-chou. On 843 IX 13 *Liu-hou-yüan* is used for a similar Base Office at the capital, in the charge of a Base Office Guard Officer (*Liu-hou-ya-ya*).

[722] *Ya-liang-fan-shih* 押兩蕃使, presumably another title for the Regional Commander of Ch'ing-chou, perhaps signifying his theoretic supervision over Korea and P'o-hai, since embassies from these countries normally went by way of this region to the capital. See note 695.

[723] The character 於 occurs at the corresponding point in Ennin's letter dated III 3, which is quoted almost verbatim in the first part of this document.

the ocean wastes from the land of their birth and forgetting their beloved land on this ocean shore. They now wish to go to various regions to worship at the holy sites and to seek teachers and to study the Law, but they fear that everywhere in the prefectures and subprefectures, the barriers and fords, the passes and market places, and the monasteries and temples, their reasons for traveling will not be honored, and so they humbly hope that they will be especially granted official credentials to serve as verification.

According to our examination of the Japanese monk Ennin and the others, [we find that], as given earlier in a report by Wen-teng-hsien, the returning ships of the Japanese tributary embassy landed in the east inlet at Mt. Ch'ih in Ch'ing-ning-hsiang on the borders of that subprefecture on the twelfth day of the sixth moon of last year [724] and that they started out on the fifteenth day of the seventh moon. We subsequently received a report from the subprefecture about the monk Ennin and his three followers who had been abandoned by the returning Japanese ships. The prefectural officers previously stated the matter in full, reporting it to the [Regional] Commander. It is respectfully stated as above.

We wonder whether or not to give them official credentials. Since the Prefect, the Administrative [Officers], and the prefectural officers lack the authority on which to issue official credentials, we are passing on the records [725] to the President of the Ministry [620] for him to make the decision and, accordingly, are sending the monk to bring the documents himself and see the President of the Ministry to get a decision.

Respectfully stated as above. We have not [previously] reported this to the [Regional] Commander and asked for a decision, but [now] forward to him the full statement. Respectfully recorded and presented. Respectfully written.

Written on the ninth day of the third moon of the fifth year of K'ai-ch'eng by the Scribe of the Government General 府史, *K'uang Ts'ung-chih* 匡從制.

Presented in full.

To the President of the Ministry.

---

[724] The date was actually VI 7, but here we may have the date of the Wen-teng-hsien document reporting their arrival.

[725] 安錄, presumably a graphic abbreviation of 案錄.

A single [720] *document issued(?)* 行囯 *on the tenth day by the Intendant, K'uang Ts'ung-chih.*

It was officially countersigned (?) 官復言 and had two seals.

12*th* DAY　We started at dawn, going thirty *li* west to the home of Hsien Ch'ing 羨慶 in Wang-hsü-ts'un 王徐 and took our midday rest. Then we started out again and went forty *li* to the home of Shao Yün 少允 in Chiu-li-chan-ts'un 九里戰 in the territory of Huang-hsien [572] and spent the night. Our host was lacking in courtesy. In my dreams I saw Abbot Enchō. [399]

13*th* DAY　We started out early in the morning, going twenty *li* west to Chan-chai-kuan 戰齋 and had our forenoon meal in the home of Tung Huan 東桓. Our host was extremely niggardly. We had to ask for a dish of vegetables several times before he would give it to us. After our forenoon meal we started out again and went west twenty-five *li* to Ch'eng-fu-kuan 乘夫, where we drank tea and then went twenty-five *li* to the home of Chiang P'ing 姜平 in Hsü-sung-ts'un 徐宋 in the territory of I-hsien in Lai-chou [482] and spent the night. Our host was an upright man. In my dreams I saw Gishin Kashō. [726]

14*th* DAY　We started out and went thirty *li* to the Wang household at T'u-ch'iu-kuan 圖丘 and took our midday rest. Our host on first seeing us was unwilling [to take us in], and we had trouble getting anything, but finally he gave us pickled vegetables in great abundance. After our forenoon meal we went ten *li* to the Wang household at Ch'iao-ts'un 喬 and drank tea and then went twenty *li* to Chung-li-ts'un 中李. There are over twenty houses there, and we went past five or six homes, looking for a place to stay,

---

[726] On 839 II 25 Ennin had been told of the Ch'ang-an monk, I-chen, whose name is written with these same characters (see note 377), but it is improbable that he would have dreamed of this man after having not mentioned him again for over a year. The dream about Enchō the preceding night suggests that here we have Gishin, the first Abbot of the Enryakuji (see note 400).

but each house had many [727] sick persons and would not let travelers stop for the night. At the very end [of the village] we came on a single house, but they would not let us stay there either and reviled us repeatedly, so we went on to the home of T'eng Feng [728] and spent the night. Our host was a religious man 道心.

15th DAY We went fifteen *li* to the Ch'eng 程 household in P'ing-hsü-ts'un 平徐 and took our midday rest. Our host was very cordial. After our forenoon meal we went fifteen *li* to Lai-chou. The walled city is one *li* from east to west [729] and more than two *li* from north to south. With the outskirts [730] it must extend three *li* in both directions. The walled town is crowded with houses and buildings. We went out of the walled town to the southeast to the Lung-hsing-ssu [256] and spent the night. In front of the Buddha Hall is a thirteen-story brick pagoda with its base crumbling away.[730a] The surrounding corridors are dilapidated, and the monastery is without any congregation of monks, having only two monks. The Rector and the Controller [81] are by nature common men and do not know the proper etiquette toward guests.

Lai-chou controls four subprefectures: I-hsien, Ch'ang-yang-hsien, and Chiao-shui-hsien.[731] A market place is located

---

[727] Both *DBZ* and *KIK* omit 多. At this point (*Tōji* 109.6) one must insert 113.6-115.2, as printed in *DBZ* and *KIK*. This section in *Tōji* follows immediately the other misplaced section mentioned in note 684.

[728] 藤峯. Since the first character is not a surname, it may be an error for its homophone 滕.

[729] *DBZ* misprints "south," and *KIK* follows, though noting the possibility of an error.

[730] *Wai-lang* 外廊, apparently used for *wai-kuo* 外郭.

[730a] Soper, *op. cit.* 39, assumes from the position of the pagoda that the monastic plan was the archaic one known as Kudara 百濟 in Japan.

[731] Ch'ang-yang 昌陽 is the modern Lai-yang 萊陽, about seventy km. southeast of I-hsien, and Chiao-shui 膠水 the modern P'ing-tu 平度, about forty-five km. due south of I-hsien.

southwest of the prefectural walled city, where millet [314] [costs] fifty cash per *tou* [217] and non-glutinous rice ninety cash per *tou*.

16*th* DAY　Early in the morning the permanent residents provided us with a meal of gruel. The monastery has no rice, and each person finds his own food [732] and brings it and eats it himself without giving any to others. Each took a little of his own provisions to supply the monks. [733]

After [the meal] we started out and, after going northwest fifteen *li*, [found] on the side of the road the grave of Wang Fu-chün. [734] An inscription had been carved on a stone, but in the course of the long passage of time the inscribed stone had fallen to the ground. It was beside an inlet of the North Sea. We went on over twenty *li* to the Fa-yün-ssu in T'ai-ts'un [735] and spent the night. The innkeeper performed his function well. The T'ai Inn originally was a Buddhist monastery, but later was made into an inn, which the people nowadays call the T'ai Inn. In front of the inn are two pagodas, one twenty feet and five stories high made of carved stone, and the other ten feet high made of cast iron in seven stories. A text on a stele says:

> Wang Hsing-tse 王行則 on Imperial command went to subdue the eastern barbarians but was sunk and over one hundred men on his ship were captured by the bandits and

The fourth subprefecture was Chi-mo (see note 482) and not Lai-chou itself (which was the same as I-hsien), as stated in notes in *DBZ* and *KIK*.

[732] Here one must return from *Tōji* 115.2 to 109.6. See note 727.

[733] The statement is ambiguous, but Ennin may have meant that, since the so-called monastery had no food to give to travelers, the two resident monks gave some of their own food to the Japanese party.

[734] 王府君. *Fu-chün*, in Han times a title for the Governor of a Commandery (*Chün* 郡), began to be used in T'ang times simply as an honorific title for an ancestor.

[735] 臺, or possibly I-ts'un 壹. *Lai-chou-fu chih* (of 1740) 8 (*ssu-kuan* 寺觀).1a states that a Fa-yün-ssu 法雲 fifty *li* west of I-hsien was rebuilt in the second half of the twelfth century.

sent to Japan.[736] He alone escaped and hid. He was able to return home and on the fifteenth day of the ninth moon of the second year of Lin-te 麟德 (665) erected these noble pagodas.[737]

After the forenoon meal it rained, so we did not start out.

17th DAY [738]   At dawn we started, going southwest. By mistake we took the Mi-chou [436] road, going five *li*, but by chance a man told us [of our mistake] and we were able to reach the right road. We went fifteen *li* to the P'an 潘 household in P'an-ts'un and took our midday rest. Our host was a rough and unpleasant man and did not perform the courtesies. We asked our host for vegetables, soy sauce, vinegar, and salt, but did not get any. Finally we paid a pound of tea and bought soy sauce and vegetables, but they were not fit to eat. After our forenoon meal we started out and went forty *li* to the home of Liu Ch'ing 劉清 in San-fou-ts'un [739] in the territory of Chiao-shui-hsien [731] and spent the night. The lady of the house reviled us, but her husband explained that she was making a joke. Thirty *li* southeast of the village is Chiao-shui-hsien.

18th DAY   We went five *li* and crossed the Chiao-ho [740] ferry. In the area of Lai-chou the people are rough and the common people are starving and poor. We went along the river for fifteen *li* to the Pu 卜 household in

---

[736] Wo-kuo 倭國, a derogatory name for Japan once used by the Chinese. This incident probably was part of the wars of 662-663 when Silla, aided by T'ang, destroyed the southwestern Korean state of Paekche 百濟, which was supported by Japan. See Okada 13.1-14 and Imanishi, *op. cit.* 291-303.

[737] At this point in the text (*Tōji* 111.1-115.2; *DBZ* 52b-53b) are found the two misplaced sections translated above (see note 684 and 727).

[738] Misprinted as "16th day" in *KIK*.

[739] 三埠 (the second character is written here with the "mountain" radical), about thirty-five km. southwest of I-hsien.

[740] 膠河. Today the river is not as close to San-fou as it appears to have been in T'ang times.

[741] 北海, the modern Wei-hsien 濰, on the Tsingtao-Tsinan Railway about eighty-five km. southwest of I-hsien.

T'ien-chuang 田庄 in the territory of Pei-hai-hsien [741] in
Ch'ing-chou [540] and took our midday rest. Our host was
very cordial, [providing] vegetables for our forenoon meal
without being stingy. After the forenoon meal we went along
the Chiao-ho for thirty *li* to the Keng 耿 household in Tung-
keng-ts'un 東耿 in Fu-jung-i [742] and spent the night.

One *li* west of the Keng house is an old walled city which
the people nowadays call the walled city of Ch'ang-kuo.[743]
It is twelve *li* around the walls, and it is broad from east
to west and narrow from north to south. At present there
are thirty households of commoners living within the walls.
I asked a village elder who told me that it had been over a
thousand years since this city had been destroyed and he
did not know what king had resided there. Within the walls
one now finds in the ground, gold, silver, pearls, jade, ancient
coins, horse trappings, and the like. There are many treasures scattered in the ground, and, after each rain, they find
them. The master of the Keng household was gentle and
good.

19*th* DAY   We started at dawn, going twenty *li* to
the Chao 趙 household in Wang-nou-ts'un 王耨 and took
our midday rest. Our host was a religious man and provided
us with enough vegetables for us to eat our fill. After the
forenoon meal we went forty-five *li* to the Kuan-fa-ssu 觀
法 in Pei-hai-hsien and spent the night. The Buddha hall
and the monks' cells were dilapidated, and the images of
the Buddhas were exposed to the elements. The twelve-odd

---

[742] 芙蓉驛 (for *i* see footnote 187). There is a Fu-jung Pond
shown in *Shan-tung t'ung-chih*, map following 2B.24, about
twenty-five km. northeast of Wei-hsien.

[743] A Ch'ang-kuo 昌國 existed in Chou times northwest of I-tu,
but that was far west of where Ennin was at this time. His
site could have been the late Chou town of Pei-tien 邶殿 (known
from Han times on as Tu-ch'ang 都昌), a little west of the
modern town of Ch'ang-i 昌邑, or else the Chou towns of Han
寒 or Chin 鄩, a little more to the west. Cf. *Ch'un-ch'iu lieh-
kuo t'u* 春秋列國圖 and *Ch'ien-Han ti-li t'u* 前漢地理圖 (both
in *Li-tai yü-ti yen-ko hsien-yao t'u*).

monks in the monastery were all living in lay quarters, but one Controller monk was living in the monastery.

In the subprefecture rice [sells for] sixty cash per *tou* and " small beans " [744] for thirty-five cash per *tou*. The subprefectural walled city is two *li* from east to west and one *li* from north to south. It is the Wei-chou [741] of former times, now called Pei-hai-hsien.

20*th* DAY   We started early and went west for twenty *li*, meeting on the moors a P'o-hai [567] embassy returning home from the capital. Then we went another five *li* to the Ts'ai 采 household in Ku-shan-ts'un [745] and prepared our meal. Our host was extremely niggardly and would not give us a single pinch of salt or spoonful of soy sauce or vinegar without payment. After the forenoon meal [we went] thirty *li* to the Li 李 household in Pan-ch'eng-ts'un 半城 in the territory of Shou-kuang-hsien [746] and spent the night. Our host was avaricious and took lodging charges for putting up guests.

21*st* DAY   We started out and went thirty *li* to the Chang 張 household in Chiu-wei-tien 韭味店 and took our midday rest. Our host was a quiet person. After our forenoon meal we went thirty *li* to the Lung-hsing-ssu [256] in Ch'ing-chou-fu [540] and spent the night. The monastery recorded in detail our reasons for coming and informed the prefecture. It has been 540 *li* from Teng-chou here.

22*nd* DAY   I went to the prefectural [offices] for the morning audience and saw a Secretary in charge of judicial matters. [747] Then I went to the entrance of the official resi-

---

[744] 小豆 (written 少豆 on IV 2 and 25 in *Tōji*) now means " lentils " in China, but " red beans " in Japan (see note 485).
[745] *Shan-tung t'ung-chih*, map following 2B.7, shows a Mt. Ku (Ku-shan) 孤 a little southeast of the modern town of Ch'ang-lo 昌樂 (about thirty km. west of Wei-hsien).
[746] 壽光, about forty km. northwest of Wei-hsien.
[747] This may be the meaning of *Lu-shih ssu-fa* (see note 696). A Judicial Bureau (*Ssu-fa* 司法) was one of the bureaus of a prefecture (cf. Des Rotours 698).

dence [748] of the President of the Ministry [620] and the Commissioner in Charge of the Two Barbarian Peoples,[722] intending to transmit the letter to the prefecture, but because I arrived late, the President of the Ministry had gone to the " ball field," [749] and I could not see him. I went back to the Teng-chou Base Office [721] and delivered its letter [720] from Teng-chou. At the time of the evening audience, I went to the prefectural [offices] and, going to the [Regional] Commander's [719] official residence,[748] met his general representative [708] Liu 劉 and transmitted to him the letter from Teng-chou. The general representative came out [again] and reported that he had been summoned to the [Regional] Commander's home and that the President of the Ministry sent me word that I should return to the monastery and that a decision would be taken subsequently. I returned to the monastery, and the Assistant Regional Commander,[750] the auxiliary official [390] Chang 張, came to the monastery and we met. I also saw the Administrative Officer of the Military Headquarters,[751] whose surname is Hsiao 蕭 and whose given name is Tu-chung.[752]

23rd DAY   Early in the morning, on the invitation of the Administrative Officer Hsiao, I went to his home to eat gruel. There was a complete sufficiency of medicinal broths and tea. The Administrative Officer understands the Buddhist Law and is a religious man. He loves discussions [of Buddhism], and, when he sees a monk come from a distance, he is cordial and solicitous. When I was about to have my forenoon meal, the Assistant Regional Commander sent an

---

[748] *Ya-men* 衙門.

[749] 毬場. As we see on III 24, this was an area within the prefectural government grounds. It may have been used in playing polo or " kick-ball," two games which were popular at the time.

[750] *Chieh-tu-fu-shih* 副使. Cf. Des Rotours 658.

[751] *Mu-fu p'an-kuan* 幕府判官. *Mu-fu* was not a standard official term at this time, but was probably used for the Regional Commander's office or some military unit under him.

[752] 度中, but Ch'ing-chung 慶中 in *Ikeda*.

official courier to summon me to the Petition Court [753] of the prefecture for the forenoon meal. Six or seven officials ate and drank there in accordance with the regulations.

24*th* DAY It was the day for the "Springtime Triumph Song," [754] and a banquet was held in the "ball field" [749] inside the prefectural [offices]. At dawn the Monastery Manager and Controller took us to the Korean Cloister,[755] where we were lodged.

25*th* DAY In order to ask for official credentials, I again prepared a statement and presented it to the President of the Ministry.

The Japanese monk in search of the Law, Ennin.

The said Ennin and the others, with hearts devoted to holy sites, crossed the sea in search of them and wish to go to Mt. [Wu]-t'ai to spend the summer and practice the Way [756] and later to go to various regions to look for teachers and to seek the Law, but he fears that, since the road is far and the season hot, they will not be able to accomplish their original desire. Since a prefectural letter has already reported the matter fully, he humbly hopes that the President of the Ministry in his benevolence will especially grant him official credentials. Hoping that he may accomplish his lowly but sincere desires and that he may soon proceed on his way, he humbly asks for a decision.

---

[753] *Chin-tsou-yüan* 進奏院. Cf. Des Rotours 670-71.

[754] " Ch'un-chieh p'o-chen yüeh " 春節破陣樂. Conceivably the first two characters are an error for Ch'in-wang 秦王, and we have here " Ch'in-wang p'o-chen yüeh " (" The Song of the Prince of Ch'in's Destruction of the [Enemy] Camp "), a famous piece of Tang music performed at official banquets. It is said to have commemorated the victory of Li Shih-min 李世民, the second T'ang Emperor, over a rival Liu Wu-chou 劉武周 in 620, when Shih-min was still the Prince of Ch'in. However, the date III 24 does not fit this famous battle, or rather series of battles, which took place in the fourth moon. Cf. *HTS* 21.3676b; Franke, *op. cit.* 3.367; *TCTC* 188; Waley 150.

[755] Presumably for the use of Korean embassies (see note 695) and probably in the monastery where Ennin was staying.

[756] *DBZ* corrects 進 to 道.

*Presented on the twenty-fifth day of the third moon of
the fifth year of K'ai-ch'eng by the Japanese monk in search of
the Law, Ennin.*

From Wen-teng-hsien in Teng-chou to Ch'ing-chou there
have been plagues of locusts for the past three or four years
which have eaten up the five grains so that the officials and
commoners alike have gone hungry. In the Teng-chou region
they have been using only acorns for food. It is difficult for
traveling monks passing through this rugged area to obtain
provisions. Millet [314] [costs] eighty cash per *tou* and non-
glutinous rice one hundred cash per *tou*. We are without
provisions to eat, and so I prepared a statement and sent it
to the Assistant Regional Commander, the auxiliary official
Chang, asking for provisions.

*The Japanese monk in search of the Law, Ennin, asks
to be given provisions for his meals.*
The said Ennin and others left their homeland far
away in order to search for Buddhist teachings, but, because he
is asking for official credentials, he has not yet moved on.[580]
He makes his home anywhere and finds his hunger beyond
endurance, but, because he speaks a different tongue, he is unable to beg [for food] himself. He humbly hopes that in your
compassion you will give the surplus of your food [132] to the poor
monk from abroad. You have already given him a certain
amount(?) 一中 , and he is extremely embarrassed to be troub-
ling you now again. He humbly sends his disciple Ishō to inform
you. Respectfully stated.
*Presented on the twenty-fifth day of the third moon
of the fifth year of K'ai-ch'eng by the Japanese monk in search
of the Law, Ennin.*
To the auxiliary official His Excellency,[757] with humble respect. [647]

The auxiliary official gave us three *tou* of non-glutinous
rice, three *tou* of flour, and three *tou* of millet, so I prepared
a letter to thank him.

The Japanese monk Ennin humbly states his thanks.
The auxiliary official in his benevolence has given us

---

[757] *Ko-hsia* 閣下.

grain and flour, and I am overwhelmed with gratitude and find it difficult to express my thanks. Unworthy that I am, I am overwhelmed [758] with the magnitude of my appreciation. Humbly I present this statement to express my thanks. Respectfully written in brief.[758a]

Presented on the twenty-fifth day of the third moon of the fifth year of K'ai-ch'eng by the Japanese monk in search of the Law, Ennin.

To the auxiliary official His Excellency, with humble respect.

27th DAY   I sent Ishō to the office of the Intendant in charge [759] to find out about the matter of our official credentials, and he reported about the case that a decision had already been made to give us official credentials. On the one hand they were going to give us official credentials and on the other hand, they were going to report to the throne about us. The President of the Ministry would put his name and seal [to the official credentials] at the morning audience day after tomorrow and the [Regional] Commander would then send it to me.

28th DAY   It is the beginning of summer,[633] but the sky is lowering. The Teng-chou Base Officer,[721] Wang Li-wu,[760] came to the cloister and we met. I then heard that a Prince of P'o-hai had arrived the other day on his way home and that he was waiting for an Imperial Emissary to arrive before leaving. He is holding a maigre feast in the Hsia-kung-yüan [761] in this monastery to which I am invited. I went there for my midday rest [675] and found an assembly of about fifty monks.

29th DAY   I prepared a statement and presented it to the President of the Ministry asking for provisions for our meals.

---

[758] The first character in the expression 不任 is missing in *Tōji*.

[758a] *Tōji* has 下 for 不.

[759] *Pen-tien-yüan* 本典院. See note 560.

[760] 王李武. Since Li, though a surname, is not normally used in given names, this perhaps should be corrected to Wang Chi-wu 季 or Li Wu.

[761] 夏供院 (" Summer Offering Cloister "). See notes 230 and 122.

The Japanese monk in search of the Law, Ennin, asks to be given provisions for his meals.

The said Ennin and the others crossed the boundless waves from afar intent on their search for the Buddhist teachings. Simple people though they are, they have come through good fortune to the honorable region of the President of the Ministry. Because they have had hard times in their travels 旅李,[549] they go hungry at mealtime, and, since they speak a different language, there is no one from whom to seek [food]. They humbly hope that the President of the Ministry in his benevolence will take care of the poor monks by giving them provisions. If he does, the blessings of his generosity will compare to those of Jinnyo,[762] and the virtue of his great aid will rival that of Hakku,[763] and [Ennin] will be overwhelmed by the depths of his admiration. He respectfully presents this letter to make known his request, more than ever in humble trepidation. Respectfully written in brief.

Presented on the twenty-ninth day of the third moon of the fifth year of K'ai-ch'eng by the Japanese monk in search of the Law, Ennin.

To the President of the Ministry

His Excellency,[757] with humble respect.

I sent my disciple Ishō to present this statement, and he received a notice in reply, stating that the decision would be made tomorrow.

30*th* DAY I went to the home of the retired scholar [764] Hsiao at his invitation for the midday rest and heard that the Regional Commander had recorded the reasons why we monks in search of the Law had come and had made a report to the throne.

---

[762] *KIK* suggests that this is Anyakyōjinnyo 阿若憍陳如 (Skr. Ājñāta-kauṇḍinya), one of the original five disciples of the Buddha.

[763] *KIK* suggests that this is Hakkura 薄拘羅 (Skr. Vakkula), one of the Buddhist saints (*rakan* 羅漢, Skr. *arhat*).

[764] *Ch'u-shih* 處士, a title for an unemployed scholar, probably used as a courtesy title for the official Hsiao, mentioned on III 22 and 23 and IV 2.

FOURTH MOON: 1st DAY [765]   At the morning audience
I received our official credentials, and the President of the
Ministry gave us three lengths [766] of cloth and six pounds of
tea. At the time for the forenoon meal, they had a maigre
feast in this monastery. Today is the birthday of the son
of the President of the Ministry, and accordingly a " long
life " [767] maigre feast was held.

2nd DAY   Early in the morning I ate gruel at the
house of Hsiao, the Administrative Officer, and then went
to the prefectural [offices] to present a letter thanking the
President of the Ministry for his gifts and to take leave of
him.

The Japanese monk in search of the Law, Ennin, has
humbly received from the President of the Ministry in his
benevolence a gift of three lengths of cloth and six pounds of
tea. Unworthy that he is, he is overwhelmed with gratitude
and respectfully presents this letter to express his thanks. Respectfully written in brief.
     *Presented on the second day of the fourth moon of the
fifth year of K'ai-ch'eng by the Japanese monk in search of the
Law, Ennin.*

The President of the Ministry summoned me to his offices
and sent word to me that what he had given was trifling
and did not merit mention and that he thanked me for
coming and I might now go. I next went to the offices of
the Assistant Regional Commander, the auxiliary official
Chang, to take leave of him. He summoned me into his
office and gave me tea and cakes to eat. We sipped our tea,
and then I bade farewell to the auxiliary official and went
to the monastery. I was invited for the forenoon meal to the
home of Chao Te-chi 趙德濟. At sunset the Administrative
Officer of the Military Headquarters [751] gave me two *tou* of

---

[765] May 6, 840.
[766] *Tuan* 端, a measure of cloth equal to almost fifty feet. Cf.
Des Rotours 471.
[767] *Ch'ang-ming* 長命.

grain as provisions and two *tou* of "small beans" [744] as fodder for the donkey. At dusk I went to the home of the Administrative Officer of the Military Headquarters and thanked him for giving us provisions for the road and took leave of him.

3rd DAY   At dawn we started. The Administrative Officer of the Military Headquarters sent an official courier to accompany us past the city gate. Ever since we first met, [the Administrative Officer of] the Military Headquarters has been extremely courteous, and while we were at the monastery, daily bestowed gifts on us and inquired kindly after us all the time. Now that we were starting, he sent a man to accompany us and show us the road.

Today the President of the Ministry, the Military Inspector,[144] and the various shrines 神廟 are praying for rain. From the monastery northwest past the city wall and ten *li* out in the country is Mt. Yao,[768] on top of which stands the Shrine of King Yao 堯王廟. When long ago King Yao passed through this area, he built this shrine. I am told that, whenever they pray for rain [here], the rains fall in response.

We went out of the walled city and went north for twenty *li* to the Ch'en 陳 household in Shih-yang-ts'un [769] in I-tu-hsien [540] and ate. Our host was a quiet man. After the forenoon meal we went northwest fifteen *li* to Tzu-shui-i in Lin-tzu-hsien [770] and then twenty-five *li* west to the Wang household east of Chin-ling-i [771] and spent the night. Our host was

---

[768] 堯, a famous hill a short distance northwest of I-tu, which, according to legend, had been climbed by the mythical Emperor Yao, whom Ennin calls King Yao below.

[769] *Shan-tung t'ung-chih*, map preceding 2B.1, shows a Shih-yang 石羊 about ten km. north and a little west of I-tu.

[770] Lin-tzu 臨淄 is almost twenty-five km. northwest of I-tu, and the Tzu-shui 淄水 flows in a northeasterly direction a short distance south and east of it.

[771] Chin-ling-chen 金嶺鎮 is at present a station on the Tsingtao-Tsinan Railway about thirty km. northwest of I-tu.

a good and upright man, and when he saw guests, he was courteous. Far to the west we could see Mt. Ch'ang-pai.[772]

4th DAY We started at dawn, going sixteen *li* southwest,[772a] where we entered a small road from which we could see Mt. Ch'ang-pai in the distance, and then we went five *li* westward to the Chao household in Chang-chao-ts'un 張趙 in Tzu-ch'uan-hsien in Tzu-chou [773] and ate. Our host was extremely poor and had no food for us to eat, but he was not a bad man at heart. After the forenoon meal we went northwest for thirty *li* to the . . . household in Ku-hsien-ts'un in Ch'ang-shan-hsien [774] and spent the night. Our host was a metal-worker, originally from P'ei-chou.[775] He was a quiet and religious man.

5th DAY We started early, going ten *li* northwest to Ch'ang-shan-hsien, and from the subprefecture we went ten *li* west to Chang-li 張李 and took our midday rest. Our host was courteous. After the forenoon meal we went fifteen *li* west to the east side of Mt. Ch'ang-pai. It was almost 4 P. M. when we drank tea at the Shih 史 household at Pu-ts'un [776] in front of the Hermit's Terrace 仙人臺 and asked for the Li-ch'üan-ssu.[777] Our host replied that, if we went fifteen *li*

---

[772] 長白, now Mt. Ch'ang, an isolated mountain rising about 2,575 feet a little distance north of the Shantung massive and about eighty km. west of I-tu.

[772a] *DBZ* and *KIK* misprint " west."

[773] 淄, the modern Tzu-ch'uan (see note 570), which was the name of the local subprefecture in T'ang times. It is about forty-five km. due west of I-tu.

[774] 長山, about sixty km. northwest of I-tu. *Shan-tung t'ung-chih*, map following 1A.19, shows a Ku-hsien 故 (written 古 in our text) some four or five km. southeast of Ch'ang-shan.

[775] Probably an error for P'ei-hsien 沛, a short distance northeast of the modern town of that name in the northwestern corner of Kiangsu. This area as well as the part of Shantung in which Ennin was then traveling are both known to have deposits of iron ore.

[776] 不, probably a copyist's error for some other character.

[777] 醴泉. *Li-ch'üan* means a spring of pure water. See below IV 6. This name may be connected with the modern Mt. Li in the

due west of Pu-ts'un, we would reach it, so we went straight west into the mountains. We went over ten *li* on the wrong road. There were many different roads, and we did not know where they led. Since night was falling, we returned to the Shih household in Pu-ts'un and spent the night. All night long the dogs barked, and we were afraid and could not sleep.

6th DAY   Early in the morning our host gave us gruel, and he also sent a man to accompany us and point out the road. We went due west into a valley, passing a high ridge, and then, going west down a slope, came on the fruit gardens of the Li-ch'üan-ssu and drank tea there. Then we went south another two *li* and came to the Li-ch'üan-ssu, where we took our midday rest.

After the forenoon meal we made a pilgrimage around the monastery and worshiped the representation of Chih-kung Ho-shang.⁷⁷⁸ It was placed in the Lapis Lazuli Hall.²⁰⁰ The doorjambs and steps were all made of blue-green stone, and precious banners of unusual colors and rarities from the whole world were spread out in the hall. Chih-kung Ho-shang was a manifestation of the Eleven-Faced Bodhisattva.⁷⁷⁹ His history is engraved on a stele. He was of the Chu family ⁷⁸⁰ and was from Chin-ch'eng.⁷⁸¹ His spirit descended to Mt. Ch'ang-pai. After his death it was not known where his body had gone, but they made this representation of him, and the whole land paid him reverence.

In the valley west of the buildings is the Li-ch'üan well,⁷⁷⁷

---

foothills north of Mt. Ch'ang, a short distance southwest of the modern town of Tsou-p'ing 鄒平. Cf. *Shan-tung t'ung-chih*, map preceding 1A.17.

⁷⁷⁸ Chih-kung 誌公 was a title of respect for Pao-chih 寶誌 (418-514), one of the great Buddhist priests of the Six Dynasties Period.

⁷⁷⁹ Jūichimen Bosatsu 十一面芉, one of the forms of Kannon (see note 6).

⁷⁸⁰ 朱代, the second character obviously being a copyist's error for 氏.

⁷⁸¹ 金城, an earlier name for the town in southwestern Shensi known in T'ang times and at present as Nan-cheng 南鄭.

where formerly the spring bubbled up fragrant and sweet of taste. Those who drank of it avoided illness and prolonged their lives. [The monastery], accordingly, is called the Li-ch'üan-ssu. After the Priest's death the spring waters dried up, and there was merely the empty well as now. Over the well stands a small building where another representation of the Priest has been made. In front of it and inside the building is the stone well some five or more feet deep. At present there is no water in it.

A peak on the south side of the monastery, called the Dragon Terrace 龍臺, stands out alone above the other peaks. It is recorded on our map that once a dragon danced on this peak and that this was reported to the throne. An Imperial order was received changing the name [of the monastery] to the Lung-t'ai-ssu ("Dragon-Terrace Monastery"), but later it was changed to the Li-ch'üan-ssu because of the spring. There are high mountains forming a wall [around the monastery] on the east, west, and south, but on the north it is open with no heights.

The monastery buildings are dilapidated, and there is not much "purified eating." [782] The holy sites are gradually going to ruin, and there is no one to repair them. Some of the monastery's fifteen estates [remain] today. Originally there were about a hundred monks,[783] but they have now scattered in accordance with their destinies, and at present [only] thirty-odd live in the monastery. The Controller [81] monk took us to the Korean Cloister [755] and lodged us there.

7th DAY We ate our gruel early in the morning in the [dining] hall and then started out. The Controller and the other monks tried to detain us, saying that tomorrow the monastery would hold a great maigre feast, and why did we have to leave so soon, but, because we wished to reach Mt. [Wu]-t'ai quickly, we did not stay. Going out of the gate of the monastery, we went fifteen *li* north to an

---

[782] 淨喫, meaning that the monks did not observe the Buddhist rules limiting both the time of meals and the diet.
[783] In 僧途 the second character may be used for its homophone 徒.

estate of the Li-ch'üan-ssu and took our midday rest. Then
we went twenty *li* due west to Chang-ch'iu-hsien [784] and from
the subprefectural [town] went west fifteen *li* and crossed
by ferry over the Chi-ho.[785] The people nowadays call
[the place] Chi-k'ou 濟口. From the ferry we went a half *li*
northwest to the Wang household and spent the night. Our
host was a quiet man.

    8*th* DAY We started early and went due west for
twenty-five *li* to Lin-chi-hsien,[786] where we went to the Yin
尹 household and took our midday rest. Then we started out.
A merchant gave us five *sheng* [217] of grain. We passed the
market place and went due west for thirty *li* and at 4 P. M.
reached the Chang household in Chih-lung-ts'un 雙龍 in
Lin-i-hsien.[787] In the evening it rained. Our host was a quiet
man.

    9*th* DAY It was raining in the morning, and we could
not start. After the forenoon meal the rain stopped, so we
started, going fifteen *li* due west to the old subprefecture,
that is, the old walled town of Lin-i-hsien. It was going to
pieces and had not a single official building. The monasteries of former ages were in ruins, with the images of the
Buddhas exposed to the elements, and [the city] had reverted
to cultivated fields. It was most melancholy. We went due
west for fifteen *li* to the ferry across the Yüan-ho [788] and,
crossing the river, went ten *li* to the Li Fu 里甫 household

---

[784] 章丘 (correctly 邱), about fifteen km. west of Mt. Ch'ang.

[785] 濟河, which approximated the modern course of the Yellow
River, though at this point it obviously was a few km. to the
east of it.

[786] From these statements we see that the town of Lin-chi 臨
濟, which no longer exists, was due west of Chang-ch'iu and
across the Chi-ho from it. *TTLCT* shows it north by northwest
of Chang-ch'iu, and on the same side of the river.

[787] 臨邑, about thirty km. north of Tsinan and about the same
distance southeast of the modern town of Lin-i.

[788] 源河, which obviously is a copyist's error for Lei-ho or
Lei-shui 濼水, a river which flowed northwest of Lin-i in T'ang
times.

in Yen-t'ang-ts'un 燕塘 in Yü-ch'eng-hsien [789] and spent the night. Our host was a religious man.

10th DAY We started at dawn, going forty li due west, and at 2 P. M. reached Yü-ch'eng-hsien. In the market place of the subprefecture millet [costs] forty-five cash for one tou, non-glutinous rice one hundred cash for one tou, " small beans " [744] fifteen cash per tou, and flour seventy or eighty cash. We passed the walled town and went west for ten li to the Chao household in Hsien-kung-ts'un 仙公 and spent the night. All night long there was thunder and lightning, and hail and rain fell. At dawn the thunderstorm stopped. Our host was not a religious man.

11th DAY We started at 6 A. M., went due west for thirty li, and at noon reached the ferry across the Yellow River.[790] The people nowadays call [this place] Yüeh-chia-k'ou 藥家口. The water is yellow and muddy [791] in color and flows swift as an arrow. The river is about one chō and five tan [792] wide and flows east. The Yellow River originates in the K'un-lun Mountains [793] and has nine bends, six of which are in the land of the Tibetans [794] and three in China. There are ferry stations on both banks on the north and south, each with walled enclosures more than four chō from north to south and about one chō from east to west. This Yüeh-chia-k'ou has many boats which are anxious to carry travelers. It costs five cash for each person and fifteen for a

---

[789] 禹城, about forty-five km. northwest of Tsinan. In the name of the household, Li Fu 里甫 probably is a copyist's error for the surname Huang-fu 皇甫.

[790] Indicating that the Yellow River flowed about twenty km. due west of Yü-ch'eng, as shown in *TTLCT*.

[791] *Ikeda* corrects 渥 to 泥.

[792] *Tan* (Ch. *tuan*, see note 766), like *chō* (see note 21), is used more as a measure of distance in Japan than in China. According to one system, a *tan* is one-tenth of a *chō*, which would make the width of the Yellow River at this point only something over five hundred feet.

[793] 崑崙, the great ranges south of the Kansu panhandle.

[794] T'u-fan 土蕃, but more commonly 吐蕃.

donkey. [The area] south of the river is under Yü-ch'eng-
hsien in Ch'i-chou [574] and north of the river belongs to the
southern part of Te-chou.[795]

After crossing the river we took our midday rest on the
north bank. Each one of the four of us ate four bowls of
porridge. Our host was astonished and was afraid that if
we ate so much cold stuff we would not digest it. Then
we went thirty-five *li* due west and at 4 P. M. reached the
Chao household in Chao-kuan-ts'un 趙館 in P'ing-yüan-
hsien [796] in Te-chou and spent the night. Our host was not
a religious man.

12*th* DAY We started early and went due west for
forty *li* to the Chao household in Hsing-k'ai-ts'un 形開 in
Hsia-ching-hsien [797] in P'ei-chou and took our midday rest.
Our host was a religious man and gave us a maigre feast,
and we ate our fill of vegetables.[798] After the forenoon meal
we started out and went thirty *li* west to the Sun household
in Meng-chia-chuang 孟家莊 in Hsia-ching-hsien and spent
the night. Our host was a religious man.

13*th* DAY We started out and went thirty-five *li* west
to the Wang household in Wang-yen-ts'un 王淹 and took
our midday rest. Our host was quite a religious man and
gave us a maigre feast. After our forenoon meal we went
thirty-five *li* west and at 4 P. M. reached the K'ai-yüan-
ssu [55] within the walled city of T'ang-chou [799] and spent the
night.

---

[795] 德, the present Ling-hsien 陵, about eighty km. northwest of Tsinan.

[796] 平原, about thirty km. northwest of Yü-ch'eng.

[797] 夏津, about sixty km. due west of Yü-ch'eng. It was in Chü-
chou 具 , the modern Ch'ing-ho 清河 (the name of the local
subprefecture in T'ang times) in southeastern Hopeh about
forty km. west and a little north of Hsia-ching. P'ei-chou (see
note 775) must be a copyist's error.

[798] *DBZ* misprints 疏 for 蔬 .

[799] Presumably a copyist's error for Chü-chou (see note 797),
since there was no T'ang-chou 唐 in this part of China.

I am told that the Vice-President [of the Tribunal of Censors] [418] informed the Regional Commander that an [ordination] platform [198] would be newly opened in the K'ai-yüan-ssu and posted notices on the streets and at the cross-roads so that people would learn about it. There were over four hundred monks who came from various prefectures to receive ordination. Yesterday the platform was closed, and the newly ordained monks all scattered. I saw a mere thirty-odd of them who had not yet gone.

The Monastery Administrator [119] recorded in detail the reasons why we Japanese monks had come and reported to the Vice-President [of the Tribunal of Censors].

14th DAY I went to the prefectural [offices] at the morning audience and called on the Vice-President. In the residence of the Vice-President a maigre feast had been arranged for ten monks, and at the invitation of the Vice-President I partook of the maigre feast in the official residence 使宅, after which I went back to the monastery to stay. In the evening I went to the cloister where the ordination platform was and saw the newly established platform. It has two levels of brick paving, the lower one twenty-five feet square and the upper fifteen feet square. The lower level is two and one-half feet high and the upper two and one-half feet [above the lower]. The platform is blue-green in color. The people nowadays speak of it as standing for a lapis lazuli color.[200]

15th DAY I took my midday rest at the Liu [48] household inside the city. The food was in accordance with the regulations. After the forenoon meal, I went to the Shan-kuang-ssu 善光 and saw the ordination platform for nuns. Banners had been hung in the hall and seating mats spread around. The ground was marked off with ropes, and they had not erected a platform. The level ground had been laid out as an ordination platform. Beginning tomorrow they will walk around [the Buddhist images] [626] and perform ordinations. I went to the prefectural [offices] for the evening audience and took leave of the Vice-President.

16th DAY We started at dawn and went twenty li

west to the Liu household at Ho-chang-liu-ts'un 合章流 in the territory of Ch'ing-ho-hsien [797] and took our midday rest. We ate a soup of " elm " leaves. Although our host did not understand Buddhism, of his own accord he served us maigre food at our midday rest. After the forenoon meal we started out and went forty *li* northwest to the Chao household in Chao-ku-ts'un 趙固 in the territory of Nan-kung-hsien in Chi-chou [800] and spent the night. Our host was an upright man.

17*th* DAY Early in the morning our host gave us gruel, and then we went fifteen *li* straight north and fifteen *li* northwest to Nan-kung-hsien. We went to the Chang household inside the city for our midday rest. We went out of the city and northwest for fifty *li*. There were few houses. We reached T'ang-yang-hsien [801] and went to the Chüeh-kuan-ssu 覺觀 inside the town and spent the night. The monastery buildings are dilapidated, and there is no group of monks but only one monk in charge of the monastery. When he saw guests, he was not courteous. He did not attend at all to fixing up the rooms and beds.

18*th* DAY We started at dawn and, heading due west, went thirty *li* to Hsin-ho-k'ou.[801] We went to the Nan 南 household inside the walls and took our midday rest. We went out the west gate and, crossing the Hsin-ho Bridge, went thirty *li* due west. The level plain stretched wide and far, and houses were very scarce. Reaching the T'ang-ch'eng-ssu 唐城 east of Ning-chin-hsien [801] in Chao-chou,[802] we

---

[800] Nan-kung-hsien 南宮 is about forty km. northwest of Ch'ing-ho, and Chi-chou 冀 is about thirty km. northeast of Nan-kung. [801] From this passage we see that T'ang-yang 堂陽 (T'ang here is written with its homophone 唐) was near or the same as the modern town of Hsin-ho 新河, about twenty-five km. northwest of Nan-kung. This would mean that the Hsin-ho-k'ou 口 (" Crossing of the Hsin River ") mentioned on IV 18 was west of the modern Hsin-ho and about halfway between it and Ning-chin 寧晉, which is about thirty km. west and a little north of Hsin-ho. [802] 趙, about twenty km. northwest of Ning-chin.

stopped for the night. The monastery was extremely poor, and the monks were common and vulgar.

19*th* DAY [803]   At 8 A. M. we started out from the walled town and went fifteen *li* northwest to the Liu household in Ch'in-ch'iu-ts'un 秦丘 and took our midday rest. Although our host was poor, he provided us with a maigre meal. At noon we started out and went twenty-five *li* northwest. The heat was like steam. Reaching the K'ai-yüan-ssu south of Chao-chou, we stopped for the night. The buildings were dilapidated, but the Buddhist images were impressive. The monks were rustics at heart and were nervous at seeing guest monks.

20*th* DAY   At dawn we ate our gruel and then went forty *li* northwest to the Sun household outside the walled town of Luan-ch'eng-hsien [804] in Chen-chou [578] and took our midday rest. Then we went thirty *li* northwest to the Liu household at Tso-hu-i 作護驛 in Ta-k'uo-hsien [805] and stopped for the night. Our host had the heart of a bandit and cheated people.

21*st* DAY   We started early and went thirty *li* due north to the headquarters of the Regional Commander of Chen-chou and went to the Chin-sha-ch'an-yüan 金沙禪 in the southwestern part of the city but found [no place] to stop for a rest. Two monks, on seeing us guests, railed at us and drove us off several times, but we forced our way into the cloister and prepared our food, and our hosts had a change of heart and themselves made noodles for us guest monks.

---

[803] Ono and Hibino 293-338 give an annotated translation into Japanese of virtually all of the diary covering the period 840 IV 19 to VII 12.

[804] 欒城 (*luan* here is written with its homophone 巒), shown in *TTLCT* a little north of the present town of that name, which is a little less than twenty km. northeast of Chao-chou.

[805] Since there was no prefectural name resembling Ta-k'uo-hsien 大廓 in this part of China, this may be an error for Ta-kuo 大郭, which at present is the first station on the railway west of Shih-chia-chuang. Cf. Ono and Hibino 294.

After our forenoon meal, we headed due north for twenty *li* to the Yang 楊 household on the [Regional] Commander's estate and spent the night. This estate belonged to the General of the Armies,[806] Wang 王, the former Regional Commander of Chen-chou, and the General of the Armies' grave and ancestral hall is located on it. The members of the household of the Regional Commander Wang[807] guard the grave, and at present a military officer[360] called Liu takes charge of the grave and ancestral hall with great care. One *li* to the south has been erected a stele hall built with high walls, and they will not let it be opened up. They say it has been three generations since the death of the General of the Armies. Our host was a religious man and was courteous to his guests.

22nd DAY   Early in the morning our host gave us gruel, and then, heading due north, we went twenty *li* to the Liu household in Nan-lou-ts'un[808] and took our midday rest. Our host had become a believer some time ago and had long been preparing maigre meals which he offered to [passing] monks, regardless of their number. Not long after we entered the house, he served us with food, and his wife came out and inquired solicitously of us several times. After we had eaten, we drank tea, and then, heading due north, we went twenty-five *li* to Hsing-t'ang-hsien[809] in the territory of Chen-chou and went to the Hsi-ch'an-yüan 西禪 inside the walled town and spent the night. There were over twenty Zen monks who were extremely unruly men at heart.

---

[806] According to Ono and Hibino, this was Wang Wu-chün 王武俊 (735-801), who was appointed Regional Commander in 784 (cf. also *HTS* 221). General of the Armies (*T'ai-wei* 太尉, here again with *ta* written for *t'ai*), was one of the Three Dukes (*San-kung* 三公), three exalted but not necessarily powerful honorary advisors of the Emperor. Cf. Des Rotours 19.
[807] *DBZ* corrects 主 to 王.
[808] 南樓, which appears on the map in *Chi-fu t'ung-chih* 畿輔通志 (of 1884) 50.27a. The second character has been interpreted as 接 or 楼 in the printed texts.
[809] 行唐, about thirty km. north of Chen-chou (Cheng-ting).

23rd DAY Early in the morning we ate our gruel and then, heading northwest, went twenty-five *li* to the Pa-hui-ssu of Mt. Huang [810] and took our midday rest, eating millet. [811] The people nowadays call it the Shang-fang Common Cloister. [812] For a long time there has been rice and gruel there, and, when men come there, regardless of whether they are clerics or laymen, they are lodged and, if there is any food, it is given to them, and if there is none, none is given. Since neither clerics nor laymen are prevented from coming and lodging there, it is called a common cloister. At the cloister there are two monks, one of whom is pleasant of disposition and the other dour. There is [also] a yellow-haired dog. When it sees a layman, it growls and snaps, with no fear of blows from a stick, but when it sees a monk, whether he be its master or a guest, it wags its tail very submissively.

After our forenoon meal, heading northwest, we entered the mountains, following along a valley. The people nowadays call them the Kuo-hsin 國信 Mountains. From Shang-fang we went on for twenty *li* to the Liu-shih 劉使 Common Cloister and stopped for the night. We then met I-shen 義深 and other monks of the Chin-ko-ssu [813] of Mt. Wu-t'ai who

---

[810] 黄, a little south of Ch'ü-yang 曲陽 (about twenty km. north of Hsing-t'ang), where a Pa-hui-ssu 八會 once stood (cf. Ono and Hibino 269).

[811] *DBZ* suggests 黍飯 for 隶飯.

[812] Shang-fang 上房 appears on the map in *Chi-fu t'ung-chih* 50.40a. From the following description and the subsequent mention of similar common cloisters (*p'u-t'ung-yüan* 普通院), they appear to have been a type of Buddhist inn erected on the approaches to Mt. Wu-t'ai for the convenience of clerical and lay pilgrims. Cf. Ono and Hibino 61-67. It is worth noting that one of the common cloisters Ennin stayed at on the way from Mt. Wu-t'ai to the capital was also called the Shang-fang Common Cloister (see **VII** 5).

[813] 金閣 "Monastery of the Golden Balcony," or "Golden Pavilion," as it is rendered in the case of the famous Japanese Kinkakuji. The Chin-ko-ssu still stands on the northern slope

had been to Shen-chou [814] to get oil and were returning to the mountains with fifty donkeys loaded with hempseed oil 油麻油.

We also saw the monk Chü-chien 巨堅 and three others from the Kuo-ch'ing-ssu [93] of [Mt.] T'ien-t'ai, who are going to Wu-t'ai. They told us that a Japanese monk and his one disciple novice and one servant are at present living at the Kuo-ch'ing-ssu of T'ien-t'ai.[815]

24th DAY It was cloudy. We started out along the mountain valley, going twenty-five li northwest. We met a shepherd driving some five hundred sheep along. Crossing a ridge we reached the Liang-ling 兩嶺 ("Twin Ridge") Common Cloister. The master of the cloister was not there, so we prepared our food ourselves. They have not had gruel or rice at the cloister for some time, and because there has been a plague of insects in recent years, they do not have any provisions now. After our forenoon meal we went up a mountain valley, going thirty li northwest to the Kuo-yüan [816] Common Cloister, where we stopped for the night. It thundered and rained.

---

of the so-called southern terrace of Mt. Wu-t'ai. See map at back of Ono and Hibino. There is a detailed description of the "Golden Balcony" itself below on VII 2.

[814] 深, the modern Shen-hsien, almost 90 km. east of Cheng-ting and over 110 km. air-line distance from where Ennin then was.

[815] This was obviously Ensai and his followers.

[816] 菓菀. The second character is usually pronounced wan, but here it appears to be yüan and used for its homophone 園, making a name meaning "Fruit Orchard," which still appears as a place name southeast of the modern town of Fou-p'ing-hsien 阜平 in the valley of the Sha-ho 沙河 about sixty km. northwest of Hsing-t'ang. Cf. Chi-fu t'ung-chih 50.32b. The Liang-ling ("Twin Ridges") Common Cloister was probably located near the ridge which today forms the border between Fou-p'ing-hsien and the northwestern corner of Hsing-t'ang-hsien. For its location and also references to the famine described in this and the following passage, cf. Ono and Hibino 297.

25th DAY   It rained. Since here, deep in the mountains, there is no gruel or rice, they eat "small beans"[744] for food at the common cloister. From Chao-chou all the way here they have had plagues of locusts the past three or four years, and the five grains have not matured, and provisions are hard to obtain.

After the forenoon meal the rain stopped, and we followed a valley to the west, going thirty *li* to the Chieh 解 Common Cloister. A party of more than a hundred monks, nuns, women, and men on a pilgrimage to Mt. Wu-t'ai lodged with us in the cloister.

26th DAY   It was clear. After eating our gruel, we went twenty *li* along a mountain valley to the Ching-shui 淨水 Common Cloister where we prepared our meal. The cloister was impoverished, and the mountain wind was quite cold. Green pines stood along the ridges. We crossed a double ridge and went thirty *li* west to the T'ang-ch'eng 塘城 Common Cloister. Passing the cloister, we went on west. The ridges are high and the valleys deep. The verdant peaks spew forth clouds, and the valley streams flow in green courses.[817] We went fifteen *li* west from T'ang-ch'eng and at 4 P.M. reached the Lung-ch'üan ("Dragon Spring")[818] Common Cloister, where we stopped for the night. From within the Dragon Hall on a hill behind [the cloister] issues a spring, clear and cold. Since the cloister is close to this spring, they call it the Lung-ch'üan ("Dragon Spring") Common Cloister. The cloister has rice and gruel.

27th DAY   We started out, going west along a mountain valley for twenty *li* to the Chang-hua 張花 Common Cloister, where with nine [other] monks we took our midday rest. The cloister had gruel and rice. After our forenoon meal we went ten *li* along a valley to the Ch'a-p'u 茶鋪

---

[817] Reflecting the green of the wooded slopes. These passages show how well wooded in T'ang times were these now desolate mountains.

[818] 龍泉, probably in the vicinity of the modern Lung-ch'üan-kuan 關, on the headwaters of the Sha-ho just across the border into Hopeh from Mt. Wu-t'ai.

("Tea Shop") Common Cloister. Passing the cloister, we went ten *li* west, crossing Ta-fu 大復 Ridge. East of the ridge the valley streams flow east, and west of the ridge they flow west.[819] We crossed the ridge and descended gradually, sometimes going west and sometimes south. The groves of pines on the peaks and the trees in the valleys grow straight and tall; groves of bamboos and fields of flax are not comparable to them [in straightness]. The mountain cliffs are precipitous and about to touch the Milky Way. The green of the pines reflects the blue [820] of the skies. West of the ridge the leaves are not yet out, and the grass is not yet four inches high. From Ch'a-p'u we went thirty *li* and at dusk reached the Chüeh-shih 角詩 Common Cloister, where we spent the night. The cloister has no gruel or rice.

28th DAY [821]   We entered an open valley and went west for thirty *li*, arriving at the T'ing-tien 停點 Common Cloister at 10 A.M. Before entering the cloister we saw toward the northwest the central terrace,[550] and bowing to the ground, we worshiped it. This then is the region of Monjushiri.[309] There are no trees to be seen on the rounded heights of the five summits, and they look like overturned bronze bowls. On looking at them from afar, our tears flowed involuntarily. The trees and strange flowers are unlike those anywhere else, and it is a most unusual region. This then is the gold-colored world of Mt. Ch'ing-liang,[822] where Monjushiri manifested himself for our benefit.

---

[819] The modern Hopeh-Shansi border follows this watershed, but it is not the divide between the central Shansi valley system and the Hopeh Plain, for the streams that flow west from this ridge actually curve around to the south and cut through the mountains and out to the Hopeh Plain a little north of Shih-chia-chuang.

[820] The frequent identification of blue and green in the Far East makes this a reasonable figure of speech to Chinese and Japanese.

[821] The remainder of the second scroll is repeated in large part at the beginning of the third scroll.

[822] 清凉, another name for Mt. Wu-t'ai. "Gold-colored world" (*konjiki sekai* 金色世界) is a term for the paradise of Monju.

We then entered the T'ing-tien Common Cloister and worshiped the image of the Bodhisattva Monjushiri. In so doing we saw on the wall of the western pavilion an inscription reading, "Reisen,[823] a Japanese Court Priest [824] and Scripture Translating Reverence,[825] reached this monastery [550] on the fifteenth [day] [825a] of the ninth moon of the fifteenth year of Yüan-ho (820)." The monks in the monastery marveled when they saw us Japanese monks arrive and showed us the inscription on the wall. Accordingly, I copied it down. At noon we had our forenoon meal in the dining hall, after which we saw several tens of monks going off toward the southern terrace. At sunset it thundered and rained.

Since we entered the mountains at 4 P. M. on the twenty-third day up until today we have been going along mountain valleys for a total of six days and, without getting through the mountains, have reached Wu-t'ai. Since we left the Mt. Ch'ih Cloister on the nineteenth day of the past second moon right up until now we have gone over 2,300 *li*. Leaving aside rest days, we have been on the road exactly forty-four days and fortunately have been entirely free of illness on the way.

29*th* DAY The T'ing-tien Cloister held a maigre feast for one hundred monks [826] and invited us to take part. Since

[823] 靈仙, mentioned in *SNK* 842 III 6 and IV 12. There we learn that at some earlier date the Japanese Emperor had sent 100 ounces (*liang*) of gold to him at Mt. Wu-t'ai through a P'o-hai embassy but that he was found to have died before the gold reached him. (For more about this incident see below under VII 3.) Reisen went to China with the Japanese embassy of 804 and studied in Ch'ang-an before going to Mt. Wu-t'ai. Cf. Tsuji Zennosuke 辻善之助, *Zōtei Kaigai kōtsu shiwa* 増訂海外交通史話 (Tōkyō, 1932) 73-74.

[824] *Nei-kung-feng* 內供奉 (J. *Naigubu*), a Buddhist office created by the T'ang in 756 and copied by the Japanese in 772. On 841 I 9 Ennin mentions a Taoist Court Priest.

[825] *Hongyō Daitoku* 翻經大德, not a standard title. See note 248.

[825a] *DBZ* and *KIK* print 日 but it is missing in *Tōji*.

[826] There is an extra 齋 in this clause.

Chü-chien, the monk from the Kuo-ch'ing-ssu of T'ai-chou,[93] is returning to his home monastery, I gave him two letters for Ensai Shōnin.[827] After the maigre feast we saw several tens of monks go off on a pilgrimage to the southern terrace.[828] The whole way up it was clear, but the heavens suddenly clouded over. The wind was violent and the clouds dark, and rain and hail fell. In the evening we saw them return with their straw hats smashed by the hail.

FIFTH MOON: 1*st* DAY [829]   It was clear. Intending to go on a pilgrimage of the terraces, we left the donkey we had brought with us at the T'ing-tien Cloister and instructed the Prior monk to arrange for its fodder. From T'ing-tien we went seventeen *li* west and then went fifteen *li* north across a high ridge and, reaching the Chu-lin-ssu,[830] took our midday rest.

After the forenoon meal, we made a pilgrimage around the monastery buildings. There is a place for practicing *hanju.*[831] Formerly a certain Fa-chao Ho-shang [832] called on

---

[827] 上人, a title of respect for a monk.

[828] In the third scroll the following incident is related under the twenty-eighth, indicating that the two references in the second scroll to " several tens of monks " going to the southern terrace on both the twenty-eighth and twenty-ninth may be duplicate statements of a single incident.

[829] June 4, 840. The preceding moon had only twenty-nine days.

[830] 竹林, " Monastery of the Bamboo Grove," which still stands about seven km. south of the western terrace. Cf. Ono and Hibino 57-61 and map at back.

[831] *Hanju dōjō* 般舟道場. *Hanju* or *hanju-zammai* is another name for *jōgyō-zammai* 常行三昧, one of the four traditional religious practices (*zammai*). In this practice the devotee walks for ninety days and nights around an image of Amida while meditating on Amida and calling on his name. Cf. note 284 and Coates and Ishizuka 457. Ennin was to erect a famous hall for the performance of *jōgyō-zammai* within a few years after his return to Japan (cf. Soper, *op. cit.* 151-52, 164).

[832] 法照, who had founded the Chu-lin-ssu. Cf. Ono and Hibino 58, and Coates and Ishizuka 444.

the Buddha's name in this hall. An Imperial rescript gave him the posthumous name of Ta-wu Ho-shang 大悟. He died two years ago.[833] They have now made a representation of him, which they have placed in the hall. They have also drawn a picture of Buddhapāla [834] arriving at Mt. [Wu]-t'ai in the first year of I-feng 儀鳳 (676) and seeing an old man.[835] In the hall of the Hua-yen-yüan 花嚴 there is a single *Kongōkai Mandara*.[277]

2nd DAY   We went to the Chen-yüan [836] Chieh-lü-yüan 戒律 (" Commandments Cloister ") and, ascending to the balcony, worshiped the *mandara* of seventy-two sages, saints, and deities [307] [made] for the benefit [407] of the nation. The coloring is exquisite. Next they opened up the Wan-sheng 萬聖 (" Myriad Saints ") Ordination Platform.[198] It is made of jade and is three feet high and octagonal. The base is filled in with plaster [made from powdered] incense 香泥, and on the platform is spread a silk carpet, fitting the platform perfectly in size. The beams, rafters,[837] and pillars are painted exquisitely. We called on the venerable monk [170] in charge of the platform. His Buddhist name is Ling-chüeh 靈覺, and he is one hundred years old, having been a monk for seventy-two years. His visage is unusual, and he is indeed a Consecrated Reverence.[838] When he saw his guests, he was courteous. I am told that during the sixth moon last year

---

[833] A gloss in *Tōji* suggests that this should be " 200," which *Ikeda* follows. *DBZ* and *KIK* suggest that it might be an error for " 20." Actually Fa-chao had gone to the Wu-t'ai region about seventy years before. Cf. also Ono and Hibino 301.

[834] Also known as Buddhapāli (J. Butsudahari 佛陀波利), a monk originally from Kashmir. Cf. Waley 138, and Coates and Ishizuka 444.

[835] See the story of his meeting Monju in the guise of an old man, recorded on V 23.

[836] Presumably referring to the Chen-yüan period (785-805).

[837] *DBZ* suggests 椽 for 樣.

[838] *Tōdan Daitoku. Tōdan* 登壇, " to mount the platform," means ordination. For *Daitoku* see note 248.

three monks of the Nālanda Monastery [839] in India came to Wu-t'ai and saw a nimbus in the form of a five-colored cloud [840] shining about his person, after which they returned to India.

The Chu-lin-ssu has six cloisters: the Lü-yüan 律 (" Rules Cloister "),[841] the K'u-yüan 庫 (" Living Quarters Cloister "),[118] the Hua-yen-yüan, the Fa-hua-yüan (" Lotus Cloister "), the Ko-yüan 閣 (" Balcony Cloister "), and the Fo-tien-yüan 佛殿 (" Buddha Hall Cloister "). The whole monastery has about forty monks. This monastery does not belong to Wu-t'ai.

FIFTH MOON: 5th DAY   In the monastery they held a maigre feast for 750 monks,[842] which is also being held by various [other] monasteries. The whole thing has been provided by a patron from the Ling-yen-ssu [843] of Ch'i-chou.

THE RITE OF WORSHIPING BUDDHA AT A MAIGRE FEAST IN THE CHU-LIN-SSU.[844]

At noon they struck a bell, and the congregation of monks entered the hall. After the full monks, novices, laymen, children, and women had been seated in rows according to their

---

[839] J. Naranda 那蘭陀, a famous Indian monastery in Magadha.

[840] *Goshikiun enkō* 五色雲圓光. There are various listings of the five colors in Buddhism, but one of the commonest is blue-green, yellow, red, white, and black.

[841] Earlier he called it the Chieh-lü-yüan.

[842] The number 750 is presumably for all the monasteries participating, and not for the Chu-lin-ssu alone. As we see below, laymen, women, and children were also included.

[843] 靈巖 (the second character is miswritten 嚴 in the corresponding place in the third scroll), a famous monastery east of Ch'ang-ch'ing 長清, which is about thirty km. southwest of Ch'i-chou (the modern Tsinan; see note 574) and one of its subprefectures. Cf. *Chi-nan-fu chih* 濟南府志 (1840 ed.) 18.67b and maps at *t'u* 24a and 38b and Ono and Hibino 304.

[844] This and the following section as far as " 14th day " are not found in the third scroll.

ranks, the Leader in Worship [845] struck a mallet and chanted, "Let all be worshipful and pay reverence to the three eternal treasures; [236] let all be widely reflective 普念." Then two junior monks of the monastery, holding golden lotus flowers in their hands, struck gourd-[shaped] cymbals, and three or four men chanted together in Sanskrit.[234] The patron burned incense, and everyone, regardless of whether he was a cleric or layman, man or woman, took his turn at burning incense. After that the Leader in Worship first read the text of offering by the patron and then offered praises [to the Buddha]. Then he chanted, "Let all be widely reflective," and the full monks chanted together, "*Maka-hannya-haramitsu.*" [621]

Next he chanted the names of Buddhas and Bodhisattvas, and the congregation repeated the words, "Together we worship the Buddha Shakamuni,[214] the Buddha Miroku,[655] the Bodhisattva Monjushiri,[309] His Holiness [552] the Bodhisattva Fugen,[286] the myriad Bodhisattvas, the Bodhisattva Jizō,[846] and all the Bodhisattvas and Great Sentient Beings.[847] On behalf of Taishaku, Bonnō, and the other [rulers] of the twenty-eight heavens,[848] we pay reverence to the three

---

[845] *Hyōtanshi* 表歎師, literally, "Express Admiration Leader." Cf. Ono and Hibino 304.

[846] 地藏 (Skr. Kṣitigarbha), especially revered in Japan as the redeemer of the souls of children.

[847] *Makasatta* 摩訶薩 [埵] (Skr. *Mahāsattva*), a term for Bodhisattvas, as the greatest of the sentient beings who have not yet become Buddhas. The third character is missing in *Tōji* the second time the term appears but is printed in *DBZ* and *KIK*.

[848] The twenty-eight Buddhist heavens are the six of the *yokkaiten* 欲界天 (Skr. *kāmadhātu*), the eighteen of the *shikikaiten* 色界天 (Skr. *rūpadhātu*), and the four of the *mushikikaiten* 無色界天 (Skr. *ārūpyadhātu*). Taishaku 帝釋 (here given only as Shaku; Skr. Śakra) is the ruler of the second heaven of the *yokkaiten* (Tōri 忉利; Skr. Trāyastriṃśa), and Bonnō is an abbreviation of Daibontennō 大梵天王, the ruler of the Daibonten (Skr. Mahābrahmā), the third heaven of the *shikikaiten*. Cf. Coates and Ishizuka 93-97.

eternal treasures; on behalf of the lasting prosperity of the holy reign [of the dynasty] 聖化無窮 , we pay reverence to the three eternal [849] treasures; on behalf of the manifold grandeur of today's patron, we pay reverence to the three eternal treasures; on behalf of the monks and our fathers and mothers and all sentient beings of the universe of the Law,[850] we pay reverence to the three eternal treasures."

[The Leader in Worship] struck a mallet and chanted, " Let the prayer for the presentation of food be said," and a monk in a raised seat said the prayer, after which they served the food. The noble and humble, the old and young, clerics and laymen, men and women, all were provided for equally.

After the congregation of monks had eaten the maigre feast, they purified themselves ritually with water,[233] rinsing out their mouths. Then a mallet was struck, and they called on the names of the Buddhas. The Leader in Worship struck the mallet and said, " On behalf of the grandeur of today's patron and the sentient beings of the universe of the Law, we call on the *Maka-hannya-haramitta*," [621] and the crowd said in unison, " We call on the Buddha Shakamuni, the Buddha Miroku, His Holiness the Bodhisattva Monjushiri, the myriad Bodhisattvas, and all the Bodhisattvas and Great Sentient Beings." [847] And so on, repeating his words and calling on the Buddhas together. After they had finished calling on the names of the Buddhas, a mallet was struck, and the congregation dispersed at will.

At sunset it thundered and hail and rain fell.

The Ko-yüan has set up a place of ritual [284] to make offerings to seventy-two sages and saints.[307] Ch'ang-ch'in 常欽, the Prior monk, sent a letter around to inform the various cloisters of this and at the same time invited us Japanese monks. In response to the invitation we went to the ritual place and saw the religious arrangements for worship 禮念法事. Along the walls inside the hall were placed

---

[849] *DBZ* misprints 往 for 住 .
[850] *Hōkai* 法界 (Skr. *Dharmadhātu*) .

in order the portraits of the seventy-two sages and saints. Valuable banners and jewels in all the beautiful colors of the world were spread out and displayed, and carpets of varied colors covered the whole floor. Flowers, lamps, fine incense, tea, medicines, and food had been placed in offering to the saints.

After dusk the full monks assembled, and one of them, mounting to the seat of worship 禮座, first struck a gourd-[shaped] cymbal and then explained the exalted reasons for [holding] this service. One by one he chanted the names of the patrons and the nature of the things they had given, and he called on the names of the Buddhas and Bodhisattvas on behalf of the patrons. Then he supplicated the seventy-two sages and saints, pronouncing the name of each one. Each time, after he had pronounced one of their names, [the monks] would all chant the words, " We merely pray that you be benevolent and pity us and descend to our place of ritual and receive our offerings." After they had stood in worship seventy-two times, he then left his seat for the first time.

Then another monk mounted to the seat [of worship] and offered praises and called on the names of the Buddhas. He supplicated the various Buddhas and Bodhisattvas, saying, " With our whole heart we supplicate the Great Teacher,[140] the Buddha Shakamuni; with our whole heart we supplicate the Buddha Miroku who is to descend and be born [in the world], the Lapis Lazuli Shining Buddha Yakushi of the Twelve Noble Vows,[622] His Holiness the Bodhisattva Monjushiri, His Holiness the Bodhisattva Fugen, and the myriad Bodhisattvas." At the beginning of all [of the supplications] he said, " With our whole heart we supplicate." They then chanted in unison the text for scattering flowers in offering 散花供養之文.[618] There were several tunes.

Next a nun also offered praises exactly as the monk had. Then a monk chanted praises together with the other monks. Then they struck a gourd-[shaped] cymbal and chanted together, " We call on the name of the Buddha Amida." [273] Then they stopped, and next the group of nuns, in place of [851] the monks, did the same thing. Alternating [851] in this manner, they gave praise to the Buddhas. Just at midnight they stopped, and together they left the place of ritual and dispersed on their way back. I have separately copied the texts for the supplications and praises.

7th DAY   The Ko-yüan has a patron who has arranged for a " seventh-day " maigre feast for monks.[852] At the time of the maigre feast the religious procedures were on the whole the same as the previous day, but in the offertory 供養音聲 in the place of ritual at the time of the burning of incense the Leader in Worship did not chant, " Let all be worshipful," etc., but stood and offered praises, and there was another monk who struck the mallet. They performed the other ceremonies and ate according to the rules.

14th DAY   At night Ishō and Igyō,[852a] together with several tens of novices who had come from afar, received full ordination [853] on the white jade [ordination] platform.

16th DAY   Early in the morning we left the Chu-lin-ssu and, following a valley, went ten *li* east and ten *li* toward the northeast to the Ta-hua-yen-ssu [854] and entered the K'u-yüan (" Living Quarters Cloister ") and lodged there. After the forenoon meal we went to the Nieh-p'an-yüan 涅槃 (" Nirvana Cloister ") and saw Abbot [Fa-chien] [855] lectur-

---

[851] *DBZ* suggests 替 for 贊.

[852] Or possibly a " seven-day " maigre feast. Another possibility is that 日 is a copyist's error for 百, and we have " a maigre feast for seven hundred monks." Cf. the opening lines under V 5.

[852a] The first character in Igyō's name is missing in *Tōji* but is printed in *DBZ, KIK,* and *ZZGR.*

[853] *Gusokkai* 具足戒 (Skr. *upasaṃpada*), the full 250 rules for monks.

[854] The ridge running between the northern and eastern terraces is called Hua-yen Ridge (cf. map at back of Ono and Hibino), and from what Ennin tells us of his approach to the Ta-hua-yen-ssu 大花嚴 and his trip from there to the central terrace (V 20), it would seem to have been near this ridge.

[855] Here and in the corresponding place in the third scroll we have

ing on the *Maka-shikan* [331] in a fairly high [two]-storied hall. More than forty monks seated in rows were listening to him lecture. We then saw the Tendai Abbot Chih-yüan Ho-shang [856] in the lecture congregation listening to the *Shikan*. It was impressive and beautiful in the hall beyond description.

When the Abbot said, " I have completed lecturing on the fourth scroll," we waited [857] until he had come down from the lecture [seat] and then went to the room of Chih-yüan Ho-shang to pay him reverence. The Priest inquired after us and was courteous. Abbot Fa-chien,[855] who has recently come from the Western Capital (Ch'ang-an), and Abbot Wen-chien,[856] who has long been at this mountain, and the more than forty auditors at the lecture are all of the Tendai Sect. Meeting together, we inquired after one another and rejoiced over meeting at the place (?) [41] of lecture.

Chih-yüan Ho-shang of his own accord said, " The Learned Doctor [596] Saichō [333] of Japan went to T'ien-t'ai in the twentieth year of Chen-yüan (804) in search of the Law. Lord Lu,[858] the Prefect [412] of T'ai-chou,[93] himself provided him with paper and scribes, and they copied several hundred scrolls which he gave to the Learned Doctor [Sai]chō. The Learned Doctor, on obtaining the commentaries, returned to his native land." Then he asked about the prosperity of the Tendai [Sect] in Japan, and I related in brief how Nan-yo Ta-shih [243] was [re]born in Japan.[335] The congregation rejoiced greatly, and the Abbot [Chih]-yüan, on hearing me

---

the single character *hsien* 賢, but this apparently is the Abbot Fa-chien 法堅 mentioned below, who in the corresponding place in the third scroll is referred to as " the Abbot who had been lecturing." The Nieh-p'an-yüan is not listed among the cloisters of the Ta-hua-yen-ssu on V 2.

[856] On 839 VII 23 Ennin, while at the Mt. Ch'ih Cloister, had been told about Chih-yüan and also Wen-chien, who is mentioned below.

[857] A carelessly copied 待 is misprinted 侍 in *DBZ* and *KIK*.

[858] 陸公, whose full name was Lu Shun 淳 (cf. Ono and Hibino 307).

tell of the [re]birth of Nan-yo Ta-shih [858a] in Japan and the spread of Buddhism there, was extremely happy.

All the monks of the fifteen cloisters of the Ta-hua-yen-ssu regard the Abbot [Chih]-yüan as their master 首座.[81] He receives no alms 施利 and eats but once a day. He never misses the six times for worship and repentance, and he constantly performs the *hokke-zammai*.[284] With his whole heart he has made the " three views " [859] his basic attitudes. Every one of the venerable monks [170] of the monastery pays him honor.

After drinking tea we went to the Nieh-p'an (" Nirvana ") Place of Ritual and worshiped the representation of [the Buddha attaining] Nirvana. The sixteen-foot figure [of the Buddha] lying on his right side beneath a pair of trees in the grove, the figure of Māyā [859a] swooning to the ground in anguish, the Four [Heavenly] Kings [97] and the eight classes of demigods,[241] and a crowd of saints, some holding up their hands and weeping bitterly, some with their eyes closed in an attitude of contemplation, everything that was described in the scriptures, was completely portrayed in these figures.

Next we went to the Pan-jo-yüan 般若 (Hannya-in) and paid reverence to the Abbot Wen-chien. He is of the Tendai Sect and has lectured on the *Shikan* several times and has painted a picture of T'ien-t'ai Ta-shih [140] and has long made offerings to it. We conversed, and he inquired kindly after us and was very courteous.

We also saw a picture of Ta-hsieh Ho-shang,[860] who form-

[858a] The first character in Ta-shih is missing in *DBZ*, *KIK*, and *ZZGR*.

[859] *Sangan* 三觀, which in Tendai are the view that the world is unreal (*kūkan* 空觀), that the world is a temporary phenomenon (*kekan* 假觀), and the middle view that the world is neither unreal nor a temporary phenomenon (*chūkan* 中觀).

[859a] 摩耶, the Buddha's mother.

[860] In the third scroll the name is written 大鞋, which is obviously correct, for the story that follows calls for a name meaning " large shoes," but in the second scroll the second character is written with the forty-fourth radical.

erly performed Buddhist practices on this mountain. He made fifty pilgrimages around the five terraces and lived on the summit of the central terrace for three years, both winter and summer, without descending. Finally, with the aid of His Holiness [Monju],[552] he was able to put on some large shoes. They were a foot high and a foot and a half long, and the larger pair was twenty-five pounds [127] and the smaller ten pounds. At present they are placed in front of the picture. The Priest formerly made 15,000 robes and gave them to 15,000 monks, and he arranged 75,000 offerings [of food for monks].[122] Now [860a] they have made his picture and put it in a high balcony and make offerings to it.

At this Mt. Ch'ing-liang [822] the nights of the fifth moon are very cold, and one normally wears robes lined with wadding.[861] On the ridges and in the valleys trees grow straight, and there is not a single crooked tree. When one enters this region of His Holiness [Monju], if one sees a very lowly man, one does not dare to feel contemptuous, and if one meets a donkey, one wonders if it might be a manifestation of Monju. Everything before one's eyes raises thoughts of the manifestations of Monju. The holy land makes one have a spontaneous feeling of respect for the region.

[END OF] SECOND SCROLL OF THE RECORD OF A PILGRIMAGE
TO CHINA IN SEARCH OF THE LAW

Collated with the manuscript Ken'in[862]

[860a] The character printed 令 in *DBZ, KIK,* and *ZZGR* might better be interpreted as 今.

[861] *Mien-ao-tzu* 綿襖子. This last paragraph is not found in the third scroll.

[862] 兼胤, the copyist of the *Tōji* manuscript. The name and statement of collation do not appear in the printed texts.

RECORD OF

A Pilgrimage to China
in Search of the Law

III

Third Scroll

OF THE RECORD
OF A PILGRIMAGE TO CHINA
IN SEARCH OF THE LAW

28th DAY [821]   We entered an open valley and went west
for thirty *li*, arriving in front of the T'ing-tien Common
Cloister at 10 A. M., and for the first time we saw the summit of the central terrace. This then is Mt. Ch'ing-liang [822]
where Monjushiri resides, the central terrace of Wu-t'ai. We
bowed to the ground and worshiped it from afar, and our
tears rained down involuntarily. The summit of the terrace
as seen from a distance is high and rounded, and there are
no trees to be seen on it.

We then entered the T'ing-tien Common Cloister and
worshiped the image of Monju. We saw on the wall of the
western pavilion an inscription reading:

Reisen,[823] a Japanese Court Priest [824] and Scripture-
Translating Reverence,[825] reached this monastery [550] on the fifteenth day of the ninth moon of the fifteenth year of Yüan-ho
(820).

At noon we went to the dining hall for our forenoon meal.

We saw an image of Monju placed in the seat of the head monk but did not see Binzuru [863] in any seat. Surprised at this, we asked the monks, and they said the various paintings in this mountain were like this.

After the forenoon meal we saw several tens of monks going off toward the southern terrace. The whole way up it was clear, but the heavens suddenly clouded over. The wind was violent and the clouds dark, and hail and rain fell mixed together. In the evening we saw them return with their straw hats smashed by the hail and their whole bodies soaking.[828]

Since we first entered the mountains at 4 P.M. on the twenty-third day of this moon, up until now we have been daily going along mountain valleys, and after six days of this we reached this Wu-t'ai for the first time. Since we left the Mt. Ch'ih Cloister on the nineteenth of the past second moon right up until now we have gone over 2,300 li. Leaving aside rest days, we have been on the road exactly forty-four days, and fortunately the party has been entirely free from illness.

29th DAY There was a maigre feast for one hundred monks in the cloister, and we also attended on invitation. Since Chü-chien, the monk from the Kuo-ch'ing-ssu of T'ai-chou,[93] is returning to his home monastery after a pilgrimage to the terraces, I gave him two letters for Ensai Shōnin.

FIFTH MOON: 1st DAY [829] It was clear. Starting off on our pilgrimage of Wu-t'ai, we went about seventeen li west from the T'ing-tien Common Cloister and then went fifteen li northward across a high ridge and, reaching the Chu-lin-ssu,[830] took our midday rest. We saw several tens of novices who had come from the various prefectures to receive ordination and were waiting at the monastery for the day.

---

[863] 賓頭盧 (Skr. Piṇḍola), the first of the sixteen saints (*rakan*; see note 763). In China and Japan an image of Binzuru was traditionally placed in the dining halls of Buddhist monasteries, but this was not the practice at Mt. Wu-t'ai at this time. Cf. Ono and Hibino 300.

After the forenoon meal we made a pilgrimage around the monastery. There is a place for practicing *hanju*.[831] Formerly a certain Fa-chao Ho-shang [832] performed the religious practice of calling on the Buddha's name (*nembutsu-zammai*) in this hall. An Imperial rescript gave him the posthumous name of Ta-wu Ho-shang. It is close to two years since he died.[833] They have now made a representation of him, which they have placed in the hall. They have also drawn a picture of Buddhapāla [834] arriving at the entrance to the mountains in the first year of I-feng (676) and seeing an old man.[835] In the Buddha Hall of the Hua-yen-yüan there is a single *Kongōkai Mandara*.[277]

2nd DAY We went to the Chen-yüan [836] Chieh-lü-yüan and, ascending to the balcony, worshiped the *mandara* of seventy-two sages, saints, and deities [made] for the benefit of the nation. The coloring is exquisite. Next they opened up the Wan-sheng Ordination Platform, and we looked around. It is made entirely of white jade and is three feet high and octagonal. The base of the platform is filled in with plaster [made from powdered] incense, and on the platform is spread a silk carpet of five colors, also octagonal and made to fit the platform exactly. The venerable monk [170] in charge of the platform has the Buddhist name of Ling-chüeh, and he is one hundred years old, having been a monk for seventy-two years. His visage is unusual, and he is indeed a Consecrated Reverence.[838] When he saw his guests, he was courteous. I am [told] [863a] that during the sixth moon last year three Learned Doctors [596] from the Nālanda Monastery [839] in India came on a pilgrimage to Wu-t'ai and saw a nimbus in the form of a five-colored cloud [840] shining about his person, after which they returned to India.

The Chu-lin-ssu has six cloisters, the Lü-yüan,[841] the K'u-yüan, the Hua-yen-yüan, the Ko-yüan, and the Fo-tien-yüan.[864] The whole monastery has about forty monks. This monastery does not belong to Wu-t'ai.

[863a] 說 is missing in *Tōji*, though it appears in the printed texts.
[864] The Fa-hua-yüan is omitted in this listing. See the corresponding passage in the second scroll.

FIFTH MOON: 5th DAY   They had a maigre feast for 750 monks,[842] which is also being held in various [other] monasteries. The whole thing has been provided by a patron from the Ling-yen-ssu [843] of Ch'i-chou. In the evening they performed the act of adoration.[865]

14*th* DAY   At night Ishō and Igyō, together with several tens of others, received full ordination [853] on the white jade [ordination] platform.

16*th* DAY   Early in the morning we left the Chu-lin-ssu and, ascending a valley, went ten *li* east and more than ten *li* toward the northeast to the Ta-hua-yen-ssu [854] and entered the K'u-yüan and lodged there. After the forenoon meal we went to the Nieh-p'an-yüan and saw Abbot [Fa-chien] [855] lecturing on the *Shikan* [331] from a high upper story. He was about to finish lecturing on the fourth scroll. More than thirty monks were listening to him together. We then saw Chih-yüan Ho-shang [856] in the lecture congregation listening to the *Shikan.* The inside and outside of the hall were impressive and beautiful beyond description.

We waited until [the lecturer] had come down from the lecture [seat] and then paid reverence to Chih-yüan Ho-shang and the Abbot who had been lecturing [855] and the monks who had been listening. They inquired kindly after us and were courteous. The Abbot has recently come from the Western Capital (Ch'ang-an). Abbot Wen-chien, who has long been at this mountain, has previously lectured on the *Shikan* and the *Lotus Sutra* several times. The auditors are the disciples of [Chih]-yüan Ho-shang, and no auditors seem to have come from anywhere else.

Chih-yüan Ho-shang said, " In the twentieth year of Chen-yüan (804) I saw the Learned Doctor Saichō of Japan go to T'ien-t'ai in search of the Law. Lord Lu,[858] the Prefect of T'ai-chou, himself provided him with paper, ink, and scribes, and they copied several hundred scrolls, which he gave to the Learned Doctor [Sai]chō. The Learned Doctor also ob-

---

[865] *Zuiki* 隨喜, to rejoice in the good works of others, the third of the five acts of penitence (*goke* 五悔).

tained [official] seals [for them] [866] and returned to his homeland." Then he asked about the prosperity of the Tendai Sect
in Japan. Accordingly, I related in brief about Nan-yo Ta-
shih's [243] [re]birth in Japan [335] and the spread of Buddhism.
[Chih]-yüan Ho-shang and the group were extremely happy.

All the many monks of the twelve [867] cloisters of the Ta-
hua-yen-ssu regard [Chih]-yüan Ho-shang as their master.
The Priest receives no alms and eats but once a day. His
observance of the rules is pure and noble; he never once
misses the six times for worship and repentance; and he constantly performs the *hokke-zammai*.[284] With his whole heart
he has made the " three views " [859] his basic attitudes. His
spirit surpasses the bounds of mere matter. Every one of the
venerable monks [170] of the various monasteries of the whole
mountain pays him honor. The fundamental purpose of his
whole life is to be able to see the Bodhisattva Fugen and
to bear witness [to the efficacy of] *hokke-zammai*.

After drinking tea we went to the Nieh-p'an (" Nirvana ")
Place of Ritual and paid reverence to the representation of
the Buddha attaining Nirvana. The sixteen-foot figure [of
the Buddha] lying on his right side beneath a pair of trees,
the figure of Lady Māyā [859a] swooning to the ground in anguish, the Four [Heavenly] Kings,[97] the eight classes of demi-
gods,[241] the heavenly beings 天人, and a crowd of saints,
some holding up their hands and weeping bitterly, some with
their eyes closed in an attitude of contemplation—everything
was made [868] as in the scriptures.

Next we went to the Pan-jo-yüan and paid reverence to
Abbot Wen-chien and to the picture of T'ien-t'ai Ta-shih.[140]

---

[866] *Inshin* 印信 can mean the seal-printed formulae and designs
of Esoteric Buddhism, but, from the use of this word twice in
connection with somewhat similar documents on V 18, it would
seem to mean the official seal of the Prefect of T'ai-chou.
[867] " Fifteen " in the second scroll.
[868] Four times within four pages *Tōji* has 作 preceded by a character interpreted as 祖 in *DBZ* and *KIK* and as 担 in *ZZGR*.
Since in its last three uses the combination clearly refers to the
making of a figure in the round, it may be a copyist's erroneous

Abbot [Wen]-chien rejoiced without end [over our coming] and said, " This monastery holds two lectures to propagate Tendai teachings. I had a feeling that we should see monks from distant lands coming here to seek Tendai teachings, and there has indeed been a great fulfillment of my premonitions."

We also saw a picture of Ta-hsieh Ho-shang,[860] who formerly performed Buddhist practices on this mountain. He made fifty pilgrimages around the five terraces and also once lived on the summit of the central terrace for three years, both winter and summer, without descending. Finally, with the aid of His Holiness [Monju],[552] he put on some large shoes. They were a foot and a half high,[869] and the larger pair was twenty-five pounds [127] and the smaller ten pounds. They are to be found in front of his picture. The Priest once made 15,000 robes and gave them to 15,000 monks, and he arranged 75,000 offerings [of food for monks].[122] Now [860a] they have placed his picture in a high balcony and make offerings to it.[870]

17th DAY I presented to Chih-yüan Ho-shang the thirty questions [400] from the Enryakuji, asking him for explanations, but [Chih]-yüan Ho-shang said that, since he had been told that Mt. T'ien-t'ai had already resolved these doubts, it would not be proper to resolve them again, and so he was not willing to accept them.[871]

In the evening I went with several other monks up to the P'u-sa-t'ang-yüan 苹堂 (" Cloister of the Bodhisattva Hall ")

---

rendition of 揑 " to knead." (Cf. the writing of 湼 in *Tōji* 8.3.) In that case, the portrayal of the Nirvana scene was also a plastic work of art rather than a painting. In the case of the image of Monju, the story clearly has reference to a casting process.

[869] Obviously a contraction of " a foot high and a foot and a half long," as given in the second scroll.

[870] This concludes the section which largely duplicates the second scroll.

[871] On 839 II 27 Ennin recorded that he had entrusted these questions to Ensai to take to Mt. T'ien-t'ai. On 840 V 18 we learn that the answers had been sent to Mt. Wu-t'ai, apparently to inform the branch monasteries of the decisions of the home monastery.

and saw the Devotions Priest.[337] He is seventy years old, but at first glance could be around forty. They say that his being ripe of age but hale and hearty is because he has the power of " devotion." [337] We opened the hall and worshiped an image of His Holiness [872] the Bodhisattva Monju. Its appearance is solemn and majestic beyond compare. The figure riding on a lion fills the five-bay [873] hall. The lion is supernatural. Its body is majestic, and it seems to be walking, and vapors come from its mouth. We looked at it for quite a while, and it looked just as if it were moving.

The venerable monk told us that, when they first made the Bodhisattva, they would make it and it would crack. Six times they cast [868] it, and six times it cracked to pieces. The master [874] was disappointed and said, " Being of the highest skill, I am known throughout the empire, and all admit my unique ability. My whole life I have cast [868] Buddhist images, and never before have I had them crack. When making the image this time, I observed religious abstinence [875] with my whole heart and used all the finesse of my craft, wishing to have the people of the empire behold and worship it and be specially moved to believe, but now I have made it six times, and six times it has completely cracked to pieces. Clearly it does not meet the desire of His Holiness [Monju]. If this be correct, I humbly pray that His Holiness the Bodhisattva Monju show his true appearance to me in person. If I gaze directly on his golden countenance, then I shall copy it [876] to make [the image]." When he had finished

---

[872] The 聖 is misplaced in *DBZ* and *KIK*. See note 552.

[873] 五間, indicating a building with a length of five bays between six main columns.

[874] *Po-shih* (J. *hakase*; see note 424), normally a title for official scholars, is on occasion used for other " experts," such as the sculptor or bronze-caster in this case. The man's name is supposed to have been An-sheng 安生 and the incident to have occurred around 710 (cf. Ono and Hibino 311).

[875] *Saikai* 齋戒.

[876] An illegible character, looking like an abbreviation for 與, appears at this point.

making this prayer, he opened his eyes and saw the Bodhi-sattva Monju riding on a gold-colored lion right before him. After a little while [Monju] mounted on a cloud of five colors [840] and flew away up into space. The master, having been able to gaze on [Monju's] true appearance, rejoiced, [but also] wept bitterly, knowing then that what he had made had been incorrect. Then, changing the original appearance [of the image], he elongated or shortened, enlarged or diminished it [as necessary], so that in appearance it exactly resembled what he had seen, and the seventh time he cast [868] the image it did not crack and everything was easy to do, and all that he desired was fulfilled. After he had made this image, he placed it in the hall, and with tears welling up in his dewy eyes, he said, " Marvelous! What has never been seen before, I have now been able to see. I pray always to be the disciple of Monjushiri, generation after generation and rebirth after rebirth." And so saying, he died.

Later this image emitted light from time to time and continually manifested auspicious signs. Each time there was a sign, it was recorded in detail and reported to the throne, and on Imperial command Buddhist scarves [188] were bestowed. The one which is at present seen draped on the body of the Bodhisattva is one of these. Because of this, each year an Imperial Commissioner 勅使 sends one hundred Buddhist scarves, which are bestowed on the monks of the monastery, and each year the Imperial Commissioner on separate Imperial command sends incense, flowers, precious baldachins, pearl-[decorated] banners and baldachins, jades, jewels, precious crowns of the " seven treasures," [877] engraved golden incense burners, large and small mirrors, flowered carpets, white cotton cloth,[878] marvelous imitation flowers and fruits, and the like. A great many of these have already accumulated and are displayed in the hall. But this is not all, the

[877] 七寶, which now means cloisonné, in traditional Buddhist terminology meant the seven precious metals and stones, such as gold, silver, and lapis lazuli.
[878] *Pai-tieh* 白氎, thought to have been a type of cotton fabric which was imported into China in T'ang times.

remainder being in the storehouse, put away for the present. The things sent yearly by various other official or private patrons from the provinces, prefectures, or regional commanderies 府 are quite beyond count. When the monasteries of Wu-t'ai now make images of the Bodhisattva Monju, they always [make them] resembling this holy [879] image, but they all are no more than one-hundredth [as grand]. So we were told.

Inside [880] the hall a baldachin of the " seven treasures " hangs over the head of the Bodhisattva, and flowered banners of rare colors and strange bejeweled chaplets and the like are displayed all over the hall, and there are large and small mirrors of gorgeous design quite beyond count.

We went out north of the hall, where we saw in the distance the northern and eastern terraces, with their rounded summits soaring high, completely devoid of trees. The short grass has coloring, and seen from a distance there are autumn colors in the midst of summer. We went back to the front of the hall and saw in the distance the southern terrace which is also without trees. The summit of the terrace stands out alone, touching the blue sky and towering above the other peaks. The western terrace is cut off by the central terrace and cannot be seen.

In front of the Bodhisattva Hall and on the edge of a cliff is a three-bay pavilion. It is floored with boards, and on the four sides are high railings. Below the pavilion is a thousand-fathom [881] precipice. The venerable monk told us that long ago the Japanese Learned Doctor [596] Reisen [823] saw a myriad of Bodhisattvas from this pavilion.

After we had made our rounds of worship, we went to the Ko-yüan and saw Abbot Hsüan-liang 玄亮 , who has been lecturing on the *Lotus Sutra* and T'ien-t'ai [Ta-shih's] commentaries on it [331] since the fourth moon. The group of

---

[879] *DBZ* corrects *Tōji* by reversing the order of 聖此.

[880] The 外 in this phrase may be a copyist's error.

[881] *Jen* 刃, standing for its homophone 仞 (as printed in *DBZ* and *KIK*), a measure sometimes defined as eight feet.

auditors numbers more than forty, all of whom are disciples of [Chih]-yüan Ho-shang. In the morning session they lecture on the *Lotus Sutra* in the Ko-yüan and in the evening session on the *Shikan* [331] in the Nieh-p'an-yüan. The congregations of both cloisters go back and forth to listen, and a great many come from various other cloisters to listen. Hung-chi 洪基, the Superior [81] monk of the monastery, after consulting with [Chih]-yüan Ho-shang, asked the two Abbots [882] to hold these two [sets of] lectures. One can truly speak of the Ta-hua-yen-ssu of Mt. Wu-t'ai as in the Tendai tradition 流.

We went up to the balcony with a group of monks and paid reverence to the relics.[407] Inside and outside, the balcony was impressive, and the many treasures all resembled those in the Bodhisattva Hall. We saw the skull of a Byakushi Buddha.[883] It is white and black in color and in appearance resembles Japanese pumice stone, but the inside of the bones is hard. It was roughly as large as a bowl of [a capacity of] two large *sheng*.[217] We saw it to be the skull above the forehead, on top of which white hair was growing about five inches long, apparently grown out since it had been shaved. It had been brought by a monk from the Western Lands [884] during the Chen-kuan 貞觀 period (627-650). There also was a *Lotus Sutra* in Indian format,[885] bones of the Buddha placed in a lapis lazuli bottle, a *Lotus* [*Sutra*] in golden characters, and a *Lotus* [*Sutra*] in small characters. They were most exquisite. In front of the balcony stands a two-storied octagonal pagoda,[730a] which is very impressive and beautiful. Beneath it, buried in the ground, is placed a

---

[882] Presumably Hsüan-liang and Fa-chien (the latter having been mentioned on V 16).

[883] *Byakushi-butsu* 辟支佛 (Skr. *Pratyeka-buddha*), "self-enlightened ones," one of the four categories of enlightened beings. Cf. Coates and Ishizuka 428.

[884] *Hsi-kuo* 西國, meaning India and other lands west of China.

[885] *Bonkō* 梵夾, a text written on *tāla* leaves and placed between boards in the Indian manner. Such a book naturally must have come from India.

pagoda of King Aśoka,[886] which they do not let people see. It is one of the 84,000 pagodas made by King Aśoka.

Next we went to the Shan-chu-ko-yüan 善住閣 and performed the act of adoration.[865] There are more than fifty Zen monks, all of whom have woolen robes and priestly staves 錫杖. All have come from various other places on pilgrimages.[887] On Imperial command a Place of Ritual for the Protection of the State [887a] has been established here, and a monk of the Tendai Sect is lecturing there on the *Shibun-ritsu*.[330] He too is a disciple of [Chih]-yüan Ho-shang.

18*th* DAY At the invitation of the Prior of the Shan-chu-ko-[yüan], we went there and had our midday rest and saw a letter brought from the Kuo-ch'ing-ssu of T'ai-chou. The thirty questions [400] from the Enryakuji to Mt. T'ien-t'ai, which I, when previously at Ch'u-chou,[871] had entrusted to the Student Monk Ensai Shōnin,[827] have already been settled by Abbot ... hsiu [888] of the Kuo-ch'ing-ssu.[93] Then the seal [866] of T'ai-chou was asked for, and the Prefect affixed his seal to it. Abbot Ching-wen of the Hsiu-ch'an-ssu [888a] had copied this in detail and sent it to Mt. [Wu]-t'ai to spread the virtues of Tendai. Abbot ... hsiu of [Mt.] T'ien-t'ai had also settled [889] [the questions in] the letter which Mugyō Kashō [115]

---

[886] 阿育王, the great Indian champion of Buddhism of the third century B.C.

[887] *DBZ* suggests that the first of the two 者 which end the sentence may be an error for 看.

[887a] Chen-kuo-tao-ch'ang 鎮國道場 (see note 284 and cf. Ono and Hibino 311).

[888] Probably the Abbot Kuang-hsiu of the Ch'an-lin-ssu, about whom Ennin was told on 839 Int. I 19.

[888a] Probably the same Ching-wen whom Ennin met in Yang-chou and who, after following Ennin from Yang-chou to Ch'u-chou, returned to Yang-chou on 839 III 4 in order to accompany Ensai to Mt. T'ien-t'ai. Hsiu-ch'an-ssu 修禪 was an old name for the Ch'an-lin-ssu (cf. Ono and Hibino 312), which Ennin recorded as Ching-wen's home monastery on 839 Int. I 19 and III 3.

[889] The printed texts have dropped the character 及 from this passage.

had sent to [Mt.] T'ien-t'ai.[404] The letter asking for the seal of the prefecture, the decision of the Prefect of T'ai-chou, and the words of the seal [866] had all been copied in detail and sent here.

20*th* DAY For the first time we went on a trip to the terraces. From the [Ta]-hua-yen-ssu we went west up a slope for about seven *li* to the Wang-tzu-ssu, where we drank tea, and then westward up a slope for six or seven *li* to the Wang-hua-ssu,[889a] and again west up a slope for over ten *li* to the central terrace. On the southern side of the terrace stands the Ch'iu-yü-yüan 求雨 ("Cloister for Seeking Rain"). From the cloister we went about a half *li* up to the summit of the terrace. On the summit toward the south are three iron pagodas, all without stories, finial rings, or the like. In shape they are exactly like inverted bells. It would take four men to reach around them. The central pagoda is square and about ten feet high, but the two on either side are round, and both are about eight feet high. They were built by the Empress 天子, Dame Wu,[890] to guard Wu-t'ai. Dame Wu was the Empress Tse-t'ien.

North of the iron pagodas is a hall of four bays in which are placed images of Monjushiri and the Buddha. A *li* and a half north of here is the center of the summit of the terrace, where there is the Jade Flower Pool.[889a] Its four sides are each about forty feet, and it is called the Dragon Pool 龍池.[472] In the center of the pool on a small island is a little hall in

[889a] *Shan-hsi t'ung-chih* 山西通志 (1734) 57.5b identifies the Wang-tzu-ssu 王子 as the later Shou-ning-ssu 壽寧. Wang-hua-ssu 王花 probably is an error for Yü-hua-ssu 玉 ("Jade Flower Temple"; see the "Jade Flower Pool" mentioned later in the account), which is mentioned as being on the central terrace in *Shan-hsi t'ung-chih* 57.8a. Cf. also Ono and Hibino 316.

[890] 武婆, evidently a vulgar name for Tse-t'ien 則天, who is also known as the Empress Wu. She was a great patron of Buddhism and the virtual ruler of China from about 656 until shortly before her death at the age of eighty-three (Chinese count) in 705. She even attempted to supplant the ruling house of T'ang with her own family, and she reigned in her own name after 690. Cf. Ono and Hibino 316.

which is placed an image of Monju. The people nowadays
call it the Dragon Hall. The water of the pool is clear and
about three feet deep. From the bank one sees through it to
the sand on the bottom, and it is clear, without any dirt or
grass.

The summit of the terrace is level, and the circumference
might be something over one hundred *chō*.[21] Soaring high,
it rises alone, sticking out like an awl.[891] The terrace is
round and lofty. From it one can see the other four terraces in the distance. The western and northern terraces are
rather close to the central terrace. If you go down from the
central terrace and northward up a slope, you will come to
the southern edge of the northern terrace, and if you go
down from the central terrace and westward up a slope, you
will come to the eastern edge of the western terrace. The
three terraces are close together and connected, but the
eastern and southern terraces are both about fifty *li* from
the central terrace.[892] From the eastern foot of the central
terrace a long ridge continues with ups and downs and various twists for fifty *li* toward the south, where it connects
with the northwestern foot of the southern terrace. At the
northeastern foot of the northern terrace a ridge sinks and
then rises again and continues up and down unevenly for
over forty *li* toward the east, where it connects with the
western foot of the eastern terrace.

Thus, the five terraces are high and stand out above the
mass of ridges. The five terraces are five hundred *li* in circumference, and out beyond them there are high peaks, one
after the other, rising high above the intervening valleys.
They are in the form of a wall around the five terraces. These
peaks vary [in height], but they are densely wooded, and only
the five summits are quite bare of trees from halfway up to
the top.

---

[891] The figure is as unusual as the character for awl 雙, which,
however, is clearly written.
[892] Actually they are about eight and eighteen km. respectively
air-line distance from the central terrace.

Now, the central terrace [893] is in the center of the [other] four terraces. All over the terrace water bubbles up out of the ground and soft [893a] grass grows over an inch long, luxuriant and thick, covering the ground. When one treads on it, it gives, but when one raises one's foot, it springs up again. At each step the water dampens [one's feet], and it is as cold as ice. Here and there are small hollows, all filled with water. All over the terrace are sand and stones, and there are innumerable stone pagodas scattered about. The fine and soft grass grows between the moss. Although the ground is damp, there is no mud, and because of the luxuriance of the spreading roots of the moss and soft grass, the shoes and feet of the traveler are not soiled.

There are rare flowers of strange colors blooming all over the western slope. From the valley to the summit there are flowers everywhere, like a spread-out brocade. Their incense is fragrant and perfumes men's clothing. They say that in the present fifth moon it is still cold, and the flowers are not fully out, but that in the sixth and seventh moons the flowers will be even more luxuriant. To see the colors of these flowers is a new experience for man. From the summit of the terrace eastward down the slope about a half *li* is the P'u-t'i-ssu.[894] In summer it has gruel and rice to offer to clerics and laymen going around the terraces.

From in front of the iron pagodas we went west on a gradually descending path for over ten *li* and then down an abrupt slope for about two *li* and then up a slope again toward the west for about a half *li* and reached the Offering Cloister [895] of the western terrace. Behind the cloister are

---

[893] *DBZ* corrects 堂 to 臺.

[893a] A copyist's repetition of 地上軟 is not shown in the printed texts.

[894] 菩提 (J. *bodai*; Skr. *bodhi*), meaning "enlightenment." In *Tōji* the characters for P'u-t'i are actually written with a single abbreviation for the two.

[895] Kung-yang-yüan (J. Kuyōin) 供養院 , apparently a name for the hospices near the summits of the various terraces, where "offerings" of food were provided for monks and other pilgrims. See note 122.

three large and precipitous peaks. The three rise up together, steep and straight. They are called the Incense Mountains.[896] Long ago an Indian monk came and, on seeing these three peaks, said, " When I was in the Lands of the West,[884] I lived for long in the Incense Mountains. Now, arriving here, I again see the Incense Mountains. Have they suddenly manifested themselves here? "

From the Offering Cloister we went westward up a slope for five or six *li* to the summit of the western terrace. The summit of the terrace is level, and it is about ten *chō* [21] in circumference. In shape the terrace is narrow from north to south and broad from east to west. The east and west ends look across at each other, the east end narrow and the west end broad. In the center of the terrace summit there is another Dragon Pool, which might be about fifty feet on each of its four sides. In the center of the pool there is a four-bay Dragon Hall, in which an image of Monju has been placed. Southeast of the pool is one of Tse-t'ien's [890] iron pagodas, round in shape and without stories. It is about five feet high and about twenty feet in circumference. The moss, soft grass, boulders,[897] stone pagodas, and strange flowers and grasses are no different [from those] on the central terrace. Water bubbles up from the ground and lies hidden under the grass or collects in hollows. On three sides are steep slopes, but on the eastern side it falls away gradually and connects with the base of the central terrace.

We went westward from the terrace down a slope for five or six *li*. On the brink of a valley is the place where Monju talked with Yuima.[898] Two large cliffs rise high, facing each other, one on the south and one on the north. They are each about thirty feet high. Both are flat on top, and both have great stone seats. Tradition has it that this is the place where

---

[896] Kōsen or Kōzan 香山, a name which appears in Buddhist texts and which has been identified with various different ranges in northern India and Tibet. Cf. Ono and Hibino 316.

[897] *KIK* suggests that the first character in 槃石 stands for its homophone 磐.

[898] Cf. Ono and Hibino 317-18 and see note 138.

the Bodhisattva Monjushiri saw and talked with Yuima.
Between the two stone seats on the rocks below are the foot-
prints of a lion, trod into the surface of the rock about one
inch deep. In front of the cliffs is a storied building of six
bays, built facing the east, in the south end of which has been
placed an image of Monju riding on a pair of lions.

At the east end has been placed an image of Yuima seated
on a square seat. He has the appearance of an old man. The
hair of his head is tied in two bunches, and the color of his
hood [898a] is pure white. It hangs over toward the front, as if
he were wearing a lotus blossom on his head. He wears a
yellow and scarlet robe and a white skirt, and a fur garment
is thrown over his robe. The color of the fur is variegated,
being red (brown), white, and black. His two arms are not
in the sleeves of the fur. His right knee is bent, and [his
right foot] rests on the seat, while his left knee is straight,
and [his left foot] placed on the ground.[899] His right elbow
rests on a stand [900] with the palm of his hand upwards and
the five fingers extended. His left hand holds a chowry,[611]
and the arm presses down on his left knee. He has his mouth
open, showing his teeth, looking as if he were talking or
laughing. Right in front of his seat there is an angel [901] on
the west side and a Bodhisattva on the east side, standing
and holding in his hand an alms bowl filled with food.

In front of this storied building and facing it is another
storied building of six bays. People say that it was made after
they had seen how things looked at the time of the manifestation [of Monju]. About one hundred paces east of the storied

---

[898a] *DBZ* suggests that 懂 is an error for 幒.

[899] 座上 presumably is an error for 座下 or 地上, because, if
seated, he could not have had one leg straight and at the same
time placed on the seat.

[900] *DBZ* suggests 案 for the same character written with the
" hand " radical in *Tōji*.

[901] *Tennyo* 天女 (Skr. *devakanyā*), " heavenly females," the
feminine creatures of the six heavens of the *yokkaiten* (see note
848).

building there is the Pool of the Eight Virtues.[902] The water bubbles out from the base of the great cliff. We went around looking [at everything] until night and then went back to the Offering Cloister [895] and spent the night.

21st DAY   After the forenoon meal we went back to the P'u-t'i-ssu of the central terrace and drank tea. We saw far off to the northeast a whitish silver color covering an area of several tens of chō,[21] deep at the bottom of a valley. People said that this is snow which does not melt year after year and remains frozen for a thousand years and piles up in a frozen mass. The valley is deep and shaded, and the rays of the sun are cut off by the cliff in front, so that they never shine on [the snow]. As a result, ever since antiquity there has never been a time when the snow melted at all. The ridge in front of the valley is the eastern foot of the central terrace.

From the P'u-t'i-ssu we went north along the eastern edge of the central terrace and continued on down a slope for about ten li and then again went up a slope for over ten li to the northern terrace. The summit of the terrace is about six chō in circumference and is round in shape. On the south side of the summit [903] is a Dragon Hall, and in the hall there is a pool. Its waters are deep and black, filling the hall, pure and limpid, and dividing it into three parts. The central section is the Palace of the Dragon King 龍王宮,[472] and an image of the Dragon King has been placed looking down on the waters of the pool. A bridge has been built across the pool to the Dragon King's seat. He is the King of the five hundred poisonous dragons 毒龍 of the five terraces. Each terrace has one hundred poisonous dragons, and all of them regard this Dragon King as their master. This Dragon King and his people (i. e., the poisonous dragons) were subjugated by Monju and, being converted, do not dare to do evil, it is

---

[902] Pa-kung-te-ch'ih (J. Hachi-kudoku-chi) 八功德池, the name of a pool in paradise. A Pa-kung-te-shui 水 is shown on the east side rather than the west of the western terrace on a map in Shan-hsi t'ung-chih 1.27a.

[903] Tōji has an erroneous mark of repetition following 頂.

said. To the right and left of the Dragon Palace but separated from it by board fences are placed images of Monju.

In front of the Dragon Hall is an Offering Cloister,[895] where we saw a monk who has not eaten rice 不飯 for three years and eats but once a day, consuming mud and earth for his forenoon meal. He has vowed not to come down from the summit of the terrace for three years. He has several disciples. In front of the cloister one looks down into a deep valley.[904] The side of the summit is rugged and might be a thousand fathoms [881] [deep]. This valley is the place where Monju once made manifest the "Treasured Tower of the Golden Bell" 金鍾寶樓 . At present they call it the Bell Tower Valley. The western end of the valley is the base of the eastern edge of the central terrace. South of the valley is a high ridge, the northern edge of which is extremely steep and plunges to the valley floor. The ice of a thousand years lies in the shady depths, glistening brightly. Toward the southeast we saw at a distance the Ta-hua-yen-ssu.

In the center of the terrace is an iron pagoda of Tse-t'ien,[890] and there are many stone pagodas around it. Soft grass and moss cover the ground everywhere, and every three or four paces one comes on small pools, which are numberless. They are called Dragon Pools. The water bubbles up from their sandy bottoms, clear and shallow.

Due north and due east the sides [of the terrace] are steep and high, looking down into deep valleys. The valley on the north is called Sung Valley.[550] This is the place where formerly a monk, in accordance with [the teachings of] Chih-che [905] of T'ien-t'ai, performed *hokke-zammai* [284] and [other] religious

---

[904] The translation of these last two sentences is based on the assumption that the second 院 is an erroneous duplication. The punctuation in the printed texts, however, calls for the following translation: "There are several subsidiary cloisters (or 'cloisters for disciples' 弟子院). The front cloister looks down into a deep valley." It seems improbable that, if there were several cloisters on top of the terrace, Ennin would have had no more to say about them than this.

[905] 智者, a name for Chih-i (T'ien-t'ai Ta-shih). See note 140.

practices and, worshiping and repenting, was able to see the Bodhisattva Monju and a Many Treasured Pagoda.[906]

Although the southern face [of the terrace] is steep,[907] there is a path up which one can scramble. The northwestern side slopes down gradually, forming a skirt ending in a deep valley. On the eastern end of the summit of the terrace is a high mound called the Terrace of the Saints.[763] The whole terrace is devoid of trees.

From the Terrace of the Saints we went down toward the southeast. Beside the path are many burnt rocks covering the ground. Both square and round, they are in the form of a stone wall which is piled high with burnt stones. This is a place which was turned into a Hell. In ancient times a Prefect of Tai-chou [908] who was violent in character did not believe in karma. He had heard that there were Hells, but he did not believe it. While he was wandering in appreciation [of nature] around the terraces, looking about, he came to this place. Suddenly [909] he saw violent flames consuming the cliffs and rocks and black smoke billowing up to heaven. The burning rocks and fiery coals, glowing brightly, made a wall around him, and devils [910] appeared before him, angry and lamenting. The Prefect was afraid and submitted to the will

---

[906] *Tahōtō* 多寶塔, a pagoda containing the remains of a Buddha known as Tahō Nyorai (see note 237), which is said to have appeared floating in the air while the Buddha was preaching on the *Lotus Sutra*. When *Tahōtō* are erected in imitation of the original one, they are usually constructed with a square lower story and a rounded upper story.

[907] The first 路 in this sentence is probably a copyist's error.

[908] 代, the present Tai-hsien, about sixty km. west of the Wu-t'ai region and in T'ang times, the prefectural capital for the area. Tai is also used as a general name for the northern Shansi area. Variant accounts of this "Hell" on Mt. Wu-t'ai are told in Ono and Hibino 319.

[909] An unusual character in *Tōji* is interpreted as 忩 in *KIK* and 急 in *ZZGR*. From the context it would seem to be the latter or else a variant of 忽.

[910] 獄率 is undoubtedly an error for its homophone *gokusotsu* 獄卒, which the printed texts give without comment.

of His Holiness the Bodhisattva Monjushiri, whereupon the fierce flames disappeared, but their remains are still here today. The burnt rocks are piled up into a wall, which is about fifty feet in circumference and is filled with black stones.

22nd DAY After our [morning] gruel, we went along the eastern side of the northern terrace toward the northeast, continuing down a slope and along a ridge to the east for about twenty *li* to the Shang-mi 上米 Common Cloister. In the hall I suddenly saw five beams of light 五道光明, shining straight into the hall, and then suddenly they were no more to be seen. Ishō, Igyō, and the others were with me in the hall, but they all said that they saw nothing, and they marveled without end.

After the forenoon meal we followed the ridge toward the east, going up a gradual slope for twenty *li* to the eastern terrace. At the eastern end of the terrace is an Offering Cloister,[895] and we entered it and drank tea. Going south up a slope for about two *li*, we reached the summit of the terrace, where there is a hall of three bays. Piled-up stones form a wall in a square about fifty feet on each side and about ten feet high. In the hall has been placed an image of Monjushiri. Close to the hall on the northwest are three of Tse-t'ien's iron pagodas,[890] in shape like those on the other terraces. There is no Dragon Pool on the summit of the terrace and no water on the surface of the ground, but the grass is rather deep. The circumference of the summit of the terrace might be about one hundred feet on each of the four sides, and its shape is rather long from north to south and narrow from east to west. The northern shoulder 根 is about a *li* long, and south of the terrace there is a ridge which continues up and down for about three *li*, but the summit of the terrace towers most high and has no trees.

At a place straight down a half *li* to the east from the summit of the terrace there is a grotto in the face of the cliff called the Naraen [911] Grotto. People say that in ancient times

---

[911] 那羅延 (Ch. Na-lo-yen, Skr. Nārāyana), defined either as a heavenly protector of Buddhism or else as another name for

the Naraen Buddha performed religious practices in this grotto and later went to the west. Inside the grotto it is damp, and water drips down. The entrance is six feet wide, and it is pitch black inside the grotto. It would do for a dragon's hideaway.

As it was late in the day we returned to the Offering Cloister and spent the night. Just before dusk, the heavens suddenly clouded over, and white clouds massed in the bottoms of the valleys to the east. Now red, now white, they swirled upwards, and the thunder sounded, rumbling loudly. The disturbance was in the deep valleys, while we on the high peak lowered [912] our heads to see it. The wind blew, and rain fell mixed with hail. Late at night it stopped.

23rd DAY   After the forenoon meal we went down from the terrace and back to the Shang-mi Common Cloister. Then we went straight down a slope to the south for about eighteen *li* into a valley and then southeast for another three or four *li* and then for about one more *li* into a valley to the west till we reached the Chin-kang [913] Grotto. The grotto is on the side of the valley. Buddhapāla,[834] a monk of the Western Lands,[884] came empty-handed to the entrance to the mountains, and Monju, appearing in the guise of an old [914] man, would not let him enter the mountains but instructed him to go to the Western Lands and get the *Butchō-sonjō-darani-kyō*.[915] The monk went back to India and got the scripture and came back to this mountain, whereupon

Daibontennō (see note 848), but not as the name of a Buddha as he is called below. Cf. Ono and Hibino 321.

[912] An unusual character should perhaps be interpreted as 低, as in *ZZGR*.

[913] J. Kongō 金剛, meaning " diamond " and used as an equivalent for the Sanskrit *vajra*, a popular symbol in Buddhism. The grotto is shown south of the northern terrace in *Shan-hsi t'ung-chih* 1.26a.

[914] *DBZ* suggests 老 for 者. See the mention of Buddhapāla meeting an " old man " on V 1.

[915] 佛頂尊勝陀羅尼經　(Skr. *Uṣṇīṣa-vijaya-dhāraṇī-sūtra*). One of the extant translations of this work was made by Buddhapāla. See note 950.

Monju led him and entered with him into this grotto. When [Buddha]pāla entered, the entrance of the grotto closed of itself, and it has not opened to this day.

The grotto wall is hard and has a yellow tinge, and there is a high tower [against the face of the cliff] where the mouth of the grotto would be. The grotto [916] mouth is at the base of the tower, but no one can see it. East of the tower is an Offering Cloister. Up in the tower at the grotto entrance is a revolving repository 轉輪藏 made as a hexagon.[917]

I saw in the records of the grotto that in the grotto there are many saintly relics from India. In the time of the Buddha Yuie,[918] the Great Recluse Mari [919] of the Incense Mountains [896] made three thousand kinds of musical instruments out of the " seven treasures," [877] and, after the death of this Buddha, Monjushiri brought them here and put [920] them in this grotto. In the time of the Buddha Kurushin,[921] Tosotsu-

---

[916] The character rendered 嵋 in the printed texts obviously stands for 窟.

[917] This is one of the earliest mentions of revolving bookcases to hold Buddhist scriptures. Cf. L. Carrington Goodrich, " The Revolving Book-Case in China," *Harvard Journal of Asiatic Studies* 7.135-36. Goodrich is probably incorrect in assuming that the following phrase, " I saw in the records of the grotto," has reference to the revolving repository. The general context as well as the small 云云 ten lines later in *Tōji* indicate that this is the opening statement about the wonders concealed in the grotto.

[918] 維衞 (Skr. Vipaśyin), one of the names for the first of the Seven Buddhas of the Past. The Seven Buddhas include the historical Buddha Shaka and six mythical predecessors, whose teachings he is supposed to have synthesized. Cf. also Ono and Hibino 322-23.

[919] 摩利 (Skr. Malikā), the name of the wife of a certain Persian King, though here it does not appear to be used for any truly historical person. *Daisen* 大仙 (Skr. *Maharṣi*), " Great Recluse," is a Buddhist term of honor.

[920] *DBZ* suggests 收 for 取.

[921] 拘留秦, more commonly Kuruson 孫 (Skr. Krakucchanda), the fourth of the Seven Buddhas of the Past.

tennō [922] made a bell which could hold 120 bushels,[217] and those who heard its toll either obtained the "four fruits" or the "first zone" [of enlightenment].[923] After the Buddha's death, Monjushiri brought this bell here and placed it in the grotto. In the time of the Buddha Kashō,[924] a silver harp [925] was made which had 84,000 notes, and each of the 84,000 notes cured one of the worldly passions. After the Buddha's achievement of Nirvana, Monjushiri brought this harp here and put it in the grotto. The Bodhisattva Monju brought a treasured pagoda of 1,300 stories for the whole body of the second Buddha of the future kalpa,[926] and put it in the grotto. The Bodhisattva Monju [also] put golden writing on silver paper of the land of Cathay [927] and a billion forms of writing of the four continents 四天下文字 in this grotto, so it is said.

About a hundred paces up a slope from the grotto, there are a Monju Hall and a Fugen Hall. This then is the place where Ta-chao 大超 Ho-shang saw the "gold-colored world." [822] Since it was late in the day, we went back to the Ta-hua-yen-kang-wei-ssu [928] and were taken to the Nieh-p'an-yüan and placed in a room under the balcony. It is the

---

[922] 兜率天王, the ruler of the Tosotsu (Skr. Tuṣita) Heaven, the fourth heaven of the *yokkaiten* (see note 848).

[923] The "four fruits" (*shika* 四果) are the four stages on the way to enlightenment. Cf. Coates and Ishizuka 360. The "first zone" (*shoji* 初地) is the first of the "ten zones" (*jūji* 十地), which are the fifth set of ten stages on the way to enlightenment, according to another enumeration. It is, thus, the forty-first stage out of fifty-two, there being two final stages added to the five sets of ten. Cf. *ibid.* 179-180.

[924] 迦葉 (Skr. Kāśyapa), the sixth of the Seven Buddhas of the Past and the one directly preceding the historical Buddha.

[925] *K'ung-hou* 箜篌, an instrument with twenty-three strings.

[926] There are three kalpas or Buddhist eons of time, one of the past, one of the present, and one of the future. This last is called *shōshukugō* 星宿劫.

[927] Shintan 振旦, one of the many transcriptions of Cīna, the Sanskrit name for China.

[928] See note 854. For *kang-wei* (J. *kōi*) see note 119.

room of Abbot Hsüan-liang Shang-jen,[929] who is lecturing on the *Lotus Sutra*. Because of his lectures the Abbot is residing temporarily at the Ko-yüan. The cloisters of [Chih]-yüan Ho-shang and Abbot Wen-chien [856] are full of writings of the Tendai teachings, and on the twenty-third we started copying Tendai writings which are not yet to be found in Japan.

SIXTH MOON: 6th DAY [930]   An Imperial emissary came to the monastery, and the congregation of monks all came out to meet him. As a rule, each year clothing, alms bowls, incense, flowers,[931] and the like are sent on Imperial order. An emissary is sent to the mountain to give to the twelve great monasteries [932] 500 fine robes, 500 packages [184] of silk floss, 1,000 lengths [766] of cloth for Buddhist scarves [188] dyed a blue-green color, 1,000 ounces [127] of incense, 1,000 pounds [127] of tea, and 1,000 hand cloths, and at the same time he goes around the twelve great monasteries with Imperial provisions to arrange for maigre feasts.

7th DAY   They held a maigre feast on Imperial order in this monastery. After the maigre feast they read [203] the *Kegon-kyō* [933] through once. In the evening the Imperial emissary went with several tens of monks up to the Bodhisattva Hall to seek a manifestation [of Monju],[934] and they went to the Nieh-p'an-yüan and paid reverence to [Chih]-yüan Ho-shang.

8th DAY   The Imperial emissary held a maigre feast for one thousand monks.

---

[929] Mentioned above on V 17. *Shang-jen* is the Chinese pronunciation of *Shōnin* (see note 827).

[930] July 8, 840. The previous moon had only twenty-nine days.

[931] Perhaps a copyist's error for " tea." See below.

[932] *DBZ*, on the basis of the text below, corrects 事 to 寺. The two characters are homophones in Japanese.

[933] 花嚴, one of the major scriptures of Far Eastern Buddhism. *Kegon* is the Japanese pronunciation of the *hua-yen* in the name of the monastery where Ennin was then staying.

[934] Ennin described in detail the wonderful image of Monju in the Bodhisattva Hall (P'u-sa-t'ang) on V 17.

9th DAY   After the forenoon meal the Imperial emissary went to the Chin-ko-ssu.[813]

11th DAY   It was the birthday[935] of the present Emperor. On Imperial order to the several monasteries of Wu-t'ai, birthday maigre feasts were arranged. The various monasteries simultaneously rang their bells, and five or six eminent monks in the highest seats rose from their places and burned incense. I heard that the Imperial emissary burned incense at the Chin-ko-ssu and then returned to the capital.

21st DAY   The heavens were beautiful and clear and the sky blue in color without a single speck of shade, but together with Ishō, Igyō, and several monks from the cloister I saw from the courtyard in front of the cloister balcony a colored cloud, shining bright and luminous. Its colors were especially beautiful and bright as it drifted through the air up to the summit [of the mountain] and then after a while melted away. The several tens of monks of the cloister who did not come out did not get to see it.

Now there is a mendicant[592] monk of Fen-chou[936] called I-yüan 義圓, who for ten years has been a solicitor of offerings[937] for the twelve monasteries and the common cloisters[938] of Wu-t'ai. Since he had come to deliver this year's offerings,

---

[935] Wu-tsung's birthday is given as the first, eleventh, or twelfth day of the sixth moon, according to different sources, and the official name for the day is given as Ch'ing-yang 慶陽. Cf. Yeh Te-lu 葉德祿, " T'ang-ti tan-ch'en chu-ho k'ao " 唐帝誕辰祝賀考, *Fu-jen hsüeh-chih* 輔仁學誌 9 (No. 1) .141. Ennin's notices on this day in 840, 841, 842, and 843 show that it was undoubtedly the eleventh. On three of these occasions he specifically names the day, and each time it is clearly written Te-yang 德陽 and not Ch'ing-yang. Ono and Hibino 324 are incorrect in saying that this was Wen-tsung's birthday.

[936] 汾, the modern Fen-yang 汾陽, in central Shansi about 250 km. southwest of Mt. Wu-t'ai.

[937] *Kuyōshu* 供養主, repeated on VII 1 and in abbreviated form 供主 on VII 2 and later. On 842 III 12 he is called a 求供. See note 122.

[938] Here called *p'u-t'ung-lan-jo* 普通蘭若. See notes 812 and 550.

he saw the shining manifestation[939] together with us and, shedding tears, he said, "For ten years since I, I-yüan, developed faith, I have yearly delivered offerings to the whole mountain without fail, but I have never before seen a single sign. Now in the company of the foreign Learned Doctor[596] I have seen a shining cloud, and I know indeed that, even though our places of birth are in different regions, in that we have been favored with a manifestation of His Holiness [Monju], we may have the same karma. Henceforth in the future we shall together establish karma affinities[940] and for long shall be the 'family' of the Bodhisattva Monjushiri."

29th DAY   We completed copying the Tendai teachings. I made a catalogue [of the texts we had copied] and, presenting it to [Chih]-yüan Ho-shang, had him write his Buddhist name on it.

SEVENTH MOON: 1st DAY[941]   In order to go to Ch'ang-an we put our baggage in order. I am told that from Wu-t'ai to Ch'ang-an one goes southwest for over two thousand *li* to reach Ch'ang-an. Before the forenoon meal, we paid our respects to the venerable monk [Chih]-yüan and to the two Abbots who are lecturing on the *Shikan* and *Mongu*[331] of T'ien-t'ai [Ta-shih] and to the congregation [of monks], after which Kuang-ch'u 廣初, the Prior[565] monk, arranged a farewell maigre feast.[130] After the forenoon meal, then, we started, and the congregation [of monks] of the cloister saw us off, going out past the gate [of the monastery].[942] Brushing aside our tears and grasping hands, we parted.

We took the Chu-lin road, passing in front of the Chu-lin-ssu, and, going southwest across a high ridge, reached the

---

[939] *Kōzui* 光瑞, defined as the nimbus emanated by a Buddha when he is about to preach.

[940] *DBZ* suggests the deletion of the sign of repetition after the first character in *kechien*. See note 289.

[941] August 2, 840. The preceding moon had thirty days.

[942] Here called figuratively the *sammon* 三門, "three gates."

Chien-ku-p'u-sa-yüan [943] of the Pao-mo-chen-kuo [944] Chin-ko-ssu and spent the night. The monk I-yüan, the solicitor of offerings [937] for the whole of [Wu]-t'ai, is also returning to Fen-chou, and he followed us today from the [Ta]-hua-yen-ssu and lodged in this cloister.

A monk of the cloister told us at tea, "Long ago the Learned Doctor [596] Reisen [823] of Japan lived in this cloister for two years, after which he moved to the Ch'i-fo-chiao-chieh-yüan ('Cloister of the Teachings and Prohibitions of the Seven Buddhas [of the Past]'),[945] where he died. This Learned Doctor himself peeled off [a piece of] skin from his arm, four inches long and three inches wide. He drew a picture of the Buddha on it and fashioning a gilt bronze pagoda, placed [the drawing] in it. At present it is under the Golden Balcony [813] of this monastery, and throughout the year offerings are made to it."

2nd DAY With I-yüan, the solicitor of offerings, and several monks of the monastery, we opened the Golden Balcony and worshiped the holy image of His Holiness the Bodhisattva Monju riding on a lion with blue-green fur. The countenance of golden hue is majestic beyond compare. We also saw the picture of the Buddha on the skin from the arm of Saint [946] Reisen and the gilt bronze pagoda. We also saw

---

[943] 堅固幵, the "Cloister of the Bodhisattva Kengo," presumably standing for the Bodhisattva Kengoi 意 (Skr. Dṛdhā-dhyāśaya).

[944] 保磨鎮國, an additional part of the name of the Chin-ko-ssu (see note 813). The second character may be an error, and the four together perhaps should mean something like "protect the nation and defend the land."

[945] 七佛教誡. On VII 3 Ennin visited this cloister and also the Ling-ching-ssu 靈境, which we learn was the actual spot where Reisen (see note 823) died. The Ling-ching-ssu, which Ennin once calls the Ta-li Ling-ching-ssu, indicating that it was probably built or rebuilt in the Ta-li period (766-799), still stands about four km. south of the southern terrace, and the cloister was a short distance north of the monastery. (Cf. Ono and Hibino 334 and map at back.) For the Seven Buddhas see note 918.

[946] *Shōnin* 聖人.

a tooth of a Byakushi Buddha [883] and relics of the body of
the Buddha. A baldachin of the " seven treasures " [877] hangs
above the head of the Bodhisattva. It was given on Imperial
order. The balcony has nine bays and three stories and is over
a hundred feet high.[946a] There is no place without paintings
on the walls, eaves, beams, or pillars. Inside and out it is
very impressive, and it has all the rarities of the world. It
stands out alone and majestic above the cryptomeria grove.
The white clouds roll below it, and the blue [roofs of its]
upper stories soar high above them.

Next we went up to the second story and worshiped the
images of the five Buddhas of the *Kongōchō-yuga*.[947] These
were put up by the Learned Doctor Amoghavajra [948] on behalf of the nation and were made after the manner of [those
in] the Nālanda Monastery [839] of India. Each Buddha has
two flanking Bodhisattvas,[949] and they all stand in a row
on the platform of planks.

Next we ascended to the third story and worshiped the
golden images of the five Buddhas of the *Chōrinnō-yuga-e*.[950]

[946a] Soper, " Hsiang-kuo-ssu, an Imperial Temple of Northern
Sung," *Journal of the American Oriental Society* 68.32, makes
reference to this description.

[947] 金剛頂瑜伽, which in this case is used as a variant name for
the *Kongōchō-kyō* (see following note), an important scripture
of Esoteric Buddhism.

[948] Ch. Pu-k'ung 不空 (705-774), a Ceylonese by birth who came
to China by sea at an early age. He later returned to India and
brought back to China various texts of Esoteric Buddhism. He
was one of the great translators of Buddhist texts into Chinese,
including one version of the *Kongōchō-kyō*, and is considered to
have introduced Esoteric Buddhism to China.

[949] *Kyōji* 脇士.

[950] The exact meaning of the term is not clear. *E* 會 can mean a
meeting, and for *yuga* (Skr. *yoga*) see note 947. Chōrinnō 頂
輪王 is another name for Konrin-butchō or Konrinnō-butchō
金輪王佛頂, a variant name for one of the five Butchōson 尊,
five Buddhas which are pictured as appearing beside the Buddha
Shaka and are supposed to represent certain of his attributes.
The reference might actually be to some part of the *Konrinnō-*

Each Buddha has one flanking Bodhisattva. Two images of Bodhisattvas, with their hands joined together [as in prayer], stand in front of the Buddhas facing south. The mudras [951] and facial expressions of the Buddhas and Bodhisattvas all are different from those of the images on the second floor. On the inner surface of the whitewashed walls are drawn *mandara* [277] of the various deities, but the colors have not yet been completely filled in. These, too, were made by Amoghavajra [948] on behalf of the nation.

After we had reverently gazed on them, we descended from the balcony and went to the Fugen Place of Ritual [284] and saw the balcony for storing scriptures 經藏閣. There is a Tripitaka in more than six thousand scrolls, all in gold and silver characters on dark blue paper with rollers of white sandalwood, [213] jade, and ivory. I saw the subtitle by the man who had vowed [to have this work done]. It said:

I, Cheng Tao-chüeh 鄭道覺, a man of Ch'ang-an, on the fourteenth day of the fifth moon of the fourteenth year of Ta-li 大曆 (779), while going around the five terraces, personally saw His Holiness [the Bodhisattva Monju] and the Myriad Bodhisattvas and the " gold-colored world " [of Monju] [822] and accordingly developed faith and copied six thousand scrolls of the Tripitaka in gold and silver characters.

There also is painted a thousand-spoked wheel impression of the [Buddha's] foot. [952] Under the footprint is written:

An envoy taking Buddhist scarves [188] from the Emperor T'ai-tsung during the Chen-kuan period (627-650) went to India and saw an old monastery of King Aśoka, [886] where on a stone was a footprint of the Buddha one foot and eight inches long

---

butchō-yōryaku-nenju-hō 要略念誦法, a work translated by Amoghavajra. See also note 915.

[951] *Shuin* 手印, the symbolic positions of the fingers and hands of Buddhist images and pictures.

[952] *Senfukurinsō* 千輻輪相, one of the thirty-two stigmata of the Buddha. A copy of the impression of the Buddha's foot in India, showing the thousand-spoked wheel, was brought to Ch'ang-an in 649. Cf. Ono and Hibino 331.

and six inches wide. He took a rubbing 打得 of the Buddha's footprint and brought it back, and it is now in the capital, and a copy has been made and placed here.

Next we opened the " Place of Ritual of the *Mandara* of Devotions " [953] and worshiped the images of the deities. This is where Han-kuang,[954] a disciple of the Learned Doctor Amoghavajra,[948] on Imperial command performed the ritual of devotion [337] on behalf of the long continuation of the glorious destiny of the Li family.[955] The surface of the platform where he performed the religious practice is three elbow-lengths [long] and has been covered with " white sandalwood " sap mixed with mud. Each time the wind blows, its fragrance can be detected at a distance. There are very many gilt bronze ritual utensils, all of which are on the platform.

Next we opened the Fugen Hall and worshiped the image of the Bodhisattva Fugen. Three elephants [956] stand side by side, and on their backs is placed a single image of the Bodhisattva. The hall both inside and outside is very impressive, and its colored paintings and carvings cannot be described in detail. I do not have time to record in detail the scripture boxes of the " seven treasures," [877] the pearl-embroidered Buddhas, on which pearls have been strung on threads and embroidered onto silk cloth with marvelous results, and all the other things. After looking at them reverently, we went back to the cloister and had our midday rest.

After the forenoon meal, making a party with the solicitor of offerings,[937] the mendicant monk I-yüan, and several others, we started for the southern terrace. Five *li* west of

---

[953] Jinen-mandara-dōjō. See notes 284 and 337. The term is an unknown one.

[954] 含光, the author of a work named after him, the *Kankō giki* (see note 339). Cf. Ono and Hibino 331.

[955] Meaning the Imperial line.

[956] The character is rendered 霄, " deities," in *ZZGR*, but in *Tōji* and *DBZ* we find a character which appears to be a variant for 象, " elephant."

the Chin-ko-ssu is the Ch'ing-liang-ssu,[957] which at present
is in charge of the southern terrace. The whole of Mt. Wu-
t'ai is called Mt. Ch'ing-liang, and, since this monastery was
the first to be built on the mountain, it is called the Ch'ing-
liang-ssu. In the monastery there is a Ch'ing-liang Rock, so
I am told. Under the guidance of the mendicant, we went
toward the southern terrace and did not get to go to this
monastery.

Going out of the gate [942] of the Chin-ko-ssu, we followed a
ridge toward the south, going up a slope for twenty *li* to the
western end of the southern terrace, and then went east along
the southern edge of the terrace for four or five *li* to its summit, where there were no trees at all. On the southeastern
side of the terrace there is an Offering Cloister,[895] and about
three hundred paces up a slope to the north from the cloister
one reaches the summit of the terrace. In a three-bay hall
has been placed an image of the Bodhisattva Monju made
of white jade and riding on a white jade lion. The soft grass
is luxuriant, and orchid-like [958] flowers smell fragrantly over
the whole terrace. As for the shape of the terrace, to the
northwest and southeast long ridges stretch into the distance,
rising and falling; and on the east, west, and north sides steep
cliffs hang over deep valleys.

From the summit one sees at a distance toward the north
the [other] four terraces, one after another before one's eyes.
Turning one's head, one sees all of the five summits, high
and round and rising far above the many other peaks. A
thousand peaks and a hundred ridges, densely covered with

---

[957] The Ch'ing-liang-ssu (see note 822) still stands about four
km. northwest of the Chin-ko-ssu. Cf. map at back of Ono and
Hibino. It was built by the Emperor Hsiao-wen of the Northern
Wei (see note 965), and south of it still stands the Ch'ing-liang
Rock which Ennin mentions. Cf. *Shan-hsi t'ung-chih* 57.5a. (This
and subsequent references to the *Shan-hsi t'ung-chih* are to the
1892 edition.)

[958] *Ling-ling-hsiang* 零陵香 (the second character here is written
凌) is the name of a type of orchid, but in this case it appears
to be used in a more general sense.

pines and cryptomerias, stand out at varying heights below the five summits. One cannot see the floors of the deep ravines and profound valleys, and one hears only the sound of the flowing [waters] in their hidden springs and mountain streams. Strange birds soar at [different] levels above the many peaks, mounting high on their feathered wings, but there are few which fly up to the summit of the terraces. Outside the 500-*li* area of the five summits, high peaks stretch out in all directions, hemming in the five terraces for perhaps a thousand *li*. With their pointed blade-[like peaks] in rows, they have the appearance of serried (walls) [959] encircling us. There are peaks and valleys, one after the other, for I don't know how many rows. Approaching Mt. [Wu]-t'ai from the east, one goes among the mountains and valleys for 500 *li*, up to the summits of precipitous crags and down to the floors of deep valleys, often taking seven days before reaching the area of Mt. Wu-t'ai. From the other three cardinal directions and four points of the compass [960] the way is also far across mountains and valleys before one reaches Wu-t'ai. One indeed realizes that Mt. Wu-t'ai is at the center of a myriad of peaks.

Five hundred poisonous dragons hide themselves in the mountains and spew forth wind and clouds. During the four seasons and eight periods [of the year] [961] it [never] [962] stops thundering and hail constantly falls. When the heavens suddenly clear, the traveler does not see a long stretch of clearness. Each time that it is clear one sees on the five terraces a pale yellow light, and then one suddenly sees on the terraces a speck of cloud rise, and all of a sudden heavy clouds cover the mountains.

Those who enter these mountains naturally develop a spirit of equality. When maigre feasts are arranged in these mountains, whether one be cleric or layman, man or woman,

---

[959] The character 壚 does not fit the context.

[960] *Ssu-wei* 四維, the directions *NE, SE, NW,* and *SW*.

[961] *Pa-chieh* 八節, which, like " four seasons," is a term meaning the whole year.

[962] The omission of the negative is probably a copyist's error.

great or small, food is offered to all equally. Regardless of
rank or position, here all persons make one think of Monju.
Long ago, the Ta-hua-yen-ssu held a great maigre feast, and
commoners, both men and women, and beggars and the destitute all came to receive food, but the patron was displeased
and said, " My intention in coming here far up the mountain
slopes and holding a maigre feast was merely to provide for
the monks of the mountain, and it was not my intention
that these worldly laymen and beggars should all come and
receive my food. If such beggars are to be provided for, then
maigre feasts can be arranged in their native places. Why
should I come all the way to this mountain [to feed them]? "
The monks persuaded him to have food given to all. Among
the beggars was a pregnant woman, heavy with child, and,
when at her seat she received her full portion, she demanded
a portion for the child [963] in her womb. The patron cursed
her and would not give it to her. The pregnant woman said
several times, " Although the child in my womb has not
yet been born, he counts as a person, so why don't you give
him his food? " The patron said, " You are a fool. Even
though the child in your belly should count as one, he does
not come out to ask for it. If he gets the food, to whom
should we give it to eat? " The woman replied, " If the child
in my belly does not get food, then I too should not eat,"
and, rising, she left the dining hall. Just as she went out of
the door of the hall, she was transformed into Monjushiri,
emitting light which filled the hall with dazzling brightness.
With his bright jade-[like] countenance and seated on a lion
with golden hair and surrounded by a myriad of Bodhisattvas, he soared up into the sky. The whole assembly of several
thousand persons rushed out together and fell dumbfound-
ed [964] and insensible to the ground. They raised their voices
in repentance and wept bitterly, raining down tears, and
called out together, " His Holiness Monjushiri," until their

---

[963] Apparently 嫁 in *Tōji*, but printed 姟 in *DBZ* and *KIK* and
obviously standing for 孩, as printed in *ZZGR*. For other versions of this story cf. Ono and Hibino 331.
[964] *DBZ* suggests 茫然 for 忙然.

voices gave way and their throats were dry, but he never deigned to turn around and grew indistinct and then disappeared. The whole assembly had no appetite for the food, and each one of them made vows. Thenceforth, when offerings were sent and maigre feasts arranged, all were provided for equally, regardless of whether they were clerics or laymen, men or women, great or small, noble or lowly, poor or rich. Accordingly, the custom of the mountain is to have a system of equality. There have been many other miracles of divine manifestation besides this one, of which the whole empire knows.

At present at maigre-feast gatherings they have in the dining hall a row of men, a row of women, some of them holding babies [963] who also receive a portion, a row of children, a row of novices, a row of full monks, and a row of nuns, and all receive their offering [of food] on their benches. The patron gives out the food equally. When people demand more than their share, they do not blame them but give them all [they ask for], whatever it may be.

There is much cold [weather] in the mountains, but during the fifth, sixth, and seventh moons rare flowers spread out in bloom like a brocade over all the 500 *li* of Wu-t'ai, filling the mountains and valleys with an incense which is very fragrant. On each of the terraces grow many leeks 葱韭. Of old the Emperor Hsiao-wen [965] lived at Wu-t'ai, wandering and admiring [the beauty]. The Bodhisattva Monju changed himself into the guise of a monk and asked the Emperor for the land [covered by] one sitting-mat.[208] The Emperor granted it to him. When the monk had been granted this, he spread out a single mat and covered 500 *li* of land. The Emperor, surprised, said, " I merely gave him the land [covered by] a single mat, but this monk has spread a single mat over all

---

[965] 孝文皇帝, the ruler and reformer of the Northern Wei (reigned 471-499). Since the Wei capital at his accession was not far from Mt. Wu-t'ai, Ennin's statement that he lived at Wu-t'ai and later left the mountains may have reference to the shift of his capital to Lo-yang in 493. Cf. Waley 276 and Ono and Hibino 331.

the five terraces. This is most wonderful, but I do not want him [966] to live here." Accordingly, he scattered leeks over the five terraces and then left the mountains. The monk, remaining behind, scattered orchid-like flowers [958] over the leeks, causing them to lose their odor. At present leeks grow all over each of the terraces, but they have no odor at all, and orchid-like flowers grow luxuriantly all over the terraces, and their fragrance is heavy. It is said that the 500 *li* of Wu-t'ai is the land on which a single mat was spread out.

At present, together with the mendicant and several tens of others, we sought a manifestation of His Holiness [Monju] on the southern terrace, but by night we had seen none, and so we finally returned to the cloister and spent the night. Early in the night, in the sky above a ridge across a valley east of the terrace,[967] we saw that there was a holy lamp. The group of us saw it together and worshiped it. The light of the lamp at first was about as large as an alms bowl, but later it gradually grew as large as a small house. The crowd was greatly moved and with loud voices chanted the name of His Holiness. There was another lamp which appeared close to the valley. It too at first was like a straw rain hat [in size] but later grew gradually larger. The two lights, when seen from a distance, were about one hundred feet apart and blazed brightly. Just at midnight they died out and became invisible.

3rd DAY   After the forenoon meal we made up a party with the mendicant and others. The mendicant said that he would accompany us right to Fen-chou [936] and that on the way he would act as host to us. From the summit of the terrace we went toward the south down some seventeen *li* into a valley. There is a cloister there with dilapidated buildings and no inhabitants, which is called the Ch'i-fo-chiao-chieh-yüan (" Cloister of the Teachings and Prohibitions of

---

[966] A dubious character in *Tōji* is interpreted as 共 in all three printed texts, but this does not fit the context.

[967] *DBZ* points out that the sign of repetition after the word " terrace " appears to be an error.

the Seven Buddhas [of the Past] ") .[968] The inscription on the cloister reads: Pa-ti-ch'ao-lan-jo 八地超蘭若.[550] The Japanese monk Reisen formerly lived here and died here. A poem by a P'o-hai[567] monk Chen-su 貞素 lamenting over Reisen Shōnin[827] is written on a board nailed to the wall. I copied it as follows:

A poem lamenting over the Japanese Court Priest [824] *and Reverence* [248] *Reisen Kashō* [115] including a preface, *by Chen-su, a monk of the land of P'o-hai.*

He who first awakened me was called Ying-kung 應 公. [Ying]-kung as a child [969] studied [Buddhism] and, following his master, went to Japan,[970] where he grew up and distinguished himself in the community of monks. I, for my part, came [to China] with my books to study the Buddhist scriptures.[971]

In the late fall of the eighth year of Yüan-ho (813) I met [Reisen] in my travels. With a single word we were in rapport, and we discussed matters from our hearts. [I, Chen]-su, became his assistant. How could I have done otherwise? Before long we had established the greatest of brotherly love for each

---

[968] See note 945. *DBZ* points out that the 名 preceding the cloister name is probably an erroneous repetition.

[969] 仆 should perhaps be corrected to 幼, which it more closely resembles in *Tōji* than might be judged from the printed forms. This whole composition is full of dubious points. Some of them may have been the result of Chen-su's inadequate command of Chinese, but most of the difficulties probably stemmed from Ennin's inability to make out the inscription, which must have become somewhat weathered during the twelve years it had stood.

[970] Here 浮桑, which in Japanese is a homophone for 扶桑 Fusō, a mythical land in the sea east of China often used as an elegant name for Japan.

[971] *Pa-yeh* 覇葉 (not 業 as given in the three printed texts), possibly a variant writing for *pei-yeh* 貝葉, the palmyra leaves on which Indian, and therefore Buddhist, books were written. In this section Chen-su probably wished to establish the fact that he came to China after studying with Ying-kung, presumably after Ying-kung had returned from Japan, where, as we learn subsequently, he had studied under Reisen.

other.⁹⁷² My heart was overflowing 足痛乃心. This [Rei]sen Daishi ¹⁴⁰ was the master of our Ying-kung, and his profound understanding has been manifested to the people.

In the second year of Ch'ang-ch'ing ⁹⁷³ (822) he took up residence at Wu-t'ai, ever neglectful of his gangrenous body and keeping his mind from hearing the cries of the white monkeys. In the fifth year of Ch'ang-ch'ing (825) the King of Japan sent him from afar one hundred [ounces of] gold, which came to Ch'ang-an. I received the gold and the letter for him and sent them to T'ieh-ch'in.⁹⁷⁴ When [Rei]sen Daishi had received the gold, he entrusted me with ten thousand grains of Buddhist relics,⁹⁷⁵ two new scriptures, and five Imperial communications,⁹⁷⁵ᵃ . . . and asked me to go to Japan to express his thanks for the King's benevolence to him. I agreed.

When I had once given my promise, how could I have shrunk from ten thousand *li* of serried billows? I was able to accomplish my . . . mission.⁹⁷⁶

When I was about to return, they entrusted another hundred [ounces of] gold to me. On the seventh day of the fourth moon of the second year of T'ai-ho (828) I returned to the Ling-ching-ssu ⁹⁴⁵ and sought out [Rei]sen Daishi, but he had long since died.⁹⁷⁷ I wept ⁹⁷⁸ tears of blood and was overwhelmed by misery.

---

⁹⁷² 早向鴒原鶺鴒之至. The lark-like bird known as the *ling* or *chi-ling* and the phrase, "the moor of the *ling*," are metaphors for brotherly love.

⁹⁷³ 長慶. The second character is miswritten 廣 in *Tōji*.

⁹⁷⁴ 鐵懃, which we learn below is the name of a monastery where Reisen frequently stayed. Cf. Ono and Hibino 334. *Shan-hsi t'ung-chih* 57.11b locates it sixty *li* southwest of the western terrace.

⁹⁷⁵ *Shari* 舍利, supposedly the bones of the Buddha, are usually in the form of small pebbles, for which the numerary adjunct *li* 粒, "grains," is used.

⁹⁷⁵ᵃ In 造勑五通, the first character may be an error for 告.

⁹⁷⁶ The sentence 得遂鍾无外緣 is itself not fully clear, and it is followed by another, 期乎遠大, which does not fit here in its normal meaning of "to expect great things."

⁹⁷⁷ *DBZ* corrects 巳 to 亡, which Ono and Hibino 332 print without comment.

⁹⁷⁸ *DBZ* corrects 位 to 泣, which Ono and Hibino 332 print without comment.

That when I floated on the dark and all encompassing deep, I looked upon death as but a return home, and that . . . 連五同行李 took no longer than the time for a meal, is all because of my connection with Ying-kung. . . .[979]

> Alas my worldly heart,
>   but my tears involuntarily flow.[980]
>
> My spirit, because of my Buddhist insight,
>   dwells on the nether world.[981]
>
> If tomorrow [someone] should inquire
>   about our friend [from across] the seas,
>
> Tell him that, leaving his shoes,
>   he returned home barefoot.[982]

Written on the fourteenth day of the fourth moon of the second year of T'ai-ho (828).

In a small grotto are placed representations of the Seven Buddhas.[918] At the mouth of the grotto is a hall, and south of it stands a small priestly dwelling. Underneath the hall are two rooms. Everything is dilapidated, and the courtyard is overgrown and deserted. In ancient times the Seven Buddhas appeared in front of this grotto.

We went about three *li* south to the Ta-li Ling-ching-ssu [945] and inquired of a venerable monk where the Learned Doctor Reisen had died. He told us that the Learned Doctor Reisen had formerly stayed for the most part at the T'ieh-ch'in-lan-jo [974] and the Ch'i-fo-chiao-chieh-yüan [945] but later had

---

[979] The remainder of the preface reads: 吾信始而復終願靈凡兮 表悉空留澗水嗚咽千秋之聲仍以雲松惆悵萬里之行四月冪落如 一首途望京之耳 . Although phrases in this section clearly refer to his deep sorrow and indicate that during the second half of the fourth moon he intended to make the long, sad trip to the capital, the text does not seem to be in good enough shape to warrant translation.

[980] Meaning that, if he were not so worldly, he would be able to rejoice that his friend and master had achieved Nirvana.

[981] 情因法眼奄幽泉 is at best of doubtful meaning.

[982] Meaning that he departed this world unencumbered by worldly ties.

come to this monastery and resided in the Yü-shih-yüan 浴
室 ("Bath House Cloister"), where he was poisoned by
someone and died, and they did not know where his disciples
had buried him.

On either side of the gate of the monastery are images
of the Saintly Guardian Bodhisattvas.[983] Of old Guardian
Deities appeared in the three regional commanderies of
T'ai-yüan, Yu, and Cheng,[984] and they themselves said, " We
are the Buddha Rushi [985] in the form of local deities to
guard the Buddhist Law. We were buried in the ground and
over the years crumbled to dust, but we were rediscovered
and are at present inside the gate of the Ling-ching-ssu of
Mt. [Wu]-t'ai." The Regional Commanders of the three
prefectures were amazed and recorded in detail the appearance [of the apparitions]. Each sent a messenger to make
inquiries, and [they discovered] there were two Guardian
Deities on the left and right of the monastery gate which in
appearance and bearing were exactly like the apparitions in
their own prefectures. The messengers returned to their provinces and reported this. Thereupon the three prefectures
sent messengers here especially to repair the old images, and
there were many divine signs. I have copied it all down
separately just as it is related in detail on a stele inscription.

---

[983] *Shō-kongō-bosatsu* 聖金剛丼 (later called *Kongō-shin* 身 and
simply *Kongō*). A *Kongō* is a Buddhist guardian deity who is
represented grasping a *kongōsho* 杵 or *vajra*, an Indian weapon
symbolizing the thunderbolt.
[984] The T'ai-yüan-fu 太原府 (here again *t'ai* is written *ta*) of
the T'ang, which at various times was known as the Northern
Capital and was one of the nine superior prefectures known as *fu*
(see VII 13 and cf. Des Rotours 680-82), is the present T'ai-
yüan-hsien. It is about twenty km. southwest of the modern
T'ai-yüan-fu, which is the present capital of Shansi Province.
Yu-chou 幽 was a city in the environs of the modern Peking,
and Cheng-chou 鄭 is now an important railway junction in
Honan between K'ai-feng and Lo-yang.
[985] Rushi-butsu 樓至佛 (Skr. Rucika), the last of the thousand
Buddhas of the present kalpa (*kengō* 賢劫). See note 926.

Near the northwest corner of the gate stands a mountain elm with a grotto hollowed out under its roots. It is called the Grotto of the Holy Bell 聖鍾窟. In the grotto from time to time can be heard the tolling of a bell. When it tolls forth, the mountain summits quiver. Tradition has it that this is a manifestation of His Holiness Monju, and this is traditionally called the Valley of the Holy Bell.

More than ten *li* due east of the monastery there is a high peak called Pao-shih-shan 寶石 ("Jewel Mountain"). In [its] grottoes there are many pebbles, all of which have a five-colored nimbus. This too is the result of a manifestation of the Saint.[946]

4th DAY   After the forenoon meal we went southwest into the valley and across a ridge for fifteen *li* to the Ta-li Fa-hua-ssu.[986] A storied pavilion has been constructed on a steep prominence with precipices on all sides. All of the buildings are beautiful, and they stand close together, though on different levels of the ground. The scriptures, images, and treasures are lovely beyond description. We went around looking at the various cloisters and then entered the Fa-hua-yüan ("Lotus Cloister") to see the picture of Shen-tao Ho-shang.[987] This Priest during his lifetime conducted himself in accordance with the practices of the Tendai *hokke-zammai*.[284] Constantly he recited the *Lotus Sutra*, and for forty-three years he did not leave the cloister. He achieved insight into purification from the six roots [of evil] 六根清浄 and entered Nirvana some years ago. His picture, the *Lotus Sutra* he had, and his manner of performing concentration, and also the great chair where he sat when gaining insight into concentration are all still preserved. Fifteen *li* northwest of the Fa-hua-ssu stands the Fo-kuang-ssu.[988]

5th DAY   After the forenoon meal we went two *li* southwest to the Shang-fang Common Cloister [812] and spent the night.

---

[986] For more about the Fa-hua-ssu 法花, which no longer remains, cf. Ono and Hibino 335. For Ta-li see note 945.
[987] 神道, identified by Ono and Hibino 335 as Shen-ying 神英.
[988] 佛光. Cf. *Shan-hsi t'ung-chih* 57.11a.

6th DAY   We started early and went southwest about five *li*. Toward the south we saw at a distance a high ridge with lofty peaks rising steeply, but with a large hole in its center, through which one sees daylight on the other side.[989] Seen from a distance the hole is about the size of a rain hat. This is the place through which Emperor Hsiao-wen [965] shot an arrow.

We went about seven *li* southwest to Ssu-yang Ridge.[990] It is the place where long ago, in the first year of I-feng (676), Buddhapāla,[834] an Indian monk of the western regions,[599] coming here and raining down tears as he worshiped Mt. [Wu]-t'ai from afar, perceived His Holiness [Monju] in the form of an old man and was ordered to return to India and get the *Butchō*.[915] A banner has now been erected on which is inscribed the *Butchō darani* with a preface recording the story of [Buddha]pāla meeting the old man.

From Ssu-yang Ridge we went thirteen *li* southwest to Ta-hsien Ridge,[991] where we took our midday rest at the common cloister. The road goes over the ridge, and at the top of the ridge there are double towered gates which are the southern gates of Mt. Wu-t'ai.

After the forenoon meal we went about five *li* southwest to Wu-t'ai-hsien [199] under the jurisdiction of Tai-chou.[908] We went thirty *li* southwest across the Hu-t'o River [992] to the Chien-an-ssu [993] and spent the night.

8th DAY   After the forenoon meal we went thirty *li* southwest to the Ch'i-yen-ssu 七巖 in Ting-hsiang-hsien in Hsin-chou [994] and spent the night.

---

[989] *Na-pan* 那畔, obviously a variant for the modern colloquial *na-pien* 那邊.

[990] 思陽嶺 , now written 虒陽, the name of a river in this area. Cf. Ono and Hibino 336 and map at back.

[991] 大賢, still one of the entrances to the Mt. Wu-t'ai region. Cf. Ono and Hibino 335 and map at back and *Shan-hsi t'ung-chih* 3.20a.

[992] 胡陀河, but more properly written as 滹沱 .

[993] Chien-an 建安 still appears as a place name across the Hu-t'o River southwest of Wu-t'ai-hsien. Cf. *Shan-hsi t'ung-chih* 3.20a.

9th DAY   We started early and went about thirty *li* southwest to the Hu-ts'un [995] Common Cloister and took our midday break and rested.

10th DAY   We started early and went about thirty *li* [996] to the Sung-ts'un [997] Common Cloister and took our midday rest. We went thirty-five *li* to the Nan-kuan-t'ou 南關頭 ("Southern Entrance of the Pass") Common Cloister at Ming-ling-chen [998] and spent the night.

11th DAY   We started early and went about twenty *li* to the Ta-kan [999] Common Cloister and took our midday rest. We went twenty-five *li* to T'a-ti-tien [1000] and spent the night.

12th DAY   We started in the fifth watch (4 A. M.) and went thirty-five *li* to the Pai-yang [1001] Common Cloister and took our midday rest. Then we went fifteen *li* further to San-chiao-i [1002] and rested. Next we went to the estate of the Ting-chüeh-ssu 定覺 and saw the water-[powered] mill 水碾. It is called the San-chiao mill. Then we went fifteen *li* further to the Ku-ch'eng [1003] Common Cloister and spent the night.

---

[994] Ting-hsiang-hsien 定襄 is almost forty km. southwest of Wu-t'ai-hsien, and Hsin-chou 忻 is about twenty km. on beyond it. Cf. Ono and Hibino 336.

[995] 胡村 ("Hu Village"). Cf. Pei-hu and Nan-hu in *Shan-hsi t'ung-chih* 3.14b and Ono and Hibino 337.

[996] *Tōji* has "twenty" as a gloss.

[997] 宋 ("Sung Village"). There is a Ta-nan-sung 大南宋 southeast of Hsin-chou (cf. *Shan-hsi t'ung-chih* 3.14b and Ono and Hibino 337).

[998] 名嶺鎮, clearly an error for Shih-ling-chen 石, a name for Shih-ling-kuan ("Rocky Ridge Barrier"), a pass on the road Ennin was following about thirty-five km. air-line southwest of Ting-hsiang-hsien.

[999] 大干, probably an error for Ta-yü 大盂, about eight km. south of Shih-ling-kuan.

[1000] 躍地店 . Cf. Ono and Hibino 337.

[1001] 白楊 ("White Willow"). Cf. Ono and Hibino 338.

[1002] 三交驛 . Cf. Ono and Hibino 338.

[1003] A Ku-ch'eng 古城 ("Old City") is shown just north of the

13*th* DAY We started at dawn and went fifteen *li* to T'ai-yüan-fu.[984] It belongs to Ho-tung-tao [1004] and is the Northern Capital, over two thousand *li* from the Western Capital (Ch'ang-an). [Entering] the north gate, we lodged at the Lower Hua-yen-ssu. We met the South Indian monk Fa-ta 法達, who had come here before us from Mt. [Wu]-t'ai. He told us that he was a descendant in the third generation of the Learned Doctor Kumārajīva.[1005] All the monks of the Ta-hua-yen-ssu [1006] of Mt. Wu-t'ai who come down here from the mountain are under this monastery, and consequently they call it the Lower Hua-yen-ssu.

The solicitor of offerings,[937] the mendicant I-yüan, brought us to this monastery. The mendicant himself has accompanied us from Mt. [Wu]-t'ai and the whole way has made arrangements for our gruel, rice, and tea, without ever stinting us.

15*th* DAY We were invited by the head of the Ssu-chung-ssu 四衆 and went with the mendicant to the monastery to have our forenoon meal, after which we went to the Tu-t'o-ssu 度脫 and worshipfully observed the All Souls' Festival.[1007] We also went into the prefectural headquarters and saw the Dragon Spring 龍泉. Next we went to the Ch'ung-fu-ssu [1008] and went around paying reverence to the

---

modern town of T'ai-yüan-hsien (see note 984) in *Shan-hsi t'ung-chih* 2.5a.

[1004] 河東道, a province corresponding roughly with the modern Shansi.

[1005] 鳩摩羅什 . See note 139. By descendant the man may have meant a disciple, but he could scarcely have been a disciple in the third generation, because Kumārajīva died in 413.

[1006] See note 854. 花 here is miswritten 莊, making it the name of a famous Ch'ang-an monastery (see note 1141).

[1007] *Urabon* 盂蘭盆 (the last character is written 瓫 here; Skr. *Ullambana*), a Buddhist festival on behalf of the souls of the dead, held on the fifteenth day of the seventh moon. See note 544.

[1008] 崇福, which was first erected in 551. Cf. *Shan-hsi t'ung-chih* 57.16b.

Buddha Hall, Balcony, and other Cloisters. All had arranged displays. Their lustrous beauty was dazzling, and the displays were most wonderful. Everybody in the whole city had come to look respectfully at them. In the evening [the people] carried on wantonly.

16th DAY We went to the K'ai-yüan-ssu and went up to the balcony and looked out over [the city]. In the balcony is an image of the Buddha Miroku [655] cast in iron. It is gilded on the surface, and the Buddha's body is over thirty feet tall [1008a] and is seated on a jeweled seat. The various monasteries have spread out [offerings before it], each selecting its finest articles.

17th DAY We were invited to the home of Hu 胡, an Assimilated Colonel [379] in the regional commandery and, together with the solicitor of offerings, the monk I-yüan, went to his house and had the forenoon meal. The All Souls' Festival of the various monasteries starts on the fifteenth day and ends on the seventeenth day.

18th DAY At the quarters of Fa-ta, the Learned Doctor from South India, I copied down inscriptions recording the divine manifestations at Mt. Wu-t'ai. We had intended to leave for Ch'ang-an on the eighteenth day, but the mendicant monk I-yüan has now hired a master [874] and has himself provided a . . . [1009] for the painting of a picture of the manifestation at Mt. Wu-t'ai, intending to send it by me to Japan, and so we are not able to start because we are waiting for the painting to be completed.

19th DAY At the invitation of a woman disciple, Chen-ju-hsing 眞如性, we went with the mendicant to her home for the midday rest. She was now our hostess because she had gone with him around [Mt. Wu]-t'ai.

22nd DAY We went with the mendicant to the home of the nun Chen-ju-hsin 眞如心 for the forenoon meal. She too had accompanied him around Wu-t'ai.

[1008a] Since this refers to the height of the standing figure, and the Buddha was seated, the actual image was by no means this high.
[1009] 帔襖子一領, presumably a piece of cloth for the picture, rather than an item of clothing as the characters suggest.

23rd DAY   We went with the mendicant to the Lü-ta-te-yüan 律大德 (" Cloister of the Reverence of the Vin-aya ") [248] of the nunnery, the Chen-ju-ta-yeh-ssu,[1009a] for the forenoon meal. Three reverend nuns also had accompanied the mendicant around [Mt. Wu]-t'ai.

26th DAY   The painting of the picture of the manifestation was completed, and the mendicant said, " I rejoice that I encountered you, a Learned Doctor from Japan, and accompanied you around [Mt. Wu]-t'ai and saw with you the manifestation of His Holiness [Monju]. Now I have painted for you a picture of the manifestation and ask you to take it back to Japan and present it in offering, that those who see it will develop faith and those with karma affinities will develop these affinities and be reborn together in Monju's great congregation 大會."

After the forenoon meal, we bade farewell to the monks of the cloister [where we had been staying] and at last started for Ch'ang-an. The mendicant said, " With my whole heart I would like to accompany you right to Fen-chou [936] and be your host on the way, but since arriving here I have not yet finished my business and I must stay here ten days or more and therefore cannot fulfill my wish."

Ling-ya 令雅, a monk who had accompanied him around [Mt. Wu]-t'ai, said, " I wish that I were able to accompany you to Ch'ang-an," and the mendicant told him, " In my place take diligent care of their baggage [1010] and do your best to wait upon them, so that these travelers from afar will not be lonely [1011] on their way." And so we started out together.

The mendicant said to us, " I shall accompany you out of the city and go with you on a pilgrimage to the Western Hills." [1012] So we went together out of the west gate of the

---

[1009a] 尼眞如大業寺. The first three characters are omitted from DBZ and KIK.

[1010] The 里 in this word must be a copyist's error.

[1011] In place of 寂寞 Tōji appears to have the same phonetics written with radical 116.

[1012] 西山, the hills immediately west of the old city of T'ai-yüan-fu.

city and went three or four *li* west to a rocky mountain called
Chin-shan 晉. There is coal all over the mountain, and all
the people from prefectures near and far come and get it to
burn. For cooking meals it has a great amount of heat. We
saw where the rocks of the cliff had been scorched to coal,
and people told us that it had been burned by lightning 天
火, but I thought to myself that it was not necessarily so
and that this had been brought about as a reward to sentient
beings.[1013]

At the entrance to the mountain was a small monastery
called the Shih-men-ssu 石門 ("Stone Gate Monastery"),
in which there was a monk who for many years had been
reciting the *Lotus Sutra*. Recently some Buddhist relics[975]
were revealed to him, and everybody in the whole city
came to make offerings. The monastery was overflowing with
monks and laymen. I don't know how many there were.

The origin of the discovery of the relics [was as follows]:
The scripture-reciting monk was sitting in his room at night,
reciting the scriptures, when three beams of light shone in
and illumined the whole room and lighted up the whole
monastery. Seeking the source of the light, [he discovered
that] it came from the foot of the . . .[1014] cliff west of the
monastery. Each night it lighted up the room and the monastery. After several days the monk followed the light to the
cliff and dug down into the ground for over ten feet and
came upon three jars of relics of the Buddha. In a blue
lapis lazuli jar were seven grains[975] of relics, in a white lapis
lazuli jar five grains of relics, and in a golden jar three
grains of relics. He brought them back and placed them in
the Buddha Hall and made offerings to them. The noble and
lowly, and the men and women of T'ai-yüan[984] city and
the various villages, and the officials, both high and low, all

---

[1013] 衆生果報所感. In other words, Ennin did not believe in
this naturalistic explanation of the formation of coal and felt
instead that it was another example of the working of the principle of causality.

[1014] An illegible character.

came and paid reverence [1015] and made offerings. Everyone said, "This has been revealed because of the wondrous strength of the Priest in his devotion to the *Lotus Sutra.*" The people coming from the city to the mountain filled the roads and in great crowds worshiped and marveled.

From the Shih-men-ssu we went westward up a hill about two *li* to the T'ung-tzu-ssu [1016] where Tz'u-en Fa-shih,[166] avoiding the Korean monk Hsüan-ts'e Fa-shih, came here from Ch'ang-an and first lectured on the *Yuishiki.*[1017] A two-storied hall is filled with large Buddhist images. We saw a stele with an inscription reading:

> Of old . . . li 禮, a Master of Meditation [249] of Chi-chou,[800] came and resided at this mountain. He suddenly saw a cloud, shining in five colors,[840] rise into the air from the ground and cast its light over all. In this shining cloud were four children

---

[1015] The second character is missing in the word 頂禮.

[1016] 童子, "Monastery of the Children," founded in 556, ten *li* west of the modern town of T'ai-yüan-hsien. Cf. *Shan-hsi t'ung-chih* 57.17a.

[1017] The reference is to a famous story told in the biographies of K'uei-chi (Tz'u-en Ta-shih, see note 166) and of a monk of the Hsi-ming-ssu of Ch'ang-an (see note 223) called Yüan-ts'e 圓測, both of which are to be found in the *Sung kao-seng chuan* 宋高僧傳 4. Yüan-ts'e secretly listened to Hsüan-tsang's lectures on the *Yuishiki-ron* 唯識論 (Skr. *Vijñaptimātratāsiddhi-śāstra*) given especially for K'uei-chi and then immediately assembled a congregation and lectured on the text, thereby stealing a march on his rival, but Hsüan-tsang comforted the latter by telling him that there were points that Yüan-ts'e did not understand and by giving K'uei-chi further information not known to others. Subsequently K'uei-chi traveled to the T'ai-yüan and Mt. Wu-t'ai areas, where marvelous revelations were made to him.

Ennin's use of the name Hsüan-ts'e 玄測 suggests that Yüan-ts'e is a later form of the name, coined to avoid a taboo character. The *Sung kao-seng chuan* makes no reference to his Korean origin, saying merely that his origin is not known. In this passage Ennin calls K'uei-chi, Tz'u-en T'ai Fa-shih (see note 7). The T'ai 臺, if not a copyist's error, is presumably an additional honorific of some sort.

seated on green lotus seats [1018] and playing. The sound shook the
earth, and cliffs crumbled and fell. An image of the Buddha
[A]mida [273] appeared where a bank had fallen away. People came
to worship from all over the Three Chin,[1019] and there were many
wonders. The Master of Meditation recorded this in detail and
reported it, asking that a monastery be erected, and finally this
monastery was built. Because of the miracle, they called it the
T'ung-tzu-ssu ("Monastery of the Children"). An image of
the Buddha [A]mida was respectfully carved revealing his appearance, majestic of countenance, radiant and dignified 皓玉
端麗, and seated cross-legged. It is 170 feet high [1008a] and 100 feet
wide.[1020] The Kannon [6] and Taisei [1021] [on either side] are each
120 feet [tall].

27th DAY After our gruel, we started out, thereupon
parting from the solicitor of offerings, the mendicant I-yüan.
Making a single party with Ling-ya, the monk who had
accompanied him around [Mt. Wu]-t'ai, we went together
toward the Western Capital (Ch'ang-an). We went south
across a ridge from the T'ung-tzu-ssu to the Yü-hua-ssu 雨
花 and took our midday rest. From the Yü-hua-ssu we went
southwestward out of the mountains for forty li to Ch'ing-
yüan-hsien [1022] and lodged at the common cloister. The Prior
did not understand the proper courtesy between host and
guest.

28th DAY We went fifteen li southwest to Chin-
ts'un-chia 晉村家 and took our midday rest. We went
twenty-five li southwest to Shih-kao-ts'un and lodged at
the Shih-hao-yüan.[1023]

[1018] The lotus flower was the usual throne for a Buddha.

[1019] 三晉, a term for the three successor states of the old feudal
state of Chin and thus a flowery term for the Shansi area.

[1020] From the dimensions, it would appear that these figures were
carved out of the face of the cliff.

[1021] Taiseishi 大勢至, or more commonly Seishi (Skr. Mahāsthāmaprāpta), a popular Bodhisattva who, with Kannon, often
flanked Amida.

[1022] 清源 (here miswritten Ch'ing-liang-hsien 涼, see note 822),
twenty km. southwest of the T'ang T'ai-yüan-fu.

[1023] I suspect that the second character of the village name, Shih-

29th DAY   We went twenty-five *li* southwest to the
Li 李 household in Wen-shui-hsien [1023] and took our midday
rest. This was [the home of] a close disciple of the mendicant
I-yüan, and our meal was in accordance with the [Buddhist]
Law. After the forenoon meal we went forty *li* to Kuo-cha-
ts'un 郭柵 and lodged at the village monastery. The Prior
monk was not happy to see guests.

EIGHTH MOON: 1*st* DAY [1024]   We went twenty-five *li*
southwest to the Chung-hsiang-ssu 衆香 of Fen-chou [936] and
took our midday rest. East of the monastery is the Fen River
Lake.[1025] The Fen River, flowing to this place, spreads out
broadly, and consequently they call it a lake. It is about a
thousand *chō* [21] in circumference. Then it veers to the south
and enters the Yellow River in Ho-chung-fu.[1026]

We went five *li* west from the Chung-hsiang-ssu to the
west side of the South Gate 南行門 of the city of Fen-chou
and lodged at the Nieh-p'an-yüan (" Nirvana Cloister ") of
the Fa-ching-ssu 法津. This cloister is that of the solicitor

kao-ts'un 石高, should be made to correspond with the second
character of the cloister name, Shih-hao-yüan 毫, which may
reflect an earlier name for the modern Shih-hou-chen 侯鎮,
northeast of Wen-shui-hsien 文水, itself about forty km. southwest of Ch'ing-yüan-hsien. Cf. *Shan-hsi t'ung-chih* 2.10a.
[1024] August 31, 840. The preceding moon had only twenty-nine
days.
[1025] 汾河泊水. The Fen is the main river of Shansi, flowing in a
generally southwesterly direction through the middle of the
province until it empties into the Yellow River. At present the
main branch of the river flows more than twenty km. southeast
of Fen-yang, but a smaller branch makes a sharp turn to the
south a little east of the city.
[1026] 河中府, the modern Yung-chi 永濟 in the extreme southwestern corner of Shansi, was one of nine superior prefectures
known as *fu* as well as the capital of a regional commandery.
Cf. Des Rotours 682-88. Although the confluence of the Fen and
Yellow Rivers is about eighty km. northeast of the city, it was
in its area of jurisdiction in T'ang times.

of offerings for Mt. [Wu]-t'ai, the mendicant I-yüan. At T'ai-yüan he had earnestly entreated us to be sure to go to the cloister to rest when we reached Fen-chou, and so we went to the cloister and lodged there.

The Guard Officer [449] of the prefecture, Ho 何 by name, came to the monastery and met and comforted us. He is a disciple of the mendicant I-yüan, and, on seeing us travelers from afar, he acted as our host most courteously.

West of the city and fifty *li* from the monastery there is in the mountains a Kuang-ch'eng-yüan 廣城 where Abbot Hsien-wu 仙悟 lectures on the *Shikan* [331] of T'ien-t'ai [Ta-shih].[140] Over fifty of his disciples are in the city at present. Eighty *li* south of the city Mt. Pao-fu 寶福 rises high. People say that it is where the Buddha Kūō [1027] performed Buddhist practices, and even today there are very many holy sites there.

2nd DAY   It rained. Early in the morning we went to the home of Ho, the Guard Officer, and had tea and conversed. The Guard Officer arranged our midday rest. After the forenoon meal we started out and went thirty *li* south to Hsiao-i-hsien.[1028] One *li* north of the town is the grave of Marquis Wen of Wei.[1029] We went to the Nieh-p'an-yüan (" Nirvana Cloister ") in the city and spent the night. The Abbot Kuei-lun 桂輪 was not pleased when he first saw us, but later we talked and he finally became happy. Formerly he lectured on the *Nirvana Sutra* several times, and he also understands the secular classics 外典. He is now compiling *A Summary of the " T'ang Rhymes "* and a *Sounds of the Tripitaka* in eight scrolls,[1030] which he intends to present to the Emperor, but he has not yet completed his labors.

[1027] 空王, one of the Buddhas of the past mentioned in the *Lotus Sutra* and other scriptures.

[1028] 孝義, almost twenty km. south of Fen-yang.

[1029] Wen-hou 文侯 in 403 B.C. founded the feudal state of Wei 魏, one of the three succession states of Chin in Shansi. *DBZ* and *KIK* misprint 候 for 侯.

[1030] 唐韻略及大藏經音八卷. The *T'ang Rhymes* (*T'ang-yün*) was a famous book compiled on the basis of earlier works about

3rd DAY   We started early and went fifteen *li* south to the Wang-t'ung-yüan in Wang-t'ung-ts'un [1031] and took our midday rest. After the forenoon meal we went thirty *li* south to Leng-ch'üan-tien [1032] and spent the night. Our host was attentive.[1033]

4th DAY   After gruel we followed the Fen River down a mountain valley, going thirty-five *li* to the Li household in Hsiao-shui-tien 小水 and took our midday rest. After the forenoon meal we followed the Fen River southwestward for ten *li* to Ling-shih-hsien.[1032] Passing the town we followed the Fen River southward twenty *li* to Yin-ti Barrier,[1034] and the barrier officer checked us through. Passing the barrier, we went south ten *li* to the Tiao [1035] household in T'ao-liu-tien 桃柳 and spent the night. The village borders the Fen River, and has five or six families. Our host was gentle of spirit.

5th DAY   At dawn we went ten *li* south to the Fen River Barrier at Ch'ang-ning-i 長寧驛, and the barrier officer checked us through. It is the northern border of Ho-chung-fu [1026] and is in the jurisdiction of Fen-hsi-hsien in Chin-chou.[1036] We went twenty *li* south to Yung-ch'ing-i 永清 and took our midday rest. After the forenoon meal we went

───────────────────────────────

a century before Ennin's time. It is no longer preserved in its entirety.

[1031] 王同, possibly the modern Wang-t'un 王屯. Cf. *Shan-hsi t'ung-chih* 2.45b.

[1032] Probably the modern Leng-ch'üan-chen 冷泉鎮 on the east bank of the Fen and north of Ling-shih-hsien 靈石, which is itself about twenty-five km. south of Hsiao-i-hsien.

[1033] The word is best written as 周匝, but on VIII 3 and 24, *Tōji* has the inner element of the second character written with radical 162 (not the character 通 as *DBZ* states under VIII 3), and on VIII 10 *Tōji* has 周帀 (not 帀 as stated in *DBZ*).

[1034] 陰地, given as Yin-t'ou-kuan 頭 in *TTLCT*. The Fen River Barrier 汾水 mentioned on VIII 5 is probably the Nan-kuan 南關 which appears on modern maps.

[1035] 掉, which is not a regular surname.

[1036] Fen-hsi-hsien 汾西 is west of the Fen River a little more

twenty *li* south to Huo-i-hsien [1037] in the jurisdiction of Chin-chou. Just west of the town wall is the Pai-chih-ch'üan 白雉泉 ("White Pheasant Spring"). Of old, Emperor Hsiao-wen of Wei [965] was passing west of the city when he saw a white pheasant fly from under some rocks to the mountains, and this spring bubbled forth [from the same place]. Three *li* south of the city is the "nose of the golden dog." [1038] Emperor Wen of the Han (180-157 B. C.) [returning] from T'ai [908] was passing south of here when he saw a golden dog barking on this "nose." The above two stories are recorded on a wooden [sign]. The "nose of the golden dog" [consists of] three hills in a row looking like overturned bowls. The hills are high and on the north and west are steep, facing the town on the north and on the west the Fen River. The town is 350 *li* from T'ai-yüan [984] to the north, 910 *li* from the capital to the south, and 160 *li* from Chin-chou [1036] to the south.

We went fifteen *li* west [1039] from the town to Ma-chia-tien 馬家 in Huo-ch'ang-ts'un 霍昌 and spent the night. Our host was a ruffian.

6*th* DAY   After gruel we went fifteen *li* south to I-ch'ang-i [1040] and took our midday rest. Although our host was a religious man, he was very poor. After the forenoon meal we went thirty *li* south to Chao-ch'eng-hsien.[1040] We

---

than thirty km. southwest of Ling-shih-hsien, and Chin-chou 晉, the modern Lin-fen 臨汾, is on the east bank of the Fen River about ninety km. south of Ling-shih-hsien.

[1037] 霍邑, the modern Huo-chou, a little more than thirty km. south of Ling-shih-hsien.

[1038] 金狗鼻. The second character appears in a variant form. The use of "nose" is not common in Chinese place names but here refers to a sort of ridge. The *Huo-chou chih-li-chou chih* (1825) 4.4a tells of a Stone Nose Valley 石鼻谷 five *li* south of the city, which may be connected with this same place name.

[1039] Presumably an error for "south," which it somewhat resembles in *Tōji*.

[1040] 益昌, a short distance north of Chao-ch'eng-hsien 趙城, itself almost twenty *li* south of Huo-chou. Cf. *Shan-hsi t'ung-chih* 3.46a.

went fifteen *li* south from the town to the Ta-li-ssu 大曆 [945] in Ch'ü-hsiang-ts'un [1041] and spent the night.

7th DAY   In the morning we went twenty *li* south to Hung-tung-hsien [1042] and took our midday rest. After the forenoon meal we went sixty *li* [1043] south to the Shih-hsi 市西 ("West of the Market Place") Common Cloister in the city of Chin-chou [1036] and spent the night.

8th DAY   Early in the morning we went out the west gate of the city and went thirty *li* southwest to Chin-ch'iao-tien 晉橋 ("Chin Bridge Store") where we took our midday rest. We went twenty-five *li* south to Ku-kuan-tien 故關 ("Old Barrier Store") and, crossing the river, lodged at the Ching-yün 景雲 Common Cloister. North of the river is the southern boundary of Hsiang-ling-hsien [1044] of Chin-chou, and south of the river is the northern boundary of T'ai-p'ing-hsien of Chiang-chou.[1045]

9th DAY   In the morning it thundered and rained, but soon the rain stopped, and we went twenty-five *li* south to T'ai-p'ing-hsien and took our midday rest. We went out of the south suburb [1046] gate, going southwest fifty *li* to Tsung-chia-tien 宗家 at Ch'ang-ch'iu-i 長秋 and spent the night. About fifteen *li* north of the post station is Mt. Ma-t'ou.[1047]

10th DAY   We started early and went thirty *li* west

[1041] 屈項, which *DBZ* corrects to Ch'ü-ting 屈頂.

[1042] 洪洞, almost twenty km. south of Chao-ch'eng.

[1043] Possibly a copyist's error, because this is much longer than Ennin's usual afternoon march, and the total distance of ninety-five *li* between Chao-ch'eng and Chin-chou is somewhat excessive for an air-line distance of only twenty-five km.

[1044] 襄陵, on the Fen River about fifteen km. southwest of Lin-fen.

[1045] T'ai-p'ing-hsien 太平, the modern Fen-ch'eng 汾城, is northwest of the Fen River about twenty km. southwest of Hsiang-ling, and Chiang-chou 絳, also known as Hsin-chiang 新, is on the Fen River about sixty km. southwest of Lin-fen.

[1046] 廓 is presumably an error for 郭.

[1047] 馬頭 ("Mt. Horse Head"), a high peak twenty-five km. due west of Fen-ch'eng.

and took our midday rest at Chi-shan-hsien.[1048] From the
town we saw Mt. Chi [1049] in the distance. At a point fifteen
li from the town, locusts [1049a] were swarming over the road,
and in the houses in town there was no place to put your
foot down.[1050] After the forenoon meal we went sixty-five
li [1050a] west. Locusts swarmed over the roads. They had eaten
up all the grain 粟穀, and the people were in distress. At
dusk we reached Lung-men-hsien [1050a] and lodged at the
Chao-t'i-yüan 招提. The Prior monk was not attentive.[1033]

11th DAY   After the forenoon meal we went sixteen *li*
southwest to Hsin-ch'iao-tu 新橋渡 (" New Bridge Crossing ") and crossed the Fen River, going from [1051] the west
bank to the east bank. We went thirty-five *li* due south to
Ch'in-ts'un 秦 in the jurisdiction of Pao-ting-hsien [1052] and
lodged at the village monastery.

12th DAY   We started late. Toward the south we saw
at a distance the Yellow River. We went twenty-five *li* south
to Pao-ting-hsien and took our midday rest at T'ien-wang-i
天王邑. After the forenoon meal we went forty *li* south to

[1048] 稷山, on the north bank of the Fen about thirty km. west
of Chiang-chou.

[1049] About twenty km. south of the town, to which it has given
its name. The character 山 after 縣 in this sentence is presumably a copyist's error.

[1049a] *Huang-ch'ung* 黃虫, " yellow insects," here stands for its
homophone 蝗蟲, " locusts."

[1050] 宿, which follows this statement in *Tōji*, is perhaps a copyist's error and does not appear in the printed texts.

[1050a] Again this is a longer afternoon's march than usual (see
note 1043), but Lung-men-hsien 龍門 (the first character is
miswritten 瀧), the present Ho-chin 河津, is actually close to
thirty km. west of Chi-shan.

[1051] *DBZ* suggests that 從渡 be reversed.

[1052] 寶鼎 (the second character appears in a variant form) the
modern Jung-ho 榮河 on the Yellow River about twenty km.
southwest of the mouth of the Fen River and thirty-five km.
from Ho-chin.

the Sung 宋 household in Fen-tien [1053] in Lin-chin-hsien [1054] and spent the night. Our host was a religious man.

13th DAY We started early and went forty li south to Hsin-i-tien-t'ou 辛驛店頭 and took our midday rest. After the forenoon meal we went thirty-five li south to the Ho-chung regional commandery.[1026] The Yellow River flows southward to the west of the city.[1055] North of Ho-chung-fu the Yellow River flows southward, but when it comes south of the city it turns to the east. Coming from the north one goes through the Shun-hsi 舜西 Gate, and then comes to the P'u-chin Barrier. Reaching the barrier, we were checked in, and then we crossed the Yellow River. Floating boats have been formed into a bridge about two hundred paces long. Bridges are built [across] the western branch of the Yellow River at two places. Not far to the south the two branches unite and pass Ch'i-ch'ung-men 七重門 . We went five li toward the west to the Pa-chu-ssu 八柱 in Ho-hsi-hsien [1055] and spent the night. The monastery is a little over [1056] a hundred paces west of the town.

14th DAY We rested.

15th DAY Starting out, we went thirty li west to

[1053] 粉 (" Flour Store "). DBZ suggests that the first character be corrected to 汾 .

[1054] 臨晉, about twenty km. south of Jung-ho.

[1055] From Ennin's statements we see that at this time the main east branch of the Yellow River flowed immediately east of Yung-chi (Ho-tung-fu), close to the present boundary between Shansi and Shensi, which at this point is about ten km. east of the present course of the river. Ho-hsi-hsien 河西 (" West of the River "), which he describes as five li west of the river, must have been close to the modern P'ing-min 平民, but TTLCT shows it considerably further west. Ch'ao-i-hsien 朝邑 , which Ennin says was thirty li west of the river, is on the west bank of the present river, about fifteen km. southwest of Yung-chi. The P'u-chin Barrier 蒲津 , which Ennin describes as at or near Ho-tung-fu, is shown in TTLCT on the west bank of the Yellow River some distance northwest of the city.

[1056] DBZ suggests 來 for 未 .

Ch'ao-i-hsien [1055] and took our midday rest at a store 店·
After the forenoon meal we went thirty-five li west to T'ung-
chou [1057] and lodged at the T'ien-wang-yüan 天王 in the Mi-
hua Ward 靡化坊. It rained at night.

16th DAY In the morning the rain stopped, and we
started out, going west ten li and crossing the Lo River.[1058]
We went west ten li to the Wang household at Wang-ming-
tien 王明 in An-yüan-ts'un 安遠 in P'ing-i-hsien [1057] and
took our midday rest. It rained,[1059] and we did not go on,
lodging in the village monastery. Westward from the Lo
River the grain sprouts have all been consumed by the
locusts,[1049a] and the people of the countryside are in great
distress.

17th DAY The rain stopped, and we went fifteen li
west to the Kao 高 household in Fan-i-tien 蕃驛 and took
our midday rest. We went forty li west to Ku-shih-tien [1060]
and lodged at the T'ien-wang-yüan.

18th DAY We started late and went twenty-five li
west to Yung-an-tien 永安 and took our midday rest. After
the forenoon meal we went thirty-five li west to Hsin-tien
新 ("New Store"). We passed about thirty houses, looking
for a place to stay, but found none, and so we forced our way
into the house of [a man called] Chao 趙 and spent the night.

19th DAY We went thirty li south to Ts'ao-yang-
hsien [1061] in the area of Ching-chao-fu [1062] and took our mid-

---

[1057] 同, the modern Ta-li 大荔, about twenty km. west of
Ch'ao-i. The local subprefecture in T'ang times was P'ing-i-
hsien 馮翊 (the first character is miswritten with a variant
form of 憑 on VIII 16).

[1058] 洛河, which flows in a southeasterly direction southwest of
T'ung-chou.

[1059] DBZ suggests 雨下 for 雨行.

[1060] Ku-shih-tien 故市 ("Old Market Store"), presumably the
modern Ku-shih-chen, about forty km. southwest of T'ung-chou.

[1061] 操陽, presumably an error for Yüeh-yang-hsien 櫟陽, the
modern Yüeh-yang-chen, about fifteen km. northeast of Kao-
ling 高陵, itself about thirty-five km. northeast of Ch'ang-an.

[1062] 京兆府, the prefecture of the capital city (see note 984).

day rest. On the south side of the town we saw the Commissioner for the Imperial Mausoleum 山陵使 returning to the capital. He was the Commissioner who had buried the K'ai-ch'eng Emperor (Wen-tsung).[676] The tomb builders [1063] and soldiers stretched out for five *li*. Soldiers stood facing each other on either side of the road, but did not interfere with the people or horses and carts going along the road. The mausoleum 陵頭 is in the mountains eighty or ninety *li* west of the town and over two hundred *li* east of the capital. [1064]

Passing through the midst of the military encampment, we went thirty-five *li* south to the Wei Bridge [1065] in Kao-ling-hsien.[1061] The river is about one *li* wide and the bridge likewise. A garrison [29] faces the Wei River on the north bank. The Wei River originates in Tibet [794] and flows far to the east to the Yellow River. We crossed the bridge and went five *li* south to the Buddha Hall 佛殿 in San-chia-tien 三家 and spent the night.

20*th* DAY [We started] early and went south twenty-five *li* to Pa-ch'iao-tien (" Pa Bridge Store ") [1066] in Wan-

---

[1063] 營幕 is presumably an error for 營墓. Cf. Des Rotours 417.
[1064] Since the mausoleum is about ten km. northwest of Fu-p'ing 富平, it is actually about thirty km. north of Yüeh-yang which is about sixty-five km. northeast of Ch'ang-an. Cf. note in the *Zoku kokuyaku kambun taisei* 續國譯漢文大成 edition of *TCTC* 14.193. *TCTC* 246 records the interment on VIII 19.
[1065] 渭橋. There is still a " Wei Bridge " south of Kao-ling-hsien across the Wei River, the main river of southern Shensi, flowing almost due east to the Yellow River at the great bend. In T'ang times this was the easternmost of three bridges across the Wei near the capital and was known as the Eastern Wei Bridge. Cf. Adachi 191-92 and map section in *Hsü-hsiu Shan-hsi-sheng t'ung-chih k'ao* 續修陝西省通志稿 (1934).
[1066] 灞橋. The Pa River and Ch'an River 滻水, which parallels the Pa on its northward course, join a short distance north of where Ennin crossed them and then continue another ten km. northward to the Wei. The present Pa Bridge and Ch'an Bridge are somewhat south of where Ennin crossed these rivers. He

nien-hsien [1067] and took our midday rest. The Pa River originates in the Chung-nan Mountains [201] and empties into the Wei River. After the forenoon meal we went fifteen *li* south from the Pa Bridge to the Ch'an River Bridge.[1066] The Ch'an River comes from the Chung-nan Mountains and empties into the Wei River. The Pa and Ch'an Rivers both flow north and are clear in color, but I have not yet found out about the Ching River.[1068] We went ten *li* west to the front of the Chang-ching-ssu [591] east of the city of Ch'ang-an and rested. The monastery is east of the city outside the T'ung-hua Gate.[591] From outside the T'ung-hua Gate we went about three *li* south to the Hsi-ch'an-yüan 西禪 in the Chen-kuo-ssu 鎮國 outside the Ch'un-ming Gate [1069] and spent the night.

22nd DAY   At noon the Commissioner for the Imperial Mausoleum returned through the T'ung-hua Gate. After the forenoon meal we left the Chen-kuo-ssu and, entering the Ch'un-ming Gate, lodged in the Hsi-ch'an-yüan in the Ta-hsing-shan-ssu.[1070]

23rd DAY   After the forenoon meal we went to the Inspection Office of the Commissioner of Good Works for the

---

seems to have followed a route which is still the main road between Ch'ang-an and Kao-ling. Cf. map section in *Hsü-hsiu Shan-hsi-sheng t'ung-chih k'ao* and maps in Adachi.

[1067] 萬年. Wan-nien and Ch'ang-an were the names of the two subprefectures located at the capital and controlling the eastern and western halves of the city plus some surrounding territory.

[1068] 涇水. This river flows from the northwest into the Wei only a short distance west of the point where Ennin crossed the Wei. He probably mentioned it here because it was known as a muddy river in contrast to the clear Wei.

[1069] 春明門, the middle of the three eastern gates of the capital.

[1070] 大興善 (also called Hsing-shan-ssu), which was near the center of the T'ang city (in the fifth ward south of the Imperial Palace on the east side of the central thoroughfare), but over a mile and a half south of the southern gate of the greatly shrunken modern city of Hsi-an 西安. Cf. Adachi 220 and map opposite 136.

Streets of the Left [1071] and saw the Inspector Guard Officer and Censor of Outside Inquiries.[1072] His surname was Chao 趙 and his given name Lien 鍊. I gave him a document requesting that we [be allowed to] reside in the monasteries of the capital and seek teachers. The document is as follows:

> *Ennin, a Japanese monk in search of the Law, his disciple monks Ishō and Igyō, and his attendant Tei Yūman.*
> *Also enclosing official credentials from Ch'ing-chou.*[1073]
> It is stated that the said Ennin and the others came with a tributary embassy in the third year of K'ai-ch'eng (838) in order to seek Buddhist teachings and that in the third moon of this year they asked for official credentials from Ch'ing-chou to go to Mt. Wu-t'ai to worship at the holy sites and then to come here to study the holy Law.
> They humbly request that [they be permitted to] reside in the monasteries of the capital and seek teachers and listen to their instruction. Respectfully stated in full as above. They humbly await your decision.
> The statement of the matter is as given above. Respectfully written.

[1071] 左街功德巡院. There were two *Ta-kung-te-shih* 大功德使 (Commissioners of Good Works), who were in control of the monks of the capital. One was in charge of the "streets of the left" (*tso-chieh*), the half of the capital east of the main central thoroughfare, and the other in charge of the "streets of the right" (see note 318). Since the Ta-hsing-shan-ssu was east of the central thoroughfare, Ennin naturally came under the Commissioner of Good Works for the Streets of the Left. The Commissioners of Good Works traditionally were eunuchs, as in this case. See note 1075 and cf. J. K. Rideout, " The Rise of the Eunuchs during the T'ang Dynasty," *Asia Major* (New Series) 1.56.

[1072] *Chih-hsün Ya-ya Chien-ch'a-shih-yü-shih* 知巡押衙監察侍御史, obviously a subordinate in the office of the Commissioner of Good Works. Ennin later calls him by various parts of this title, including *Shih-yü* 侍御, a term for a Censor. For *Chien-ch'a-yü-shih* cf. Des Rotours 309. Also see note 418.

[1073] Obviously the document Ennin received at Ch'ing-chou (see note 540) on 840 IV 1.

Written on the twenty-third day of the eighth moon of the fifth year of K'ai-ch'eng by Ennin, the Japanese monk in search of the Law.

The Inspector Censor [1072] sent an Inspection Officer 巡官 to have us placed in the Tzu-sheng-ssu. [1074]

24th DAY   At 8 A. M. the Guard Officer [1072] of the Inspection Office [1071] wrote an order and sent an Inspection Officer to bring us to the Commissioner of Good Works, [1071] [who is] Ch'iu Shih-liang, [1075] the Commissioner of Good Works for the Streets of the Left, the Commander of the [Left] Guard Army [of Inspired Strategy], [1076] a *K'ai-fu-i-t'ung-san-ssu*, [1077] and the Grand General in Charge of the Steward's Department of the Palace, [1078] enfeoffed with 3,000 households. We monks followed the Inspection Officer Censor northward from the monastery past four wards and through

[1074] 資聖, apparently in the northeastern part of the city from the description of the route from the monastery to the Commissioner's office on VIII 24.

[1075] 仇士良 , whose biography is to be found in *HTS* 207. He was a eunuch from Kwangtung who exercised great power under Wen-tsung and is generally considered to have played a leading role in the disturbance of 835 (see note 207). He is also credited with the chief responsibility for having obtained the throne for Wu-tsung.

[1076] *Hu-chün Chung-wei*, an abbreviation of *Tso Shen-ts'e-chün Hu-chün Chung-wei* 左神策軍護軍中尉, the Commander of a capital army created in 753 and commanded by eunuchs after 786. Ch'iu Shih-liang had first been appointed to this post in 835 V, and it and his position as Commissioner of Good Works for the Streets of the Left were his two major official posts. Cf. Des Rotours LVIII, LIX, 565-69, 844 ff. and *TCTC* 245.

[1077] 開府儀同三司, the highest of the twenty-nine titles without function for civil officials. It was given to officials of the second class of the first rank. Cf. Des Rotours 35.

[1078] *Chih-nei-sheng-shih Shang-chiang-chün* 知內省事上將軍. Since Des Rotours 863 cites the case of a eunuch who in 796 was simultaneously appointed to be *Chih-nei-shih-sheng* 知內侍省 and *Tso Shen-ts'e-chün Hu-chün Chung-wei, Chih-nei-sheng-shih* here is probably an error or variant for *Chih-nei-shih-sheng*.

the Wang-hsien Gate.[1079] Next we entered the Hsüan-hua
Gate 玄花 and, passing the gate of the Commissioner of the
Crown Prince's Secretariat [1080] and the Bureau of the Director
General of the Imperial Parks,[1081] entered another gate and
arrived at the south gate of the Commissioner's quarters. Inside the gate was the gate for the foot and mounted [soldiers]
of the Left [Army] of Inspired Strategy.[1076] In all we passed
through six gates. Arriving before the Commissioner's Desk
案頭, we presented our documents and asked for a decision.
They inquired in detail about our reasons for coming, and I
made out another document to explain [1082] the matter, which
is as follows:

> The Japanese monk Ennin, his disciple monks Ishō and
> Igyō, and his attendant Tei Yūman.

The said Ennin and the others, accompanying the Japanese Tributary Embassy, boarded ship in the fourth moon [691]
of the third year of K'ai-ch'eng (838) and crossed the sea. On
the second day of the seventh moon they reached Pai-hu-chen [42]
in Hai-ling-hsien in Yang-chou and during the eighth moon
reached Yang-chou, where they resided in the K'ai-yüan-ssu,
spending one winter there. In the second moon of the fourth year
of K'ai-ch'eng (839) they left Yang-chou and went to Ch'u-chou,
where they resided in the K'ai-yüan-ssu. In the seventh moon
they went to the Mt. Ch'ih Cloister [523] in Wen-teng-hsien in
Teng-chou, residing there one winter. In the second moon of this

---

[1079] 望仙, the second from the east of the five gates leading from
the south into the Ta-ming Palace 大明宮, which was outside
the northern wall of the city proper. Cf. Adachi 171 ff. and map
opposite 136.

[1080] Nei-she-shih 內舍侍 is an unidentified title, but it closely
resembles that for one of the officials in the Crown Prince's
Secretariat (Ch'un-fang 春坊). Cf. Des Rotours 582 and 597.

[1081] Tsung-chien-yüan is an abbreviation of Kung-yüan Tsung-
chien-yüan 宮苑總監院. The Ta-ming Palace occupied a part
of the great Imperial Park which stretched from Ch'ang-an
northward and westward to the Wei and Ch'an Rivers. Cf. Des
Rotours 432 and Adachi 171.

[1082] DBZ suggests 令知 for 合知.

year they left Teng-chou and in the third moon reached Ch'ing-chou, where they provisionally resided in the Lung-hsing-ssu. For ten days [1083] they made petitions to the Regional Commander, the President of the Ministry Shou,[620] and finally obtained official credentials. On the first day of the fifth moon they reached Mt. Wu-t'ai and made pilgrimages to the holy sites. On the first day of the seventh moon they left Wu-t'ai and reached the capital on the twenty-third day of this moon.[1084]

They now request [to be permitted] to reside provisionally in the monasteries in the city, to seek teachers and listen to their instruction, and to return to their homeland. Respectfully stated in full as above. They humbly request a decision.

The statement of the matter is as above. Respectfully written.

Written on the twenty-fourth day of the eighth moon of the fifth year of K'ai-ch'eng by Ennin, the Japanese monk in search of the Law.

Because the *K'ai-fu* [1085] did not come, we were unable to present the document. The Administrative Officer [38] Ho 何 of the [Commissioner's] Desk escorted us to the Nei-hu-kuo-t'ien-wang-ssu 內護國天王 ("Inner Monastery of the Heavenly Kings, Protectors of the Nation") and settled us there. The monastery is north of the " ball field " [749] of the Left Army of Inspired Strategy and across a wall from the Imperial Palace 大內, thus being in the northeastern corner inside the inner wall of the Imperial City.[1086] They always have two [sets of] seven monks there to read [203] scriptures. When the monks saw us guests, they were attentive.[1033]

[1083] 十日巳來 normally would mean " from the tenth day on," but actually they first made application to the President of the Ministry on III 22 and received their credentials on the tenth day from the twenty-second (Chinese count), that is, on IV 1.
[1084] 今月廿三日 has been misprinted in *DBZ* as 今三月廿日 and has consequently been misinterpreted in *KIK*.
[1085] Although *K'ai-fu* was a title for certain military officers (cf. Des Rotours XXIX, 7, 520), here it is an abbreviation of *K'ai-fu-i-t'ung-san-ssu* (see note 1077) and therefore refers to Ch'iu Shih-liang.
[1086] Huang-ch'eng 皇城, the wall-enclosed administrative area

25th DAY   After the forenoon meal a messenger came from the Commissioner's Office to summon us monks, and we followed him to the Commissioner's Quarters, where we received a document from the Commissioner of Good Works. It stated that we were provisionally to stay at the Tzu-sheng-ssu [1074] and to rely on the Monastery Administrator [119] for provisions. The Inspector Censor, in conformity with the Commissioner's document, notified the Tzu-sheng-ssu and dispatched an Inspection Officer to accompany us to the monastery, where we were settled in the K'u-hsi-t'ing 庫西亭 ("Western Pavilion of the Storehouse").

26th DAY   It rained. In the evening the Monastery Administrator prepared quarters for us in the Ching-t'u-yüan 淨土 ("Paradise Cloister") and placed us there. Shih-an 師安, the Prior monk, was a religious man, and when he saw us guest monks he inquired about us kindly. Each time we asked the monks about the men who were devoted to and knew the [Buddhist] Law, we could learn nothing definite.

NINTH MOON: *5th* DAY [1087]   At night I concentrated 繋念 on Bishamon,[1088] praying that he would show me men who knew the Law.

I have heard that Li Te-yü,[92] the Regional Commander [1089] of Yang-chou, was given an Imperial command to come to the capital and that on the third day of the ninth moon he went to the Palace and was appointed Minister of State.[1090]

6th DAY   Early in the morning the monk Huai-ch'ing 懷慶 of this cloister, who occupies himself with devotions,

---

in the north central part of Ch'ang-an immediately south of the Imperial Palace.

[1087] The first day of the moon was September 30, 840. The previous moon had thirty days.

[1088] 毘沙門 (Skr. Vaiśravaṇa), one of the Four Heavenly Kings (see note 97).

[1089] Followed by a superfluous character 繋.

[1090] *TCTC* 246 records Li Te-yü's arrival at the capital on IX 1 and his appointment as Minister of State on IX 4.

brought five grains of relics [975] of the Buddha and had us worship them. He told us [the following]:

If we wish to observe the Esoteric Law, he knows well those in the whole city who understand the great Law. [Fa]-jun Ho-shang [1091] of the Ch'ing-lung-ssu [357] understands the *Taizō[kai]* [277] and has completely mastered the whole practice. Everyone in the city admits his skill. Although there is a monk from the Western Lands [884] at that monastery, he does not yet understand much of the [Chinese] language. The practices of devotion are not very hard to understand. Master [333] Wen-wu 文悟 of the Ta-hsing-shan-ssu [1070] understands the *Kongōkai*,[277] and [everyone] in the city [admits] his skill. I-chen Ho-shang [377] of the Ch'ing-lung-ssu [understands] both of the two [*mandara*].[277] At the Ta-hsing-shan-ssu is Yüan-cheng 元政 Ho-shang who has a deep understanding of the *Kongōkai* and understands both the phenomenal and the noumenal.[1092] Although there is a Learned Doctor [596] Nanda [1093] from the Western Lands at this monastery, he does not know much Chinese. At the Ta-an-kuo-ssu 大安國 is Master Yüan-chien 元簡 who understands and is skilled in the *Kongōkai* and also knows the Sanskrit letters,[1094] their drawing, and how to write Sanskrit 梵字. Fa-ch'üan [1095] Ho-shang of the Hsüan-fa-ssu 玄法 has a deep understanding of the Triple Great Law.[1096]

[1091] 法潤, a disciple of the famous Hui-kuo (see note 377).

[1092] *Jiri* 事理, which, while implying something of the dichotomy understood in the terms "noumenal" and "phenomenal," actually stands for the Buddhist metaphysical terms *uihō* 有爲法 (Skr. *saṁskṛta-dharmas*), "conditional elements," and *muihō* 無爲法 (Skr. *asaṁskṛta-dharmas*), "unconditional elements," which in combination produce the impermanent phenomena of the universe. Cf. Coates and Ishizuka 149-150.

[1093] 難陀, an Indian name which appears frequently in Buddhist literature.

[1094] *Shittan* 悉曇 (Skr. *siddham*), the study of the Sanskrit system of writing.

[1095] 法全, a famous disciple of Hui-kuo (see note 377) and

The new Emperor has rebuilt a monastery in the Hsüan-yang Ward,[1097] but he has not yet granted it its name plaque.[1098] It was erected by the Empress Dowager of the Yüan-ho [period].[1099] The present Emperor specially ordered the Empress Dowager to rebuild it and ordered the monasteries of the capital to select more than fifty monks and assign them to this monastery.

7th DAY   At the time of the forenoon meal Chao Lien, the Inspector Guard Officer of the Commissioner of Good Works for the Streets of the Left, came to this monastery and selected seven monks.[1100]

From the twenty-sixth day of the eighth moon until the tenth day of the ninth moon it rained continuously without clearing.

14th DAY   I wrote a letter inquiring about the health of the Inspector Censor, as follows:

As late autumn gradually grows colder, I humbly hope that much happiness will bless the Censor's person and actions. I, Ennin, have received your benevolence, but, limited by being a traveler, I have not been able to come to see you. There is nought to which I can compare the depth of my devotion. Since my trifling affairs have caused you much trouble, I had hoped to come to thank you now that I have obtained quarters, but, because it has rained without clearing for some

---

teacher of Esoteric Buddhism, who is usually associated with the Ch'ing-lung-ssu (see note 357).

[1096] *Sambu daihō* 三部大法, the triple division of Esoteric Buddhism into the *Taizōkai, Kongōkai* (see note 277), and *Soshitsujihō* 蘇悉地法. This last as explained in the scripture, *Soshitsujikyō*, is a way of uniting the other two. Ennin himself subsequently wrote a commentary on this scripture.

[1097] 宣陽坊 , near the southeastern corner of the Imperial City (see note 1086).

[1098] 額, to be hung over the main gate. In other words, it had not yet been named.

[1099] 元和上太后. Yüan-ho (806-820) was the year period of Hsien-tsung, the grandfather of Wen-tsung and Wu-tsung.

[1100] Presumably for the new monastery. See IX 6.

tens of days, I have not yet been able to accomplish this desire. I am abjectly fearful [1101] and humbly beg you not to blame me. I shall soon come to see you, but [meanwhile] I am thinking of you all the more.[1102]

I am respectfully sending my disciple monk Ishō to present this letter of inquiry. Respectfully written in brief.

Presented on the fourteenth day of the ninth moon of the fifth year of K'ai-ch'eng by Ennin, the Japanese monk in search of the Law.

To the Inspector Censor His Excellency, with humble respect.[647]

The Censor's letter in reply is separately [recorded]. I also received oral word from him asking us how we were now that we were here and stating that, since the monastery had no institutional meals,[1103] our meals could not be in accordance with the [Buddhist] Law, so we should write and bring him a letter and he would pass it on to the K'ai-fu,[1085] who would place us in a monastery having institutional meals.

18*th* DAY I wrote a letter and presented it to the Censor:

Ennin, the Japanese monk in search of the Law.

The said Ennin a few days ago humbly received your esteemed message. You have especially deigned to put him at ease. Insignificant as he is, he is not worthy of your gracious kindness.

Now, Ennin and the others, arriving suddenly, have already benefited from the kind offices of the Commissioner's Office 使司 and have provisionally been placed in this monastery. Their appreciation is humble and profound, and there is nothing more they wish. If they were to ask to be moved to a monastery with institutional meals,[1103] they would be apprehensive lest they cause trouble to the great officials. They now ask to [be allowed to] reside in the Tzu-sheng-ssu and to go to the various monasteries in order to find teachers and listen to

---

[1101] 悚 and a second character which appears to be an error for 疚.
[1102] *DBZ* suggests the addition of 增 to make the phrase 增馳結, as in the letter of X 17.
[1103] 堂飯, "hall meals," presumably meaning meals prepared by the monastery kitchen in accordance with the Buddhist regulations for monks.

their instruction, seeking the [Buddhist] Law as they wish, and to return at night to this monastery. They humbly request that the Censor benevolently arrange this and specifically grant them his permission.

Respectfully stated in full as above. They humbly ask for his decision. The statement of the matter is as above. Respectfully written.

Written on the eighteenth day of the ninth moon of the fifth year of K'ai-ch'eng by Ennin, the Japanese monk in search of the Law.

The Censor sent us the oral message that he left the matter up to us and, if we wanted anything else, we were to let him know and it would be no trouble for him to arrange it for us.

TENTH MOON: 13*th* DAY [1104]   I sent Ishō to the Ch'ing-lung-ssu [357] with Master Huai-ch'ing to see those who knew the [Buddhist] Law. At the Tung-t'a-yüan 東塔 ("Eastern Pagoda Cloister") is I-chen Ho-shang,[377] who understands the *Taizō[kai]*.[277] Master [En]gyō [123] of Japan studied the [Buddhist] Law here. There also is Fa-jun Ho-shang,[1091] who understands the *Kongōkai*. He is seventy-three years old and is palsied and senile.

16*th* DAY   I sent them to the Ta-hsing-shan-ssu [1070] to select men who knew the [Buddhist] Law for me. In the Fan-ching-yüan 翻經 ("Scripture Translation Cloister") is Master Yüan-cheng, who understands the *Kongōkai* and is well provided with literature on devotions. The Learned Doctor Nanda [1093] of India does not understand much Chinese. Master Wen-wu [1105] is not up to Master [Yüan]-cheng.

17*th* DAY   I sent a letter inquiring about the health of Master [Yüan]-cheng and also asked to borrow the *Methods of Reciting Religious Formulae*.[1106]

For long I have admired you, but never having had any

[1104] The first day of the moon was October 29, 840.

[1105] Misprinted 文語 in *DBZ* and *KIK*. See IX 6.

[1106] *Nenju hōmon* 念誦法門, which from the following references to it would seem to be a specific book or body of writings. Ennin uses the term *nenjuhō* on 841 IV 22 (see under IV 28).

contact with you, it is hard for me to express in words the depth of my admiration. I was most grateful for your esteemed inquiries yesterday and that you especially consoled my stupid self. As the early winter gradually grows colder, I humbly hope that much happiness will bless your holy self and actions.

I, Ennin, have gone far from my homeland 本縁 to seek out the Buddhist teachings and have wandered to this city, but I still do not have [a teacher] to serve under. I have humbly heard that you are renowned for virtue and are eminent in the [Buddhist] Way, that you have penetrated deeply into the repositories of the Law and have revealed the true teaching. Although I, Ennin, have not yet met you, I look up to your spirituality. As a stranger here, I have not been able to call on you, and so all I could do was to admire you [from afar]. I shall see you before long, but [meanwhile] I think of you all the more.

I am respectfully sending my disciple monk Ishō to present this letter in my place. Respectfully stated in brief.

Presented on the seventeenth day of the tenth moon of the fifth year of K'ai-ch'eng by Ennin, the Japanese monk.

To [Yüan]-cheng Ho-shang of the Hsing-shan-ssu

His Reverence, with humble respect.

At the Mt. Ch'ih Monastery [523] I had dreamed that I had bought a set of scales [1107] and the man who sold me the scales had said, " These are scales on which is weighed the weight of the three thousand myriad worlds," [1108] upon hearing which I greatly rejoiced.[1109] I was able to borrow the *Methods of Reciting Religious Formulae*.[1106]

[1107] *Ch'eng* 秤 , a " steelyard," in which the balancing weight is slid along a graduated rod.

[1108] *Sanzen daisen sekai* 三千大千世界, a term for the numberless worlds of Buddhist cosmology. *Daisen,* which I have rendered " myriad," is defined as 1,000,000,000.

[1109] The small 云云 at this point may be a copyist's erroneous repetition of the same characters at the end of the quotation, which *DBZ* omits. Ennin may have mentioned this dream here because he felt that it was a prophecy that he would be initiated into the mysteries of Esoteric Buddhism and that this prophecy was being fulfilled through his borrowing of the *Methods of Reciting Religious Formulae* from Yüan-cheng.

18*th* DAY   I started copying them.

29*th* DAY   I went to the Ta-hsing-shan-ssu and, entering the Ch'ih-fan-ching-yüan 勅翻經 (" Imperial Scripture Translation Cloister "), called on Yüan-cheng Ho-shang and for the first time received instruction in the Great Law of the *Kongōkai*. Entering the Imperially Established Baptistry 勅置灌頂道場, I worshiped the various great *mandara*,[277] made offerings, and received baptism. On the walls of the Fan-ching-t'ang 堂 (" Scripture Translation Hall ") are painted portraits of the Priest [115] Vajrabodhi [1110] and the Learned Doctor Amoghavajra.[948] South of the Fan-ching-t'ang is the Reliquary Pagoda of Ta-pien-cheng-kuang-chih, the Priest Amoghavajra.[1111] The two Learned Doctors, Vajrabodhi and Amoghavajra, formerly translated scriptures in this cloister.

On the night of the twenty-ninth day of the twelfth moon [1112] of the fifth year of K'ai-ch'eng I [dreamed] [1113] that I drew a *Kongōkai Mandara*, and, when I reached Japan, the Great Teacher,[140] on spreading out the *mandara*, rejoiced greatly. I started to pay reverence to the Great Teacher, but he said, " I dare not receive your reverence. I now pay you reverence." And with great courtesy he rejoiced that I had drawn the *mandara*.

ELEVENTH MOON: 3rd DAY [1114]   It snowed.

13*th* DAY   It snowed.

[1110] 金剛智, a southern Indian monk, well versed in Esoteric practices, who arrived in China via Canton in 719 and died in 732 at the age of seventy-one.

[1111] 大弁正廣智不空和尙舍利塔, presumably containing Amoghavajra's " relics," that is, his ashes. Ta-pien-cheng-kuang-chih is an official posthumous title he was given. The character 弁 is more properly written 辯.

[1112] Presumably an error for " tenth moon."

[1113] *DBZ* and *KIK* add this word (cf. X 17), but fail to indicate that it is missing in *Tōji*.

[1114] The first day of the moon was November 28, 840.

26th DAY   It was the festival of the winter solstice.[1114a] The monks exchanged felicitations, saying, " I humbly hope that you will long be in the world and will be in harmony with all creatures." The ordained and the novices in speaking to the Superior [81] observed exactly the regulations of the written codes of conduct. The novices touched their right knees to the ground in front of the monks and spoke words of congratulation on the festival. When we ate our gruel, they served us dumplings [1115] and fruit.

TWELFTH MOON: 8th DAY [1116]   On Imperial command the various monasteries burned incense and held maigre feasts. In this monastery the Minister of State Li Te-yü [92] and an Imperial Commissioner 勅使 burned incense. It was the memorial day of Hsüan-tsung, the Emperor of the Ta-li [period].[1117] The maigre feast was arranged completely with government goods. The Debater of the Three Teachings [1118]

[1114a] In the calendar under I 15 the winter solstice was dated on XI 20, which fits in better with the other subseasons.

[1115] Hun-t'un 餛飩 (the first character is miswritten with the phonetic 昆), which are usually stuffed with pork, though in this case they must have been vegetarian dumplings.

[1116] The first day of the moon was December 28, 840.

[1117] DBZ corrects the word order from 大曆玄宗忌日皇帝 to 大曆玄宗皇帝忌日, but does not indicate that a change has been made. A still better word order might be 大曆皇帝玄宗忌 日 . Ennin here has made a double mistake. This was the memorial day of Ching-tsung 敬宗 (reigned 824-826; see 838 XII 8 and note 265), who was the brother and predecessor of both Wen-tsung and Wu-tsung. Ching-tsung was murdered on 826 XII 8. Hsüan-tsung (reigned 712-756) died on 762 IV 5, and the Emperor of the Ta-li period was not Hsüan-tsung but Tai-tsung 代宗 (reigned 762-779), who died on 779 V 21.

[1118] San-chiao T'an-lun 三教談論, presumably one who had been honored by being invited to participate in the official debates at court between Buddhists, Taoists, and Confucianists. Ennin himself subsequently mentions several debates between the first two categories. In this title he sometimes uses Chiang 講 in place of T'an.

and Reverence [248] of the Palace Place of Ritual,[1118a] Chih-hsüan 知玄 Ho-shang of this monastery, offered praises.

22nd DAY   I had Wang Hui 王惠 of the Yung-ch'ang Ward [1119] start drawing four copies of the *Kongōkai Great Mandara.*

25th DAY   Since we were once again entering a new year, the congregation of monks went to the hall and ate gruel, dumplings,[1115] and mixed fruits. While the congregation of monks was eating gruel, the Monastery Administrator,[119] Controller,[81] and Manager [641] read before the assembly the books of the uses of money and goods [1120] for the monastery's estates 諸庄, its trade 交易, its provisions [1121] for guests, and various expenses.

K'AI-CH'ENG · SIXTH YEAR

hsin-yu

FIRST MOON: 1*st* DAY [1122]   Monks and laymen celebrated the new year. At the monastery food was provided for the monks for three days.[1123]

4th DAY   It was a national anniversary for the preceding Emperor.[676] An Imperial command ordered the Chien-fu-ssu [1124] to burn incense, and one thousand monks were invited.

[1118a] *Naidōjō* (Ch. *Nei-tao-ch'ang*) 內道塲   (see note 284).

[1119] 永昌, in the northeastern part of the city just east of the Imperial Palace.

[1120] 用錢物帳. Cf. 用途帳 on 838 XII 29 in a similar passage.

[1121] *DBZ* suggests a graphic variant of 料 for what seems to be 斷.

[1122] January 27, 841. *Hsin-yu* 辛酉 is fifty-eighth in the sixty-year cycle.

[1123] See 839 I 1.

[1124] The Ta-chien-fu-ssu 大薦福 (also known as the Chien-fu-ssu) stood almost in the center of the T'ang capital a little south of the Imperial City. Thirteen stories of the fifteen-story pagoda built there in T'ang times still stand as a prominent land-

6*th* DAY   It was the festival of the beginning of spring.[633] Hempseed cakes 胡餅 were given by the Emperor, and at the time for gruel the monastery served the hempseed cakes. All the lay households did likewise.

A special Imperial order has appointed a Grand General of the *Chin-wu* Guards of the Left.[388] He is an Imperial relative, being the maternal uncle of the present Emperor. Originally he was destitute and last year went to the city wards and monasteries, carrying turnips, chrysanthemums, violets, and the like to sell. Recently he has received Imperial favor and been made a Grand General of the *Chin-wu*. He went to the Palace and received the appointment, and when he came out, twenty pairs of armored [men] led his horses, some fifty or sixty mounted soldiers blocked the streets with staves, and a hundred-odd foot soldiers guarded his carriage. The foot soldiers all wore embroidered hats and embroidered robes.[1124a] The robe, headgear, and shoes which the Grand General wore were all embroidered with a design of birds holding auspicious plants in their mouths.[1125] After worshiping in the southern suburb,[1126] he was appointed Regional Commander of Feng-hsiang-fu.[1127]

mark about one mile south of the southern gate of the present city. The pagoda is now known as the Hsiao-yen-t'a 小雁塔, "Little Wild Goose Pagoda." Cf. Adachi 214-16 and map opposite 136.

[1124a] The 來 in this sentence may be a copyist's error.

[1125] In 鳥衙瑞草之文 *DBZ* suggests that the second character be corrected to 衡.

[1126] In 南郡 here and on I 9 and in 南郡壇 on I 8, *DBZ* corrects the second character to 郊, since the Altar of Heaven (*T'ien-t'an* 天壇) was in the southern suburb of the city and the reference appears to be to it. Perhaps this sentence is a later interpolation and is to be understood, "After [the Emperor] had worshiped in the southern suburb [on I 8 and 9], he appointed [his maternal uncle] to be Regional Commander of Feng-hsiang-fu."

[1127] 鳳翔府, north of the Wei River and about 180 km. west of Ch'ang-an.

7th DAY   The present Emperor went to the T'ai-
ch'ing Palace [1128] and had a maigre feast.

8th DAY   Early in the morning the Emperor went
out of the city and proceeded to the Altar [of Heaven] in the
southern suburb.[1126] The Altar is in front of the Ming-te
Gate.[1129] A crowd of two hundred thousand guards and
soldiers of the left and right accompanied him. The many
wonders [of the occasion] were quite beyond count.

9th DAY   After completing his worship in the southern
suburb in the fifth watch (4 A. M.), the Emperor returned
to the city early in the morning and, proceeding to the Tan-
feng Tower,[1130] changed the year period, making the sixth
year of K'ai-ch'eng into the first year of Hui-ch'ang 會昌.

An Imperial order was sent to seven monasteries in the
left and right streets [1071] to hold lectures for laymen 俗講.
Four of these places [are] in the left streets: the Tzu-sheng-
ssu [1074] had Hai-an 海岸 Fa-shih of the Yün-hua-ssu 雲花, a
Reverence Granted the Purple,[1131] lecture on the *Kegon-
kyō*; [933] the Pao-shou-ssu 保壽 had T'i-hsü 體虛 Fa-shih, Archbishop of the Streets of the Left,[1132] a Debater of the Three
Teachings,[1118] a Reverence Granted the Purple, and an Attendant Priest,[1133] lecture on the *Lotus Sutra*; the P'u-t'i-ssu

---

[1128] 太清宮, an official temple to Lao-tzu, the reputed founder
of Taoism. Cf. Des Rotours 14, 387, 390. Probably the maigre
feast the Emperor had at this temple was a Taoist version of
the Buddhist meal.

[1129] 明德, the central southern gate of the city at the southern
end of the great central thoroughfare leading from the Imperial
Palace and Imperial City.

[1130] 丹鳳樓, the tower over the Tan-feng Gate, the central southern gate to the Ta-ming Palace (see note 1079).

[1131] 賜紫. Only courtiers of the fifth rank were entitled to wear
robes of this color. Therefore it was a mark of special favor for
a monk to have been granted this privilege. See note 248.

[1132] *Tso-chieh-seng-lu,* a government appointee. See note 317.

[1133] *Yin-chia* 引駕, standing for *Yin-chia Ta-shih,* one of the four
honorary titles of *Ta-shih* (see note 140) granted monks by the
T'ang and meaning something like " Great Teacher Who Leads
the Carriage of the Emperor."

菩提 [894] had Ch'i-kao 齊高 Fa-shih of the Chao-fu-ssu 招福, a Reverence who is a Court Priest [824] and a Debater of the Three Teachings, lecture on the *Nirvana Sutra*; [203] the Ching-kung-ssu 景公 had Kuang-ying 光影 Fa-shih lecture. Three of the places [are] in the right streets: the Hui-ch'ang-ssu [1134] had Wen-hsü 文漵 Fa-shih, who is a Court Priest, a Debater of the Three Teachings, a Reverence Granted the Purple, and a Personal Attendant Priest,[1135] lecture on the *Lotus Sutra*. He was the first Priest to give lectures for lay-men in the city. I have not yet obtained the names of lec-turers at the Hui-jih-ssu 惠日 and the Ch'ung-fu-ssu 崇福.

Also on Imperial command, lectures on Taoism were held. In the left streets they had Chü-ling-fei 矩令費, who had recently been summoned on Imperial command from Chien-nan-tao [1136] to be the Court Priest [824] of the T'ai-ch'ing Palace,[1128] lecture at the Hsüan-chen-kuan 玄眞觀 on the *Nan-hua* [1137] and other scriptures. I have not yet got the name of the one place [where lectures on Taoism were held] in the right [1138] streets.

All of these were lectures on Imperial command. Since the ninth year of T'ai-ho (835) they have held no lectures, but the new Emperor has started them again. They started on the fifteenth day of the first moon and ended on the fifteenth day of the second moon.

[1134] Since Hui-ch'ang was the name of the new year period, this must have been a recently given name, but it could not have been the unnamed monastery mentioned on 840 IX 6, because that was in the streets of the left (see note 1097).

[1135] Here *ch'i-chü* 起居, meaning one's personal activities or health, is appended to *Yin-chia* (see note 1133).

[1136] See note 160. *Tōji* actually has 釰南道, but the first char-acter may be a copyist's error or a graphic variant for 劍, and the third is corrected in *Ikeda* to 道.

[1137] 南花, standing for the *Nan-hua-ching* 南華經, a term for the great Taoist classic, the *Chuang-tzu* 莊子.

[1138] The printed texts have "left," but the character in *Tōji* appears to be "right," as the context demands.

SECOND MOON: 8th DAY [1139]   The drawing of the *Kon-gōkai Mandara* was completed.

On Imperial command Ching-shuang 鏡霜 Fa-shih of the Chang-ching-ssu [591] transmits the *nembutsu* teachings of the Pure Land of Amida [1140] in the various monasteries. From the twenty-third day until the twenty-fifth day he transmitted the *nembutsu* teachings in the Tzu-sheng-ssu. He also goes around to the various other monasteries, [staying] three days at each monastery. He continues his rounds without stopping month after month.

The Ta-chuang-yen-ssu [1141] held an offering to the tooth of the Buddha Shakamuni from the eighth day of the third moon [1142] until the fifteenth day. The Chien-fu-ssu [1124] held an offering to the tooth of the Buddha. From the eighth day to the fifteenth day Lan-t'ien-hsien [1143] had tea and food without restrictions,[1144] and monks and laymen came from every direction to eat. T'i-hsü Fa-shih, the Archbishop of the Streets of the Left,[1132] served as the head of the festival.[1145] The

---

[1139] The first day of the moon was February 25, 841.

[1140] *Amida jōdo nembutsu kyō* 阿彌陀淨土念佛教 . The Pure Land is the name of Amida's paradise, and *nembutsu* means " to call on the name of Buddha " (see notes 273 and 510). The whole term smacks strongly of the popular faith concepts which were to come to the fore in Japan in the twelfth and thirteenth centuries.

[1141] 大莊嚴, in the extreme southwestern corner of the city. Cf. Adachi map opposite 136.

[1142] This apparently is not an error for " second moon," even though it is recorded under II 8, and later date notations indicate that Ennin was still writing about the second moon. Ennin makes reference again to this festival on 842 III 8, indicating that it was an annual event which began each year on III 8. Possibly the two following references to the second moon are errors for " third moon."

[1143] 藍田, about forty km. southeast of Ch'ang-an.

[1144] 无㝵茶飯. Cf. *muge daie* 無礙大會 , a great maigre feast for all monks and laymen without restrictions on participants.

[1145] *DBZ* suggests 會主 for 會至.

various monasteries took part, each arranging fine offerings. All sorts of medicines and foods, rare fruits and flowers, and many kinds of incense were carefully prepared and offered to the Buddha's tooth. They were spread out beyond count in the gallery around the storied offering hall 供養樓. The Buddha's tooth was in the . . .[41] in the storied hall. All the Reverences [248] of the city were in the storied hall adoring [865] it and making praises. The whole city came to worship and make offerings. One man donated one hundred bushels [217] of non-glutinous rice and twenty bushels of millet.[314] Another man provided biscuits [1146] plentifully and without restrictions. Another man donated enough cash for the miscellaneous needs of the meals without restrictions 无礙供雜用錢. Another man provided thin cakes without restrictions, and another donated enough for the meals of the Reverences and venerable monks [170] of the various monasteries. In this way each one made his vows and offered his alms, making a glorious festival of the Buddha's tooth. People tossed cash like rain toward the storied hall of the Buddha's tooth.

We monks in search of the Law went on the tenth day and performed adoration.[865] We went up into the storied hall of the Buddha's tooth and saw the Buddha's tooth ourselves and reverently held it 頂戴 and worshiped it. We also entered the Fan-ching-yüan (" Scripture Translation Cloister ") and saw the portrait of the Learned Doctor I-ching.[1147] On the wall was painted [1148] [a picture of the Buddha] touching the Learned Doctor's head in ordination.[1149]

The Hsing-fu-ssu 興福 west of the Sung-shu-chieh 松樹街

[1146] *Nieh-t'ou* 捻頭.

[1147] I-ching (635-713) went to India in 671 and after twenty-five years there returned to China to become a famous translator of Buddhist scriptures (see note 530). Since much of his work of translation was done at the Chien-fu-ssu and he ultimately died there, it is probable that Ennin was recording what he saw at that monastery rather than at the festivals held simultaneously at the Ta-chuang-yen-ssu and Lan-t'ien-hsien.

[1148] *DBZ* suggests 畫 for 書.

[1149] *Machō* 摩頂.

("Pine Tree Street") also holds an offering to the Buddha's tooth from the eighth day to the fifteenth day of the second moon,[1142] and the Ch'ung-sheng-ssu [1150] holds another offering to the Buddha's tooth. In all there are four teeth of the Buddha in the city. The Buddha's tooth at the Ch'ung-sheng-ssu was brought from heaven by Prince Nata [1151] and given to the Preceptor [1152] [Tao]-hsüan of the Chung-nan Mountains.[201] The Buddha's tooth at the Chuang-yen-ssu was brought from India in the flesh of a [person's] thigh. The Protector of the Law 護法, the deity Kabira,[262] was able to bring it. Another was brought by Fa-chieh 法界 Ho-shang from the land of Khotan,[1153] and another was brought from Tibet.[794] So has run the tradition since early times, and at present in the city the four monasteries make offerings [to the teeth].

SECOND MOON: [1142] *13th* DAY　My instruction in the Great Law of the *Kongōkai* was concluded, and I made offerings to the *Kongōkai Mandara* and received Baptism as a Transmitter of the Law.[1154] Five jars of water were poured on my head. At night I made offerings to the Twelve Heavens.[1155] Everything went auspiciously. I also mounted the pagoda of the Tz'u-en-ssu.[1156]

[1150] 崇聖, in the west central part of the city. Cf. Adachi map opposite 136.

[1151] Prince (太子 here but 天子 on III 25) Nata 那吒 (Skr. Naṭa) is the son of Bishamon (see note 1088).

[1152] *Risshi* 律師 (Ch. *Lü-shih*), an appropriate title for the systematizer of the Rules Sect (see note 330).

[1153] Yü-tien 于闐, in the southern part of the Tarim Basin.

[1154] *Dembō Kanjō* 傳法灌頂, for those competent to teach Esoteric Buddhism. See 840 X 29. Coates and Ishizuka 172-73 list the various forms of baptism.

[1155] *Jūniten* 十二天, a listing which includes the heavens of Taishaku, Bonnō, and Bishamon (see notes 848 and 1088). Ennin may have made this particular offering because pictures of the Twelve Heavens commonly surround a Baptistry.

[1156] The Tz'u-en-ssu 慈恩, one of the greatest of the Ch'ang-an monasteries in T'ang times, stood in the southeastern part of the city. Its great pagoda, erected by Hsüan-tsang (see note

15th DAY The Hsing-t'ang-ssu 興唐, on behalf of the nation, held a Baptism Ritual [284] from the fifteenth day to the eighth day of the fourth moon.[1157] Those with affinities [for the Law] came and received the Baptism to Establish Affinities.[1158]

THIRD MOON: 25th DAY [1159] I went to the Ch'ung-sheng-ssu [1150] and worshiped at the festival of the tooth of the Buddha Shakamuni.[214] I was repeatedly told that [Tao-hsüan], the Priest [115] of the Chung-nan Mountains,[330] obtained it from the Prince of the Bishamon Heaven and that Prince Nata [1151] had brought it from heaven and given it to the Priest. At present it is placed in the monastery where offerings are made to it.

FOURTH MOON: 1st DAY [1160] The Fan-ching-yüan ("Scripture Translation Cloister") of the Ta-hsing-shan-ssu [1070] held a Baptism Ritual [284] on behalf of the nation. It went right on until the twenty-third day before stopping.

4th DAY I went to the Ch'ing-lung-ssu [357] and, entering the Tung-t'a-yüan ("Eastern Pagoda Cloister"), examined the various *mandara* in detail.

7th DAY I went to the Ta-hsing-shan-ssu and, entering the Baptistry, performed adoration.[865] I also mounted the Balcony of His Holiness Monju.

---

166), still stands about two miles south of the southeastern corner of the modern city and is known as the Ta-yen-t'a 大雁塔, "Big Wild Goose Pagoda." See note 1124 and cf. Adachi 203 ff. and map opposite 136. It was because of his long residence in the Tz'u-en-ssu that K'uei-chi received the appellation Tz'u-en Ta-shih (see note 166).

[1157] The latter date is the traditional birthday of the Buddha.

[1158] *Kechien Kanjō* (see notes 289 and 1154), a baptism given to laymen whether or not they were believers in Esoteric Buddhism. By "those with affinities" 有緣 Ennin means those who because of their karma were willing to receive baptism. See also note 1169.

[1159] The first day of the moon was March 27, 841.

[1160] The first day of the moon was April 25, 841.

9th DAY   The *K'ai-fu* [1085] dedicated 迎 a stele cele-
brating his glorious deeds and virtuous administration. It
was taken from the Ta-an-kuo-ssu through the Wang-hsien
Gate [1079] and was erected in [the grounds of] the Left Army
of Inspired Strategy.[1076] The inscription read, " Stele of the
Glorious Record and Virtuous Administration of Lord 公
Ch'iu." [1075] The soldiers and their mounts at the dedication
of the stele and the various grand preparations were beyond
enumeration. The present Emperor looked on from the
Wang-hsien Tower.[1161]

13th DAY   I summoned the painter Wang Hui and
conferred over the price for painting the *Taizō[kai]* pictures.

15th DAY   After finishing the forenoon meal, in my
sleep I saw an old monk of this monastery bring in forty
bolts [192] of silk and say, " Some patrons know that you intend
to make a representation of the *Taizō[kai]*, and therefore
they have brought these alms." About ten laymen were in
the room, expressing their admiration, and they said, " You
are soon going to have a *Taizōkai Mandara* made. We are
overflowing with wealth and have nowhere to put it, so
please accept these goods."

I also dreamed that a monk brought me a letter and said,
" I have come from Mt. Wu-t'ai. The mendicant [592] who
lives on the northern terrace gave me a letter inquiring after
the Japanese Priest." I then opened the envelope and looked
at the letter. The opening 初注 said, " We had never met in
our lives, but some time ago I saw you at Wu-t'ai." The
main message 具問詞 [said], " I am sending you a sash of
white silk and a knife. I have long treasured them both, so
please accept them. Salutations."

In the evening the master [874] [Wang] Hui came, and we
settled on the price for the drawings. For fifty strings of
cash [191] he was to make five drawings.

28th DAY   He started drawing the *Taizō* pictures.

[1161] The tower over the Wang-hsien Gate. Brief mention of this
incident is made under the date of 841 II in *CTS* 18A. Cf. also
Okada 11.484.

As early summer gradually grows hotter, I humbly hope that much happiness will bless the Priest's person.

I, Ennin, have received your kind tolerance and have been allowed to undertake this copying. Since I have not been able to meet you often, I am most apologetic [1101] and shall make a special visit in a day or two. I shall soon pay you my respects, but [meanwhile] I think of you all the more. I am respectfully sending my disciple monk Igyō to present respectfully this inquiry. Respectfully written in brief.

Presented on a day in the fourth moon of the first year of Hui-ch'ang by [En]nin, the Japanese Shaman [1162] in search of the Law.

To [I]-chen Ho-shang [377] of the Ch'ing-lung-ssu [357]

His Honor, with humble respect. [1163]

Three bolts [192] of silk.

Though the above goods are insignificant, I respectfully apply them to the expenses of your protective power.

I, Ennin, have been a traveler for many years. Because I am poor, even though my attendance on you has been close, I am without goods to offer you. With the above trifling goods, I respectfully manifest my deep feelings, and I humbly hope you will accept them without scorning their insignificance. Respectfully stated in brief.

Presented on a day in the fourth moon of the first year of Hui-ch'ang by Ennin the monk in search of the Law.

To [I]-chen Ho-shang of the Ch'ing-lung-ssu His Reverence.

I finished copying the newly translated scriptures of the Hsing-shan-ssu and the *Methods of Reciting Religious Formulae* [1106] on the twenty-second day of the fourth moon. [Yüan-cheng] Ho-shang said to me, " I have told you all that I understand about the Great Law of the *Kongōkai*, and you have copied down all of these practices. If there is anything further that you lack, you should seek it elsewhere." All the gold which I gave at one time or another to Yüan-cheng Ho-

---

[1162] *Shamon* 沙門 (Skr. Śramaṇa), a term sometimes used for Buddhist priests.

[1163] 座前謹空. *DBZ* misprints 識 for the third character. See note 647.

shang amounted to twenty-five ounces.[127] Besides this [there were other things] not within this limit.

> *Ten strings of cash.*
> The above, although insignificant, respectfully manifests my deep sincerity. I humbly hope you will examine and accept it.
> I, Ennin, have come from afar because of the Law and, fortunately meeting you, have learned from you the Great Law of the *Taizō[kai]*. I humbly ask that your grace especially descend upon me, and I humbly vow to propagate widely the Buddhist Law to benefit sentient beings. I am overwhelmed by my gratitude to you. Respectfully I present this letter, respectfully making this statement.
> *Presented on the twenty-eighth day of the fourth moon of the first year of Hui-ch'ang by Ennin, the Japanese monk in search of the Law.*
> *To [I]-chen Ho-shang of the Ch'ing-lung-ssu His Reverence.*

28th DAY   We set about drawing the *Taizō* pictures.

30th DAY [1164]   At dusk [1165] we consulted over the price for drawing the *Kongōkai Kue* [1166] *Mandara* and settled on sixty cash [1167] excluding the silk for the drawings. A lay convert of [I]-chen Ho-shang gave me forty-six feet of silk to be used for the drawings.

[1164] *Ikeda* has "29th day," possibly because there were only twenty-nine days in this moon in the Japanese calendar, although there were thirty in the Chinese calendar. This is one of several small indications that *Ikeda*, instead of representing an independent transmission of the text, is merely a copy of *Tōji* with certain corrections (and an occasional miscorrection) made by a reasonably intelligent copyist.

[1165] *Ikeda* corrects 黃 to 黃昏.

[1166] *Kue* 九會, meaning "nine assemblies," refers to the fact that the *Kongōkai Mandara* is divided into nine equal squares, each with an assemblage of Buddhas and lesser divinities.

[1167] This probably should be "sixty strings of cash" or else "6,000 cash" (六千 instead of "sixty" 六十, as on V 3), which would be more in line with the price of fifty strings of cash for five copies of the *Taizōkai Mandara* (10,000 cash each) agreed

FIFTH MOON: 1st DAY [1168] I sent my attendant Tei Yūman with my thanks [to I-chen].

Yesterday I humbly received your esteemed opinions, and I am delighted beyond measure that everything is about to be accomplished. I deeply thank the Priest's convert for having given me forty-six feet of silk for the good work of drawing [the *mandara*]. His benevolence is very great, and I, Ennin, am overwhelmed with gratitude. With the hot nights of summer here, I hope that much happiness will bless the Priest's person.

I, Ennin, have received your kind tolerance, but because of minor matters I have not been able to come in person to state my thanks. I am abjectly embarrassed and shall come especially to your cloister some day in the future. I shall thank you in person before long, but [meanwhile] I think of you all the more. I am overcome with the greatness of my awe and happiness.

I am respectfully sending Tei Yūman to present this letter humbly stating this. Respectfully written in brief.

Presented on the first day of the fifth moon of the first year of Hui-ch'ang by Ennin, the monk in search of the Law.

To [I]-chen Ho-shang of the Ch'ing-lung-ssu

His Reverence, with humble respect.

FIFTH MOON: 1st DAY On Imperial command lectures were held. There were lectures on Buddhism in ten monasteries in the two halves of the city [1071] and lectures on Taoism in two temples. Ssu-piao 嗣標 Fa-shih, a Court Priest [824] and a Debater [1118] Reverence of this monastery, lectured on the *Diamond Sutra* [292] in this monastery. Yüan-ching 圓鏡 Fa-shih of the Ch'ing-lung-ssu [357] lectured on the *Nirvana Sutra* [203] in the P'u-t'i-ssu. I cannot record in detail the others.

3rd DAY We started the drawing of the five *Kongōkai Kue* [1166] *Mandara.* Aside from the silk for the drawings, the cost of the drawings was 6,000 cash. [1167] On this day I made

---

upon on IV 15. These obviously were different *Kongōkai* paintings from the four commissioned on 840 XII 22 and completed on 841 II 8.

[1168] May 25, 841.

offerings at the Ch'ing-lung-ssu. Then I received baptism and cast a flower [1169] in the Imperially Established Life Star Baptistry.[1170] I started to receive instruction in the *Taizō[kai]* and the Great Law of the *Birushana-kyō* [1171] and also in the Great Law of *Soshitsuji*.[1096]

FIFTH MOON: 14*th* DAY   I ate some melons [1172] which were delicious and ripe.

SIXTH MOON: 11*th* DAY [1173]   It was the birthday of the present Emperor, and a maigre feast was arranged in the Palace. The [Buddhist] Reverences and Taoist priests from the two halves of the city who were being served assembled and discussed their [respective] scriptures in a four-cornered debate.[1174] The two Taoist priests were granted the purple,[1131] but none of the Buddhist Reverences was permitted to wear it.

The Learned Doctor Ratnacandra [1175] of Southern India

[1169] 抛花 for *tōge* 投華. In the *Kechien Kanjō* (see note 1158) the participant threw a flower on a *mandara*, and whichever one of the many portraits of deities it landed on was then considered to be his patron deity with whom he had " established affinities." Ennin probably was performing these ceremonies in preparation for the new course of instruction he was undertaking.
[1170] *Hommyō Kanjō Dōjō*. In 850 Ennin was to establish on Mt. Hiei a place of ritual on the model of the Life Star Place of Ritual (*Hommyō Dōjō*) of the Ch'ing-lung-ssu, in which prayers were made to the Emperor's life star (*hommyō-sei* 本命星) for the preservation of the state. Cf. Ennin's biography in the *Genkō shakusho* 元亨釋書 3 (*DBZ* 101.173b), a series of biographies of famous Japanese monks compiled by Shiren 師錬 (1278-1346).
[1171] 毘盧遮那經 (or *Dainichi-kyō* 大日), the *Mahāvairocana-sūtra*.
[1172] 苽 appears to be an error for 瓜.
[1173] The first day of the moon was June 23, 841.
[1174] 四對論議. Since two Taoists were rewarded, it is possible that one Buddhist and one Taoist from each of the two halves of the city took part in the debate.
[1175] Ch. Pao-yüeh 寶月. Cf. Waley 154.

went to the Palace and, confronting His Majesty, drew out a statement from his bosom and presented it, asking to [be allowed to] return to his homeland. He did this rash act [1176] without previously consulting the *K'ai-fu*.[1085] He was detained by the military for five days and charged with the crime of going over the heads of the officials. As a result, Ratnacandra's three disciples [1177] were each sentenced to seven strokes of the rod, and his interpreter monk was sentenced to ten strokes of the rod, but the Learned Doctor was not beaten, nor was he allowed to return to his homeland.

EIGHTH MOON: 7th DAY [1178]   In order to return to my homeland, I prepared a document and presented it to the Commissioner.[1179]

> *Ennin, the Japanese monk in search of the Law at the Tzu-[sheng]-ssu, his disciple monks Ishō and Igyō, and his attendant Tei Yūman.*
> The said Ennin and the others arrived in the city from Mt. Wu-t'ai on the twenty-third day of the eighth moon of last year and humbly received the good offices of the *K'ai-fu*, who had them provisionally settled at the Tzu-sheng-ssu. They now intend to return to their homeland, but they dare not do so on their own.
> Respectfully stated in full as above. They humbly ask for his decision. The statement of the matter is as above. Respectfully written.

[1176] *DBZ* suggests 急發 for 惡發.

[1177] *DBZ* expands 弟 to 弟子, making " younger brothers " into " disciples."

[1178] The first day was August 20, 841.

[1179] Undoubtedly referring to Ch'iu Shih-liang, whom the Indian monk had bypassed with such disastrous results. The printed texts interpret the recipient of the document as the 使賚寺 (ostensibly the name of a monastery), but obviously the last two characters are instead the beginning of the letter and are a corruption or abbreviation of the name of the Tzu-sheng-ssu, where Ennin was staying.

Respectfully written on a certain day in the eighth moon of the first year of Hui-ch'ang by Ennin, the Japanese monk in search of the Law.

NINTH MOON: 1st DAY [1180]   An Imperial order was given to the various monasteries of the two halves of the city to hold lectures for laymen.

7th DAY   I heard that the Japanese monk Egaku [1181] and his disciples, three persons [in all], had arrived at Mt. Wu-t'ai. The master had vowed that, in order to seek his alms in all directions, he would return to his homeland, but he is having his two disciples stay at Mt. [Wu]-t'ai.

23rd DAY   There was a heavy snowfall for a whole day and a whole night, and the trees were broken down [with the weight].

ELEVENTH MOON: 1st DAY [1182]   It was the festival of the winter solstice. A comet appeared [1183] and several days later gradually grew larger. The officials asked the various monasteries to read scriptures.

TWELFTH MOON: 3rd DAY [1184]   We moved to the Hsi-yüan 西 ("West Cloister").

4th DAY   The moon and Venus [1185] were in conjunction, and they moved along close together.

8th DAY   It was a national anniversary,[1117] and this monastery held an official maigre feast, and the various monasteries in the city arranged baths. The comet gradually disappeared.

[1180] September 19, 841.

[1181] 惠蕚 (the first character is more properly written 慧), a Japanese monk who made in all four round trips to China. This was his first trip (839-847), on which he visited both Mt. Wu-t'ai and Mt. T'ien-t'ai. He returned to Japan from his last trip in 864.

[1182] December 17, 841.

[1183] Cf. 838 X 22.

[1184] The first day was January 16, 842.

[1185] 大伯星 is presumably an error for 太白星.

HUI-CH'ANG · SECOND YEAR

jen-hsü

FIRST MOON: 1st DAY [1186] All the households erected bamboo poles and hung banners from them and made New Year's prayers for long life. The various monasteries held lectures for laymen.

SECOND MOON: 1st DAY [1187] On Imperial order the *K'ai-fu* Ch'iu was appointed to be the Army Inspector Commissioner [1188] and was also put in charge of the military affairs of the empire.

17th DAY It was the Cold Food Festival.[347] With the day before and after, there was a three-day holiday. All the households paid reverence to the [family] graves.

19th DAY It was the "clear and bright" festival.[633]

29th DAY I began to receive instruction in the Great Law of the *Taizō[kai]* at the place of Master [333] Fa-ch'üan of the Hsüan-fa-ssu. Also, at the place of Master Yüan-chien [1189] of the Ta-an-kuo-ssu, I carefully checked over again the rules of the Sanskrit letters.[1094]

THIRD MOON: 3rd DAY [1190] Li, the Minister of State,[1191] petitioned the throne to have the monks and nuns regu-

---

[1186] February 14, 842. *Jen-hsü* 壬戌 is fifty-ninth in the cycle.

[1187] March 16, 842.

[1188] *Kuan-chün-jung-shih* 觀軍容使. Cf. Des Rotours 824, 844, 848. *TCTC* 246 records this appointment in 841 VIII.

[1189] *Tōji* has 箇 for the second character. Fa-ch'üan and Yüan-chien were first mentioned on 840 IX 6.

[1190] The first day was April 15, 842.

[1191] Okada (12.150-51) argues that this must be Li Te-yü, whom Ennin had met in Yang-chou, and not Li Shen 李紳, who had been appointed a Minister of State in 841 and was one of Li Te-yü's chief allies in the factional disputes at court. The chief reason Okada puts forward is Ennin's reference to the man

lated,[1192] and an Imperial order was issued, dismissing the "nameless monks without protection"[1193] and prohibiting the appointment of boys as novices.

8th DAY The Chien-fu-ssu[1124] held an offering to the Buddha's tooth. I visited the monastery, performed adoration, and made offerings. The Hsing-fu-ssu west of the street[1194] held [an offering] to the Buddha's tooth.

---

merely as "Li, the Minister of State." However, on 842 X 9 Ennin refers to "the petition of the Minister of State Li Shen." Very possibly the first time he heard of the petition he was confused over the identity of the author, assuming that it was the Minister of State Li whom he already knew, but subsequently discovered that it was a different man. In any case, Ennin's diary contains enough indications of Li Te-yü's friendliness toward Buddhism to more than offset Okada's examples to the contrary. Furthermore, statements Ennin makes on 846 VI 29 and X 2 indicate that the persecution of Buddhism was particularly severe in Huai-nan-tao at a time when Li Shen was the local Regional Commander. Consequently, it is not safe to accept Okada's judgment that Li Te-yü was the author of this petition and therefore a major instigator of the Buddhist persecution which followed.

[1192] *T'iao-liu* 條流, a T'ang term which seems to have sometimes had the connotation of "to limit" or "to weed out." It is often confused with a related term, *t'iao-su* 條疏, "to register" and hence sometimes "to blacklist," and is printed as such in *DBZ* and *KIK*. Cf. Okada 12.161-62. Under 843 IX 3 *Tōji* has *su-li* 疏理 and under 845 III 3 *tieh-liu* 牒流, both, apparently, with much the same meaning as *t'iao-liu*.

[1193] *Pao-wai wu-ming seng* 保外無名僧. Monks in T'ang times were divided into *pao-wai* and *pao-nei* categories. Foreign monks belonged to the former group, but the exact distinction between the two is not clear. Cf. Okada 12.162. Perhaps this term, like the term "nameless," refers to those who were not officially registered and therefore not officially protected. The term "nameless," is expanded on 843 IX 13 to the fuller and clearer phrase, "those whose names were not in the public registers" 公案无名者.

[1194] Possibly meaning west of the main central thoroughfare and

The Inspection Office [1071] *informs the Hsing-shan-ssu, the Ch'ing-lung-ssu, and the Tzu-sheng-ssu.* [1195]

Foreign monks and Learned Doctors.

The above has received a decision of the Army Inspector. [1196] The said foreign monks are all asked to be at ease, as they cannot be dismissed. The matter must be reported to them, and each should be fully informed in accordance with this decision.

We transmit the notice in accordance with the document.

Written on the fifth day of the third moon of the second year of Hui-ch'ang.

The Inspector Guard Officer [1072] *Ho Kung-chen.* [1197]

11*th* DAY Visiting the Hsing-fu-ssu, I worshiped the Buddha's tooth and spent one night.

12*th* DAY Because I-yüan the solicitor of offerings [937] for Mt. [Wu]-t'ai was returning to the mountain, in the evening we sent by him an offering [for meals] for 150 monks.

Ennin, the Japanese monk in search of the Law, his disciple monks Ishō and Igyō, and his attendant Tei Yūman respectfully send to Mt. Ch'ing-liang [822] *an offering [for meals] for 150 monks.*

The reason that the said Ennin and the others are arranging this offering is that in seeking the Law they may be successful, that in crossing the sea they may avoid disaster and arrive safely, bring wide benefits to all creatures [1198] and kalpa after kalpa and birth after birth be eternally in the family of

---

therefore in the right half of the city, but see the reference to this monastery on 841 II 8.

[1195] This sentence is not given as part of the document in the printed texts.

[1196] *Chün-jung* 軍容 is an abbreviation of the new title Ch'iu Shih-liang had received (see note 1188). Here as elsewhere the second character closely resembles 客 and is so printed in *DBZ* and *KIK*.

[1197] 何公貞, possibly the Ho in Ch'iu Shih-liang's office mentioned on 840 VIII 24.

[1198] *DBZ* corrects 郡主 to 群生.

His Holiness Monju, bring benefit to all around, and that all those with souls in the universe of the Law may likewise be favored with these blessings. Respectfully stated.[1199]

Respectfully stated on the twelfth day of the third moon of the second year of Hui-ch'ang by Ennin, the Japanese monk in search of the Law, and the others.

The Uighur [1200] army has entered China, invading the frontiers, and at present is at Ch'in-fu.[1201] The nation has drawn troops from six regional commanderies and is sending them to the Uighur frontier. There are several hundred Uighurs in the capital, and they have all been executed in accordance with an Imperial command. The same is also being done in the various prefectures and commanderies.[1202]

The Inspection Office [1071] *informs the Tzu-sheng-ssu.*
The Japanese monk Ennin and his disciples Ishō and Igyō and his attendant Tei Yūman.

The above has received a document from the Commissioner to the effect that " guest monks without protection " [1193] be dismissed and put out of the monasteries. We did not venture on our own to dismiss this Ennin and the others, and we have received a decision from the Army Inspector [1196] that we need not dismiss them. In accordance with the above, you are to take custody of them.

[1199] In true Oriental fashion, no mention is made of the real reason for this present, which was to make some payment for the hospitality the four had received while at Mt. Wu-t'ai almost two years before.

[1200] Hui-hu 回鶻 (the first character is written 廻), a powerful Turkish people of Central Asia.

[1201] 秦府, which Okada (12.282) proves is an error for Chen-wu, standing for the Chen-wu-chün 振武軍, the army command in northern Shensi and southern Sui-yüan centered at Chin-ho 金河, which was about halfway between the modern Sui-yüan city and the Yellow River. Ennin's account of the Uighur disturbances, though garbled, does help date the incursion accurately.

[1202] Okada cites corroborating evidence to Ennin's statement that men were drawn from various regional commanderies and sent to the frontier (12.285-86), but he finds the statement about the executions hard to accept (12.286-87).

We have made this statement [1202a] in accordance with the document. We have informed the monastery in conformity with the Commissioner's decision.

Stated on the tenth day of the third moon of the second year of Hui-ch'ang.

The Guard Officer Inspector Ho Kung-chen.

I have been told that the troops of the Uighurs have entered the city of Ch'in-fu,[1201] that the Regional Commander has fled, and that the newly appointed Regional Commander is on the road but dares not enter [the city].[1203]

Abbot Fa-ch'üan of the Hsüan-fa-ssu understands the Triple Great Law.[1096] He gave me for the propagation [of the faith] abroad a *Taizō dai giki* [1204] in three scrolls, and also a *Besson-hō* [1205] in three scrolls, and the *Taizō* mudras.[1206] I sent him a letter expressing my thanks.

Having come in contact with you, my devotion is difficult to. . . . With summer . . .[1207] I humbly hope that much happiness will bless the Abbot's person.

I, Ennin, have received your kindness, but because of petty reasons I have not been able to call on you. I am humbly apologetic.[1101]

I thank the Abbot for graciously bestowing on me six scrolls of the holy teachings for the propagation [of the faith]. Overcome with awe, I shall transmit it abroad in response to this

---

[1202a] 帖巡, which is reversed without comment by *DBZ* and *KIK*, may be corrupt.

[1203] Okada (12.287) states that this passage corroborates the change of Regional Commanders at this time, but he does not accept the rumor that the original Regional Commander had fled. He suggests that the 住 before the first *Chieh-tu-shih* is an error for 舊.

[1204] " The Great *Giki* of the *Taizōkai*." See note 339.

[1205] 別尊法, here clearly the name of a text, though the term itself merely means " the worship of one deity at a time."

[1206] 手契, presumably the same as *shuin* (or *inkai* 印契). See note 951. This too was presumably a text or series of pictures.

[1207] 接近勤渴難令夏契 is apparently corrupt. The fourth character may be an error for 竭 , and some characters may be missing.

holy grace. But having made you no offering, my trepidation is intense. Within a day or two I shall come myself to your cloister. Although I shall thank you in person before long, [meanwhile] I think of you all the more.

I am respectfully sending my disciple [561] to present this letter. Respectfully written in brief.

Written on a day in the fourth moon by Ennin, the Japanese Shaman [1162] *in search of the Law.*

To Abbot [Fa]-ch'üan   His Reverence, with humble respect.

FOURTH MOON: 23rd DAY [1208] The Emperor in his Imperial tower 御樓 was presented with an honorific title.[1209] The troops of the various armies 諸司軍 were drawn up in front of the tower, and the many officials, monks, and Taoist priests were in ordered ranks. The Ministers of State presented the honorific title.

FIFTH MOON [1210] On Imperial command, lectures for laymen were held at five places in each of the two halves of the city.

25th DAY Ninsai,[1211] the attendant monk of the Student Monk Ensai, came and I received [En]sai Shōnin's [827] detailed statement [1212] of the eighteenth day of the twelfth moon of the first year of Hui-ch'ang (841) to the effect that the Japanese Ambassador to China and Consultant Counselor [392] had died after returning to the Japanese capital; [1213]

[1208] The first day was May 14, 842.

[1209] *Tsun-hao* 尊號. *HTS* 8 and *TCTC* 246 record that on this day the Ministers presented the Emperor with the honorific title of Jen-sheng Wen-wu Chih-shen Ta-hsiao Huang-ti 仁聖 文武至神大孝皇帝. *TCTC* indicates that the ceremony was held in the Tan-feng Tower (see note 1130).

[1210] The first day was June 13, 842.

[1211] 仁濟, not to be confused with Ninkō, another disciple of Ensai (see note 7) first mentioned in a document on 838 VIII 4 and who appears again in the text on 844 II.

[1212] There is no 書 preceding 委曲 as printed in *DBZ*.

[1213] *DBZ* corrects 六薨 to 亡薨. According to *SNK*, Fujiwara

that the Administrative Officer Naga[mine] had become the Vice-Governor of Iyo; [1214] that a Secretary had become a Junior Recorder of the Left; [1215] that the Secretary Taka[oka] had become a Clerk of Dazai[fu]; [1216] that the Emperor Junna had died in the seventh moon of last year; [1217] and that the second ship had floated to the land of naked men and had been smashed. The goods of the persons on board were all destroyed, and [only] thirty-odd men managed to escape alive. They broke up [1218] the large ship and made small boats and were able to reach Japan.[1219]

There also was a letter of the first day of the second moon of this year sent through Ninsai from Yu Sinŏn, the Korean Interpreter of Ch'u-chou, saying that the [Korean] helmsmen [427] and sailors who had accompanied the tributary em-

---

no Tsunetsugu (see note 5) died on 840 IV 23, less than a year after returning to Japan.

[1214] According to *SNK*, Nagamine no Takana, first mentioned by Ennin on 838 VII 2, was appointed, not Vice-Governor of Iyo 伊豫, but Provisional Vice-Governor of Ise (*Ise Gon no Suke* 伊勢權介) on 839 X 25 and was made Governor of Yamashiro 山城守 on 840 VIII 22.

[1215] *Sashōshi* 左少史, a minor official serving in a liaison capacity under the Controller of the Left in the Council of State (see note 383).

[1216] *Dazai Sakan* 典, the fourth-ranking category of officers in Dazaifu (see note 2). Takaoka no Momooki was first mentioned by Ennin on 838 VII 2 and is mentioned by *SNK* on 839 VIII 25 as having arrived back in Japan.

[1217] Junna 淳和 , who reigned 823-833, died on 840 V 8 according to *SNK*. In "last year" Ennin probably is quoting a phrase from the letter, which itself was written in 841, but in any case he has the month wrong.

[1218] *DBZ* corrects 圻 to 折 .

[1219] From *SNK* 9 (840 IV 8, 15, VI 5, 18) we learn that the group eventually reached Japan on two boats arriving separately. On the second was Yoshimine no Nagamatsu (see note 470), proving that the vessel lost was the second of the original four and not the second of the nine smaller ships obtained in China.

bassy had returned to their homes [1220] in the autumn of the year before last. Master Gensai [1221] was at present at Yu Sinŏn's place with letters and twenty-four small ounces [127] of gold dust. Egaku [1181] Kashō [115] went to Ch'u-chou by ship, having already made [a pilgrimage] around Mt. Wu-t'ai. He was intending to return home this spring, and [Yu] Sinŏn had arranged for someone's ship [to carry him], but [E]gaku Kashō stayed briefly last autumn at [Mt.] T'ien-t'ai, and [Yu Sinŏn] received a letter during the winter [from him], saying that he intended to avail himself of the ship of Li Lin-te Ssu-lang [1222] to return to his homeland from Ming-chou,[185] but that, since his valuables and clothing as well as his disciples were all at Ch'u-chou and someone's ship had already been arranged for, he was still depending on [Yu Sinŏn to arrange] for their being sent from there [to Japan].

[En]sai Shōnin's detailed statement said that the monk Gensai had brought twenty-four small ounces of gold and that there were letters from various people, which had been given to T'ao Shih-erh-lang [1223] on his return to China. These things are now at the home of Yu Sinŏn.

25th DAY   A document from the Commissioner inquired into the accomplishments of the foreign monks.

[1220] Since the men, though Korean, were from the Ch'u-chou region, we may assume that China and not Korea is meant.

[1221] 玄済, who seems to have been a monk from Japan, though nothing more is known of him. Although *Tōji*, which usually has no paragraph divisions, makes one at this point, this and the following items seem to be taken from Yu Sinŏn's letter. The use of 弊所 (the first character standing for 敝) in this sentence (translated " Yu Sinŏn's place ") indicates a direct quotation from the letter.

[1222] 李隣徳四郎. The second character appears as 驎 on 845 VII 5 but as here on 846 I 9. Since each time we hear of this man it is either from or in connection with the Korean Yu Sinŏn, it is probable that he too was a Korean, but, lacking definite proof, I have given his name in Chinese pronunciation.

[1223] 陶十二郎, with the last character miscopied 部 in *Tōji*. This apparently is the person called T'ao Chung 中 on 842 X 13 and 846 I 9. He too was probably a Korean, and the reason Japanese

The Inspection Office [1071] *informs the Yang-hua Group.* [1224]

The foreign monks who are supposed to be in the various monasteries of the Group.

The above has been notified by the Commissioner to find out from what countries [the foreign monks] have come, the dates they reached the city, the monasteries they live in, their ages, and what accomplishments they are versed in, and to record their names and report them. Notice of this matter is to be given to the Group.

You are ordered to make out the statement. We await your report which must be made without delay or error. [1225] Notice is given the Group in accordance with the document.

Stated on the twenty-fifth day of the fifth moon of the second year of Hui-ch'ang.

The Guard Officer Inspector Ho.

The Japanese monk Ennin of the Tzu-sheng-ssu aged fifty; versed in lecturing on the Lotus Sutra *and his disciples, the monk Ishō* aged thirty *and the monk Igyō* aged thirty-one; both are versed in the Lotus Sutra.

They have received a notice inquiring into the country from which they come, the date they reached this city, the monastery they live in, their ages, [1226] and what accomplishments they are versed in.

The said Ennin and the others, in order to copy missing scriptures and transmit these to their country, came to Yang-chou with a Japanese tributary embassy in the seventh moon of the third year of K'ai-ch'eng (838). They reached this city on

---

travelers were interested in his whereabouts (according to Ennin 846 I 9) was not because he was a Japanese but because of his connection with missing Japanese funds.

[1224] 揚化團. From the distinctly Buddhist name of the P'u-t'i Group (see note 894) mentioned in the document of 843 V 25 and from the functions of these " groups," one may assume that they were groupings of monasteries or else suboffices under the Commissioner of Good Works.

[1225] *DBZ* suggests 遲達 for 遲速. See the closely parallel document under 843 V 25.

[1226] Here we find only the second character of the phrase used in the preceding document.

the twenty-third day of the eighth moon of the fifth year of K'ai-ch'eng (840) and, on notice from the Commissioner, resided provisionally in the Tzu-sheng-ssu and received instruction.

Respectfully stated in full as above. Respectfully written. The matter is as stated above. Respectfully stated.

Respectfully written on the twenty-sixth day of the fifth moon of the second year of Hui-ch'ang by the Japanese monks, Ennin and the others.

Starting on the 16*th* DAY *of the FIFTH MOON*, I again studied the Sanskrit letters [1094] at the place of Ratnacandra,[1175] the Indian Learned Doctor, at the Ch'ing-lung-ssu and personally learned from his mouth the correct sounds.

29*th* DAY   There was an Imperial order abolishing twenty Court Priest [824] Reverences [248] from each of the two halves of the capital.

SIXTH MOON: 11*th* DAY [1227]   It was the Emperor's birthday.[935] In the Palace they held a birthday [1228] maigre feast. Reverences of the two halves of the city debated with the Taoist priests in the Imperial presence. The two Taoist priests received the purple,[1131] but the monks were not allowed to wear the purple.

SEVENTH MOON: 21*st* DAY [1229]   Ninsai, the attendant of the Student Monk [Ensai], returned to [Mt.] T'ien-t'ai, and I sent Ishō to accompany him as far as Ch'u-chou to get the letters from our homeland.

EIGHTH MOON: 16*th* DAY [1230]   At night there was an eclipse of the moon.

TENTH MOON: 13*th* DAY [1231]   Ishō returned to the capital from Ch'u-chou, and I received two letters from the

---

[1227] The first day was July 12, 842.
[1228] There is an extra 降 written in *Tōji*.
[1229] The first day was August 10, 842.
[1230] The first day was September 8, 842.
[1231] The first day was November 6, 842.

national government 大國, one letter from the Ryōgon'in,[1232] one letter from . . . -kō 高 Shōnin, and four knives. The twenty-four small ounces of gold which had been entrusted to T'ao Chung [1223] had already been used [1233] by Yu Sinŏn, the Interpreter of Ch'u-chou, and [Ishō] did not get any at all and returned empty handed. I received a note from the Interpreter saying that he had already used [the gold] in accordance with Master Ensai's instructions.[1234] The letters, boxes, and envelopes had already been broken open.

On the 9th DAY of the TENTH MOON an Imperial edict was issued [to the effect that] all the monks and nuns of the empire who understand alchemy, the art of incantations, and the black arts,[1235] who have fled from the army, who have on their bodies the scars of flagellations and tattoo marks 鳥 文 [for former offenses, who have been condemned to] various forms of labor, who have formerly committed sexual offenses or maintain wives, or who do not observe the Buddhist rules, should all be forced to return to lay life. If monks and nuns have money, grains, fields, or estates, these should be surrendered to the government. If they regret [the loss of] their wealth and wish to return to lay life [in order to retain it], in

---

[1232] Or more fully the Shuryōgon'in 首楞嚴院 , one of the subdivisions of the Enryakuji (see note 7).

[1233] 月 is obviously a copyist's error for 用 , which appears in a closely parallel passage in the next line.

[1234] Waley 154 suggests that Ensai had appropriated it to pay his own debts.

[1235] This is the only known rendition of this important document, but it is so abbreviated and garbled in parts as to be scarcely intelligible. However, Okada (12.164-66) has interpreted it on the basis of the somewhat similar edict against Buddhism issued by Shih-tsung of the Chou dynasty 周世宗 almost three centuries earlier. (The latter document is the eleventh in Ch'üan T'ang wen 全唐文 125.) Okada interprets 燒練呪術禁氣 by equating it with two passages from Shih-tsung's edict, 燒臂鍊 指 and 符禁左道 , which refer to magical practices, including self-mutilation, which was particularly abhorrent to Chinese intellectuals.

accordance with their wishes,[1236] they are to be forced to return to lay life and are to pay the " double tax "[1237] and perform the corvee. The text of the Imperial edict is separately [recorded].

The Commissioners of Good Works for the two halves of the capital notified the monasteries not to let the monks and nuns out, and they kept the monastery gates closed.

The monk Hsüan-hsüan [1238] made a memorial to the throne [to the effect] that he would make a " sword wheel "[1239] and would himself lead the troops to defeat the land of the Uighurs.[1200] An Imperial edict ordered him to try to make the " sword wheel," but he did not succeed. It was because of the petition of the Minister of State Li Shen [1191] that this regulation [1192] [of the clergy] was started. The monk Hsüan-hsüan [1238] was guilty of falsehood, and he has been decapitated in accordance with Imperial command.[1240]

The Commissioners of Good Works for the Streets of the Left and Right have notified the monasteries, investigated the monks and nuns and their wealth, and regulated them in accordance with the Imperial edict. It has been generally the same throughout the land. The various prefectures and

---

[1236] *DBZ* suggests 亦壬意 for 玄亦壬.

[1237] *Liang-shui* 兩稅, the chief land taxes during the second half of the T'ang period.

[1238] Here 眩玄, but Lüeh-hsüan 晗玄 below.

[1239] *Kenrin* or *kenrinhō* 劍輪法 was a Buddhist magical practice intended to subdue evil forces.

[1240] Ennin apparently meant to indicate either that it was the unfortunate incident regarding Hsüan-hsüan which inspired Li Shen's petition (first mentioned on III 3) or that the two together were the immediate causes of the persecution. Beginning with the words " and he has been decapitated " and carrying through the words " notified the monasteries and investigated " in the next paragraph, the translation is based on seventeen small characters written on the margin of *Tōji* 137. These are lacking in *Ikeda*, and *DBZ* does not know where to insert them, but Okada 12.167 suggests that they be added between the characters 誑 and 隸, where a small circle appears in *Tōji*, and where they make good sense.

commanderies have been notified by the Imperial Secretariat and Imperial Chancellery [92] and are carrying out [the edict].

In the capital the Army Inspector Ch'iu [1196] opposed the Imperial edict and did not wish to regulate [the clergy]. Because of the Emperor's desires, this was not permitted, but he was allowed to request a stay of one hundred days, and he notified the monasteries not to let the monks and nuns leave the monasteries.

The Commissioner of Good Works for the Streets of the Left made a memorial to the throne [to the effect] that in the regulation of monks and nuns in accordance with the Imperial edict, aside from those who were decrepit with age and those who were strict in their observance of the rules, there were in all 1,232 [monks] and nuns who, because they valued their wealth, had voluntarily returned to lay life. The Commissioner of Good Works for the Streets of the Right memorialized the throne that, in the regulation of the monks and nuns in accordance with the Imperial edict, aside from those who were already decrepit with age and those who were strict in their observance of the rules, there were in all 2,219 monks and nuns who, because they valued their wealth, returned to lay life of their own volition.[1241]

Receiving the Imperial edict, the Commissioners of Good Works for the Streets of the Left [1241a] *and Right memorialize the throne:*

As for the monks and nuns who, in accordance with the Imperial edicts of the seventh and sixteenth days of the tenth moon of last year,[1242] have been regulated and forced to

---

[1241] This statement, of course, could not have been written until after the completion of the regulating, which Ennin records on 843 I 18, when he again gives the figure of 1,232 for the left streets but 2,259 for the right streets.

[1241a] The printed texts omit 左.

[1242] Since the first of these is presumably the edict Ennin described on 842 X 9, this document also clearly dates from 843. Okada (12.168-69) feels that, although this document is ostensibly a petition, the bulk of it sounds more like an edict, indicating that part of the text has been lost at this point and two

return to lay life, those who, because they value their wealth, wish to return to lay life should be handed over to their respective places of origin and should be included among the payers of the " double tax." [1237] Hereafter, cases such as this in the various provinces should all be handled in this manner.

As for the slaves they possess, monks may retain one male slave and nuns two female slaves. The others are to be returned and given over to the custody of their original families. Those who have no family should be sold by the government. Likewise, aside from their clothes and alms bowls, the wealth [of the monks and nuns] is to be stored up and its disposition is to await [1242a] subsequent Imperial decree. If among the slaves retained by monks and nuns there are those who [are versed in] the military arts or understand medicine or the other arts, they may not be retained at all, nor may their heads be shaved in secret.[1243] If there are violations [of these orders], the Monastery Administrators [119] and Supervisors [557] are to record them and notify the government. The other property and money should all be turned over to the Commissioners of Good Works to be regulated by them. So it is petitioned.

HUI-CH'ANG · THIRD YEAR

kuei-hai

IN THE CYCLE OF YEARS

FIRST MOON: 1*st* DAY [1244]

17*th* DAY   The Commissioners of Good Works notified the monasteries that the monks and nuns involved in the regulating were all to be returned to lay life. In the Tzu-sheng-ssu thirty-seven [were defrocked].

---

different documents have thus been run together. It may, however, be that Ennin, in paraphrasing or abbreviating the document, inadvertently changed its tone from a petition to that of an edict.

[1242a] 侍 in *Tōji* is a copyist's error for 待, which is given in the printed texts.

[1243] That is, non-official ordination. *DBZ* suggests 剃 for 削.

[1244] February 3, 843. *Kuei-hai* 癸亥 is last in the sixty-year cycle.

18*th* DAY   Early in the morning this return to lay life was completed. In the left half of the city there were in all 1,232 monks and nuns who returned to lay life, and in the right half of the city there were in all 2,259 [1241] monks and nuns who returned to lay life.

27*th* DAY   There was a notice from the Army Inspector summoning the foreign monks in the monasteries in his half of the city.

28*th* DAY   Early in the morning we went to the military. Five men from the Ch'ing-lung-ssu, [including] the South Indian Learned Doctor [1244a] Ratnacandra; [1175] one man from the Hsing-shan-ssu, the North Indian Learned Doctor Nanda; [1093] a monk of the land of Ceylon from the Tz'u-en-ssu; [1156] we three Japanese monks from the Tzu-sheng-ssu; Korean monks from various monasteries; and also a monk of the land of Kucha [1245] whose name I did not get, in all twenty-one men gathered in the quarters of the Army Inspector at the Left Army of Inspired Strategy. [1076] After drinking tea, we saw the Army Inspector, who personally consoled us, and on the same day we all returned to our own monasteries.

29*th* DAY   A Korean traveler from Ch'u-chou arrived, and I received a letter from the Ch'u-chou Interpreter Yu Si[nŏn] and a letter from Master Junshō. [1246]

SECOND MOON: 1*st* DAY [1247]   A notice from the Commissioner stated that the monks and nuns who had already returned to lay life could not go into monasteries or stay there. Moreover the monks and nuns " without protection " [1193] who had been dismissed were not permitted to reside in the capital or enter the garrison areas. [1248]

[1244a] On 845 V we learn that Ratnacandra had four Indian disciples with him.

[1245] Chiu-tzu 龜玆, on the northern side of the Tarim Basin in Chinese Turkestan.

[1246] *SNK* 843 XII 9 records the return to Japan on board a Korean ship of " Ninkō and Junshō 順昌, disciples of Ensai."

[1247] March 5, 843. The preceding moon had thirty days.

SECOND MOON: 25th DAY   The Princess Who Makes Peace with the Barbarians [1249] entered the capital. The officialdom and three thousand troops went out of the city to meet her and escort her through the T'ung-hua Gate [591] and into the Palace, where she was received in audience. On Imperial decree she was settled at the Southern Palace.[1250] This is the T'ai-ho Princess.[1249] In order to make peace with the land of the Uighurs, the T'ai-ho Emperor [1251] married her to the Uighur King, but now, because the law of the King of that land has collapsed and armed disturbances have arisen, the Princess has fled back to her homeland. None of the Uighurs who accompanied the Princess [1252] were allowed

---

[1248] It is not clear exactly what is meant by *chen-nei* 鎮內, but it might refer to certain strategic military areas.

[1249] This was the daughter of Hsien-tsung and aunt of Wu-tsung who in 821 had been given in marriage by her brother Mu-tsung to the Uighur Khan (see note 1200). During the disturbances that followed the latter's death she fled back to China, as recorded here. She is usually known as the Ting-an 定安 Princess or the T'ai-ho 太和 Princess (as Ennin calls her later, though *Tōji* again substitutes *ta* for *t'ai*), but here she is called the Hofan Kung-chu 和蕃公主, which is descriptive of her function as a symbol of amity between the Chinese and their powerful nomadic neighbors. *CTS* 18A records her return to the capital under the third moon, and *TCTC* 247, though recording it under the second moon, gives a cyclical date which corresponds to III 1. Both texts state that the Princess was met at the Chang-ching-ssu (see note 591), which was outside the T'ung-hua Gate, which Ennin mentions. Okada 12.288-291 discusses this passage in detail.

[1250] Nan-nei-yüan 南內院, presumably meaning the Nan-nei, another name for the Hsing-ch'ing 興慶 Palace, which is thought to have been located in the ward of the same name just inside the Ch'un-ming Gate (see note 1069). Cf. Adachi 178-79.

[1251] Since the Emperor of the T'ai-ho period was Wen-tsung, Okada suggests that this is an error for Yüan-ho, referring to Hsien-tsung, in whose reign the Uighur Khan first asked for the Princess in marriage.

[1252] The second character of *Kung-chu* is missing.

in the city. A Uighur Prince had accompanied her, but she herself killed him on the way.[1253]

FOURTH MOON: MIDDLE TEN DAYS [1254] An Imperial edict was issued [ordering] [1255] the Manichaean priests of the empire to be killed. Their heads are to be shaved, and they are to be dressed in Buddhist scarves [188] and made to look like Buddhist Shamans [1162] and are to be killed. The Manichaean priests are highly respected by the Uighurs.

FIFTH MOON: 25th DAY [1256] The Commissioner sent a notice inquiring into the origins of the foreign monks in the various monasteries.

> *The Inspection Office [1071] informs the P'u-t'i Group.[1224]*
> *The foreign monks who are supposed to be in the various monasteries.*
> The above has been ordered by the Commissioner to find out from where [the foreign monks] have come, the dates of their arrival in the city and their residence in the monasteries, their ages, and what accomplishments they are versed in, and to record their names and organize [the materials] and report them without delay or error.
> You are ordered to make out the statement, and we depend on you for it. Notice is given the Group in accordance with the document.
> *Fifth moon, twenty-fifth day.*
> *The Acting [383] Guard Officer Inspector, Ho.*

[1253] Okada reserves judgment on this surprising statement, because there is no reference to it elsewhere in Chinese literature.

[1254] The first day of the moon was May 3, 843.

[1255] Okada, who discusses the passage in detail (12.291-94), suggests that 夸 should be 弇. He points out that, while the Manichaeans were being severely persecuted at this time, there is no other evidence that their priests were actually executed, though he feels that Ennin may well be correct on this point.

[1256] The first day was June 2, 843.

Ennin, the Japanese monk in search of the Law aged [1257]
fifty-one; versed in lecturing on the Lotus Sutra and his disciples, the monk
Ishō aged thirty-one *and the monk Igyō* aged thirty-two, *both of whom*
are familiar with the Lotus Sutra.[1258]

The said Ennin and the others, in order to seek the
Buddhist teaching, crossed the sea with a tributary embassy. On
the twenty-third day of the eighth moon of the fifth year of
K'ai-ch'eng (840) they received the Commissioner's decision and
were provisionally lodged in the Tzu-sheng-ssu.

Respectfully stated as above. Respectfully written. The
matter is as stated above. Respectfully written.

Respectfully written on the twenty-sixth day of the
fifth moon of the third year of Hui-ch'ang by Ennin, the Japa-
nese monk in search of the Law.

[END OF] THIRD SCROLL OF THE RECORD OF A PILGRIMAGE

TO CHINA IN SEARCH OF THE LAW

Collated with the manuscript   Ken'in [862]

[1257] 年 has been omitted in *DBZ* and *KIK*.
[1258] Not in small characters as printed in *DBZ* and *KIK*.

RECORD OF

A Pilgrimage to China
in Search of the Law

IV

Fourth Scroll

OF THE RECORD
OF A PILGRIMAGE TO CHINA
IN SEARCH OF THE LAW

HUI-CH'ANG · THIRD YEAR

SIXTH MOON: 3rd DAY [1259]   The Army Inspector [1196] resigned his offices and returned home. Five or six times previously he had presented petitions, seeking to retire, but the
Emperor had not released him. He again presented a petition
making the request, and in the fifth moon there was an Imperial edict releasing him to return home. He moved his
household goods, and on the third day the Army Inspector
resigned his offices and returned home. An Imperial edict
appointed a new Commander, assigning Yang Ch'in-i, a
Great Official of the Palace and a *T'e-chin,* [1260] to be the Commander of the Left Guard Army of Inspired Strategy [1076] and

---

[1259] The first day was July 1, 843.
[1260] See note 144. Since Yang Ch'in-i, like his predecessor, was

the Commissioner of Good Works for the Streets of the Left.[1071] He assumed his post on this very day.

11th DAY   It was the present Emperor's birthday,[935] and a maigre feast was held in the Palace. Reverences [248] and Taoist priests from the two halves of the capital debated in the Imperial presence. Each of the two halves [of the city] has abolished twelve Reverences [as Court Priests].[1261] The Commissoners of Good Works notified the Inspection Offices to select seven Reverences from each of the two halves of the city. As of old, they went to the Palace, and the Reverences [1262] debated with the Taoist priests. Two Taoist priests were granted purple robes on Imperial decree, but none of the Reverences was allowed to wear the purple.

Fifteen days before the Emperor's birthday, [1263] several officials from the Palace 內宮 went to various monasteries to arrange maigre feasts as offerings for [the Emperor's] long life. The General Manager of the Crown Prince's Household, Wei Tsung-ch'ing,[1264] compiled a commentary on the *Nirvana Sutra* [203] in twenty scrolls and presented it to the throne. When the Emperor saw the commentary, he burned it and issued a decree, ordering the Imperial Secretariat and Imperial Chancellery [92] to go to [Wei's] house and find the original draft and burn it. The text of this edict is as follows:

---

a eunuch, the term " Great Official of the Palace " (*Nei-chang-kuan* 內長官), probably refers to his post as an important palace eunuch. *T'e-chin* 特進 was an honorary title for an official of the first class of the second rank. Cf. Des Rotours 35. Okada 11.479 points out that this is the only indication we have that Yang Ch'in-i received this appointment so early.

[1261] See 842 V 29.

[1262] The first character in *Daitoku* is missing in *Tōji*.

[1263] A careless reading of this phrase caused Okada (12.170) to place the following incident under the date VI 15. In *Tōji* 白 appears for 日 but is corrected without comment in the printed texts.

[1264] 韋宗卿, who was the *T'ai-tzu Chan-shih* 太子詹事. Cf. Des Rotours 574.

AN IMPERIAL EDICT.

Wei Tsung-ch'ing, a *Yin-ch'ing-kuang-lu-ta-fu*,[1265] the Provisional [384] General Manager of the Crown Prince's Household, a Grand Pillar of the State,[1266] and a Baron Founder of the Realm of Hua-yin-hsien with an estate of three hundred families,[1267] stands among those of honorable degree and should conform to the Confucian way of life, but he is drowned in evil doctrines, which stir up depraved customs. He has opened the door to delusions and has gone completely against the doctrines of the sages. How deep is the depravity among those of high office! So much the more should We proscribe that which is not the words of the sages. Why should foreign religions be propagated?

We should like to overlook [his offense], but this may do injury to public morality. He is to be demoted, and We are still to be called magnanimous [in doing this]. He is to be made the Prefect of Ch'eng-tu-fu [1268] and is to be rushed there by the post stations.

[Wei] [1268a] Tsung-ch'ing, the General Manager of the Crown Prince's Household, has presented to the throne *The Three Virtues as Culled from the Buddhist Nirvana Sutra* in twenty scrolls and *An Abstract of the Imperially Commissioned Complete Mirror to the Letter " I "* in twenty scrolls.[1269] These have been carefully examined.

[1265] 銀青光祿大夫 , an honorary title for officials of the second class of the third rank. Cf. *ibid*. 35-36.

[1266] *Shang-chu-kuo* 上柱國 , the highest of the honorary titles of merit. Cf. *ibid*. 50-51.

[1267] *K'ai-kuo-nan* 開國男, the ninth and lowest rank of nobility, theoretically entitling the owner to an estate worked by three hundred families. Cf. *ibid*. 44. Hua-yin-hsien 花陰 is in the Wei Valley about one hundred km. east of Ch'ang-an and about twenty km. southwest of the great bend of the Yellow River.

[1268] Ch'eng-tu 成都, the modern capital of Szechuan, was one of the nine superior prefectures (see note 1026), and as such its Prefect was called a *Yin* 尹 .

[1268a] The character, though missing in *Tōji*, is printed in *DBZ* and *KIK*.

[1269] 佛教涅槃經中撰成三德廿卷奉勅大圓伊字鏡略廿卷. Neither title is attested elsewhere, and their exact meanings are not entirely clear. *I-tzu* 伊字 was the Chinese name for the letter *i* in the Sanskrit alphabet.

The Buddha was a western barbarian in origin, and his teachings spread the doctrine of "non-birth" 不生. Confucius, however, was a Chinese sage, and the Classics provide words of profit. Wei Tsung-ch'ing, while being an ordinary Confucianist, a scholar, an official, and [a man of] distinguished family, has not been able to spread [the teachings of] Confucius and Mo-tzu,[1270] but, on the contrary, believes blindly in Buddhism and has foolishly made compilations from barbarian writings and has rashly presented them. How much more have the common people of China been steeped for long in these ways! In truth, their delusions should all be stopped, and they should be made to return to their pristine simplicity. But [Wei Tsung-ch'ing] assembles mystical falsehoods and in turn misleads the stupid people. Ranking as he does among the courtiers, should he [not] [1271] be ashamed of himself?

The scriptures he presented have already been burned in the Palace. The Imperial Secretariat and Imperial Chancellery [92] are commissioned to find the original drafts and burn them, so that he cannot pass them on to others.

ISSUED ON THE THIRTEENTH DAY OF THE SIXTH MOON OF THE THIRD YEAR OF HUI-CH'ANG.

23rd DAY　The Army Inspector Ch'iu died, and the Emperor sent mourning clothes.[1272]

25th DAY　Four Secretaries [1273] under the Army Inspector Ch'iu, the Vice-President [of the Tribunal of Censors] [418] Cheng 鄭, and His Excellency the Chief [of the General Court of Censors] Chang,[1274] and [two] others were

---

[1270] The Chou philosopher Mo-tzu 墨子, though not at all as popular as Confucius, was sometimes linked with him as a native philosopher of the scholarly tradition.

[1271] *DBZ* and Okada (12.170) suggest the insertion of the negative, as given in *Ikeda*.

[1272] This is the modern meaning of *hsiao-i* 孝衣, but from the context it is possible that ceremonial robes for the corpse are meant.

[1273] *K'ung-mu-kuan* 孔目官 were archival and secretarial officers in the two Armies of Inspired Strategy. Cf. Des Rotours 567.

[1274] Chang 張, whose title of *Tuan-kung* 端公 was a term of respect for one of the categories of Censors. Cf. Des Rotours 298.

decapitated on Imperial command and their men and women and their slaves were all killed and their houses destroyed.

27th DAY   In the third watch of the night (midnight) fire broke out in the Eastern Market [1275] and burned over four thousand houses in twelve alleys westward from the gate of the Controller of the Eastern Market. Public and private money and gold, silver, silks, and drugs were all destroyed.

28th DAY   In the third watch of the night a fire broke out in the Palace and burned the Shen-nung-ssu.[1276]

29th DAY   Fire broke out outside the Ch'ang-lo Gate [1277] and burned a hayloft. Previously there had been an Imperial edict to burn the Buddhist scriptures in the Palace and also to bury the images of the Buddhas, Bodhisattvas, and Heavenly Kings.[97] Later fire broke out in two places and still later, on two nights, fire broke out again in several places in the Eastern Market.

> *The Japanese monk Ennin, his disciple monks Ishō and Igyō, and his attendant Tei Yūman.*
>
> Aside from these four, there are no other guest monks, novices, or lay guests in their rooms.
>
> They have received a notice from the monastery office saying, "We have received a document [1278] from the Commissioner's office notifying us that we can by no means keep [monks] 'without protection,' [1193] novices, and lay guests." If subsc-

---

[1275] The Eastern Market (*Tung-shih* 東市) was a large area some six hundred paces square southeast of the Imperial City. Cf. Adachi 144-49 and map opposite 136. It was balanced by a Western Market in the right half of the city. The alleys (*hang* 行) in the market were not necessarily individual streets but rather groups of merchants in the same type of business gathered in a single alleyway.

[1276] 神濃. *Ikeda* corrects the second character to 農, making the name of one of the mythical Emperors of China. More probably this is an error for Ssu-nung-ssu 司農寺, the Ministry of Agriculture (cf. Des Rotours 418), which was located near the center of the Imperial City (cf. Adachi 123).

[1277] 長樂, the easternmost of the three gates leading from the Imperial City into the Imperial Palace.

[1278] *DBZ* corrects 久 to 文.

quently someone reports that they have concealed [others] in their rooms, they will ask for severe punishments.

Humbly they request your decision. The matter is as stated above. Respectfully written.

Written on the second day of the seventh moon [1279] *of the third year of Hui-ch'ang by the Japanese monk Ennin.*

My disciple monk Igyō was ill from the first day of the twelfth moon of last year until the seventh moon of this year. In all he was ill for eight moons, and he died at the end of the second watch of the night (11 P. M.) on the 24th DAY *of the SEVENTH MOON* of the third year of Hui-ch'ang which corresponds to the tenth year of Jōwa in Japan.

Igyō, the disciple monk of the Japanese monk Ennin.

The said disciple monk Igyō for long has suffered from illness, and he died at the end of the second watch last night. I have respectfully recorded the matter and informed you, and I ask for a decision. The matter is as stated above. Respectfully written.

Written on the twenty-fifth day of the seventh moon of the third year of Hui-ch'ang by the Japanese monk Ennin.

The death of Igyō, the disciple monk of the Japanese monk Ennin.

The said disciple monk Igyō, aside from his personal clothing, had no money, cloth, or grain in his room. If subsequently someone reports that the said deceased monk did have other money and the like in his room, his teacher monk Ennin and his fellow student monk Ishō will ask to be punished.

Respectfully stated as above. They humbly ask for a decision. The matter is as stated above. Respectfully written.

Respectfully written on the twenty-fifth day of the seventh moon of the third year of Hui-ch'ang by the Japanese monk Ennin.

Igyō the deceased disciple monk of the Japanese monk Ennin.

The said disciple monk has died, and I have no money at all to buy a [grave] plot. I humbly beg that the monastery

---

[1279] The first day was July 31, 843.

officer priests [81] in their benevolence grant me a grave plot in which to inter him.

Respectfully stated as above. I humbly request a decision. The matter is as stated above. Respectfully written.

Respectfully written on the twenty-fifth day of the seventh moon of the third year of Hui-ch'ang by the Japanese monk Ennin.

The Monastery Administrator [119] assigned us a grave plot.

27th DAY   We layed him away temporarily [1280] in the north corner of the brick-kiln grounds of the Tzu-sheng-ssu east of the Chen-kuo-ssu outside the Ch'un-ming Gate. [1069]

29th DAY   We covered over the grave. The monks Hui-chien 惠見 and Tsung-hsin 宗信 of this cloister [1281] arranged the whole burial. The monk Huai-an 懷安 of the Ching-t'u-yüan ("Paradise Cloister") provided the meals for those in the funeral procession. The monks in the funeral procession were Ssu-pien 思辯, Ching-chung 敬中, Huai-yüeh 懷約, Hui-chien, and Tsung-hsin. Chih-hsüan Fa-shih, [1282] a Reverence of this monastery, who is a Court Priest [824] and a Debater of the Three Teachings, [1118] sent his fellow student monk K'o-ts'ung 可從 to accompany the funeral procession. There were in all over ten monks and laymen who went in the funeral procession out of the city. At the grave, before burying him, I asked the seven monks [1283] to call on the names [of the Buddhas] ten times and to recite incantations. [110]

EIGHTH MOON: 13th DAY [1284]   In our attempt to return to our homeland, we are relying on Li Yüan-tso 李元佐, a Guard Officer [449] of the Left Army of Inspired Strategy. [1076] He is a personal 親事 Guard Officer for the Com-

---

[1280] 殯葬, awaiting formal interment two days later when the casket in the open grave was covered over with earth 覆墓.

[1281] Presumably the Hsi-yüan of the Tzu-sheng-ssu, to which they had moved on 841 XII 3 (see 840 VIII 26).

[1282] See 840 XII 8.

[1283] These must have been the six listed plus Ishō.

[1284] The first day was August 29, 843.

mander of the Left Army. He believes in Buddhism and is very religious, and he is of Korean origin. His home is in the Yung-ch'ang Ward.[1285] One enters the north gate [of the ward] and turns to the west at the first corner, and [his house] is against the south wall, at what is the northwest corner of the rear wall of the Hu-kuo-ssu. I went to his house and met him, and he agreed to confer with me.

15th DAY   We held the "three-sevens day" maigre feast [1286] for Igyō. That night there was an eclipse of the moon.

29th DAY   It was the "five-sevens day" maigre feast.

NINTH MOON: 13th DAY [1287]   It was the "seven-sevens day" maigre feast. Each time we invited the Court Priest.[1282]

The Imperial son-in-law, Tu Ts'ung,[1288] was appointed Regional Commander of Huai-nan to serve as Commissioner of the Iron and Salt of the Empire,[1289] and Li Shen,

---

[1285] See note 1119. These wards were surrounded by walls with either two or four gates. Apparently the Hu-kuo-ssu occupied part of the southern end of the Yung-ch'ang Ward and consequently the south wall of the residential part of the ward formed the north wall of the monastery. For more about Li Yüan-tso see 845 V 14.

[1286] 三七日齋 , coming on the twenty-first day after Igyō's death (twentieth day Western count). The "five-sevens day" and "seven-sevens day" mentioned later are similar. The next service after that of the forty-ninth day is on the hundredth day, and after that they occur annually. The hundredth day actually was XI 6, but *Tōji* has XI 3, 三 being a common copyist's error for 六 .

[1287] The first day was September 28, 843.

[1288] 杜悰, given in *Tōji* as 枡埬 and printed in *DBZ* and *KIK* as 拙琮. *Fu-ma* (here miswritten 附馬) is an abbreviation of *Fu-ma tu-wei* 駙馬都尉, a title for Imperial sons-in-law (cf. Des Rotours 374). He was the husband of a daughter of Hsien-tsung. For more about this man see 844 VII 15, where his surname is given correctly.

[1289] *T'ien-hsia Yen-t'ieh Shih* 天下鹽鐵使 . Cf. the comparable offices cited in Des Rotours 14. Occasionally Ministers of State

the [former] Regional Commander of Huai-nan and the Vice-President [of the Department of State],[1290] was sent to the capital on Imperial command to become a Minister of State.

Liu Ts'ung-chien, the Regional Commander of Lu-fu in Ho-pei Province, has revolted.[1291] An Imperial edict was sent to various prefectures and commanderies to levy a total of 50,000 troops to attack Lu-fu. They were unable to penetrate its borders but maintained a guard on the borders. Two hundred thousand strings of cash [1292] are needed daily to supply the armies, and what the various provinces send is not enough, so they transport grain from the storehouses in the capital without end.

---

were given special charges of this sort. The salt and iron monopolies were among the oldest state economic enterprises in Chinese history.

[1290] Li Shen (see note 1191) is known to have held these posts, but this particular shift is not listed in his biographies (cf. CTS 173 and HTS 181). The Vice-Presidents (P'u-yeh 僕射) of the Department of State (see note 224) were Ministers of State (cf. Des Rotours 4-5, 27). The second character in Chieh-tu-shih is missing in his title.

[1291] 劉從諫 (the last character is miswritten with a homophone 簡 by Ennin), was the Regional Commander of the Chao-i Army (Chao-i-chün Chieh-tu-shih 昭義軍節度使 ; cf. Des Rotours 658). He had his base at Lu-chou 潞 (which Ennin miswrites Lu-fu 路府), the modern Ch'ang-chih 長治 (or Lu-an 潞安) in southeastern Shansi. Although Lu-chou was north of the Yellow River (Ho-pei 河北), it was not in Ho-pei Province (roughly the same as the modern Hopeh) as Ennin says, but in Ho-tung Province (see note 1004).

Liu Ts'ung-chien had been estranged from the court for some time, and when he attempted to pass on his position to his nephew Liu Chen 稹 before his own death in the fourth moon of 843, the Emperor, on Li Te-yü's advice, refused to recognize the appointment, forcing Liu Chen into rebellion. The story is told in some detail in TCTC 247-48, beginning in 843 IV, but the account there differs greatly in tone from what Ennin reports from time to time as capital gossip about the campaign.

[1292] 廿万貫錢, 200,000,000 cash, is a fantastic figure, but Ennin repeats it under 844 VII 15.

The Lu-fu Base Office [721] is in the P'ing-k'ang Ward [1293] in the left half of the city, and the Lu-fu Guard Officer, Chiang Sun,[1294] has been there handling the affairs of the province. An Imperial edict ordered his arrest, but he fled, and his whereabouts is not known. They looked for him in various places but did not catch him. They could only seize his wife and children, whom they beheaded, and they destroyed his house.

Someone reported that the Lu-fu Base Office Guard Officer, Chiang Sun, had shaved his head and was at present hiding among the monks in the city, so an Imperial edict ordered the Commissioners of Good Works of the two halves of the city to regulate [1192] the monks in the city and elsewhere. Those whose names were not in the public registers [1193] were all forced to return to lay life and were sent [1295] to their places of origin. It was the same in the various provinces, prefectures, and commanderies. Monks who had recently [come to] live in the monasteries and whose origins were not clear were all seized by Ching-chao-fu.[1062] Those monks who had recently wrapped up their heads [1296] were handed over to the prefectural government, and over three hundred were executed. Those who fled and hid did not dare walk in the streets.

The army of the land of the Uighurs suffered a great defeat. The provinces involved then memorialized the throne, and all the soldiers from the various prefectures and commanderies returned to their own provinces.

[1293] 平康, at the southeastern corner of the Imperial City, between it and the Eastern Market.

[1294] 畺孫. Chiang, however, is not a standard surname.

[1295] *DBZ* suggests that 遞 and 俗 be reversed in order, as in a similar passage under 844 X.

[1296] *Katō* 裏頭 is a term for a monk when he wraps up his head for warmth or to conceal his shaved pate and therefore his clerical status. Ennin seems to use it for monks who had been recently defrocked as well as for those in disguise.

ELEVENTH MOON: 3rd DAY [1297]   It was the hundred-day maigre feast for Igyō.[1286]

TWELFTH MOON [1298]   I received a letter from Yu Sinŏn, the Korean Interpreter of Ch'u-chou, saying that the Student [Monk] Master Ensai at Mt. T'ien-t'ai had reported that he had petitioned to have his two disciple monks returned to Japan. The disciples had come to Sinŏn's place, looking for a ship, and Sinŏn had arranged for a ship for them and had sent them off. They left in the ninth moon of this year.[1246]

HUI-CH'ANG · FOURTH YEAR

chia-tzu

IN THE CYCLE OF YEARS

SECOND MOON [1299]   A military Guard Officer of Yüeh-chou [1300] by the name of P'an 潘, having been commissioned to deliver medicines to the court, brought me a letter from Master Ensai. The letter said that, because he had run out of clothes and provisions, he had sent his two disciple monks, Ninkō and another, to Japan to ask for clothes and provisions.[1246] The Guard Officer P'an said that [En]sai Shōnin wished he could come to the capital and was making a request for documents from Yüeh-chou, which he had entrusted to [P'an] to present to the Imperial Secretariat and Chancellery.[92] Recently [P'an] had been carefully waiting for a chance to present the document to the Imperial Secretariat, but a Minister of State had decided against it and would not let him present the petition, so the *Shōnin's* [827] affair did not succeed.

[1297] The first day was November 25, 843.

[1298] The first day was December 25, 843.

[1299] The new year started on January 24, 844, the second moon on February 22. *Chia-tzu* 甲子 is first in the sixty-year cycle.

[1300] 越, the modern Shao-hsing 紹興 in northern Chekiang on the way from Mt. T'ien-t'ai to the north.

THIRD MOON [1301]   An Imperial edict was issued to the
effect that the Emperor wished to proceed to the Eastern
Capital [201] and the officialdom was to be informed that, if a
courtier admonished him [against doing so], he would be
executed and his family wiped out.

An Imperial edict has forbidden offerings to the teeth of
the Buddha. An edict was also issued saying that, whereas
festivals had been held for the Buddha's finger [bones] in
the monasteries at Mt. Wu-t'ai in Tai-chou, the P'u-kuang-
wang-ssu 普光王 of Ssu-chou,[194] the "Five Terraces" 五臺
in the Chung-nan Mountains, [201] and the Fa-men-ssu 法門
of Feng-hsiang-fu,[1127] no offerings or pilgrimages [to these
places] were to be permitted. If someone presents a single
cash, he is to receive twenty strokes of the cane on his back,
and, if a monk or nun at the said places accepts a single
cash, he is to receive twenty strokes of the cane on his back.
If in the various provinces, prefectures, and subprefectures
there should be those who make offerings, they are to be
seized on the spot and given twenty strokes of the cane on
the back. Because of this, no one comes to these four holy
areas or makes offerings. In accordance with the Imperial
edict, the monks of these places were questioned, and those
lacking official credentials were all executed on the spot and
their names recorded and presented to the Emperor. They
fear that the Base Guard Officer of Lu-fu [1291] is hiding in
these places in the guise of a monk.

The Ministers of State Li Shen and Li Te-yü memorialized
the throne to abolish the moons of the three long [fasts],[1302]
and, following the teachings of the Taoist priests, they recently established [in their place] the "moons of the three
beginnings," [1303] the first moon being the "upper beginning,"

[1301] The first day was March 23, 844.
[1302] *Sanchōgatsu* or more fully *sanchōsaigatsu* 三長齋月, which
were the first, fifth, and ninth moons, when according to Buddhist rules no food was to be eaten after noon. See note 204.
[1303] *San-yüan-yüeh* 三元月, referring to the *san-yüan*, which
according to one way of calculation are the fifteenth days (full

the sixth moon being the "middle beginning," and the tenth moon the "lower beginning." In China the regular rule has been that life must not be taken in the moons of the three long [fasts], but the present Emperor does not observe this.

In order to destroy Lu-fu,[1291] the Emperor summoned eighty-one Taoist priests [to perform sacrifices]. He also had a "ritual place of the nine heavens"[1304] constructed in the open on the Palace grounds. Eighty benches were piled up high and covered with elegantly colored [drapes], and at the twelve hours [of the day][1305] ceremonies were held and sacrifices made to the heavenly deities.[1306] Dried meats, wine, and meat were used in the sacrifices to the Huo-lo Heaven.[1307] [The ceremony] started on the 1st DAY *of the FOURTH MOON* and lasted until the fifteenth day of the seventh moon.[1308] Since the place of ritual was not in a building and the ceremonies were performed in an open court, when it was clear the sun burned down [on the priests] and when it rained they were drenched, and many of the eighty-one men fell sick.

The present Emperor is a biased believer in Taoism and hates Buddhism. He does not like to see monks and does not wish to hear about the "three treasures."[236] Buddhist images

---

moons) of the first, seventh (not sixth as Ennin says), and tenth moons. These are called respectively the "upper beginning" 上元, "middle beginning" 中元, and "lower beginning" 下元.

[1304] *Chiu-t'ien tao-ch'ang* 九天道場 (see note 284). *TCTC* 246 mentions the construction of a "ritual place of the nine heavens" on 841 VI. The "nine heavens" are the heavenly areas of the center and the eight directions, which have been worshiped in China since ancient times.

[1305] Since each hour corresponded to two Western hours, this means all day and all night.

[1306] *T'ien-tsun* 天尊, the heavenly deities of Taoism.

[1307] 火羅天, which also apppears in Buddhist mythology (*Kara-ten*) and is thought to have been derived from the Sanskrit *horā*, a word meaning time. Buddhist terms were commonly borrowed by the Taoists.

[1308] April 22 to August 2, 844.

and scriptures have been placed since early times in the place of ritual inside the Ch'ang-sheng Hall,[1309] and three sets of seven monks who are versed in devotions [337] have been drawn from the monasteries of the two halves of the city and assigned in rotation to perform devotions there each day without cease, both day and night. However, the present Emperor has had the scriptures burned and the Buddhist images smashed. He has routed out the monks and sent them back to their respective monasteries and in the place of ritual has put images of the heavenly deities [1306] and of Lao-tzu [1310] and has had Taoist monks read [203] Taoist scriptures and practice Taoist arts.

It is a national custom each year on the Emperor's birthday to invite from the two halves of the city Reverences who are Court Priests [824] and Debaters [of the Three Teachings] [1118] and also Taoist priests to hold a maigre feast and burn incense in the Palace. The monks are invited to discuss the scriptures [1311] and a debate is held between Buddhism and Taoism. This year they only invited Taoist priests and did not invite monks. It would appear that hereafter they do not want monks to enter the Palace.

Taoist priests memorialized the throne, stating, " Confucius says, ' With the eighteenth son of the Li family, its grand destiny will be exhausted, and black-robed Emperors will rule the land.' [1312] We personally believe that the black-robed ones are the monks." The Emperor accepted what they said and because of this hated the monks and nuns. The meaning

---

[1309] 長生殿 (" Hall of Long Life "), a building in the Hua-ch'ing Palace 華清宮 constructed around the hot springs on Mt. Li 驪, about thirty km. due east of Ch'ang-an. Cf. Adachi 181-82 and Des Rotours 425-26.

[1310] 老子 (here Lao-chün 老君), the supposed founder of Taoism.

[1311] *DBZ* suggests the deletion of the 對 which follows.

[1312] This quotation could possibly have been in the Confucian apocrypha. In any case, it is based on a still current pun on the character *li* 李, which is made up of graphic elements meaning " eighteen sons " 十八子. Since the family name of the T'ang Emperors was Li, this pun could be interpreted as applying to

[of the quotation] is that the character Li being " eighteen sons," the present Emperor comes as the eighteenth reign [of the T'ang], and the destiny of the Li family may be exhausted and the black robes may usurp the throne.

The Commissioners of Good Works notified the monasteries that, in accordance with an Imperial edict, monks and nuns are not allowed to be abroad in the streets at the time of the bell [for their forenoon meal].[1313] If they have gone out, they must all return home before the bells of the various monasteries have sounded. Furthermore, they are not allowed to stay overnight in another monastery. If monks and nuns are in the streets at the time of the bell or go to another monastery and spend a single night, they are guilty of having violated an Imperial edict. Hitherto they have not been allowed to go out of the monasteries after noon, but now they are not allowed to be out at the time of the bell.

In the second moon the Emperor went to the Chin-hsien-kuan 金仙觀 [84] in the right half of the capital. It is a Taoist nunnery, and it has a Taoist priestess who is extremely pretty. The Emperor summoned her into his presence and saw fit to bestow on her one thousand bolts [192] of silk. Then he ordered the Palace Officers [1314] to reconstruct the convent, connecting it with the Palace,[1315] and to construct a Chin-hsien-lou 樓 (" Tower of the Golden Immortal "). The con-

---

them. Actually Wu-tsung was only the fifteenth Li Emperor, but, if one were to include the Empress Wu (see note 890) and two predynastic ancestors, as was the common practice, Wu-tsung could have been considered the eighteenth ruler.

[1313] The phrase is *fan-chung-sheng* 犯鐘聲, literally " to transgress the sound of the bell." The second character is erroneously copied in places in *Tōji* as 鍾 and is consistently printed as such in *DBZ*. In a reference to the same ruling under 845 I 3 we find it called *fan-chai-chung* 犯齋鐘 " to transgress the bell for the forenoon meal." From the context it is clear that this means to be outside of the monastery at that time, which was presumably somewhat before noon.

[1314] *Chung-kuan* 中官, here probably referring to eunuchs. Cf. Des Rotours 191.

[1315] This seems to be the most reasonable interpretation of 便通

vent had been dilapidated, but he had it reconstructed and beautified, and the Emperor frequently goes there.

Later the Emperor went to the Hsing-t'ang-kuan 興唐觀 in the left half of the city. It is a Taoist monastery. He bestowed one thousand bolts [of silk] on it also and had it reconstructed and cast a figure of himself in bronze. The Imperial figure was made majestic [1316] and mysterious.

On the 15th DAY of the SEVENTH MOON [1308] the various monasteries of the city made offerings [for the All Souls' Festival].[1007] The monasteries made flowery candles,[1317] flowery cakes, artificial flowers, fruit trees, and the like, vying with one another in their rarities. Customarily they spread them all out as offerings in front of the Buddha halls, and [people of] the whole city go around to the monasteries and perform adoration. It is a most flourishing festival. This year the offerings displayed by the various monasteries surpassed those of normal years, but the Emperor ordered all the flowers, medicines, and the like which were offered at the Buddha halls of the monasteries to be taken to the Hsing-t'ang-kuan and offered as sacrifices to the heavenly deities. On the fifteenth day the Emperor went to the Taoist monastery and summoned the people to see [the display], but the people cursed him, saying that since he had seized the offerings to the Buddhas and presented them to the spirits 鬼神, who would be willing to look at them? The Emperor [1318] was surprised that the people did not come. The monasteries were extremely [1319] distressed because their offerings had been seized.

The army attacking Lu-fu [1291] has not been able to penetrate its borders and is only at the boundary. There were frequent Imperial edicts of importunement, expressing sur-

---

內, but without knowing the location of the Chin-hsien-kuan, one cannot be certain.

[1316] *DBZ* prints 莊嚴 where *Tōji* has 莊校. Cf. Okada 12.173 for an explanation of this word.

[1317] *Hua-la* 花蠟, perhaps flower-scented candles.

[1318] *DBZ* prints 天子 where *Tōji* has only the first character.

[1319] *DBZ* prints 甚 where *Tōji* has 其.

prise at the lack of news and wondering why, after so many punitive expeditions, there had been no word at all of the chastisement [of the rebels]. The soldiers, fearing [the Imperial wrath], seized the herdsmen and farmers of the border region and sent them to the capital, claiming that they were captured rebels. The Emperor gave ceremonial swords,[1320] and right in the streets [the prisoners] were cut into three pieces. The troops of the two armies [1321] surrounded and slaughtered them. In this way they kept sending [prisoners], and there was no end of troops. The slaughtered corpses constantly littered the roads, while their blood flowed forth and soaked the ground, turning it into mud. Spectators filled the roads, and the Emperor from time to time came to see, and there was a great profusion of banners and spears.

I have been told that those who were sent were not rebels against T'ang but were the herdsmen and farmers of the border region who had been wrongfully seized and that the government troops had never penetrated the borders, but, fearing that the ruler would blame them for their lack of results, had wrongfully seized innocent men and sent them to the capital. The legionaries [1322] of the two armies,[1321] each time they killed a man, cut out his eyes and flesh and ate them, and the people of the wards all said that this year the people of Ch'ang-an were eating human beings.

An Imperial edict sent the Imperial son-in-law Tu,[1288] the Regional Commander of Huai-nan, to the capital. The Minister of State, Li Shen, desired to be the [Regional] Commander of Huai-nan, and in accordance with the Imperial

---

[1320] *Feng-tao* 封刀, occurring in a similar passage under 844 VIII, may mean swords which symbolized the Imperial authority with which the executions were endowed.

[1321] *Liang-chün* 兩軍, which from a passage under 844 IX-X we find is used by Ennin to mean the Left and Right Armies of Inspired Strategy. See note 1076.

[1322] *Chien-erh* 健兒, who, as Des Rotours (XLIV, XLVIII, 671, etc.) points out, were permanent professional soldiers. I have translated *chün-chien* 軍健 and *chien* used later in the text in the same way.

rescript,[1323] he was sent to be the Regional Commander.[1323a]
The Imperial son-in-law Tu reached the capital, and on the
day [1324] he was received in audience, he was made a Minister
of State and was put in charge of salt, iron, and the public
revenues.[1325] The officials were all surprised, for since early
times an Imperial son-in-law had never been appointed a
Minister of State. It was a national custom to bestow [the
title of] Minister of State on Grand Overseers.[92] Li Te-yü
presented a memorial to the throne, saying that an Imperial
son-in-law who has been made a Minister of State should
not ride in a carriage.[1326] The Emperor hesitated over this
point, and, lacking an Imperial edict, the Imperial son-in-
law could not ride in a carriage.

The troops attacking Lu-fu [1291] are using 200,000 strings
of cash [worth of supplies] every day.[1292] What the various
prefectures send is not enough, and the storehouses in the
capital are on the point of giving out, so there was an Imperial edict assessing sums from the officials.[1327] They paid
much or little money in accordance with their rank, and it
was used for supplies for the army attacking Lu-fu. The
officials of the various provinces, prefectures, and commanderies all did the same.

[1323] *DBZ* suggests that 勅依 be reversed in order. This appointment is mentioned as the first item in *TCTC* 248 under the date
of 844 Intercalary VII 11.
[1323a] 節矣 in *Tōji* is an obvious error for 節度 and is printed as
such in *DBZ* and *KIK*.
[1324] *DBZ* suggests 日 for 曰.
[1325] The story of this appointment is the final item in *TCTC* 247
under the date of 844 VII 23. There the title is given more fully
as *Tu-chih-yen-t'ieh-chuan-yün-shih* 度支鹽鐵轉運使, "Commissioner of Public Revenues, Salt, Iron, and Transportation."
Cf. Des Rotours 902 and see note 1289.
[1326] Li Te-yü may have put his protest against the appointment
in this way in order to make a verbal play on the title *Fu-ma*
(see note 1288), which means an extra horse harnessed alongside the team.
[1327] This is apparently the meaning of *fen-ch'ien pai-ssu p'an-
ch'ien* 分欠百司判錢, but the terms are not familiar ones.

Another Imperial edict was issued ordering that throughout the land the mountain monasteries,[1328] the common Buddha halls,[1329] and the fasting halls at the public wells and in the villages [1330] which were less than two hundred *ken* [1331] [in size] and not officially registered,[1332] were to be destroyed and their monks and nuns all forced to return to lay life and to perform the local corvee 邑役. [The results] were to be drawn up in detail and reported to the throne.

In the wards within the city of Ch'ang-an there are more than three hundred Buddha halls. Their Buddhist images, scripture towers,[1333] and so forth are as magnificent [1316] as [those described] in the Law, and all are the work of famous artisans. A single Buddha hall or cloister rivals a great monastery in the provinces. But in accordance with the edict they are being destroyed. I do not know how many Buddha halls and cloisters of the land in the various provinces are being done away with. There [also] was an Imperial edict ordering the destruction of all the revered stone pillars and the grave monuments of monks. [Another] Imperial edict called upon the University for Sons of the State,[1334] the

---

[1328] 山房蘭若 . See note 550.

[1329] 普通佛堂 may have had reference to places like the common cloisters (see note 812) which were for the use of all persons.

[1330] 義井根邑齋堂 is an obscure phrase, but like those which precede it, seems to refer to small and unofficial Buddhist structures.

[1331] *Chien* 間 (J. *ken*) I have usually translated as "bays" in connection with the size of buildings (see note 873), for the latter were commonly described in terms of the number of bays between their main columns, but in this case a measure something like the Japanese *ken* of six feet is probably meant, and the reference is to the over-all area of the buildings or grounds.

[1332] 不入寺額 . Cf. the term *jōgakuji* 定額寺, meaning an officially registered monastery.

[1333] 經樓, small two-storied structures housing the Buddhist scriptures.

[1334] *Kuo-tzu-chien* 國子監 . Cf. Des Rotours 442 ff.

Scholars,[1335] those who had achieved the status of Accomplished Literati [1336] of the land, and those of learning, to take up Taoism, but so far not a single person has done so.

Beginning this year, each time that there was little rain the Commissioners of Good Works, on Imperial command, notified the various Buddhist and Taoist monasteries to read scriptures and pray for rain. But, when in response it rained, the Taoist priests alone received rewards, and the Buddhist monks and nuns were left forlorn with nothing. The people of the city laughingly said that, when they pray for rain, they bother the Buddhist monks, but, when they make rewards, they only give them to the Taoist priests.

During the *EIGHTH MOON* [1337] the Empress Dowager died. She was of the Kuo family and was the T'ai-ho Empress.[1338] Because the Empress Dowager was religious and believed in Buddhism, each time the monks and nuns were regulated she always admonished the Emperor. The Emperor killed her by giving her poisoned wine.

The Empress of the I-yang Hall 義陽殿 of the Hsiao family is the present Emperor's " mother " [1339] and is very beautiful. The present Emperor ordered her to be his Consort, but the Empress Dowager refused. The Emperor drew his bow and shot her. The arrow penetrated her bosom and she died.

Three thousand troops of T'ai-yüan-fu [984] who had been

[1335] *Hsüeh-shih* 學士, a title for the scholars of the Han-lin Academy 翰林院. Cf. *ibid.* 17.

[1336] *Chin-shih* 進士, the most respected of the examination degrees under the T'ang and later dynasties.

[1337] The first day was September 16, 844. The eighth moon was preceded by an intercalary seventh moon.

[1338] The T'ai-ho Empress should be the wife of Wen-tsung, the Emperor of the T'ai-ho period. However, the only Kuo 郭 Empresses or Consorts listed in *CTS* 52 and *HTS* 77 were married to Hsien-tsung, Ching-tsung, and an Emperor who had at this time not yet come to the throne.

[1339] *A-niang* 阿孃. This may have been the Hsiao 蕭 Empress of Mu-tsung, Wu-tsung's father, who was the mother of Wen-tsung but not of Wu-tsung himself. Her death is recorded in 847 in *HTS* 77 but *CTS* 52 records it in the Hui-ch'ang period.

on guard on the Uighur frontiers for three years returned
home upon their defeat of the Uighurs this year, but before
many days had passed and before they had seen their dear
ones, the Regional Commander dispatched them again, [this
time] against Lu-fu.[1291] The legionaries [1322] appealed several
times, saying that they had suffered and become weary during the three years they had fought the Uighurs and they
had but recently returned home and had not yet seen their
dear ones and parents. They humbly asked that other troops
be sent, but the Regional Commander was not willing to
do so. The three thousand men were all indignant and
attacked [1340] the city. The Regional Commander reported
this to the throne and seizing them, sent them to the
capital. The Emperor had the troops questioned in detail.
Those [making the inquiry] stated that, because of their good
work fighting the Uighurs, they did not deserve to be killed.
They recorded the matter in detail and reported it to the
throne, but the Emperor did not follow the report, and,
giving ceremonial swords,[1320] had them cut into three pieces.
They were executed on a mound in the north street of the
Eastern Market.[1275] The captured legionaries [1341] from Lu-fu
are always executed here.

NINTH MOON [1342] Lu-fu was completely defeated, and
the Guard Officers and Generals captured there were sent to
the capital, and executions were held six or seven times. Later
the decapitated head of the rebel chief, Liu Ts'ung-chien,[1343]
arrived. It was stuck on a three-bladed spear, and his name
was displayed at the top of a pole over thirty feet high. It

[1340] *DBZ* suggests 迫 for an indistinct character.
[1341] See note 1322. Here Ennin seems to have forgotten his
previous assertion (see 844 VII) that these men were merely
herdsmen and farmers. The repetition of 來 preceding "legionaries" is a copyist's error.
[1342] The first day was October 16, 844.
[1343] See note 1291. Although he had died almost a year and a
half earlier, it is possible that his body had been dug up and
decapitated.

was first taken around the two markets [1275] and then taken
into the Palace. The Emperor, seated in the tower above the
Yin-t'ai Gate [1344] looked on and, laughing loudly, said, " Now
that Chao-i [1345] has been smashed, the only [1346] ones that We
have not yet got rid of are the monasteries of the land. We
are not yet completely finished regulating the monks and
nuns. Are you aware of this, Our lords? "

Some tens of days later, on Imperial command, the wealth,
money, treasures, and household goods of the Liu family of
Lu-fu were presented to the throne. Seven or eight gold-
decorated carts were loaded at a time and sent to the capital
and put in the Palace storehouses.

The Private Counselor [1346a] in charge of the Steward's
Department of the Palace,[1078] who was the son of the Army
Inspector Ch'iu,[1347] drank some wine, and getting completely drunk, offended the Imperial person by saying, " Although the Emperor is so revered and noble, it was my
father [1348] who set him up." The Emperor was angered and
struck him dead on the spot, and an Imperial edict ordered
that his wife and womenfolk be seized and sent into exile
and, with their hair shaved off, be made to guard the Imperial mausoleums. Then the Palace Officers [1314] were ordered

---

[1344] There were a left and right Yin-t'ai Gate 銀臺 at the northern ends of the two parks in the southeastern and southwestern
corners of the Ta-ming Palace. See note 1079 and cf. Des Rotours
map IV at end.

[1345] Miswritten 照儀, but obviously referring to Liu Ts'ung-
chien. See note 1291.

[1346] 准 is probably an error for 唯.

[1346a] *Ch'ang-shih* 常侍. Cf. Des Rotours 141, 631.

[1347] *TCTC* 246 under the date of 840 XI confirms that Ch'iu
Shih-liang had an adopted son. *HTS* 207, *CTS* 18A, and *TCTC*
247 all record the posthumous disgrace of Ch'iu Shih-liang this
year and the latter two texts date it in the sixth moon. Okada
12.484-86 discusses this discrepancy at some length. Ch'iu Shih-
liang's disgrace was presaged by the destruction of four of his
henchmen, which Ennin recorded on 843 VI 25.

[1348] *DBZ* and *KIK* print *a-yeh* 阿爺 where *Tōji* has 阿耶.

to take over the wealth of the family. Elephant tusks filled
the rooms; jewels, gold, and silver completely filled the storehouses; and the cash, silk, and goods were beyond count.
Each day thirty carts transported [the treasure] to the Palace
storehouses, but they did not complete transporting it within
a month. The remaining treasures and rarities were [still]
beyond count. The Emperor went to the Palace storehouses
to see [the treasures] and, striking his hands together in
surprise, he said, " Our storehouses have never before con-
tained such things," and the high functionaries bowed their
heads and did not speak.

The Taoist priests, Chao Kuei-chen [1349] and others, made
a memorial to the throne, saying:

The Buddha was born among the western barbarians
and taught " non-birth." " Non-birth " is simply death. He converted men to Nirvana, but Nirvana is death. He talked much
of impermanence, pain, and emptiness, which are particularly
weird [doctrines]. He did not understand the principles of spon-
taneity and immortality.[1350]

Lao-tzu, the Supreme,[1351] we hear, was born in China.
In the Tsung-p'ing-t'ai-lo Heaven [1352] he roamed about and
spontaneously and naturally became transformed. He concocted
an elixir [1353] and, taking it, attained immortality and became one
of the realm of spirits and produced great benefit without limit.

[1349] 趙歸眞 , a famous Taoist who became active at court shortly
after Wu-tsung's accession and was finally beaten to death in
846 IV shortly after Wu-tsung's death. He appears frequently in
the standard historical sources. (Cf. for example *CTS* 18A
under 845 I and *TCTC* 246-48 under 841 VI, 844 IV, 845 VII,
and 846 IV.)

[1350] *Wu-wei* 无爲 (" non-doing ") and *ch'ang-sheng* 長生 (" long
life "), two basic concepts of Taoism.

[1351] T'ai-shang 太上 Lao-chün. See note 1310.

[1352] 宗平太羅之天 . The last part of this name bears a close
graphic resemblance to the characters for Huo-lo Heaven (see
note 1307).

[1353] *Fei-lien hsien-tan* 飛練仙丹. For terms similar to these and
others used in this section, cf. Henri Maspero, " Les procédés
de ' nourrir le principe vital ' dans la religion Taöiste ancienne,"

We ask that a terrace of the immortals [1354] be erected in the Palace where we may purify [1353] our bodies and mount to the heavenly mists and roam about the nine heavens [1304] and, with blessings for the masses and long life for the Emperor, long preserve the pleasures of immortality.

The Emperor accordingly [1355] ordered the two armies [1321] to build a terrace of the immortals in the Palace 150 feet high.[1356] It was started in the *TENTH MOON*,[1357] and each day he had three thousand legionaries [1322] of the Left and Right Armies of Inspired Strategy [1076] transport earth to build it. The Emperor earnestly desired to have it constructed quickly, and there were daily edicts urging on the construction. The General Supervisors [1358] of the two armies held sticks and oversaw [the work]. When the Emperor went to inspect it, he asked the Great Officials of the Palace [1260] who the men holding sticks were. They told him that they were the General Supervisors of the Guard Armies,[1359] managing

---

Journal asiatique 229 (1937) .177-252, 353-430. On page 232 Maspero points out the frequent use of 練 in place of its homophone 鍊 " to smelt, to refine."

[1354] *Hsien-t'ai* 仙臺.

[1355] *DBZ* suggests 依奏 for 宜依.

[1356] *HTS* 8 and *TCTC* 248 both mention the building of a " terrace for viewing the immortals " (*wang-hsien-t'ai* 望仙臺) in the southern suburb (see note 1126) on 845 I 3, the former in connection with the Emperor's worshiping in the southern suburb on that day. *CTS* 18A mentions the " terrace for viewing the immortals " (with 儑 as the second character) on 845 I 1, again in connection with the Emperor's worshiping at the Altar of Heaven. On 845 I 3 Ennin tells about the terrace again immediately after his account of the Emperor's worshiping in the southern suburb. All these references would indicate that Ennin was wrong here in stating that the terrace was in the Palace grounds.

[1357] The first day was November 14, 844.

[1358] *Tu-yü-hou* 都虞候 (the printed texts give 侯 as the last character). Cf. Des Rotours 647, 857.

[1359] *Hu-chün*, part of the full name of the Left and Right Guard Armies of Inspired Strategy. See note 1076.

the construction of the terrace. The Emperor told them, " We do not want you [1360] to hold sticks and manage [the work]. You yourselves should be carrying earth." And he had them transport earth. Later the Emperor went again to the place where the terrace was being built and he himself drew a bow and for no reason shot one of the General Supervisors, which was a most unprincipled act.

Since last year the [Buddhist] lectures in the two halves of the capital have been stopped.

Ever since his accession, the Emperor has enjoyed going out [of the Palace] on trips, and, in addition to [his scenery-viewing trips during] the four seasons and eight periods [of the year],[961] he goes out every two or three days. Each time he goes out with his retinue, he orders the monasteries to arrange benches, mats, and carpets, to tie flowered curtains to their towers, and to set out cups and saucers, trays, and chairs. For a single one of his trips with his retinue, each monastery spends more than four or five hundred strings of cash.

An Imperial edict ordered the destruction of the small monasteries of the land. Their scriptures and images were taken to the large monasteries, and their bells were sent to the Taoist monasteries. Those monks and nuns of the destroyed monasteries who were unrefined in their conduct or did not observe the rules, regardless of their age, were all forced to return to lay life, were sent back to their places of origin, and made to perform the local corvee. Those who were old and observed the rules were assigned to the great monasteries, but those who were young, even though they observed the rules, were all forced to return to lay life, going back to their places of origin. In the city thirty-three small monasteries were destroyed and their monks regulated, exactly in accordance with the Imperial edict.

ELEVENTH MOON [1361] An Imperial edict was issued saying that, since the Chao-i [1345] bandits had been destroyed,

---

[1360] *DBZ* and *KIK* print 儞 for 你.
[1361] The first day was December 13, 844.

the Emperor was selecting the first moon of next year to again worship in the southern suburb [1126] and that orders were to be given to the official bureaus and instructions to the offices to put things in order quickly. In accordance with the edict, the officials repaired the bridges, roads, and streets, and men, horses, carts, and oxen were kept off them. The Altar [of Heaven] in the southern suburb of the city and the special road leading to it were rebuilt. Flowered curtains were spread around all sides of the Altar, and towers and walls laid out, making it look just like the interior of the city. The officials were harassed without end.

HUI-CH'ANG · FIFTH YEAR

i-ch'ou

IN THE CYCLE OF YEARS

FIRST MOON: 3rd DAY [1362] [The Emperor] worshiped in the southern suburb.[1356] The ceremonial objects and rites were just like those of the first year [of Hui-ch'ang].[1363] They did not permit monks and nuns to look on.[1363a] For long there has been a regulation that monks and nuns are not permitted to leave their monasteries after noon, and they are also not permitted to be abroad [at the time] of the bell for the fore-noon meal [1313] or to go to another monastery and spend the night. Therefore a monk cannot see the southern suburb.

The construction of the terrace of the immortals was about to be completed,[1356] and an Imperial edict ordered the Taoist priests to concoct an elixir.[1353] Chao Kuei-chen, [1349] the head of the Taoist priests, sent a memorial to the throne, saying that there was a certain drug of immortality which does not

---

[1362] The year started on February 11, 845. *I-ch'ou* 乙丑 is second in the sixty-year cycle.

[1363] See 841 I 8-9.

[1363a] 者 in *Tōji* may be an error for 看, printed in *DBZ* and *KIK*.

exist at all in this country but was to be found in the land
of Tibet, and he asked to go to Tibet himself to get the drug.
The Commanders of the two armies [1321] would not permit
this, memorializing the throne to send another man to get it,
for Chao Kuei-chen was the head of those who sought immortality and it would not be proper for him to go himself.
The Emperor, in accordance with the memorial from the
Commanders, did not let him go.

An Imperial edict inquired what drugs were used in the
search for immortality and [ordered the priests] to record
their nature and report on them. The Taoist priests [1364] reported the names of the drugs [as follows]: ten pounds of
plum skins 李子衣, ten pounds of peach fuzz, ten pounds of
the membranes of living chickens,[1364a] ten pounds of tortoise
hairs, and ten pounds of rabbit horns. The Emperor ordered
that these be sought in the medicine stalls [1275] of the markets,
but they all said that they had none. Consequently documents were issued for [the merchants] to be beaten. But [the
Emperor's] worry was not assuaged, and they finally looked
[for the drugs] in various places to no avail.

Since earlier times [the Emperor] has, in accordance with
custom, granted a seven-day holiday for the Cold Food [Fes-
tival].[347] Each day [they have had] three thousand official
legionaries as workers to construct the terrace [of the im-
mortals], and these were not let off for the Cold Food Festival. They were resentful and, holding their tools, they bowed
down, and all three thousand of them raised their voices
together. The Emperor was afraid and bestowed on each
one three bolts of silk and gave him a three-day holiday.

THIRD MOON: 3rd DAY [1365]   The construction of the

[1364] The printed texts delete without comment the middle character in 道者士.
[1364a] 生鷄膜 . This may mean " fresh hen-egg membranes," but,
since these are meant to be more or less fanciful ingredients,
possibly made even more ridiculous by the pen of a scoffiing
Buddhist, no reasonable translation may be possible.
[1365] The first day was April 11, 845.

terrace was completed,[1356] and, going to the terrace of the immortals, the ruler mounted it, and the Commanders of the two armies and the high officials and the Taoist priests followed him up. The Commanders of the two armies said to Chao Kuei-chen [1349] [and the other priests], " Today we have come to the terrace of the immortals. I wonder if you, my lords, will seek to become immortals." [Chao] Kuei-chen lowered his head and did not speak.

I have been told that the terrace of the immortals is 150 feet high. The area on top is level and [big enough] for the foundations of a seven-bay [1331] building, and on top rises a five-peaked tower. People inside and outside [the grounds] can see it from afar, soaring high like a solitary peak. They have brought boulders from the Chung-nan Mountains [201] and have made mountain cliffs on the four [sides] with grottoes and rocky paths. It is arranged most beautifully, and pines, arbor vitae, and rare trees have been planted on it. [The Emperor] was overjoyed with it, and there was an Imperial edict ordering seven Taoist priests to concoct [1353] [an elixir] and seek immortality on the terrace.

Another Imperial edict was issued to the monasteries of the land prohibiting them from establishing estates and also ordering that an inventory be made of the number of slaves of the monasteries of the land and their money, grain, and textile [holdings], which were to be ascertained in detail, recorded, and reported to the throne. The Commanders of the two armies were ordered to make an inventory of the monasteries in the city, and the inventory of those in the various prefectures and commanderies was entrusted to the Imperial Secretariat and Imperial Chancellery.[92]

The slaves of the monasteries in the city were in three classes: those with skills [1366] were handed over to the military; those who lacked skills but were young and strong were sold; and those who were old and feeble were joined to the Palace slaves. This, alas, was a time when fathers went north and sons south. The Commissioners of Good Works notified the

---

[1366] *DBZ* reverses the order of the last two characters in 藝者業.

monasteries that [every] five slaves was to constitute a single mutual guaranty group 保 and that, if a single one of the group fled, it would be fined two thousand strings of cash. The money of the monasteries and the payments [1367] for the slaves that were sold were all taken by the government to be applied to the officials' salaries. Another Imperial edict ordered all the monks and nuns under forty in the monasteries of the land to be forced to return to lay life and to be sent to their places of origin.

The ruler again mounted the terrace of the immortals and ordered a singer 音聲人 to push the Commander of the Left Army [of Inspired Strategy] off, but the singer was unwilling to push him. The Emperor asked him, " When We have you push him, why don't you obey? " The singer said, " The Commander is an important minister of the land. I dare not push him down." The Emperor became angry and gave him twenty strokes of the cane on his back.

While on the terrace [the Emperor], wondering about the Taoist priests, said, " Twice We have mounted the terrace, but not a single one of you, Our lords, has as yet mounted to immortality. What does this mean? " The Taoist priests said, " Because Buddhism exists alongside of Taoism in the land, *li* and *ch'i* are in excess,[1368] blocking the way of the immortal. Therefore it is impossible to mount to immortality." The ruler told the Commissioners of Good Works of the two halves of the city, " We wonder if you realize, Our lords, that We do not want any [Buddhist] teachers at all, whoever they may be."

Several days later an Imperial edict was issued to the effect that monks and nuns of the land under fifty were all to be forced to return to lay life and to be sent back to their places of origin. Later there was an Imperial edict which said:

[1367] *DBZ* corrects 續 to 贖.

[1368] *Li ch'i yüeh-chu* 里氣越著 is not clear, but the first character is probably an error for 理, giving us the two words, *li* and *ch'i*, which express the noumenal and phenomenal dichotomy of Chinese philosophy. The whole phrase then would mean that these two were not in proper balance.

The monks and nuns of the land over fifty who lack documents from the Bureau of Sacrifices [590] are all to be forced to return to lay life and are to be sent back to their places of origin. Those with documents from the Bureau of Sacrifices are to be questioned by their prefectures or subprefectures, and those with irregularities are all to be forced to return to lay life and are to be sent back to their places of origin. The monks and nuns in the city are to be regulated [1192] in this same way by the Commissioners of Good Works.

The Imperial Secretariat and the Imperial Chancellery [92] have notified the various provinces in accordance with the edict. The regulation of the monks and nuns within the city by the Commissioners of Good Works has been extremely strict. They examined the group of monks and nuns who lacked documents from the Bureau of Sacrifices and made a detailed record of them and reported it to the throne. Then the monasteries were notified that they should send on their household goods. Those with documents from the Bureau of Sacrifices were all taken to the military and questioned, and if there were the slightest smudge on their documents from the Bureau of Sacrifices or if the birth year differed from that entered by the offices of the Commissioners of Good Works on their " protection documents," [1369] they were put among those to be returned to lay life. [The documents which] showed no discrepancies were taken by the military offices and were not returned, thus putting the monks and nuns of the various monasteries in the position of lacking credentials 告身. Everyone said that the failure to return the credentials was a plot to get rid of the monks and nuns and the taking of the slaves and money of the monasteries was a foreshadowing of their destruction.

The Emperor announced, " The pit from which they took the earth [1370] [for the terrace of the immortals] is very deep and makes people afraid and uneasy. We wish that it could be filled up. On a day for sacrifice to the terrace, you should falsely state that a maigre feast is being held to pay rever-

---

[1369] *Pao-tieh* 保牒. See note 1193.
[1370] *DBZ* suggests 土 for 云 in *Tōji* and 出 in *Ikeda*.

ence to the terrace and should gather all the monks and
nuns of the two halves of the city at the Left Army [of
Inspired Strategy] and should cut off their heads and fill the
pit with them." An acting Privy Councilor [1371] said to the
Emperor, "The monks and nuns basically are ordinary
people of the state, and if they are returned to lay life and
each makes his own living, it will benefit the land. I submit
that you need not drive them [to extinction]. I ask that you
order the offices concerned to force them all to return to lay
life and to send them back to their places of origin to perform the local corvee." The Emperor nodded his head, and
after quite a while he said, "As you say." When the monks
and nuns of the various monasteries heard about this, their
spirits lost confidence, and they did not know where to turn.

I, Ennin, sent a letter,[1372] stating that I desired to return
to lay life and go back to my homeland. The Commissioner
of Good Works has received the letter, but there has not yet
been any decision. There have, however, been repeated letters
of consolation.

The Commissioners of Good Works notified the monasteries that, in accordance with an Imperial edict regulating
the monks and nuns and not permitting them to go out of
the monasteries, they would have to send five or six of the
members of their households to guard the gates of the
monasteries and that they could not let the monks and nuns
go out of their monasteries. If there were violations, the
Monastery Administrators,[119] "three elders," Controllers,
and Managers [1373] as well as the men guarding the gate would

---

[1371] *Chien Shu Pu Mi* 撿樞卜密 is apparently corrupt. The powerful Privy Council (*Shu-mi-yüan* or *Ch'u-mi-yüan* 樞密院) of
Sung times was the outgrowth of the *Shu-mi-shih* 使 of T'ang
times, who were first appointed in 765 and were usually eunuchs.
Cf. Des Rotours 184. *Chien* probably stands for *Chien-chiao*
(see note 387). Pu, unless a simple error, may be a misplaced
surname.

[1372] *DBZ* corrects 收 to 狀.

[1373] 三老典直. "Three elders" appears again in conjunction
with *Sankō* (see note 81) on 845 V 13, while the last two char-

each be sentenced to twenty strokes of the cane on the back, and the monk or nun who had gone out of the monastery would be executed on the spot.

The Left and Right Armies of Inspired Strategy are the Guard Armies [1359] of the Emperor. Each year they have 100,000 soldiers. Since olden times the rulers constantly suffered from rebellions by their ministers and so they created these armies, and since then no one has dared usurp the throne. The Emperor gives them seals. Each time a Commander is first appointed, on Imperial command he leads forth his troops and receives his seal. They conduct official business on their own and are not under the civil administration. [1374]

At the beginning of the *FOURTH MOON* [1375] of this year there was an Imperial edict demanding the seals of the two armies, but the Commanders were not willing to surrender the seals. There were Imperial edicts demanding them several times. The Emperor's idea was to demand the seals of the Guard Armies and give them to the Imperial Secretariat and Imperial Chancellery so that they would jointly control the two armies, and he intended to have them handle everything. The Commander of the Left Army agreed to surrender his seal, but the Commander of the Right Army was not willing to surrender his seal. Finally he sent a memorial to the throne, saying that since on the day he received his seal he had led forth his troops to receive it, on the day he surrendered his seal [1376] he should also muster his troops to surrender it. The Commander's idea was that, if the Emperor agreed, through this stratagem he would muster his troops and start something. He then ordered those in charge

---

acters may be abbreviations for *Tenzo* (see note 81) and *Chissui* (see note 641).

[1374] *Nan-ssu* 南司, a term in T'ang times for the three main organs of the civil administration: the Department of State (*Shang-shu-sheng*), the Imperial Secretariat (*Chung-shu-sheng*), and the Imperial Chancellery (*Men-hsia-sheng*). See notes 92 and 224.

[1375] The first day was May 10, 845.

[1376] *DBZ* corrects 迎 to 印.

to put his forces secretly in order, but the ruler was alarmed and gave in, and [the seal] was not surrendered.[1377]

I have been told that, in regulating the monks and nuns and returning them to lay life, the Commissioners of Good Works arranged stages. After ordering those under thirty [1378] to return to lay life, they next ordered those under [1379] fifty to return to lay life. Then they ordered those over fifty who lacked documents from the Bureau of Sacrifices [590] to return to lay life. As a third step they ordered an investigation of the documents from the Bureau of Sacrifices, and those with discrepancies in them were ordered to return to lay life. Thus, the monks and nuns are being exterminated. The scheme is generally the same throughout the land.

Because it was being carried out on Imperial order, beginning on the first day of the fourth moon the monks and nuns under forty returned to lay life and were sent back to their places of origin. Each day three hundred monks returned to lay life, and on the fifteenth day the monks and nuns under forty had all disappeared. Beginning on the sixteenth day the monks and nuns under fifty returned to lay life, and by the tenth day of the *FIFTH MOON* [1380] they

---

[1377] This passage, which finds no parallel in the standard histories, indicates clearly that Wu-tsung did make an effort to deprive the eunuchs of power by gaining control over the Armies of Inspired Strategy. Okada, who has made a detailed study of this incident (11.477-483), assumes that the attempt was made at this time because the eunuchs had lost some strength since the death of the powerful Ch'iu Shih-liang two years earlier. Okada points out that Yang Ch'in-i (see note 144 and 843 VI 3), the Commander of the Left Army, was close to Li Te-yü and the civil officials and hence was understandably amenable to the demand, but that Yü Hung-chih 魚弘志, the Commander of the Right Army, was a eunuch more in the tradition of Ch'iu Shih-liang.

[1378] An error for "forty," as is to be seen from Ennin's statements in the next paragraph.

[1379] 下 is missing in *Tōji*, and *DBZ* follows the erroneous correction of *Ikeda* in printing 上, "over."

[1380] The first day was June 9, 845.

had all disappeared. Beginning on the eleventh day those over fifty who lacked documents from the Bureau of Sacrifices returned to lay life.

Since year before last [1381] in regulating the monks and nuns they chose those of unrefined conduct and those who did not conform to their own religion and returned them to lay life and sent them back to their places of origin. But this year they did not distinguish between those of lofty and those of unrefined conduct and, paying no heed to whether they were accredited monks,[1382] Reverences,[248] or Court Priests,[824] had them return to lay life when their time came. The Emperor repeatedly inquired how many had already returned to lay life and how many had still not returned to lay life, thus urging them [to increase] the number [of those defrocked].

Foreign monks had not yet been included in the regulating, but the Commissioners of Good Works made special inquiry of the throne, and a decision was made, and an Imperial edict stated that, if they lacked documents from the Bureau of Sacrifices, the foreigners too were to be forced to return to lay life and were to be sent back to their homelands. Nanda,[1093] a Learned Doctor [596] of Northern India in the Western Lands, who is at the Ta-hsing-shan-ssu, and Ratnacandra,[1175] a Learned Doctor of Southern India, together with his four disciples, who mastered the Buddhist practices in Central India [1383] and are all versed in the great art of devotion,[337] meticulous in their observance of the regulations and broadly versed in the scriptures, and who are at the Ch'ing-lung-ssu,[357] all lack documents from the Bureau of Sacrifices of China. Most of the Korean monks also lack documents of the Bureau of Sacrifices. We Japanese monks, Ennin and Ishō, don't have documents from the Bureau of Sacrifices of China either. The Commissioners of Good Works, in accord-

---

[1381] Ennin recorded the first actual defrockings on 843 I 18.

[1382] *DBZ* and Okada 12.179 correct 驗增 to 驗僧.

[1383] Only the first two characters of 中天竺 appear in the text. Elsewhere Ratnacandra is said to have come from South India. See 841 VI 11 and 843 I 28.

ance with the Imperial edict, included us in the return to lay life. They also notified the monasteries that, if a monk or nun does not submit to being returned to lay life, he is guilty of disobedience to an Imperial edict and will be condemned to death on the spot.

On hearing this I bound up my written materials, wrapping up all the scriptures I had copied, the teachings on devotion, and my *mandara*.[277] In all I had four hampers of writings and clothes. Then I bought three donkeys and waited for a decision [on my case]. I do not regret my return to lay life. I merely regret that I shall not be able to take with me the holy teachings I have copied. Buddhism has been proscribed on Imperial order, and I fear that, [were I to take the writings with me], on my way the various prefectures and commanderies would examine me and, discovering the truth, would accuse me of disobedience to an Imperial edict.

13*th* DAY A notice came from the Commissioner. There are thirty-nine monks in the monastery who lack documents from the Bureau of Sacrifices, and among this number are the names of us two Japanese monks.[1384]

Lin Tsung-hsin,[1385] a monk who previously returned to lay life, saw and consulted with us and asked to be allowed to accompany us to Pien-chou,[1386] which is 1,400 *li* from the capital. Seeing how great was his concern, I did not oppose his desire.

The monastery officers [81] and the " three elders " [1373] came and grieved with us, saying, " You have come here from afar

---

[1384] This number was probably in addition to the thirty-seven monks from the Tzu-sheng-ssu defrocked on 843 I 17-18. See also 843 VII 29.

[1385] Presumably the monk Tsung-hsin who took part in Igyō's funeral on 843 VII 29, but now given with his family name Lin 林. *DBZ* and *KIK* split the four characters 林宗信觀 to make two priestly names. Since nothing more is heard of Tsung-hsin, it appears that he did not make the trip to Pien-chou after all.

[1386] 汴, the modern K'ai-feng 開封 in Honan on the direct route from Ch'ang-an to the coast.

to search for the Law and having encountered this difficulty
with the ruler, cannot avoid being defrocked. Since ancient
times until now those in search of the Law have indeed had
their troubles. We beg you to remain calm. If it were not because of this difficulty, there would be no way for you to
return to your land, and we rejoice that you will be able to
return to your land with the holy teachings, as was your
original intention." The *Tsuina* [81] monk, Fa-yü 法遇, gave us
a sandalwood box and image as an offering for our return
home. In the evening we bade farewell to the monks of the
whole monastery and then put on lay clothes.

14*th* DAY   Early in the morning we went to Ching-
chao-fu [1062] and asked for official credentials, fearing that
without official credentials we might run into difficulties on
the way. Seven Learned Doctors from the Western Lands [1387]
were also with us at the prefectural government, asking for
official credentials. The prefectural officials gave us documents for two provinces,[1388] ordering those on our way to
let us through.

Now, since the first year of Hui-ch'ang (841) I had sent
letters through the Commissioner of Good Works more than
one hundred times, asking to [be allowed to] return to our
homeland, and through several powerful persons I had used
bribery and schemed, but we had not been allowed to go.
Now, because of the trouble over the return to lay life of
the monks and nuns, we could suddenly return to our homeland. There was both sorrow and joy.

With regard to our return to our homeland, for close to
two years I had relied on and consulted with Li Yüan-tso,[1389]
the Guard Officer of the Left Army of Inspired Strategy, a
Yin-ch'ing-kuang-lu-ta-fu,[1265] the acting [387] Rector of the
University for Sons of the State,[1390] a Censor of Palace and

---

[1387] See 843 I 28.

[1388] Probably referring to Ho-nan-tao 河南道, which stretched
from the bend of the Yellow River to the coast, and Huai-nan-
tao south of it (see note 11).

[1389] See 843 VIII 13.

[1390] *Kuo-tzu Chi-chiu* 祭酒. See note 1334 and Des Rotours 442.

External Affairs,[1391] and a Grand Pillar of the State.[1266] He was most friendly at heart and had always helped me whenever, far from home, I had been in want of something. Because the Commissioner of Good Works was an irreligious man, when [Li] had inquired about our returning to our homeland, he had been unable to get permission. While we were at the prefectural government, [Li] provided us with food and blankets and again solicitously aided us.

15th DAY We left the prefectural government and went to Wan-nien-hsien.[1067] The prefectural government sent a man to accompany us to Yang Ching-chih 楊敬之, the President of the Supreme Court [1392] and a *Chung-san-ta-fu*,[1393] who had been granted the purple [1131] and a bag for the fish [tally] of gold.[1394] He had been appointed to be a Vice-President of the Tribunal of Censors.[418] He had a special representative come and question us about what day we would leave the city and what route we would take, and he also gave us a string of brick tea.[1395]

While at the subprefecture I prepared a letter to express

[1391] *Tien-chung-chien-ch'a-shih-yü-shih* 殿中監察侍御史. Cf. *ibid*. 307 and 309 and see note 1072.

[1392] *Ta-li-ch'ing* 大理卿. Cf. *ibid*. 404.

[1393] 中散大夫, an honorary title for an official of the first class of the fifth rank (cf. *ibid*. 36), though his post was that of an official of the second class of the third rank.

[1394] 賜紫金魚袋. A "fish bag" (*yü-tai*) was a bag made to contain a half tally in the form of a fish with which high officials identified themselves when entering the Palace grounds. The bag was a badge of distinction, and its color as well as the type of fish tally it held were indicative of rank. Cf. *ibid*. 166-67. Des Rotours has made a detailed study of the fish tallies and other tallies used by the T'ang in "Les insignes en deux parties (*fou* 符) sous la dynastie des T'ang (618-907)," *T'oung pao* 41.1-148. On pp. 70-73 Des Rotours quotes *HTS* 24, showing that all those who had been granted the purple (see note 1131) were also entitled to have a "fish bag." He interprets "gold" as modifying "fish" rather than "bag" (see p. 70).

[1395] 團茶一串, which must have been several bricks of tea strung together.

my thanks to a [certain] Court Priest [824] and Debater [1118] Reverence from whom I had not heard since he returned to his home last year, but who had now secretly wrapped up his head [1296] and was hiding at the home of Yang, the President [of the Supreme Court]. He had his acolyte Ch'ing-liang 清凉 bring me a letter, in which were veiled words of parting. It was tragic.

Yün-hsi 雲栖, an Abbot of our monastery who had lectured on the "Hundred Laws of Yuima," [1396] and the Abbot Ling-chuang 靈莊, who had lectured on the *Nirvana Sutra*,[203] had previously returned to lay life in the group of those under forty. Now, with their heads wrapped up and garbed in lay clothing, they came, and we saw each other at the subprefecture.

The Censor Li [1389] came with his sister's son, Yüan Shih-san-lang,[1397] and inquired after us. They took charge of our baggage and went around buying us felt hats and the like, and they also went to the monastery and looked over our hampers of writings. Abbot Yün-hsi also took charge of our hampers, and together they put them in order, but I fear that we shall not be able to take them with us.

In the evening we left the city. The subprefectural office sent a man to accompany us to Chao-ying-hsien,[1398] eighty or ninety *li* from the capital. The Censor Li and the Abbot [Yün]-hsi accompanied us outside the Ch'un-ming Gate,[1069] where we drank tea. Yang, the President [of the Supreme Court], sent a man with a letter, saying, "I, your disciple, have written five documents and notes in my own hand for the officials I have known of old in the prefectures and subprefectures on your route. If you take these letters, they should help you get through."

[1396] *Yuima hyappō* 百法. See note 138.

[1397] 阮十三郎. *DBZ* suggests the first character in place of 忨 here and in place of 既 at the end of the account of this day.

[1398] 昭應 (the first character is miswritten 照), the present Lin-t'ung 臨潼, about twenty-five km. northeast of Ch'ang-an, thus being not much more than half as far from the capital as Ennin believed.

Yang Lu-shih 楊魯士, who was the Senior Secretary of the Regional Military Office [1399] and had been granted a " fish bag " of dark red,[1394] had previously come to see me and, when I was at the monastery, had been courteous and solicitous. Several times he had come to the monastery to see how I was and had given me silk and woolen shirts and trousers. Now he had his son bring me letters and see me off. I received from him two bolts of silk, two pounds of tea, a string of brick tea,[1395] two strings of cash, and two letters for [persons] on my route. And there was also a letter [for me].

Yang 楊, my patron from the market place, sent a man with one bolt of silk, one length [766] of woolen cloth, and one thousand cash for use on our trip. I cannot record all the others who saw us off. All of them bade us farewell outside the Ch'un-ming Gate, saying, " Stay a while longer." [1400]

The representative of Yang, the President [of the Supreme Court], and the Censor Li were unwilling to go back and accompanied us to the head of Ch'ang-lo Slope,[319] five *li* from the city, and spent the night with us talking in a store. The Censor Li's farewell presents to us were ten bolts of *shao-wu* damask 少吳綾, one piece of fragrant sandalwood, two sandalwood boxes with images, a bottle of incense, a five-pronged silver *vajra*,[1401] two felt hats, one scroll of the *Diamond Sutra* [292] in silver characters at present a Palace possession,[1402] a pair of soft slippers, and two strings of cash. The list is on a separate sheet.

He made his sorrowful farewell with politeness and said, " Your disciple has had much good fortune in his life in having met you who came from afar in search of the Buddhist Law and in having made presentations to you for

---

[1399] *Chih-fang Lang-chung* 職方郎中 (the first character is miswritten 織). Cf. Des Rotours 109 and see note 224.

[1400] 留期分, the second character being *DBZ*'s substitution for 斯.

[1401] J. *bazara* 縛曰羅, here written 拔折羅. See *kongōsho* in note 983.

[1402] Presumably a later gloss indicating the final disposition of this particular treasure in Japan.

several years, but my heart is not yet satisfied, and I do not want to be separated from you my whole life. You now have encountered this difficulty with the ruler and are going back to your homeland. Your disciple believes that it is not likely that he will see you again in this life, but certainly in the future in the paradises of the various Buddhas I shall again be your disciple, as I am today. When you attain Buddhahood, please do not forget your disciple."

Again he said, "I ask that you leave with your disciple the Buddhist robe and scarf you wore that I might take them home and burn incense and make offerings to them for the rest of my life." Upon these words, I gave them to him. Yüan Shih-san-lang [1397] also showed his affinities with me most sincerely.

16th DAY   Early in the morning we parted and set out. We went together with nineteen Chinese monks. In the evening we reached Chao-ying-hsien [1398] and spent the night.

In our group there was a monk twenty years of age who was a native of the city of Ch'ang-an and whose parents, brothers, and sisters were still alive. At an early age he entered the church and at the Ta-chien-fu-ssu [1124] had been an attendant to a Korean monk who was his teacher. Because of the persecution of monks he had been given a Korean monk's name and had thus been able to live at the monastery. The government, in accordance with his official credentials, was sending him off to Korea. At the prefectural government he had tried everything to present his case, but could not escape being sent. His dear ones wailed, taking leave of him in the street, but finally he was shipped off to Chao-ying-hsien. He had spent the night together with us, but, when we all started in the fifth watch (4 A.M.), he secretly fled away. No one in the party was aware of this, and it was discovered [1402a] only when we reached Chao-ying-[hsien]. Two of the three government hirelings, taking different roads, went to look for him, and searched for him all day without success. Believing that he had already gone to

---

[1402a] The first two characters should probably be reversed in 明即知.

his home in the city and was hiding there, the subprefectural government notified the prefecture to search for and apprehend him.

22nd DAY   We passed the T'ung Barrier.[1403] It is the throat [leading] to the capital. I had letters from Yang, the President [of the Supreme Court], to Wei-nan-hsien,[1404] Hua-yin-hsien,[1267] and Yung-ning-hsien [1405] and delivered them all.

SIXTH MOON: 1st DAY [1406]   We reached the home of the Grand Tutor [1407] Ts'ui 崔 in the Eastern Capital [201] and presented the letter from Yang, the President [of the Supreme Court]. The Grand Tutor's special representative came and transmitted to us his words of comfort and gave us a bolt of silk cloth.

9th DAY   We reached the place of the Senior Secretary [of the Imperial Secretariat],[1408] Li 李, the Prefect [412] of Cheng-chou.[984] I had a letter for him from Yang, the President [of the Supreme Court], and also one for the Administrative Officer,[38] Jen 任. I took the letters to the prefectural government and saw the Prefect and Administrative Officer, and they both put us at ease courteously.

Hsin Chiu-yü 辛久昱, the Chief Administrator [1409] of the

[1403] 潼, the narrow pass between river and mountains on the south bank of the Yellow River near the great bend, which, as Ennin says, was the strategic " throat [leading] to the capital " from the east.

[1404] 渭南, on the main road to the east about fifty-five km. northeast of Ch'ang-an.

[1405] 永寧, which in T'ang times was about forty km. northeast of the present town of Yung-ning (or Lo-ning 洛寧, about eighty-five km. southwest of Lo-yang). The Yung-ning of T'ang times was about 150 km. beyond the T'ung Barrier and considerably south of the present main route to Lo-yang.

[1406] July 8, 845.

[1407] *T'ai-fu* 太傅, one of the Emperor's Three Preceptors (*San-shih* 三師), who were exalted though not necessarily powerful personages. Cf. Des Rotours 19.

[1408] *She-jen* 舍人. Cf. *ibid.* 180.

[1409] *Ch'ang-shih* 長史, the third-ranking officer in a prefecture.

prefecture and a Censor of Palace and External Affairs,[1391] who had been granted the purple [1131] and a bag for the fish [tally] of gold,[1394] while at Ch'ang-an had long provided me with funds for food and had been most kind in his attitude toward me. Last year he had become the Chief Administrator [1409] of Cheng-chou and had come to this post. Now we met at the prefectural government, and sorrow and joy were mixed together. He inquired most solicitously about us and invited us to his house, where we took our midday pause and rested.

The Prefect gave us two bolts of silk. People all told us that, since this was the great road from the two capitals, there were floods of those asking for his hospitality, and he could not [always] do the proper thing for them. If it were not a great official but an ordinary official or client [705] who came, when he was being very courteous to them, they would receive one or two bolts [of cloth]. That I received two bolts showed the great depth of his kindness.

The Administrative Officer Jen gave us a bolt of tie-dye cloth.[506] When the Chief Administrator Hsin appeared, he had woolen shirts made for us. After the forenoon meal we left the prefectural government and returned to our inn, and a special representative of the Chief Administrator Hsin came and gave us a bolt of silk, a stomach wrap, light shirts and woolen shirts, and a letter saying that since he was coming later to bid us farewell, he wished we would wait a little longer. However, because the subprefectural government had already sent men . . . 貧祥, we could not wait and so started forth.

After fifteen *li* I turned around and saw the Chief Administrator Hsin far to the west, coming after us on a horse . . . dashed up the road.[1410] We had tea with him in a wayside store and talked for a long time. When we parted he said, " Buddhism no longer exists in this land. But Bud-

Cf. *ibid.* 725. The term appears five times in this section, but the first two times the second character is miswritten 吏.
[1410] 三對行官遏道走來 is not fully clear, but contains the term " official courier."

dhism flows toward the east. So has it been said since ancient times. I hope that you will do your best to reach [1411] your homeland and propagate Buddhism there. Your disciple has been very fortunate to have seen you many times. Today we part, and in this life we are not likely to meet again. When you have attained Buddhahood, I hope that you will not abandon your disciple."

13*th* DAY We reached Pien-chou.[1386] I had a letter from the Senior Secretary [1399] Yang to the Senior Secretary [224] P'ei,[1412] who was the Assistant Regional Commander,[750] and a letter from Yang, the President [of the Supreme Court], to Chu 竹, the Commissioner of Troops,[78] and I delivered them both. The Senior Secretary P'ei inquired about us kindly and sent an official courier to arrange for a boat [1413] to send us on. The Commissioner of Troops was not at the prefectural government, and we were not able to see him. The Senior Secretary P'ei hired a boat, and we went directly to the anchorage west of Ch'en-liu-hsien [1414] and waited for a document from the subprefecture, but before it came we had to give up waiting because of the various government and private cargo boats, and so we started off on the Pien River. Along the way we ourselves had to hire a [new] boat at each subprefecture. The people along the banks of the river from Pien-chou on are evil at heart and not good. One could compare them to the swift and turbid waters of the Pien River, which they drink. Since our documents from

---

[1411] *DBZ* interprets a dubious character in *Tōji* as 建, but suggests 達 for it.

[1412] 裴, twice misprinted 斐 in *DBZ*.

[1413] *DBZ* suggests 船 for 般.

[1414] 陳留, about twenty km. southeast of Pien-chou (K'ai-feng), down the modern Hui-chi River 惠濟河, which flows into the Kuo River 渦河, which in turn flows into the Huai River in north central Anhwei. In T'ang times more than one waterway connected Pien-chou with the Huai, but they all drew water from the Pien River 汴河, which in turn drew from the Yellow River some distance west of Cheng-chou. Ennin appears to have descended the Kuo River to the Huai.

the capital said nothing about our provisions on the way, we
had to bring our own food on the journey.

22nd DAY   We reached Ssu-chou.[1415] This prefecture
is under the jurisdiction of the regional commandery of
Hsü-[chou].[426] The P'u-kuang-wang-ssu of Ssu-chou is famed
throughout the land, but at present its estates,[1416] money,
and slaves have all been confiscated by the government, and
the monastery is desolate and no one comes there. The prefectural government is about to destroy it in accordance
with an Imperial edict.

23rd DAY   We crossed the Huai [River] and reached
Hsü-i-hsien,[1417] which is two hundred *li* from Ch'u-chou [146]
to the east. Our original intention had been to go from here
to Ch'u-chou to look for a ship on which to cross the sea,
but the subprefectural government directed us to Yang-
chou [11] instead.[1418] We presented statements giving our case,
but the Subprefect [77] was unreasonable, and we had to go to
Yang-chou. From Hsü-i-hsien to Yang-chou there are nine
post stations with no water route, and at each post station
we hired donkeys for our hampers of writings.

On the way we met the Senior Secretary [of the Imperial
Secretariat],[1408] P'ei,[1419] who had formerly served as Prefect
of Hai-chou [107] but who had been put out this spring and

[1415] See note 194. *Tōji* has 西 here and 洒 two sentences later
(printed as 泗 in *DBZ* and *KIK* the second time), but the
reference to the P'u-kuang-wang-ssu, which Ennin mentioned
under 844 III, shows clearly that Ssu-chou is meant.

[1416] *DBZ* suggests the deletion of the middle character in 庄
國園.

[1417] See note 194. The first character is written with homophones,
煦 here and 昫 later in the passage (but printed with the first
character both times in the printed texts). The T'ang Hsü-i-
hsien is placed north of the Huai River and Ssu-chou south of
the river in *TTLCT* 41a, but this passage indicates that their
positions were probably the reverse.

[1418] *Tōji* has 對, where *DBZ* and *KIK* print 剛, with a footnote
to the effect that 對 appears in *Ikeda*.

[1419] Not to be confused with the Senior Secretary (*Lang-chung*)
of the same surname they had met at Pien-chou.

demoted to Chief Administrator [1409] of T'ai-chou.[93] There also was a Han-lin Professor [1420] who had been degraded to Senior Administrator [1421] of a distant prefecture. When he met us he said, " On the twenty-ninth day of the fifth moon I left Ch'ang-an. While I was in the city, the return to lay life of the monks and nuns in the city was completed. In accordance with an Imperial edict, the monastery officers [81] were left in each monastery to make an inventory of its money and wait until the government had collected it, after which they were to be returned to lay life. The destruction of the monasteries has been started, and the Chang-ching-ssu,[591] the Ch'ing-lung-ssu,[357] and the [Ta]-an-kuo-ssu are being incorporated into the Imperial parks."

28th DAY We reached Yang-chou and saw the monks and nuns of the city being sent back to their places of origin with their heads wrapped up.[1296] The monasteries [1422] are to be destroyed, and their money, estates, and bells are being confiscated by the government. Recently a document came on Imperial command saying that the bronze and iron Buddhas of the land were all to be smashed and weighed and handed over to the Salt and Iron Bureau [1423] and a record made of this and reported to the throne.

Chiang-tu-hsien [1424] dispatched men to take us to Chiang-yang-hsien,[151] but, using bribery, we asked to go to Ch'u-chou, and the subprefectural government then sent us to Ch'u-chou. We passed through Kao-yu-hsien [154] and Pao-ying-hsien.[370]

[1420] *Po-shih* (see notes 424 and 874), a title for various professorial and scholarly officers in the T'ang government, but not for any in the Han-lin Academy (see note 1335).

[1421] *Ssu-ma* 司馬, ranking after the Chief Administrator in a prefectural government. Cf. Des Rotours 725.

[1422] 寺舍 is misprinted 寺金 in the printed texts, but correctly in Okada 12.183.

[1423] *Yen-t'ieh-ssu* 鹽鐵司 . See notes 1289 and 1325 and 845 VIII 27.

[1424] See note 11. Here the first character is miswritten 紅.

SEVENTH MOON: 3rd DAY [1425]   We were able to reach Ch'u-chou. First we went to the Korean ward and saw Sŏl, the General Manager [of the ward] [1426] and an Assimilated Colonel [379] of this prefecture, and the Korean Interpreter Yu Sinŏn. On meeting, they inquired courteously about us. Our hampers of writings were taken by boat to the Interpreter's home. Then we went to Shan-yang-hsien [373] and presented a document stating our intentions, namely, that since the Japanese tributary embassies all boarded ship here to cross the sea and return home and since I, Ennin, and the others had been sent here to return home, we asked to cross the sea from here, but the subprefectural government refused, saying, " At this prefecture you are not yet out on the sea, and, since you are being sent through on Imperial order, we dare not detain you, and therefore you should be sent to the land's end in Teng-chou, [419] where you can board ship and return home."

The Korean Interpreter Yu Sinŏn himself went to the subprefectural government and, using bribes, conferred with them about the original proposal, trying to get them to agree. They told him that this was an area of law and order and within the jurisdiction of the Minister of State, Li Shen, [1427] and it would be a violation of the Imperial edict if those being sent through on Imperial command should tarry a day or two. The subprefectural government was not willing to be reasonable.

The Commissioner Sŏl [1426] and the Interpreter Yu then

[1425] The first day was August 7, 845.

[1426] *Tsung-kuan* 惣官. See the use of this term on 839 II 26. The surname in *Tōji* appears to be Sal 薩, but this is clearly the same man who is referred to five times later as " the Commissioner 大使 Sŏl 薛," on 846 VI 17 as " Sŏl Chŏn 詮, the General Manager and Assimilated Colonel of Ch'u-chou," and on 847 VI 10 as " the former General Manager, Sŏl Chŏn." *DBZ* prints 薛 in this last instance and *KIK* 辟. The other Korean Ennin called on, Yu Sinŏn, was an old friend who first appeared in the diary on 839 III 22.

[1427] See note 1191 and 844 VII 15.

went to the prefectural government to talk it over, but they opposed it too. For two days they tried everything without success, and we had to be sent on through. The Shan-yang-hsien office was moved by the earnest appeals of the Interpreter Yu, but his every effort came to nought. They said to us, " If you wish to go south, then we shall send you south, and if you wish to go north, then we shall send you north, but it is beyond the powers of the subprefectural government to let you stay here looking for a ship." There was nothing more to be said in words, so we asked to go to Teng-chou, which is the northeastern extremity of China over 1,100 *li* from Ch'u-chou. The subprefectural government issued documents and dispatched men to take us to Teng-chou. The Commissioner Sŏl and the Interpreter Yu had wished to be able to keep us and settle us in the Korean ward and send us home from here, and they were made unhappy over their inability to keep us because of the sub-prefecture's refusal.

5th DAY   At dawn we went with some government hirelings [1428] to the home of the Interpreter Yu.[1428a] The Interpreter gave three hundred cash to the government hire-lings and conferred with them privately, saying, " The monks are going on a distant trip just at the hottest time of the year, and already they are in distress. I should like to be able to keep them in my home and have them rest for two or three days. You, sirs, go home and come here early on the eighth." The government hirelings [1428] agreed to the suggestion and returned home. The Commissioner and the Interpreter did all they could to take care of us.[1429]

I have been told that the road from Ch'u-chou to Teng-chou is all mountains and wilderness, the trees and grasses

---

[1428] 家下, which *DBZ* corrects to *chia-ting* 家丁, on the basis of the use of this latter term elsewhere in this passage and on 845 V 16.

[1428a] The last two characters in 譯宅語 should be reversed, as they are in *DBZ* and *KIK*.

[1429] The 養 of *Tōji* may be preferable to the 發 of *Ikeda*, which *DBZ* follows. In *Tōji* the 使 in " Commissioner " is miswritten 便.

are high and thick, and the mosquitoes and horseflies like rain. All day long one crosses mountains and moors, and the village stockades are far apart. Dwellings are rarely to be seen, and the people are evil at heart. One goes seventy or eighty *li* before coming across a house or two, and people are frightened [when one does meet them]. If we were to take our hampers of writings with us and call them our goods, we would be despoiled by the people, and I fear that we would fail. Moreover,[1430] since Buddhism is banned by Imperial edict and has been completely proscribed and since the people of the prefectures and subprefectures to the north are evil at heart, if we were discovered taking Buddhist images with us, they would surely make obstacles for us, and our crime would be that of disobedience to an Imperial edict. Therefore, I consulted with the Interpreter Yu and put all four of the hampers of holy teachings, pious pictures,[407] and clerical clothing which we had brought from the capital, into the Interpreter's house and entrusted them to him, bidding him take charge of them. Earnestly I charged him, saying, "If I reach Teng-chou and can stay there, then please bring my books. If not, let your chief concern be to take care of them and not let them get lost." The Interpreter agreed and put our baggage in order in a special [1431] place.

The Commissioner Sŏl gave us three pairs of socks, and the Interpreter Yu [gave us] nine bolts of silk, ten Korean knives, five pairs of socks, and besides these, a lot of provisions.

The people of the subprefectures of Yang-chou and Ch'u-chou in Huai-nan-tao [11] are evil at heart and very hard to trust.

At present the Interpreter has a man who informed us, saying, "Two ships which came over from Japan together, have landed in the Ch'ang-chou [1432] region in Chiang-nan-

[1430] The character printed 今 in the printed texts is miswritten 令 in *Tōji*.

[1431] *DBZ* suggests 特 for 持.

[1432] 常, the present Wu-chin 武進, south of the Yangtse River

[tao] [156] over three thousand *li* from here. They intend to sell their ships and hire Chinese ships to transport their things here. I suspect that these may be the ships which took Master Ensai's disciples in the third year of Hui-ch'ang (843) and have now returned [to China]. [1246] We now wish to send a man to find out about this. Also, the Japanese Master Egaku, [1433] who worshiped at Mt. Wu-t'ai in the second year of Hui-ch'ang (842), returned to Japan on the boat of Li Lin-te [1222] to seek provisions for [Mt.] Wu-t'ai. Year after year he has brought provisions, but now he has encountered the national difficulties and has returned to lay life and is at present in Ch'u-chou." I asked especially for news of Ensai, but no one knew about him.

8th DAY We started. The Interpreter Yu had letters for his compatriots 鄉人 along the way up to Teng-chou, bidding them to care for us and to act as our patrons and the like. We boarded a boat and embarked on the Huai.

9th DAY At the time for the forenoon meal we reached Lien-shui-hsien. [425] It is under Ssu-[chou]. [194] Because the Ch'u-chou Interpreter had a letter for his Lien-shui compatriots bidding them to care for us and to see about keeping us when we reached the subprefecture, we first went to the Korean ward, but when we met the people of the ward they were not courteous to us. We went to the General Manager [of the ward] [1426] and others and earnestly sought their recognition but found everything difficult to accomplish.

We ran into Ch'oe Un Sibirang, [1434] who formerly was the

---

about midway between Shanghai and Nanking. The distance from Ch'u-chou to Ch'ang-chou was really only about four hundred *li*.

[1433] See note 1181. *DBZ* and *KIK* suggest that the 子 after his name be expanded to 弟子 (" disciples "), but on 842 IV 25 we were told that it was Egaku himself who was returning to Japan from Ming-chou on the ship of Li Lin-te, while his disciples were apparently returning on a different ship from Ch'u-chou.

[1434] 崔暈十三郎 . See note 541. The 第 which appears here after Un in his name is not repeated elsewhere. The 隅 which precedes the name is corrected by *DBZ* to 遇 and by *KIK* to 偶.

Commissioner of Troops [78] of Ch'ŏnghaejin.[438] When we
were at the Mt. Ch'ih Cloister [523] in Teng-chou, we had
met him once, and he had written his name for us to keep,
saying, " When you monks return to your homeland from
your search for the Law, you must take this paper with my
name to Lien-shui, and I, Un, shall do my best to accompany
you back to Japan." Later [1435] he returned to Korea, met
with some political difficulties, and fled to Lien-shui to
live.[1436] Now we met and recognized each other and felt
close to each other. He did all he could to plan for our
remaining there, and he earnestly sought for our recognition.[1437] The [General] Manager and the others thought it
all over.

We wrote out a statement and went to the subprefectural
government to see the Chief Official [77] and ask to stay in the
Korean ward of this subprefecture searching for a ship on
which to return home. When the Chief Official saw us, he
took pity on us and summoned an orderly [1438] to take charge
of us. He had him arrange for tea and food for us to drink
and eat and then had him bring us to see the Chief Official,
who asked us, " Do you have previous acquaintances in the
Korean ward? " We replied, " When the Japanese tributary
embassy left from Ch'u-chou for home in the fourth year of
K'ai-ch'eng (839), it obtained all its men from Ch'u-chou
and this subprefecture, and consequently we must have
acquaintances." The Chief Official instructed the orderly to
take us to the Korean ward and, if we were recognized, to

[1435] *DBZ* suggests 期 for 斯 .

[1436] Okada (13.27-28) believes that this refers to the death of
Chang Pogo (see note 438) and confirms the date of 841 given
in *SNK* 842 I 10, rather than the date of 846 which appears in
the Korean sources for Chang Pogo's death.

[1437] *Shih-jen* 識認, which apparently is used in this passage to
mean the formal acceptance of responsibility for Ennin and
his companions by the leaders of the Korean community.

[1438] *Chih-ch'eng-jen* 祗承人 , literally " one who respectfully
receives [orders] from above." *DBZ* and *KIK* interpret the first
character as 祇, but *ZZGR* prints it correctly.

have [the Koreans] make out an affidavit, which he was to bring back, but, if no one recognized us, to bring us back here.

We then went with the representative to the [Korean] ward. The General Manager and the others intended to accept us, but there was also a Special Officer 專知官 there, who refused. Consequently, they would not make out the affidavit, and we returned to the subprefectural government. The Chief Official decided to lodge us temporarily in the Ta-shan-ssu 大善, letting us stay there and rest for three days. Ch'oe Sibirang provided for us as our patron.

We obtained a subprefectural document and a man to accompany us and started for the prefecture.[1439] Ch'oe Sibirang had hired a boat and had put in order our provisions for the road, our bowls, plates, vegetables, and the like. After all was prepared, we took leave of each other, and he said, "Your disciple wishes that he were able to keep you and send you home from here, but, because the group refused and the official document has expired, my efforts [1440] have been to no avail, and I cannot fulfill my wish. After the autumn I intend myself to go to the Teng-chou region, and I hope to see you then."

15th DAY   We reached Hai-chou and went to the subprefectural government and presented a statement, asking to stay there a little while. [It said:]

The ships of the Japanese tributary embassy landed here and started back to Japan from here. We, Ennin and the others, came with the embassy to China and are now returning to our homeland and have been sent here in due course.[1441] Since

---

[1439] This should mean Ssu-chou (see note 194), for Ennin was correct above in placing Lien-shui-hsien under its jurisdiction, but from what follows he obviously meant Hai-chou (see note 107).

[1440] *DBZ* corrects 奴 to 努.

[1441] The correction of 節級 to 節度 , "regional commandery," in *DBZ* and *KIK* appears unjustified by the context or by the facts. In the document of VIII 27 the word is miscopied 節仍.

this is the seacoast, we humbly beg to stay for a little while in this prefecture to look for a ship on which to return home.

The Chief Official [77] said, " Recently a Korean monk too was sent here from Ching-chao-fu [1062] and asked to stay in this prefecture temporarily, but the Magistrate [619] [of the prefecture] refused, and so he was sent on. It would be difficult, [thus, to grant] your request to stay here. The subprefectural government is not free in the matter, and you must present your statement through the Magistrate."

16th DAY We went to the Prefect and asked to return home from this prefecture, [1442] but he was unreasonable. He gave his decision, saying, " You are to be sent on, in accordance with the Imperial edict. The prefectural government does not dare keep you. You have been notified."

17th DAY We started out. From Hai-chou northward there is no water route. Although we went alongside the sea marshes, [1443] we did not see the sea. All day long we crossed waste lands and then entered the mountains.

18th DAY We reached Huai-jen, [1444] which is under the jurisdiction of Hai-chou. The people were proper in their attitudes, and when they saw travelers, they were very courteous and accepted us without ado. The subprefectural government was sympathetic and good.

20th DAY We started out, going through mountains and waste lands. The grass and trees were tall and thick, and we rarely met anyone. All day long we went up mountains and into valleys, treading in mud and water and suffering without end.

21st DAY We reached Chü-hsien, [1445] which is under the jurisdiction of Mi-chou. [436] The subprefectural government and the people were rough and evil.

[1442] 常州 (see note 1432) is clearly a copyist's error for 當州.

[1443] The correction of 海汙 to 海行 suggested by DBZ appears unnecessary.

[1444] 懷仁, about forty km. north of Hai-chou and a little west of the modern town of Kan-yü 贛楡.

[1445] 莒, in southeastern Shantung about 120 km. north and a little west of Hai-chou.

26*th* DAY We reached Mi-chou. The people were rough and evil, and gentle ones were rare.

EIGHTH MOON: 2*nd* DAY [1446] We reached Kao-mi-hsien.[1447] The people were gentle.

6*th* DAY We reached Chi-mo-hsien,[482] which is under the jurisdiction [1448] of Lai-chou.[482] The people were polite and could put their guests at ease.

10*th* DAY We reached Ch'ang-yang-hsien,[731] which is under the jurisdiction of Lai-chou. The people were pleasant.

16*th* DAY We reached Teng-chou [419] and saw His Excellency Hsiao 蕭 the Chief [of the General Court of Censors],[1274] who had recently come to his post.

There has been an Imperial edict, saying that prefectural and subprefectural governments are to peel the gold off the gilt bronze Buddhist images throughout the land and are to weigh it and present it to the throne.

The road from Hai-chou up to Teng-chou is impassable. There are broad waste lands, the paths are narrow, and the grass and trees close in over them. Every few steps we got into mud, and we constantly lost our way. If we had not had someone who knew the way to guide us, we could not have gone a step. We went from waste lands into mountains, and from mountains into waste lands. The slopes are steep, the streams deep and icy, hurting us to the bone when we forded them. In the mountains, we would cross a hundred mountains and ford a hundred streams in a single day. In the waste lands, the trees were dense and the grass was thick, and if someone went a little ahead, it was difficult to see him.[1449] Only when one saw the movement of the grass

---

[1446] The first day was September 6, 845. The preceding moon had thirty days.

[1447] 高密, on the railway about sixty-five km. air-line northwest of Tsingtao and sixty km. northeast of Mi-chou.

[1448] *DBZ* and *KIK* misprint 營 for 管.

[1449] Some of the characters at this point are doubtful, but the general meaning is clear from the context.

did one know there was a man walking there. The mosquitoes and horseflies were like rain, and we did not have
enough strength to swat them. The mire beneath the grass
came to our knees or to our waists.

The prefectural and subprefectural towns along the way
were like single mounds in the wilderness. The food of the
people of the mountain villages and subprefectural towns is
coarse and hard, and they love to eat salty tea [1450] and millet.
The taste [of their food] is unbearable, and when one eats it,
one's chest hurts. The custom in the mountain villages is to
eat soup without having boiled it, and for years on end they
eat only cold dishes. The greatest politeness to an honored
guest is to give him empty cakes [1451] and cold dishes as a
fine banquet.

We went north for 1,300 li at one stretch, going all the way
through mountains and waste lands. Although we had been
close to the seashore, we had not seen the sea and only did
so when we reached Teng-chou. Teng-chou is the northeastern extremity of China. The prefectural city stands near the
North Sea and facing it. The city walls are about one or two li
from the sea. Although it is a remote place,[1452] it has been
no different from the capital in the regulation of monks and
nuns, the destruction of the monasteries, the banning of the
scriptures, the breaking of the images, and the confiscation
of the property of the monasteries. Moreover they have
peeled off the gold from the Buddhas and smashed the
bronze and iron Buddhas and measured their weight. What
a pity! What limit was there to the bronze, iron, and gold
Buddhas of the land? And yet, in accordance with the Imperial edict, all have been destroyed and have been turned
into trash.

P'eng-lai-hsien [419] made out a document and sent us to

[1450] Perhaps the character which resembles "tea" 茶 is to be
corrected to 榮, in which case we have "salty dishes."

[1451] That is, bread stuffs with no filling of chopped meat or the
like to make them more tasty.

[1452] DBZ and KIK interpret the character as 北, but it appears
to be 地, as printed in ZZGR and copied in Ikeda.

Mou-p'ing-hsien.[493] We went southeast along the seacoast. The rivers and waste lands were hard to cross, and there were mountains upon mountains.

21st DAY   We reached Mou-p'ing-hsien and, obtaining a subprefectural document, went towards [1453] the south-eastern sea[coast].

24th DAY   We reached Wen-teng-hsien.[508] After crossing mountains and waste lands, our flimsy clothing was completely worn out. We went to the subprefecture and saw the Subprefect and asked to go to the Office in Charge of Korean Affairs 勾當新羅所 in the eastern part of the subprefecture, where we would seek [sustenance] whereby to prolong our lives and would ourselves seek a ship on which to return to our homeland. The Chief Official, in accordance with our papers, wrote out a document sending us to the Office in Charge of Korean Affairs. It is seventy *li* southeast of the subprefectural town and in the jurisdiction of Ch'ing-ning-hsiang [528] in Wen-teng-hsien.

27th DAY   We reached the Office in Charge of Korean Affairs, where Chang Yŏng, the Imperially appointed 勑 Assimilated Colonel [379] of the Regional Commandery of the P'ing-lu Army [1454] and the Guard Officer in charge of military matters of Teng-chou,[531] was in charge of the Korean population of the Wen-teng-hsien area. When we reached his home and saw him, we recognized each other and rejoiced, and he inquired courteously after us. When we left for Wu-t'ai from this inlet in the fifth year of K'ai-cheng (840), we were sent off by this Commissioner, who devoted himself to arranging for our written documents and official credentials from this prefecture and subprefecture. Now that we had returned here, he was courteous and put us at ease. Then I

[1453] *DBZ* is incorrect in saying that 以 appears for 向 in *Tōji*.
[1454] The P'ing-lu Army 平盧軍, or the P'ing-lu Regional Commandery as it was also known, had originally been on the northern frontier in the present Jehol area, but in the second half of the eighth century it was moved to the Ch'ing-chou area (see note 540) and put in control of the northern part of what is now Shantung.

handed over the documents from the subprefecture and told him in detail the matters on my mind.

The Commissioner received us and took us in and permitted us to search for a ship on which to be sent home. Rejoicing, he said, "From the time you set off from here until now, I have had no news of you, and in my heart I thought that you had returned to Japan earlier. I did not think that you would come here again and to have met you again is very strange, very strange. Your disciple has great affinities with you. I shall strive to see that nothing untoward happens to you within my jurisdiction. Please be at ease and rest yourself. There is no need to worry. I wish to provide you myself with provisions for your forenoon meals each day until you return home, so eat your fill and sleep."

The Commissioner then made out a statement informing the prefecture:

We have received a document from Wen-teng-hsien, which says, "The two Japanese monks, Ennin and Ishō, have each been granted covering documents from Ching-chao-fu [1062] and, in accordance with the Imperial edict, are being sent to their homeland and in due course [1441] have been sent to this subprefecture. They ask to go to the Office in Charge of Korean Affairs to seek [sustenance] whereby to prolong their lives and to await a ship bound across to Japan, on which they would hope to return home." They are at present at this inlet.

Ten days later he received a document from the prefecture, saying, "Let the monks be at ease. If there is a ship bound across to Japan, then they may go at their discretion."

Recently there was an Imperial edict [saying]:

The black clothing of the monks and the nuns of the land who have been returned to lay life should all be collected and burned by their respective prefectures and subprefectures. It is feared that the officials . . . 覬播 have used their power to hide [monks and nuns] in their private homes and that in secret they wear their black robes. These should be ruthlessly confiscated and all burned, and the matter reported to the throne. If after the burning there be monks or nuns who wear their black

robes and have not given them all up and there be those who
protect [monks and nuns] at the time of the investigation, they
shall be sentenced to death [1455] in accordance with the Imperial
edict.

The prefectures and subprefectures, in accordance with
the Imperial edict, have notified the city wards and the cantons [29] to collect the clothing of the monks and nuns and
bring it to the prefectures and subprefectures for all of it
to be burned.

There also was an Imperial edict ordering that the rarities,
treasures, jewels, and gold and silver of the monasteries of
the empire be confiscated by the prefectures and subprefectures and presented to the throne.

Again, there was an Imperial edict, saying that the copper [1455a] utensils, bells, gongs, caldrons, pans, and the like,
used by the monks and nuns of the monasteries of the land,
should be collected into the government storehouses by the
Commissioners of Salt and Iron [1423] of the various provinces
and the matter recorded and reported to the throne.

There was an Imperial edict banning wheelbarrows [1456]
throughout the land. If after the ruling [on this matter]
someone trundles a wheelbarrow along, he is to be sentenced
to death on the spot. Since the Emperor believes in the
teachings of the Taoist priests and wheelbarrows break up
the middle of the road, he fears that the hearts of the Taoist
priests might not be at ease [if wheelbarrows were used].[1457]

There was an Imperial edict proscribing pigs, black dogs,
black donkeys and oxen, and the like throughout the empire. This was because the Taoist priests wear yellow, and

---

[1455] 處死 is misprinted 處分 in the printed texts.

[1455a] *DBZ* and *KIK* misprint " silver."

[1456] *Tu-chiao-ch'e* 獨脚車, " single-legged carts."

[1457] The prohibition was obviously based on a pun, for " center
of the road " 道中心 also means " the heart of the Way
(Taoism) ." *Ikeda*, presumably because of a misunderstanding of
the text, substitutes 士 for the second character, giving us
" the hearts of the Taoist priests."

[the Emperor] feared that, if there were much black, it might repress the yellow and cause it to be destroyed.

They have ordered the prefectures and subprefectures close to the sea to present live otters. I do not know the reason for this. Recently an Imperial edict ordered the provinces to present the hearts and livers of youths and maidens of fifteen years. This also was [because the Emperor] has been deluded by Taoist priests.

The monks and nuns of China are naturally poor. Throughout the land they have all been returned to lay life, and, now that they have been secularized, they lack clothes to wear and food to eat. Their hardships are extreme, and they cannot assuage their cold or hunger, so they enter the cantons and villages and steal the property of others, and their transgressions are very numerous. Those whom the prefectures and subprefectures are arresting are all monks returned to lay life. Because of this, the check on monks and nuns who have been regulated and have already returned to lay life is still more [severe].[1458]

NINTH MOON: 22nd DAY [1459]   The Commissioner's servant, Kosan 高山, is taking a passing ship to Ch'u-chou. I consulted with the Commissioner and wrote letters to be sent to the Ch'u-chou Interpreter Yu Sinŏn and to the Commissioner Sŏl,[1426] asking for the scriptures, writings, pious pictures,[407] and clothing which I had entrusted to them previously.

Since there were official guests without end at the house of the Commissioner, we asked him for a quiet place in which to spend the winter. Our original intention had been to live in the Mt. Ch'ih Cloister,[523] but the prefecture and subprefecture had destroyed it in accordance with the Imperial edict, and there was not a building in which we could live. The Commissioner decided to put us in a house on the monastery's estate, and he provided our food.

[1458] *DBZ* suggests the addition of the character 甚.
[1459] The first day was October 5, 845.

I Sinhye,[1460] a Korean monk who had returned to lay life, went to Dazaifu [2] in Japan in the *wei* year of Kōnin (815) [1461] and lived there for eight years. It was at the time that Prince Sui [1462] was the Governor of the Province of Chikuzen,[666] and he took pity on him. The Commissioner Chang went to Japan in the first year of Tenchō 天長 (824), and when he returned, [Sinhye] came back to China on his ship. At present he lives on the monastery's estate. Since he understands Japanese, he acts as an interpreter.

The Commissioner settled matters for our stay as guests, and we left everything for him to manage. Of his own volition he supplied us plentifully with our daily vegetables. He constantly wrote letters and sent us provisions, and he courteously put us at ease.

ELEVENTH MOON: 3rd DAY [1463]   The Commissioner came to the estate and saw us and putting us at ease, said, " On the seventh of this moon I am going to the prefectural city to see the new Prefect, His Excellency the Chief [of the General Court of Censors].[1274] I shall take this occasion to tell him in detail about my sending you to Japan and shall ask for a document from the prefecture. Next spring, then, I shall fix up a ship for you."

I am told that since the seventh moon the Tibetans have

[1460] On 840 I 15 Ennin recorded that Sinhye had lived six years in Japan, though here he says eight years and the dates he cites would make it ten or more years. Sinhye's surname is given here as 季, but *DBZ* suggests that this should be corrected to the common surname 李.

[1461] There was only one year marked with the cyclical character *wei* 未 in the Japanese year period of Kōnin (see 839 I 8; the first character here is miswritten 私), and this year was 815. *KIK* is wrong in printing 末 for *wei*, which would make it the last year of Kōnin, which was 823 or else the first four days of 824.

[1462] Since Prince Sui 須井宮 does not appear in the Japanese sources, the name is probably garbled.

[1463] The first day was December 3, 845.

made a great descent upon the Chinese borders. Also, Uighur forces have entered China and are pillaging the land. On Imperial command, troops are being drawn from the provinces [to meet the barbarians].

In the last three or four years, in accordance with Imperial edicts, the prefectures and subprefectures of the land have regulated the monks and nuns, and their return to lay life has been completed. Moreover, throughout the land the Buddha halls, monasteries,[550] and temples have all been destroyed; throughout the land scriptures, images, and clerical clothing have all been burned; throughout the land the gold on the figures of the Buddhas has been peeled off; throughout the land the bronze and iron Buddhas have been smashed, weighed, and confiscated; and the prefectures and subprefectures of the land have gathered in the money and estates of the monasteries and have taken their retainers and slaves. Only in four regional commanderies north of the Yellow River, Chen,[578] Yu,[984] Wei,[577] and Lu,[1291] where Buddhism has always been honored, they have not destroyed the monasteries, the monks and nuns have not been regulated, and Buddhism has not been in the least disturbed. There have repeatedly been Imperial Commissioners to investigate and punish them, but they say, " If the Emperor himself were to come to destroy [the monasteries] and burn [the scriptures], it could be done, but we are unable to do it." [1464]

ELEVENTH MOON: 15th DAY At dusk there was an eclipse of the moon, and as night came on the body of the moon disappeared entirely and was completely invisible. In the third watch (midnight) it gradually appeared again.

Recently there was an Imperial edict that the remote prefectures of the land where there might be monks and nuns

---

[1464] Okada (12.185-86) points out that the protection of the Buddhists in Lu-fu could only have lasted until the destruction of the Liu forces the previous year (see 844 IX). He also cites a passage from *TCTC* 248 (under the date 845 VIII 7, where this work has its chief account of the Buddhist persecution), showing

who had returned to lay life, should all order the places where they were, to keep track of their whereabouts and not to let them travel. The monk Chang Fa-man 張法滿, who had been returned to lay life, was being sent back to Tibet [1464a] by Ching-chao-fu [1062] in accordance with the Imperial edict, and he consequently was sent to the Regional Commandery of Feng-hsiang.[1127] Because the Regional Commander repeatedly petitioned the throne, the Emperor ordered Feng-hsiang-fu to take charge of him, and it was not required that he be sent to Tibet. On account of this, the monks and nuns of the remote prefectures of the land who have been returned to lay life are not allowed to travel.

In order to send us, the monks in search [of the Law, to Japan], the Commissioner in Charge [of Korean Affairs] asked this prefecture for a passport. His Excellency the Chief [of the General Court of Censors] [1274] made his decision, saying, " If they are seeking a ship themselves, it would be much better if we, in accordance with the Imperial edict, send them on through. They should not stay here and live." But the officers in charge [1465] conferred together and said, " This would be to oppose the text of the Imperial edict. We are not willing to give them official credentials."

HUI-CH'ANG · SIXTH YEAR

ping-yin

IN THE CYCLE OF YEARS

FIRST MOON: 1st DAY *kuei-mao* [1466]

9*th* DAY The Commissioner's servant Kosan, who had previously been sent to Ch'u-chou to get our writings,

---

that monks from Mt. Wu-t'ai had been fleeing to Yu-chou, which indicates that some protection was to be found there.

[1464a] Here Hsi-fan 西蕃. See note 794.

[1465] *DBZ* suggests 本曹官人 for 本當官入.

[1466] January 31, 846. *Ping-yin* 丙寅 is third and *kuei-mao* 癸卯 fortieth in the cycle of sixty.

pious [pictures],[407] and the like, came back, and I received a
letter from the Ch'u-chou Interpreter, Yu Sinŏn, saying:

> There has been an Imperial edict to burn the Buddhist
> scriptures, banners, and baldachins, and the clothing, bronze
> vases, bowls, and the like of the monks, destroying them com-
> pletely.[1466a] Those who disobey are to be punished to the limit of
> the law. I burned all the scriptures, banners, pious [pictures], and
> the like of my household and kept only your writings and the rest.
> Since the regulating has been extremely severe, I feared that at
> guarded barriers they would discover them, so I did not dare
> take them out and send them to you.

It also said that recently he had received reliable word that
the ship of Li Lin-te [1222] had returned, and added that Japanese travelers had also come to get information about T'ao
Chung,[1223] and, if there turned out to be letters from Japan,
he would be sure to send them on to us.

Kosan said that in Ch'u-chou he himself had seen a man
from the ship who said that two monks had come by this
ship solely for my sake [1467] but had now encountered the
persecution of monks and were there with their heads
wrapped up.[1296]

SECOND MOON: 5th DAY [1468]   I [decided to] send Tei
Yūman to Ch'u-chou by the ship of Yen Fang-chin 閻方金
to get the scriptures and the rest which we had entrusted to
Yu Sinŏn of Ch'u-chou. The Commissioner arranged for the
dispatching of the ship, and it set sail on the 13th DAY *of
the THIRD MOON*.[1469]

9th DAY   I received a letter from the Commissioner,

[1466a] 書 may be a copyist's error for 盡.

[1467] Since the term *Shōyaku-sō* (see note 7) is used, this could be
interpreted to mean that the two monks had themselves come
as Scholar Monks to study in China, but these were probably
the men mentioned on III 9, who apparently constituted a
search party sent to find Ennin.

[1468] The first day was March 1, 846.

[1469] The first day was March 31, 846.

saying that recently he had received information from men
on a ship from the south to the effect that one monk and
four laymen from Japan had reached Yang-chou with letters
from their homeland and that they had come solely to look
for me.

FOURTH MOON: 15th DAY [1470]   I heard that the Emperor had died [1471] and that for several moons the various
provinces, prefectures, and subprefectures are to be in
mourning and mourning clothes are to be worn. The Emperor died because his constitution had been ruined.

27th DAY   Wang Chong 王宗, a Korean, brought a
letter from Yang-chou from the Japanese Shōkai [1472] Hosshi.[7] In it he stated in detail his reasons for coming.

FIFTH MOON: 1st DAY [1473]   Since Wang Chong was returning to Yang-chou, I gave him a letter inviting Shōkai
[Hos]shi.

The new Emperor,[1471] whose surname is Li,[1312] had a great
amnesty in the fifth moon. There also was an Imperial edict
that each prefecture of the land was to build two monasteries
and that the regional commanderies were permitted to
build three, and each monastery was to have fifty monks.
The monks over fifty years of age who had been returned to
lay life last year were allowed to take Buddhist orders as

[1470] The first day was April 29, 846.
[1471] The standard historical sources as well as Ennin (VII 22)
agree that Wu-tsung died on III 23, allowing twenty-one
days for the news to reach Ennin. The new Emperor was
Hsüan-tsung 宣宗, an uncle of Wu-tsung and the latter's two
predecessors.
[1472] Shōkai 性海, who seems to have been the leader of the
search party mentioned on I 9 and III 9, is mentioned in *SNK*
848 III 26 together with Ishō as the two disciples whom Ennin
brought back to Japan with him. The first character of his name
is miswritten 悔 here but correctly on V 1. It is preceded here
by the character 壊, which is not clear in this context and has
been omitted entirely in the printed texts.
[1473] May 29, 846.

of old, and on those who had reached eighty years were bestowed five strings of cash by the state. The moons of the
three long [fasts] [1302] were re-established, and, as before,
butchering was proscribed [during these moons]. The Imperial edict was proclaimed at Ch'u-chou on the *22nd* DAY
of the FIFTH MOON.[1474]

SIXTH MOON: 17*th* DAY [1475] I received a letter from
Sŏl Chŏn,[1426] the General Manager and Assimilated Colonel [1476] of Ch'u-chou, sent through Li Kuo-yü.[1477] Then I
learned that Tei Yūman, whom I previously had sent to
the southern prefectures, was about to start back, and I
also learned that Wang Chong, who had returned to the
southern prefectures on the first day of the fifth moon, had
reached [1478] Ch'u-chou in the last ten days of the fifth moon
and then had gone on to Yang-chou. Li Kuo-yü told me this.
SIXTH MOON: 29*th* DAY Tei Yūman returned, and I
received a letter from my Ch'u-chou patron, Yu Sinŏn.
Among the pious pictures and the writings which I had
previously entrusted to him, the *Double Great Taizō and
Kongō Mandara* [277] in full colors had been burned by Yu
Sinŏn because of the severity of the Imperial orders in Huai-
nan, but [Tei Yūman] was able to bring all the other drawings, writings, and the rest. Yūman had returned because he
was unable to go to Yang-chou.[1479]

[1474] *TCTC* 248 records this amnesty involving the Buddhists on
V 5 (seventeen days before it was proclaimed in Ch'u-chou) and
also tells of the execution of the Taoist priest Chao Kuei-chen
the preceding moon (see note 1349).
[1475] The first day was June 28, 846.
[1476] The final character of *T'ung-shih-chiang* is omitted here. See
note 379.
[1477] 李國遇 , read in Chinese fashion, although he too may have
been a Korean.
[1478] 得 is perhaps to be corrected to 到. As it stands the passage
reads, " obtaining word from Ch'u-chou in the last ten days of
the fifth moon, had gone to Yang-chou."
[1479] Presumably Ennin had expected him to go to Yang-chou
to see Shōkai or to make inquiries about ships going to Japan.

SEVENTH MOON: 22nd DAY [1480]   The Imperial tumulus was completed. I have been told that the Hui-ch'ang Emperor (Wu Tsung) died on the twenty-third day of the third moon.[1471]

TENTH MOON: 2nd [DAY] [1481]   [Shō]kai Shōnin [827] arrived from Yang-chou, and we met for the first time. [I received] a document from the Japanese Council of State,[383] [a document from] the Enryaku[ji],[1482] a letter from Ono, the Deputy Vice-Governor of Dazaifu,[1483] a letter from the Private Secretary . . .-kai,[1484] and some gold bestowed on me by the Emperor. Li Shen,[1191] the Regional Commander of Yang-chou and the Grand Overseer,[1484a] did not himself dare to open the Council of State document, the Enryakuji document, and [the letter from] the Deputy Vice-Governor [O]no, because they were sealed, but sent them sealed to Ch'ang-an. The present Emperor, after examining them thoroughly, ordered the Regional Commander of Huai-nan to return them to their owner. Therefore, [Shō]kai Shōnin was able to bring them to me. I have the Imperial edict here.

TWELFTH MOON: 2nd DAY [1485]   At 10 A. M. there was an eclipse of the sun. Only one-tenth [of its surface] remained.

[1480] The first day was July 27, 846.

[1481] The first day was October 24, 846.

[1482] See note 7. 寺牒 is missing here but occurs in the second listing of the documents in this passage.

[1483] Two *Shōni* 少貮 were the third-ranking officers of Dazaifu (see note 2). This man reappears on 847 XI 25, but it is not certain which member of the big Ono 小野 family he was.

[1484] 養 is presumably only the second half of a surname. There were six Private Secretaries (*Naiki* 内記) in the Ministry of Central Affairs (*Nakatsukasashō* 中務省), the first of the eight ministries under the Council of State.

[1484a] The final character in *P'ing-chang-shih* is omitted in *DBZ* and *KIK*. See note 92.

[1485] The first day was December 22, 846.

HUI-CH'ANG · SEVENTH YEAR

ting-mao

IN THE CYCLE OF YEARS [1486]

During the *FIRST MOON* [the year period] was changed to the first year of Ta-chung 大中.

The Commissioner Chang has been building a ship since the winter of last year,[1487] and it was completed in the *SECOND MOON* of this year. It is especially intended to take me and the others back to Japan.

INTERCALARY THIRD MOON [1488]   Chin Chien-chung 金簡中, the Vice-Ambassador to Korea to announce the mourning, [to conduct] the mourning ceremonies, and to en-feoff [the King of Korea],[1489] who is a provisional Audience Secretary of the Crown Prince's Household [1490] and has been granted a dark red "fish bag," [1394] and the Administrative Officer [38] [of the Embassy], Wang P'o 王朴, have been at Mt. Ju Inlet [501] in the southern part of Mou-p'ing-hsien [493] in this prefecture for ten days and have boarded a ship to cross the sea. Someone treacherously [said] that the Assimi-lated Colonel Chang, ignoring the national regulations,[1491] intends to dispatch men from a foreign land and has been

---

[1486] The year began on January 21, 847. *Ting-mao* 丁卯 is fourth in the cycle of sixty.

[1487] Meaning the last three moons of 846.

[1488] Following the regular third moon, it began on April 19, 847.

[1489] 告　哀兼弔祭册立等副使. Although this was more than a year after the death of Wu-tsung, it could have reference to no one else, because there was no change of reign during this period in Korea. Presumably the enthronement of a new Emperor in China required a new enfeoffment of the Korean King.

[1490] *T'ai-tzu T'ung-shih She-jen* 太子通事舍人. Cf. Des Rotours 596. "Provisional" here is *shih* 試.

[1491] *DBZ* suggests that 遣國章 is an error for 遣國事. The 諸 at the beginning of the sentence may be an error for one of the characters suggested in note 1492.

selfishly building a ship for them and has not come to greet the Imperial envoys. The Vice-Ambassador and the other, on hearing these [slanderous] words,[1492] were very indignant and notified him that the regulations of the whole land did not permit anyone to send travelers on ships across the sea. The Commissioner Chang did not dare specifically oppose them, and so our plan to return home across the sea from the Wen-teng region has come to nought.

We conferred about going to Ming-chou [185] to catch the ship of the Japanese Kamioi [1493] and the others in order to return home. Because at the time [1494] there was no ship going south, we hired the wagon of the Korean, Chŏng Kaek 鄭客 for seventeen lengths [766] of cloth, to transport our clothes and went along the coast towards the Mi-chou region.[436]

INTERCALARY THIRD MOON, 2nd DAY [1495] We started out. Our patron, the Commissioner Chang, accompanied us for twenty *li* before parting from us.

17*th* DAY In the morning we reached Chiao-ma Inlet 駮馬浦 at Mt. Ta-chu [435] in the Chu-ch'eng-hsien [436] region of Mi-chou, where we happened upon the ship of the Korean Chin Ch'ung 陳忠, loading charcoal and bound for Ch'u-chou. We bargained over the boat fare, which was settled at five bolts of silk.

FIFTH MOON: 5th DAY [1496] We boarded the ship and waited for a wind.

[1492] 讚, "praise," is certainly a copyist's error for 譖,譏 (which *KIK* prints without comment), or some similar word.

[1493] 神御井. The name is probably a corruption or abbreviation.

[1494] *DBZ* corrects 自下 to 目下.

[1495] *DBZ* and *KIK* correct this to "12th day." The distance to Mt. Ta-chu, however, is 250 km. air-line and much more by road through the mountains. Therefore, it could not have been covered with a wagon in six days. Two years before, it took Ennin twenty-one days to go the somewhat shorter distance from Mi-chou to Teng-chou. See 845 VII 26-VIII 16.

[1496] The first day was June 17, 847.

9th DAY   We started. Because the wind changed to southeast, we threw out the anchor stone not far from Mt. Ta-chu between Lang-yeh Terrace and Chai-t'ang Island [1497] and spent four nights there.

13th DAY   We started out at night.

14th DAY   At dusk we reached T'ien-wan Inlet 田灣 浦 at Mt. Tung-hai [423] in the Hai-chou region and tied up, awaiting the wind.

18th DAY   We started, but midway the wind shifted unsteadily, and we floated about all day and all night.

19th DAY   We floated to the neighborhood of Tang-chiao Island 鐺脚嶋 out in the sea, where we tied up. We were suffering.

23rd DAY   We had a northeast wind. That [1498] night just before the second watch (9 P. M.) we left for Mt. Tung-hai, where we passed the night.

24th DAY   Starting early, we reached the Huai River in the third watch (midnight) but stayed out on the sea, not being able to enter the Huai because of an opposing wind and high waves. Our provisions for the trip were exhausted, and we were distressed without limit.

SIXTH MOON: 1st DAY [1499]   The wind and waves had calmed somewhat, and we finally went in on the tide.

5th DAY   We reached Ch'u-chou. A special representative of Yu Sinŏn, the General Manager of the Korean ward,[1500] met us [1501] and had a member of their group 團頭

[1497] Lang-yeh Terrace 瑯邪臺 is a rocky promontory on the southeast coast of Shantung only fifteen km. southwest of Mt. Ta-chu. Chai-t'ang 齋堂 ("Maigre Feast Hall") Island lies just southeast of it. Cf. *Ch'ung-hsiu Chu-ch'eng-hsien chih* 重脩 諸城縣志 (1764) 1.1b, 7b, 14a. There is an extra 與 between "Chai-t'ang" and "Island," resulting in curious misinterpretations in *DBZ* and *KIK*.

[1498] *DBZ* corrects 北 to 此.

[1499] July 16, 847. The preceding moon had twenty-nine days.

[1500] See note 1426. On VI 10 we learn that Yu Sinŏn had suc-

transport our hampers of clothing and settle us in a government building. On inquiry we discovered that our compatriots at Ming-chou [185] had already departed, and in view
of the road ahead of us, we clearly would not arrive in time
for that ship. We therefore asked the Commissioner Yu to
be sent home from here.

9th DAY We received a letter from the Chinese
Chiang Ch'ang 江長 and the Koreans, Kim Chabaek 金子
白, Hŭm Yanghwi,[1502] and Kim Chin 金珍, on board a Su-
chou [332] vessel, saying:

On the eleventh day of the fifth moon we started for
Japan from the mouth of the Sung River [1503] of Su-chou. After
twenty-one days we reached Mt. Lao [1504] in the Lai-chou region.[482]
Several people talked with us, [saying that] Japanese monks and
laymen were then at Mt. Ch'ih [529] in Teng-chou, so we intended
to go there to get them. On the day of our departure, just when
we were about to go, we happened to meet a man who said that
these monks [1505] had already gone to the southern prefectures
to take a Japanese ship.[1506] At present we are at Mt. Lao waiting
for you. You should turn about and return here.

ceeded Sŏl Chŏn as General Manager, entitling him to be called
the " Commissioner," as he is later in this passage.
[1501] *DBZ* corrects 專便仰接 to 專使迎接.
[1502] 欽良暉, who is mentioned in the biography of Enchin (see
note 7), the *Tendai-shū Enryakuji zasu Enchin den* 天台宗延
曆寺座主圓珍傳 (*DBZ* 28.1366), as the " Chinese " trader on
whose ship Enchin went to China in 853.
[1503] 松江, the modern Wu-sung 吳淞 River, which now flows
from Su-chou to Shanghai.
[1504] 峄山 (slight variants for the first character are printed by
DBZ and *KIK*), now written 勞, the highest coastal mountain
in Shantung (1,150 meters), standing on a promontory about
thirty-five km. northeast of Tsingtao.
[1505] *DBZ* corrects 便 to 僧.
[1506] In 往南州趁本國州趁本國船, the four repeated characters
are clearly a copyist's error, but *DBZ* and *KIK* overlook this
fact, with curious results.

In the letter it also said that Shuntarō and Shin'ichirō [1507] and the others were returning to their homeland on board the ship of Chang Chih-hsin 支信 of Ming-chou,[185] and when [the messenger] was coming here, word was received that they had started. Shuntarō originally had intended to hire this ship [1508] to return home on, but after he had gone to Kuang-chou,[1509] Shin'ichirō gave money to Chang Chih-hsin, so Shuntarō left on the Ming-chou ship. Shuntarō's son Munetake 宗健 moreover had the . . .[1510] thing and was now on this ship.[1508]

Kim Chin and the others also instructed Yu Sinŏn, the General Manager of Ch'u-chou, saying, " If the Japanese monks and men arrive there, send them over here."

10th DAY Since a chance ship was going to Mt. Lao, we prepared letters and sent them to Kim Chin and the others, telling them our news and having them especially wait for us, after which, intending to go to Mt. Lao and to cross the sea from there, we arranged our provisions for the trip. Yu, the General Manager of Ch'u-chou, attended to everything. The former General Manager, Sŏl Chŏn,[1426] Chang Chongŏn 張從彥 , the younger brother of the Commissioner Chang of Teng-chou,[531] and his daughter all saw us off.

18th DAY In the evening we boarded the ship of Wang Kach'ang 王可昌 of the Korean ward of Ch'u-chou and [started] at the end of the third watch (1 A. M.).

19th DAY It was the beginning of autumn. For the first time I ate the ship's fare.[1511]

[1507] 春太郎 and 神一郎, which are either abbreviated names or given names without surnames. These men may have been the Japanese laymen who had accompanied Shōkai to China. See 846 III 9. The second time Shin'ichirō's name appears, the middle character is written 大, but this is overlooked in *DBZ*.

[1508] Meaning the ship belonging to the writers of this letter.

[1509] Kuang-chou 廣, the Chinese name for Canton.

[1510] The copyist has left three dots, presumably for characters he was unable to decipher.

[1511] Probably Ennin meant that he was forced to abandon temporarily the Buddhist prohibitions on eating.

26th DAY We reached Chieh-chia-chuang [1512] south of Mt. Lao and looked for Kim Chin's ship, but it had already gone to Mt. Ch'ih Inlet in Teng-chou. We saw a letter they had left behind, saying that they would especially wait for us at Mt. Ch'ih. Since this was the situation, we had to go on to Mt. Ju [501] to catch the ship.

27th DAY I wrote a letter to the General Manager Yu of Ch'u-chou and sent it by the ship of the Ch'oe 崔 family and again hired the ship of the shipmaster Wang Kach'ang and headed for Mt. Ju.

28th DAY We started, but when we reached T'ien-heng Island,[1513] there was no reliable wind, and we spent fifteen days unable to start.

SEVENTH MOON: 13*th* DAY [1514] I sent Tei Yūman and also hired a man to go to Mt. Ch'ih by land and to look for the ship of Kim Chin and the others on the way.

19th DAY We had a reliable wind and started out.

20th DAY We reached the Ch'ang-huai Inlet 長淮浦 of Mt. Ju and found the ship of Kim Chin and the others. Then, loading our goods and boarding the ship, we started off.

21st DAY We reached the Teng-chou region and tied up. Chang Yŏng,[531] the Commissioner in Charge of Korean Affairs and an Assimilated Colonel, came on board and we saw each other. Those on shipboard . . . their food supplies,[1515] intending to cross the sea from here.

[1512] 桝家庄. The first character is doubtful, being printed as 枡 in *KIK* and *ZZGR*. The last character is printed 店 by *DBZ* and *KIK*, but in *Tōji* it is clearly 庄 (as usually written in that text), which is a common final component of village names in this area.

[1513] 田横嶋 (the first character is miswritten 由), one of a cluster of small islands about forty km. northwest of Mt. Lao. Cf. *Chi-mo-hsien chih* (1873) maps 3b, 9b.

[1514] The first day was August 15, 847.

[1515] The first character in 籴粮 may be a copyist's amalgamation of two characters or an error for a verb.

EIGHTH MOON: 9th DAY [1516]   We received parting letters and presents from the Commissioner Chang. The list is
separately [recorded].

15th DAY   We shaved our heads and again donned
our black robes.

24th DAY   We worshiped the spirits.

NINTH MOON: 2nd DAY [1517]   At noon we started across
the sea from [Mt.] Ch'ih Inlet.[523] We went out the Mo-yeh [542]
mouth of the Mt. Ch'ih [Inlet] and headed due east all day
and all night.

At dawn on the 3rd DAY, we saw at a distance to the
east the mountains of the western part of Korea. The wind
shifted to due north, and trimming sail, we headed southeast all day and all night.

At dawn on the 4th DAY, we saw mountainous islands
to the east stretching out in an unbroken line. When I asked
the helmsmen, they said that this was the western part of
Western Ungju [1518] in Korea and originally was Paekche
territory. All day we went southeast. Mountainous islands
were strung out to the east and to the west. Just before the
second watch (9 P. M.) we reached Koi Island,[1519] and tied
up. It belongs to the southwestern part of Muju.[1520] About

[1516] The first day was September 14, 847.

[1517] The first day was October 13, 847.

[1518] 熊州, the area around Ungjin 熊津, the modern Kongju
公州, in the central part of Ch'ungch'ŏng-namdo 忠清南道
about 125 km. south of Seoul. It had been the capital of Paekche
(see note 736).

[1519] 高移, probably a variant writing of Koi 皋夷, which Shiratori Kurakichi 白鳥庫吉 and Tsuda Sōkichi 津田左右吉
(*Chōsen rekishi chiri* 朝鮮歷史地理 1.344, 346, and map 6)
suggest may be the modern Haŭi 河衣 (or 荷衣) Island, which
is located in an archipelago almost forty km. southwest of
Mokp'o 木浦, an important port near the southwestern tip of
the Korean mainland.

[1520] 武州, standing for Mujin 武珍, the modern Kwangju 光
州, which is the capital of Chŏlla-namdo 全羅南道 in the
southwestern corner of Korea.

a hundred *li* northwest of the island is Mt. Hŭk.[1521] The mountain is visible from east or west for quite a distance. It is where the third son of a Paekche King fled to take refuge. Now there are three or four hundred families living on the mountain.

5th DAY The wind changed to southeast, and we could not start out. In the third watch (midnight) we got a northwest wind, and started.

6th DAY At 6 A. M. we reached a muddy inlet 泥浦 on Hwangmo Island 黃茅嶋 in the southern part of Muju and tied up. It is also called Kuch'o Island.[1522] There were four or five men on a mountain, so we sent a man to get them, but they ran and hid, and we could not find them. This is the place where the third Minister of State of Silla [13] pastured horses. From Koi Island to this [Ku]ch'o Island mountainous islands follow one after the other. Far to the southeast we saw Quelpart Island.[1523] This Kuch'o Island can be reached from the mainland of Korea with a good wind in one day.

Presently an island guard and two falconers 投鷹 of the household of the Governor 太守 of Muju came on board and told us that the nation is at peace. At present an Im-

---

[1521] 黑山, the modern Great Mt. Hŭk Island (Taehŭksando 大黑山島), about fifty km. west and a trifle north of Haŭi Island and ninety km. west of Mokp'o. It and its surrounding islets are known as the Mackau Group.

[1522] 丘草, apparently the modern Kŏcha 巨次 Islands (also known as the Gocha or Sylvia Group), about forty km. south of Haŭi and seventy-five km. southwest of Mokp'o. This may be the Kuch'o 葛草 Island mentioned by Shiratori and Tsuda, *op. cit.* 1.346 and map 6, and identified by them on grounds of phonetic similarity with Chija 只佐 (or 箕佐) Island northeast of Haŭi.

[1523] T'amna 耽羅 Island, the modern Cheju 濟州 Island, known in the West as Quelpart Island. Since the central mountain mass on Quelpart rises to about 6,400 feet, it could easily have been visible from the Kŏcha Islands at this time of year, even though it is about 115 km. from Kŏcha to the summit of the mountain on Quelpart.

perial Chinese Embassy of over five hundred men in all is
at the capital. During the fourth moon six commoners from
Tsushima[1524] in Japan floated here while fishing, and the
Muju [officials] took them away and had already reported
the matter to the throne, but as yet no Imperial edict had
been issued. The men were now in confinement[1525] in Muju,
waiting to be sent to their homeland, and one of the six had
sickened and died.

6th and 7th DAYS   There was no reliable wind.

8th [DAY][1525a]   We heard bad news[1526] and were extremely frightened, but since there was no wind, we could
not start. The group on board cast away mirrors and the
like in sacrifice to the spirits to obtain a wind. We monks
burned incense and recited prayers on behalf of the spirits
of the soil of this island and the spirits of the great and the
lowly, praying that we might safely reach our homeland.
Then at this place we read[203] the *Diamond Sutra*[252] in one
hundred scrolls on behalf of the spirits of this soil and the
spirits of the great and the lowly. In the fifth watch (4
A. M.), we started out even though there was no wind.
Scarcely had we gotten out of the mouth of the inlet when
a west wind suddenly blew up, so we hoisted sail and headed
east. It seemed as though the spirits were aiding us.

We went among the mountainous islands, with row upon
row of mountainous islands scattered about both north and
south of us.

[*9th*] DAY[1527]   At 9 A. M. we reached An Island[1528]

[1524] 對馬, the large island between Kyūshū and Korea.

[1525] *DBZ* corrects 因禁 to 囚禁.

[1525a] *DBZ* and *KIK* incorrectly print the character for " day."

[1526] Possibly information regarding the presence of pirates or
some other hostile force.

[1527] One or more characters seem to have been lost from the text
where 參然日 occurs. *DBZ* and *KIK* suggest the addition of
差 after the first character, but a more important omission is
probably that of " 9th " before " day." As the text stands, it
would appear that Ennin made no entry for the " 9th day,"
which is most improbable under the circumstances. Moreover, a

and rested for a short while. This is a mountain where the families of the southern part of Korea pasture horses. Close to the east is an estate of the Hwangnyongsa 黄龍寺, and here and there are two or three homes. We saw Quelpart Island far to the southwest. After noon (1 p. m.) the wind improved, and we started. We went between the mountainous islands and at a point southeast of the land of Korea went out into the open sea and headed southeast

10*th* DAY   At dawn, far to the east we saw the Island of Tsushima.[1528] At noon we saw ahead of us the mountains of Japan stretching out clearly from the east to the southwest. At nightfall we reached Shika Island in the northern part of Matsura District in the Province of Hizen [1529] and tied up.

---

five-hour run appears to have taken them to a point from which Quelpart Island was to be seen to the southwest. Such a point must have been close to a hundred km. east of the Kŏcha Islands, which would have been much too far for a five-hour run in a ship such as they had. It would, therefore, be more reasonable to assume that a whole day and night elapsed between their 4 a. m. departure and 9 a. m. arrival. As we see below (see note 1528), the actual run may have been closer to 180 km., which would have been possible in twenty-nine hours but scarcely in five.

[1528] 鴈, possibly the present An 安 Island, thirty km. south of Yŏsu 麗水 (a port and railhead near the middle of the south coast of Korea) and about 180 km. east of the Kŏcha Islands. An argument against this identification is that Ennin records seeing Quelpart Island to the southwest, and its peak is 170 km. southeast of An Island, which is not far short of the maximum distance of visibility under optimum conditions. On the other hand a run of about seventeen hours southeast from An Island brought them to a point from which low-lying Tsushima (with a maximum height of only 1,863 feet near its southern extremity) could be seen to the east and another twelve hours brought them to the coast of Japan, and both the course described and the time required for this run suggest that they started from a point about as far west as the modern An Island.

[1529] Hizen 肥前 constituted the northwestern corner of Kyūshū and adjacent islands, and Matsura District 松浦郡 was the

11*th* DAY At dawn Yamato no Musashi 大和武
蔵, a retainer of Ta[jihi] [1530] the Administrative Officer [82]
of the Province of Chikuzen, [666] together with the headman
of the island came, and we met and learned in general
about events in the country.

15*th* DAY We reached Tachibananoura. [1531]

17*th* DAY We arrived below Nokonoshima [1532] southwest of Hakata [2] and tied up.

---

extreme northwestern part of Hizen, including the northwestern
tip of Kyūshū itself, Hirado 平戸 Island just off the tip, and
the Gotō Archipelago some distance to the west (see note 3).
Shika 鹿 Island, however, has not been positively identified.
The *Nihon kōki* 12 records that a ship of a Japanese embassy to
China arrived there on 805 VI 17, and the editors of the Asahi
Shibun 朝日新聞 edition (p. 66) suggest that this may be an
error for Chika 血鹿, an old name for the Gotō Archipelago,
or a variant of Shikotsushima 色都島, an old name for the
southernmost of the larger Gotō Islands (see also Yoshida Tōgo
吉田東伍, *Dai Nihon chimei jisho* 大日本地名辭書 2.1612a).
This text rules out the first possibility, and the second is made
improbable by the course the ship was taking, which should have
brought them to the vicinity of Hirado or at the furthest west,
to the islands at the northern end of the Gotō Archipelago.
Furthermore, the Gotō Islands can hardly be considered to be
in the northern part of Matsura District. In fact, Matsura was
subdivided into Eastern, Western, Northern, and Southern Dis-
tricts, and the Gotō Archipelago formed Southern Matsura
District, while Hirado and its adjacent islands and the northwestern tip of Kyūshū constituted Northern Matsura District.
[1530] Since 丹 is not a complete Japanese name, it must be an
abbreviation for a surname such as Tajihi (see note 124), which
was rather common at this time.
[1531] The *Shoku Nihongi* 續日本紀 35 records that on 778 X 23
a ship of a Japanese embassy to China arrived at Tachibananoura 橘浦 in Matsura District. Yoshida, *loc. cit.*, believes
Tachibananoura to be in the Gotō Archipelago, but it was
obviously east of Shika Island on the way to Hakata (see
note 2).
[1532] 能舉島, now written 殘島, in the western part of Hakata
Bay.

18*th* DAY   We arrived in front of the *Kōrokan*.[1533]

19*th* DAY   We entered it and resided there.

TENTH MOON: 6*th* DAY [1534]   We borrowed eighty bolts of silk and two hundred packages [184] of silk floss from the official storehouse for winter clothing for the forty-four men on board the ship. On the sixth day ten bushels [217] of rice were sent us for our living provisions. The provincial government from the first day of the tenth moon on began to furnish [our needs].

19*th* DAY   A notice from the Council of State [383] arrived at Dazaifu [2] for Ennin and the others, five [in all],[1535] to hasten to the capital and the Chinese, Kim Chin [1536] and the others, forty-four men [in all] to be given their payment by Dazaifu. This notice is separately [recorded].

26*th* DAY   We have not received the documents for going to the capital, but we left the [Dazai]fu offices.

[1533] 鴻臚館, an official institution for the reception of foreign embassies. There were three *Kōrokan*: one in Kyōto, another in what is now the city of Ōsaka at the head of the Inland Sea, and the third under the jurisdiction of Dazaifu (see note 2). See note 318 for the corresponding institution in China, for which the *Kōrokan* were named.

[1534] The first day was November 12, 847.

[1535] The five presumably included Ennin, Ishō, Shōkai (see note 1472), and Shuntarō's son, Munetake, who on VI 9 was reported to be on this ship. It is not certain whether Tei Yūman was the fifth man. We are not told that he rejoined the vessel after being put ashore on VII 13, although there was plenty of time for him to have done so, and he may have been left in China. We know that he was either still in China or else back in China some six years later. See note 94.

[1536] This transformation upon arrival in Japan of a Korean resident of China into a regular Chinese suggests that many of the so-called Chinese traders and mariners who appear in the Japanese records were actually Koreans. *SNK* 17, in noting Ennin's return to Japan under the date of 847 X 2, states that he came back with two disciples and forty-two Chinese. See also note 1502.

ELEVENTH MOON: 7th DAY [1537]   The Superior of Mt.
[Hi]ei,[7] Chūgyō 仲曉 [Hos]shi, and the monks, Jiei 慈叡 **and**
Genkō 玄皎, arrived and said that they had come especially
to greet us.

14*th* DAY   We received a notice of the thirteenth day
of the tenth moon from the Council of State about providing
generously for the Chinese travelers, Kim Chin and the
others.

25*th* DAY   Since Ono,[1537a] the Deputy Vice-Governor,[1483] was going to the capital, I sent word by him.[1538] I
had a letter for the Grand Counselor [1539] and others respectfully addressed to Tomo, the Vice-Controller of the Right,[1540]
and to Ono, the Consultant Counselor,[1541] and gave them all
to Ono, the Deputy Vice-Governor.

28*th* DAY   In regard to the five thousand scrolls of

[1537] The first day was December 12, 847.

[1537a] 貳 is a copyist's error for 野, which the printed texts give
without comment.

[1538] The erroneous repetition of 便上 in *Tōji* is overlooked by
both *DBZ* and *KIK*.

[1539] *Dainagon* 大納言, the highest of the three categories of
Counselors of the Council of State (see notes 383 and 385).
This may have been Fujiwara no Yoshifusa 良房, who was a
Grand Counselor at this time (cf. *SNK* 845 II 5 and 848 I 10)
and who in 857 became the Prime Minister (*Dajōdaijin* 太政
大臣) and in 866 the first Regent (*Sesshō* 攝政) of non-
Imperial lineage.

[1540] *Uchūben* 右中辨 (see note 383), probably a copyist's error
for Vice-Controller of the Left (*Sachūben*), for *SNK* 847 V 27
records that a Fujiwara was the Vice-Controller of the Right,
while Tomo no Narimasu 伴成益 was the Vice-Controller of
the Left. He had been appointed Officer in Charge of Costumes
(*Shōzokushi* 裝束司) for the embassy to China when it was
first organized (cf. *SNK* 834 II 2).

[1541] *Saishō* (see note 392). This was Ono no Takamura, originally
the Vice-Ambassador of the embassy (see note 143). According
to *SNK* he was recalled from exile on 840 II 14, and on 847 I 12
was appointed a Consultant Counselor, a post he held until 848
I 13.

the *Diamond* [*Sutra*] [292] and the *Hannya-*[*kyō*],[203] about which I had prayed while at the Daisanji [1542] when I was first going to China, I had already sent a messenger there to present figured silks, and on this day in the early morning I both sent a messenger with figured silks and then read through [203] the scriptures. This same day I read through one thousand scrolls [of scriptures] on behalf of the Great God of Kamado.[1543]

29*th* DAY   Before noon I read through five hundred scrolls [of scriptures] on behalf of the Great God of Sumiyoshi.[416] After noon I read through five hundred scrolls [of scriptures] on behalf of the Famous God of Kashii.[1544]

TWELFTH MOON: 1*st* DAY [1545]   Before noon I read through five hundred scrolls [of scriptures] on behalf of the Famous God of Chikuzen.[1546] After noon I read through five hundred scrolls [of scriptures] on behalf of the spirit of the Matsura Deputy Vice-Governor.[1547]

[1542] 大山寺, presumably a local monastery where he had stayed on his way to China.

[1543] 竈門, referring to the Kamado Shrine located on Mt. Kamado (also known as Hōmanzan 寶滿山) a short distance northeast of Dazaifu. Saichō (see note 333) worshiped here on 803 Intercalary X 23 in order to insure the safe arrival of the four ships of the embassy he was accompanying to China. Cf. *Eizan Daishi den* 叡山大師傳 in *Zoku* 續 *gunsho ruijū* 8.464b. Ennin probably paid monks to do most of this pious chore of scripture reading for him. On XII 3 he specifically mentions what he paid for this task.

[1544] 香椎名神, referring to the Kashii Shrine, located on the east shore of Hakata Bay northeast of Hakata.

[1545] January 10, 848, making the last day recorded in the diary January 23, 848.

[1546] Probably the chief deity of one of the leading shrines of the province. This may have been the Emperor Ōjin 應神, the main deity of the Hakozaki 筥崎 Shrine near Hakata, which was considered to be the first shrine of the province.

[1547] In the Kagami Shrine 鏡宮 (also called the Shrine of the Illustrious Deity of Matsura 松浦名神宮), at Kagami in Mat-

2nd DAY I read through one thousand scrolls [of scriptures] on behalf of the Famous God of Kawaru.[1548]

3rd DAY I read through one thousand scrolls [of scriptures] on behalf of the Bodhisattva Hachiman.[526] The Kannon lecturers [1549] helped me in everything. My gifts to the monks who read the scriptures were two hundred packages [184] of white floss silk.

14th DAY [1545] After noon Master Nanjū 南忠 came.

[END OF] FOURTH SCROLL OF THE RECORD OF A PILGRIMAGE TO CHINA IN SEARCH OF THE LAW

---

sura District near the coast about forty km. southwest of Hakata, is enshrined the spirit of Fujiwara no Hirotsugu 廣嗣, a Deputy Vice-Governor of Dazaifu (see note 1483), who revolted in 740 and was killed in Matsura District, but who came to be worshiped as a deity because certain catastrophies were attributed to his revengeful spirit.

[1548] 香春名神, referring to the Kawaru Shrine located in the town pronounced Kawara though written with the same characters, about thirty-five km. northeast of Dazaifu. According to *SNK* 837 XII 11, Dazaifu reported that Saichō had prayed to the God of Kawaru Peak for a safe crossing to China (see note 1543) and had built a temple at the base of the mountain, with the result that this hitherto treeless mountain had become heavily wooded and the seat of a flourishing popular cult.

[1549] *Kannon kōshi* 講師 (see note 6), which *DBZ* interprets as "lecturers from the Kannonji," better known as the Kanzeonji, Kyūshū's most famous ancient monastery, located near the original site of Dazaifu.

ON A CERTAIN DAY IN THE TENTH MOON OF THE SECOND YEAR OF MEITOKU 明德 (1391), I RECEIVED ALL FOUR BOOKLETS THROUGH DIVINE GRACE. HOW JOYFUL! HOW JOYFUL!

Gembō 賢寶*, the Provisional Grand Vicar General* [1550] *of Hōin [Rank]* [1551]   *aged fifty-nine.*

[1550] *Gon-dai* 大 *-sōzu* (see notes 124 and 258). There were three ranks of Vicar Generals, of which this was the highest.

[1551] An abbreviation for *Hōin-daikashō-i* 法印大和尙位 , the highest of the honorary ranks of the Japanese Buddhist church. See note 133.

I have finished copying this, while rubbing my old eyes, on the twenty-sixth day of the tenth moon of the fourth year of Shōō 正應 *(1291) in a room in the Chōrakuji,*[1552] *copying it in accordance with the original. Later persons can collate it with corroboratory texts.*

Written by Henjō-kongō[1553] *Ken'in*[862] *of Hōin-daikashō Rank*[1551] [aged] seventy-two.

I have collated it with the manuscript,[1554] annotating only that which was doubtful. Text of Kan'en,[1555] the Bishop[316] of Second [Court] Rank.

[1552] 長樂寺, a monastery originally of the Tendai Sect, located in Maruyama 圓山 Park in Kyōto.

[1553] This was Ken'in's *kongō-myōgō* 金剛名號, a name conferred upon an initiate in Esoteric Buddhism. Henjō-kongō 遍照金剛, which was also Kōbō Daishi's *kongō-myōgō* (see note 357), was the secret name of the Buddha Dainichi-nyorai 大日如來 (Skr. Mahā-vairocana; see note 237).

[1554] Two almost illegible characters are printed 寫畢 in *DBZ* and *KIK*, but 寫本 in *ZZGR* and on page 5 of Okada's Introduction to the photographic edition of *Tōji*, in conformity with the colophons of scrolls two and three.

[1555] Two almost illegible characters are interpreted as 寬圓 in *KIK* and on page 6 of Okada's Introduction to the photographic edition of *Tōji*, but Okada (11.462) prints them as Jitsuen 實圓, *DBZ* renders them as Ken'en 憲圓, and *ZZGR* as Jitsuden 實田 (the printing itself in this last case is not clear).

CHARACTER GLOSSARY

For references, names, and terms used in the companion volume, *Ennin's Travels in T'ang China*, and not occurring in the translation or notes of this volume.

Abe no Nakamaro 阿倍仲麻呂

An'e 安惠

An Lu-shan 安祿山

Aso 阿蘇

Ason 朝臣

Awada no Mabito 粟田眞人

Kairyūō-gyō 海龍王經

Buzen 豐前

Chai 齋

Ch'an 禪

Ch'ang-li Hsien-sheng chi 昌黎先生集

Chia Chung-yao 賈鍾堯

Ch'ing 頃

Chŏng Yŏn 鄭年

Chōsen shi 朝鮮史

Daihannya-kyō 大般若經

Daijin 大臣

Daini 大貳

Erei 惠靈

Fujiwara no Kadonomaro 藤原葛野麻呂

Fujiwara no Kiyokawa.... 清河

Gagaku-tōshō-shi 雅樂答笙師

Gembō 玄昉

Gon no Hakase 權博士

Hai-k'ou-so-yu 海口所由

Han Yü 韓愈

Hōryūji 法隆寺

Hou Han shu 後漢書

Hsi-yü-chi 西域記

Hui-ch'ao 慧超

I dynasty 李朝

I-ching 醫經

Iki 壹伎

Ishi 醫師

Jikaku Daishi den 慈覺大師傳

Jimon 寺門

Jingō 神功

Jōjin 成尋

Jun-hangan 准判官

Kabane 姓

Kako no Chō 水手長

Kami 守

Kammu 桓武

Kamo 賀茂

Kampyō Nyūdō Shinnō 寬平入道親王

Kao Hsien-chih 高仙芝

Kibi no Makibi 吉備眞備

Kimiya Yasuhiko 木宮泰彦

Ki no Mitsu 紀三津

Kōchi 廣智

Kōgōgūshiki 皇后宮職

Koryŏ 高麗

Kōya 高野

Koyomi-ryūgaku-shō 曆留學生

Koyomi-shōyaku 曆請益

Lai-jih 來日

Li Po 李白

Liu Erh-lang 劉二郎

Li Wen-jao wen chi 李文饒文集

Matsukawa no Miyatsuko Sa-datsugu 松川造貞嗣

Mibu 壬生

Miidera 三井寺

Mimbu no kami 部民卿

Minamoto no Hideaki 源英明

Minamoto no Moriaki.... 庶明

Minamoto no Noboru.... 昇

Minamoto no Tōru.... 融

Ming, Emperor 明帝

Ming-jih 明日

Montoku 文德

Montoku jitsuroku.... 實錄

Munekata 宗像

Mutsu 陸奧

Naniwa 難波

Nara 奈良

Nariyo 齊世

Nihon kōsō den yōmon shō 日木高僧傳要文抄

Nihon shoki 日本書紀

Nisshi kōtsū shi 日支交通史

Nu 奴

Onjō-chō 音聲長

Onjōji 園城寺

Ono no Imoko 小野妹子

Ono no Michikaze (Tōfū).... 道風

Onyōshi 陰陽師

Ōtani Kōshō 大谷光照

Po Chü-i 白居易

Rikkokushi 六國史

Sagami 相摸

Sayomi no nuno 贄布

Seiwa 清和

Senshi 船師

Shih-huo 食貨

Shih-tsung 世宗

Shimotsuke 下野

Shintei zōho kokushi taikei 新訂增補國史大系

Shinzai 眞濟

Shiseki shūran 史籍集覽

Shishō 史生

Shitennōji 四天王寺

Shōshi 笙師

Sochi 帥

Soga 蘇我

Sugawara no Kajinari 菅原梶成

Sugawara no Michizane.... 道眞

Suiko 推古

Sui shu 隋書

Sujin 崇神

Sung shih 宋史

Taiheira 太平良

Tajihi no Fumio 丹墀文雄

Tajima 但馬

Takamine no Sukune 高岑宿禰

Takaoka 高丘

Takeuchi no Sukune 武內宿禰

T'ang Hui-ch'ang cheng-chiao ch'ung-t'u shih-liao 唐會昌政教衝突史料

Teiō hennenki 帝王編年記

Temmon-ryūgaku-shō 天文留學生

Tenchi 天智

Tendai kahyō 天台霞標

Tien 店

Tōdaiji 東大寺

Tōdai no Bukkyō girei 唐代の佛教儀禮

Tōyō bunko sōkan 東洋文庫 叢刊

Tsuga 都賀

Uda 宇多

Udaiben 右大辨

Ujing 祐徵

Wa 倭

Washio Junkei 鷲尾順敬

Yamizo-kogane-no-kami 八溝 黃金神

Yokawa 橫川

Yŏm Chang 閻長 (also 閻丈)

Zasshi 雜使

Zōhakushi 造舶使

Index

Abbot: 3n, 21, 40, 57, 79, 87, 91n-3, 137, 165n, 188, 222-4, 229-31, 234-6, 249, 251, 275, 315-6, 366; of the *Vinaya*: 58

Abstinence: 123n, 232

Abstract of the Imperially Commissioned Complete Mirror to the Letter I: 331

Ācārya: 78n

Accomplished Literati: 348

Account book: 66, 296

Accredited Monks: 362

Acolyte: 366

Acorns: 177, 196

Acting Administrative Officer: 22, 110n

Acting Controller of the Left: 88

Acting Guard Officer: 327

Acting President of the Bureau of Imperial Sacrifices: 89

Acting Secretary: 11, 32n, 110n

Acting Ship Captain: 17, 30

Adachi Kiroku: *Chōan Shiseki no Kenkyū*. XIX, 35n, 83n, 147n, 282n-3n, 286n, 297n, 300n, 302n-3n, 326n, 333n, 342n

Adhicitta: 59n

Adhiprajñā: 59n

Adhiśīla: 59n

Administrative Officer: 10-12, 15, 18, 21-2, 28, 30-2, 36, 39, 42-3, 45, 52, 60, 64, 75, 80, 82-4, 86, 93-5, 101, 109-10, 112-3, 119-21, 123, 134-5, 167, 178, 180-2, 187, 194, 199-200, 287, 317, 369-70, 394, 404

Adoration: 229, 236, 301, 303, 312, 344

Affinities: 251, 270, 303, 308n, 368, 384; *see also* Karma

Ajari: 78n

Ajñāta-kauṇḍinya: 198

Alchemy: 321

All Souls' Festival: 35n, 368-9, 344

Alms: 92, 224, 230, 301, 304; bowl: 140, 171, 179, 186, 241, 249, 260, 324; cash: 56

Altar of Heaven: 297n-8, 352n-354

Ambassador: 2, 5, 7, 9-10, 12-9, 21-4, 26, 29, 36, 39, 41-3, 64, 67, 75, 82-4, 86-8n, 90n, 93, 95, 99, 101-3, 316; Plenipotentiary: 88

Ambassador's attendant: 60, 96

Amida: 64, 183n, 216n, 221, 273, 300

Amida jodo nembutsu kyō: 300n

Amitābha: 64n

Amnesty: 47, 391-2n

Amoghavajra: 87n, 253-5, 294

An Island: 402-3n

Ancestral Hall: 210

Anchor: 6, 10, 97-8, 103, 116, 118, 120, 125, 127-9, 131, 133; stone: 133, 396

Angel: 241

Ango: 53n

An-hsiang-ts'un: 176

A-niang: 348n

Animal pictures: 67

An-lo-kuan: 85

Anniversary: 23, 53, 61, 172n, 178; national: 310

An-sheng: 232n

Anyakyōjinnyo: 198n

An-yüan-ts'un: 281

Apparitions: 264

Arannya: 137n

Āranya: 137n

Arbor Vitae: 356

Archbishop: 75; of the Streets of the Left: 298, 300

Archer: 7-9, 14-6, 18, 32, 64, 77, 81-2, 84, 116-7, 125, 135

Arhat: 198n

Armies: 316, 321, 337-8; of Inspired Strategy: 332n, 361n; – –, left: 345n, 352, 357, 359-60, 364; – –, right: 345n, 352, 360

Army Inspector, 313-4, 323, 325, 329, 332, 350; Commissioner: 311

Arrest: 49, 81-2n, 84, 105, 338, 386

Arrow: 266

Artificial flowers: 344; lotus: 62

Artisan: 64, 347

Artist: 26

Ārūpyadhātu: 219n

Aśoka, King: 236, 254

Assessment of funds: 346

Assimilated Colonel: 88, 269, 374, 383, 392, 394, 399
Assistant Judge: 181-2
Assistant Regional Commander: 194, 196, 199, 371
Assistant Subprefect: 109
Attendant: 14, 19, 26n, 44, 52, 75, 82, 84, 87, 91, 95-6n, 115, 184, 284, 286, 307, 309, 313-4, 320, 333, 368; monk: 105, 132, 140, 148, 316; Priest: 298
Audience: 81, 86, 193-4, 197, 199, 207, 326, 346; hall: 178; Secretary of the Crown Prince's Household: 394
Augury: 47
Autumnal equinox: 160
Autumn begins: 159-60n
Auxiliary official: 89, 194, 196-7, 199
Auxiliary Secretary: 148
Avalokiteśvara: 2n
Awada: 110, 112, 121, 132, 135; no Ietsugu: 60, 67, 84, 96, 135
Axe: 129
A-yeh: 350n
Azuki: 114n

Back-scratcher: 99n
Bag for the fish tally of gold: 365, 370
Baggage: 14, 29-31, 89, 93, 103-4, 106-7, 112, 138, 140, 251, 270, 366, 376
Balcony: 49, 52-3, 217, 225, 228, 231, 235, 248, 250, 253-4, 269; Golden: 252; of the Auspicious (Sandalwood) Images: 49, 68-9, 77; Cloister: 218, 269; of His Holiness Monju: 303; for storing scriptures: 254
Baldachin: 233-4, 253, 390
Ball field: 194-5, 287
Bamboo: 3, 17, 20, 65, 71n, 156, 214; box: 102; Grove, Monastery of the: 216n; poles: 311
Bandits: 163; Catcher of: 109
Banner: 62, 73, 202, 207, 221, 233-4, 266, 311, 345, 390
Banquet: 41, 195
Ban Shiman: 27, 87
Banzai: 65
Baptism: 294, 302, 308; Ritual: 303; to Establish Affinities: 303
Baptistry: 294, 302n-3, 308
Barbarians: 186, 190, 194, 326; Western: 332, 351
Barbarian writings: 332
Baron Founder of the Realm: 331
Barrier Officer: 276
Barriers: 171, 180, 187, 278, 390

Base Officer: 186n, 194, 338; Guard Officer: 186n, 340
Base Officer: 185-6n, 197
Bath House Cloister: 264
Bathing: 63, 123, 310
Bays, five: 232; four: 237, 240; nine: 253; seven: 356; six: 241; three: 234, 245, 256
Bazara: 367n
Beans: 17; red: 193n; small; 193, 200, 205, 213
Bed: 208
Beggars: 258
Begging: 147-8, 196; bowl: 106
Beginning of autumn: 159-60n
Beginning of spring: 70, 297
Beginning of summer: 197
Beginning of winter: 149
Beginnings, Moons of the Three: 340; lower: 341; middle: 341; upper: 340
Bell: 66, 106, 152, 154-5, 218, 248, 250, 343, 353-4, 373, 385; bronze: 140; golden: 243; Grotto of the Holy: 265; -shaped pagodas: 237; Tower Valley: 243; Valley of the Holy: 265
Bench: 54-5, 66, 259, 341, 353
Benediction: 156, 160
Beriberi: 105
Besson-hō: 315
Bhaiṣajyaguru: 92n
Big Wild Goose Pagoda: 303n
Bingo: 32n
Binzuru: 227
Bird: 71n, 73n, 89n, 257, 297; black: 130; pictures: 67
Birthday: 199, 250, 303n, 308, 320, 342; Emperor's 250, 320, 330, 342; maigre feast: 250, 320, 330, 342
Birushana-kyō: 308
Biscuits: 301
Bishamon: 288, 302n-3
Bishop: 74-6, 410
Bitchū: 32n
Bizen: 32n
Black arts: 321
Black clothing: 384
Black-robed Emperors: 342
Black robes: 343, 384, 400
Black sea: 68
Blanket: 90, 365
Blessing: 153, 156
Boatswain: 30
Bodai: 239n
Bodhi: 239n
Bodhisattva: 2, 10n, 26, 60-1, 64, 67n,

92, 130n, 137n, 156, 160, 165-6, 202,
215, 219-21, 230, 232-4, 241, 244-5,
248, 251-6, 258, 264, 273, 333, 408;
Hall: 234-5, 249; Hall, Cloister of
the: 231; of Wisdom; 73n
Bōen: 68n
Bolt of silk: 44, 51, 53, 80, 89, 304-5,
343-4, 355, 367, 369-70, 376, 395, 405
Bones of the Buddha: 166, 235, 262n,
340
Bonkō: 235n
Bonnō: 219, 302n
Bosatsu: 2n
Bosatsu-kai: 160n
Bottle: 367; lapis lazuli: 235
Bow: 6-7, 105, 125, 353
Bowl: 141, 206, 235, 379, 390; see also
Alms bowl
Box: 321; sandalwood: 364, 367
Boys' Festival: 41n
Branches (cyclical): 157
Breakfast: 31n
Bribery: 364, 373-4
Brick: 189, 207; -kiln grounds: 335;
tea: 365, 367
Bridge: 21, 23, 42n, 62, 85, 136, 208,
242, 278-80, 282, 354; of the Ch'in
Emperor: 136n
Bronze: 344, 381; bell: 106, 140; Bud-
dha: 373, 382, 388; -caster: 232n;
gilt: 255; jug: 140; vases: 390
Brush: 12, 15, 22, 24, 29, 35, 44-5,
49-51, 79
Buddha: 6, 49, 54-5, 60, 62-4, 66-7n,
71, 73, 92, 115, 123-4, 137n, 147,
149-50, 152-7, 161, 165-6, 169, 179-
80, 186, 192, 198, 204, 217-22, 224,
228, 230, 235, 237, 244n, 246-8, 252-
5, 263-4, 269, 271, 273, 275, 289,
300-3, 312-3, 332-3, 340, 344, 351,
368, 382, 388, 410n; bronze: 373,
382, 388; gold: 382; Hall: 71, 156,
165, 174, 183, 189, 192, 228, 271,
282, 344, 347, 388; Hall Cloister:
218, 269; iron: 373, 382, 388; of
Healing: 92n; of the Future: 165n
Buddhapāla: 217, 228, 246-7, 266
Buddha's bones: 166, 235, 262n, 340
Buddhist practices: 225, 231, 275
Buddhist robe: 368
Buddhist scarves: 233, 249, 254, 327,
368
Bureau of Ceremonies for Foreigners:
75n
Bureau of Imperial Sacrifices: 109

Bureau of Merits: 145
Bureau of Sacrifices: 146, 148n, 358,
361-3
Bureau of the Director General of the
Imperial Parks: 286
Burial: 30, 335
Burnt rocks: 244-5
Bushel: 50, 74, 131, 135, 178-9, 183,
248, 301, 405
Bussho kaisetsu daijiten: 35n, 76n
Butchering: 392
Butchō darani: 266
Butchōson: 253n
Butchō-sonjō-darani-kyō: 246
Butsudahari: 217n
Butsuden: 71n
Butsunichi: 149n
Byakushi: 235, 253; -butsu: 235n

Cakes: 14, 120, 141, 199, 301, 382;
flowery: 344
Caldron: 385
Calendar: 64, 128, 149, 157-60, 306n
Calling on the Buddha's name: 228
Canal: 16, 18, 20n, 97
Candles, flowery: 344
Cane, strokes of: 357, 360
Canton (Kwangchou): 398
Canton: 9n, 145, 385-6; elders: 139
Cargo boats: 371
Carpenters: 76
Carpet: 180-2, 217, 221, 228, 353;
flowered: 233
Carriage: 297, 346
Cart: 282, 350-351, 354
Carvings: 255
Cash: 21, 48, 56, 63-4, 71, 92, 106,
108, 177, 190, 192-3, 196, 205, 301,
306-7, 340, 351, 375; see also Strings
of cash
Casting: 231n-3, 269, 344
Catalogue: 251
Catcher of Bandits: 109
Catty: 33n
Catūrvarga-vinaya: 77n
Cavalry: 40, 50, 52
Cells: 156-7, 177, 192
Censer: 62, 155
Censor: 284n-5, 288, 290-2, 332n, 366-
7; of Outside Inquiries: 284; of
Palace and External Affairs: 364,
370
Ceremonial sword: 345, 349
Ceylon: 253n, 325
Chair: 50, 52, 111, 265, 353

Chai-t'ang Island: 396
Champa: 70
Ch'an Bridge: 282n
Ch'an River: 282n-3, 286n; Bridge: 283
Chan-chai-kuan: 188
Ch'an-chih Bridge: 23
Ch'an-chih-ssu: 23, 84-5
Chang: 178, 185, 193-4, 196, 199, 204, 208, 332
Ch'ang, Mt.: 201n-2n
Ch'ang-an: 26n, 35, 38, 44, 46n, 51n, 60, 64, 75n-6n, 83, 87n, 90, 102, 138, 147n, 188n, 215n, 223, 229, 251, 254, 262 268-70, 272-3, 281n, 283, 286, 288n, 342n, 345, 347, 368, 370, 373, 393
Chang-chao-ts'un: 201
Ch'ang-chien: 35
Ch'ang-chih: 337n
Chang Chih-hsin: 398
Ch'ang-ch'in: 220
Ch'ang-ch'ing 218n, 262
Chang-ching-ssu: 146, 283, 300, 326n, 373
Chang-ch'iu-hsien: 204
Ch'ang-ch'iu-i: 278
Chang Chongŏn: 398
Ch'ang-chou: 376
Chang Chüeh-chi: 70
Chang Fa-man: 389
Chang-hua Common Cloister: 213
Ch'ang-huai Inlet: 399
Ch'ang-hui-k'ou: 123n
Ch'ang-i: 192n
Chang-jen: 52n
Chang-kuan: 21n
Ch'ang-kuo: 192
Chang-li: 201
Chang Liang: 105-7
Ch'ang-lo: 193n; Gate: 333; Post Station: 75; Slope: 75n, 367
Chang Mao: 105
Ch'ang-mi: 44
Ch'ang-ming: 199n
Ch'ang-ning-i: 276
Ch'ang-pai Bridge and Dam: 85
Ch'ang-pai, Mt.: 201-2
Ch'ang-piao: 174
Chang Pogo: 100, 118, 131, 133n-4, 166-9n, 378n, 387
Ch'ang-shan-hsien: 201
Ch'ang-sheng: 351n; Hall: 342
Chang Shih: 108
Ch'ang-shih: 350n, 369n
Ch'ang-yang-hsien: 189, 381

Chang Yŏng: 131, 133n, 161-2, 164, 166, 169-70, 173, 383, 394-5, 398-400
Ch'an-lin-ssu: 77, 79, 92, 236n
Ch'an-lin-yüan: 79
Chan-p'o-kuo: 70n
Ch'an-shih: 57n, 93, 137
Chanting: 55, 62-3, 73, 152-5, 181, 219-21
Chao: 192, 201, 205-6, 208, 281
Ch'ao-ch'eng: 143n
Chao-ch'eng-hsien: 277
Chao-chou: 208-9, 213
Chao-fu-ssu: 299
Chao-hsien-kuan: 173-4
Chao-i: 350, 353; Army: 337n
Chao-i-chün chieh-tu-shih: 337n
Ch'ao-i-hsien: 280n-1
Ch'ao-i-lang: 108n
Chao-ku-ts'un: 208
Chao-kuan-ts'un: 206
Chao Kuei-chen: 351, 354-6, 392n
Chao Lien: 284, 290
Chao Te-chi: 199
Chao-t'i-yüan: 279
Chao Ts'an: 148
Chao-ying-hsien: 366, 368
Chaplets: 234; see also Rosary
Ch'a-p'u Common Cloister: 213-4
Charcoal: 103, 106, 395
Charity: 56
Chavannes, Édouard: Les Mémoires historiques de Se-ma Ts'ien: 136n
Che: 77
Che-hsi-tao: 72
Cheju Island: 401n
Chen: 388
Chen: 9n
Ch'en: 200
Ch'en: 158
Chen-chiang: 72n
Ch'en-ch'ien: 56n
Chen-chou: 143, 209-10
Chen-chuang-ts'un: 135, 151n
Cheng: 173, 332
Ch'eng: 189
Ch'eng (steelyard): 293n
Ch'eng (subprefectural official): 109n
Ch'eng, Mt.: 136n
Cheng-chou: 264n, 369-70
Ch'eng-fu-kuan: 188
Cheng Tao-chüeh: 254
Cheng-ting: 143n, 212n
Ch'eng-tu-fu: 331
Chen-ju-hsin: 269
Chen-ju-hsing: 269

Chen-ju-ta-yeh-ssu: 270
Chen-kuan: 235, 254
Chen-kuo-ssu: 283, 335
Chen-kuo-tao-ch'ang: 236n
Ch'en-liu-hsien: 371
Chen-nei: 326n
Chen-shun: 24, 44, 48-9
Chen-su: 261
Chen-wu-chün: 314n
Chen-yüan: 78, 80, 217, 223, 228-9
Che-tung-tao: 72
Ch'i: 357
Chi, Mt.: 279
Chia-ch'en: 160
Chia-ch'ing Hai-chou chih-li-chou chih:
  98n, 104n, 107n, 110n
Chia-hsü: 160
Chiang: 185
Chiang Ch'ang: 397
Chiang-chou: 278
Chiang-chün: 61n, 89n
Chiang-nan: 72n; -tao: 38, 376
Chiang P'ing: 188
Chiang-shih-lang: 109n
Chiang Sun: 338
Chiang-tu: 4n; -hsien: 15n, 38n, 373
Chiang-yang-hsien: 38, 84-5, 373
Chiao-ho: 191-2
Ch'iao Kai: 176
Ch'iao-lung-chen: 97
Chiao-ma Inlet: 395
Chiao-shui-hsien: 189, 191
Ch'iao-ts'un: 188
Chia-ting: 375n
Chia-tzu: 339
Chia-yin: 66
Chi-chou: 208, 272
Ch'i-chou: 143, 206, 218, 229
Ch'i-chü: 299n
Ch'i-ch'ung-men: 280
Chicken: 355
Chie: 152n
Chief Administrator: 369-70, 373
Chief of Employees: 109, 163n
Chief Official: 21, 163, 172-3, 177,
  378-80, 383
Chief of the General Court of Cen-
  sors: 332, 381, 387, 389
Chieh-chia-chuang: 399
Chieh Common Cloister: 213
Chieh-hsia: 179n
Chieh-lü-yüan: 217-8n, 228
Chieh-tu-fu: 24n, 185n
Chieh-tu-fu-shih: 194 n
Chieh-tu-shih: 11n, 24n, 315n, 337n

Chien (bay): 347n
Chien (legionary): 345n
Ch'ien, 34n, 44n
Chien-an-ssu: 266
Chien-ch'a-shih-yü-shih: 284n
Chien-chiao: 89n, 359n
Chien-chen: 59, 68
Chien-ch'u: 158n
Chien-chün-men: 37n
Chien-chün-yüan: 37n
Chien-erh: 345n
Chien-fu-ssu: 296, 300-1n, 312
Ch'ien-fu-ssu: 35, 44
Ch'ien-Han ti-li t'u: 192n
Chien-kuang: 46n
Chien-ku-p'u-sa-yüan: 252
Chien-nan-tao: 39, 299
Chi-fu t'ung-chih: 210n-2n
Ch'ih, Mt.: 129-31, 136, 138, 142-3,
  161, 167, 169, 171-2, 176-7, 180, 186-
  7, 397; Cloister: 135, 137, 139-41,
  144-5, 147n, 151-2, 162, 168n, 170,
  176, 215, 223n, 227, 286, 378, 386;
  Inlet: 129n, 134-5n, 141, 176, 399-
  400; Monastery: 293; Village: 142
Ch'ih-an-ts'un: 17
Chih-che: 243
Chih-ch'eng-jen: 378n
Chih-ch'iang: 31
Ch'ih-fan-ching-yüan: 294
Chih-fang Lang-chung: 367n
Ch'i-fo-chiao-chieh-yüan: 252, 260, 263
Chih-hou-yüan: 186n
Chih-hsüan: 296, 335
Chih-hsün: 284n
Chih-i: 36n, 56n, 77n, 243n
Chih-kung: 202
Chih-li, Gulf of: 13n, 173n
Chih-lung-ts'un: 204
Chih-nei-sheng-shih Shang-chiang-chün:
  285n
Chi-ho: 204
Ch'ih-shan: 129n; -chi: 129n; -ts'un:
  131, 142-3
Ch'i-hsia-ssu: 65n
Ch'i Hsüan-yüan: 139, 144-5n
Chih-yang, Mt.: 175n
Chih-yang-kuan: 175
Chih-yüan: 137, 223-4, 229-31, 235-6,
  249-50
Chija Island: 401n
Chiji: 139n
Chijin: 161
Chijō (senji): 9n
Chika: 404n

Ch'i-kao: 299
Chi-k'ou: 204
Chikuzen: 168, 387, 404; Famous God of: 407
Chi-ling: 262n
Ch'i-ling-ssu: 65
Chi-lo: 172
Chi-mao: 143
Chimney: 156
Chi-mo: 113n, 190n; -hsien: 381
Chi-mo-hsien chih: 399n
Chin: 33n
Chin (state): 273n, 275n
Chin (town): 192n
Chin dynasty: 142n
Ch'in Emperor, Bridge of: 136n
Ch'in, Prince of: 195n
Chi-nan-fu chih: 218n
Chin-ch'eng: 202
Chin-ch'iao-tien: 278
Chin Chien-chung: 394
Ch'in-ch'iu-ts'un: 209
Chin-chou: 276-8
Chin-ch'ung: 395
Ch'in-fu: 314-5
Ching: 57n
Ch'ing, Mt.: 136; Inlet: 141
Ching River: 283
Ching-chao-fu: 281, 338, 364, 380, 384, 389
Ch'ing-chou: 133, 142-3, 155, 163, 185-6n, 192, 196, 284, 287, 383n; -fu: 193
Ching-chung: 335
Ch'ing-ho: 206n; -hsien: 208
Ching-kung-ssu: 299
Ch'ing-liang: 366; Mt.: 214, 225-6, 256, 313; Rock: 256; -ssu: 256
Ching-lung: 39n
Ch'ing-lung-ssu: 83, 87, 289-90n, 292, 303, 305-8, 313, 320, 325, 362, 373
Ch'ing-ning-hsiang: 131, 138, 140, 142, 144-5, 171, 176, 186-7, 383
Chingong: 161
Ching-shuang: 300
Ching-shui Common Cloister: 213
Ch'ing-ts'un: 145
Ching-tsung: 51n, 61n, 295n, 348n
Ching-t'u-yüan: 288
Ching-wen: 77-9, 92-3, 236
Ch'ing-yang: 250n
Ch'ing-yüan-hsien: 273
Ching-yün Common Cloister: 278
Chin-ho: 314n
Chin-hsien-kuan: 343-4n
Chin-hsien-lou: 343

Chin-kang Grotto: 246
Chin-ko-ssu: 211, 250, 252, 256
Chin-ling-chen: 200n
Chin-ling-i: 200
Chin-sha-ch'an-yüan: 209
Chin-shan: 271
Chin-shih: 348n
Ch'in Shih-huang: 136, 173n
Chin-tsou-yüan: 195n
Ch'in-ts'un: 279
Chin-ts'un-chia: 273
Ch'in-wang p'o-chen yüeh: 195n
Chin-wu: 89n, 297; Guards of the Left: 297; Imperial Palace Guards of the Left: 89, 108
Chinzeifu-tōtoku: 88n
Chi Pin: 10
Chi-shan-hsien: 279
Chissui: 161n, 360n
Ch'iu, Lord: 304
Chiu-li-chan-ts'un: 188
Chiŭng: 161
Ch'iu Shih-liang: 285, 287n, 309n, 311, 313n, 323, 332, 350n, 361n
Chiu T'ang shu: XIX, 25n, 41n, 47n, 172n, 304n, 326n, 337n, 348n, 350n-2n
Chiu-t'ien tao-ch'ang: 341n
Chiu-tzu: 325n
Chiu-wei-tien: 193
Ch'iu-yü-yüan: 237
Chi-wei: 66
Ch'i-yen-ssu: 266
Chō: 8, 205, 238, 240, 242, 274
Ch'oe: 134, 166-7, 399; Un Sibirang: 134n, 377, 379
Chōkai: VIII
Chŏlla-namdo: 400n
Ch'ŏnghaejin: 100n, 167, 169, 378, 400n
Chŏng Kaek: 395
Chōrakuji: 410
Chōrinnō-yuga-e: 253
Chōsai: 47n
Chōshū: 82n
Chou (rice gruel): 31n
Chou (prefecture): 9n
Chou dynasty: 192n, 321n, 332n
Chou Chung-sun: 148
Chowry: 152-3, 241
Chrysanthemums: 297
Chu (surname): 202, 371
Chuang-tzu: 299n
Chuang-yen-ssu: 302
Ch'üan-ku: 44
Ch'üan T'ang wen: 321n
Ch'üan-ts'ao: 24

Ch'üan-ya: 79-80, 87
Chu-ch'eng: 99n; -hsien: 395
Chü-chien: 212, 216, 227
Ch'u-chou: 37, 45, 64, 68, 76, 81-3,
  85-8n, 90, 95-7n, 99, 102-4, 112, 137,
  163, 236, 286, 317-8, 320-1, 325, 339,
  372-4, 376-8, 386, 389-90, 392, 395-
  6, 398-9
Chü-chou: 206n
Chüeh-chiang: 5n, 16n
Chüeh-chiang-chen: 5n, 13n-4n, 30
Chüeh-chiang-ti: 12n
Chüeh-chiang-ying: 14n
Chüeh-kou: 16n
Chüeh-kuan-ssu: 208
Chüeh-shih Common Cloister: 214
Ch'u-fu: 160n
Chūgyō: 406
Ch'ü-hsiang-ts'un: 278
Chü-hsien: 380
Chūkan: 224n
Chü-ling-fei: 299
Chu-lin-ssu: 216, 218, 222, 227-9, 251
Chün: 190n
Ch'un-chieh p'o-chen yüeh: 195n
Chün-chien: 345n
Ch'un-ch'iu lieh-kuo t'u: 192n
Ch'un-fang: 286n
Chung-ch'eng: 95n
Ch'ungch'ŏng-namdo: 400n
Chung-ch'üan: 44
Ch'ung-fu-ssu: 268, 299
Chung-hsiang-ssu: 274
Ch'ung-hsiu   Chu-ch'eng-hsien   chih:
  396n
Ch'ung-hsiu Pao-ying-hsien chih: 85n
Ch'ung-hsiu Yang-chou-fu chih: 15n,
  23n, 39n-40n, 42n-3n, 59n, 68n, 76n,
  79n
Chung-kuan: 343n
Chung-nan Mountains: 46n, 77n, 283,
  302-3, 340, 356
Chung-san-ta-fu: 365
Chung-shan: 46
Ch'ung-sheng-ssu: 302-3
Chung-shu Men-hsia P'ing-chang-shih:
  25n
Chung-shu-sheng: 25n, 360n
Ch'ungsin: 161
Chün-jung: 313n
Ch'un-ming Gate: 283, 326n, 335, 366-7
Chu-pu: 109n
Chu-shih: 148n
Ch'u-shih: 198n
Ch'ü-ting: 278n

Ch'ü-yang: 211n
Cīna: 248n
Cintāmaṇicakra: 80n
Civil administration: 360
Classics, secular: 275, 332
Clear and bright: 159, 311
Clerical clothing: 376, 388
Clerk of Dazaifu: 317
Client: 181, 370
Cloisonné: 233n
Cloister: 15; Balcony: 218; Buddha
  Hall: 218; Commandments: 217;
  common: 211-5, 226-7, 245-6, 250,
  265-7, 273, 278, 347n; Eastern Pa-
  goda: 68, 292; for Seeking Rain: 237;
  Korean: 138, 156, 169, 171, 176, 180,
  186, 195, 203; Living Quarters: 218,
  222; Lotus: 218; Mt. Ch'ih: 135,
  137, 139-41, 144-5, 147n, 151-2, 162,
  168n, 170, 176, 215, 223n, 227, 239-
  40, 242-3, 245-7, 256, 286, 378, 386;
  Nirvana: 222; of the Bodhisattva
  Hall: 231; Rules: 218; Scripture
  Translation: 301, 303; southern: 151;
  T'ing-tien: 216; see also Offering
  Cloister
Cloth: 199, 249, 334, 395; coarse silk:
  124; cotton: 233; silk: 369; tie-dye:
  122, 370; woolen: 367
Clothes: 106, 138, 140-1, 171, 249, 318,
  324, 334, 339, 363, 383-6, 390, 395,
  397; blue-green: 50; clerical: 376,
  388; court: 14, dark red: 52, 94;
  green: 52; lay: 364, 366; mourning:
  391; winter: 405
Cloud Banner General: 89
Coal: 271
Coates, Harper Havelock and Ishizuka
  Ryugaku: Honen the Buddhist
  Saint, His Life and Teaching: XIX,
  67n, 216n-7n, 219n, 235n, 248n, 289n,
  302n
Coats, green: 182
Cocks: 17
Coffin: 30
Coins: see Cash
Cold days: 81
Cold dew: 160
Cold dishes: 382
Cold Food Festival: 173, 311, 355
Comet: 47-8, 310
Commander: 28, 32, 36, 93, 99, 101-2,
  123, 285, 329, 335, 355-7, 360-1n
Commanderies: 190n, 323, 338, 346,
  363

Commandments Cloister: 217
Commentaries of the Six Statesmen: 60n
Commentary: 35-6n, 40, 57, 77n, 83, 142, 223, 234, 290n, 330
Commerce ships: 133, 141
Commissioner: 14, 19, 29, 31, 125, 131, 133, 145, 166-9, 182, 233, 309, 314-5, 318-20, 325, 327-8, 363, 374-6, 383-4, 386-7, 389-90, 394-5, 397-8, 400; for Foreign Guests: 86; for the Imperial Mausoleum: 282-3; his desk: 286-7, his office: 288, 291, 333; Imperial: 388; in Charge of Korean Affairs: 389, 399; in Charge of the Japanese Embassy: 28, 30, 61, 64,; in Charge of the Two Barbarian Peoples: 186, 194; of Ch'ŏnghaejin: 100n; of Good Works: 283-5, 288, 290, 319n, 322-4, 330, 338, 343, 348, 356-9, 361-2, 364-5; of Public Revenues, Salt, Iron, and Transportation: 346n; of Salt and Iron: 385; of the Crown Prince's Secretariat: 286; of the Iron and Salt of the Empire: 336; of Troops: 133, 180-1, 371, 378; to Inspect the Ship: 30
Common Buddha Halls: 347
Common cloister: see Cloister, common
Commoner: 121, 192, 258, 402
Concentration: 67n, 72, 265, 288
Concert: 76
Conch shell: 50
Confucian (ists): 295n, 331-2
Confucius: 332, 342
Conjunction of stars: 310
Consecrated Reverence: 217, 228
Consort: 348
Consultant Counselor: 88, 90-4, 102, 124, 135, 141, 316, 406
Contemplation: 230
Controller: 21n, 66, 161, 173-4, 178, 189, 193, 195, 203, 296, 359; of the Eastern Market: 333; of the Left: 88n, 317n
Convent: 38, 52, 108, 343; see also Nunnery
Copper: 48; utensils: 385; see also Cash
Corvee: 322; local: 347, 353, 359
Cotton cloth: 233
Council of State: 88-9n, 317n, 393, 405-6
Counselor: 89n, 406n
Courtiers: 332, 340

Court Priest: 215, 226, 261, 299, 307, 320, 330, 335-6, 342, 362, 366
Courtyard: 15n, 61n-2n, 71, 77, 131, 250, 263
Cross-legged position: 73
Crown Prince: 41-2n, 78; his household: 330-1, 394; his Secretariat: 286
Crowns of the Seven Treasures: 233
Cryptomeria: 253, 257
CTS: see Chiu T'ang shu
Cup: 106, 353; lamp: 73, 92
Cupboard, iron: 166
Curse: 127
Cuttlefish: 4
Cymbals, gourd-shaped: 219, 221

Daibonten (nō): 219n, 246n
Daie: 43n-4
Daigaku: 96n
Daijō-kishin-ron: 21n
Dainagon: 406n
Dainichi-kyō: 308n
Dainichi-nyorai: 410n
Dainihon Bukkyō zensho: IX, XIX
Daisanji: 407
Daisen: 247n
Daishi: VII, 36n, 262
Daishishi: 166
Daishō: 137n
Daitoku: 57n, 217n, 330n
Dajōdaijin: 406n
Dajōkan: 88n
Damask, shao-wu: 367
Dan: 80
Dānapati: 55n
Dancing: 141
Danna: 55n
Dan'otsu: 55n
Dan'yō: 80n, 103
Darani: 114n, 246, 266
Dazaifu: 2n, 168, 317, 387, 393, 405, 407n-8n
Dazai Sakan: 317n
DBZ: see Dainihon Bukkyō zensho
Debate: 308, 320, 330, 342
Debater: 151, 153, 307, 366; of the Three Teachings: 295, 298-9
Decapitation: 322, 333, 338, 349, 359
Deities: 6, 127, 130, 217, 228, 254-5, 302, 308n, 407n-8n; of heaven and earth: 99, 122, 124; of the mountains and islands: 130
Deliverance: 152
Dembō Kanjō: 302n
Demigods: 224, 230

Dengyō Daishi: 78n
Dentō-hosshi Rank: 34-5, 167-9n
Dentō-man Rank: 35
Department of State: 52n, 155n, 337n, 360n
Deputy Secretary: 52, 74
Deputy Vice-Governor: 393, 406, 408n
Des Rotours, Robert: *Traité des fonctionnaires et traité de l'armée, traduits de la nouvelle histoire des T'ang*: XVn, XIX, 9n-12n, 14n, 17n, 24n-5n, 33n, 37n, 43n-4n, 49n, 52n, 61n, 75n, 80n, 88n-9n, 94n-5n, 105n, 108n-9n, 139n, 145n-6n, 148n, 155n, 178n, 181n, 186n, 193n, 195n, 199n, 210n, 264n, 274n, 282n, 284n-7n, 298n, 311n, 330n-3n, 336n-7n, 342n-3n, 345n-8n, 350n, 352n, 359n, 364n-5n, 367n, 369n, 373n, 394n
Des Rotours, Robert: "Les grands fonctionnaires des provinces en Chine sous la dynastie des T'ang": 139n
Des Rotours, Robert: "Les insignes en deux parties (fou) sous la dynastie des T'ang (618-907)": 365n
Devakanyā: 241n
Devils: 244
Devotions: 232, 272, 288-9, 292; 315, 342, 362-3: *Mandara*: 255; Priest: 79, 232
Dewa: 70
Dhāraṇī: 114n
Dharma: 54n
Dharmadhātu: 220n
Dharmagupta-vinaya: 77n
Dharmalakṣana: 83n
Dhūta: 147n
Diamond: 246n
Diamond Sutra: 69, 307, 367, 402, 407
Dinghy: 128, 132-3
Dining hall: 53, 55-6, 66, 73, 215, 227n, 258-9
Disciple: 83, 87n, 139, 156, 162, 165, 171, 176, 179, 184, 186, 196, 198, 229, 233, 235-6, 243, 255, 264, 268n-9, 274-5, 284, 286, 291, 293, 305, 309-10, 313-4, 316, 318, 325n, 328, 333-4, 339, 362, 366-8, 371, 377, 379, 384, 391n
Dish: 59, 188
Divination: 27, 114, 116, 127
Diviner: 114, 116-7, 125-7
Dog: 202, 211, 385; Nose of the golden: 277
Dōjō: 67n

Donkey: 107-8, 121, 183, 200, 206, 212, 216, 225, 363, 372, 385
Dōsha: 57
Double (Great Taizō and Kongō) Mandada: 65, 392
Double tax: 322, 324
Dragon: 55n, 110n, 146, 203, 242, 246, 257; Hall: 213, 238, 240, 242; -King: 242; -King of the Sea: 110, 117, 130; -Kings of the Five Directions: 114, 124; palace: 146, 243, Pool: 237, 240, 243, 245; Spring: 213, 268; -Terrace Monastery: 203
Drawings: 2, 28, 60-1, 67, 93, 296, 304, 306-7, 392; *see also* Pictures and Paintings
Dṛdhādhyāśaya: 252n
Dream: 165, 188, 293-4, 304
Dried meats: 341
Drugs: 333, 354-5
Drum: 16-7, 83, 96-7, 172
Ducks: 20
Dug channel: 5, 12
Dumplings: 295-6
Duyvendak, J. J. L.: 17n
Dysentery: 15, 21-2, 30

E: 59n
Earth-break: 159
Earth-construct: 158
Earth-even: 160
Earth God: 159
Eastern Capital: 46n, 75n, 340, 369
Eastern Market: 333, 349
Eastern Pagoda Cloister: 68, 292
East (ern) Sea: 47, 96, 136n
Eastern Wei Bridge: 282n
Ecclesiastic: 3n
Ecclesiastics Who Convert Laymen: 57
Eclipse (moon): 150, 320, 336, 388; (sun) 393
Egaku: 310, 318, 377
Egrets: 4
Eight classes of demi-gods: 55, 63, 224, 230
Eight deities: 157n
Eight Virtues: 242
Eight ship: 42n, 101-2, 112
Eizan Daishi den: 407n
Ekōmon: 153n
Elders, Canton: 139; three: 359; Village: 192
Elephant: 67n, 255; tusks: 351
Eleven-Faced Bodhisattva: 202
Elixir: 351, 354, 356

Elm: 265; leaves: 208
Embassy: 119-20, 133n, 177n, 183,
    186n, 193, 195n, 402, 404n, 405n-7n;
    see also Korean Embassies; Tribu-
    tary embassy
Embroidery: 255; on hats: 297; on
    robes: 297
Emperor: 41, 46, 61n, 67, 74, 76, 81,
    86-8n, 100n, 118n, 120, 133, 147n,
    172-3, 180, 210n, 215n, 250, 254,
    256n, 259, 266, 275, 277, 282, 290,
    295-9, 304, 308, 316-7, 320, 323, 329-
    30, 332, 337n, 340-5, 348-55, 357-60,
    362, 385-6, 388-9, 391, 393, 407n; his
    Birthday: 250, 320, 330, 342
Emperors, black-robed: 342
Empress: 61n, 237; Dowager: 290, 348;
    of the I-yang Hall: 348; Tse-t'ien:
    237
Enchin: 3n, 25n-6n, 397n
Enchō: 90-2, 188
Enfeoffment: 285, 394
Engyō: 32n, 42, 83, 87, 90n, 292
Enlightened beings: 235n
Enlightenment: 149, 152n, 180, 186,
    239n, 248
Ennin: VII
Enryakuji: 3n, 91n, 96, 149, 188n, 231,
    236, 321n, 393
Enryaku period: 23, 43
Ensai: 3n, 9, 27, 29n, 35n, 64n, 87,
    90, 92-3, 212n, 216, 227, 231n, 236,
    316, 318, 320-1, 325n, 339, 377
Envelope: 321
Envoy: 119, 133
Enza: 73n
Equality: 257, 259
Esoteric Buddhism: 65n, 80n, 230n,
    253n, 290n, 293n, 302n-3n, 410n
Esoteric Law: 289
Esoteric practices: 294n
Esquire: 162, 164, 167
Estate: 131, 203-4, 210, 267, 296, 321,
    331, 356, 372-3, 386-8, 403; see also
    Manor
Eunuch: 37n, 47n, 284n-5n, 330n,
    343n, 359n, 361n
Evangelists: 57
Examination degrees: 348n
Excited insects: 158
Executions: 173, 314, 327, 338, 340,
    345, 349, 363, 385, 392n
Exile: 36n, 350

Fa-chao: 216-7n, 228
Fa-chen: 44

Fa-chi: 44
Fa-chieh: 302
Fa-chien: 222-3, 229, 235n
Fa-chin: 60
Fa-ching-ssu: 274
Fa-ch'üan: 289, 311, 315-6
Fa-hua-ssu: 265
Fa-hua tao-ch'ang: 67n
Fa-hua-yüan: 64, 67n-8, 85, 131, 161,
    218, 228n, 265
Fa-jun: 289, 292
Fa-k'ung: 135, 151
Falconers: 401
Fa-men-ssu: 340
Famine: 212n; see also Starvation
Fa-mo-ssu: 177
Famous God of Chikuzen: 407; of
    Kashii 407; of Kawaru: 408
Fan-chai-chung: 343n
Fan-ch'e-ts'un: 174
Fan-ching-t'ang: 294
Fan-ching-yüan: 292, 301, 303
Fan-chung-sheng: 343n
Fang-chang: 136n
Fang-ch'i: 31, 36
Fang-ch'uan: 16n
Fan-i-tien: 281
Farewell maigre feast: 251
Farmers: 345
Fa-shih: 3n, 39, 51, 53, 60, 65, 272,
    298-300, 307, 335
Fasting halls: 347
Fasts: 47; three long: 340-1, 392
Fa-ta: 268-9
Fathom: 6, 116, 126, 234, 243
Fa-tuan: 44
Fa-yü: 364
Fa-yün-ssu: 190
Fei-lien-hsien-tan: 351n
Felt hat: 366-7
Fen: 34
Fen River: 274, 276-9; Barrier: 276;
    Lake: 274
Fen-ch'eng: 278n
Fen-chou: 250, 252, 260, 270, 274-5
Feng-hsiang-fu: 297, 340, 389
Feng-li-lang: 109n
Feng-tao: 345n
Fen-hsi-hsien: 276
Fen-tien: 280
Fen-yang: 250n, 274n
Ferry: 191, 204-5; stations: 205
Festival: 40, 58-9, 71, 93, 123, 135n,
    141-2n, 268-9, 295, 297, 300-1, 303,
    310, 340, 344

Fields: 321
Fifth ship: 95, 101
Figured silk: 407
Finger bones: 340
Finial rings: 237
Fire-complete: 160
Fire crystal: 117
Fire-open: 159
Fire-remove: 160
Fire signals: 2, 3
Firewood: 150, 178-9, 183
First Emperor of the Ch'in: 136, 173n
First ship: 1-2, 60, 64, 77, 95, 97, 101-2
First zone of enlightenment: 248
Fish: 120; bag: 365n, 367, 394
Fisherman: 22, 28, 32, 134n, 402
Five beams of light: 245
Five Buddhas of the *Chōrinnō-yuga-e*:
  253
Five Buddhas of the *Kongōchō-yuga*:
  253
Five-colored cloud: 218, 228, 233, 272
Five-colored nimbus: 265
Five elements: 158n
Five grains: 114-5
Five-pronged silver *vajra*: 367
Five-sevens day maigre feast: 336
Five Terraces: 137n, 231 238, 242, 254,
  257, 260, 340; *see also* Terrace; Wu-
  t'ai
Flagellations: 321
Flanking Bodhisattva: 254
Flax: 214
Flour: 109, 178-9, 182-3, 197, 205
Flowered banners: 234; carpets: 233;
  curtains: 353-4
Flowers: 214, 221, 233, 239-40, 249,
  256, 259-60, 301; artificial: 344; cast-
  ing of: 308; scattering of: 154
Flowery cake: 344; candles: 344
Fog: 115-6, 119-20, 133
Fo-kuang-ssu: 265
Food: 175, 221, 297, 382
Foot: 44n, 254; -print: 254-5; soldier:
  40, 50, 52
Fords: 171, 180, 187
Foreigners: 26, 139
Foreign Guest Court: 75-6
Foreign monk: 169, 179, 312n-3, 318-9,
  325, 327, 362
Foreign religions: 331
Forenoon meal: 24-6, 31-3, 37, 42, 44,
  48-9, 72-3, 75, 81, 89, 91, 93-4, 103,
  107, 109, 124, 132, 135, 150-1, 160,
  169, 172-3, 175-6, 178, 183, 185, 188-

9, 191-5, 199-202, 204, 206-8, 210-3,
  215-6, 222, 226-9, 242-3, 245-6, 250-
  1, 255, 260, 265-6, 268-70, 274-81,
  283, 288, 290, 304, 343n, 354, 370,
  377, 384
Formulae: 230n
Forty-two sages and saints: 72-3
Fo-tien: 71n
Fo-tien-yüan: 218, 228
Founders (for shipbuilding): 76
Fou-p'ing-hsien: 212n
Four continents: 248
Four fruits: 248
Four Heavenly Kings: 26, 60-1, 64, 92,
  224, 230, 288n
Fourth ship: 1-3, 13, 22, 28, 30-2, 81,
  84, 95, 102
Fou-t'u: 165n
Fox: 126
Franke, O., *Geschichte des Chines-
  ischen Reiches*: 48n, 195n
Frontier garrison: 9n
Fruit: 233, 295-6, 301; gardens: 202;
  orchard: 212n; trees: 344
Fu (heat): 160n
Fu (prefecture): 24n, 264n, 274n
Fu-chün: 190n
Fudaraku: 183n
Fugen: 67, 73, 137, 166, 219, 221, 230,
  255; Hall: 248, 255; Place of Ritual:
  254
Fujiwara no (Ason) Sadatoshi: 22, 60,
  64, 95; Hirotsugu: 408; Toyonami:
  36, 82, 110; Tsunetsugu: 2n, 316n;
  Yoshifusa: 406
Fu-jung-i: 192
Fukuoka: 2n
Fukushi: 23n
Full monks: 221, 259
Full moon: 77
Fu-ma tu-wei: 336n, 346n
Fund-raising statement: 69
Funeral: 363n; procession: 335
Fu-p'ing: 282n
Fur: 90; garment: 241
Fuse: 56n
Fu-shan: 175n
Fusō: 261n

Gakumon-sō: 9n
Ganjin: 60n
Garbha-dhātu: 65n
Garrison: 282; areas: 325; Commis-
  sioner: 14n, 19; office: 11-2, 18-9,
  30

Gashi: 26n
Gatekeeper: 92
Gates, double-towered: 266
Geese: 20, 150
Gejo: 94n
Gembō: VIII, 409
General: 61-3, 89, 95, 98, 181, 349;
  Manager: 374, 377-9, 392, 396-9;
  Manager of the Crown Prince's
  Househld: 330-1; of the Armies: 210;
  representative: 182, 194; representa-
  tive of the subprefecture: 106-7;
  Supervisors: 352-3
Gengaku-sō: 78n
Gengi: 79
Genkō: 406
Genkō-shakusho: 308n
Gensai: 318
Gichō: 83
Giki: 80, 315
Gilding: 269
Giles, Herbert A., *A Chinese Bio-
  graphical Dictionary*: 25n; *A Chi-
  nese-English Dictionary*: 159n
Gilt bronze Buddhist images: 381;
  pagoda: 252; ritual utensils: 255
Girdle: 94
Gishin: 91n-2n, 188
Glacier: 242-3
Gocha Group: 401n
God of Kawaru Peak: 408n
God of the thunderbolt: 130
Gogatsu Sekku: 41n
Gojō: 43n-4
Goke: 229n
Gokusotsu: 244n
Gold: 34, 103-4, 192, 215n, 233n, 261-2,
  305, 318, 321, 333, 351, 381-2, 385,
  388, 393; and silver characters: 254;
  Buddha: 382; -colored lion: 233;
  -colored world: 214, 248, 254; -deco-
  rated carts: 350; dust: 33-4, 41, 44,
  89-90, 94, 318
Golden Balcony: 211n-2n, 252
Golden Bell: 243
Golden characters: 235; *see also*: Gold
  and silver characters; Golden writing
Golden dog: 277
Golden hair: 258
Golden images: 253
Golden Immortal, Tower of the: 343
Golden incense burners: 233
Golden Pavilion: 211n
Golden writing: 248
Gomyō: 142n

Gon-dai-sōzu: 409n
Gong: 4n, 385
Gon no Jō: 32n
Goodrich, L. Carrington, "The Re-
  volving Book-Case in China": 247n
Goshikiun enkō: 218n
Gotō Archipelago: 2n, 404n
Gourd-shaped cymbals: 219, 221
Government property: 17
Government General: 24n, 75, 142,
  171, 177, 186-7
Government hireling: 368, 375
Government University: 96n
Governor: 168, 190n, 317n, 387, 401;
  General: 24, 88
Grain: 163, 197, 200, 204, 213, 279,
  281, 321, 334, 337, 356; fills: 159;
  in ear: 159; rains: 159n
Grains of Buddhist relics: 262, 289
Grand Canal: 4n, 38n, 85n
Grand Counselor: 406
Grand General: 89n, 297; in Charge
  of the Steward's Department of the
  Palace: 285
Grand Overseer: 88, 346, 393; of the
  Imperial Secretariat and Imperial
  Chancellery: 25n
Grand Pillar of the State: 331, 365
Grand Tutor: 369
Grass-boats: 16
Grave: 43, 190, 210, 275, 311, 335;
  monuments: 347; plot: 334-5
Great compassion: 156
Great God of Kamado: 407; of Sumi-
  yoshi: 407
Great heat: 159
Great Law of *Soshitsuji*: 308; of the
  Birushana-kyō: 308; of the *Kongō-
  kai*: 294, 302, 305; of the *Taizōkai*:
  306, 311
Great Mt. Hŭk Island: 401n
Great Official of the Palace: 329-30n,
  352
Great Recluse: 247
Great River in Huai-nan-chen: 11; of
  Yang-chou: 4
Great Sage 137n
Great Sentient Beings: 219-20
Great Teacher: 221, 294
Green coats: 182
Grooms: 19
Grotto: 245-8, 263, 356; of the Holy
  Bell: 265
Group, P'u-t'i: 327; Yang-hua: 319
Gruel: 31, 56, 66, 73, 107-8, 157, 172,

190, 194, 199, 202-3, 208-14, 239, 245, 268, 273, 276-7, 295-7
Guard Armies: 352, 360
Guard Captain: 14, 16, 23, 30, 107
Guard Office: 108
Guard Officer: 105-13, 119-21, 124-5, 131, 134n, 162-4, 166-7, 169-73, 183, 185-6n, 275, 282, 285, 290, 313, 315, 319, 327, 335, 338-40, 349, 364, 383
Guardian Deities: 264
Guards: 298; of the passes: 148
Guest: 181-2; monks without protection: 314; rooms: 31
Gumyō-chō: 73
Gunsho ruijū: 91n
Gusokkai: 222n
Gyō: 88n
Gyōdō: 157n
Gyōkō: 54n
Gyōryakushō: 3n, 25n
Gyōzui: 54n

Hachibushū: 55n
Hachi-kudoku-chi: 242n
Hachiman: 130, 408
Hai-an: 298
Hai-chou: 29, 95-8, 105, 108, 110n, 114n, 163, 372, 379-81, 396
Hail: 146, 205, 216, 220, 227, 246, 257
Hai-ling-chen: 14
Hai-ling-hsien: 5n, 9, 11, 13-4n, 21-2, 38, 176, 286
Hai-lung-wang-miao: 110-1
Hakase: 96n, 232n
Hakata: 168n, 404; Bay: 1n-2n, 407n
Hakku: 198
Hakkura: 198n
Hakozaki: 407n
Half cross-legged position: 73
Hall of Fugen's Counter-Wind: 67-8
Hall of the Deity Kabira: 61
Halley's comet: 47n
Hamper: 363, 366, 372, 374, 376, 397
Han (town): 192n
Hand cloths: 249
Han dynasty: 190n, 192n, 277
Hane Hōshō: 184
Hang: 333n
Hangan: 10n, 82n
Hanju: 216, 228; dōjō: 216n
Hankafuza: 73n
Han Kan: 67
Hankaza: 73n
Han-kuang: 255

Han-lin Academy: 348n, 373; Professor: 373
Hannya-in: 224
Hannya-kyō: 46, 115, 155n, 407
Han-shih: 81n
Hao-lin-ssu: 74
Haramitta: 155n
Harbor Master: 144-5
Harp: 248
Harumichi no Sukune Nagakura: 16n, 82-3
Hasetsukabe no Sadana: 18, 135
Hat: 83n, 106, 216, 227, 260, 367; embroidered: 297; felt: 366; rain 266; straw: 106, 216, 227, 260
Hata Sodatsu: 184, Umiuo: 184
Haŭi Island: 400n-1n
Hayloft: 333
Headgear: 90, 297
Headings of the scripture: 152, 154
Headman: 404
Heaven: 351; Huo-lo: 341, 351n; Prince of the Bishamon: 303
Heavenly amnesty: 159-60
Heavenly beings: 230
Heavenly deities: 341-2, 344
Heavenly Kings: 333
Heavenly protector: 245n
Heaven's Gate Cloister: 135
Heavens, nine: 352; twelve: 302; twenty-eight: 219
Heavy snow: 160
Hoihalou: 127n
Hell: 244
Helmsmen: 97, 317
Hemp: 136
Hempseed cakes: 297; oil: 212
Heng, Mt.: 55n
Heng-shan: 55n
Henjō-kongō: 410
Herdsmen: 345
Hermit's Terrace: 201
Hetuvidyā: 142n
Hexagenary cycle: 58n, 66n, 143n, 157n-8n
Hexagon: 247
Hibino Takeo: see Ono Katsutoshi
Hiei, Mt.: VIII, 3n, 99, 308n, 402
Higan: 54n
Hiki: 44n
Hikyōkeshi: 57n
Hirado Island: 404n
Hiragane: 4n
Hireling, government: 368, 375

His Excellency: 163, 169, 174, 196-8,
    291, 332, 381, 387, 389
His Holiness: 137, 219-21, 225, 231-2,
    245, 251-2, 254, 258, 260, 265-6, 270,
    303, 314
His Honor: 179, 184, 305
His Majesty: 309
His Reverence: 305-7, 316
Hitorutama: 117n
Hizen: 403
Ho: 275, 287, 319, 327
Hoar frost descends: 160
Hōben: 152n
Ho-chin: 279n
Ho-chou: 37
Ho-chung-fu: 274, 276, 280
Ho-fei: 38n
Ho-hsi-hsien: 280
Ho-chang-liu-ts'un: 208
Hoe: 165
Hoeryang: 161
Ho-fan Kung-chu: 326n
Hoffleit, Dorrit: 47n
Hōgan: 10n
Hōin Rank: 409
Hōin-daikashō Rank: 410
Hōin-daikashō-i: 409n
Hōkai: 220n
Hokke: 35n; dōjō: 67n; -enkyō: 76;
    -gengi: 77n; -kyō: 40n; -kyō shikan:
    77n; -mongu: 77n; sandaibu: 77n;
    -zammai: 67n, 137, 224, 230, 243,
    265; Zasu: 40n
Ho Kung-chen: 313, 315
Holiday: 66, 172, 311, 355
Holy land: 140, 149
Holy teachings: 363-4, 376
Hōmanzan: 407n
Hommyō kanjō dōjō: 308n
Hommyō-sei: 308n
Honan Province: 142n
Ho-nan-fu: 46n
Ho-nan-tao: 364n
Honchō kōsō den: 91n
Honey: 33
Hongyō Daitoku: 215n
Honorary ranks: 35n, 409n
Honorary titles: 32n, 50n, 57n, 59n,
    190n, 298n 316, 330n-1n
Honor guards: 52
Hopei Province: 337
Horā: 341n
Hori Ichirō: X
Horn scepter: 99

Horse: 121, 282, 354, 370, 401, 403;
    trappings: 192
Horseflies: 376, 382
Ho-shang: 31n, 40, 60, 63, 78, 80, 138,
    202, 216-7, 223-4, 228-31, 235-6,
    248-9, 251, 265, 289, 292-4, 296, 302,
    305-7
Hōshin: 60n
Hospices: 239n
Hosshi: 3n, 32, 83, 87, 92, 110, 112,
    124, 132, 135, 391, 406
Hosshōjakkū: 45n
Hosshōkū: 45n
Hossō: 83, 110, 132
Hostel: 22n
Ho-tung Province: 337n
Ho-tung-fu: 280n
Ho-tung-tao: 268
Hou-tzu: 175
Hsia-ching-hsien: 206
Hsia-kung-yüan: 197
Hsi-an: 283n
Hsiang: 9n
Hsiang-ch'i-lao: 139n
Hsiang-kung: 25n
Hsiang-ling-hsien: 278
Hsiao: 198-9, 348, 381
Hsiao-i: 332n
Hsiao-i-hsien: 275
Hsiao-kan-ssu: 68-9
Hsiao-shui-tien: 276
Hsiao Tu-chung: 194
Hsiao-wen: 256n, 259, 266, 277
Hsiao-yen-t'a: 297n
Hsi-ch'an-yüan: 210, 283
Hsi-ch'ih-ssu: 20-1
Hsieh-shan-kuan: 174
Hsien: 9n
Hsien Ching: 188
Hsien-kung-kuan: 23
Hsien-kung-ts'un: 205
Hsien-ling: 21n
Hsien-t'ai: 352n
Hsien-tsung: 47n, 51n, 290n, 326n,
    336n, 348n
Hsien-wu: 275
Hsi-fan: 389n
Hsi-kuo: 235n
Hsi-lien Island: 98n
Hsi-ming-ssu: 51, 272n
Hsin-chiang: 278n
Hsin-ch'iao-tu: 279
Hsin-ching-ssu: 108
Hsin Chiu-yü: 369-70
Hsin-chou: 266-7n

Hsing-ch'ing Palace: 326n
Hsing-ch'üan: 44
Hsing-fu-ssu: 301, 312-3
Hsing-ho Bridge: 85
Hsing-k'ai-ts'un: 206
Hsing-kuo-ssu: 107-8n
Hsing-li: 137n
Hsing-man: 78
Hsing-shan-ssu: 283n, 293, 305, 313, 325
Hsing-t'ang-hsien: 210, 212n
Hsing-t'ang-kuan: 344
Hsing-t'ang-ssu: 303
Hsing-tuan: 35
Hsin-ho: 208n; Bridge: 208; -k'ou: 208
Hsin-hsien: 108n
Hsin-i-tien-t'ou: 280
Hsin T'ang shu: XIX, 25n, 100n, 172n, 195n, 285n, 316n, 337n, 348n, 350n, 352n, 365n
Hsin-tien: 281
Hsin-yu: 296
Hsi-t'ien: 149n
Hsiu-ch'an-ssu: 236
Hsiu-ta: 31
Hsi-yüan: 310, 335
Hsü: 158, 160n
Hsüan-chen-kuan: 299
Hsüan-fa-ssu: 289, 311, 315
Hsüan-hua Gate: 286
Hsüan-hsüan: 322
Hsüan-liang: 234-5n, 249
Hsüan-su: 137
Hsüan-tsang: 40n, 272n, 302n
Hsüan-ts'e: 272
Hsüan-tsung: 15n, 51n, 59n, 295, 391n
Hsüan-yang Ward: 290
Hsü-chou: 97, 100n, 372
Hsü-hsiu Shan-hsi-sheng t'ung-chih k'ao 282n-3n
Hsü-i: 45n, 372
Hsün: 6n, 46
Hsün-chien: 49n
Hsün Nien-i-lang: 37
Hsü-sung-ts'un: 188
HTS: see *Hsin T'ang shu*
Hu: 173, 269
Hu: 50n
Hu, Mt.: 136
Hua-ch'ing Palace: 342n
Huai River: 37n, 45n, 95-8, 371n-2, 377, 396
Huai-an: 37n, 85n, 87n, 97n, 335; -hsien: 86n
Huai-ch'ing: 288, 292

Huai-jen: 380
Huai-nan: 167, 336-7, 345, 392-3; -chen: 11-2; -tao: 4n, 11n, 38-9n, 97n, 312n, 364n, 376
Huai-yüeh: 335
Hua-la: 344n
Huan-ch'ün: 53
Huang, Mt.: 211
Huang-ch'eng: 287n
Huang-ch'ung: 279n
Huang-fan: 158
Huang-hsien: 142, 188
Hua-su Fa-shih: 57n
Hua Ta: 109
Hua-yen: 249n
Hua-yen Ridge: 222n
Hua-yen-yüan: 217-8, 228
Hua-yin-hsien: 331, 369
Hu-chün: 352n
Hu Chün-chih: 139, 144, 170-1
Hu-chün chung-wei: 285n
Hu-hung Island: 98, 112
Hui-ch'ang: 298-9n, 305-7, 310-1, 313-6, 319-20, 324, 328-9, 332, 334-5, 339, 354, 364, 377, 389, 394; -ssu: 299; Emperor: 393
Hui-chao-ssu 39, 74, 99
Hui-chao-chiao-ssu: 39n
Hui-chi River: 371n
Hui-chien: 335
Hui-ch'uan Dam: 84
Hui-chü-ssu: 172-3
Hui-hai-ssu: 179
Hui-hsia: 164n
Hui-hu: 314n
Hui-jih-ssu: 299
Hui-kuo: 87n, 289n
Hui-shen: 44
Hui-ssu: 55n
Hui-wei: 76
Hui-yün: 60
Hŭk, Mt.: 401
Hu-kuo-ssu: 336
Hŭm Yanghwi: 397
Hundred-day maigre feast: 339
Hundred Laws of Yuima: 366
Hung-chi: 235
Hung-chien: 44
Hung-lu-ssu: 75n
Hung-tse, Lake: 45n
Hung-tung-hsien: 278
Hun-t'un: 295n
Huo-ch'ang-ts'un: 277
Huo-chou: 277n
Huo-chou chih-li-chou chih: 277n

Huo-i-hsien: 277
Huo-lo Heaven: 341, 351n
Hu-t'o River: 266
Hu-ts'un Common Cloister: 267
Hwangmo Island: 401
Hwangnyongsa: 403
Hwasang: 138
Hyaku-ron: 60
Hyegak: 161
Hyeil: 104
Hymn: 62-3, 152-5
Hyōtanshi: 219n

I (station): 192n
I (cyclical character): 157
I-ch'ang-i: 277
I-chen: 87, 188n, 289, 292, 305-7
I-ching: 131n, 301
I-ch'ou: 354
I-feng: 45n, 217, 228, 266
Igyō: 27, 44-5, 48n, 102-3, 132, 140,
  142, 148, 171, 176, 179, 186, 222,
  229, 245, 250, 286, 305, 309, 313-4,
  319, 328 333-4, 336, 339, 363n
I-hai: 160
I-hsien: 113n, 188-9
I-hsing: 174-5
Ikeda Chōden: VIII
Ikeda Manuscript: VIII, XIX
I-ling: 40n; -kuan: 22-3n
Image: 49, 52, 55, 68, 71n, 77, 80n,
  157, 165-6, 192, 204, 209, 216n, 226-
  7, 231n-4, 237-8, 240-3, 245, 249,
  252-6, 264-5, 269, 272-3, 333, 341-2,
  347, 353, 363, 367, 376, 381-2, 388
Imanishi Ryū: *Shiragi shi kenkyū*:
  101n, 191n
Immortality: 351-2, 354-7
Immortals: 136n; terrace of the: 352-8
Immyō-ron: 142
Imperial Bodyguard: 94n; of the Left:
  135n
Imperial Chancellery: 25n, 323, 330,
  332, 339, 356, 358, 360
Imperial City: 287, 333n
Imperial Command: 233, 236, 255, 288,
  295-6, 299-300, 307, 314, 316, 322,
  333, 337, 348, 350, 360, 373-4, 388
Imperial Commissioner: 233, 295, 388
Imperial Communications: 262
Imperial credentials: 29
Imperial decree: 324, 326, 330
Imperial edict: 147-9, 321-3, 327, 329,
  331, 333, 337-8, 340, 343-7, 350, 353-

7, 359-60, 362-3, 372-4, 376, 380-2,
  384-6, 388-93, 402
Imperial Emissary: 197, 249-50
Imperial figure: 344
Imperial guard groups: 135n
Imperial mausoleums: 350
Imperial order: 29, 40, 48, 64, 72, 79-
  80, 87, 93, 95, 203, 249-50, 253, 297-
  8, 310-2, 320, 361, 363, 374
Imperial Palace Guards: 89n, 283n,
  285, 287-8n, 333n
Imperial Parks: 286, 373
Imperial Permit: 41, 78, 90
Imperial Prince: 168n
Imperial Prohibition: 84
Imperial Regional Inspector: 80
Imperial Rescript: 180-2, 217, 228, 345
Imperial rice: 74
Imperial Scripture Translation Cloister:
  294
Imperial Secretariat: 25n, 323, 330,
  332, 339, 356, 358, 360, 369, 372
Imperial Son-in-Law: 336, 345-6
Imperial tumulus: 393
Imperially Established (Life Star)
  Baptistry: 294, 308
Ina: 21n, 152, 154
Inamasu: 98
Incantations: 114, 321, 335
Incense: 54-5, 62-3, 84, 178, 217, 219,
  221-2, 228, 233, 249-50, 259, 295-6,
  301, 342, 367-8, 402; burners: 63,
  233; cups: 62; Land of: 34n; Moun-
  tains: 240, 247
India: 49, 53n, 110n, 114n, 147n, 149,
  180, 183n, 186, 218, 228-9, 235-6n,
  240n, 246-7, 253-4, 266, 292, 294n,
  301n-2, 308; Central: 362; Northern:
  362; South(ern): 269, 294n, 308,
  362; ink: 68
Indian: 320, 325; South: 325; monk:
  240, 266, 268; monk, South: 268
Indochina: 70n
Inju: 141n
Inkai: 315n
Inn: 22-4, 26, 28, 30-2, 43, 81-2, 86,
  94-5, 174, 190, 211n, 370; Korean:
  177; P'ing-ch'iao: 42; P'o-hai: 177;
  T'ai: 190; Water: 41; -keeper: 174,
  190
Inō: 21n, 139n
Insects: 177, **212**
Inshin: 230n
Inspection Office: 283, 313-4, 219, 327,
  330

Inspection Officer: 285, 288
Inspector: 284-5, 288, 290-1, 313, 315, 319, 327
Institutional meals: 291
Intendant: 139, 144-5, 170-1, 188; in charge: 197
Interpreter: 14, 42, 84, 110, 112, 321, 339, 387; see also Korean Interpreter
Invocation: 152
Iron: 4-5, 49, 336-7n, 346; Commissioner of Salt and: 385; alms bowl: 140; Buddha: 373, 382, 388; Bureau, Salt and: 373; cupboard: 166; pagodas: 237, 239-40, 243, 245
Ise: 317
Ise Gon no Suke: 317n
I-shen: 211
Ishikawa no Ason Michimasu: 23n, 43
Ishō: 27, 32, 44n-5, 48, 61, 92, 102-3, 132, 135, 140, 142, 148, 161-2, 164, 171, 176, 179, 184, 186, 196-8, 222, 229, 245, 250, 284, 286, 291-3, 309, 313-4, 319-20, 328, 333, 335, 362, 384, 391n, 405n
I Sinhye: 387
I-ssu: 159
I-ts'un: 190n
I-tu: 133n; -hsien: 200
Ivory: 254; see also Elephant tusks
I-yang: 90n
I-yang Hall, Empress of: 348
Iyo: 317
I-yüan: 250-2, 255, 268-9, 273-5, 313

Jacket: 52n
Jade: 192, 217, 222, 228-9, 233, 237, 254, 256; lion, white: 256; ordination platform, white: 222, 229; white: 228-9
Japanese products: 12, 15, 24, 26, 28-9, 125
Japanese travelers: 390
Jari: 78n
Jars: 302; blue lapis lazuli, relics: 271; golden, relics: 271
Jen: 369-70
Jen: 234n
Jen-hsü: 311
Jen-sheng Wen-wu Chih-shen Ta-hsiao Huang-ti: 316n
Jewel: 221, 233, 351, 385; Mountain: 265; seat: 269
Jiei: 406
Jihi: 152n
Jikaku Daishi: VII

"Jikaku Daishi no nittō kikō ni tsuite": see Okada Masayuki
Jinen: 79n; Kashō: 79n; -mandara-dōjō: 255n
Jinnyo: 198
Jisetsu-daishi: 88n
Jishu: 21n
Jitsuden: 410n
Jitsuen: 410n
Jīvaṃjīvaka: 73n
Jizō: 219
Jō (magistrates): 32n
Jō (meditation): 59n
Jōbun: 152n
Jōgakuji: 347n
Jōgyō: 32, 35n, 43, 65
Jōgyō zammai: 216n
Jōjū sambō: 54n
Jōwa: 1n, 9, 66, 176, 334
Jōza: 21n
Ju, Mt.: 120, 123, 126, 399; Bay: 120n; Inlet: 166, 394
Judicial Bureau: 193n
Jug, bronze: 140
Jūichimen Bosatsu: 202n
Jui-hsiang Balcony: 49
Jui-hsiang-fei-ko: 49n
Jūji: 248n
Ju-kao-chen: 5n, 13n-4n, 16-8, 30
Ju-kao-hsien: 5n
Ju-kao-hsien chih: 14n, 17n
Jun-chou: 72, 74
Jung-ch'eng: 136n; -hsien: 129n
Jung-ch'eng-hsien chih: 129n, 134n, 136n
Jung-ho: 279n
Junior Recorder of the Left: 317
Jūniten: 302n
Junna: 317
Jun-rokuji: 11n
Jun-senshi: 17n
Junshō: 325
Jupiter: 157n

Kabira: 61, 302
Kaeriten: IX-X
Kafuza: 73n
Kagami Shrine: 407n
Kai: 59n
K'ai-ch'eng: 10, 66, 139-41, 145-6, 149, 157, 161-2, 167-71, 176-7, 179-80, 184-7, 196-9, 282, 284-7, 291-4, 296, 298, 319-20, 328, 378, 383; Emperor: 172
Kaidan: 45n

K'ai-feng: 363n
K'ai-fu: 287, 291, 304, 309, 311; -i-
    t'ung-san-ssu: 285, 287n
Kaijo: 94n
K'ai-kuo-nan: 331n
Kaimyō: 83n, 110, 112, 124, 132, 135
K'ai-yüan: 15n; -ssu: 15, 24, 26, 28,
    30-1, 35, 38, 44, 46n, 48, 59n-61, 64,
    67-8, 75, 77, 81, 86, 92, 176-8, 183,
    206-7, 209, 269, 286
Kalaviṅka: 73n
Kalpa: 248, 264n, 313
Kāmadhātu: 219n
Kamado, Great God of: 407
Kamado Shrine: 407n
Kami: 110
Kami no Noritsugu: 82
Kamioi: 395
Kan: 31n
Kan Chiang: 134, 142
Kan-ch'üan, Mt.: 39n
Kan-ch'üan-ssu: 39n
Kan'en: VIII, 410
Kanji: 31n
Kanjō: 302n-3n, 308n; -gyō: 114-5
Kankō giki: 255n
Kan-kokushin: 82n
Kannon: 2-3n, 10, 80n, 156n, 183n,
    202n, 273; Cloister: 53
Kannon kōshi: 408n
Kannon lectures: 408
Kanshin: 60n
Kansu: 31n, 139n
Kan-t'ang-i: 90
Kan-yü: 380n
Kanze: 3n, 92n -on: 3n, 156, 166;
    -onji: 408n
Kao: 281
Kao An: 175
Kao-ling-(hsien): 281n-3n
Kao-mi-hsien: 381
Kao Shu: 174
Kao-tsu: 51n
Kao-yu-hsien: 38, 85, 373
Kapila: 61n
Karaten: 341n
Karma: 34n, 68n-9, 244, 251, 270,
    303n; see also Affinities
Karyōbinga-chō: 73
Kaṣāya: 43n
Kashii: 407; Famous God of: 407;
    Shrine: 407n
Kashmir: 217n
Kashō: 31n, 78-9, 93, 147, 188, 236,
    248, 261, 318

Kāśyapa: 248n
Katō: 338n
Katsuno Ryūshin: XVI
Kawaru: 408; Famous God of: 408;
    Peak, God of: 408n; Shrine: 408n
Kechien: 69n, 251n; kanjō: 303n, 308n
Kechigan: 156n
Kegon-kyō: 249, 298
Kekan: 224n
Kekkafuza: 73n
Ken: 347
Ken'en: 410n
Keng: 160n
Keng: 192
Kengo: 252n
Kengō: 264n
Kengoi: 252n
Keng-shen: 58n, 159
Ken'in: VIII, XI, 225, 328, 410
Kenrinhō: 322n
Kesa: 43n
Kessai: 123n
Khan: 326n
Khotan: 302
Kibi: 32
Kick-ball: 194n
Kiden-ryūgaku-shō: 99n
Kim Chabaek: 397
Kim Chin: 397-9, 405-6
Kim Chŏngnam: 5, 29, 64, 76, 81n, 93,
    101-2
King: 55, 100n, 118n, 120, 134, 192,
    262; of Korea: 394; Uighur: 326
Kinkakuji: 211n
Ki no Ason Sada: 184
Ki no Harunushi: 110n, 112
Kisha no Setsu: 41n
Kishinron: 21
Kiyomine: 82, 84
Knife: 29, 50-1, 304, 321; Korean: 376
Kōbō Daishi: 83n, 410n
Kōcha Islands: 401n, 403n
Koguryŏ: 142n
Ko-hsia: 196n
Kōi: 31n, 248n
Koi Island: 400-1
Kōkechi: 122n
Kokushi: 59n
Kokuyaku issai kyō: IX-X, XIX
Kōkyō Hosshi: 69n
Komaro: 26n
Kombu: 41n
Kongju: 400n
Kongō: 246n, 264n
Kongōchō-kyō: 253n

Kongōchō-yuga: 253
Kongō-hannya-haramitsu-kyō: 69n
Kongōkai: 65n, 80, 87, 289-90n, 292, 294, 302, 307; Great Law of the: 305; *Great Mandara*: 296; *Kue Mandara*: 306-7; *Mandara*: 217, 228, 294, 300, 302
Kongō-kyō: 69n
Kongō Mandara: 392
Kongō-myōgō: 410n
Kongō-shin: 264n
Kongōsho: 264n, 367n
Kōnin: 70, 387
Konjiki sekai: 214n
Konkōmyō (-saishōō) -kyō: 131
Konoe: 94n
Konrin (nō) -butchō: 253n
Konrinnō-butchō-yōryaku-nenju-hō: 253n
Korea: 5n, 18-9, 99-101, 114, 116-7, 120, 133, 141-2n, 151, 170, 186n, 191n, 368, 378, 394, 400-1, 403; King of: 394
Korean affairs: 383-4, 389, 399; boat: 121; Cloister: 138, 156, 169, 171, 176, 180, 186, 195, 203; Embassies: 131n, 169, 195n; Inn: 177; Interpreter: 5, 14n, 29, 64, 76n, 93-4, 102, 110, 119, 121-2, 124, 131-2, 317, 321, 325, 339, 374-7, 386, 390; knives: 376; language: 151-2; monk: 137, 143, 146, 165, 272, 325, 362, 368, 380, 387; people: 70, 93-4n, 103-4, 118-9, 121-2, 150, 318n, 325, 336, 391-2n, 395, 397, 405n; population: 383; rite: 154-5; sailors: 97, 99; ship: 70n, 119, 126, 166, 325n; ward: 374-5, 377-9, 396, 398
Kōrokan: 405
Kosan: 386, 389-90
Kōsen: 240n
Kōshaku: 34n
Kōshi: 31n
Koshiki no Inamasu: 95
Kōshin- (machi): 58
K'o-ssu: 60
K'o-ts'ung: 335
Kou-tang: 28n, 61n, 63; *Jih-pen-kuo Shih*: 28n
Ko-yüan: 218, 220, 222, 228, 234-5, 249
Kōyui: 31n
Kōzan: 240n
Kōzui: 251n
Krakucchanda: 247n
Kṣitigarbha: 219n

Ku, Mt.: 193n
Kuan (hostel): 22n
Kuan (string): 44n
Kuan (Taoist monastery): 23n
Kuan River: 98n
Kuan-ch'a-shih: 80n
Kuan-chien: 14n
Kuan-chung ssu-sheng: 36n
Kuan-chün-jung-shih: 311n
Kuan-fa-ssu: 192
Kuang-ch'eng-yüan: 275
Kuang-chou: 398
Kuang-ch'u: 251
Kuang-hsiu: 79, 236n
Kuang-i: 74
Kuang-ling Inn: 43
K'uang Ts'ung-chih: 187-8
Kuang-ying: 299
Kuang-yo: 39
Kuan-nei-tao: 38-9
Kuan-yin: 2n; -yüan: 53
Kubota Ryōen: X
Kucha: 325
Ku-ch'eng Common Cloister: 267
Kuch'o Island: 401
Kudara: 189n
Kudoku: 92n, 242n
Kue: 306n
K'uei-chi: 40n, 272n, 303n
Kuei-hai: 324
Kuei-lun: 275
Kuei-mao: 160, 389
Kuei-yu: 160
Ku-hsien-kuan: 175
Ku-hsien-ts'un: 201
K'u-hsi-t'ing: 288
Kūkai: 83n, 87n
Kūkan: 224n
Ku-kuan-tien: 278
Kumārajīva: 36n, 61n, 268
Kŭmjŏng: 161
K'ung-ch'a: 76n
Kung-chu: 326n
K'ung-fan: 34n, 76n
K'ung-hou: 248n
K'ung-mu-kuan: 332n
Kungp'a: 101n
Kungpok: 101n
Kung-yang-yüan: 239n
Kung-yüan Tsung-chien-yüan: 286n
Kuni tsu mono: 9n
K'un-lun Mountains: 205
Kūō: 275
Kuo: 348
Kuo River: 371n

Lu-shan-ssu: 174
Lu-shih: 178n
Lü-shih: 302n
Lu-shih ssu-fa: 193n
Lu Shun: 223n
Lü-ta-te-yüan: 270
Lü-yüan: 218, 228

Ma-chia-tien: 277
Machō: 301n
Mackau Group: 401n
Magadha: 218n
Magistrate: 32, 155, 163, 169, 178-84, 380
Mahābrahmā: 219n
Mahākāśyapa: 147n
Mahā-prajñāpāramitā-sūtra: 155n
Maharṣi: 247n
Mahāsattva: 219n
Mahāsthāmaprāpta: 273n
Mahā-vairocana: 410n
Mahāvairocana-sūtra: 308n
Mahāyāna-śraddhotpāda-śāstra: 21n
Maigre feast: 24n, 34, 36, 53-7, 61, 63-4, 66, 73, 76, 92, 166, 174, 183, 197, 199, 203, 206-7, 215-6, 218, 220, 222 227, 229, 249-51, 257-9, 295, 298, 300n, 308, 310, 320, 330, 336, 339, 342, 358; essay: 34n-5, 54n-6
Maigre food: 208
Maigre meal: 209-10
Maigre tea: 76
Maitreya: 165n
Maka-hannya: 155; *-haramitsu*: 219-20; *-haramitsu-kyō*: 155n
Makakashō: 147n
Makasatta: 219n
Maka-shikan: 77n, 223
Malikā: 247n
Mallet: 155, 219-20, 222
Manager: 28n, 63, 77, 83, 87-9, 91, 124, 161, 174, 296, 359; of Foreign Guests: 108
Man-ching: 150n
Manchuria: 141n-2n
Maṇḍala: 65n
Mandara: 65, 80, 93, 103, 217, 228, 254-5, 289, 294, 296, 300, 302-4, 306-8n, 363, 392
Manichaean priests: 327
Manifestation: 202, 225, 233, 240-1, 243, 245, 249-51, 258-60, 265, 269-70; *see also* Sign; Miracle
Mañjuśrī: 73n
Manor: 150; *see also* Estate

Mantra: 65n
Manuscript: VII-IX, 225, 328, 410; *see also* Tōji manuscript; Ikeda manuscript
Many Treasured Pagoda: 244
Mari: 247
Market: 44, 85, 350, 355; Eastern: 333, 349; Western: 333n; place: 84-5, 171, 180, 187, 189, 204-5, 278, 367
Maruyama Park: 410n
Maspéro, Henri, "Les procédés de 'nourrir le principe vital' dans la religion Taöiste ancienne": 351n
Mast: 4-7, 10, 126-7, 133n
Master: 78, 92-3, 112, 134-5, 151, 155, 172, 212, 224, 230, 232-3, 261, 269, 289, 292, 304, 311, 318, 321, 325, 339, 377 408; of Meditation: 57, 272-3; of Sanskrit: 54; of scripture-reciting: 68
Mat: 48, 66, 260, 353; sitting: 48n, 207, 259
Ma-t'ou, Mt.: 278
Matsura, Shrine of the Illustrious Deity of: 407n
Matsura Deputy Vice-Governor: 407
Matsura District: 403-4n, 407n
Mausoleum: 282-3, 350
Māyā: 224; Lady: 230
Meat: 123n, 341
Medicine: 73, 84, 147, 194, 221, 301, 324, 339; stalls: 355
Meditation: 57n, 59n, 73n, 152, 216n; Master of: 57, 272-3
Meitoku: 409
Melons: 308
Memorial: 322-3, 338, 340, 342, 346, 351, 354-5, 360; day: 295; essay: 43
Mendicancy: 147n
Mendicant: 149, 250, 255-6, 266, 268-70, 273-5, 304
Meng-chia-chuang: 206
Men-hsia-sheng: 25n, 360n
Merchant: 11, 29, 48-9, 125, 204, 333n
Metal-collect: 160
Metal-even: 160
Metal founder: 134
Metal-grasp: 160
Metal-worker: 201
Methods of Reciting Religious Formulae: 292-3, 305
Miao: 110n
Mibu no Kaisan: 7-8
Mi-chou: 99, 102-4, 113, 191, 380-1, 395

Midday rest: 172, 174-5, 183, 188-9, 191-3, 197-8, 202, 204, 206-11, 213, 216, 227, 281, 283, 370
Mien-ao-tzu: 225n
Hi-hua Ward: 281
Miketsu: 91n
Military: 73-4, 309, 325, 356, 358; affairs: 311; aide: 32, 50, 52, 68; arts: 324; Attaché: 94, 110; detachment: 10, 13, 17; encampment: 282; Guard Officer: 131n, 161, 181, 183, 339; Headquarters: 194, 199-200; Inspector: 37n, 52, 61n, 200; Inspector's Bureau: 37; Inspector's Office: 74; Officer: 83, 111, 180-2, 210; official: 134, 180; police: 105-7
Milky Way: 214
Mill: 267; San-chiao: 267
Millet: 17, 74, 117, 135, 177, 190, 196, 205, 211, 301, 382
Mimasaka: 32n
Ming-chou: 43, 101, 318, 377n, 395, 397-8
Ming-ling-chen: 267
Ming-te Gate: 298
Ming-wang-miao: 177
Minister of State: 24-6, 28-30, 32, 36-7, 39-41, 46-7, 49-50, 52, 58, 61-4, 66, 68-9, 72, 74, 77, 82-3, 87-8, 90n, 288, 295, 311-2n, 316, 322, 336n-7, 339-40, 345-6, 374, 401
Ministry: 52n, 88n, 155n; of Agriculture: 333n; of Central Affairs: 393n; of Rites: 146n
Miracle: 259, 273; see also Manifestation; Sign
Miroku: 165-6, 219-21, 269
Mirror: 122, 233-4, 402
Miru: 41n
Mishina Akihide: "Shiragi Karō no genryū to sono hatten ": 142n
Mochi: 43n
Mo-fu: 160n
Mo-ho: 142n
Mokp'o: 400n-1n
Monastery Administrator: 31, 33, 35, 54-5, 139, 144, 149, 173, 207, 288, 296, 324, 335, 359
Monastery living quarters: 31, 36, 55, 76, 132, 150, 182
Monastery Manager: 195
Monastery officers: 21, 26, 75, 363, 373
Monastery Steward: 31, 33, 56, 66, 75
Monastery Supervisor: 31, 34, 36, 55, 75

Money: 44n, 56, 65, 68-9, 321, 324, 333-4, 346, 350, 356-8, 372-3, 388; see also Cash
Mongu: 251
Monju: 73, 137n, 214n, 217n, 225-8, 231-4, 238, 240-4, 246-9, 251-2, 254, 256, 258-60, 265-6, 270, 303, 314; Hall: 248; his great congregation: 270
Monjushiri: 73n, 165-6, 214-5, 219-21, 226, 233, 237, 241, 245, 247-8, 251, 258
Monkey: 262
Monks of Learning: 9
Moon: 310; eclipse: 150, 320, 336, 388
Morokimi: 127
Mosquitoes: 15-6, 19, 376, 382
Mo-tzu: 332
Mou-ch'eng-ts'un: 175
Mountain monasteries: 347
Mounted soldiers: 297; see also Cavalry
Mou-p'ing-hsien: 117, 142, 174, 177, 383, 394
Mourning: 172, 391, 394; ceremonies: 394; clothes: 332, 391; garb: 172
Mou-shen: 159
Mou-yin: 157-8
Mo-yeh Island: 134, 142, 400
Mu-chia: 134n
Mudra: 254
Mu-fu p'an-kuan: 194n
Muge daie: 300n
Mugyō: 92-3, 236
Muihō: 289n
Mujin: 400n
Mujō jugan: 30n
Muju: 400-2
Munetake: 398, 405n
Muraji Takesada: 184
Murakiyo: 75, 82
Murals: 67, 294, 301
Mushikikaiten: 219n
Music: 14, 76, 141, 157n, 195n; instrumental: 141
Mu-tsung: 51n, 326, 348n
Mutual guarantee system: 138n, group: 357
Myōhō-renge-kyō: 40n
Myōken: 10, 26, 60-1, 64, 92
Myŏngsin: 161
Myriad Bodhisattvas: 219-21, 234, 254, 258
Myriad Saints: 217
Mystics: 57n

Pans: 385
Pan-t'ou: 138, 144-5
P'an-ts'un: 191
Pao-chih: 202n
Pao-fu, Mt.: 275
Pao-mo-chen-kuo: 252
Pao-nei: 312n
Pao-shih-shan: 265
Pao-shou-ssu: 298
Pao-tieh: 358n
Pao-ting-hsien: 279
Pao-wai wu-ming seng: 312n
Pao-wei: 158
Pao-ying: 86n; -hsien: 85, 373
Pao-yüeh: 308n
Paper: 229, 248, 254; money: 65
Paradise: 34n, 214n, 242n, 300n, 368;
    Potalaka: 183; Western: 183; Clois-
    ter: 288, 335
Passes: 171, 180, 187
Passport: 389
Pa-ti-ch'ao-lan-jo: 261
Patriarch: 149, 180, 186
Patron: 54-6, 151-2, 156, 218-22, 229,
    234, 258-9, 304, 367, 377, 379, 392,
    395; deity: 308n; deity of ships: 117
Pavilion: 234; storied: 265
Pa-yeh: 261n
Peaches: 15, 355
Pearls, 192, 233, 255
Peasants: 177
P'ei: 371-2
P'ei-chou: 201, 206
Pei-hai: 13n; -hsien: 192-3
P'ei-hsien: 201n
Pei-tien: 192n
Pei-yeh: 261n
P'eng-lai: 95n, 136n; Mt.: 136; -hsien:
    142, 175, 177, 382
P'eng-lai-hsien chih: 177n
Penitence: 229n
Pen-tien-yüan: 197n
Permit, written: 170-1
Persia: 70; king of: 247n
Personal Attendant Priest: 299
Petition: 29, 36, 39, 41-2, 68, 72, 83,
    86-7, 169n, 195, 287, 311-2n, 322-4,
    329, 339, 389
Pheasant: 277
Phenomenal: 289, 357n
Physician: 148
P'i: 44n
Pickled vegetables: 174, 188
Picture: 3n, 26-8, 60-1, 64, 67, 71,
    73, 91-2, 217, 224-5, 228, 230-1, 252,

    265, 269-70, 304, 306; pious: 92,
    376, 386, 390, 392; see also Draw-
    ings; and Paintings
Pien River: 371
Pien-chou: 363, 371
Pig: 385
Pilgrimage: 340
Pilloring: 81
Pindola: 227n
Pine: 213-4, 257, 356; nuts: 95
P'ing-chang-shih: 25n, 393n
P'ing-ch'iao Inn: 42, 81-2
P'ing-hsü-ts'un: 189
P'ing-i-hsien: 281
P'ing-k'ang Ward: 338
P'ing-lu Army: 383
Ping-ma-shih: 21n
P'ing-min: 280n
P'ing-shan-t'ang: 65n
P'ing-tu: 189n
Ping-tzu: 159
Ping-yin: 389
P'ing-yüan-hsien: 206
Place of ritual: 67n, 216n, 220-2, 224,
    230, 254, 296, 308n, 341-2; for the
    Protection of the State: 236; of the
    Mandara of Devotions: 255
Plague: 163, 177, 196, 212-3
Plaster: 217, 228
Plates: 379
Platform: 255
Plum skins: 355
P'o-hai: 141-2, 173n, 177n, 186n, 193;
    Prince of: 197; commerce ship: 141n
    embassy: 215n; Inn: 177; monk: 261
P'o-hsieh: 173n
Poison: 264, 348
Poisonous dragon: 242, 257
Police Commandant: 105-6, 108
Police Guards: 49-52
Police Inspectors: 49
Polo: 194n
Pontoon bridge: 280
Pool of the Eight Virtues: 242
Pŏpch'ŏng: 141, 146, 148, 161, 169,
    172
Pŏphaeng: 161
Porridge: 206
Porter: 64
Portrait: 68, 72, 221, 294, 301, 308n
Po-shih: 232n, 373n
Po-ssu-kuo: 70n
Posthumous name: 217, 228
Posthumous title: 36n, 294
Post station: 278, 331, 372; inn: 86

Potalaka Paradise: 183
Pound: 33n, 48-9, 95, 199
Powdered tea: 92, 95
Praises: 55, 219, 221-2, 296, 301
Prajñā: 147, 149
Prajñāpāramitā-sūtra: 46n
Pratyeka-buddha: 235n
Prayer: 3, 55, 63, 115, 117, 123, 127, 130, 153n, 156, 200, 220, 233, 288, 348, 402, 407-8n; for long life: 311
Preceptor: 302
Prefect: 72n, 94-5n, 109, 111, 155, 174, 178n, 181n, 184-7, 223-4, 229-30, 236-7, 244, 331, 369-70, 372, 380, 387
Prefecture: 9n, 13, 94
President of the Ministry: 155, 187, 194-5, 197-200, 287
President of the Supreme Court: 365-7, 369, 371
Priest: 31n, 57, 78, 203, 223, 225, 230-1, 265, 272, 294, 299, 303-5, 307; Devotions: 79, 232
Priestess, Taoist: 343
Priests, Manichaean: 327, Taoist: 53, 181-2, 308, 316, 320, 330, 340-2, 348, 351, 354-7, 385-6, 392n
Prime Minister: 406n
Prince, Uighur: 327; of Korea: 118, 120; of the Bishamon Heaven: 303; Sui: 387
Princess Who Makes Peace with the Barbarians: 326
Prior: 141, 147n, 161, 169, 172, 185n, 216, 220, 236, 251, 273-4, 279, 288
Private Counselor: 350
Private Secretary: 393
Privy Council (or): 359
Probationary: 108
Professor: 96, 135; Han-lin: 373
Protection, monks without: 312, 314, 325, 333
Protection documents: 358
Protector of the Law: 302
Provinces: 364, 391
Provisional Audience Secretary: 394
Provisional General Manager of the Crown Prince's Household: 331
Provisional Governor General of Kyū-shū: 88
Provisional Grand Vicar General: 409
Provisional Magistrate: 32n
Provisional Professor: 96n, 135
Provisional Subprefect: 108

Provisional Superintendent of Registers: 109
Provisional Vice-Governr: 317n
Provisions: 32-3, 88, 121-2, 125, 135, 178, 196-8, 200, 212, 249, 288, 296, 339, 372, 376-7, 379, 384, 387, 396, 398, 405
Pu: 191
P'u: 85n
Public registers: 312n, 338
P'u-chin Barrier: 280
P'u-kuang-wang-ssu: 340, 372
Pu-k'ung: 253n
Pure Land of Amida: 300
Purification: 94, 113, 127, 130, 220, 265, 352; by water: 54
Purified eating: 203
Purple: 308, 320, 365, 370; Reverence Granted the: 298-9; cloth: 180; clothes: 14, 52; garments: 50; robes: 330
P'u-sa-t'ang: 249n; -yüan: 231
P'u-t'i Group: 319n, 327
P'u-t'i-ssu: 239, 242, 298, 307
Pu-ts'un: 201-2
P'u-t'ung-lan-jo: 250n
P'u-t'ung-yüan: 211n
P'u-yeh: 337n

Quelpart Island: 401, 403
Questions: 91, 93, 153, 231, 236

Rabbit horns: 355
Ragora: 166
Rāhula: 166n
Raiding General: 32
Rain: 16, 23, 58, 76, 99-100, 115-6, 119, 124-6, 128-9, 132-3, 146, 175, 185, 191-2, 200, 204-5, 212-3, 215-6, 220, 227, 246, 257, 275, 278, 281, 288, 290, 341, 348; hat: 106, 266; water: 158
Raising of funds: 68-9, 77
Rakan: 198n, 227n
Rank, record of: 43
Ratnacandra: 308-9, 320, 325, 362
Razor: 117, 179, 186
Reader: 154
Rebirth: 223-4, 230, 233, 270, 313
Reciting of the *Lotus Sutra*: 67
Reciting scriptures: 155, 271; *see also* Scripture reading
Rector: 21n, 31, 46-7, 108, 161, 165, 174-5, 189; of the University for Sons of the State: 364

Red beans: 193n
Reed: 4, 10-11n, 23; -gatherers: 16n; -sellers: 11
Regent: 406n
Regional Commander: 11n, 24n, 28, 37, 72n, 145n, 155, 181n, 185-7, 194, 197-8, 207, 209-10, 264, 278-8, 297, 312n, 315, 336-7, 345-6, 349, 389, 393
Regional Commandery: 24n, 62, 69, 143n, 234, 264, 269, 274n, 280, 314, 372, 383, 388-9, 391
Regional Military Office: 367
Registrar: 37
Regulation of clerics: 311, 322-4, 338, 348, 350, 353, 358-9, 361-2, 382, 386, 388, 390
Reischauer, Edwin O., *Ennin's Travels in T'ang China*: VII; " The Thunder Weapon in Ancient Japan ": 128n
Reisen: 215, 226, 234, 252, 261-3
Relics: 235, 247, 253, 262, 271, 289
Religious practice: 228, 243, 246, 255
Reliquary Pagoda: 294
Repeating scriptures: 155
Repeat lecturer: 153-4
Repentance: 151, 224, 230, 244, 258
Respect, with humble: 162, 169, 179, 184, 196-8, 291, 305, 307, 316
Responsive chanting: 62
Restrictions, biscuits without: 301; food without: 300
Retainer: 30, 83, 388, 404
Retired scholar: 198
Return to lay life: 338, 347, 353, 357-9, 361-4, 366, 373, 377, 384, 386-9, 391
Reverence: 57, 78, 183, 261, 270, 272, 296, 299, 301, 307-8, 320, 330, 335, 342, 362, 366; Granted the Purple: 298-9; of the *Vinaya*: 57n-8, 74
Revolving repository: 247
Ri: 2n
Rice: 50, 73-4, 117, 131, 135, 174, 178, 182-3, 190, 193, 211-4, 239, 243, 268, 405; hulled: 73; non-glutinous: 177, 190, 196, 205, 301
Rideout, J. K.: " The Rise of the Eunuchs during the T'ang Dynasty ": 284n
Right Army: 361n; of Inspired Strategy: 345n, 352, 360
Right half of the capital: 343; of the city: 325
Right Streets: 284n, 298-9, 322, 323
Ringe: 147n

Risshi: 302n
Rite, scripture-lecturing: 152; of a single-day lecture: 154; of reciting scriptures: 155; of worshipping Buddha: 218
Ritsu: 31n, 60n, 77n
Ritsu (vinaya): 57n
Ritsu-daitoku: 57n
Ritual, Baptism: 303; place of: 216, 220-2, 224, 230, 236, 254, 296, 308n, 341-2; defilement: 123n; of devotion: 255; place of the nine heavens: 341; purity: 123; utensils, gilt bronze: 255
Robbery: 163
Robe: 106, 225, 231, 241, 249, 297-8n; black: 343, 384, 400; Budhist: 368; embroidered: 297; woolen: 236
Rock crystal: 50, 117
Rod, strokes of the: 309
Rokuji: 8n
Rollers: 254
Ron (śāstra): 57n
Rosary: 50-1, 117; *see also* Chaplet
Rō (sō) shuku: 40n
Rubbing: 255
Rucika: 264n
Rudder: 6, 133; board: 132; house: 115
Rules: 45n, 58, 152; Cloister: 218; of the Bodhisattva: 160; Sect: 302n
Rūpadhātu: 219n
Ruri: 46n
Rushi: 264
Rutsūbun: 152n
Ryōbu Mandara: 65n
Ryōgon'in: 321
Ryū: 55n
Ryūgaku Hosshi: 3n
Ryūgakumon-sō: 27n
Ryūgaku-shō: 84n
Ryūgaku-sō: 3n, 9n

Sachūben: 406n
Sacrifice: 99, 127, 341, 344, 358, 402; to the earth god: 159-60
Sadaiben: 88n
Saddharma-puṇḍarīka-sūtra: 40n
Saeki no Kanenari: 30; no Matatsugu: 30
Sages: 217, 220-1, 228, 331-2; and saints: 72-3, 217, 220-1, 228
Sagyo: 161, 165
Sai: 24n, 34n
Saichō: 78-9, 223, 229, 407n-8n
Saikai: 232n

Sail: 6, 98, 103, 110, 112-5, 120, 123, 125, 127-30, 400; white: 126; -cloth: 125, 131

Sailor: 6, 11, 15-8, 25, 27, 32, 77, 80-1, 84, 93, 95, 103, 114-7, 122-3n, 125, 132, 317

Saintly Guardian Bodhisattvas: 264

Saints: 72-3, 149, 180, 186, 198n, 217, 220-1, 224, 228, 230, 252, 265; sixteen: 227n; Terrace of the: 244

Saishō: 90n, 406n

Sakon'e: 135

Śakra: 219n

Śākyamuni: 49n

Sal: 374n

Salary: 80

Salt: 20, 107, 178-9, 183, 191, 193, 336-7n, 346; and Iron, Commissioner of: 385; (and Iron) Bureau: 11-2, 20, 373

Salty dishes: 382n

Salty tea: 382

Samādhi: 59n

Samantabhadra: 67n

Sambu daihō: 290n

Sambun: 152n

Saṃgha: 54n

Samguk sagi: 100n

Samguk yusa: 101n

Sammon: 152n, 251

Saṃskṛta-dharmas: 289n

San-chiao-i: 267

San-chiao-t'an-lun: 295n

San-chia-tien: 282

Sanchō (sai) gatsu: 340n

Sandai jitsuroku: 42n

Sandals: 136

Sandalwood: 49, 254-5, 367; box: 364, 367; Images: 68, 364

San'e: 43

San-fou-ts'un: 191

Sang Island: 123, 127-8

Sangaku: 59n

Sangan: 224n

Sange: 154n

Sangi: 88n

Sangjŏk: 151, 165

Sangō: 21n

Sang-t'ien-hsiang: 9

Sangun: 94n

Sankō: 21n, 31n, 359n

San-kung: 210n

Sanne: 43n

Sanron: 31-2n, 43, 60, 65

San-shih: 369n

Sanskrit: XV-XVI, 152, 154-5, 219; hymn: 54, 62-3, 73; letters: 289, 311, 320

San-tsang: 57n

Sanuki: 32

San-yüan (-yüeh): 340n

Sanzen daisen sekai: 293n

Sanzō: 57n, 147n

Sash: 304

Sashōshi: 317n

Śāstra: 57, 142n

Sasun: 161, 165

Śata-śāstra: 60n

Saucers: 353

Scales (set of): 293

Scarves, Buddhist: 43n-4, 91, 233, 249, 254, 327, 368

Scattering of flowers: 154, 221

Scholar: 42, 332, 348; Monk: 3, 13, 21, 23, 25-7, 29, 32-4, 39, 42, 44, 49, 53-4, 78-9, 81, 83, 86-7, 90, 94-6, 102-3, 110, 116-7, 125, 132, 167, 390

Scribe: 15, 83, 85, 95, 101, 119n, 148, 187, 223, 229

Scripture: 68-9, 342; headings of the: 152, 154; box: 255; -discussion: 342; lecturer: 151; -Lecturing Priest: 69; -Lecturing Rite: 152; reading: 3, 46, 54, 56, 58, 64, 76, 114, 123-4, 287, 310, 348, 407-8; reciting: 155, 271; repeating of: 155; translated: 305; Storehouse: 156; towers: 347; Translating Reverence: 215, 226; Translation Cloister: 292, 294, 301, 303; Translation Hall: 294

Scriptures: 224, 230, 254, 262, 265, 332-3, 353, 362-3, 382, 386, 388, 390

Sea deities: 94n

Seal: 170, 188, 197, 230, 236-7, 360, 393

Sea of serpents: 68

Seat of worship: 221

Seaweed: 41

Second ship: 29, 82-3n, 93-5, 97, 99, 101-2, 106, 109, 111, 136, 248, 317

Secretary: 8-9, 11-3, 15-6, 19, 21, 32n, 42, 45, 86, 90, 108-10, 112, 121, 132, 135, 178, 180-2, 184, 317, 332; in charge of judicial matters: 193; in Charge of Rites: 109

Seeking Rain, Cloister for: 237

Sei Kyūtai: 30

Seishi: 273n

Sendō: 28n

Senfukurinsō: 254n

Seng-chao: 36

Seng-cheng: 74n
Seng-chieh-ho-shang-t'ang: 183
Seng-jui: 36n
Seng-lu: 75n
Senior Administrator: 373
Senior Secretary: 52, 74, 367, 369, 371-2
Sentient beings: 271, 306
Servant: 105, 111, 119n, 139-40, 144-5, 148, 151, 162, 171, 176, 179, 184, 186, 212, 389
Sesshō: 406n
Settō: 88n
Seven Buddhas of the Past: 247n-8n, 252, 261, 263
Seven (official) Monasteries: 20, 58
Seven-sevens day maigre feast: 336
Seventh-day maigre feast: 222
Seventh ship: 101
Seven treasures: 233-4, 247, 253, 255
Seventy-two sages and saints: 220-1; sages, saints, and deities: 217, 228
Severe cold: 160
Sexual offenses: 321
Sha-ho: 212n-3n
Shaka: 49, 247n, 253n; -muni: 49n, 55, 67n, 73n, 219-21, 300, 303
Shaman: 305, 316, 327
Shamon: 305n
Shan-chu-ko-yüan: 236
Shang-chu-kuo: 331n
Shang-fang Common Cloister: 211, 265
Shang-fang-ssu: 23n
Shang-jen: 249
Shang-mi Common Cloister: 245-6
Shang-shu: 155n; -*sheng*; 52n, 360n
Shan-hsi t'ung-chih: 237n, 242n, 246n, 256n, 262n, 265n-8n, 272n, 274n, 276n-7n
Shan-kuang-ssu: 207
Shan-nan-tao: 39
Shantung Province: 142
Shan-tung t'ung-chih: 123n, 175n-6n, 192n-3n, 200n-2n
Shan-yang-hsien: 85-6n, 374-5
Shan-yang-hsien chih: 86n-7n
Shao-fu: 163n
Shao-hsing: 339n
Shao-ts'un: 124; Inlet: 118, 120, 129
Shao-wu damask: 367
Shao Yün: 188
Shari: 262n
Shaving of heads: 44-5, 324, 327, 338, 350, 400
Sheep: 212

She-jen: 369n
Shen: 157-8n
Shen-chou: 212
Sheng: 50n, 74, 115n, 204, 235
Shen-hsien: 212n
Shen-nung-ssu: 333
Shen Pien: 32-3, 47, 50, 52, 68-9, 71-2
Shen-tao: 265
Shen-ts'e-chün: 285n
Shen-wan: 40
Shen-ying: 265n
Shen-yu: 158n
Shepherd: 212
Shibun-ritsu: 77, 236
Shibunritsu Sect: 77n
Shichijō: 43n-4
Shiganoshima: 1
Shih: 201-2
Shih (commissioner): 28n, 185n
Shih (provisional): 394n
Shih (stone): 50n
Shih-an: 288
Shih-chia-chuang: 143n, 209n
Shih-chün: 155n
Shih-hao-yüan: 273-4n
Shih-hou-chen: 274n
Shih-hsi Common Cloister: 278
Shih-jen: 378n
Shih-kao-ts'un: 273
Shih-ling-kuan: 267n
Shih-li-p'u: 76n
Shih-men-ssu: 271-2
Shih-shih: 44
Shih-tao Bay: 129n, 134n, 136n
Shih-yang-ts'un: 200
Shih-yü: 284n
Shijō: 15n
Shika: 248n
Shika Island: 403-4n
Shikan: 79, 223-4, 235, 251, 275
Shikikaiten: 219n
Shikishin: 54n
Shikotsushima: 404n
Shimei yoka: IX
Shimonoseki: 2n
Shin'eki: 3n
Shingon: 31n-2, 42, 65n, 83, 87
Shingon: 65
Shin'ichirō: 398
Shintan: 248n
Shintō deities: 6, 115, 117, 130n
Ship Captain: 17, 30
Ships, patron deity of: 117
Ship's bells: 4n
Ship's carpenters: 76

Ship's Commander: 94, 101
Ship's Masters: 9, 15-6, 84
Shiragi (Osa): 5n
Shiratori: 82, 84
Shiratori Kurakichi and Tsuda Sōkichi,
 Chōsen rekishi chiri: 400n-1n
Shiren: 308n
Shiro Ushigai: 184
Shirts, light: 370; woolen: 367, 370
Shiryō Hensan Jo: IX
Shitennō: 26n
Shittan: 289n
Shō: 115, 117
Shoes: 224n-5, 231, 263, 297
Shōgen: 94n
Shoji: 248n
Shōkai: 391-3, 398n, 405n
Shōkō: 90n
Shō-kongō-bosatsu: 264n
Shoku Nihongi: 404n
Shoku Nihon kōki: XIX, 16n, 28n-9n,
 32n, 36n, 42n-3n, 91n, 100n, 110n,
 128n, 215, 316n-7n, 352n, 378n,
 391n, 405n, 408n
Shōni: 393n
Shōnin: 216, 227, 236, 249, 261, 316,
 318, 321, 339, 393
Shōnin (saint): 252n
Shōō: 410
Shōrimon-ron: 142n
Shōshi: 139n
Shōshūhun: 152n
Shōshukugō: 248n
Shōtoku, Prince: 78n
Shou: 155, 287
Shou: 88n
Shou-cho: 10n
Shou-chou 37
Shou-kuang-hsien: 193
Shou-ning-ssu: 237n
Shōyaku Hosshi: 3n
Shōyaku-shō: 42n
Shōyaku-sō: 9n, 390n
Shōzokushi: 406n
Shrine: 125, 127, 200; of King Yao:
 200; of the Illustrious Deity of
 Matsura: 407n
Shu: 88n
Shūbi: 152n
Shuin: 254n, 315n
Shukō-kokudo: 34n
Shu-mi-shih: 359n
Shun-hsi Gate: 280
Shuntarō: 398, 405n
Shun-tsung: 51n, 178n

Shuryōgon'in: 321n
Shuso: 21n
Shu-t'ai: 175
Shūtei kanshoku yōkai: 9n
Shuzen'in: 91
Siddham: 289n
Sign: 130, 233, 251, 264; see also Mani-
 festations; Miracles
Silk: 44, 48, 53, 67, 72, 80, 89, 122,
 304-7, 333, 343-4, 351, 355, 367, 370,
 376 395, 405; eastern rough: 89;
 figured: 407; carpet: 217, 228; cloth:
 124, 255, 369; damask: 51, 53; floss:
 43, 89, 117, 120, 124, 249, 405, 408;
 -worm Palace: 158n
Silla: 5n, 100n, 141-2, 177n, 191n, 401
Silver: 50, 192, 233n, 333, 351, 367,
 385; characters: 367; harp: 248;
 paper: 248; vajra: 367
Singer: 357
Singing: 141, 152
Single-day lecture: 154
Sinhye: 161, 387n
Sinmu: 100n, 118n
Sitting mat: 48n, 207, 259
Sitting posture: 73
Six roots of evil: 265
Sixteen-foot figure: 224, 230
Sixteen saints: 227n
Sixth ship: 102
Six times for worship and repentance:
 224, 230
Skin: 252
Skirt: 241
Slaves: 100n, 324, 333, 356-8, 372, 388
Sleeve: 181-2
Slight heat: 159n
Slippers: 62, 367
Small (horn) beans: 17, 193, 200,
 205, 213
SNK: see Shoku Nihon kōki
Snow: 59, 64, 150, 294, 310
Socks: 376
Sōjō: 74n
Sŏl Chŏn: 374-6, 386, 392, 397n-8
Soldier: 10, 12-4, 38, 61-3, 105, 107,
 109, 282, 297-8, 304, 338, 345, 360
Solicitor of offerings: 250, 252, 255,
 268-9, 273-4, 313
Sŏnbŏm: 161
Sŏngnim (Hwasang): 138, 151, 161
Son-in-law, Imperial: 345-6
Sons of the State, University for: 347
Soper, Alexander C., "Hsiang-kuo-ssu,
 an Imperial Temple of Northern

Sung ": 253n; *The Evolution of Bud-dhist Architecture in Japan*: 61n, 189n, 216n
Sōroku: 75n
Soshitsuji, Great Law of: 308
Soshitsujihō: 290n
Soshitsuji-kyo: 290n
Sosŏn: 161
Sounding: 6, 116
Sounds of the Tripitaka: 275
Soup: 174, 208, 382
Southern Palace: 326
South (ern) suburb: 297-8, 325n, 354
Soy sauce: 174, 191, 193
So-yu: 17n
Sōzu: 60n
Spear: 129, 345; three-bladed: 349
Special Officer: 379
Spirits: 344, 400, 402
Spoon-and-bamboo lamp: 71
Spring (well): 203, 213, 268, 277, 342n
Spring begins: 159n, 297
Springtime Triumph Song: 195
Śramaṇa: 305n
Ssu: 157n
Ssu-chou: 45n, 340, 372, 377, 379n
Ssu-chung-ssu: 268
Ssu-fa: 193n
Ssu-hsien: 45n
Ssu-kung: 145n
Ssu-ma: 373n
Ssu-nung-ssu: 333n
Ssu-piao: 307
Ssu-pien: 335
Ssu-pu: 146n
Ssu-pu ts'ung-k'an: 137n
Ssu-wei: 257n
Ssu-yang Ridge: 266
Stabilization achieved: 158
Stand for elbow: 241
Star: 46, 157n
Starvation: 163, 177, 191, 196; *see also* Famine
Staves, priestly: 236
Stele: 68, 190, 202, 264, 272, 304; hall: 210
Stems (cyclical): 157
Stern: 6, 126; rudder house: 115
Steward's Department of the Palace: 350
Stigmata: 254n
Stomach wrap: 370
Stone-god: 128
Stone image: 165

Stone Nose Valley: 277n
Stone pillars: 347
Stone triangle: 62-3
Storehouse: 17, 74, 234, 288, 337, 346, 351; government: 385; official: 405; Palace: 350-1
Storeroom: 87
Storied building: 241; hall, two-: 272; offering hall: 301; pagoda: 240, 243; pavilion: 265
Straw (rain) hat: 106, 216, 227, 260
Streetshop: 65
Streets of the left: 75n, 284-5, 290, 298-9, 322-3, 330
Streets of the right: 75n, 284n, 298-9, 322-3
String of cash: 44, 53, 61, 64, 69-70, 77, 84, 92, 304, 306, 337, 346, 353, 357, 367, 392
Strokes of the cane: 340, 357, 360
Student: 90; monk: 3, 10, 13-5, 21, 23, 25, 27, 29, 31, 33, 35, 42-4, 49, 52-3, 65, 81, 84, 86-7, 89-91, 99, 236, 316, 320, 339; of History: 99
Subprefect: 21, 108-9, 112-3, 139, 144-5, 155n, 169n, 178n, 180, 372, 383
Subprefecture: 9n, 13
Substitute (Assistant) Subprefect: 109, 139, 144-5n
Suburb: 278; southern: 297-8, 325n, 354
Su-ch'eng-ts'un: 104, 106, 111-3
Su-chou: 78, 397
Sudarśana: 10n
Sugawara no Yoshinushi: 42n, 95
Suhye: 161
Sui: 5n, 16, 23n, 33n, 49-50n
Sui, Prince: 387
Sui-hsing: 158
Sui-p'o: 158
Sui-sha: 158
Sui-te: 157n-8
Su-li: 312n
Su-mi: 74n
Suminoe: 94n
Sumiyoshi: 94n; Great God of: 94, 98, 114, 117, 122, 130, 407
Summary of the T'ang Rhymes, A: 275
Summer begins: 159
Summer festival, first: 159, last: 160
Summer Offering Cloister: 197n
Summer retirement: 53, 79
Summer solstice: 159-60n
Sun (surname): 206, 209

Sun: 158n
Sun, eclipse of: 393
Sun-chia-shan: 104n
Sun Ch'ing: 125
Sung: 280
Sung River: 397
Sung Valley (Monastery): 137, 243
Sung Jih-ch'eng: 174
Sung kao-seng chuan: 272n
Sung-shan-ssu: 79n
Sung-shan-yüan: 79
Sung-shu-chieh: 301
Sung-ts'un Common Cloister: 267
Sun Hua-mao: 175
Sun-like Buddha: 149
Superintendent: 148; of Registers: 109, 139, 144, 170-1, 173, 180
Superior: 21n, 31, 150, 161, 165, 235, 294, 406; prefecture: 264n, 274n, 331n
Supervisor: 139, 324; of the National Tribute Articles: 82-4
Supplementary goods: 9n
Supplications: 152
Sūtra: 57
Suvarṇa-prabhāsottama-rāja-sūtra: 131n
Sword: 46, 48, 129, 134, 142; ceremonial: 345, 349; of Authority: 88n; wheel: 322
Sylvia Group: 401n

Ta-an-kuo-ssu: 289, 304, 311, 373
Taboo: 27, 163; characters: 155; name: 33, 51
Ta-chao: 248
Ta-chiang-chün: 89n, 157
Tachibananoura: 404
Ta-chien-fu-ssu: 296n, 368
Ta-chu, Mt.: 99, 101, 113, 395-6
Ta-chuang-yen-ssu: 300-1n
Ta-chung: 394
Taehŭksando: 401n
Tael: 33n
Ta-fu: 50, 52, 111
Ta-fu Ridge: 214
Tahō Nyorai: 244n
Ta-hsieh: 224, 231
Ta-hsien Ridge: 266
Ta-hsing-shan-ssu: 283-4n, 289, 292, 294, 303, 362
Ta-hua-yen-kang-wei-ssu: 248
Ta-hua-yen-ssu: 222, 224, 229-30, 235, 237, 243, 252, 258, 268
T'ai: 272n

T'ai Inn: 190
T'ai-ch'ang-ch'ing: 89n
T'ai-ch'ang-ssu: 89n
T'ai-ch'ing Palace: 298-9
Tai-chou: 244, 266, 277
T'ai-chou: 25-7, 29, 38-41, 43, 64n, 72, 83, 87, 90, 216, 223, 227, 230n, 236-7, 340, 373
T'ai-fu: 369n
T'ai-ho: 45, 47n, 262-3, 299; Emperor: 326, 348; Princess: 326
Tai-hsien: 244n
T'ai-hsien: 5n
Tailor: 44
T'ai-p'ing-ch'iao: 42n
T'ai-p'ing-hsien: 278
Taiseishi: 273n
Taishaku: 219, 302
T'ai-shang Lao-chün: 351n
Taishi: 2n
T'ai-shih: 131n
T'ai-sui: 157-8n
T'ai-ts'un: 190
Tai-tsung: 51n, 295n
T'ai-tsung: 51n, 254
T'ai-tzu chan-shih: 330n
T'ai-tzu t'ung-shih she-jen: 394n
T'ai-wei: 210n
T'ai-yin: 157
T'ai-yüan: 271, 275, 277; -fu: 268, 270n, 348; -hsien: 264n, 272n
Taizō mudras: 315
Taizō pictures: 306, 392
Taizō dai giki: 315
Taizōkai: 65n, 80, 87, 289, 290n, 292, 308, 315n; Great Law of the: 306, 311; *Mandara*: 93, 304, 306n
Tajihi: 404; no Takanushi: 32n
Takakusu: "Le voyage de Kanshin en Orient ": 60n
Ta-kan Common Cloister: 267
Takaoka no Sukune Momooki: 11, 42, 317n
Ta-kung-te-shih: 284n
Ta-kuo: 209n; -hsien: 209
Tāla leaves: 235n
Ta-li: 252n, 254, 263, 265, 281n, 295
Ta-liang: 67n
Ta-li-ch'ing: 365n
Ta-li-ssu: 278
Ta-ming Palace: 286n, 398n, 350n
Ta-ming-ssu: 65n
T'amna Island: 401n
Tamp'yo: 161
Tan: 205

Tan Inlet, Mt.: 133
Tan-feng Gate: 298n; Tower: 298, 316n
T'ang Rhymes, A Summary of the: 275
T'ang-ch'eng Common Cloister: 213
T'ang-ch'eng-ssu: 208
Tang-chiao Island: 396
T'ang-chou: 206
T'ang-hui-yao: 178n
Tangle: 41
Tango: 41n
T'ang-ti-li-chih t'u: XIX, 37n, 96n, 204n-5n, 209n, 276n, 280n, 372n
T'ang-yang-hsien: 208
T'ang-yang-t'ao-ts'un: 117-8
T'ang-yün: 275n
Ta-nien: 147
T'an Tan: 145
T'an-yu: 44
Tao-ch'ang: 67n
T'ao Chung: 318, 321, 390
Tao-hsüan: 77n, 302-3
Taoism: 57n, 298n-9, 307, 341, 348, 357
Taoist Court Priest: 215n; monastery: 344, 348, 353; monks: 342; nunnery: 343; priest: 53, 181-2, 308, 316, 320, 330, 340-2, 348, 351, 354-7, 385-6, 392n; priestess: 343; scriptures: 342; temple: 110n
Taoists: 57n, 295n
Tao-jung: 36
T'ao-liu-tien: 276
Tao-sheng: 36
T'ao Shih-erh-lang: 318
Tao-wu: 64
Ta-pien-cheng-kuang-chih: 294
Target-Shooting Festival. 41
Tarim Basin: 302n, 325n
Ta-shih: 14n, 28n, 36n, 131n, 223-4, 230, 234, 251, 275, 298n, 303n
Tate Hikkan: 184
Tathāgata: 54n
T'a-ti-tien: 267
Tatto marks: 321
Ta-wu: 217, 228
Taxes: 322, 324
Ta-yen-t'a: 303n
Ta-yü: 267n
TCTC: see Tzu-chih t'ung-chien
Tea: 52, 92, 95, 108, 132, 178, 188, 191, 194, 199, 201-2, 210, 221, 224, 230, 237, 242, 245, 249, 252, 268,

275, 300, 325, 365-7, 370, 378, 382; brick: 365, 367
Teachers: 27, 40, 71, 77-8n, 87n, 140, 147, 152n, 161, 179-80, 186-7, 195, 284, 287, 291, 334, 368
Teachings: 251, 293, 300, 315, 340, 376; holy: 363-4; Three: 295, 298-9, 342; on devotion: 363
Tea Shop Common Cloister: 214
Teashops: 18
T'e-chin: 329-30n
Te-chou: 206
Tei Kachikomaro: 25-6n
Tei Man: 25n-6n
Tei Yūman: 25n-7, 102-3, 140, 148, 171, 176, 179, 186, 284, 286, 307, 309, 313-4, 333, 390, 392, 399, 405n
Temple of the Dragon-King of the Sea: 110
Ten (scanning scriptures): 46n
Ten (heavenly beings): 55n
Tenchō: 387
Tendai: VIII, 3n, 25n, 31n, 44, 56n, 67n, 77n-8, 91n, 137, 223-4, 230-1, 235-6, 249, 251, 265, 410n; Lotus Sect: 35, 40n
Tendai-shū Enryakuji zasu Enchin den: 397n
Tendai zasu no ki: 91n
Teng-chou: 95, 117, 130, 142-3, 155, 171, 174, 176-7, 186, 193-4, 196-7, 286-7, 374-9, 381-3, 397-9
T'eng Feng: 189
Teng-shih-lang: 109n
Tengyō: 46n
Tennen: 46n
Tennyo: 241n
Tenryū-hachibu: 55n
Tent: 121, 124
Tenzo: 21n, 139n, 360
Ten zones: 248n
Terrace; central: 214, 222n, 225-6, 231, 237-40, 242-3; eastern: 234, 238, 245; northern: 137, 234, 238, 245-6n, 304; southern: 212n, 215-6, 227, 234, 238, 252n, 255-6, 260; western: 234, 238-40, 242n, 262n; *see also* Five Terraces
Terrace for viewing the immortals: 352n; of the immortals: 352-8
Terrace of the Saints: 244
Te-tsung: 51n
Textile: 356
Te-yang: 250n
Thai: 90n
Third ship: 95, 97, 101, 112n-3

Thirty-two stigmata: 254n
Thousand Buddhas of the present kalpa: 264n
Thousand-spoked wheel impression of the Buddha's foot: 254
Three beginnings: 340
Three chief officers: 174
Three Chin: 273
Three Dukes: 210n
Three elders: 359, 363
Three (eternal) treasures: 54, 62-3, 155, 219-20, 341
Three Great Lotus Works: 77n
Three learnings: 59
Three long fasts: 340-1, 392
Three parts (of scripture headings): 152, 154
Three praises: 153
Three Preceptors: 369n
Three-sevens day maigre feast: 336
Three Teachings: 295, 298-9, 342
Three thousand myriad worlds: 293
Three views: 224, 230
Three Virtues as Culled from the Buddhist Nirvana Sutra, The: 331
Thunder: 15-6, 76, 98, 106, 111, 124-6, 129-30, 146, 175, 205, 212, 215, 220, 246, 278; -bolt: 126, 128n-9, 264n; -bolt, god of the: 130, -god: 128n
Ti: 12n
Tiao: 276
T'iao-liu: 312n
T'iao-su: 312n
Tibet: 240n, 282, 302, 355, 398; people of: 205, 387
Tie-dye cloth: 122, 370
T'ieh-ch'in: 262; -lan-jo: 263
Tieh-liu: 312n
Tien: 139n
T'ien-ch'ang-hsien: 38
T'ien-chou: 90
T'ien-chuang: 192
Tien-chung-chien-ch'a-shih-yü-shih: 365n
T'ien-heng Island: 399
T'ien-hsia yen-t'ieh shih: 336n
T'ien-men-yüan: 135, 151n
T'ien-she: 159n
T'ien-t'ai: 55, 79, 136, 138, 223, 229, 234, 243; Mt.: 25n, 45, 72, 77-8, 81, 91-3, 102, 137, 212, 231, 236-7, 310n, 318, 320, 339; Sect: 25n; Ta-shih: 36, 53, 64, 67, 70, 77, 224, 230, 243n, 251, 275
T'ien-t'an: 297n

T'ien-tsun: 341n
T'ien-wan Inlet: 396
T'ien-wang-i: 279
T'ien-wang-yüan: 281
T'i-hsü: 298, 300
Ti-i-kuo-ch'in: 89n
Tiller: 6n
Ting: 25n
Ting-an Princess: 326n
Ting-ch'ou: 159
Ting-chüeh-ssu: 267
Ting-hsiang-hsien: 266-7n
Ting-hsien-yüan: 26
Ting-mao: 394
T'ing-tien Common Cloister: 214-6, 226-7
Ting-wei: 159
T'ing Yen: 176
Tobimo: 95
Tōdan Daitoku: 217n
Tōge: 308n
Tohyŏn: 111-2, 119, 121-2, 124, 132, 134
Tōji (manuscript): VII-VIII, XI, XIX
Tojin: 161
Tokiwa Daijō, *Shina Bukkyō shiseki tōsa ki*: 65n
Tokō: 154n
Tomb builders: 282
Tomo: 95; no Narimasu: 406n; no Sugao: 32n, 42; no Sukune: 102
Tonjung: 151, 161
Tooth: 253, 300-3, 313, 340
Tōri: 219n
Tortoise hairs: 355; shell: 127
Tosotsu Heaven: 248n
Tosotsu-tennō: 247
Tou: 50n, 74, 109, 177-9, 183, 190, 193, 196, 199-200, 205
Tou Wen-chih: 138
Tower: 243, 247, 316, 350, 353-4, 356
Townsmen: 70
Tōyō bunko ronsō: VIII, XIX
Tōyō gakuhō: Xn, XIX
Trade: 70, 83, 100n, 134, 296
Translated scriptures: *see* Scripture
Transmitter of the Law: 302
Travel documents: 140
Traveler: 22, 143, 162-4, 166, 177
Trays: 353
Trāyastriṃśa: 219n
Treasured pagoda: 248
Treasured Tower of the Golden Bell: 243
Treasures: 72, 235, 265, 350-1, 385;

seven: 233-4, 247, 253, 255; three eternal: 54, 62-3, 155, 219-20, 341
Tribunal of Censors: 95n, 365
Tributary embassy: 19, 89, 102, 105-6, 121, 124, 126, 135, 140, 171, 176, 184, 187, 284, 286, 317, 319, 328, 374, 378-9
Tribute: 9n; articles: 9, 13, 18, 22, 28, 82-4
Trīni śiksani: 59n
Tripitaka: 57n, 147n, 254
Triple Great Law: 289, 315
Troops: 38, 314-6, 322, 326, 337, 345-6, 348-9, 360, 388
Trousers: 367
Ts'ai 193
Tsai-hsiang: 25n
Ts'an-chün: 94n
Ts'an-kung: 158
Ts'ao-yang-hsien: 281
Tseng-hsiu Kan-ch'üan-hsien chih: 65n
Tseng-hsiu Teng-chou-fu chih: 123n, 129n, 134n, 136n, 174n-5n
Tse-t'ien: 240, 243, 245; Empress: 237
Tsinan: 143n, 218n
Tso-chieh: 75n, 284n; -seng-lu: 298n
Tso Chin-wu Wei: 89n
Tso-erh-chiang-shih-chiang: 108
Tso-hu-i: 209
Tso Shen-ts'e-chün Hu-chün Chung-wei: 285n
Tsou-p'ing: 202n
Tsuchinoto hitsuji: 66
Ts'ui: 134, 369
Tsui: 21n
Ts'ui-chia-ch'an-ssu: 92
Ts'ui Chün-yüan: 109
Tsuina: 21n, 31, 364
Tsuji Zennosuke, Zōtei Kaigai kōtsu shiwa: 215n
Ts'un: 9n
Ts'un-cheng: 145n
Tsung-chia-tien: 278
Tsung-chien-yüan: 286n
Tsung-hsin: 335, 363n
Tsung-jui: 51
Tsung-kuan: 374n
Tsung-p'ing-t'ai-lo Heaven: 351
Ts'ung-shih: 44
Tsun-hao: 316n
Ts'un-pao: 138, 145
Tsushima: 402-3
TTLCT: see T'ang ti-li-chih t'u
Tuan: 199n, 205n
Tuan-kung: 332n

Tuan Ch'eng-shih: 137n
Tu-ch'ang: 192n
Tu-chiao-ch'e: 385n
Tu-chih-yen-t'ieh-chuan-yün-shih: 346n
Tu-ch'iu-kuan: 188
T'u-fan: 205n
Tumulus, Imperial: 393
T'un: 43n
T'ung Barrier: 369
T'ung-chih-lang: 109n
T'ung-chou: 281
Tung-hai: 29n, 104; Mountains: 98, 105, 111, 113n, 396; -hsien: 96-8, 111-3, 121
Tung-hsi: 144n
T'ung-hua Gate: 147n, 283, 326
Tung Huan: 188
Tung-keng-ts'un: 192
Tung-lang Water Gate: 83, 85
Tung-liang-feng-ts'un: 9-14, 16
Tung-p'ing: 143n
T'ung P'ing-chang-shih: 25n
Tung-shih: 333n
T'ung-shih-chiang: 83n, 88n, 392n
Tung-t'a-yüan: 68, 292, 303
T'ung-tzu-ssu: 272-3
Tungus: 141n-2n
Turnips: 150, 297
Tu-shih: 182n
Tusita: 248n
Tu-t'o-ssu: 268
Tu Ts'ung: 336, 345-6
Tu-tu: 24n; -fu: 24n
Tu-yu-chiang: 105n
Tu-yü-hou: 352n
Tu-yu-i (-shih): 105n
Twelve great monasteries: 249
Twelve great vows: 156
Twelve Heavens: 302
Twelve Noble Vows: 221
Twin Ridge: 212
Two armies: 345, 352, 355-6, 360
Two halves of the capital: 322, 330, 353, 357, 359; of the city: 307-8, 310, 316, 320, 338, 342
Tzu-chih t'ung-chien: XIX, 25n, 41n, 48n, 172n-3n, 195n, 282n, 285n, 288n, 311n, 316n, 326n, 337n, 341n, 346n, 350n-2n, 388n, 392n
Tzu-chou: 201
Tz'u-chou: 142-3
Tzu-ch'uan: 142n, 201
Tz'u-en: 40, 272; Ta-shih: 303n
Tz'u-en-ssu: 302-3n, 325
Tzu-hsün chün-chung: 105n

Tz'u-pu: 146n
Tzu-sheng-ssu: 285, 288, 291, 298, 300,
    309, 313-4, 319-20, 324-5, 328, 335,
    363n
Tz'u-shih: 94n
Tzu-shui-i: 200

Uchūben: 406n
Uighur: 314-5, 322, 326-7, 338, 349,
    388; King: 326; Prince: 327
Uihō: 289n
Ukushima: 2
Ullambana: 268n
Ungjin: 400n
Ungju: 400
Universe of the Law: 220, 314
University, Government: 96n; for Sons
    of the State: 347
Upasaṃpada: 222n
Upper beginning: 340-1n
Urabon: 268n
Usa: 130n
Uṣṇīṣa-vijaya-dhāraṇī-sūtra: 246n

Vaiśravaṇa: 288n
Vajra: 246n, 264n, 367
Vajrabodhi: 294
Vajracchedikā-prajñā-pāramitā-sūtra:
    69n
Vajra-dhātu: 65n
Vakkula: 198n
Valley of the Holy Bell: 265
Varṣa: 53n
Vases, bronze: 390
Vegetables: 188, 191-2, 206, 379, 387;
    pickled: 174, 188
Venerable monk: 40, 62-3, 76, 217,
    224, 228, 230, 234, 251, 263, 301
Venus: 310
Vernal equinox: 159
Vicar General: 60, 409
Vice-Ambassador: 23, 36, 43, 134, 394-
    5, 406n
Vice-Chief of Employees: 139, 144,
    170-1
Vice-Controller of the Left: 406n; of
    the Right: 406
Vice-Governor: 317, 407
Vice-President of the Department of
    State: 337; of the Tribunal of Cen-
    sors: 95, 207, 332, 365
Vijñaptimātratāsiddhi-śāstra: 272n
Village directors: 145; elder: 104, 192;
    headman: 105; manager: 122
Vimalakīrti: 35n

Vimalakīrti-nirdeśa sūtra: 35n
Vinaya: 57-8, 270
Vinegar: 174, 178-9, 183, 191, 193
Violets: 297
Vipaśyin: 247n
Visser, M. W. de: *The Dragon in
    China and Japan*: 110n
Viśvabhadra: 67n
Vows: 26, 92, 115, 117, 130, 140, 168,
    243, 254, 259, 301, 306; twelve
    great (noble): 156, 221

Wada Hidematsu: *Shutei kanshoku
    yōkai*: 9n, 168n
Wadding: 225
Wagon: 395
Wajō: 31n
Wake (surname): 110, 135
Wake: 58n
Waley, Arthur, *The Real Tripitaka
    and Other Pieces*: Xn, XIX, 2n-
    3n, 25n-7n, 30n, 34n, 37n, 48n,
    195n, 217n, 259n, 308n, 321n
Wando: 100n
Wang: 134, 172, 188, 200, 202, 204,
    206, 281; An: 108-9; Changmun:
    150; Ch'ang-tsung: 183; Chiao-yen:
    120; Chong: 391-2; Ch'ŏng: 70; Fu-
    chün: 190; Hsing-tse 190; Hsün: 122,
    124, 131; Hui: 296, 304; Hyŏn: 165;
    Kach'ang: 398-9; K'o: 29; Liang:
    104-5; Li-wu: 197; P'o: 394; Shou-
    ch'eng: 47n; Tso: 139, 144-5, 170-1,
    175; Wu-chün: 210n; Yai: 48n; Yu-
    chen: 28-31, 61, 64, 83, 87-9, 91
Wang-hai-k'ou (Wang-hai-ts'un): 123
Wang-hsien gate: 286, 304; Tower: 304
Wang-hsien-hsiang: 175
Wang-hsien-t'ai: 352n
Wang-hsü-ts'un: 188
Wang-hua-ssu: 237
Wang-ming-tien: 281
Wang-nou-ts'un: 192
Wang-t'un: 276n
Wang-t'ung-ts'un: 276
Wang-t'ung-yüan: 276
Wang-tzu-ssu: 237
Wang-yen-ts'un: 206
Wan-nien-hsien: 282, 365
Wan-sheng Ordination Platform: 217,
    228
Wan-sui: 65n
Ward: 148, 283, 285, 297, 336, 347,
    385; Hsüan-yang: 290; Korean: 374-
    5, 377-9, 396, 398; Mi-hua: 281;

P'ing-k'ang: 338; Yung-ch'ang; 296, 336
Watchmen: 17
Water bottle: 106
Water-break: 159
Water-buffalo: 16-20
Water-close: 159
Water-even: 159
Waterfowl: 20
Water gate: 23, 83, 85
Water Inn: 41
Water-powered mill: 267
Water tank: 115
Waterway: 11-2, 14-5, 18-20
Wei: 158, 387
Wei, Marquis Wen of: 275
Wei Bridge and River: 282-3, 286n
Wei-chou: 143n, 193, 388
Wei-chüan: 79
Wei-fu: 143
Wei-hsien: 191n
Wei-nan-hsien: 369
Wei Tsung-ch'ing: 330-2
Well: 202-3, 347
Wen: 44n
Wen of Han, Emperor: 277
Wen of Wei, Marquis: 275
Wen-ch'en: 65
Wen-chien: 137, 223-4, 229-31, 249
Wen-hou: 275n
Wen-hsi: 35-6
Wen-hsü: 299
Wen-hsüan: 60
Wen-shui-hsien: 274
Wen-teng-hsien: 123n, 129n, 131, 142-3, 162-3, 170-4n, 176, 180, 186-7, 196, 286, 383-4, 395
Wen-teng-hsien chih: 123n, 129n
Wen-tsung: 41n, 51n, 172-3n, 282, 285n, 326n, 348n
Wen-wu: 289, 292
Western Barbarian: 332, 351
Western Capital: 223, 229, 268, 273
Western Chiang-nan-tao: 38
Western Hills: 270
Western Lands: 235, 240, 246, 266, 289, 362
Western Market: 333n
Western Paradise: 183
Western pavilion: 87, 215, 226
Western Ungju: 400
Whale: 47
Wheelbarrow: 385
White dew: 160
White jade lion: 256

White jade ordination platform: 222, 229
White Pagoda Monastery: 40n, 60
Willow: 18
Wine: 14, 89, 94, 109, 117, 120, 123n, 341, 348; party: 94
Winter begins: 160
Winter clothing: 405
Winter sacrifice: 160
Winter solstice: 58-9, 81n, 150, 160, 295, 310
Wo-kuo: 191n
Wooden mallet: 54
Woolen cloth: 367; robes: 236; shirts: 367, 370
Worlds, three thousand myriad: 293
Worship, Leader in: 222
Worshiping: 151, 156-7, 166, 218, 220, 224, 230, 244, 253, 255, 260, 266, 272-3, 294, 297, 301, 303, 313, 352n, 354, 377, 400, 408n
Worship platform: 153
Wrapping up of heads: 338, 366, 373, 390
Writings: 140, 248-9, 363, 366, 372, 374, 376, 386, 390, 392
Wu: 157-8
Wu: 134, 142; Dame: 237; Empress: 343n
Wu Ch'eng-lo: *Chung-kuo tu-liang-heng shih*: 33n, 50n
Wu-chin: 376n
Wu Chüeh: 155, 174
Wu-feng: 45
Wu-lei-tao Bay: 117n
Wu-liang-i-ssu: 35, 64, 71
Wu-sung River: 397n
Wu-t'ai: 179-80, 212, 215, 217-8, 227-8, 234, 237, 250-2, 259-60, 262, 304, 383; Mt.: Xn, 45, 137-8, 143, 149, 167, 185-6, 195, 203, 211-5n, 217, 226-7n, 231n, 235-6, 250, 256-7, 264, 266, 268-70, 272n-3, 275, 284, 287, 304, 309-10, 313-4n, 318, 340, 377, 389n; -hsien: 46n, 266-7n
Wu-tsei-pei (Wu-tsei-yü): 4n
Wu-tsung: 173n, 178n, 250, 285n, 343n, 351n, 361n, 391n, 393-4n
Wu Tzu-ch'en: 133
Wu-wei: 351n

Yabuuchi Kiyoshi, *Zui Tō rekihō shi no kenkyū* 158n
Ya-kuan: 14n, 181n

Yakushi: 92, 156, 221; -ruri-kōbutsu: 156n
Ya-liang-fan-shih: 186n
Yamashiro: 317n; no Ujimasu: 9n, 13, 16; no Yoshinaga: 82
Yamato no Itomaru: 17, 30n;
Yamato no Musashi: 404
Ya-men: 194n
Yang: 58
Yang: 210, 367; Ching-chih: 365-7, 369, 371; Ch'in-i: 37n, 329-30n, 361n; Lu-shih: 367, 371
Yang-chou: 4-5, 9, 11, 15n, 22n-5n, 28, 37-9, 43n, 47, 49, 59n-60, 65n, 67, 72, 74-5, 81n, 85-7, 89-93, 112, 163, 166, 176, 236n, 286, 288, 311n, 319, 372-3, 376, 391-3
Yang-fu: 24, 26, 29-30, 37-8, 40, 56
Yang-hua Group: 319
Yanghyŏn: 143, 161
Yang Lien-sheng, "Numbers and Units in Chinese Economic History": 33n-4n
Yang-ti: 5n, 16, 23n, 49
Yangtse River: 4n-5n, 11n, 13n, 37n, 38n, 101
Yang-tzu-hsien: 38
Yao, Mt.: 200
Yao-chi: 37n
Yao-wang-miao: 200
Ya-ssu Lu-shih: 108n
Ya-ya: 105n, 284n
Year period: VIII, 10, 298, 394
Year-star: 157n
Yeh-hsien: 113n
Yeh Te-lu, "T'ang-ti tan-ch'en chu-ho k'ao": 250n
Yellow paper: 180
Yellow River: 98n, 143, 204-5, 274, 279-80, 282, 369n, 388
Yellow Sea: 13n, 173
Yen Fang-chin: 390
Yen-hai-hsiang: 19
Yen-hai-ts'un: 13, 19
Yen-hsing Gate: 83n
Yen-kuan: 11n
Yen-kuang-ssu: 76
Yen-t'ang-ts'un: 205
Yen-t'ieh-ssu: 373n
Yen Ts'o: 111
Yin: 204
Yin (cyclical character): 158
Yin (female principle): 58
Yin (prefect): 331n
Yin-chia (Ta-shih): 298n-9n

Yin-ch'ing-kuang-lu-ta-fu: 331, 364
Yin-fu: 160n
Ying, Mt.: 136
Ying-chou: 136n
Ying-kung: 261-3
Ying-yu-shan: 98n
Yin-t'ai Gate: 350
Yin-ti Barrier: 276
Yin-t'ou-kuan: 276n
Yoga: 253n
Yokkaiten: 219n, 241n, 248n
Yoko: 30n
Yŏnghyŏn: 161, 165
Yoshida Tōgo, Dai Nihon chimei jisho: 404n
Yoshimine no Nagamatsu: 109n-10, 112-3, 317n
Yŏsu: 403n
Yu: 388
Yüan: 15n
Yüan-chang: 185
Yüan-cheng: 289, 292-4, 305
Yüan-ch'eng: 63
Yüan-chien: 289, 311
Yüan-ching: 307
Yüan-ho: 14n, 47, 108n, 147-8, 204, 215, 226, 261, 290, 326n
Yüan Hsing-ts'un: 12
Yüan Shih-san-lang: 366, 368
Yüan-wai-chih T'ung-cheng-yüan: 89n
Yüan-wai-lang: 148n
Yüan-yü: 15
Yü-ch'eng-hsien: 205-6
Yu-chi-chiang-chün: 32n
Yu-chou: 264n, 389n
Yüeh-chia-k'ou: 205
Yüeh-chou: 339
Yüeh-yang-hsien: 281n
Yü-hou: 49n
Yü-hua-ssu: 237n, 273
Yü Hung-chih: 361n
Yuie: 247
Yuigyō: 27n
Yuijō: 27n
Yuima: 35n, 240-1, 366
Yuima hyappō: 366n
Yuima kanchū-sho: 48
Yuimakitsu-shosetsu-kyō: 35n
Yuima-kyō: 35-6n
Yuima-kyō gengi: 36n
Yuima-kyō kanchū shoki: 35n
Yuima-kyō ki: 35n
Yuima-kyō monsho: 36n
Yuishiki-ron: 272n
Yün: 33

Yün-chou: 143
Yung-an-tien: 281
Yung-ch'ang Ward: 296, 336
Yung-chi: 274n, 280n
Yung-ch'ien-wu-chang: 66n
Yung-ch'ing-i: 276
Yungnak: 161
Yung-ning-hsien: 369
Yung-t'u-chang: 66n
Yün-hsi: 366
Yün-hua-ssu: 298
Yün-hui Chiang-chün: 89n
Yü-shih-t'ai: 95n
Yü-shih-yüan: 264
Yu Sinŏn: 94-5, 317-8, 321, 325, 339, 374-7, 386, 390, 392, 396-9
Yü-tai: 365n

Yü-tien: 302n
Yu-yang tsa-tsu: 137n

Zage: 53n
Zagu: 48n
Zammai: 216n
Zasshiki: 42n
Zasu: 21n
Zen: 31n, 44, 161, 210, 236
Zenji: 57n, 90
Zoku gunsho ruijū: 407n
Zoku kokuyaku kambun taisei: 282n
Zoku zoku gunsho ruijū edition: IX, XIX
Zuda: 147n
Zuiki: 229n
ZZGR: *see Zoku zoku gunsho ruijū*

Date Due

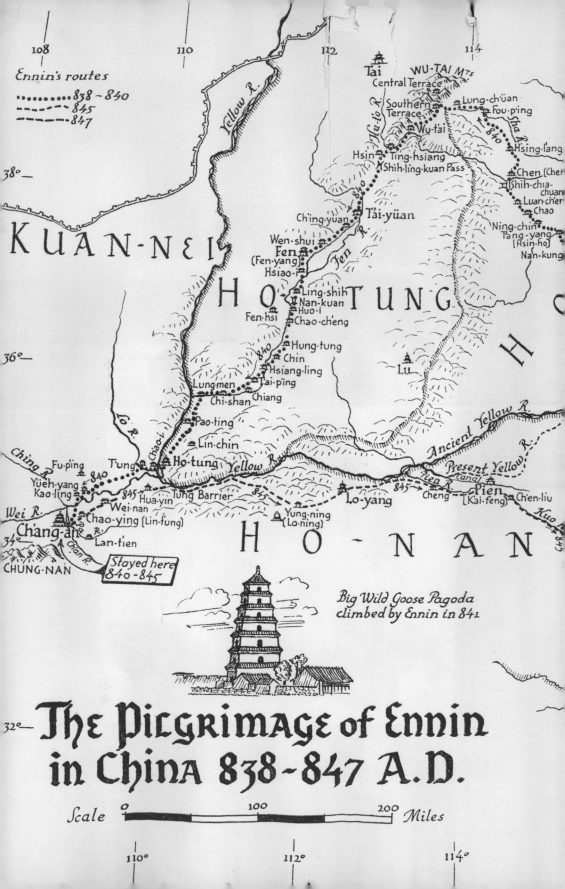

Ennin's routes
•••••••• 838 – 840
– – – – 845
– – – – 847

108   110   112   114

38° —

Yellow R.

KUAN-NEI

36° —

HO — TUNG

34° —

Wei R.
Ch'ang-an
CHUNG-NAN
Stayed here
840-845

Ching R.
Fu-ping
Yüeh-yang
Kao-ling
Wei-nan
Chao-ying (Lin-fung)
Lan-tien

Tung
Ho-tung
Lin-chin
Pao-ting
Chi-shan
Lung-men
Tai-p'ing
Chiang
Hsiang-ling
Chin
Hung-tung
Chao-ch'eng
Huo-i
Nan-kuan
Fen-hsi
Ling-shih
Hsiao-i
Fen
(Fen-yang)
Wen-shui
Ch'ing-yüan

Hua-yin
Tung Barrier
Yellow R.
Yung-ning
(Lo-ning)

HO - NAN

Lu

T'ai-yüan

Fen R.

Hu-to R.

Shih-ling-kuan Pass
Ting-hsiang
Hsin
Wu-t'ai
Southern
Terrace
Central Terrace
T'ai
WU-TAI Mts

Lung-ch'üan
Fou-p'ing
Hsing-t'ang
Chen (Chen
Shih-chia-
chuang
Luan-ch'en
Chao
Ning-chin
Tang-yang
[Hsin-ho]
Nan-kung

Ancient Yellow R.
Present Yellow
canal
Tien R.
Lo-yang
Cheng
Pien
[Kai-feng]
Ch'en-liu
Kuo R.

Big Wild Goose Pagoda
climbed by Ennin in 841

32° —

The Pilgrimage of Ennin
in China 838 - 847 A.D.

Scale   0   100   200   Miles

110°   112°   114°